Microsoft®

OLAP

SECOND EDITION

Timothy Peterson
James Pinkelman
et al.

SAMS

Unleashed

Microsoft® OLAP Unleashed

Copyright © 2000 by Sams Publishing

International Standard Book Number: 0-672-31671-4

Library of Congress Catalog Card Number: 99-61409

Printed in the United States of America

First Printing: October 1999

01   00   99   4   3   2   1

Trademarks

Warning and Disclaimer

ASSOCIATE PUBLISHER
Michael Stephens

EXECUTIVE EDITOR
Rosemarie Graham

ACQUISITIONS EDITOR
Carol Ackerman

DEVELOPMENT EDITORS
Heather Goodell
Marla Reece-Hall

MANAGING EDITOR
Charlotte Clapp

PROJECT EDITOR
George Nedeff

COPY EDITORS
Maryann Steinhart
Geneil Breeze

INDEXER
Kevin Fulcher

PROOFREADERS
Cynthia Fields
Wendy Ott
Mary Ellen Stephenson

TECHNICAL EDITORS
Alex Baronian
Alexander Berger
Bob Pfeiff
Campbell Gunn
David Owen
Irina Gorbach
Jim Klein
Kevin Viers
Matt Ambrose
Mosha Pasumansky
Shane Swamer
Sundar Rajan
Ted Daley
T.K. Anand

SOFTWARE DEVELOPMENT SPECIALIST
Craig Atkins

INTERIOR DESIGN
Gary Adair

COVER DESIGN
Aren Howell

COPY WRITER
Eric Borgert

LAYOUT TECHNICIAN
Timothy Osborn
Mark Walchle

Contents at a Glance

Contents

12 Programming with the DTS Object Model   289

28 Advanced MDX Queries   713

Foreword

Microsoft has decided to expand into new solutions possibilities with the release of SQL Server 7.0. Including a robust online analytical processing (OLAP) server with SQL 7, and bundling the client side engine of the OLAP services in the PivotTable Service in Office 2000 will undoubtedly have an impact on how organizations perceive a business intelligence solution in terms of cost. I have had the privilege of meeting and talking with the people who built this impressive set of products. They are uniquely talented and thoroughly dedicated to making this product work well for those of us who use it every day.

Microsoft OLAP Unleashed is a comprehensive guide to using Microsoft's data warehousing tools. It brings a wealth of information together that, to date, has been virtually impossible to find in one place. The authors have combined concepts with practical step-by-step examples and code segments to enable readers to explore business intelligence solution possibilities offered in Microsoft SQL Server 7.0.

Industry analysts and experts have predicted that OLAP vendors will have to react to Microsoft's entry into the market and that their presence will put downward pressure on the cost of OLAP tools and solutions. SQL 7 has been criticized and praised in various trade journals and other fora, but the long and short of it is that the tools that ship with SQL 7 offer some compelling functionality.

This book discusses Microsoft's entry into the business intelligence/data warehousing world along with discussion of OLAP solutions in general. Examples abound that you can build on as you enter this fascinating solution area.

The sections of this book take you through the entire data warehouse environment. You will work through probably the most challenging aspects of a data warehouse solution[md]building a database structure to support the queries required to answer business questions, and populating this structure from source data. Star schema, or dimensional database, design techniques are discussed here. Data Transformation Services are covered in detail.

Cube building is covered including creating, processing and partitioning capabilities. You will follow practical examples to become familiar with and build cubes in the OLAP Manager. Use of the Decision Support Objects (DSO) programming interface, PivotTable Service and third-party tools are covered as well.

Building client solutions using tools like Microsoft Visual Basic, Active Server Pages, and Excel 2000 is covered, again with practical examples. The OLE DB for OLAP specification and ActiveX Data Objects, Multidimensional (ADO MD) are discussed. Some of the leading third-party OLAP presentation products are covered too.

Multidimensional Extensions (MDX) for OLAP, the query language of the OLAP Server, is covered. This extremely flexible and fairly complex language is described in two chapters that show the reader how MDX queries are structured and provide practical code examples.

Managing the data warehouse environment is covered in the last section. Performance and security are discussed. Metadata management issues and use of the Microsoft Repository are included as well.

I've had experiences, both good and bad, with solutions aimed at decision support. The architecture of systems that strive to facilitate easy analysis of data from disparate source systems is different from typical "line of business" operational systems. Study of the differences between operational and analytical systems is key to succeeding with this kind of solution. Microsoft's tools will make such solutions more affordable and common. Use this book to bring the techniques and tools together before proceeding on a Microsoft-based business intelligence solution.

Bob Pfeiff, MCSD, MCT, MVP

Contributing Editor for *MS SQL Server Magazine*

About the Authors

Tim Peterson is a Microsoft Certified Software Engineer and a Microsoft Certified Trainer. He is also a Charter participant in the Microsoft Certified Solution Developer program, being one of the first individuals to earn the MCSD certification in April 1995.

Tim is one of the owners and is the chief consultant at SDG Computing, Inc., a Microsoft Solution Provider dedicated to making multidimensional data analysis a reality for a broad range of organizations, using SQL Server 7.0, the Data Transformation Services, and the OLAP Services. You can visit the company's Web site at www.sdgcomputing.com.

Tim has taught five of the official Microsoft SQL Server courses—Overview, Administering, Developing Applications, Performance Tuning and Optimization, and Data Warehousing. He currently teaches one week a month for Mindsharp Learning Centers in Bloomington, Minnesota.

Tim has provided SQL Server consulting or worked on SQL Server projects for a variety of organizations and companies, including Thrifty Car Rental, ITI Technologies, the University of Minnesota, Fisher-Rosemount Systems, and the Microsoft Corporation. He started working on his first data-warehousing project using SQL Server 6.0 in 1995.

Dr. James Pinkelman has six years of programming experience with front, middle, and back-end applications for database systems, Internet applications, and custom solutions. Most of his skills have been built up using Microsoft development tools and the COM interface on the Windows NT operating system. Prior to his entry into the software development business, Jim acquired some expertise in linear regression analysis and digital signal processing as an engineer on space and aircraft systems.

Currently, Jim is vice president of technology for Geppetto's Workshop L.L.C. (www.geppetto.com), a small software technology firm that specializes in innovative data access components for developers building applications for relational and multidimensional databases. Jim is also a senior lecturer at Loyola University–Chicago. He teaches statistics and computer systems courses in the Management Sciences department of the Undergraduate Business School.

Dr. Russell Darroch is owner, senior consultant and director in charge of systems and training of Accord IT Solutions (www.accord-it.com.au), an MCSP and MS CTEC in Australia. Accord IT provides specialized training, consulting, and support to clients. He is a Microsoft Certified Software Engineer, Microsoft Certified Database Administrator, Microsoft Certified Professional, and Microsoft Certified Trainer. He has extensive experience with MS SQL Server and MS OLAP.

Kevin Viers is manager of the Enterprise Technologies Group at Keiter, Stephens Computer Services, Inc. and a graduate of James Madison University. He has more than six years of consulting experience, specializing in designing, developing, and implementing enterprise solutions. Kevin began programming with PowerBuilder 1.0 and has since developed a broad development background including SAP, Active Server Pages, and Visual Basic, and most recently has concentrated on implementing OLAP technologies in an enterprise environment.

Kevin lives with his wife, Pam, and his boxer, Alli, in Richmond, Virginia. He can be reached via the Internet at `kviers@kscsinc.com`.

Ted Daley (`tdaley@ciber.com`), is a senior consultant/teacher and member of the Data Warehousing Practice at CIBER Inc., a company specializing in sophisticated data warehousing and business intelligence solutions. Ted is a Microsoft Certified Systems Engineer (MCSE), Microsoft Certified Database Administrator (MCDBA), and Microsoft Certified Trainer (MCT) who brings more than 11 years of experience to the computer industry. His current consulting and teaching efforts focus exclusively on decision support and data warehousing.

Dr. Shane Swamer is the program manager of the Business Intelligence initiative for WinResources Computing. Born in Appleton, Wisconsin, he graduated with a Ph.D. in Cognitive Psychology. After completing his graduate research on recurrent neural networks, Shane moved to warmer climates and started his career as a datbase administrator for an internet startup company. Now he applies his data mining and database administration skills at WinResources Computing where he is the primary specialist for data warehousing, SQL Server optimization, and business intelligence.

Dedication

To my wife, Donadee, and our children, Nathan, John, and Elise—Tim Peterson

This book is dedicated to my wonderful and beautiful wife, Kate, and our two incredible children, Colleen and Killian—James Pinkelman

Acknowledgments

I would like to thank all those who took on extra work so that I could devote the time needed to write this book: most of all to the faithful staff at SDG Computing, Inc. and also to the people at Mindsharp Learning Centers and Arlington Hills Lutheran Church.

I would also like to thank those who have helped me learn and given me the opportunities to learn database development: Donadee Peterson, Earl and Lorraine Peterson, Don Mussfeldt, Dave Larson, Stu Erdenberg, Dave and Roxanne Thorson, Greg Miller, Dave Fletcher, Tina Rankin, Jack Reichert, Kevin Mixter, Nathan Peterson, Chris Horgen, and all of my students.

Thanks to the folks at Macmillan for giving me this opportunity. Thanks to Carol Ackerman, Marla Reece-Hall, Heather Goodell, co-author Jim Pinkelman, my in-house editor Donadee, and everyone else who has worked hard on the project.

Special thanks to Chris Horgen, for writing much of the programming code in Chapters 18, 19, and 20.

And, most importantly, I want to thank my family for their patience and support.

—*Tim Peterson*

I would not and could not have done this without the support and understanding of my wife, Kate. Thank you.

Thanks, John Grace and the rest of the team at Geppetto's Workshop, for the continual pleasure of working with you and allowing me the freedom to tackle this particular task. From Macmillan, I would like to thank Carol Ackerman for her patience, encouragement, expertise, and for the opportunity to participate in this effort. I would also like to thank Heather Goodell and the technical editors for straightening out the winding course of my writings.

—*Jim Pinkelman*

jim@pinkelman.com

Tell Us What You Think!

As the reader of this book, *you* are our most important critic and commentator. We value your opinion and want to know what we're doing right, what we could do better, what areas you'd like to see us publish in, and any other words of wisdom you're willing to pass our way.

As Associate Publisher for Sams, I welcome your comments. You can fax, email, or write me directly to let me know what you did or didn't like about this book—as well as what we can do to make our books stronger.

Please note that I cannot help you with technical problems related to the topic of this book, and that due to the high volume of mail I receive, I might not be able to reply to every message.

When you write, please be sure to include this book's title and authors as well as your name and phone or fax number. I will carefully review your comments and share them with the authors and editors who worked on the book.

Fax: 317-581-4770
Email: office_sams@mcp.com
Mail: Michael Stephens
          Sams Publishing
          201 West 103rd Street
          Indianapolis, IN 46290 USA

Introduction

We are writing this book because of two convictions:

- Microsoft has provided excellent tools for OLAP in SQL Server 7.0.
- There is a need for practical, technical information to help people use those tools.

The primary authors of this book are developers and teachers. Lead author, Tim Peterson, is a teacher of the Microsoft Official Curriculum Course, #1502, "Developing and Implementing a Data Warehouse Using Microsoft SQL Server 7.0." Jim Pinkelman teaches data warehousing at local colleges and develops data warehouse systems as a consultant. We, the authors, have seen the potential in the SQL Server 7.0 OLAP tools. We have also seen the lack of detailed technical knowledge.

The 9,000 pages of SQL Server 7.0 product documentation give a lot of good information. The SQL Server 7.0 Data Warehousing course provides an introduction to the tools. But there has been nowhere to go to find the additional help that developers often want. We hope this book helps fill the need for that additional information.

The Rise of OLAP and Data Warehousing

People have been doing multidimensional analysis of business data with computers since the 1960s. OLAP and data warehousing are terms that were both first used in the 1990s to describe this process.

Some people use the terms OLAP and data warehousing almost interchangeably. In general, though, OLAP refers to the tools that are used to store multidimensional data and the tools that are used to present a multidimensional view of data to the end user. Data warehousing is a broader term, referring to the whole process of assembling an organization's data so that it can be used for business analysis.

The term OLAP was first used in a September 1993 whitepaper by E. F. Codd entitled "Providing OLAP (On-Line Analytical Processing) to User-Analysts: An IT Mandate." By the time Microsoft released its first version of OLAP Services with SQL Server 7.0 in early 1999, there were at least 100 different companies providing OLAP tools.

The term data warehousing was first used by Bill Inmon in his 1992 book *Building the Data Warehouse*. Besides the OLAP end-user tools, software companies have created specialized tools for data extraction, data cleansing, and the managing of metadata.

The Range of Topics in *Microsoft OLAP Unleashed*

The focus of this *Unleashed* book is Microsoft's SQL Server 7.0 OLAP tools, but we also decided to include a limited discussion of data warehousing. Whenever you set up an OLAP system, you do many of the things that you would do when setting up a full data warehousing system. For example, you almost always have to do some preparation of the data before you can build OLAP cubes.

This book covers all the SQL Server 7.0 tools that can be used for OLAP and data warehousing:

- Preparing the data with Data Transformation Services
- Creating and managing cube structures with the OLAP server
- Creating client applications for OLAP
- Querying multidimensional structures with MDX
- Using other SQL Server 7.0 tools for managing a data warehouse

This is a book for developers and programmers. Many programming languages and object models are covered:

- The Data Transformation Services (DTS) Object Model
- The VB Scripting Language, as it is used in DTS
- The SQL NameSpace Object Model (SQL-NS)
- The Decision Support Object Model (DSO)
- The Multidimensional Extensions to ADO (ADO-MD)
- Programming with PivotTable Services
- Structured Query Language (SQL)
- Multidimensional Expressions (MDX)

Recommended Reading

SQL Server 7.0 is a powerful database that comes with many convenient tools. As you create an OLAP system, you will be using many of SQL Server's general tools and features. We are not attempting in this book to give a full description of the capabilities of SQL Server 7.0. Many other books take on that task, including two in the Unleashed series:

Microsoft SQL Server 7.0 Unleashed

Microsoft SQL Server 7.0 Programming Unleashed

There is also much important information about OLAP and data warehousing that is not covered in this book. We recommend reading the following books to gain a broader understanding of data warehouse design, dimensional modeling, and data mining:

The Data Warehouse Toolkit by Ralph Kimball

The Data Warehouse Lifecycle Toolkit by Ralph Kimball, Laura Reeves, Margy Ross, and Warren Thornthwaite

Data Warehouse Design Solutions by Christopher Adamson and Michael Venerable

Corporate Information Factory by W. H. Inmon, Claudia Imhoff, and Ryan Sousa

Data Mining Techniques by Michael Berry and Gordon Linoff

Keeping Up With the Changes

Many of these OLAP tools and technologies are new or have been applied in new ways in SQL Server 7.0. We expect many will be modified or extended in the months and years ahead. As we have been in the process of writing this book, Service Pack 1 for SQL Server 7.0, the Add-In Kit for OLAP Manager, and the DTS Task Kit 1 have all been released.

We have attempted to present the most current information possible, but we recognize that some of the things we have written will be out of date by the time you read them. We expect that everyone in this field will be learning a lot in the next couple of years. We hope this book will help you in that on-going challenge.

Conventions Used in This Book

The following conventions are used in this book:

- Code lines, commands, statements, objects, methods and any text you type or see on the screen appears in a `computer` typeface.

- Placeholders appear in an *`italic computer`* typeface. Replace the placeholder with the actual filename, parameter, or whatever element it represents.

- Sometimes a line of code is too long to fit as a single line in the book, given the limited width of the book. Long lines in VB and VBScript code listings break with an underscore and continue on the next line.

- As part of the *Unleashed* series, this book also contains notes, tips, and warnings to help you spot important or useful information more quickly. We have also introduced troubleshooting sidebars to give you troubleshooting tips.

All source code referenced in this book can be found on the accompanying CD-ROM.

The New OLAP Paradigm—MS OLAP Services in SQL Server 7.0

PART

I

IN THIS PART

Microsoft's Entry into the World of OLAP

by Tim Peterson

IN THIS CHAPTER

CHAPTER 1

OLAP is On-Line Analytical Processing—a software tool that provides a multidimensional view of data for the purpose of business analysis. OLAP systems have been called Decision Support Systems and Business Intelligence Systems. OLAP can transform a large quantity of rarely used data into strategic information that improves business processes.

"Multidimensionality for the Masses!" is one of the slogans that's been used by Microsoft's OLAP development group. Microsoft SQL Server 7.0 is making the multidimensional reality of OLAP available to more organizations than ever before.

SQL Server 7.0 and the New Financial Equation for OLAP

A 1996 survey showed that the average cost of a data-warehousing project was $2–5 million. The hardware, the specialized software tools, the development time, and the end-user training all came together to make data warehousing a possibility only for larger companies and organizations.

Speakers at data warehousing conferences have focussed a lot of attention on how to justify and win support for massive data warehousing projects. When data warehousing projects were successful, they often produced a very significant return on investment (ROI). Many projects failed because the job was more complex than originally envisioned, results could not be delivered quickly enough, or the project could not be completed within budgetary constraints. Data warehousing consultants have invested a lot of effort in creating methodologies to attempt to increase the chance of success.

In response to the high cost of data warehousing projects, many vendors in 1997 and 1998 started to promote the notion of cheaper, quicker, smaller data warehouses, which were often called data marts. Instead of building a data warehouse for $2 million, you could build a data mart for $200,000. Some consultants began to talk about a data warehouse as being a collection of data marts with conformed dimensions and facts.

The release of Microsoft's SQL Server 7.0 continues the trend toward lower prices. OLAP systems, data marts, and full data warehousing projects are more accessible than ever before. Consider these factors in the accessibility of a Microsoft OLAP system:

- SQL Server 7.0 is a powerful database system that can handle data in the terabyte range, but it is available for an initial investment of less than $2,000.

- All the tools you need to develop a complete OLAP or data warehousing system are sold as a part of the SQL Server 7.0 package. Users don't have to pay extra for a data transformation tool or an OLAP server. The key new data warehousing tools included with SQL Server 7.0 are:

- Data Transformation Services—A tool for preparing data for OLAP.
- OLAP Server—The multidimensional server in OLAP Services.
- PivotTable Services—The client tool in OLAP Services.
- MDX—The multidimensional expressions provided with OLAP Services to manipulate OLAP data.
- The Repository—A tool to store metadata.
- English Query—A tool to access data using normal language.

- OLAP client applications can be built using Excel 2000, Active Server Pages, or Visual Basic.

- Because they already own the tools, companies are going to be able to experiment with OLAP and data transformations without making a significant initial commitment of financial resources to a new project.

- Because SQL Server 7.0 is widely distributed, business analysts are going to be exposed to the possibilities of OLAP.

- Because the tools are available, there will also be a far greater number of database developers who will be learning how to develop OLAP systems.

- Microsoft has developed standards for building cubes, querying cubes, and storing metadata. These standards are being supported by a growing number of companies, so that the time and investment you put into developing a SQL Server 7.0 OLAP system isn't wasted, even if you decide in the future to use an OLAP server from another vendor. (See Chapter 21, "Other OLE DB for OLAP Servers.")

You still must make an investment of time and money to set up a SQL Server 7.0 OLAP system:

- Transforming data and creating OLAP cubes can be very processor-intensive and time-consuming operations. If you're doing a major OLAP project, you'll probably need to invest in new hardware.

- There are a number of additional tools that you can purchase from other companies to enhance your OLAP system. Some of those tools are discussed in this book and there are some samples on the book's CD-ROM. Chapter 14, "Other Data Transformation Tools," and Chapter 26, "Third Party Clients and Tools," discuss some of these.

- The preparation of data for OLAP often involves a considerable amount of data transformation, cleansing, and homogenization. SQL Server 7.0 provides excellent tools for doing this, but the process of deciding how data should be transformed can still be very time-consuming. It takes time for business users to decide how their data should be organized and for developers to set up the required data transformations. If the data is inconsistent, it can take a lot of time to create and implement a strategy for correcting those inconsistencies.

The overall cost of a SQL Server 7.0 OLAP system will almost certainly be less than the cost of an OLAP system built with any other product. But the revolutionary change in SQL Server 7.0 is not the overall cost, but in how cheap it is to start an OLAP project. If you own SQL Server 7.0, you already own the OLAP tools. You can start experimenting. You can start learning. You can create a small sample OLAP application with almost no investment. You can use the results of that sample application to help determine the scope and plan for the whole project. And if you later decide to do a full data warehousing system, you will have already acquired much of the knowledge you need to implement it.

Can a Big Company Use SQL Server 7.0's OLAP Solution?

I teach a SQL Server 7.0 course about one week a month. A few months ago, I was looking over the list of my students for the Microsoft Official Curriculum Course 1502, "Designing and Implementing a Data Warehouse Using SQL Server 7.0." I noticed that one of them worked for a company that has built one of the biggest and best data warehouses in American industry. This company has a staff of at least 50 people working fulltime to maintain and further develop its data warehouse.

My student was the manager of an Information Systems group that served five of this company's divisions. I asked him why he was interested in SQL Server 7.0 data warehousing when his company had already made such a big investment in the field using other technology.

He told me that the corporate data warehouse wasn't filling the needs of his departments. When users requested that new information be added to the warehouse, it took about three months for the changes to be approved and implemented. They needed a data warehouse that was closer to the people actually using it—a data warehouse that could be modified to meet changing business needs.

He couldn't ask his company to invest in another data warehouse, because they had already spent tens of millions of dollars building one of the best. He needed the OLAP and data transformation capabilities of Microsoft SQL Server 7.0, so he could start building on his own.

Can a big company use SQL Server 7.0's OLAP solution? It certainly can. SQL Server 7.0 is powerful enough to build terabyte-size data warehouses. But the real power of SQL Server 7.0 is in how it can bring OLAP to the smaller organizations. That's true even for the big companies. With SQL Server 7.0's OLAP, you

can implement an OLAP project that's close to the end-users.
"Multidimensionality for the Masses!"

--tep

What You Need to Get Started with SQL Server 7.0's OLAP Capabilities

You have SQL Server 7.0, with DTS, OLAP Services, and the other data warehousing tools. What more do you need before you can develop an OLAP system? You need some understanding and knowledge of OLAP, including

- A sense of what OLAP can accomplish. Chapter 2, "How OLAP Is Used in the Real World," describes how OLAP can be used for a variety of business purposes.

- A basic understanding of the purpose of each of the tools in SQL Server 7.0. How can the tools be used to create an OLAP system? The rest of this chapter addresses that question. Chapter 3, "The Keys to a Successful OLAP System," also explains what is needed to be successful in using OLAP.

- The knowledge and skill to use those tools. That's the focus of the rest of this book.

Here's a brief description of the special OLAP and data warehousing tools that are included with SQL Server 7.0:

- Data Transformation Services (DTS) is a tool for transforming and cleansing data. DTS can be used to prepare data for OLAP.

- The OLAP server builds the multidimensional data cubes, stores the cube data, and provides access to that data to clients.

- PivotTable Service is used by client applications to retrieve data from the multidimensional cubes.

- The Multidimensional Expressions (MDX) language is used to query multidimensional cubes.

- The Microsoft Repository is a tool for storing metadata about databases and data transformations.

- Microsoft English Query is a tool that can be used to create client applications that convert English questions into database queries.

> **Note**
>
> The SQL Server 7.0 OLAP tools are easy to learn and easy to use. What can be difficult is the amount of new information that you need to assimilate as you start using OLAP:
>
> New terminology
>
> New business goals
>
> New development goals
>
> New database schemas
>
> New tools
>
> New object models
>
> OLAP brings a new perspective on database reality—a new paradigm for organizing information. The goal of this book is to help you feel at home in the multidimensional world of OLAP.

Data Transformation Services (DTS)—Preparing the Data

The biggest challenge for OLAP and data warehousing is getting the data ready for multidimensional analysis. That's why a large portion of this book, Part II, is devoted to this preliminary work. Most of the chapters in Part II focus on the Data Transformation Services (DTS):

Chapter 4, "Enterprise Data Structure and Data Flow"

Chapter 5, "The Star Schema"

Chapter 6, "Microsoft Data Transformation Services Overview"

Chapter 7, "The Core Data Transformation Tasks"

Chapter 8, "Using Other DTS Tasks"

Chapter 9, "DTS Packages"

Chapter 10, "Using the DTS Import and Export Wizards"

Chapter 11, "Writing ActiveX Scripts"

Chapter 12, "Programming with the DTS Object Model"

Chapter 13, "Using the Repository in Data Transformations"

Chapter 14, "Third-Party Data Transformation and Repository Tools"

You don't have to use DTS in your OLAP system. You can build your cubes directly on your operational data—but if you do, you could face the following problems and limitations:

- It is difficult to map fields from a typical normalized data schema to the dimensions and measures of an OLAP cube.
- It is more difficult if data needs to be pulled from more than one database.
- It becomes almost impossible if that data needs to be cleansed, homogenized, or modified in any way before it is used in the cubes.
- You can experience resource conflicts if you try to build OLAP cubes on data that is being used by other processes at the same time.

It's deceptively easy to create a cube using FoodMart, the sample database that's installed with OLAP Services. It's easy because the data in FoodMart is already organized in the dimensional schema that is used for OLAP and data warehousing—the star schema. It's a lot harder to use the OLAP Manager on a typical normalized relational database.

DTS gives you the tools you need to prepare your data for OLAP. You can move data between different databases and data formats. You can transform the data as it's being moved—checking for errors and making it consistent. You can move the data into a schema that can be directly used to build OLAP cubes.

These data transformation tools are available programmatically in the DTSPackage Object Library and the DTSDataPump Scripting Library. Most of the functionality of DTS is also available in a user interface called the DTS Package Designer, which can be opened from within the SQL Server Enterprise Manager.

OLAP Server—Preparing the Cubes

The OLAP server is one of the components that are installed with OLAP Services. Part III, "Creating OLAP Cubes," and Part IV, "Programming the OLAP Server," describe the functionality of this tool.

The OLAP server provides a model for constructing multidimensional OLAP cubes. It also includes a specialized multidimensional storage format for cube data. Most OLAP products implement data storage in one of these three ways:

- ROLAP—Storing OLAP data in a relational database.
- MOLAP—Storing OLAP data in a specialized multidimensional structure which optimizes storage space, aggregate calculation, and retrieval speed.

- HOLAP—A combination of the ROLAP and MOLAP strategies. Data is stored with ROLAP while aggregations are stored with MOLAP.

One of the strengths of Microsoft's OLAP server is that it provides all three of these types of OLAP data storage as options. You can even divide your cube so that one partition is stored in one of the data formats and another partition is stored in a different format. And if you want to try a different storage mechanism, your storage choice can be changed to one of the other two options with no need to change the cube's fundamental design.

The OLAP server's functionality is available in the Decision Support Objects (DSO), the topic of Chapter 18, "Decision Support Objects." Most of this functionality is also available in the OLAP Manager, the user interface that is provided as a part of OLAP Services. The use of the OLAP Manager is discussed in these chapters:

Chapter 15, "Creating Cubes"

Chapter 16, "Processing and Browsing Cubes"

Chapter 17, "Partitioning Cubes and Administering OLAP Server"

Chapter 19, "Developing an Add-In Program for OLAP Services"

PivotTable Service—Delivering the Cubes

The client portion of the OLAP Services is called the PivotTable Service. A fully functional client program for browsing cubes is not provided with SQL Server 7.0. Instead, Microsoft provides an OLAP client with Excel 2000 and the tools for building custom OLAP clients. Microsoft also encourages third-party vendors to create and market OLAP client applications.

The various options for client applications are discussed in the following chapters:

Chapter 23, "Implementing Microsoft Excel as an OLAP Client"

Chapter 24, "Building an OLAP Web Client"

Chapter 25, "Building an OLAP Client Application with Visual Basic"

Chapter 26, "Third-Party OLAP Clients"

Additional programming details for using the PivotTable Service are discussed in Chapter 20, "The PivotTable Service," and Chapter 22, "Programming Access to the OLAP Data Sources."

MDX—Querying in a Multidimensional World

The OLAP Services implements a language for querying cubes. This language is called the Multidimensional Expressions or MDX. A subset of MDX is used to create calculated members in the cubes. The full language is used for querying the data that is stored in cubes. MDX is described in Part VI, "Querying with Multidimensional Expressions (MDX)." The chapters of Part VI include:

Chapter 27, "Building an MDX Query"

Chapter 28, "Advanced MDX Queries"

Chapter 29, "Using SQL Queries on the OLAP Server"

Chapter 30, "MDX Reference"

MDX is a powerful language, with many specialized functions. You can use MDX to drill down, drill up, drill across, combine multiple dimensions on one axis, join members of a dimension in a combined view, summarize data, look at year-to-date value, find the highest values or lowest values, and perform calculations.

Microsoft Repository— A Centralized Location to Store Metadata

Metadata is information about data. Metadata includes information such as table definitions, field names, data constraints, and descriptions of data transformations. The Microsoft Repository is a place to store metadata in a standardized format. A centralized metadata store allows a variety of different database systems and database tools to be used together cooperatively.

The Repository is integrated with the Data Transformation Services. Metadata describing both databases and data transformations can be automatically stored by DTS. Metadata can be retrieved from the repository to describe the data that is being manipulated.

There are two chapters that focus on the Repository and the use of metadata:

Chapter 13, "Using the Repository in Data Transformations"

Chapter 34, "Metadata"

Microsoft English Query—Asking Questions in English

Microsoft English Query is a tool that can be added to client applications. It allows users to request database information using normal English questions. English Query takes these questions, translates them into SQL, queries the database, and sends the data back to the user. If the question cannot be interpreted, a reasonable English response is returned to the user indicating the piece of information that is missing.

> **Note**
>
> You can use English Query to ask questions of a relational database. You cannot use English Query to retrieve data from an OLAP cube. Microsoft has demonstrated the next version of English Query, which is able to query cubes. In fact, it can translate queries for cubes into either MDX or SQL, using the language that will be more effective in each particular situation.
>
> Hopefully, the OLAP-enabled version of English Query will be available soon. Because it was not available at the time this book was written, English Query is not covered except here in Chapter 1.

One of the sample applications for English Query is built with the Northwind database. Using this sample database you can ask the question, "Who are the contacts?" You will receive a list of all the contact names and contact titles from the company table, because the application has been taught that the word "contacts" is associated with those two fields.

A user of the application might have used a different word for contacts and asked the question, "Who are the representatives?" The sample application does not return any data in response to that question. Instead, the following statement is sent back to the client, "I haven't been given any information on representatives."

Users who have gained some experience in using an English Query application will recognize that the problem with their question was the use of a word that the application had not yet been taught to understand. Hopefully, they can find a synonym that can be understood, so that the proper information can be retrieved.

When English Query cannot answer a question, that question is entered into a log file for a developer to review. If the developer sees a word that was not understood and can identify what entity or relationship was being queried by the end-user, that word can be added to the application. If the developer adds the word "representative" as a synonym of "contact," future users will receive the correct response to the question, "Who are the representatives?"

"This Is Getting Silly!"

English Query is smart. It's also kind of fun. With English Query you can start having a reasonably intelligent conversation with your database. Microsoft doesn't emphasize the hints of artificial intelligence that come in English Query. It wants to position this software as a practical business tool, which it certainly is. There are numerous practical applications for English Query today and the possibilities will be exponentially greater when our computers all become speech-enabled.

Here's a sample conversation I recently had with my database using English Query:

Question: "How many customers are there?"

Response: "91"

Question: "Why?"

Response: "The information was in the database."

Question: "Why?"

Response: "I don't know how I know the information was in the database."

Question: "Why?"

Response: "This is getting silly."

--tep

Other SQL Server 7.0 Tools

You need an understanding of how to use SQL Server's other tools as you build an OLAP system. The basic use of SQL Server's tools is not discussed in this book. How SQL Server capabilities can be used for OLAP and data warehousing is discussed in Part VII, "Managing a Data Warehousing System":

Chapter 31, "Performance Issues"

Chapter 32, "Indexing"

Chapter 33, "OLAP Security"

Summary

OLAP Services, Data Transformation Services, the Repository, and English Query are all in their first release in SQL Server 7.0. They are powerful tools now and their functionality is being continually extended.

You can use these tools to bring the power of multidimensional analysis to your organization. You can prepare your data for OLAP, create multidimensional cube structures, and build client applications. You can query your cubes now with MDX. In the future you will be able to provide your clients with the ability to query your cubes in English. You can use the Repository to integrate a variety of different database systems and database tools. You can build an OLAP system or a full data warehousing system.

The next chapter, "How OLAP Is Used in the Real World," will show you some of the ways OLAP is being used by companies today.

"Multidimensionality for the masses!"

How OLAP Is Used in the Real World

by Tim Peterson

CHAPTER 2

IN THIS CHAPTER

The first section of this chapter shows the general process of OLAP browsing. If you are familiar with OLAP, this section will not have much value for you. But if you've never done any OLAP browsing, here's a chance to see what it's like.

The rest of this chapter gives real-world scenarios for the application of OLAP tools. Anything you analyze now with a spreadsheet, you can probably do more effectively with OLAP. The companies that are taking advantage of these new analytical possibilities are changing the face of today's business.

The Goal of OLAP

I think the best place to start explaining OLAP is to describe how an OLAP tool actually works. Businesses use spreadsheets to describe their activities. I have seen monthly reports that contain a stack of spreadsheets an inch thick. This pile of spreadsheets takes a significant amount of effort to create, it's difficult to use them to find the particular pieces of information you need, and there's always additional information that hasn't been included.

An OLAP tool provides the business analyst with a million spreadsheets at a time. These spreadsheets are available in a logical, hierarchical structure. The analyst can quickly move to a higher or lower level of detail or look at the data from additional perspectives.

For example, an analyst using the PivotTable in Excel 2000 is examining sales of various products in various states (data shown in Figure 2.1). He might be curious about the level of sales for one of the product departments, such as Canned Foods.

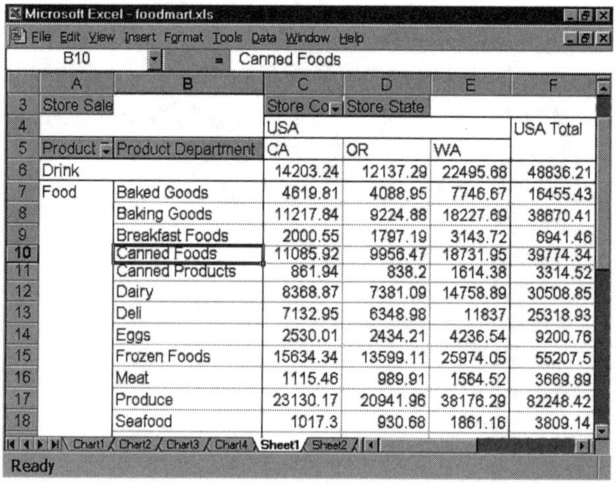

	A	B	C	D	E	F
3	Store Sale		Store Co	Store State		
4			USA			USA Total
5	Product	Product Department	CA	OR	WA	
6	Drink		14203.24	12137.29	22495.68	48836.21
7	Food	Baked Goods	4619.81	4088.95	7746.67	16455.43
8		Baking Goods	11217.84	9224.88	18227.69	38670.41
9		Breakfast Foods	2000.55	1797.19	3143.72	6941.46
10		Canned Foods	11085.92	9956.47	18731.95	39774.34
11		Canned Products	861.94	838.2	1614.38	3314.52
12		Dairy	8368.87	7381.09	14758.89	30508.85
13		Deli	7132.95	6348.98	11837	25318.93
14		Eggs	2530.01	2434.21	4236.54	9200.76
15		Frozen Foods	15634.34	13599.11	25974.05	55207.5
16		Meat	1115.46	989.91	1564.52	3669.89
17		Produce	23130.17	20941.96	38176.29	82248.42
18		Seafood	1017.3	930.68	1861.16	3809.14

FIGURE 2.1
This is a view of OLAP data using the PivotTable in Excel 2000.

By double-clicking that product department, the analyst can immediately view the sales for each of the product categories within that department (shown in Figure 2.2) and see that Canned Soup is a big seller.

FIGURE 2.2

The analyst can drill down to Product Category, a lower level of detail.

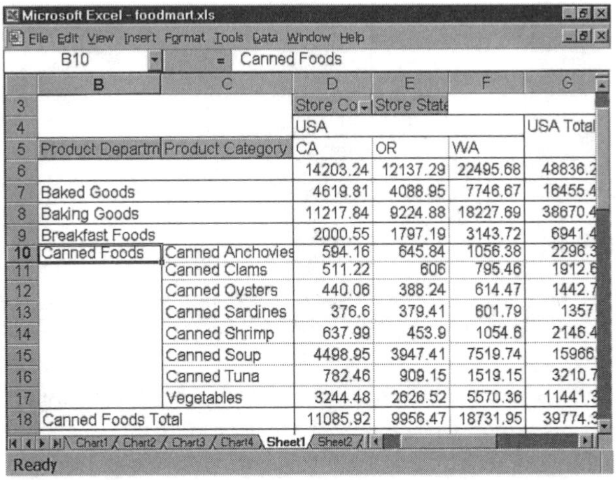

FIGURE 2.3

The drilling down continues from Product Category to Product Sub-Category, Brand Name, and Product Name.

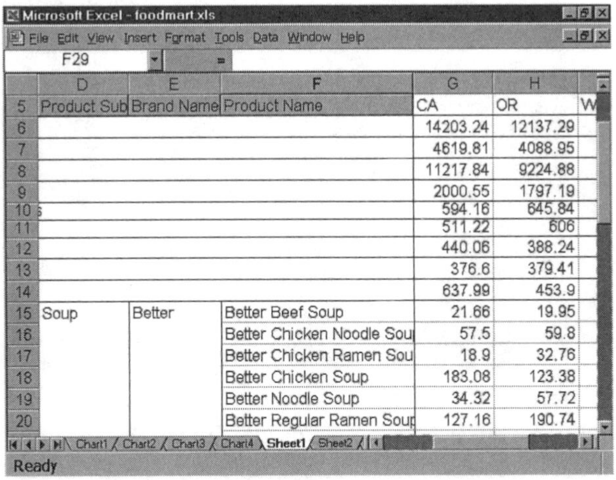

If the analyst wants to see more specific data, he can keep drilling down to greater detail, as shown in Figure 2.3.

Then the analyst might want to see how the sales of those particular products have varied, not by state, but by the range of income of the customers. Figure 2.4 shows the column headings changed from state to income range.

FIGURE 2.4
The analyst has changed from viewing sales by product by state to sales by product by customer income range.

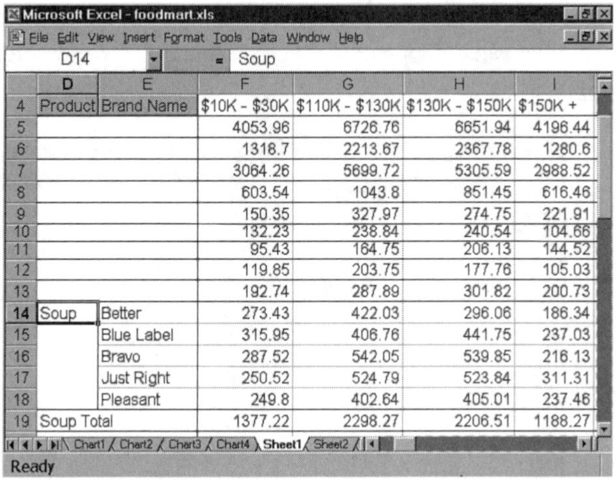

	D	E	F	G	H	I
4	Product	Brand Name	$10K - $30K	$110K - $130K	$130K - $150K	$150K +
5			4053.96	6726.76	6651.94	4196.44
6			1318.7	2213.67	2367.78	1280.6
7			3064.26	5699.72	5305.59	2988.52
8			603.54	1043.8	851.45	616.46
9			150.35	327.97	274.75	221.91
10			132.23	238.84	240.54	104.66
11			95.43	164.75	206.13	144.52
12			119.85	203.75	177.76	105.03
13			192.74	287.89	301.82	200.73
14	Soup	Better	273.43	422.03	296.06	186.34
15		Blue Label	315.95	406.76	441.75	237.03
16		Bravo	287.52	542.05	539.85	216.13
17		Just Right	250.52	524.79	523.84	311.31
18		Pleasant	249.8	402.64	405.01	237.46
19	Soup Total		1377.22	2298.27	2206.51	1188.27

If the analyst wants to see the income range of customers for all the products, he can return to a higher level of detail. Figure 2.5 shows product by customer income range at the product department level.

FIGURE 2.5
The analyst can drill up to higher levels of detail while still viewing the data from the perspective of income range.

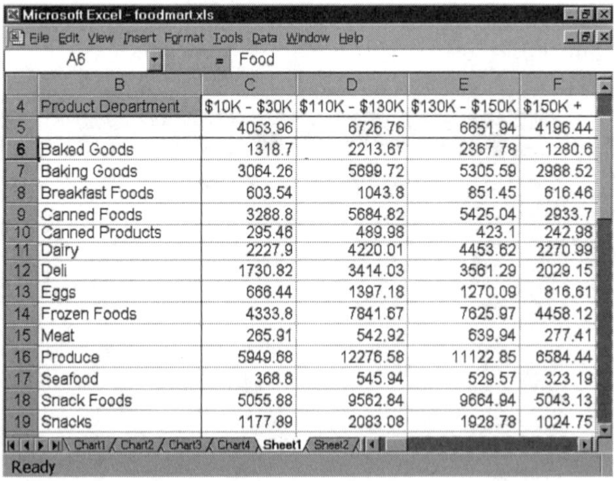

	B	C	D	E	F
4	Product Department	$10K - $30K	$110K - $130K	$130K - $150K	$150K +
5		4053.96	6726.76	6651.94	4196.44
6	Baked Goods	1318.7	2213.67	2367.78	1280.6
7	Baking Goods	3064.26	5699.72	5305.59	2988.52
8	Breakfast Foods	603.54	1043.8	851.45	616.46
9	Canned Foods	3288.8	5684.82	5425.04	2933.7
10	Canned Products	295.46	489.98	423.1	242.98
11	Dairy	2227.9	4220.01	4453.62	2270.99
12	Deli	1730.82	3414.03	3561.29	2029.15
13	Eggs	666.44	1397.18	1270.09	816.61
14	Frozen Foods	4333.8	7841.67	7625.97	4458.12
15	Meat	265.91	542.92	639.94	277.41
16	Produce	5949.68	12276.58	11122.85	6584.44
17	Seafood	368.8	545.94	529.57	323.19
18	Snack Foods	5055.88	9562.84	9664.94	5043.13
19	Snacks	1177.89	2083.08	1928.78	1024.75

Additional criteria can be used to filter the results. Figure 2.6 shows how those criteria can be selected.

FIGURE 2.6

Additional filters can be used. In this case, the analyst is choosing to view the data for one particular city.

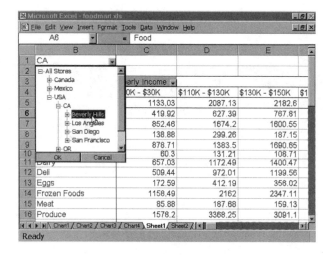

All of these different views of the data can be reached with simple, intuitive actions. A double-click on any item drills down to lower levels of detail. Or, if lower levels of detail are already being viewed, a double-click returns to the higher-level view. What is shown on the rows, on the columns, or in the data cells can be changed by dragging a different item from the PivotTable palette. Figure 2.7 shows an additional item, cost, has been added to the data cells.

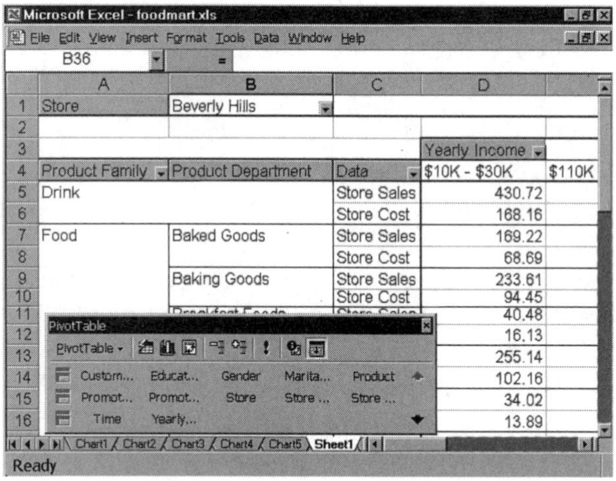

FIGURE 2.7

The PivotTable palette can be used to add or replace what is shown in the worksheet.

Could you do this kind of analysis with an inch-think stack of spreadsheets? Maybe, but there would very likely be some views of the data that are missing. And even if all the information is there, it takes a significant effort to know where to find the right piece of paper. Most people who use spreadsheets become more productive when using a good OLAP tool.

Bring on the Multi!

I don't think the term "OLAP" is very effective in communicating the benefits of this new technology. It doesn't mean anything to anybody until you explain what it is, and even then it doesn't mean much. This is a typical conversation I've been having lately:

"You're writing a book on what?"

"On OLAP."

"OLAP? What's that?"

"It's short for On-Line Analytical Processing."

"Oh."

In the Beta versions of SQL Server 7.0, the OLAP Services were called the Decision Support Services. Some vendors have been using the term Business Intelligence for their OLAP products. Those words at least say something, though Business Intelligence has the drawback of implying that businesses haven't been very intelligent in the past.

I would like to propose a new word for OLAP, or at least a new word for an OLAP client application. I propose the word "multi," which can be used like this:

"Let's take a look at the data with the multi."

Isn't that better than saying the following?

"Let's take a look at the data with the OLAP tool."

If anyone asks, we can say that multi is short for "multidimensional, multilevel, multiperspective analytical software tool." After that, they'll be glad that we just call it a multi.

I think OLAP deserves to have a less geeky label as it enters into everyday use. After we've successfully renamed OLAP, then we can try to find better terms for "data warehouse" and "data mart."

Let's bring on the multi!

--tep

Sales Trends

OLAP has been used more frequently for the analysis of sales data than for any other purpose. Retail stores, distributors, and manufacturers all need to know what products are selling. Sales information can be used to:

- Assure that an adequate supply of product is on hand.
- Reduce the level of unsold or returned merchandise.
- Manage distribution channels.
- Move merchandise between locations based on need.
- Analyze trends for future sales potential.

Sales trends are especially important for seasonal merchandise. All levels of the supply chain need to know as soon as possible whether or not a particular product is selling. If more of a particular product is needed, there often isn't much time available to obtain it. If a product isn't selling at an adequate level, it needs to be offered at a discount or replaced with other merchandise as quickly as possible.

Helping the Retail Stores

The Hewlett-Packard Company has implemented a SQL Server 7.0 OLAP system for its sales representatives so that they can help the retail stores where their printers and other products are sold. The system includes information about market share, customer demographics, pricing, advertising results, sales rate, channel activity, and profitability.

The sales representatives can see detailed information from the previous week about product sales and inventories. They can see what stores are running low on inventory. They can identify stores where sales are above or below average and use that information to help individual retailers identify ways to better market HP products.

This OLAP system is valuable because it brings strategic knowledge. In the highly competitive world of retail sales, HP's sales representatives understand all the factors that are affecting the profitability of the retail stores selling their products. They are in a position to give the best possible assistance to these retailers.

Effectiveness of Promotions

Retailers can also use OLAP to measure how well their promotions are doing. The effectiveness of a promotion is based on several factors:

- At what rate was the product selling before the promotion?
- At what rate did the product sell during the promotion?
- At what rate did the product sell after the promotion had ended?
- Did the promotion have a positive effect on the sale of any other products?
- Did the promotion have a negative effect on the sale of any other products?
- What was the economic benefit of the promotion in comparison to its costs?
- How did the results of this promotion compare to other promotions?

OLAP browsing can answer many of these questions. Some of the more complex ones, such as the effect on the sales of other products and the long-term effect of the promotion, need more sophisticated data mining tools to be adequately addressed.

Customer Demographic Analysis

OLAP analysis is also useful for analyzing your customer demographics. Customer information is usually gathered for the purpose of profiling—to determine which demographic groups are most likely to respond to a particular marketing effort. The types of customer demographic information that can be valuable include

- Income range
- Type of occupation
- Marital status
- Number of children
- Age
- Gender
- Geographic location
- Education level
- Previous purchasing behavior

"Who Are My Customers?"

All of this customer demographic information can be useful, but the first issue for many businesses is to determine who their most frequent customers actually are. There are many companies that have been recording the names and addresses of their customers but never use that information for any type of analysis.

Three and a half years ago I worked on a project for a major car rental company. All the company's franchises were reporting car rental information on a regular basis to the corporate headquarters. This data was being stored in flat files. The company had access to the details of each rental transaction but was not able to do any analysis, including such simple questions as, "Which customers rented cars from our company more than five times in the previous year?"

We moved the company's data into SQL Server and made it available for a variety of different kinds of analysis. But the most important result of all is that the company can now identify who its customers are, communicate with those customers, encourage their loyalty, and try to figure out how to get more customers like them.

--tep

Businesses have different opportunities for collecting demographic data. Some of it can be purchased from information brokers, although concerns about privacy are limiting the availability from that source. It can be gathered through the return of warranty cards or by having customers sign up for a special promotion. Customer loyalty cards that offer a discount on merchandise can be especially valuable for this purpose.

Sometimes general demographic information can be useful. If you don't know the income range of your customers, but you know their addresses, you can do some analysis based on the average income of people living in a particular area.

Internet retailers have the best opportunities to analyze their customers. Not only can they track previous purchase behavior of customers, but they can also track what types of products those customers are considering, as they browse their online stores.

Customer Satisfaction Analysis

OLAP Analysis can help identify patterns in customer satisfaction—and dissatisfaction. Information about returned merchandise, refunds given, and customer complaints can be captured and organized for analysis. This information can be profitably viewed from the following dimensions:

- Product, product line, and manufacturer
- Time—Are complaints increasing or decreasing when viewed across time periods?
- Store location
- Sales person
- Demographic description of customer

It is often useful to classify complaints or product return information into various categories of problems. If a particular type of problem is recurring, a set of problems can be addressed at the same time. It's also important to keep the individual details regarding each complaint so that an analyst can see in detail what the customers who have a particular type of complaint are saying.

Location Analysis

OLAP can be used to help retailers answer the critical questions about location. Which store locations are the most profitable? What factors are the most important when considering the location of future stores? Which stores are becoming marginally profitable or unprofitable? How does the location of a store affect its sales of a particular product or product line?

Location inside a store can also be very significant. Retailers have always recognized the benefit of placing a product in a strategic location and placing certain products close to each other. In-store location can be one of the dimensions used in OLAP analysis, so that the actual effect of moving merchandise to a new spot can be measured.

Capacity Management

Many businesses can only be profitable if they are operating at or close to capacity. Hotel rooms and airline seats lose their value very quickly if they are not used, for example. Companies use a variety of marketing and pricing techniques to ensure that they achieve the highest possible level of utilization.

OLAP can help companies achieve their goal of maximum utilization. The various factors that affect capacity can be monitored and analyzed. Comparisons can be made between similar time periods. Trends can be spotted early so that prices can be raised or lowered and marketing strategies can be modified appropriately.

Further OLAP analysis can be done on the particular marketing strategies, to determine which are most effective and most profitable. As the capacity management strategy is analyzed over the long term, the average rates paid by the customers should be included, so that the actual profitability of various marketing strategies can be considered.

Inventories and Warehousing

OLAP can help a business manage the critical factors for effective inventory management:

- The amount of the product currently on hand at each location
- How fast the product is being used
- How long it will take to get more of the product
- How long it will take to move the product from one location to another
- The velocity of the inventory—how fast the inventory is moving through the warehousing system
- The cost of storing the product in the warehouse

An OLAP system for managing inventories tracks the products in the warehouses. It also tracks the available warehouse space, so that products can be stored and moved in a way that brings the greatest benefit to the business. For some businesses, the greatest benefit is in maintaining a high inventory velocity—always moving merchandise through the system quickly. For other businesses, the goal is to always have an adequate supply of each particular product on hand so that the customers can be served promptly. OLAP analysis can help optimize a system for either of these goals.

Costing in Manufacturing Processes

OLAP is also used for analyzing manufacturing processes, although it has not been used there as much as it has with sales and customer analysis. One key area where OLAP can be helpful for manufacturers is in inventory control, as was discussed in the previous section. Another key area is in cost analysis of the manufacturing process.

If a company is producing a product at several different plants or on several different lines within a plant, the input and output for each production unit can be examined and compared. Production can be compared for various time periods—last year versus this year, or last month versus. this month. Comparisons can also be made by the day of the week or by the hour within a day. Production can be compared at times when different individuals or groups of individuals are working.

If the company is using a system of costing, where each individual's time and each machine's time is added into the cost of the product, then OLAP can be used to compare the relative profitability of different products and different manufacturing processes.

OLAP analysis can also be applied to analyze shortcomings in the manufacturing process—looking at what types of situations are correlated with a higher level of system failure, for example.

Data from the Manufacturing Process

I have worked on the analysis of data for a factory control software package that could record several hundred megabytes of data per day. Opportunities for OLAP analysis included the following:

The average length of time for various processes

The average number of system alerts

The average length of time it took operators to respond and fix alerts

Which pieces of equipment were used for which process

The amount of raw materials used for input

The amount of product produced

The number of processes that were completed in a particular time period

All of this data was already being recorded by the operational system. If there was a problem with a particular batch of product, the data regarding its processing could be examined. Besides that, though, the data was never used. An OLAP system gives the possibility of using all the available data on an on-going basis to improve the manufacturing process.

--tep

Household Analysis and Customer Loyalty

The greatest benefit of an OLAP system for a banking or financial services company is usually in the area of customer loyalty. One of the challenges for these companies is to identify which accounts represent the same customer. A family can have several accounts that are registered in different names. What is most important to a bank is to recognize what accounts represent the same household, because it wants to target its customer loyalty efforts at the household level. This keeps the bank from duplicating its efforts and also enables it to analyze the value of each particular household as a customer.

Many financial service companies believe that the most effective strategy for encouraging customer loyalty is to make each household a multiple customer. Studies have shown that people are much less likely to change banks if they have two or more accounts at one institution. Financial institutions are using customer demographic data and current account information to determine what additional services a particular household might need. They can then use targeted marketing in an attempt to turn single-account households into multiple-account households.

Some institutions have also started analyzing the profitability of each of their households as customers. Households are ranked in terms of their value as customers. Customer service representatives are given access to these rankings as they handle customer inquiries and complaints. If a member of a very profitable household is having a problem, an extra effort is made to see that the issues are satisfactorily resolved.

These business strategies depend on good data, especially for determining which accounts are included in which households and in calculating the impact of each account on profitability.

"The Daughter"

There's a story that I've heard several times in data warehousing circles about a bank that started using a system that discriminated between profitable and unprofitable customers. A young woman called in, asking for assistance. A deposit had not been credited quickly enough to her account and one of her checks had been refused payment due to insufficient funds.

The customer representative saw that the woman was listed in the unprofitable category, having been a customer for several years with only a checking account. She had recorded several overdrafts in that time period. The bank representative followed the guidelines for an unprofitable customer, offering little assistance and ending the conversation quickly.

The next day the bank's management heard from the woman's father, who was one of the bank's biggest customers.

Any company that is trying to discriminate between profitable and unprofitable customers tries to do it on the basis of households rather than on the basis of individuals or individual accounts. A profitable household, from a bank's perspective, might have several unprofitable accounts. All of a household's accounts have to be treated well if the bank wants to keep its profitable households happy.

Profitability

The bottom line for any kind of business information, of course, is profitability. These are the kinds of questions that can be asked with OLAP browsing in a sales environment that can help to analyze and improve profitability:

- Which products are producing the greatest return in comparison to the floor space they are using in the store?
- Which products are producing the greatest return when compared to the money used to maintain them in inventory?
- Which products are causing the most expense in terms of customer dissatisfaction and returns?
- What is the overall profitability of each of our products?
- Which products are unprofitable?
- What types of promotions deliver the greatest improvement on profitability?
- At what point does the cost of promotions and discounts outweigh the benefits of increased business?
- Which of our customers or types of customers are unprofitable, because of a low level of purchases or a high level of maintenance?
- Who are our most profitable customers?

All of these questions can be asked from a variety of different perspectives. These perspectives are called dimensions, levels of dimensions, and attributes. They can be viewed separately or in any combination when browsing an OLAP cube:

- Time—Year, quarter, month, week, day, day of week, day of month, day of year, time of day, shopping season, characteristics of day such as holiday status
- Location—Country, region, district, state, city, neighborhood, store, store characteristics such as store size, department, product location within the store
- Customer—Location of residence, group membership, demographic characteristics such as income range
- Employee—Department, shift, supervisor, individual
- Product—Product family, product line, product group, individual product, product packaging, particular product characteristics such as color
- Promotion—Promotion type, specific promotion, promotion characteristics such as cost range

Targeting Direct Mail

One of the best uses of customer demographic data is to target direct mail. If a company knows which individuals are more likely to respond favorably to a mailing, it can mail only to the targeted individuals, reducing the number of pieces that are mailed. This makes the company happy, by reducing expenses. It

2

makes the rest of us happy, by reducing the amount of junk mail in our mailboxes.

The improvement in results based on demographic analysis is called "lift." You calculate the lift by dividing the number of responses you obtain when using demographic analysis by the number of responses you would have obtained with a random mailing. If an average of 2 people out of 100 normally respond to a mailing, but you are able to raise the response rate to 5 out of 100, you have achieved a lift of 2.5.

Lift can be shown on a chart that plots the new level of response with the average level of response that would have been obtained without using any demographic analysis (see Figure 2.8). The greatest lift occurs at the lowest levels of mailing, where you are sending only to the most likely customers. A business analyst uses the information from a chart showing the lift to determine what the best level of mailing is for a company in a particular situation. In this particular case, the selected cutoff point was at 60% of the mailings. At this point, 90% of the total positive responses were obtained, for a lift of 1.5. The company gave up 10% of its sales, but saved 40% of its mailing expenses. At lower levels, they would have achieved a higher lift, but would have given up an unacceptably high portion of the potential business. To achieve 100% of the potential return, the company would have to mail 100% of the mailings and give up the benefit of lift, and this kind of analysis, altogether.

FIGURE 2.8

The lift is the ratio between the results of a targeted mailing and the straight-line return from a mass mailing.

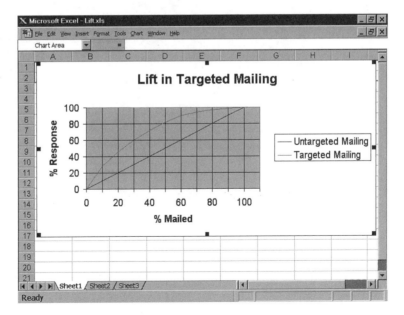

Summary

OLAP is a logical extension of the spreadsheet analysis used in business. This tool for multidimensional analysis helps people find useful patterns in the mountains of data that are generated by modern society.

"Multidimensionality for the masses!"

"Let's bring on the multi!"

The Keys to a Successful OLAP System

by Tim Peterson

IN THIS CHAPTER

CHAPTER 3

There are several keys in building a successful OLAP system. These factors are important no matter what OLAP development tools you choose to use. I discuss these issues in this chapter.

A Business Purpose

Software projects need a business purpose. That's been especially true for the typical data warehousing project in the past, when the price tag has been running in the millions of dollars and the return on the investment was not received until 12 to 24 months afterward.

It's easier to find an adequate business purpose for a SQL Server 7.0 OLAP system, because the initial cost is so little. You still could be investing a significant amount of time and money, though. Here are some of the tasks you have to accomplish:

- Find out what data the users want and need in their OLAP browsing.
- Transform data from several OLTP systems into a star schema.
- Cleanse the OLTP (On-Line Transaction Processing) data.
- Build the multidimensional cubes.
- Invest in hardware for the data transformation, cube processing, and data storage.
- Build or purchase OLAP client applications.
- Set up a strategy for updating the data.
- Train the OLAP users.

How much will it cost and how much time will it take? That depends on a lot of factors. You can accomplish a lot with SQL Server's OLAP capabilities with $30,000. But if you have a lot of data sources to integrate and a lot of data cleansing to do, the cost can easily escalate into the hundreds of thousands of dollars.

How do companies judge the value of OLAP to their businesses' success? Some companies focus on a calculation of the Return On Investment (ROI). They look at how the OLAP system will save money, either through reduced inventories, a lower level of returns, a reduction of personnel time spent in creating reports, or an increased level of sales.

Other companies see the benefits of an OLAP system in a more general context. They recognize that the knowledge they obtain from OLAP browsing helps them run their businesses better in a number of ways that can't easily be translated into a particular dollar figure. The need for an OLAP system could also be driven by a recognition that rival companies are using OLAP to gain a competitive advantage over them.

If the business justification is present but not altogether persuasive, you still have the possibility of implementing an OLAP system with SQL Server. Start with a small project. Use one data source and one subject area. Find a subject that the business analysts in the company are concerned about. After you implement a small project, it will be easier for the decision-makers to properly judge whether a more comprehensive OLAP system would be worth the investment.

Rapid OLAP Browsing

Rapid browsing for the end users is essential to the success of an OLAP system.

Nigel Pendse and Richard Creeth, authors of the *OLAP Report*, have developed what they call the FASMI (Fast Analysis of Shared Multidimensional Information) test to judge whether or not an application qualifies to be an OLAP tool. An OLAP tool should provide:

- Fast—Browsing must be consistently fast. In their opinion, fast normally means less than five seconds to respond to any query.
- Analysis—The application should contain analytical tools both for the developer and for the end user. Client tools are discussed in the next section.
- Shared—The cubes must be able to handle the security requirements of sharing confidential information. Security requirements are discussed in the last section of this chapter.
- Multidimensional Information—OLAP is defined by its presentation of multidimensional data.

If an OLAP browsing query takes longer than five seconds, the business analyst assumes something is wrong and will often abort the request. A speed of less than two seconds will give the user a sense that the data is being returned immediately. As Nigel and Pendse indicate in their definition, rapid response is more than a goal. It is, in fact, an essential, defining characteristic of OLAP.

There are many techniques for assuring rapid browsing in a Microsoft OLAP system. These techniques are discussed in numerous places in the book. The easiest way to achieve rapid speed for all queries is to use the MOLAP storage method, as discussed in Chapter 16, "Processing and Browsing Cubes." Optimizing the client caching is also very important and it is discussed in Chapter 20, "The PivotTable Service."

An Intuitive OLAP Client Tool

You have a lot of choices in selecting a client for your SQL Server OLAP System. You can use Excel 2000, create a Web client, create a Visual Basic client, or purchase an OLAP client from a third-party vendor. These choices are discussed in Chapters 23 through Chapter 26.

Whether you create or purchase an OLAP client, consider the following criteria for an effective client:

- It should be easy for the end users to learn and should provide an intuitive method for choosing different measures, switching dimensions, viewing multiple dimensions simultaneously, drilling up, drilling down, and adding additional filters.
- It should provide the capabilities that the end users need, whether that's the ability to calculate values, use particular MDX functions, perform "what if" analysis, create graphical views of the data, or create reports.
- The clients should deliver rapid performance.
- The clients must support the security of the OLAP system.

Rapid Initial Development

Rapid progress in the initial development of an OLAP system can be critical in building support and acceptance of the effort. In situations where OLAP is new to an organization, it's helpful to provide people with an initial view of what OLAP browsing looks like. People often need to see an example of OLAP before they are able to know what they would like to see included in a system.

The graphical tools provided in the OLAP Manager make it easy to quickly build dimensions and cubes. Getting the data ready for the OLAP Manager can be more time-consuming.

The most important factor in achieving swift initial development is to limit the complexity of the source data. Try to include data from only one source. Use data that doesn't require extensive transformations. Keep the total volume of data in a range that can be easily handled by your hardware.

If you're not using too much data and you're not doing any data cleansing, you can build the OLAP demonstration without doing any data transformations at all. You can build cubes based directly from your production data. Techniques for doing this are described in Chapter 5, "The Star Schema." You will have no conflicts between your online system and your OLAP system, if these three things are true:

- You use the MOLAP cube storage method.
- You do a full refresh of your cubes when you want to include new data.
- You have the time to process the cubes when the database isn't being used.

If you haven't selected an OLAP client tool, you can start by using Excel 2000 with very little time investment. It's also very easy to build a Web page using the PivotTable to view the cubes. If you want a full-featured client, the fastest strategy is to purchase a third-party OLAP client tool.

An Extensible Development Strategy

Whatever the size of your OLAP or data warehousing project, it is very likely to get larger in the future. Businesses change and, even when they stay the same, business analysts often want to see new perspectives on the data. One of the biggest challenges in extending OLAP systems can come when two companies are merged.

Keep the possibility of new requirements in mind as you design your OLAP system. Here are some of the ways you may be asked to extend your system:

- Include a lower level of detail for the current data.
- Add new data fields from the current data.
- Provide more calculated values for the data.
- Integrate new data sources.
- Add more users.
- Add more departments.
- Distribute the OLAP data to dispersed users.
- Refresh the data in the cubes more frequently, so that more current information is available.
- Provide more historical data.
- Include more data from sources outside the organization.
- Provide Internet/intranet access to the cubes.
- Provide new client capabilities. It might be necessary to modify the existing client application or switch to a new client.

You can't get ready ahead of time for all the potential changes, but there are a few general strategies you can follow that will help you be as prepared as possible:

- Develop an enterprisewide perspective. Consider how your OLAP project is related to other OLAP or data warehousing efforts. Chapter 4, "Enterprise Data Structure and Data Flow," discusses these issues.

- Save the lowest possible level of detail in your OLAP system—the atomic facts. You can easily add new data summaries in the future. But if you don't include the atomic level of data in your OLAP system, that information will always be unavailable unless you rebuild your whole system.

- Include all the fields that could possibly be needed in data transformations.

- Use system-generated unique keys for your data. This allows you to integrate data together from different data sources

- Use a central repository to store the data about the databases and data transformations used in the OLAP system. This will assist in automating the incorporation of new data sources and new software tools.

- Reach the broadest level of agreement on the meaning on the structures used in the system. Chapter 4 discusses the use of conformed dimensions and conformed measures. If you can achieve a broad level of agreement within your organization on the definition of these structures, it will be much easier to extend your system into new areas.

Note

This key to a successful OLAP system, "An Extensible Development Strategy," is often in conflict with the previous key, "Rapid Initial Development." The conflict comes in the need to have agreement on data structures and data definitions. Reaching agreement on these issues isn't a technical challenge. It's an organizational, managerial, political challenge.

If you wait until everybody agrees on all the data structures, you'll probably never get started. If you start development before everybody agrees, you will likely have problems later on when you're extending your system to new departments or merging your OLAP system with an OLAP system that somebody else has built somewhere else.

You sometimes won't be able to fully resolve this conflict. In areas where there is some disagreement, try to keep your options open. If, for example, there's disagreement between different departments on the date that should be used for a completed sale, try to include all the possibilities in your data structure. If there's disagreement on how a value such as profit should be calculated, try to include all the factors that are needed for the calculations, so it can be calculated either way. If there's disagreement on the level of detail that should be kept, try to keep the lowest level. It can always be summarized later.

Keeping the Smallest Detail

I always recommend that people keep all the data they could possibly imagine using and also keep it at the lowest level of detail. I can think of too many cases where the users thought they'd never be interested in using a certain field for analysis, only to be asking for it the next month. Users can't imagine all the possibilities of OLAP browsing until they actually start doing it.

If you summarize data, you can take away some of your best possibilities for OLAP. If, for example, you summarize sales by product by store by day, then you'll never be able to do customer analysis or market basket analysis (analysis of what products tend to be purchased at the same time). Sales data is much more valuable when it is saved at the lowest possible, atomic level—the individual detail of each individual sale.

Still, there are exceptions to this rule. I was once making the argument for keeping the lowest level of detail when a person who worked for an electrical utility company asked if that would be appropriate for them. This company had the capability to read the electrical usage of its customers in 15-minute intervals or less. Should that level of detail be saved for OLAP browsing?

I don't know. In situations where data is continuous, the atomic level of data does not exist. You have to make a decision to divide the continuous flow of reality into discrete pieces of data. I recommend that, in making this decision, you consider the smallest possible level that an analyst might want to consider and then divide the data into pieces one order of magnitude smaller than that.

There will come a time in the future when someone will find a reason to examine even smaller units of data.

--tep

Assuring Quality Data

It can be difficult to assure the quality of data in an OLAP system. Many operational systems do not check for the validity of data as it is being entered. Data can be missing, data can be inconsistent, and data can be incorrect.

The process of data improvement is often called data cleansing. Your data might need to be cleansed in a number of different ways. Here are some typical examples:

- Customers, suppliers, or other data entities could have duplicate records in the source systems. These duplicate records could have the same spelling or they could be spelled differently. They could have the same or different addresses. The process of removing duplicate records is sometimes called deduplicating or *deduping*.

- A specialized form of deduping is needed when records are being assigned to households. The benefits of householding are discussed in Chapter 2, "How OLAP Is Used in the Real World."

- Codes are sometimes used in place of data values. Different source systems often use different codes. The replacement of these diverse codes with consistent values is sometimes called *data homogenization*.

- Fields can be used for more than one purpose or for an undocumented purpose. If possible, the different pieces of information should be extracted and placed in separate fields.

- Required data fields can be empty or null in some of the records. If they can be determined, the correct values should be inserted into these fields. If not, the data should have a consistent way of displaying unknown values.

- Sometimes when operators don't know the value for a field they're required to enter, they will enter a meaningless string of characters. These invalid strings must be removed from the data.

- The data could be incorrect. If the data values can be checked against other known data values, some of these errors can be removed. An obvious place this can be done is in checking the zip codes of addresses against a list of actual zip codes.

There are three general courses of action you can take when you are data cleansing:

- Change the data in the source database and implement procedures in the data collection process so the same errors will not occur again.

- Change the data as it is being entered into the OLAP system. Chapter 4 discusses several places where you can cleanse the data in an OLAP system.

- Leave the inaccurate or incomplete data as it is. Document the data problems so that the users are aware of the situation.

It's certainly best to fix the data problems in the source systems, but that's often not practical. If you are setting up a data transformation to load data into your OLAP system, it can be convenient to include data cleansing as a part of the transformation process. Unfortunately, it is also often necessary to leave some inaccurate or incomplete data in the OLAP system. Data cleansing is costly and time-consuming. The quality of the data can usually be improved, but the data will probably still not be perfect.

I like the way the data-cleansing process is summarized in *The Data Warehouse Lifecycle Toolkit*. The authors suggest that the goal of data cleansing is "the truth, the whole truth, and nothing but the truth." You want to give your users as much data as you can. You want the data to be as accurate as possible, considering the resources you have available. Data problems should be thoroughly documented. If you make data corrections or fill in missing data values, that data cleansing process also should be fully documented so that your users can judge the accuracy of the data for themselves.

Providing Informative Metadata

The data elements in an OLAP system need to be understandable. This data is often consolidated from several different source systems. OLAP users need to have an explanation of what it is they are viewing. They should have access to information about where this data has come from and how it has been modified along the way. They also need to know how accurate the data is and what has been done to correct data inconsistencies.

Metadata provides the description of the various data elements. Metadata is the data about the data. It's helpful to distinguish two kinds of metadata in an OLAP system:

Technical metadata fully describes the data from a technical perspective.

Business metadata is the description of the data provided to the person browsing the OLAP data.

Metadata is discussed in Chapter 13, "Using the Respository in Data Transformations," and Chapter 34, "Metadata."

Maintaining a Secure System

Many people have suggested that data-warehousing system designers often do not pay enough attention to security issues. The goal of OLAP and data warehousing is to get information to users. Security concerns can sometimes make that job more difficult. A database administrator might not want to give permission to access some of the data that is needed for the OLAP system. One department might not want to have its data visible to users in other departments.

An OLAP system must be able to accommodate a variety of security requirements. It may have some data that can be visible to the public, other data that is visible only to employees in a particular department, and other data only visible to employees with special permissions. Security needs to be considered for all of the following:

- Data transformations
- Data storage
- Data archiving
- OLAP cube creation
- Access to OLAP cubes for browsing
- Storage of the OLAP cubes

Security is discussed several times in this book. Security in the Data Transformation Services is discussed in Chapter 9, "DTS Packages." Security of cubes when working with the OLAP Manager is discussed in Chapter 17, "Partitioning Cubes and Administering OLAP Server." These issues are discussed most fully in Chapter 33, "OLAP Security."

Using Adequate Hardware

The processes of transforming data and building OLAP cubes are both processor- and memory-intensive. Unless you have a very small project, you should consider dedicating hardware resources to your OLAP system.

Here are some of the hardware issues to consider:

- The SQL Server 7.0 database server engine, the Data Transformation Services, and the OLAP Services are all multithreaded applications. They will run faster on machines with multiple processors.
- SQL Server and OLAP Services both benefit from a large amount of memory. Queries will run significantly faster if all the data they are accessing is already in the data cache.
- OLAP clients also benefit from having a large amount of memory because they can cache cube data locally.
- OLAP systems can require large amounts of disk space. Space is needed for the data staging area, the relational data marts, and the OLAP cubes. If space and adequate processing time are available, a greater number of cube aggregations can be created, which increases the browsing speed for end users.
- Take into account what hardware you are going to use for archiving data. If you have more than 100 GB of data, you might want to contemplate archiving some of the older, less-used data into a cheaper, less-accessible storage system.
- You will need hardware for backing up your system.

Summary

This chapter started with a discussion of the importance of having a business purpose for your OLAP system. I think it's appropriate to end the chapter with that same theme.

There's a lot of work and expense involved in setting up an OLAP project. There's a lot of learning involved with the new concepts and the new tools. You need a reason to make the effort to set up an OLAP system.

Your reason must be a business purpose. If your business needs its data transformed into information, then you have a reason to create an OLAP system. If your business analysts see the million convenient spreadsheets available in an OLAP tool and they need the information in those spreadsheets to run the business effectively, then you have a reason to create an OLAP system. You have a reason to work through the rest of this book—to learn how to use Data Transformation Services, OLAP Services, OLAP clients, and MDX. Your business has the reason to invest the money and the effort it will take to make OLAP a reality for you.

3

THE KEYS TO A
SUCCESSFUL
OLAP SYSTEM

Preparing Data
for OLAP

PART

II

IN THIS PART

CHAPTER 4

Enterprise Data Structure and Data Flow

by Tim Peterson

IN THIS CHAPTER

Before you can build OLAP cubes, you have to get your data ready for OLAP. The best way to start is to consider the big picture—the enterprise data structure for your organization.

In the days of centralized computing, organizations typically had a fairly simple data structure. A few applications generated data that was stored in a central location. With the rise of personal computers and client/server computing, the enterprise data structure became more diverse and fragmented. Many applications stored data in many different locations, and that data could be controlled by different departments.

One of the goals of the data warehousing movement has been to bring order to the chaos of diverse data. Various data warehousing practitioners have envisioned this organizing process in somewhat different ways. This chapter discusses the concepts and the strategies that have been proposed to bring conceptual order to the diversity of data reality.

The Inmonites and the Kimballites

Two of the most prominent data warehousing practitioners are Bill Inmon and Ralph Kimball. Bill Inmon has written several books, including the first book to use the term "data warehouse" back in 1992, *Building the Data Warehouse*. Ralph Kimball has written some popular data warehousing guides, including *The Data Warehouse Toolkit* in 1996.

Several years ago, people started referring to the followers of these two authorities as Inmonites and Kimballites. Both individuals have downplayed their differences, but the perception that there are two schools of data warehousing thought has persisted.

A couple of years ago, I heard Bill Inmon respond to a question about the differences between his views and Kimball's. In his reply, Inmon said there really weren't any differences. After all, how could Ralph or anyone else disagree with the completely obvious things he was saying about the structure of a data warehousing system?

I think there are some significant differences between Inmon and Kimball in their presentation of data warehousing reality. There are some different concepts and some different emphases. Here's a summary of the most important differences, based on two books both published in 1998:

> *Corporate Information Factory* by Bill Inmon, Claudia Imhoff, and Ryan Sousa
>
> *The Data Warehouse Lifecycle Toolkit* by Ralph Kimball, Laura Reeves, Margy Ross, and Warren Thornthwaite

Inmon describes the centralized data warehouse as the place where an enterprise achieves its data integration. Kimball describes a data warehouse bus architecture that unifies data marts as the marts share common dimensions and measures on the data warehouse bus.

Inmon states that the data warehouse must be the source of data for all the data marts. Kimball describes the data warehouse as a virtual concept. When you look at all the data marts along the data warehouse bus, you are seeing the data warehouse.

Inmon insists that the data warehouse must have a normalized design, while Kimball insists that the data warehouse must not be normalized.

Inmon's enterprise data structure includes a component called an operational data store (ODS). The ODS is similar to a data warehouse but is used for the enterprise's immediate operational needs for data analysis. Kimball does not believe that the ODS should be a separate structure. The immediate data needs should be either provided by the operational systems themselves or from the data warehouse directly.

It seems to me, in general, that the primary goal of an Inmonite data warehouse is to have an enterprisewide, unified source of data. On the other hand, the primary goal of a Kimballite data warehouse is to make data available for analysis to the users as quickly and as efficiently as possible.

Should you be a Kimballite or an Inmonite? Bill Inmon was the first person who introduced data warehousing to me. His views have helped me see the big picture of an enterprise's information structure. But I think Ralph Kimball's views are more practical for the majority of data warehousing situations. I think the goal of getting the data to the users quickly and efficiently far outweighs the goal of a fully unified enterprise data structure.

--tep

Looking at the Whole Enterprise

Bill Inmon, Ralph Kimball, and other data warehousing authors all emphasize the need to look at all the data in the enterprise when planning a data warehousing system. It's possible to build data marts outside of a comprehensive data warehousing system. This kind of strategy is discussed later in this chapter as the non-architected data marts. Although this may be the best option in certain limited situations, the overall success of data warehousing requires a more comprehensive view.

Your data warehousing system should have a business purpose. Your system should take into consideration all the needs of the enterprise. You should consider all the possible sources of data.

Business Drivers for the Enterprise

The first question in building any decision support system should be the question of business purpose. These are a few of the many appropriate questions:

- Why do you need a data warehouse?
- Why do you need OLAP browsing?
- How will this software benefit the business?
- Will this system help the company increase sales?
- Will this software help the company cut costs?
- Will this software help the company provide better customer service?
- Will this software help the company remain competitive?
- How will this software help the company be more efficient?
- Is the potential benefit of this software worth the potential cost of developing it?

Considering All the Needs of the Enterprise

You have determined there is a business purpose that can drive development of a data warehousing system for your company. The following questions focus on the needs of the whole enterprise:

- How many departments would benefit from a data warehousing system?
- In what ways is data currently being used for business analysis?
- Can the data warehousing system be designed so that it can be used for multiple purposes?

Data in the Enterprise

It's also important to take an enterprise perspective on the available data, with questions like these:

- What are all the potential sources of data for the data warehousing system?
- What operational systems have data that could be used? How often does that data get changed? How often is new data added?
- What historical or archived data could be included in the system? How accessible is that data?

- What external sources of data could be included in the system?
- How reliable is the data in each source?
- How much data cleansing will have to be done for each source?
- What data will need to be merged?
- What is the total volume of data that will be used?

OLTP Systems and OLAP Systems

On-Line Transaction Processing (OLTP) systems are the applications that run an organization's basic operations. They are the order-taking programs, the systems that store information from cash registers, and the software that runs the factory. OLTP systems use data in the following ways:

- They generate data in the ongoing process of conducting business.
- They store data in a format that optimizes the retrieval and updating of individual records.
- They generate a limited number of reports that summarize the events that have taken place.

OLAP systems are created for the purpose of analyzing an organization's data.

- They import data from the OLTP systems and other sources, including sources from outside of the organization.
- They store data in a format that optimizes analytical queries. These queries often summarize information from many records and many tables.
- The goal of an OLAP system is to provide a browsing tool that allows an analyst to view the data from all useful perspectives.

The easiest place to run analytical queries is directly on the databases used by the OLTP systems. This rarely provides adequate performance, for the following reasons:

- OLTP systems have to deliver results as quickly as possible. As an order is being processed, both the customer and the order-taker are wasting valuable time. Analytical queries can significantly slow OLTP systems because they are using processor time and memory resources. Both the online processing and the analytical queries can also be slowed by record-locking conflicts between them.
- Databases used for OLTP are usually normalized, a process that optimizes a database for the retrieval and updating of individual records. In a normalized database each piece of information is only stored once, so it can be updated in a single location. The analytical queries used in OLAP run much more quickly when the

database schema is designed for querying multiple records. This design strategy is called dimensional modeling and the result is referred to as a star schema. This OLAP modeling strategy is described in Chapter 5, "The Star Schema."

- OLTP systems work more efficiently when the tables have a limited number of targeted indexes. Each index has to be modified with every data modification. Having too many indexes can slow the normal OLTP process of updating records. OLAP systems work best when there are a lot of indexes. The data is not being updated as it is being analyzed, so there is no problem wasting time in the process of updating a large number of indexes.

- You don't want to calculate summary values in an OLTP system, because the individual records are changing and each time a record changes, all the summary values will have to be changed. You want a lot of summarization in an OLAP system, so that the aggregated values can be presented to the analyst immediately, no matter what combination of factors the analyst chooses to view.

- The most efficient data store for an OLTP system is a relational database system. This type of database system has, in fact, been developed specifically to meet the goals of OLTP systems. The data used for an OLAP system can be stored in a relational database system, but you also have the possibility of gaining performance by storing the data in multidimensional data structures. Multidimensional database systems have been created to meet the specialized needs of analytical querying, as is used by OLAP.

The goals for data manipulation are very different for OLTP and for OLAP. It is possible to use the same database for both OLTP and OLAP queries, but it is impossible to optimize a single database for both. There are different strategies for optimizing these two types of queries and those strategies are in opposition to each other. If you need the best possible performance from both your OLTP system and your OLAP system, you will have to separate them into individual databases. The remainder of this chapter and the next chapter explain how to do that.

The Data Warehouse and the Data Marts

The data warehouse and the data marts are defined and used in distinct ways in different data warehousing systems. It's hard to define these words in a way that is meaningful but is also broad enough to cover all the ways people use them. Here is an attempt at some definitions:

- Data warehouse—The collection of all the data in the enterprise that is used for business analysis queries.

- Data mart—A smaller collection of data that is used for the business analysis queries of a single department or workgroup.

The rest of this chapter discusses the various pieces of the corporate information factory, with special focus on an effective implementation of OLAP in the enterprise.

When I Use a Word...

I have been involved in data warehousing conversations where there seemed to be very little communication between the participants. The problem often seems to be in the definition of the terms that are used.

Bill Inmon has had a powerful influence in the world of data warehousing. There are many people who have accepted his definition of data warehousing as the right and true way to use that term. It's good to know Inmon's data warehouse definition (which is described in the next section) because there are people who will say that you don't really have a data warehouse unless you meet the specifications of his definition.

There are also problems with other words that are used in this field. I have heard people use the terms "star schema" and "dimensional modeling" in ways totally different from the way they really should be used—in my very humble opinion, of course.

The term data mart is probably the most confusing word of all. What is a data mart? How is a data mart different from a data warehouse? Is it just a matter of size? Does a data mart become what it is because of a particular relationship to a data warehouse? Can you have a data mart without a data warehouse? If you do, how do you know it's a data mart and not just a small data warehouse? Are data warehouses good and data marts bad? Or is it the other way around?

I will make an attempt to address these questions in the next section. But I think it's good to keep a proper perspective on the limitation of words. People will use words to mean what they want those words to mean.

My favorite source of linguistic perspective is Humpty Dumpty in Lewis Carroll's book *Through the Looking-Glass.*

"I don't know what you mean by 'glory,'" Alice said.

Humpty Dumpty smiled contemptuously. "Of course you don't—till I tell you. I meant 'there's a nice knock-down argument for you!'"

"But 'glory' doesn't mean 'a nice knock-down argument,'" Alice objected.

continues

> "When *I* use a word," Humpty Dumpty said, in rather a scornful tone, "it means just what I choose it to mean—neither more nor less."
>
> *--tep*

Enterprise Data Structure for Business Analysis

There are an unlimited number of ways that an enterprise can structure its data for use in business analysis. The three enterprise data structures described in this section are representative examples of all the possibilities:

- The non-architected structure—Independent data marts. This is the data warehousing structure that develops in the absence of a plan.
- The dependent data mart structure—The central data warehouse with dependent data marts. This is the structure that has been proposed by Bill Inmon.
- The data warehouse bus structure—Data marts along the data warehouse bus. This is Ralph Kimball's vision of data warehousing reality.

The data warehouse and the data mart are viewed differently in each of these enterprise structures. For all three of these structures, the cubes built with Microsoft's OLAP Services can be seen in two different ways:

- The cubes can themselves be considered to be the data marts.
- The data marts can be built as tables in the relational database, and the cubes can be based on the data marts.

The Non-Architected Structure

In the non-architected business analysis structure there is no data warehouse. Independent data marts are created. There is no attempt to view the data from the various data marts in an enterprise-wide perspective. Figure 4.1 illustrates the data marts of a non-architected business analysis structure, with OLAP cubes based on those data marts.

Figure 4.2 shows the same structure with the cubes themselves being the data marts.

This structure is appealing because it is the quickest to build. You don't have to reach agreement with people in other departments about the definition of your data elements. When vendors talk about building a data mart in three weeks or three days or three hours, they are talking about an independent data mart in a non-architected business analysis structure.

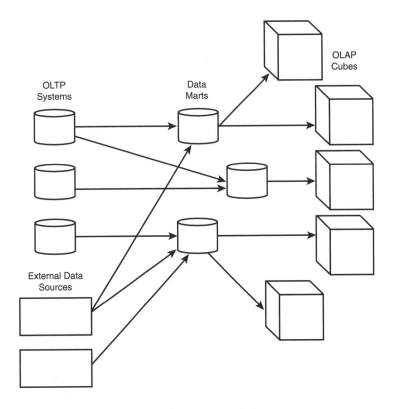

The drawback of this structure is that it falls short of a goal that many people have had for data warehousing—a unified presentation of enterprise data. It is often very difficult to merge data marts that have been created independently. If you ever want to view your data together with data from other departments, you will have to transform your data so that it fits into one of the other structures. Unfortunately, much of the work you have done for your original data mart will probably not transfer into the new architecture.

The Dependent Data Mart Structure

Bill Inmon coined the term data warehouse. He saw the need to transfer data from the diverse OLTP systems into a centralized place where that data could be used for analysis. His definition of the data warehouse has been widely used in the data warehousing industry. By this definition, a data warehouse contains data with the following characteristics:

- Subject-oriented—Data is organized in subject areas that have relevance for the analyst. An OLTP system might divide data by different regions or different time periods. A data warehouse stores the same information by subject areas such as orders, shipments, accounts, customers, and products.

FIGURE 4.2

OLAP cubes can be independent data marts in the non-architected structure.

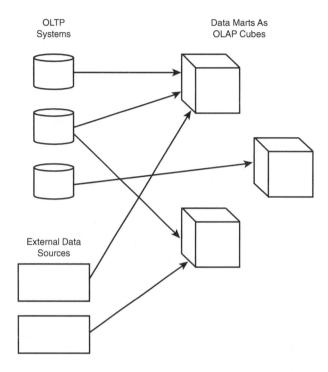

- Integrated—Data is brought into the data warehouse from many sources. As the data warehouse is loaded, the inconsistencies in the data from those various sources is removed. The data warehouse has data that has been integrated into a single format.

- Time-variant—Data in a data warehouse always has a time component. The data warehouse contains information that represents the state of business at a particular time. Inventory information, for example, would be stored as a series of data snapshots, each snapshot representing the state of the inventory at that particular time.

- Nonvolatile—Data in a data warehouse is not changed. When an address changes in an operational system, many applications will simply overwrite the previous record. In a data warehouse, the data is entered and never changed, except to correct errors. In the case of a changed address, both the new and old addresses will be left in the warehouse, each reflecting the state of reality at a particular point in time.

- Detailed and summarized—The data warehouse stores the atomic level of detailed data that describes the operation of the business. The data warehouse also contains summarized views of the same data.

Bill Inmon describes data marts as subsets of the data warehouse that are built for individual departments. The data marts receive their data from the data warehouse. Each data mart is optimized for the analysis needs of the particular department for which it was created. Figure 4.3 shows the relationship between the data warehouse and the data marts.

FIGURE 4.3

The data marts are derived from the data warehouse in the dependent data marts structure.

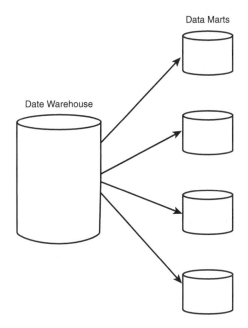

The Data Warehouse Bus Structure
==================================

The Data Warehouse Bus Structure

I was first introduced to the concept of the data warehouse bus by *The Data Warehouse Lifecycle Toolkit*. In this model, each data mart is a part of the data warehouse because it is connected to the data warehouse bus. This bus contains the common data elements that are used by all the data marts. These common elements consist of the conformed dimensions and the conformed measures that have been defined for the enterprise. Conformed dimensions and measures are discussed in Chapter 5. If each data mart uses these common elements, you will be able to query all of the data marts together. The data marts, the data warehouse, and the data warehouse bus are shown in Figure 4.4.

When you use the data warehouse bus architecture, the data warehouse is more of a virtual reality than a physical reality. All the data marts could be located on one server and, if they were, the data warehouse would be on that server. More often, though, the data marts would be located on servers spread across the enterprise and the data warehouse

FIGURE 4.4

The bus contains the common elements in the data marts when using the data warehouse bus structure.

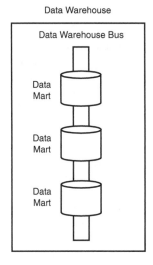

Data Warehouse

would only have a virtual existence, being nothing more than the totality of all the individual data marts.

You can consider cubes created by OLAP Services either to be the data marts themselves (see Figure 4.5) or you can create the data marts in SQL Server and build the cubes on top of them (see Figure 4.6). In both cases, you can use the shared dimensions that are available in the OLAP database structure for the conformed dimensions.

FIGURE 4.5

OLAP cubes can be the data marts on the data warehouse bus.

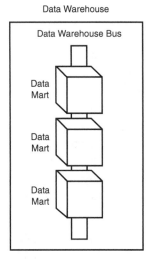

Data Warehouse

FIGURE 4.6

OLAP cubes can be based on SQL Server data marts. Both the cubes and their source data marts have conformed dimensions.

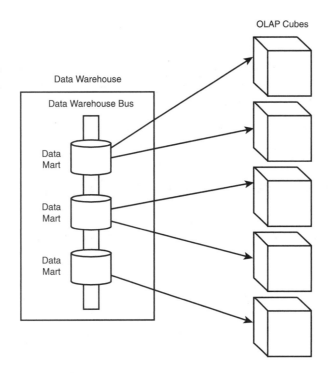

Choosing a Data Structure for Business Analysis

I have already indicated my general preference for the data warehouse bus architecture. My preference for this architecture is influenced by the following factors:

- This model strikes a good balance between centralized control and localized flexibility.

- Data marts can be delivered more quickly with this model than with the dependent data mart model, because the whole data warehouse structure does not have to be built before the data marts are created.

- The shared data structures along the bus eliminate the repeated effort expended when building multiple data marts in a non-architected structure.

- The conformed dimensions along the bus fit very well with the shared dimension and virtual cube capabilities of Microsoft's OLAP Services.

There are a couple of situations in which the non-architected structure is the best.

- When rapid development of an individual data mart is more important than the development of the enterprise data warehousing system.

- When OLAP browsing is needed for a set of data that has almost nothing in common with any other sets of data that need to be analyzed.

The dependent data mart structure could be considered in situations where it is important or convenient to maintain centralized control of the data. Centralized control could be preferable in the following situations:

- Data is being collected from several remote locations.
- A high level of security needs to be maintained.

Assembling Data for OLAP

There are three different ways that you can assemble data for OLAP analysis. I am going to discuss these three ways from the perspective of the data warehouse bus architecture. If you use a different data warehousing structure, you will have the same three options for assembling your data.

- Build the OLAP cubes directly from operational data. This is the quickest and least flexible solution.
- Load the operational data into the staging area and build the OLAP cubes from that data.
- Load the operational data into the staging area and load the data marts from that data. Build the OLAP cubes from the data in the data marts. This solution provides the best opportunity for data cleansing. It also is the best way to integrate data from multiple sources.

In the first two strategies, the cubes themselves are the data marts. In the third strategy the data marts are built as sets of tables in the relational database and the OLAP cubes are seen as a method of presenting the data in the mart to the end-user.

The two most important SQL Server 7.0 tools for moving data are replication and the Data Transformation Services.

You can use replication in situations where the data is already in SQL Server and is not being changed as it is moved. This could be the best method for moving data from the operational system into the staging area.

The Data Transformation Services (DTS) is used in other situations:

- If data needs to be transformed or cleansed as it is being moved. Transformations can be done as the data is loaded into the staging area, but it would be more common to transform the data after it is in the staging area or is being moved from the staging area to the data marts.

- If data is being loaded from flat files. DTS has a Bulk Insert Task that is designed for this task. The functionality of this task is also available in the Transact-SQL Bulk Insert statement and the bcp utility program.
- If data is being loaded from other types of data sources. DTS is able to import data from any data store that has an OLE DB provider or an ODBC driver.

The use of DTS is discussed in Chapters 6 through 13.

Figure 4.7 shows replication and DTS being used to load data into the data staging area, DTS being used to load the data marts, and OLAP Services being used to create OLAP cubes from the data marts.

FIGURE 4.7

SQL Server 7.0 tools are used to move data in the data warehouse bus architecture.

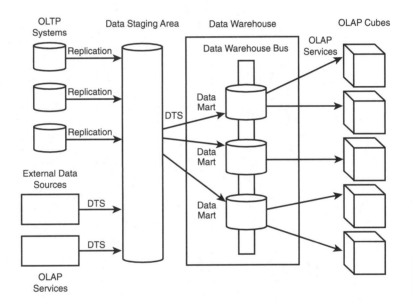

Delivering the OLAP Data to the Users

OLAP client applications are needed to bring the OLAP data to the end-users. Different types of clients such as the following can be used to deliver the data:

- Client applications that access OLAP cubes across the network.
- Mobile clients, using cubes that have been loaded on to each local machine.
- Internet, intranet, or extranet clients that access the cubes through an Internet browser.

The data in a data warehousing system will usually be used for more than just OLAP browsing. Users will also need

- Applications that generate reports.

- Business management applications that use analytical data to help manage a business more effectively.

- Data mining tools that examine the data to find complex patterns that could be missed by an analyst. Data mining tools are discussed in a section later in this chapter.

Figure 4.8 shows the client applications with the data warehouse bus system.

FIGURE 4.8

A variety of client applications can use the data from a data warehousing system.

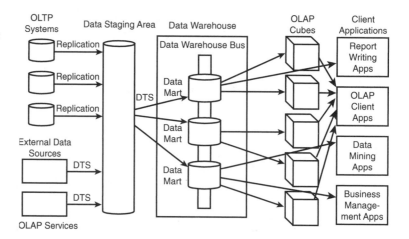

Metadata

Metadata is involved with each stage of the movement of data in the enterprise.

- The existing metadata is updated. DTS, for example, can automatically update the metadata as it is transferring data. If there has been any change in the data structures of the databases being used by DTS, those changes will be made to the metadata in the Repository.

- The existing metadata is used to transform the data. The processes that are moving and transforming the data need information to properly match data fields and data types.

- The metadata is used by the client applications. The following types of information can be provided to the end-users:

Data definition

Data sources

Data transformations

Data reliability

- Metadata describing the data movement is recorded while the data is being moved.

DTS has a significant advantage over replication and other data movement tools in a data-warehousing environment in the handling of metadata. DTS Package information can be stored in the Microsoft Repository. When it is, the metadata describing the data movement is automatically saved each time the package is executed. The use of metadata with DTS is described in Chapter 13, "Using the Repository in Data Transformations."

Figure 4.9 shows the metadata being created, updated, and used in the process of moving data.

FIGURE 4.9

The Microsoft Repository can be used to store the metadata that is needed in data movement.

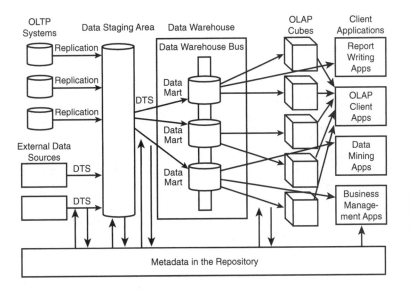

Monitoring Data Use and Archiving Data

Data warehousing systems often need a method of archiving historical data. Data needs to be moved out of the data warehouse into an archive for two reasons:

- There is too much data to fit in the space available for online storage.
- The large amount of data in the data warehouse or data mart is hurting performance.

Before archiving data, it can be helpful to monitor the data that is actually being used. Most data warehouses contain a large amount of data that is rarely or never accessed. A monitoring tool can identify what data can be archived without interfering with ongoing OLAP browsing capabilities.

Data that is being archived is usually saved in a summarized form in the online storage.

If there's a problem with not having enough storage space for the cube structures created by OLAP Services, you can use cube partitioning to reduce the space. Divide your cube into separate partitions, with the data that is rarely used in a separate partition. Use the HOLAP or ROLAP storage method with few or no aggregations. The cube structures will take virtually no space if there are no aggregations. Your performance when browsing this data will be very slow, but that will not have much of an impact on your users if they are rarely using that portion of the data. Cube partitioning is described in Chapter 17, "Partitioning Cubes and Administering OLAP Server."

Partitioning cubes to save storage space can be used in place of or in addition to archiving. This strategy is usually a lot easier to implement and can be cheaper than archiving. If there's a need to reduce the amount of base data in online storage, archiving is the only option.

> **Note**
>
> Data warehouses can become huge. Keeping the atomic level of detail can result in a massive amount of data after a period of time. Additional space can be consumed by storing summarized views of the data. The largest amount of space is consumed by indexes—sometimes 5 to 10 times the amount of space taken by the data itself.
>
> What's the resulting size of the data warehouse? For WalMart, a company that has invested hundreds of millions of dollars in data warehousing, the size is 30 terabytes.

Data Mining

Data mining is the process of examining data to find complex patterns that could be missed by an analyst. The following are some of the things that you can do with data mining:

- Perform market basket analysis, the process of examining the products that are typically sold together.

- Find likely candidates for cross-selling, products that particular customers are likely to purchase because of previous purchasing patterns.

- Identify profitable and unprofitable customers.

- Search for unusual insurance claims patterns that could indicate fraud.

- Analyze stock market behavior.

- Develop algorithms for predicting future inventory needs.

Data mining is a complex topic that does not receive a full discussion in this book. However, it is important to be aware of the opportunities for data mining when you are developing an OLAP system. You may want to include fields in your data mart for the purpose of using them later in data mining applications.

Summary

As you consider the best way to organize your enterprise data, remember your business goals. Your company needs a corporate information factory to provide the data for critical corporate decisions. If you build OLAP cubes directly on OLTP data or if you choose to use a non-architected data warehousing system, you can achieve quicker results. Those choices, though, could result in limited flexibility in the future. The business goal is to build the type of solution that will be most effective in meeting your organization's particular needs.

The next chapter teaches you how to convert your relational database into the dimensional schema used in OLAP. The following chapters tell how to use DTS, the tool that Microsoft has provided with SQL Server 7.0 for moving and transforming data in a data warehousing environment.

4

ENTERPRISE DATA
STRUCTURE AND
DATA FLOW

The Star Schema

by Tim Peterson

CHAPTER 5

It's easy to open the OLAP Manager and make a cube from FoodMart, the sample database that is installed with OLAP Services. It's easy because FoodMart has the design of a star schema, the logical structure for OLAP.

It's a lot harder when you have to use the OLAP Manager with data from a typical normalized database. The tables in a relational database present data in a two-dimensional view. These two-dimensional structures must be transformed into multidimensional structures. The star schema is the logical tool to use for this task.

The goal of this book is to teach you how to use Microsoft's OLAP tools. The goal of this chapter is to teach you multidimensional modeling. You can use the star schema to design multidimensional reality in a relational database. When you have done that, your data will be ready for OLAP.

Many concepts are used in multidimensional modeling. Here are some of the ones that are covered in this chapter:

- The fact table and the dimension tables
- The use of primary and foreign keys in star schema tables
- Measures and whether a measure is fully additive, semi-additive, or non-additive
- Fact-less facts
- Fields that hold the levels of the dimension hierarchy
- Multiple hierarchies within one dimension
- Fields used as attributes of a dimension
- Time dimensions and lineage dimensions
- Degenerate dimensions and junk dimensions
- Dividing dimensions to minimize updating
- Using a weighting table in a dimension
- Snowflaking the dimension tables
- Type 1, 2, and 3 strategies for updating dimension records

The rules used for data modeling in the star schema differ from the rules used in a relational database. Multidimensional Modeling Concepts boxes are used throughout this chapter to give you a summarized view of these different rules.

Multidimensional Modeling Concept #1: The Star Schema

The star schema is a logical tool for designing multidimensional reality in a relational database.

The Design of the Star

The star schema receives its name from its appearance. It has several tables radiating out from a central core table, as shown in Figure 5.1.

FIGURE 5.1

A star schema has a core table in the center. Several other tables radiate out from the center to form the points of the star. This example of a star schema is adapted from FoodMart, the sample database included with the OLAP server.

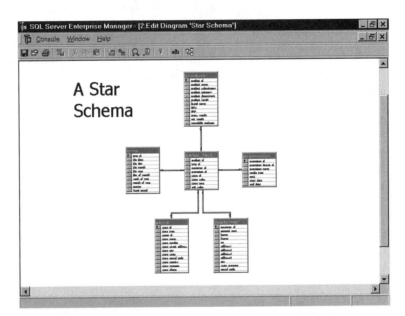

The fact table is at the core of the star schema. This table stores the actual data that is analyzed in OLAP. Here are the kinds of facts you could put in a fact table:

- The total number of items sold
- The dollar amount of the sale
- The dollar amount of discounts on the item sold
- The cost of the item sold
- The profit on the item sold
- The number of minutes taken for an activity
- The account balance before the transaction
- The account balance after the transaction
- The number of days the item was on the shelf
- The number of days from order to delivery
- The number of units produced

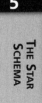

Multidimensional Modeling Concept #2: The Fact Table

The fact table is at the core of the star schema and holds the actual data that will be analyzed with OLAP.

The tables at the points of the star are called dimension tables. These tables provide all the different perspectives from which the facts are going to be viewed. Each dimension table will become one or more dimensions in the OLAP cube. Here are some possible dimension tables:

- Time
- Product
- Supplier
- Store Location
- Household
- Customer
- Customer Demographic
- Promotion
- Status
- Customer Representative
- Employee

Multidimensional Modeling Concept #3: The Dimension Tables

The dimension tables are the points of the star, providing a variety of perspectives for viewing data with OLAP.

Differences Between Relational Modeling and Multidimensional Modeling

There are several differences between data modeling as it's normally applied in relational databases and the special multidimensional data modeling that prepares data for OLAP analysis. Star schema modeling doesn't follow the normal rules of data modeling. Here are some of the differences:

- Relational models can be very complex. The proper application of the rules of normalization can result in a schema with hundreds of tables that have long chains of relationships among them.

- Star schemas are very simple. In the basic star schema design there are no chains of relationships. Each of the dimension tables has a direct relationship (primary key to foreign key) with the fact table.

- The same data can be modeled in many different ways using relational modeling. Normal data modeling is quite flexible.

- The star schema has a rigid structure. It must be rigid because the tables, relationships, and fields in a star schema all have a particular mapping to the multidimensional structure of an OLAP cube.

- One of the goals of relational modeling is to conform to the rules of normalization. In a normalized database each data value is stored only once.

- Star schemas are radically denormalized. The dimension tables have a high number of repeated values in their fields.

- Standard relational models are optimized for On Line Transaction Processing. OLTP needs the ability to efficiently update data. This is provided in a normalized database that has each value stored only once.

- Star schemas are optimized for On Line Analytical Processing. OLAP needs the ability to retrieve data efficiently. Efficient data retrieval requires a minimum number of joins. This is provided with the simple structure of relationships in a star schema, where each dimension table is only a single join away from the fact table.

The rules for multidimensional modeling are different because the goals are different.

The goal of standard relational modeling is to provide a database that is optimized for efficient data modification. The goal of multidimensional modeling is to provide a database optimized for data retrieval.

Multidimensional modeling prepares data for OLAP.

Multidimensional Modeling Concept #4: Data Modeling Rules

The rules followed in multidimensional modeling vary considerably from the rules followed in standard relational modeling. The rules are different because the goal is different—rapid data retrieval rather than efficient updating.

> **Note**
>
> This chapter discusses how to derive fact tables and dimension tables from a relational database. You need to understand all the information in this chapter if you are going to build a star schema in a SQL Server database.
>
> There are times when you may be using the OLAP Server to build cubes directly from your relational data. You still need to understand most of what this chapter says about star schemas. All OLAP cubes are based on the star schema structure, even if that star schema isn't physically created in a database.
>
> Microsoft has made it easy to create cubes directly from relational data. You can join tables in the OLAP Manager as you are creating your dimensions. But if your fact table is based on more than one table in your relational database, you have to make some preparations before you use the OLAP Manager. The easiest thing to do is to create a SQL Server view that can then be the basis for the fact table in your cube.

The Fact Table

The fact table is the heart of the star schema. This one table typically contains 97% to 99.9% of the space used by the entire star because it holds the records of the individual events that are stored in the star schema.

Fact tables are designed for growth, with new records being added weekly, daily, or even hourly. For example, the nightly import could add a new record in the Sales Fact table for each line item of each sale during the previous day.

Fact table records are never updated, unless a mistake is being corrected or a schema change is being made. Fact tables records are never deleted, except when old records are being archived.

> **Multidimensional Modeling Concept #5: Fact Table Characteristics**
>
> The fact table contains 97% to 99.9% of the total data in the star schema. New fact records are added regularly and existing fact records are left unchanged.

The fact table has two kinds of fields—*keys* and *measures*.

- The fields containing the facts in the fact table are called *measures*. These fields are nearly always numeric.

- There is a foreign *key* field in the fact table for each of the dimension tables.

Multidimensional Modeling Concept #6: Measures

The fields that hold the factual data in a fact table are called measures.

The fact table usually does not have a separate field for a primary key. The primary key is a composite of all the foreign keys.

If you use a primary key constraint on the fact table, you are required to set all the foreign key fields to not allow null values. Even if you don't use this constraint, it's still a good idea to not allow null values in the fact table's key fields. You can eliminate nulls by using the following procedure:

1. Identify the various situations that could result in a null value in one of the key fields of the fact table. For each dimension, consider whether it's possible that a value could be unknown or might not be applicable.

2. Add a record for each one of these situations into the appropriate dimension table. You could have a sales fact table with a key to a customer representative dimension. If there are times when the customer representative is unknown, you could put a record in the dimension table with Unknown in all its fields. If you have sales that are not associated with a particular customer representative, you could put a separate record in the dimension table with Not Applicable as the data in all its fields.

3. Use the key values for these new records in the fact table records that would have had null values.

Multidimensional Modeling Concept #7: Fact Table Keys

A fact table has a foreign key field for each of the dimension tables. The fact table's primary key is a composite of all the foreign keys. Null values should not be allowed in these key fields.

A simple fact table is shown in Figure 5.2.

FIGURE 5.2

The two basic types of fields in a fact table are keys and measures.

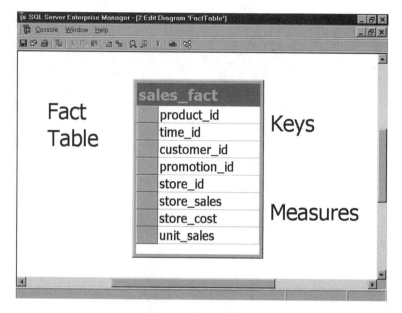

> **Tip**
>
> In most fact tables, unique values are guaranteed by the combination of dimension foreign keys. If that is not the case, I recommend adding an extra field to assure uniqueness in the fact table. This extra field could be a key value from the source data schema, as discussed later in this chapter in the section on degenerate dimensions.

Fully Additive, Semi-Additive, and Non-Additive Measures

The most important characteristic of a measure is the degree to which it can be aggregated. If you can't roll up your measures into meaningful values, you lose the whole purpose of OLAP. Measures are fully additive, semi-additive, or non-additive.

Here is a simple example to illustrate the three kinds of additivity.

In this example you are analyzing the business of selling apples at four stores for a period of three days. You have an AppleSales star schema with two dimension tables—time and store.

The records in the time dimension are shown in Table 1.

TABLE 5.1 Sample Data in the Time Dimension

TimePK	DayOfWeek
1	Monday
2	Tuesday
3	Wednesday

The records in the store dimension are shown in Table 2.

TABLE 5.2 Sample Data in the Store Dimension

StorePK	StoreLocation
1	Alexandria
2	Bloomington
3	Cottage Grove
4	Downsville

The fact table in this example has three measures:

- A fully additive measure—Apples sold
- A semi-additive measure—Apples in stock at beginning of day
- Non-additive measure—Average number of apples sold per sale

The records in the fact table are shown in Table 3.

TABLE 5.3 Sample Data in the Fact Table

TimeFK	StoreFK	ApplesSold	ApplesInStock	AvgApplesPerSale
1	1	100	875	6.0
1	2	75	1000	7.5
1	3	200	500	6.5
1	4	80	800	7.7
2	1	150	845	7.9
2	2	105	1000	6.5
2	3	40	600	8.0
2	4	100	900	7.3
3	1	120	1000	8.0

continues

TABLE 5.3 continued

TimeFK	StoreFK	ApplesSold	ApplesInStock	AvgApplesPerSale
3	2	125	900	5.5
3	3	200	600	8.3
3	4	120	800	6.5

ApplesSold is fully additive because you can aggregate over all (in this case, both) dimensions. You can add (aggregate) the values in the appropriate records and receive accurate answers to the following questions:

- How many apples were sold on each day for all the stores?

  Monday: 455, Tuesday: 395, Wednesday: 565

- How many apples were sold at each store for the whole time period?

  Alexandria: 370, Bloomington: 305, Cottage Grove: 440, Downsville: 300

- How many apples were sold at all the stores for the whole time period?

  1,415

Note that we can add (aggregate) all the answers from either of the first two questions to get the correct answer to the third question: 455+395+565=1,415 and 370+305+440+300=1,415.

ApplesSold is semi-additive because you can aggregate over the store dimension, but not over the time dimension. Consider the corresponding three questions:

- How many apples were in stock on each day for all the stores?

  Monday: 3,175, Tuesday: 3,345, Wednesday: 3,300

- How many apples were in stock at each store for the whole time period?

  Alexandria: 2720, Bloomington: 2900, Cottage Grove: 1700???, Downsville: 2500

- How many apples were in stock at all the stores for the whole time period?

  9820

The first question is answered correctly, but the values do not add correctly for the second and third questions. The problem is that many of the apples that are in stock at a store on Monday are still in stock on Tuesday. When the aggregation takes place over time, many apples are counted twice or even three times.

AvgApplesPerSale is non-additive. There is no logical situation in which these numbers have any significance when added together.

- What was the average number of apples sold per sale on each day for all the stores?

  Monday: 27.7, Tuesday: 29.7, Wednesday: 28.3

- What was the average number of apples sold per sale at each store for the whole time period?

  Alexandria: 21.9, Bloomington: 19.5, Cottage Grove: 22.8, Downsville: 21.5

- What was the average number of apples sold per sale at all the stores for the whole time period?

  85.7

None of the questions is answered correctly. Average values, along with most other calculated values, are totally non-additive.

Fully Additive Measures

The ideal measure in a star schema is fully additive. A *fully additive measure* will aggregate to a correct value no matter what levels and dimensions are queried. Fully additive measures can be pre-aggregated when cubes are created, so that the most rapid OLAP browsing can be achieved.

Multidimensional Modeling Concept #8: Fully Additive Measure

A fully additive measure can be aggregated correctly across all dimensions.

Semi-Additive Measures

A *semi-additive measure* is one that aggregates correctly with certain combinations of dimensions and levels, but fails to aggregate correctly with other combinations.

A typical example of a semi-additive measure is shown in Figure 5.3. The Inventory Star Schema has four dimensions—Time, Product, Warehouse, and Supplier. The fact table has one inventory record for each day. Two of the measures, Quantity Received and Quantity Shipped are fully additive. The other measure, Quantity On Hand, is only semi-additive. This measure will not aggregate correctly across the time dimension.

FIGURE 5.3

Quantity On Hand is a semi-additive measure because it can be aggregated for most dimensions but cannot be aggregated across the time dimension.

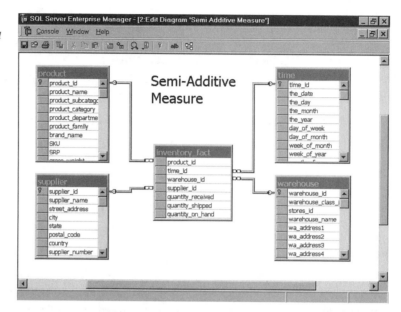

Multidimensional Modeling Concept #9: Semi-Additive Measure

A semi-additive measure can be aggregated correctly across some dimensions but cannot be added across at least one dimension. Inventory facts, such as quantity on hand, are semi-additive because they cannot be added across the time dimension.

Semi-additive measures can be replaced with calculated measures when they are used in OLAP browsing. The Quantity on Hand measure could be changed into Average Quantity on Hand Per Day. This average value is non-additive and cannot be aggregated. But once it has been calculated, Average Quantity on Hand Per Day can be successfully queried across all the dimensions. This strategy is discussed more thoroughly in the section on calculated measures in Chapter 15, "Creating Cubes."

Non-Additive Measures

A non-additive measure is one that will not aggregate across any dimension. Average values, percentages, and most other measures based on mathematical formulas are non-additive.

It is never useful to store the values of non-additive measures in a star schema or to pre-aggregate these measures in a cube. For example, the average of 5 and 15 is 10. The average of 20, 30, and 40 is 30. The combined average of 10 and 30 is 20, but the average of these two sets of numbers is 22. All non-additive measures must be directly calculated from the data at every particular intersection of dimensions, levels, and attributes.

It can be very useful to pre-aggregate the values that make up non-additive measures. If you know the total of a group of numbers at every point and the count of those numbers at every point, you can derive the average by doing a simple division of those two pre-aggregated values.

> **Multidimensional Modeling Concept #10: Non-Additive Measure**
>
> A non-additive measure cannot be aggregated correctly across any dimension. Average values and many other values derived from calculations are non-additive.

> **Note**
>
> The values that are pre-aggregated for the purpose of later calculating a non-additive measure are often not very useful when viewed by themselves. There are times when these values can be misleading. In the OLAP Manager, you can set the Is Internal property to Yes to prevent a measure from being seen by OLAP clients.

Fact-Less Facts

A *fact-less fact* is a measure that doesn't have a value in the source data. It exists because the intersection of dimensions has meaning in itself.

You could build a star schema that has a Customer Contact Table and dimensions for Time, Customer, Employee, Product, Initiation Type, Resolution Type, and Comment as shown in Figure 5.4. The only fact in this table is the count of the customer contact. The value for this fact is 1 for every record in the fact table.

There are two ways to implement fact-less facts. You can add a field to the fact table that is always filled with a value of 1. This field can then be counted or summed like any other measure. The other method is to define the fact-less fact as the COUNT of any of the non-null fields in the fact table.

FIGURE 5.4

Count of Customer Contacts is a fact-less fact because its only significance is that it exists. It can have no other possible value than 1.

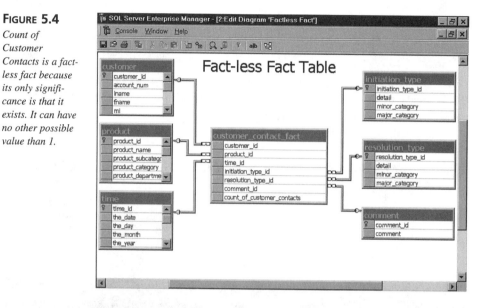

Tip

I can't see any reason not to use this second strategy when building a star schema for use with the Microsoft OLAP Server. The OLAP Manager allows you to define a fact-less fact as a regular measure and have it pre-aggregated like any other measure. You also can define a fact-less fact as a calculated measure and not have its values be pre-aggregated. Once they're defined, these fact-less facts are treated like regular measures. I don't think there's any performance improvement by creating a fact-less fact as a separate field.

Multidimensional Modeling Concept #11: Fact-less Facts

A fact-less fact is a measure that always has a value of 1.

The Dimension Tables

By themselves, the facts in a fact table would have little value. The dimension tables provide the variety of perspectives from which the facts become interesting.

Compared to the fact table, the dimension tables are nearly always very small. For example, there could be a Sales data mart with the following numbers of records in the tables:

- Store Dimension—One record for each store in this chain—14 records
- Promotion Dimension—One record for each different type of promotion—45 records
- Time Dimension—One record for each day over a two-year period—730 records
- Employee Dimension—One record for each employee—2,500 records
- Product Dimension—One record for each product—31,000 records
- Customer Dimension—One record for each customer—47,000 records
- Combined total for all of these dimension records—81,289 records
- Sales Fact Table—One record for each line item of each sale over a two-year period—60,000,000

While the fact table always has more records being added to it, the dimension tables are stable. Some of them, like the time dimension, are created and then rarely changed. Others, such as the employee and customer dimension, are slowly growing.

Dimension table records can be updated, but those updates can complicate OLAP cube creation and browsing. Various strategies for updating dimension tables are discussed at the end of this chapter. One of the goals of star schema design is to minimize the need for dimension table updates.

> **Multidimensional Modeling Concept #12: Dimension Table Characteristics**
>
> Dimension tables are relatively small. Records in dimension tables can be updated, but good star schema design minimizes the need for those updates.

Dimension tables have three kinds of fields—a *primary key* field, *hierarchy level* fields, and *attribute fields*, as shown in Figure 5.5. The following sections describe each of these types of fields.

The Primary Key in a Dimension Table

The primary key of a dimension table should be a single field with an integer data type.

FIGURE 5.5

A typical dimension table has a primary key, two to five hierarchy level fields, and 10 to 70 attribute fields.

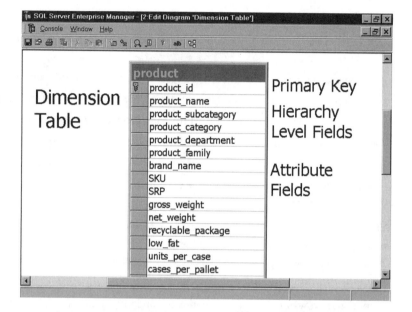

Tip

Fields with a smallint data type (2-byte signed) are often adequate for the dimension table primary keys. You will not generally be concerned about the size of your dimension tables, but using these half-size key values can significantly reduce the size of the fact tables, which can get very large. Smaller key fields also make indexes work more efficiently. But don't use the 2-byte integer unless you are absolutely certain that it will be adequate now and in the future.

Primary key values from the source data should not be used as the key values in the dimension tables. All key values should be generated automatically.

Creating New Keys for Your Star Schemas

You may be tempted to use key values that already exist in your source database to define the relationships between the fact and dimension tables in your star schema.

Don't do it! One of the primary purposes of building a data warehouse is to integrate data from various sources. If you use keys that exist in one of your sources in your star schema, it will be very hard to import other data in the future.

There are other advantages to generating new key values. You can guarantee that those key values will be unique. You also can gain performance by using the smallest possible data type for the joins in your star schema—a 4-byte or a 2-byte integer.

The consensus among data warehousing professionals is to always create new keys to define the relationships in a star schema.

You can keep existing key fields in your star schema, if you want to, as attributes in the dimension table. Existing key values can also become degenerate dimensions, which are discussed later in this chapter.

This advice does not apply in situations where you are building a logical star schema so that you can query your relational data with OLAP. In those cases the source key values are all you have, so use them!

--tep

Tip

The Identity property creates an auto-incrementing field. SQL Server provides a number of convenient tools to use with the Identity. There's a global system variable called `@@identity`, which holds the most recent value generated by an identity field on your connection. You can use `@@identity` when you are adding new dimension records and need the dimension primary key value for your new fact record. You also have the ability to use `Identity_Insert` to overrule the automatic generation of a new value.

Multidimensional Modeling Concept #13: Dimension Table Primary Keys

Integer values should be used as the keys of the dimension tables. Key values from the source system should not be used as keys in a data warehouse.

Levels of the Dimension Hierarchy

The levels of the dimension hierarchy are modeled in the star schema with individual fields in the dimension tables. The names of these fields are the levels of the hierarchy.

> ### Multidimensional Modeling Concept #14: Dimension Table Hierarchy Fields
>
> Dimension tables have a field for each level of the dimension's hierarchy. The names of these fields are typically used as the names of the levels in the hierarchy.

Table 5.4 shows what data look likes in the hierarchy fields of a product dimension table. This example is adapted from the FoodMart sample database. The field names are the four levels of the product hierarchy. Note all the repeated values in the fields at the higher levels of the hierarchy.

TABLE 5.4 Sample Data in the Time Dimension

Family	Category	Department	Product_name
Food	Canned Foods	Canned Shrimp	Blue Label Canned Shrimp
Food	Canned Foods	Canned Shrimp	Better Large Canned Shrimp
Food	Canned Foods	Canned Shrimp	Bravo Large Canned Shrimp
Food	Canned Foods	Canned Soup	Blue Label Vegetable Soup
Food	Canned Foods	Canned Soup	Blue Label Noodle Soup
Food	Canned Foods	Canned Soup	Better Regular Ramen Soup
Food	Canned Foods	Canned Soup	Better Turkey Noodle Soup
Food	Canned Foods	Canned Soup	Better Beef Soup
Food	Canned Foods	Canned Soup	Better Rice Soup
Food	Canned Foods	Canned Soup	Pleasant Noodle Soup

The data values placed in the hierarchy fields are called the members of each level of the hierarchy. In the data displayed in the previous example, the only member of the Family level is Food. The members in the Department level are Canned Shrimp and Canned Soup. The members in the Product Name level are Blue Label Canned Shrimp, Better Large Canned Shrimp, and so on.

> ### Multidimensional Modeling Concept #15: Members of a Level in a Hierarchy
>
> The data values in the hierarchy fields are the members of that particular level of the hierarchy.

One dimension table can have more than one dimension hierarchy stored in it. Dimensions often are viewed from a variety of different perspectives. Rather than choose one hierarchy over another, it is usually best to include multiple hierarchies. The fields containing the levels of multiple hierarchies in a dimension can be distinguished by using compound names such as Sales District, Marketing District, Sales Region, and Marketing Region.

Figure 5.6 shows a Location dimension table with two hierarchies, one for marketing and one for sales. At the two lowest levels, these hierarchies are the same—Neighborhood and City. But for State/Province, Region, and District, the hierarchies are different. This allows cities to be included with differing State/Provinces, the States/Provinces to be rolled up into different Regions, and the Regions to be rolled up into different Districts. At the highest level, Country, the two hierarchies come back together.

FIGURE 5.6

A dimension table with two hierarchies, one for the Sales department and one for the Marketing department. Note that both hierarchies use some of the same levels.

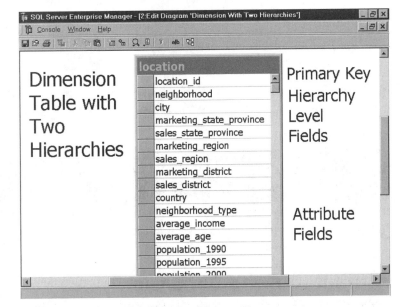

Note

Microsoft's OLAP Services has a significant (but poorly documented) difference between the server tools and the client tools in handling multiple dimensions within one hierarchy.

continues

When you use the client tools, ADO MX and the PivotTable Service, you can have multiple hierarchies for a dimension. In the ADO MX object model the Dimension object contains a Hierarchies collection. Each Hierarchy object contains a Levels collection.

When you use the OLAP server tools, the OLAP Manager and the Decision Support Objects (DSO), you can only create a single hierarchy per dimension. The DSO object model has a Dimension object that contains a Levels collection. This object model does not have a Hierarchy object.

But there is a way to work around this limitation on the server side. If you use a two-part naming convention for the dimension you create with the server tools, the client tools will recognize the first part of the name as the dimension and the second part of the name as the hierarchy.

To implement the example in Figure 5.6, create the two hierarchies in the OLAP Manager (as discussed in Chapter 15) as if they were completely separate dimensions. Give these dimensions the following two-part names:

Location.Sales

Location.Marketing

When you access your cube with the OLAP client tools, you will find one dimension, Location, that contains two hierarchies, Sales and Marketing.

Multidimensional Modeling Concept #16: Multiple Hierarchies in One Dimension Table

If a dimension has more than one hierarchy, fields for levels of both hierarchies should be included in the dimension table.

Attributes of the Dimension

Attribute fields give additional information about the members of a dimension. These fields are not part of the hierarchical structure of a dimension.

The attributes in a product dimension could include fields such as Size, Weight, Package Type, Color, Units Per Case, Height, and Width. Attributes most often use one of the string data types, but they can also use numeric, datetime, or Boolean data types.

Attributes usually apply to members at the lowest level of the dimension, but they can be used at higher levels. For example, if there is a geographic dimension where District is one of the levels, District Population could be included as an attribute for that level of the dimension.

Rich, detailed attributes add value to the star schema. Each attribute provides a new perspective from which the cube can be browsed.

Some of the attribute fields in the Customer dimension of the FoodMart sample database are

- Total Children
- Number Children at Home
- Marital Status
- Education
- Yearly Income
- Gender

Figure 5.7 shows all these Customer fields from FoodMart being used for OLAP browsing in the Preview Cube Data view of the OLAP Manager's Cube Editor. Gender and Education are shown in the rows, while yearly income is shown in the columns. A particular marital status (M), Number of Children at Home (3), and Total Children (3) have been picked in the list boxes in the slicer pane at the top of the screen. The Cube Editor is discussed in Chapter 15.

FIGURE 5.7

Various attribute fields of the Customer dimension are browsed in the OLAP Manager's Cube Editor.

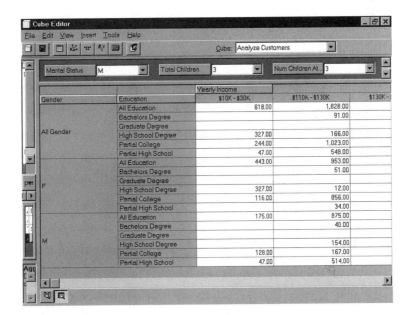

> ### Multidimensional Modeling Concept #17: Attribute Fields
>
> Attribute fields provide additional information about the members at one of the levels of the dimension's hierarchy.

The Time Dimension

Almost all star schemas have a time dimension. Data warehouse information is, by definition, gathered with respect to particular periods of time. The data reflects the state of reality at various times in history.

A time dimension often has more than one hierarchy built into it, because time can be aggregated in a variety of ways. The lowest level of the time hierarchy varies greatly. It could be the day, the shift, the hour, or even the minute. The lower levels would be included only if there were some valid reason to query at those levels of detail.

Significant attributes for a time dimension could include

- A Special Day field, which could have the names of various holidays and other days of significance for an organization
- A Selling Season field, which could have a particular company's self-defined significant periods in the year
- Boolean fields indicating special types of days, such as Is Weekend, Is Holiday, Is School Year, Is First Day Of Month, Is Last Day Of Month, and so on

Figure 5.8 shows part of a time dimension.

> ### Modeling Concept #18: Time Dimension
>
> Nearly all star schemas have a time dimension so that measures can be aggregated and compared for various time periods.

A Dimension for Data Lineage

Regardless of the subject matter of your data, it's a good idea to add an additional dimension table, called data lineage, to a star schema for tracking purposes. Lineage fields are stored in a star schema so that the transformation process used to create each record can be identified. Data transformation packages are often changed over time. The lineage variables produced by the Data Transformation Service (DTS) are an essential

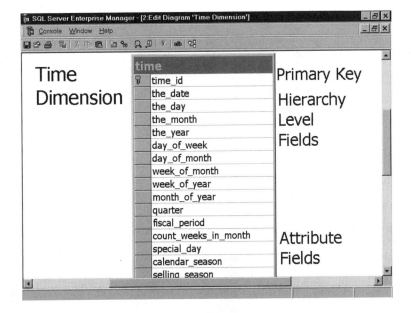

FIGURE 5.8

A time dimension is nearly always included in a star schema.

part of the technical metadata needed to fully document the creation of star schema data. If you store these variables with the data that has been transformed, you are able to identify the version and the execution time of the DTS Package that created each record.

Figure 5.9 shows a data lineage dimension, which would have one record for each table receiving new records in one execution of a particular DTS Package. The two DTS lineage variables (lineage_full and lineage_short) fully identify the transformation. You can retrieve additional information about a transformation and the databases involved with that transformation from the Repository, if you know the values of the lineage variables.

> **Note**
>
> Each record in the fact table would, of course, have a foreign key value tying it to the Data Lineage dimension. A foreign key to the Data Lineage dimension should also be used in all dimension tables that are receiving new records, so that the lineage of each of the dimension records is preserved.

FIGURE 5.9

A data lineage dimension stores information about the data transformation that was used to load a particular record into the star schema.

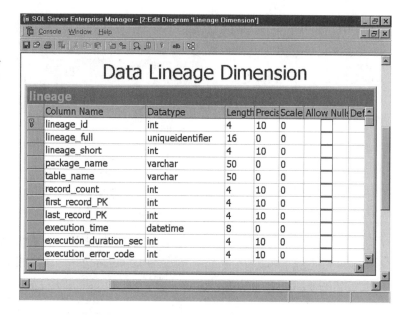

The DTS lineage variables consist of the following:

Variable	Data Type	Description
DTSLineage_Full	unique identifier	Uniquely identifies the DTS package version used for the transformation
DTSLineage_Short	integer (4-byte)	Uniquely identifies the date and time a DTS package was executed

Multidimensional Modeling Concept #19: Lineage Dimension

A lineage dimension table can be used in a star schema to keep track of the lineage variables. The lineage dimension provides the history for each record in the star schema's tables.

The storage of lineage variables and the use of DTS Package metadata are discussed more fully in Chapter 13, "Using the Repository in Data Transformation."

Degenerate Dimensions

A *degenerate dimension* is a field that should be its own dimension, but is allowed to remain as a field in the fact table, because it's the only piece of information for that dimension.

The most common degenerate dimension is a key value from the table in the source database that contains the same level of detail as you have chosen to store in the fact table. Key values are important because they provide a way to tie the star schema back into its source database.

Multidimensional Modeling Concept #20: Degenerate Dimension

A single field that is not a part of any dimension can be included in the fact table of your star schema as a degenerate dimension.

Junk Dimensions

OLAP's multidimensional perspective is the natural method of analyzing business data. There are many kinds of information that fit very naturally into a multidimensional schema, with hierarchies and levels, drilling up and drilling down.

Unfortunately, there are usually also some pieces of data that are left over after the fact table and the dimension-tables have been created. These separate pieces of unrelated information could each be used to create a separate dimension table or they could be left in the fact table as degenerate dimensions. But another possibility is to put these leftovers into their own separate dimension table. This strategy produces what is called a *junk dimension*.

A junk dimension typically does not have a hierarchy. All its fields are attributes. These attributes don't necessarily have some connection with one another.

Tip

Many relational data structures include fields for comments. A nonhierarchical dimension similar to a junk dimension can be used for comments. Because of the general star schema rule of not allowing null values, this dimension would include a record such as "None" or "No Comment" to be used for all those fact table records that did not have a comment.

There is no piece of data in this relational schema that has to be eliminated when you create a star schema. If you want to include a piece of data that doesn't seem to fit, put it in a junk dimension.

> **Multidimensional Modeling Concept #21: Junk Dimensions**
>
> If you have a set of fields that don't fit into any dimension, you can create a junk dimension, which is used to hold a group of unrelated attributes.

Dividing a Dimension to Manage Change

There are several strategies for handling change in dimension tables, which are discussed at the end of this chapter. The most important goal in managing change in dimensions is to avoid changing fields that are used for OLAP browsing. When you can identify a set of these fields where change is expected to occur, you can avoid change by moving those fields into a separate dimension.

The most obvious place this occurs is in a Customer dimension. The customer has a number of changeable attributes that could be of interest to the marketing department—income range, age, marital status, and so forth. You could track these changeable characteristics in a Customer Demography dimension. You could create a Customer Identity dimension that would have fields not being used for OLAP browsing, such as account number, name, and street address. Some fields, such as city, state, and country, could be put in both tables, because they are of interest in OLAP browsing and also logically fit with the address information in Customer Identity.

Figure 5.10 shows the divided Customer Dimension. Both the Customer Identity dimension and a Customer Demography dimension are treated as regular dimension tables, with their primary key values saved as foreign keys in the fact table. There is also a relationship saved between the two tables, indicating the current demographic description for each customer. When the demographic description for a customer changes, the only field that needs to be updated in the Customer Identity table is the Customer Demographic ID Current foreign key field. If that new demographic profile already exists in the Customer Demographic table, nothing else has to be done. If the change results in a new combination of demographic variables, then a new record is added to Customer Demographic.

FIGURE 5.10

The Customer dimension divided into two tables, to manage the frequent changes that normally take place in the Customer table. All frequently changing fields being used for multidimensional analysis have been moved to Customer Demographic. Other fields used in demographic analysis, such as gender, have also been moved to Customer Demographic.

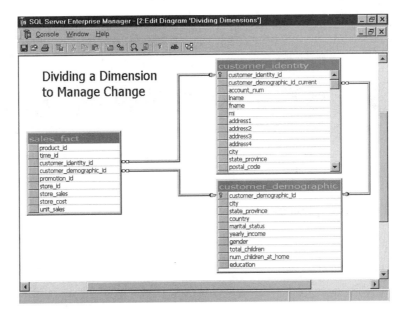

Multidimensional Modeling Concept #22: Dividing Dimensions to Reduce Change

The need to frequently update dimension records can be reduced by creating a new dimension out of the fields used for OLAP browsing that are most likely to change.

Creating a Weighting Table to Resolve Many-to-Many Relationships from Facts to Dimensions

A *weighting table* helps in situations where one fact table record is associated with more than one dimension table record. A product could be included in more than one promotion at the same time. The foreign key in the fact table points to a set of records in the weighting table—one record for each of the promotions in effect. These weighting table records, in turn, would point to a table containing the actual promotion records.

The weighting table has a field that assigns a weighting factor to each of the records in the set. The weighting factor allows the star to be queried in two different ways. The

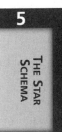

relative impact of each promotion can be determined by including the weighting factor in aggregates. The total usage of particular promotions can be determined by ignoring the weighting factor when calculating the aggregates.

> **Tip**
>
> When I create a cube based on a star schema that has a dimension with a weighting table, I make two separate dimensions out of that dimension—one new dimension includes the weighting factor and the other ignores it.

Table 5.5 is an example of the data entered into a weighting table.

TABLE 5.5   Sample Data for a Weighting Table

Promotion_group_id	promotion_id	weighting_factor
0	0	1.00
1	1	.25
1	10	.25
1	13	.25
1	20	.25
2	1	1.00
3	2	1.00
4	1	.50
4	2	.50
5	1	.75
5	2	.25
6	1	.334
6	5	.333
6	10	.333

The sum of the weighting factors for a particular group must equal 1.00. A weighting factor of 1.00 is assigned to groups that have only one element. Promotion groups 4 and 5 illustrate a situation in which two different groups have the same members but differ in the relative weight given to those members.

When using a weighting table, you usually need one other additional table. A particular group of weighting records could be used by several different records in the fact table.

This results in a many-to-many relationship between the fact table and the weighting table.

Figure 5.11 shows this many-to-many relationship being resolved by a join table called *promotion_group*, which has only one field—the primary key for the group of records that are being weighted together. If the join table were omitted, it would be impossible to use constraints to enforce the proper integrity between the fact table and the weighting table.

FIGURE 5.11

A weighting table is used to attach one fact record to several records in a dimension. The influence of each element in the dimension is fully additive if the weighting factor is included.

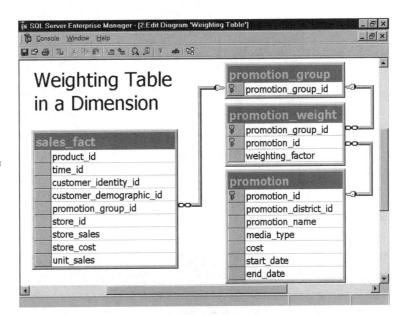

Multidimensional Modeling Concept #23: Using a Weighting Table

A weighting table is used to resolve many-to-many relationships between the fact table and a dimension table and to allow for the relative contribution of different dimension members to be accurately assigned in aggregations.

Snowflaking the Dimension Tables

One of the strategies in building the dimensions of a star schema is a technique called *snowflaking*. In snowflaking, some of the repeated fields in the dimension tables are broken off into separate tables with a one-to-many relationship back to the dimension table. Figure 5.12 shows snowflaking in the levels of the dimension hierarchy.

FIGURE **5.12**

Snowflaking is a modification that normalizes some of the repeated fields in the basic star schema.

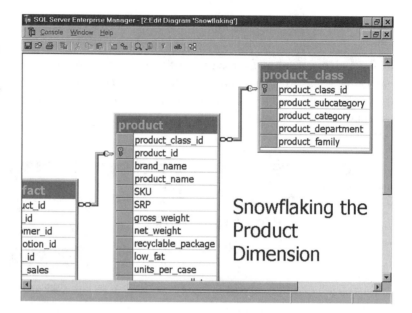

Snowflaking reduces data storage space by eliminating repeated fields. This really isn't much of an advantage, though, because the dimension tables are taking up only a very small portion of the star schema's storage space.

> **Note**
>
> I don't use snowflaking in my star schema designs. I don't think my multidimensional models are improved by adding a little normalization back into them. But if you want to snowflake, the OLAP Manager is designed to assist you in joining your snowflaked tables back into a unified dimension. This is extremely useful when building a cube on top of a relational schema. The logical star schema must have a fact table physically created as a view, but that isn't necessary for the dimension tables. Just tell the OLAP Manager's Dimension Wizard you are using a snowflaked dimension, and you are allowed to join on-the-fly whatever tables you need. The Dimension Wizard is discussed in Chapter 15.

> **Multidimensional Modeling Concept #24: Snowflaking the Dimension Tables**
>
> Snowflaking is an optional design technique that normalizes or partially normalizes the fields holding the levels of the dimensions.

Deriving a Fact Table from a Relational Database

You are starting with an OLTP database with hundreds of tables joined with all kinds of relationships. You know that you want to build a multidimensional structure for your OLAP browsing. How do you map your existing tables and fields into a collection of star schemas? How do you move your data from a normalized database into the star schemas? How can you update your star schemas when changes take place in your OLTP system?

The place to start is at the heart of the star—with the facts.

> **Tip**
>
> The rest of this chapter focuses on the transformation of an existing relational database into a star schema. You are looking for the fields to include in your star schema. All this analysis needs to be done with an understanding of the business purpose for the OLAP browsing that you are creating. Be creative in finding data to include in your OLAP cubes, but don't fill your star schema with data that is irrelevant to your particular users.

Choosing the Measures

Some of the fields you choose as measures in your star schema are obvious. If you want to build a star that examines sales data, you will want to include Sale Price as one of your measures, and this field will probably be evident in your source data.

After you have chosen the obvious measures for your star, you can look for others. Keep the following tips in mind for pulling out other fields:

- Consider other numeric fields in the same table as your obvious measures.
- Consider numeric fields in related tables.
- Look at combinations of numeric fields that could be used to calculate additional measures.
- Any field can be used to create a counted measure. Use the COUNT aggregate function and a GROUP BY clause in a SQL query.
- Date fields can be used as measures if they are used with MAX or MIN aggregation in your cube. Date fields can also be used to create calculated measures, such as the difference between two dates.

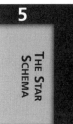

5

THE STAR
SCHEMA

- Consider averages and other calculated values that are non-additive. Include all the values that will be needed later to calculate these non-additive values.

- Consider including additional values so that semi-additive measures can be turned into calculated measures that can be evaluated from every dimension.

Choosing the Level of Summarization for the Measures

Measures can be used either with the same level of detail as in the source data or with some degree of summarization. Maintaining the greatest possible level of detail is critical in building a flexible OLAP system. Summarizing data is sometimes necessary to save storage space, but consider all the drawbacks:

- The users will not be able to drill down to the lowest level of the data.

- The connection between the star schema data and the source data is weakened. If one record in the star schema summarizes 15 records in the source data, it is almost impossible to make a direct connection back to those source records.

- The potential to browse from particular dimensions can be lost. If sales totals are aggregated in a star schema for a particular product per day, there will be no possibility of browsing along a customer dimension.

- Merging or joint querying of separate star schemas is much easier if the data is kept at the lowest level of detail. Summarized data is much more likely to lead to independent data marts that have no communication with each other.

- The possibilities for future data mining can be limited. Saving only the total sales per product per day eliminates the possibility of ever using the popular data mining strategy known as market basket analysis.

Summarizing data in a star schema makes the most sense for historical data. After a few years, the detail level of data often becomes much less frequently used. Old unused data can interfere with efficient access to current data. Move the detailed historical data into an off-line storage area, where it's available for the occasional need. Create a summarized form of the historical data for continued on-line use.

A cube created with summarized historical data can be joined together with cubes based on current data. You join cubes together by creating a virtual cube. As long as two or more cubes have common dimensions they can be joined together, even if they have a different degree of summarization.

> **Tip**
>
> If you want to summarize current data in the star schema to improve performance, one possibility is to create two stars that are identical except for the level of aggregation. But before going to the extra work of doing this, consider all the various possibilities for aggregation when using the OLAP Server. One of the primary benefits of using the OLAP Server is its ability to create aggregations, which are summarizations of the data on multiple levels. Whenever it's possible, I leave the work of summarization to the OLAP Server.

> **Multidimensional Modeling Concept #25: Level of Detail in the Fact Table**
>
> It is usually best to keep the lowest possible level of detail in the fact table. A summarized version of the fact table data is often kept online when older data is archived.

Calculating Measures

In addition to summarizing data, there are many possibilities for calculating and storing fully additive measures as a part of the star schema structure. The following are some measures that work well:

- Profit as the difference between the Purchase Cost and the Selling Cost.
- The change in the level of inventory from one time to the next.
- Actual Price as the product of Sales Price and Percent Discount.
- The difference between two dates, as in Ship Date less Order Date.

> **Tip**
>
> I create most of my calculated measures when I create my cubes rather than when I create my star schemas. The OLAP Server provides many opportunities for calculating measures: when creating measures, when creating calculated members, and in the PivotTable Services. Calculating measures in a star schema is usually beneficial only when the fields used in the calculation are themselves not being included in the star.

> **Multidimensional Modeling Concept #26: Using Calculated Measures**
>
> Calculated data can be used in measures in a fact table. Before you calculate values, consider the range of possibilities provided for calculating measures with OLAP Services.

Adding Fact Table Records

Most star schemas have a time dimension and new records are usually loaded into a star schema for a particular range of time.

The most important issue in adding new records into the star schema is to determine what records have not been previously loaded. This determination is straightforward if the records have a sequential key value that is saved in the star schema or if the records are always loaded from a particular time period, such as the previous day.

> **Note**
>
> If it's impossible to distinguish between new records and those that have been previously loaded, the fact table has to be emptied and rebuilt with every import.

Updating Fact Table Records

You typically do not update fact table records. If data changes over time, you still want a record of the reality at previous times. The unchanging fact table records give you that sense of history.

These are the special situations when you update a fact table:

- There is an error in the data in the fact table and you are making a correction.
- You are adding a new dimension table. You are inserting an additional key value into all the existing fact records for that new measure.
- You are adding a new measure. You are adding a value for that measure to all the existing fact records.
- You are changing the level of detail in the records of one of the dimension tables. This change requires some of the foreign key values in the fact table to be changed.

> **Caution**
>
> Making these kinds of changes to a fact table can be very difficult, especially changes resulting from a different level of detail in a dimension table. It might be impossible to update the fact table without going back and reloading it from the source data.
>
> The most difficult change to make in a star schema is increasing the level of detail in the fact table. That kind of change almost always requires a total rebuilding of the fact table and rewriting the programs that are loading the fact table. I recommend, as I did earlier, that you use the lowest level of detail possible in your fact table.

Deriving the Dimension Tables from a Relational Database

As you've learned from the preceding sections, the fact table provides the information and the dimension tables provide the perspectives from which to view the information. You can create dimension table fields from almost all the fields in the source database—including the fields that you have already used for measures. The only fields that are not candidates for consideration in creating the dimension tables are those fields that are being used exclusively for primary and foreign key relationships.

Conformed Dimensions

The most important overall strategy to remember when designing dimensions is to use conformed dimensions. A *conformed dimension* is a dimension that is shared by two or more star schemas. There are several advantages in using conformed dimensions:

- Using conformed dimension tables saves work and effort because one table is being used for several purposes.

- You can join fact tables from different star schemas if they have conformed dimensions.

- Most importantly, your data marts will fit together logically into a virtual data warehouse. People using different star schemas and the OLAP cubes based on them will all be viewing data with dimensions that have the same hierarchies, levels, and members.

> **Tip**
>
> Microsoft makes it very convenient to use conformed dimensions. They are called shared dimensions in the OLAP Manager. Whenever a new cube is created, shared dimensions can be added to the cube's structure by selecting them from a list. Shared dimensions are discussed in Chapter 15.

> **Multidimensional Modeling Concept #27: Conformed Dimensions**
>
> A conformed dimension is one that is used for more than one star schema. Fact tables that share conformed dimensions can be joined together.

Choosing the Dimensions

As with measures, some dimensions are fairly obvious. Time, product categorization, geographical location, and organizational structure are the most common. These types of dimensions have clear hierarchical relationships, with well-defined levels and members.

Other dimensions are more difficult to define. The goal is to include data elements within the dimension that have some logical connection to one another. If the fields don't have any connection, you have created a junk dimension. Junk dimensions are often useful, but they should always be your last choice.

You can bring fields from many tables to create a dimension. These fields are usually textual, although you can also use numeric fields. You import some fields directly from the source table. In other cases, especially when numeric or datetime fields are used, you transform the data from discrete points into specific ranges, as is illustrated later in this chapter.

Effective OLAP cubes usually have between 5 and 15 dimensions. If you have fewer than 5 dimensions, you're not giving your analysts many opportunities for browsing. If you have a very large number of dimensions, the amount of time and space needed for aggregations can become a problem.

Choosing the Hierarchies

Viewed from the top down, the ideal hierarchy is a set that can be divided into five to eight subsets. All of these subsets can themselves be divided into five to eight subsets. These neat divisions continue until you reach the basic level at the bottom of the hierarchy.

Note

The elements in the subsets at each level in an OLAP hierarchy are called members, as in "The members of the product category level of the product hierarchy are grocery, meat, produce, toiletries, and paper products."

Hierarchies are usually more confusing than that. Here are some of the challenges:

- There are times when two sales representatives could be working with one customer. If those sales representatives have different superiors, then the credit for those sales will have to be properly divided.

- There are products that can be categorized in different ways. You could have a level called Product Family, which would include members such as Food, Beverage, and Dry Goods. The next lower level could be called Product Category. Members of Product Category under Food could include Bread, Soups, and Dairy. Members under Beverage could include Soft Drinks, Beer, and Dairy. The Dairy category doesn't uniquely fit in either the Food family or the Beverage family.

- Some levels have too many members. If a country has 50 states, it will be hard to display all those members at the same time.

- Some levels have too few members or only one member. In a geographical hierarchy for store location, there may be five stores per city in five cities in one state, and only one store in one city in another state.

Tip

One thing to always remember when you are looking for hierarchies in existing data—they're often not there! Traditional relational systems have not handled the notion of data hierarchies very effectively. The construction of hierarchies is much more dependent on what the OLAP consumers actually want, rather than on what currently exists in the data. After the truly useful hierarchies have been established with the users, then the analyst can try to find out if those hierarchies exist in the data. It may be necessary to create some new lookup tables to use in the transformation process, so that particular records can be attached to the correct level of a newly defined or refined hierarchy. These lookup tables associate a particular member in the hierarchy with a particular combination of values that exists in the data.

Working together with the OLAP users and the source data, you create the hierarchical reality for the dimension. Sometimes there are too many members in a dimension, such as having 50 states in one country. When this happens you can create an intermediate level for the hierarchy. You can divide the states into 7 regions, each of which has 5 to 9 states. In doing this you would, of course, try to find groupings that make logical sense to the users.

> **Tip**
>
> You can create calculated dimensions with the MDX language that enable users to skip levels that have been defined in the hierarchies. For example, if you persuade your users to try 7 regions rather than always looking at 50 states, you can still provide them with a calculated measure that skips the region level and gives them all 50 states in one grouping. This is done with the MDX function Descendants. The following code gives all the descendants of the member USA at the level State. This provides your users with the same situation they had before you created the region level.
>
> ```
> Descendants(USA, State)
> ```

The other problem that almost always occurs in hierarchical design is the inconsistency in the definition of the membership of particular levels. This can sometimes be handled by defining more than one hierarchy within one definition. If the data has a fiscal year and a calendar year, include both a fiscal year hierarchy and a calendar year hierarchy. If a city is included in one region by the sales department and another region by the service department, create two geographical hierarchies for the customers, each of which reflects the actual reality for the particular department.

> **Tip**
>
> The messiness of dimensional design can seem to be one of the more subjective aspects of moving from a relational to a star schema—and it is. But this isn't a problem for the star schema—it's a problem for the relational databases that are being transformed. Star schema dimensional design can help an organization understand its own individual, particular hierarchical reality.

Adding Attribute Fields

Add as many attribute fields to each dimension as is possible and useful. Each additional field takes up very little storage space unless that field is used to create aggregate values when the cubes are created.

In the source data, the fields that are used for attributes often contain values that are abbreviated or encoded. An important part of the transformation process is to write out all the fields in the clearest possible way. This is especially important in situations where data is coming from multiple systems. It makes no sense to transform the codes from one system into the codes of a different system.

> **Tip**
>
> ID Numbers in the source system can often be the source of additional informa-tion for the attribute fields. In the days when data storage was expensive, much information was often encoded into identification numbers. You can extract this information as you build the star schema.

Using Ranges of Values

You can use attribute fields and dimension fields to hold ranges of data values. These ranges can then be used to divide a continuous reality into discrete segments.

A range of values could be used for any of the following:

- Salary ranges {[0–$20,000], [$20,001–$40,000], [$40,001–$60,000]}
- Age ranges {[0–9], [10–19], [20–29], [30–39]}
- Time/date ranges that fall outside the typical time hierarchy {[Jan 1–Jan 10], [Jan 11–Jan 20], [Jan 21–Jan 30]}
- Cost of products purchased {[$.01 $1.00], [$1.01 $2.00], [$2.01 $3.00]}

You can transform numerics from a discrete value in the source data to the appropriate range value. Use the CASE clause in a standard SQL statement:

```
SELECT 'SalaryRange' =
CASE
  WHEN (salary <=20000)
    THEN '0-20000'
  WHEN (salary> 20000 and salary <=40000)
    THEN '20001-40000'
  WHEN (salary> 40000 and salary <= 60000)
    THEN '40001-60000'
```

```
WHEN (salary> 60000)
   THEN '60001+'
WHEN (salary is null)
   THEN 'Salary Unknown'
END
from customer
```

> **Note**
>
> The previous SELECT statement handles the Is Null condition. There should be no null values in the star schema. Remember to handle all the possibilities with some reasonable string that informs the end user that a value is unknown.

One of the decisions that has to be made when converting discrete data into range data is whether or not the exact data value must be saved. If it must be, you can save it as a measure or as a degenerate dimension in the fact table.

When analysts find interesting data in the OLAP cube, they often drill down to lower levels. They want to understand the pieces of information that are coming together to create this interesting data. They often, in fact, want to see the exact details of the original data.

You can include all the information from the source data in your star schema. But if the data isn't going to be used in multidimensional analysis, it doesn't have much purpose being there. If it's possible to maintain a link with the original data, that link will provide the most efficient way to retrieve the exact values that have been summarized into ranges.

> **Tip**
>
> Here's one more encouraging reason for keeping the keys to link back to the original data. It may not be possible to maintain the link forever and for all users. But in the development and early usage stage of a data warehousing system, a link back to the base data can help build credibility for the whole project. Multidimensional analysis often brings out information in a new and unusual perspective. The analysts may need to be convinced that this information is accurate. A link back to the base data can help provide that proof. Of course, if you have made a mistake in your data transformation, a direct link back to the original data also becomes an indispensable debugging tool.

Multidimensional Modeling Concept #28: Converting Data to Ranges

Data is often transformed from discrete points into ranges because a fairly small number of range values is more effective in OLAP browsing than a large number of exact values. The best way to provide access to the exact values is to maintain a link back to the original data.

Adding Records to the Dimension Tables

Some dimension tables contain a set of records that continually expands. Other tables have a known set of records that can be entered in advance.

The customer dimension is an example of the first type. As new customers are entered into the OLTP system, those new customer records must also be added to the customer dimension of the star schema.

The time dimension is an example of a dimension that can have its records entered in advance because the values are already known. There is a gain in processing efficiency if they are added all at once.

Tip

The records in most junk dimensions could also all be added in advance—with one record included for every possible combination of all the constituent attributes. This strategy provides the quickest import of new records into the star schema, but it could also result in a large amount of wasted disk space. The possible junk dimension records could be in the millions, with only a few thousand actually being used. If that is the case, it is better to check the junk dimension table every time a new fact record is being added. If there is a corresponding record already in the junk dimension table, enter its primary key into the new fact record. Add that particular combination of values if it does not yet exist. Then add the appropriate foreign key of this new dimension record to the new record in the fact table.

Updating the Dimension Tables

Updating the dimension tables can be the hardest part of maintaining a star schema. There are three basic strategies for updating the data. These strategies are known as Type 1, Type 2, and Type 3.

Note

I first saw these three strategies referred to as Type 1, Type 2, and Type 3 in *The Data Warehouse Toolkit* by Ralph Kimball.

Tip

The best strategy for dealing with the updating of dimension tables is to avoid the update altogether—or if it can't be avoided, minimize it. That's the primary reason for splitting a dimension table into its more static and its more dynamic components, as discussed earlier in this chapter. Planning for dimension table updating in advance is a key component in building a maintainable data warehousing system.

Type 1 Changing Dimensions—Replace Data

The Type 1 strategy for handling a changing dimension is to change the dimension record when the underlying OLTP data changes. This is usually the best way in the following situations:

- You are changing the dimension record to correct an error that was previously made. This is the most obvious reason to use a Type 1 strategy, but it still could cause a problem. There could be reports that have been prepared based on the previous condition of the data. If those reports are now regenerated, they will change, and there won't be any apparent reason for those changes.

- You are changing a field that has no effect on multidimensional analysis. A person or a company could have a name change. If that change is made in the dimensional record, it won't affect the results of multidimensional analysis across any particular time period. Again, there is the problem of changes to previously prepared reports.

The Type 1 strategy is not appropriate for changes that affect multidimensional analysis:

- If the sales territory boundaries for a company are changed, you should not make those changes directly in the dimension records. The browsing of the historical data will no longer be accurate. Instead of seeing sales performance by the territories the way they were at a particular time, the user can only view the past results from the perspective of the current boundaries. The previous reality has been lost.

- If all the customer information is maintained in one table and a customer moves to a new income bracket, you should not make that change directly to the record.

Historical sales analysis will no longer be accurate. When a user is browsing the 1997 spending patterns of people in a $100,000 income bracket, individuals who are currently in that income bracket but had only half that income two years ago must not be included.

Caution

Writing a new value in any dimension table field that is used for multidimensional analysis will result in inaccurate OLAP browsing across the time dimension.

Multidimensional Modeling Concept #29: Type 1 Strategy for Handling Dimension Changes

The Type 1 strategy for handling dimension change is to replace the existing data with the new data. This strategy can result in incorrect information when browsing historical data.

Type 2 Changing Dimensions—Create New Record

The Type 2 strategy for handling a changing dimension is to create a new record with the changed information. The new record is used when new facts are entered into the fact table. The previous record remains in the table with its links to older facts in the fact table.

Browsing is maintained for the historical data, because the old combinations of facts and dimensions are not changed.

The challenge with using the Type 2 strategy is in building an accurate view of the past combined with the present. If you add a new record to the customer table when a customer moves into a new income record, you won't be able to view the organization's interactions with that single customer across time. The one customer will now appear theoretically as two customers. The accuracy of historical browsing is maintained, and no prepared reports are invalidated, but you can no longer accurately combine the past and the present.

> **Tip**
>
> You can join two customer records back into one record by creating a calculated member in the cube. It's easy to do this on an occasional basis. But it would be an administrative nightmare to do use this as the typical method of handling change.

> **Multidimensional Modeling Concept #30: Type 2 Strategy for Handling Dimension Changes**
>
> The Type 2 strategy for handling dimension change is to create a new record. This strategy maintains the accuracy of historical browsing, but makes it impossible to give a consistent view of data browsed across time.

Type 3 Changing Dimensions—Create Separate Fields

The Type 3 strategy calls for creating separate fields to record the previous and the present values for a piece of data. This is an impractical strategy for all but a few specialized situations.

Figure 5.13 shows a product dimension where a corporation is reorganizing its product hierarchy. The existing fields that hold the levels of the dimension are marked as Previous. The new levels of the hierarchy are marked with Current. The data can be browsed both from the perspective of the previous hierarchy and the perspective of the new hierarchy.

This strategy maintains both the accuracy of historical browsing and the validity of browsing across the past and the present. The problem with this solution is that it is unwieldy. If there are frequent changes to a dimension table, there are more complications. How many changes to one field should be kept? Should the date the change was made also be stored? Are the cube browsers going to be given both previous and current perspectives indefinitely? Are calculated measures going to be created to combine previous and current values in one view?

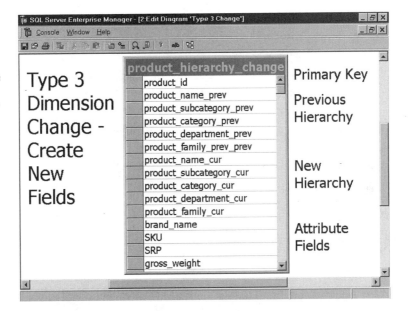

FIGURE 5.13
*In the Type 3
dimension change
strategy, new
fields are added in
the dimension
tables to hold cur-
rent and previous
values.*

Multidimensional Modeling Concept #31: Type 3 Strategy for Handling Dimension Changes

The Type 3 strategy for handling dimension change is to create separate fields for the old and the new data. This strategy maintains the accuracy of all OLAP browsing. The drawback with this strategy is that it is the most difficult to implement.

Changing Dimensions—A Comprehensive Strategy

The following list suggests a comprehensive strategy for handling changing dimensions:

1. Correct errors in the dimension tables by updating the record. This is a Type 1 strategy.

2. Move all fields that are being used for OLAP browsing into separate dimension tables unless they are guaranteed never to change or the impact on the accuracy of your OLAP aggregates will be negligible if they do change. Take care of changing dimensions ahead of time with creative star schema design. This is a proactive strategy.

5

THE STAR
SCHEMA

3. Update the dimension record for all attribute fields not being used for OLAP browsing. This could include fields used for names and some address information. This is a Type 1 strategy.

4. When there is a major reorganization of a dimension, to the extent that users want to see both the past and present perspectives, create separate fields to hold previous values and current values. This is a Type 3 strategy.

5. If you still have a problem with a changing field in a dimension table, write a new record and tie the two records together as a calculated member when you create your OLAP cube. But don't let this happen very often! This is a Type 2 strategy.

Summary

Designing the star schema is the central creative task in developing an OLAP system. It's the place to use your imagination. Find out what the users want. Look at what's in the data. Imagine the multidimensional possibilities for that data.

This chapter has outlined the logical path for moving from a relational database to a multidimensional structure ready for OLAP. The following chapters present SQL Server's tool for physically moving your data—the Data Transformation Services.

CHAPTER 6

Microsoft Data Transformation Services (DTS)

by Tim Peterson

IN THIS CHAPTER

Microsoft has created an integrated environment for extracting, moving, cleansing, and transforming data. This programming environment, the Data Transformation Services (DTS), is helping make SQL Server 7.0 a robust platform for OLAP and data warehousing.

The following DTS topics are introduced in this chapter and are discussed fully in the ensuing chapters:

The Capabilities of DTS

Data Transformation Services is a data pump that allows data to be transformed as it's being moved from a data source to a data destination. DTS provides a way to bring data together from a variety of data sources. The main components of DTS are shown in Figure 6.1.

FIGURE 6.1

The DTS data pump moves data from a source to a destination, with the option of transforming each record of data as it is being moved.

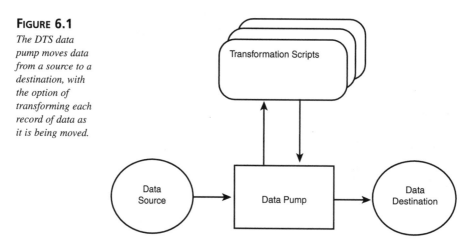

Here are some of the capabilities of DTS:

- You can use almost any kind of data store as the source or as the destination for the data.
- You can organize all the pieces of your data transformation process into one unit with a DTS package.
- You can perform complex data manipulation on each row of data using scripts written with VBScript, JScript, or PerlScript.
- You can update star schema dimension tables with a specific DTS tool—the Data-Driven Query task.
- You can import text file data into SQL Server at high speeds by using the Bulk Insert task.

Microsoft Data Transformation Services (DTS)

CHAPTER 6

117

6

MICROSOFT DATA
TRANSFORMATION
SERVICES (DTS)

- You can integrate existing data transformation programs into a DTS package.
- You can move SQL Server objects from one server to another.
- You can move database schema and data (but not indexes and other objects) from other relational databases into SQL Server.
- The capability for storing the lineage variables provides a historical record of how your data has been manipulated.
- The schema of the source databases being used by DTS can be stored in the Repository, and the metadata of these databases is available to client applications.
- DTS has a built-in package versioning system, which allows you to track modifications that are made to a transformation package.
- DTS is integrated into SQL Server and Visual Basic. You can control DTS from either the client or the server. DTS can call both server functions and client functions.
- Microsoft provides DTS as part of the SQL Server product, at no extra charge.

There are many others tools that can be used for importing, transforming, and manipulating data. Some of those tools are discussed in Chapter 14, "Third-Party Data Transformation and Repository Tools."

Sources and Destinations for Data

DTS solves the problem of connecting SQL Server to a variety of data sources. You can move data stored in a text file into an Oracle database. Data stored in Oracle can be transferred to Microsoft Access.

You can use any data store as the data source or the data destination, as long as you have an OLE DB provider or an ODBC driver for that particular data store. Use the data sources and destinations in any combination. Some of the DTS capabilities, such as the Bulk Insert task and the Transfer SQL Server Objects task, are written especially for SQL Server. But you can employ the core data transformation capability without having SQL Server as either the data source or the data destination.

> **Note**
>
> Microsoft is in the process of replacing ODBC with OLE DB. While ODBC provides connectivity to a wide variety of different relational database sources, OLE DB also provides access to non-relational data stores such as text files.

Data Sources Available for DTS

Figure 6.2 shows the Data Connection Palette in the DTS Designer, along with connections that have been made to eight different data sources.

FIGURE 6.2

Select different types of available data sources on the Data Connection Palette.

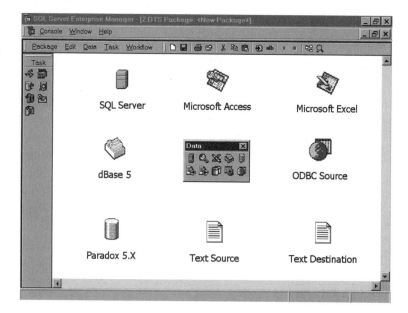

The OLE DB provider for ODBC allows DTS to be used with any relational database that currently has an ODBC driver. The ability to use all ODBC databases allows for a wide range of databases to be used for DTS right now, without having to wait for OLE DB providers to be written.

Note

All the tasks have similar names when used by the DTS Designer and when used in code, except for the Transform Data task. In code, the Transform Data task is referred to as the DataPumpTask object. SQL Server Books On Line consistently refers to this task as the Transform Data task or the Data Transformation when discussing the DTS Designer interface. But when discussing how this task is used in code, it is called the Data Pump task. I have chosen to always refer to this task as the Transform Data task, except for situations when I am specifically referring to the DataPumpTask object.

Text Files and Other Non-Relational Data

DTS provides a consistent way of dealing with relational and non-relational data.

All non-relational types of data can be processed in a Data Pump task or Data-Driven Query task in the same way as data stored in relational databases. This is true of data as diverse as text files, Excel worksheets, and data from a Data Link.

When you import data from a text file into SQL Server, you also have the option of using a Bulk Insert task. The Bulk Insert results in quicker processing but eliminates the possibility of transforming data as it's being imported.

DTS Packages

The DTS package is the executable programming unit for DTS. The package is the highest level object in the DTS object hierarchy. Chapter 9, "DTS Packages" discusses the details of setting up DTS packages.

Four kinds of objects are included in a DTS package:

- A connection defines a data source or a data destination.
- A task defines a specific action that is being accomplished.
- A step defines the control of flow among the tasks within the package. The precedence of a step provides for conditional branching in a package. Figure 6.3 shows the three types of precedence—On Completion, On Failure, or On Success.

  When a task fails, an On Failure workflow object sends processing to the Send Mail task, to inform the Information Systems Manager. When a task succeeds, an On Success workflow object sends processing to the next step. After the Mail to Manager task, whether or not it is successful, an On Completion object sends processing to the Send Mail task to inform the Manager of the IS department that the package has finished.

- A global variable can be used throughout a package so that information can be shared among tasks and ActiveX scripts.

DTS packages are executed in a variety of ways:

- Through the user interface—in the Enterprise Manager, the Data Designer, and the DTS Import and Export Wizards.
- As a scheduled task using the `dtsrun` utility.
- From the command line, using the `dtsrun` utility.
- From a client program, by using the Execute method of the DTS package object.

FIGURE 6.3

This DTS package includes two connections, five tasks, and the three types of precedence.

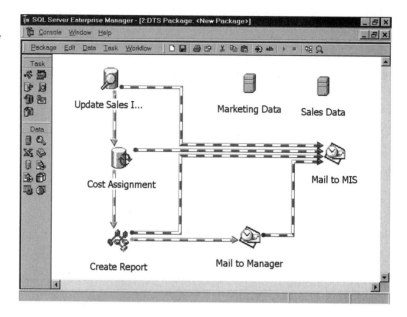

The DTS package can be saved in three different ways:

- In the Microsoft Repository. This is the preferred method of storage because it provides an opportunity to save metadata, track package versioning, and use lineage variables for identifying the transformation that was used for a particular record.

- In SQL Server, but not in the Repository. This method provides the fastest method of accessing a DTS package.

- In the file system. This method allows users to share DTS packages with other users.

DTS Tasks

The units of work in DTS are called tasks. There are eight types of tasks built into DTS. It is also possible to create a custom task with Visual Basic or C++. Figure 6.4 shows the Task palette and the icons for seven tasks that can be chosen from it.

Transform Data Task

The Transform Data task is the basic task used in DTS. It is not listed with the other tasks in the DTS Designer but is displayed by itself. And it isn't referred to as a task, but as a "data transformation." Figure 6.5 shows the Transform Data task as it appears in the DTS Designer. Instead of having a freestanding icon, this task is shown as a black arrow leading from the data source to the data destination.

FIGURE 6.4

The Task palette contains seven DTS task icons that are used in the DTS designer to designate those tasks.

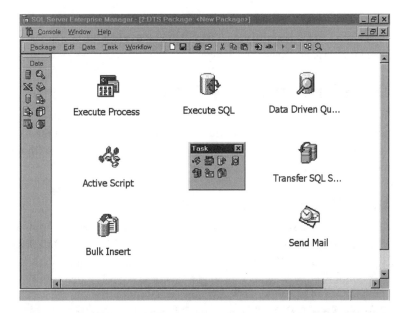

FIGURE 6.5

Transforming data task from Sales Data to Sales Data Mart.

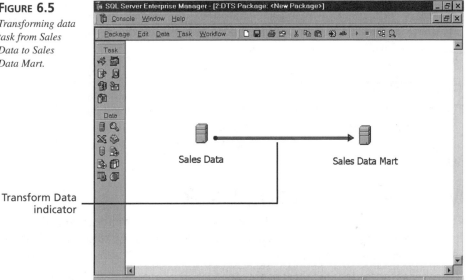

Transform Data indicator

There are two basic variations of the Transform Data task. In the first, the fields in the data source are copied directly into the fields of the data destination. In the second, ActiveX scripts are used to transform each data record as it's being imported.

The first two tasks, Transform Data and Data-Driven Query, are the subject of Chapter 7, "The Core Data Transformation Tasks." The other six tasks are discussed in depth in Chapter 8, "Using Other DTS Tasks."

Data-Driven Query Task

The Data-Driven Query task has all the functionality of the Transform Data task but gives the ability to update or delete destination records, based on the data in an individual record. Because the data from each processed record is used to fill query parameters, these queries are said to be data-driven.

Bulk Insert Task

The Bulk Insert task provides the quickest way to import records from a text file into SQL Server. It offers the same functionality as the SQL Server Bulk Insert command (which is new for SQL Server 7.0). The functionality of a Bulk Insert is similar to that of the bcp (bulk copy program) command line utility, but is much faster.

Transfer SQL Server Objects Task

This task provides the ability to transfer database objects and data from one SQL Server database to another SQL Server database. Tables, indexes, constraints, views, stored procedures, rules, defaults, and logins can all be transferred.

Execute SQL Task

This task executes one or more SQL commands in a database being used by DTS. You can use the Execute SQL Task with a variety of SQL. The OLE DB driver passes the SQL commands directly to the connected database, so you can use a variety of types of SQL in this task.

Microsoft ActiveX Script Task

This task executes an ActiveX script. The scripts can be created with Microsoft Visual Basic Scripting Edition, Microsoft JScript, or PerlScript. Any COM objects can be referenced from inside these scripts.

Writing ActiveX scripts is the topic of Chapter 11.

Execute Process Task

This task executes an external program. It provides an opportunity to integrate DTS tasks with other programs that are being used as a part of the data transformation process.

Send Mail Task

This task sends an email message using SQL Mail. Messages can be created that are sent on failure, on success, or on completion of one or more of the tasks.

Custom Task

New tasks for use with DTS can be created using Visual Basic or C++. After these tasks are registered with DTS, they function in the same way as the tasks that are shipped with the product. They can be fully incorporated into the user interface and also used through COM.

Saving Metadata with DTS

One of the most important features of DTS is the ability to save metadata. You can save the structure of the databases, tables, and fields involved with the transformation. You can also save all the information about each transformation process, including what records were processed during a particular execution of the transformation package. All of this metadata is saved in the Microsoft Repository, the topic of Chapter 13, "Using the Repository in Data Transformations."

The physical location of the Repository is a set of system tables in the msdb database. The metadata is not intended to be viewed directly in these tables. Instead, the Repository structure provides a consistent way of retrieving this data.

The goal of the Repository is to provide a uniform storage place for metadata, so that applications created by different vendors can be used interchangeably.

There are three types of metadata that can be saved with DTS:

- The lineage variables—These two fields uniquely identify a DTS package, the package version, and the particular time that package was executed. The values of the lineage variables are intended to be saved with the records that have been created by the execution of a DTS package. If these variables are saved, then the source of that transformation can be examined.

- The package definition—If a DTS package is saved to the repository, then every version of that package is also archived. When the lineage variables are used to examine the source of a record, the particular version of the package can be retrieved and examined. You have a permanent record of what action was taken by every particular transformation.

- The schema of the tables used by the DTS package—It's possible that changes could be made in the databases you are using as the source for a DTS transformation. DTS can be programmed to check for those changes every time the package is executed. If a change has been made, that change is recorded in the repository. This complements the saving of the versions of the DTS packages. A complete historical record of the transformations is maintained.

Using the DTS Designer

You can start using all these tools in the DTS Designer, the graphical user interface that Microsoft has provided with DTS. It's easier to create a Package using the DTS Import/Export Wizard. You have more control when you create a package using the DTS Object Model. But the DTS Designer gives you the highest level of control, without being very hard to use.

The use of the DTS Designer is discussed in Chapters 7, 8, and 9.

The DTS Designer displays connections, tasks, and steps as icons. There are palettes of task objects and connection objects. Step objects are located in the Workflow menu. Objects are added to the package by clicking the appropriate icon on the toolbars or in the menu. Steps of the correct precedence are added by selecting two tasks and selecting the appropriate precedence icon from the workflow menu.

You can view the properties for any object being used in a package by double-clicking its icon.

> **Note**
>
> The Transform Data task is not listed with the other tasks on the Task palette and it is not on the Task menu. It has its own icon on the toolbar, or can be added by choosing Add Transform from the Workflow menu.

Figure 6.6 shows the schematic presentation of a Transform Data task and a Data-Driven Query task. They look quite different, although they function in almost exactly the same way.

You can execute DTS packages that you have created and saved. You can also execute DTS packages while you are developing them inside the Data Designer Choose Package, Execute or click the Execute icon on the toolbar.

FIGURE 6.6

A Transform Data task and a Data-Driven Query task appear quite dissimilar in the Data Designer, even though they are actually very alike in operation.

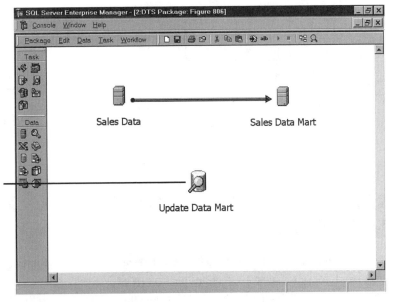

Using the DTS COM Interface

Microsoft has provided a COM interface with DTS. Everything that you can do with the Data Designer, you can do with the COM interface—and more.

There are separate code libraries for DTS packages and for the data pump:

- The Microsoft DTSPackage Object Library is implemented in dtspkg.dll. Visual Basic and other libraries that support OLE Automation can use this library.

- The Microsoft DTSDataPump Scripting Object Library is also called DTSPump. It is implemented in dtspump.dll. This library uses a COM interface without OLE Automation, so it cannot be used by Visual Basic. DTSPump allows C++ programmers to create custom transformations by directly programming the data pump.

The higher levels of the DTS Object model are illustrated in Figure 6.7.

The DTS object model is presented in Chapter 12, but the names of the COM objects, their properties, and their methods are also pointed out as DTS functionality is discussed in Chapters 8 through 9.

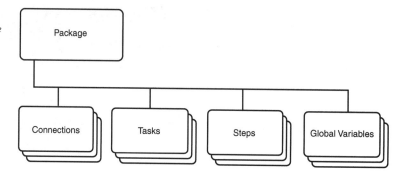

FIGURE 6.7

The package is the highest level of the DTS object hierarchy and has four constituent objects.

Using the DTS Import and Export Wizards

The DTS Import Wizard and the DTS Export Wizard are provided with DTS. They are the main topic of Chapter 10. Besides the Enterprise Manager menu, you can reach the wizards by right-clicking on Data Transformation Services in the Enterprise Manager's console tree, choosing All Tasks and then Import Data or Export Data. You can also call them from other locations:

- Choose Import and Export Data from the Microsoft SQL Server 7.0 menu on the Start Menu.
- Through the dtswiz utility from the command line.
- Through SQL NameSpace, the SQL-NS object library. This allows you to call the wizards with Visual Basic or C++ code.

The DTS wizards implement much of the functionality of the Data Pump task. In addition, they set up Execute SQL tasks for creating tables and deleting all the records from those tables.

Running the DTS Import or Export wizard creates a DTS package. At the end of the process you can choose whether or not to run the package immediately. You can also choose whether or not to save the package.

> **Tip**
>
> The DTS Import and Export wizards are among the most useful wizards provided with SQL Server 7.0. I like the wizards in SQL Server, although many of them don't really make your work much faster. But if you are importing and

exporting data from many tables at the same time, these wizards can save you a tremendous amount of time.

I find that the quickest way to set up a DTS package is often to start with the Wizard, save the package, and then add additional functionality with the DTS Designer.

Executing DTS Packages with Dtsrun

A DTS package can be executed with the dtsrun utility, which is used when a DTS package is scheduled with SQL Server Agent. Dtsrun can also run a DTS package from the command line or in a batch file.

Many of the dtsrun parameters are encrypted. Encryption can be used for the server name, user password, user name, filename, repository database name, package name, package password, Package ID and Version ID. An encrypted parameter is indicated by placing a tilde ~ before the argument.

Here is the syntax for dtsrun:

```
dtsrun [{
/? |
{/[~]S server_name
{/[~]U user_name [/[~]P password] | /E} |
 {/[~]F filename/[~]R repository_database_name} }
{/[~]N package_name [/[~]M package_password] |
[/[~]G package_guid_string] | [/[~]V package_version_guid_string]}
[/!X] [/!D] [/!Y] [/!C]
}]
```

The dtsrun utility arguments are:

- /S   Show an explanation of all the dts parameters
- ~   Parameter is being used in encoded format.
- /S   The network name of the computer running SQL Server where this package is being run.
- /U   The login ID used to connect to SQL Server.
- /P   The password for the login ID.
- /E   A trusted connection is being used. A password is not needed when this argument is chosen.

- /N   The DTS package name. This argument is not required if the /G argument is included.

- /M   The DTS package password. DTS packages can but do not have to have passwords. If the DTS package has been given a password, then this argument is required.

- /G   The DTS package ID. This is one of the two lineage variables that uniquely identify the DTS package. This argument is not required if the /N argument is used.

- /V   The DTS version ID. This is the other lineage variable. It uniquely identifies the version and the instance of execution of a DTS package. Without this argument, the most recent version of the package is used.

- /F   The filename of a DTS package stored as a file. If this argument is used together with /S, the Server Name, the contents of this named file are replaced with the DTS package stored on the named SQL Server.

- /R   The repository database containing the DTS packages. Without this argument, the default database name is used.

- /!X   Overwrites the contents of a file with a DTS package stored in SQL Server. The package is not executed when this argument is used.

- /!D   Deletes a DTS package stored in SQL Server. The package is not executed when this argument is used.

- /!Y   Displays an encrypted command. The package is not executed when this argument is used.

Here is an example of dtsrun used with a package saved as a file:

```
Dtsrun /S ServerName /U UserName /P UserPassword
/N PackageName /M PackagePassword
/F c:\temp\StarImport.dts
```

To use dtsrun with a package saved in SQL Server, follow this sample code:

```
Dtsrun /S ServerName /U UserName /P UserPassword
/N PackageName /M PackagePassword
```

You can use dtsrun with a package saved in the repository with code like this:

```
Dtsrun /S ServerName /U UserName /P UserPassword
/N PackageName /M PackagePassword /R msdb
```

Here is an example of dtsrun used with a package saved in the repository, using a trusted connection, referenced by the lineage variables:

```
Dtsrun /S ServerName /E /R msdb
```

```
/G {9F99EE87-FE2F-11D2-91A8-00E0980134A1}
/V -943767260
```

The following sample code shows an example of an encrypted `dtsrun` command:

```
Dtsrun /~S 0xBD02B5BE90E2B90926828A12F24175AA
/~N 0xEF81FBEFE60680AA013ED967BE41F0D31E621291E96E
D2597717AD9B12DE4BFB /E
```

Summary

A database administrator recently told me that he purchased SQL Server just because he needed to use the Data Transformation Services!

You now have an introduction to the capabilities of DTS, but the power of DTS is found in the details. In upcoming chapters we will examine each of the DTS tasks, what is involved in setting up DTS packages, and the capabilities of the DTS wizards. You will see how to use this functionality both in the graphical user interface and through the programmable COM interface.

The goal is to prepare data for OLAP. You can import your data from any source. You can cleanse your data. You can move your normalized data into a star schema.

And even if you decide not to use OLAP, you still may find several ways to use the Data Transformation Services.

The Core Data Transformation Tasks

by Tim Peterson

IN THIS CHAPTER

CHAPTER 7

There are two DTS tasks that are used to set up data transformations. The Transform Data task is the basic tool used for data transformations. The Data-Driven Query task provides the same capabilities as the Transform Data task. It also has the ability to make data modifications to existing records in the destination table and run different queries based on different values in the data.

This chapter begins with a discussion of data connections. You can use DTS to connect to a variety of different database systems and file-based data storage systems. These connections are used as the source and the destination of transformations.

The chapter continues with a discussion of the Transform Data task and the Data-Driven Query task. These tasks provide the core functionality of Data Transformation Services. The Transform Data task is the primary tool for importing and transforming data. The Data-Driven Query task is the tool to use when your data import also involves an update of existing data.

Tips for Using COM with DTS

In this chapter I discuss the capabilities of the two data transformation tasks and show you how to work with these tasks in the DTS Designer. I will also give you some COM Tips, showing you how the user interface aligns with the objects, collections, properties, and methods contained in the DTS Object Model. You can find a DTS COM reference in Chapter 12. Chapter 11 has many examples of using COM in ActiveX scripts.

Creating and Modifying Data Connections

Connection objects define data sources or data destinations. They are needed for four of the built-in DTS tasks:

- Transform Data task
- Data-Driven Query task
- Bulk Insert task
- Execute SQL task

A unique ID number identifies each connection within the DTS Package. The Connection ID is used to tie particular connections together with particular tasks. This ID number is automatically assigned when a connection is created in the DTS Designer. As a connection is selected for use with a task, this number is also automatically associated with that task.

Tips for Using COM with DTS

The Connection ID must be manually assigned when creating connections in code. It is the ID property of the `Connection` object and has an integer data type. The programmer must assure that a unique value is assigned to it. This value is assigned to the `DestinationConnectionID` and `SourceConnectionID` properties of `DataPumpTask` and `DataDrivenQueryTask` objects. It's also assigned to the `ConnectionID` property of the `BulkInsertTask` and the `ExecuteSQLTask` objects.

Connections can be made to any data source that has an available OLE DB provider, including all database systems that have ODBC drivers. The definition of a connection object varies depending on the type of connection that is being made.

The performance of your DTS package can be improved by using connections efficiently. Connecting to databases is time consuming and can be a significant use of resources. You have the following control to optimize the use of connections:

- One connection in a DTS package can be used for several different tasks, or you can create several separate connections to a data source, one for each time it's used for a task.
- You have the choice of opening all connections when the execution of a package is started or opening each connection when it's needed. The default is to open as needed. This option cannot be changed in the DTS Designer.
- You can choose whether or not to close a connection when a task is finished. The default is to leave the connection open. This setting is set in the Workflow Properties of the task, discussed in Chapter 9, "DTS Packages."
- You can open and close connections programmatically in the ActiveX scripts included in your package.

Tips for Using COM with DTS

The `ConnectionImmediate` property of the `Connection` object determines whether or not a connection is opened immediately when a package is executed. The default value is False.

continues

> The CloseConnection property of the Step object associated with a particular task is used to close a connection immediately when the task is finished. The default setting is True, causing connections to be left open.
>
> You can open and close connections programmatically in an ActiveX script by using the AcquireConnection and ReleaseConnection methods of the Connection object.

Creating Data Connections

Data connections are created in the DTS Designer with the following procedure:

1. Click one of the data source icons on the data connection palette, choose one of the items on the Data menu, or right-click the design sheet and choose Add Data Connection.

2. Use the option buttons to indicate whether you want to create a new connection or use an existing connection. If you choose to use an existing connection, you don't have to do anything else. A new icon on the design sheet is created for a connection that already exists. Creating new icons for a connection can make the workflow lines in a package diagram easier to read.

3. Choose the appropriate data source.

4. Provide the additional information that is needed for the particular type of connection being created. The information needed to access a text file is different from what is needed to access an Oracle database.

Setting the Properties of a SQL Server OLE DB Provider

Figure 7.1 shows the Connection Properties dialog for a SQL Server connection.

You can choose a different data source provider by selecting a new item in the list. The additional information that is displayed for SQL Server changes to the information needed for the other data provider.

Here is the additional information you need to set for SQL Server connections:

- The name of the server, which can be picked from a list.
- Whether to use Windows NT authentication or SQL Server authentication.
  If you choose SQL Server authentication, a User name and a Password are required.
- The name of the database, which you can also pick from a list.

FIGURE 7.1

The Connection Properties dialog displays different information for different OLE DB Providers. Here the dialog is shown for the OLE DB provider for SQL Server.

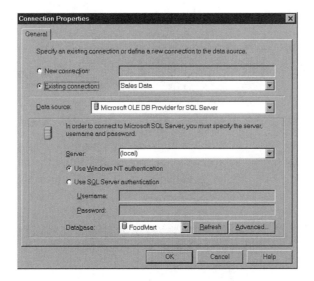

Open the Advanced Properties dialog, shown in Figure 7.2, by clicking the Advanced button in the Connection Properties dialog. It displays additional settings that are available for each specific OLE DB provider.

FIGURE 7.2

The Advanced Properties dialog for a SQL Server OLE DB connection presents additional opportunities for configuration.

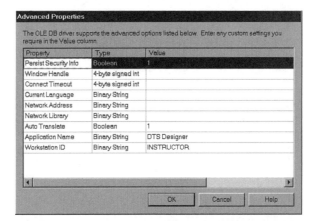

Tips for Using COM with DTS

The DTS package object has a collection that contains all the connections that have been created in a package. Each connection object itself has one

continues

collection, OLEDBProperties. The OLEDBProperties collection contains the specific values for each OLE DB provider. These are the values that are set in the Connection Properties dialog and the Advanced Properties dialog.

Setting the Properties for Text File Connections

When you create a connection for a text file, you have to choose between Text File (Destination) and Text File (Source). All other providers can use the same connection for both destination and source. The Connection Properties dialog for a text file is shown in Figure 7.3.

FIGURE 7.3

The Connection Properties dialog for a text file looks the same for Destination and Source text files, but the Properties button leads to different options.

The Properties button brings up the Text File Properties dialog. The dialog's choices differ depending on whether or not the connection is being used for import or for export. Figure 7.4 shows the Text File Properties dialog for a destination connection.

The choices for specifying a file format for a destination include the following:

- Whether the fields are to be separated with a specified delimiter or a fixed field width is going to be used.

- Whether or not to include the column name in the export, using the column names as the fields of the first row.

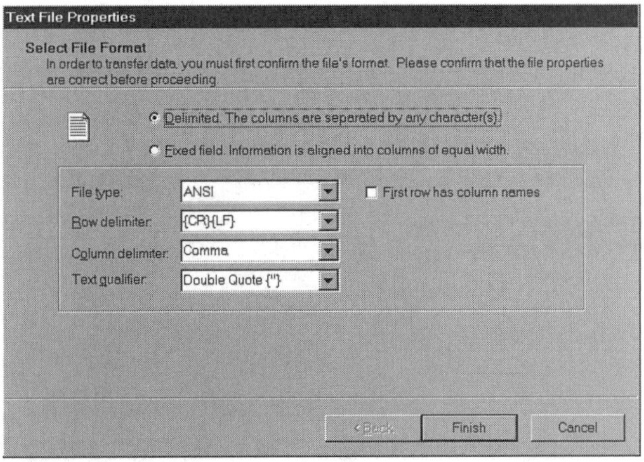

FIGURE 7.4

There is only one screen for the Text File Properties dialog when it is used for a destination connection.

- The type of text file to be created. The available choices are ANSI, OEM, or Unicode. ANSI is the default choice.
- What character, if any, is to be used for a row delimiter.
- What character is to be used for a column delimiter.
- What character, if any, is to be used for a text qualifier. This choice is not available when fixed-length fields are used.

> **Note**
>
> Choosing a column delimiter should also not be an available choice when fixed-length fields are used. You are allowed to choose a column delimiter for a destination connection that is using fixed-length text fields, but your choice is ignored when the data is exported.

For a source connection there are at least two and sometimes three screens in the Text File Properties dialog. The dialog uses Back and Next buttons to navigate between the screens. The first screen is shown in Figure 7.5.

Several of the source text file properties selected on this first screen are the same as the choices for the destination text file properties:

- Delimited or fixed fields.
- First row has column names.
- File type.

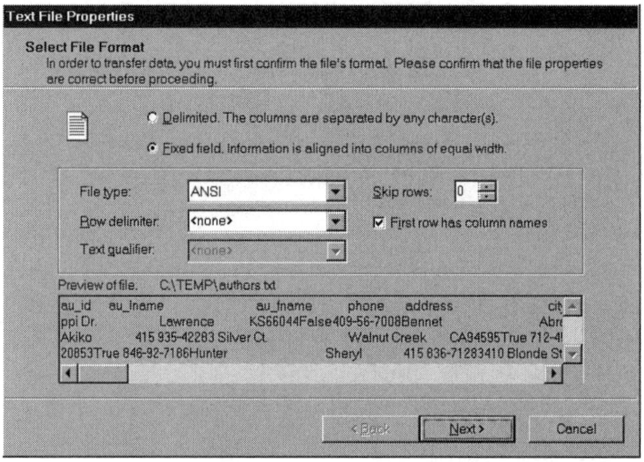

FIGURE 7.5

The first screen of the Text File Properties dialog for a source connection has some of the same options as the one for a destination connection.

- Row delimiter. (The column delimiter is chosen on the last screen of the dialog.)
- Text qualifier.

In addition, there is a spin box to enter the number of rows at the top of the file that are to be skipped. A value of 9 for Skip rows means that this connection sees the 10th record in the file as the first.

The text file can be previewed in a box at the bottom of the dialog's first screen.

If this is a fixed-length field and there is no row delimiter, the second screen gives the opportunity to specify the total length of the fields. You see the contents of the file and you move a red line to divide the first and second records, as shown in Figure 7.6. Alternatively, you can specify the total length of fields in a row by entering a value in the spin box.

Figure 7.7 shows the last screen of the Text File Properties dialog, as it appears when fixed-length fields are used. This screen is used to set the widths of each field. The field dividing lines are created with a single click, are deleted with a double click, and can be dragged to the proper place.

For text files with delimited fields, the last screen of the Text File Properties dialog shows a sample of the file and gives an opportunity to select the correct field delimiter.

FIGURE 7.6

The second screen of the Text File Properties dialog is only used for a connection source that has fixed-length fields and no row delimiter. The purpose of the screen is to designate the width of each row.

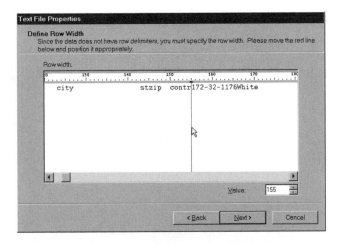

FIGURE 7.7

The last screen of the Text File Properties dialog is used to set the widths of fixed-length fields.

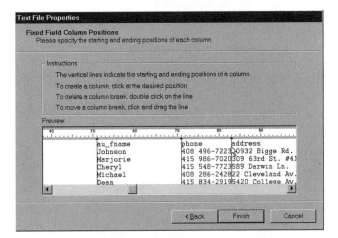

Setting the Properties for the OLE DB Provider for ODBC Data Sources

The Connection Properties dialog for the OLE DB Provider for ODBC is shown in Figure 7.8. You can choose an existing User, System, or File Data Source Name (DSN), or you can create a new User or System DSN. The New button opens up the Create New Data Source Wizard.

Setting the Properties for Other Data Sources

The Connection Properties dialogs for other data sources are similar. The dialog for the Oracle DB Provider is very similar to the one for SQL Server. A Microsoft Data Link connection requires either the loading of a *.udf file or setting the appropriate properties for an OLE DB provider. Microsoft Access, Microsoft Excel, dBase, and Paradox connections require a filename and security information. A Connection Properties dialog for Microsoft Access is shown in Figure 7.9.

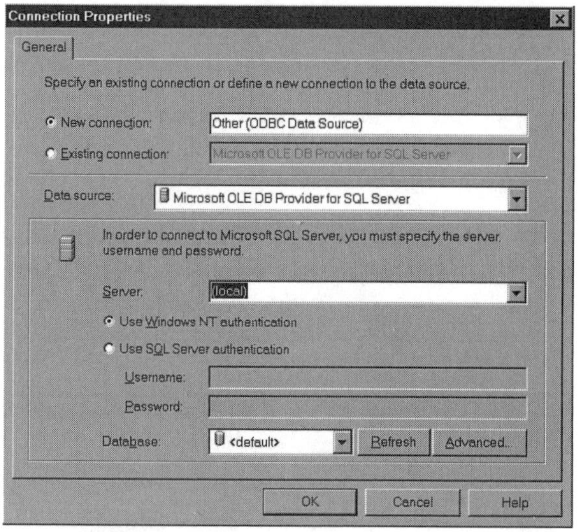

FIGURE 7.8

Choose an existing DSN or create a new one with the Connection Properties dialog for the OLE DB Provider for ODBC.dialog for the OLE DB Provider for

FIGURE 7.9

A Microsoft Access data connection requires a filename and appropriate security information.

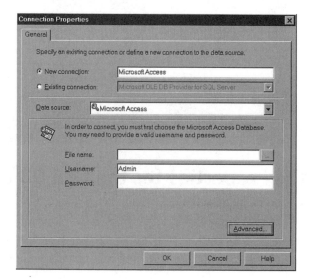

Modifying Data Connections

Connections are modified in the interface by selecting the connection's icon, modifying any of the properties in the dialog, and saving those changes.

Connections can be modified while a DTS Package is running. This allows you to simplify your code by using the same connection for several different databases.

The following code fragment checks to see if a connection is currently in use. This code could be used in either an ActiveX script task (discussed in Chapter 8, "Using Other DTS Tasks") or a Workflow ActiveX Script (discussed in Chapter 9). The connection is closed, the name of the database used in the connection is changed, and the connection is reopened, now connected to a different database.

```
With oConnectSQL

    .ReleaseConnection
    .Catalog = "Sales1998"
    .AcquireConnection

End With
```

7
THE CORE DATA
TRANSFORMATION
TASKS

Tips for Using COM with DTS

The database used for a connection is referenced by the `Catalog` property of the `Connection` object.

The Transform Data Task

The Transform Data task is the primary task in DTS. It is the task that you will use most often for importing data into your star schemas.

The Capabilities of the Transform Data Task

There are three main parts to the Transform Data Task—a data source, a data destination, and a data transformation. The data source is a particular table or query from the source connection. If it's a query, it can be based on one or several tables.

The data destination is a particular table from the destination connection. There are two choices for the data transformation. The simple choice is to copy the data in the columns from the source to the destination. The more complex choice is to use an ActiveX script to transform the data row by row, as it's being imported.

If you use ActiveX scripts for a data transformation, there are many more possibilities:

- You can create and reference global variables.
- You can look up values in other tables by using the `Lookup` object.
- You can manipulate other COM objects.
- You can create new rows in the destination that are not in the source data.

- You can combine two or more rows in the source into one row in the destination.
- You can skip some of the rows in the source data (not include them in the destination).

Choosing to Use the Transform Data Task—Or Something Else

Microsoft has given us this tool called Data Transformation Services which comes with lots of tasks, one of which seems to have almost the same name as the tool itself—the Transform Data Task, the Data Transformation Task, or the DataPump Task—whatever it happens to be called.

How can you decide which task is most appropriate for a particular import? You use the Transform Data task most often. The main thing you do with Data Transformation Services is Transform Data. But consider these specialized situations where other tasks are more effective:

- If you are transferring database objects from a SQL Server to a SQL Server database, use a Transfer SQL Server Objects task.
- If you are updating or deleting records in the destination data based on the records in the source data, use the Data-Driven Query task. You can use a Data-Driven Query task for updating dimension tables in a star schema.
- If your data source is a text file, your data destination is SQL Server, you are not transforming the data as it's being imported, and you want the fastest possible speed for your data transfer, use the Bulk Insert task.

In all other cases, use the Transform Data task to transform your data.

--tep

Creating a New Transform Data Task

A new Transform Data task is created in the DTS Designer with the following procedure:

1. Create two connections, one for the data source and the other for the data destination.
2. Click the connection that is going to be used as the data source.
3. Press the Shift key and click the connection that is going to be used for the data destination.
4. Click the Transform Data icon on the toolbar or select Add Transform from the Workflow menu.

Figure 7.10 shows a Transform Data task being created. The two data connections are selected and Add Transform is chosen from the Workflow menu.

FIGURE 7.10

Create a Transform Data task by highlighting two connections and selecting Add Transform from the Workflow menu. You have to select your data source connection first.

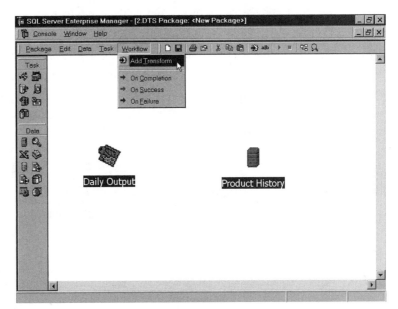

The description for this task is set at the top of the first tab of the Data Transformation Properties dialog. It appears as a tool tip for the Transform Data task in the DTS Designer.

Setting the Source for a Transform Data Task

The source for a Transform Data task is set on the first tab of the Data Transformation Properties dialog. The source connection cannot be changed at this point without deleting the task and starting over.

If the data source is a text file, you don't have any more choices to make on this tab. The file as it is specified in the connection will be the source for the transformation.

If the data source is a relational database, choose between using a table or a query as the source for the transformation. A list shows the names of all the tables. SQL Server views and Microsoft Access queries are included in this list.

If you elect to use a query as the transformation source, you have three options for creating the query:

- Type the query into the box on the Source tab.

- Choose the Browse button to find a file that has a SQL statement in it.

- Choose the Build Query button and design the query in the Data Transformation Services Query Designer.

There is also a Parse Query button which checks the query syntax and the validity of all the field and table names used.

The Data Transformation Services Query Designer is shown in Figure 7.11. It is the same query designer that is available in the Enterprise Manager for looking at table data and for creating a view.

FIGURE 7.11

The Data Transformation Services Query Designer provides an interactive design environment for creating queries.

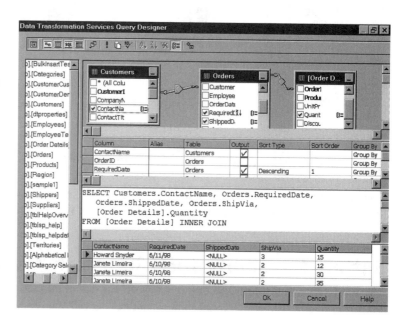

There are four panes in the Query Designer:

- The Diagram pane is shown at the top of Figure 7.11. Any changes that you make in this box are immediately reflected in the Grid and the SQL panes. In the Diagram pane, you can

  Drag tables into the pane from the table list at the left.

  Join tables by dragging a field from one table to another.

  Right-click the join line to choose a dialog for setting the properties of the join.

  Select fields to include in the query output.

Right-click a field and choose it for sorting.

Highlight a field and pick the group by icon on the toolbar.

- The Grid pane provides a more detailed view for specifying how individual columns are used in the query. Changes in this pane are immediately reflected in the Diagram pane and the SQL pane.

- The SQL pane shows the text of the SQL statement that is being generated for this query. Changes here are not made in the Diagram and Grid panes immediately, but they are made as soon as you click any object outside the SQL pane.

- The Results pane shows the results of running the query you are designing. The effect of the changes you make in the query design are not reflected until you re-run the query by pressing the Bang(!) symbol on the toolbar.

> **Tip**
>
> Right-clicking in any of the panes brings up the Properties dialog for the query. Here's where you can use the new SQL Server 7.0 syntax for choosing the TOP X or TOP X PER CENT of the records in a result set.

> **Tip**
>
> I like the ability the Query Designer gives me to switch back and forth between visual and textual design. I have been able to get it confused, but not very often. One more thing—it's a tool that needs a big monitor if you want to see all the pieces at the same time.

Setting the Destination for a Transform Data Task

The destination for a Transform Data Task is set on the Destination tab of the Data Transformation Properties dialog. You have two choices: select one of the tables in the drop-down list box or create a new table.

When you select the Create New button, the Create Destination Table dialog opens, as shown in Figure 7.12. The Create Table SQL statement is generated automatically for you, matching the fields of the source that have been chosen. Edit this SQL Statement to create the table the way you want it to be. Click OK in the Create Destination Table and the new table is created immediately in the Destination database.

FIGURE 7.12

Create a new table to serve as the destination of a Transform Data task by using the Destination tab of the Data Transformation Properties dialog and the Create Destination Table dialog.

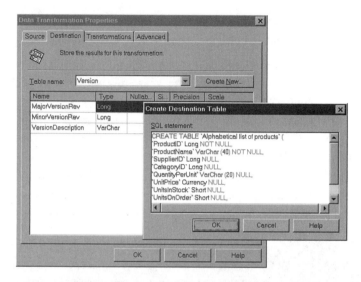

Caution

When you select OK in the Create Destination Table dialog, the new table is created immediately in the Destination database. Make sure the Create Table SQL statement is correct before you leave this dialog. You cannot drop the table you have created from within the DTS Designer.

When you are using a text file as the destination for a transformation, the Destination tab has a button that opens the Define Columns dialog (shown in Figure 7.13). The columns needed to match the columns from the source are automatically selected. Click the Execute button to set these columns as the ones to be used for the data destination.

Caution

Defining the columns for a text destination is a very quick task, but don't forget to do it. If you change the table you are using for the source of the data, you also have to go to the destination tab and define the columns again. The new choice for the source isn't automatically carried over to the destination.

FIGURE 7.13

The Define Columns dialog is used to set the destination columns for a text file in a Transform Data task.

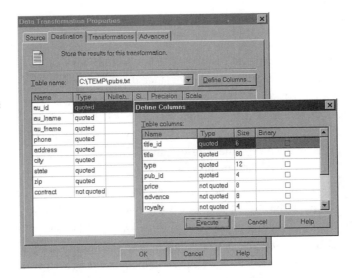

7

THE CORE DATA
TRANSFORMATION
TASKS

Setting the Advanced Properties for a Transform Data Task

The Advanced Properties for a Transform Data Task are set on the Advanced tab of the Data Transformation Properties dialog, as shown in Figure 7.14.

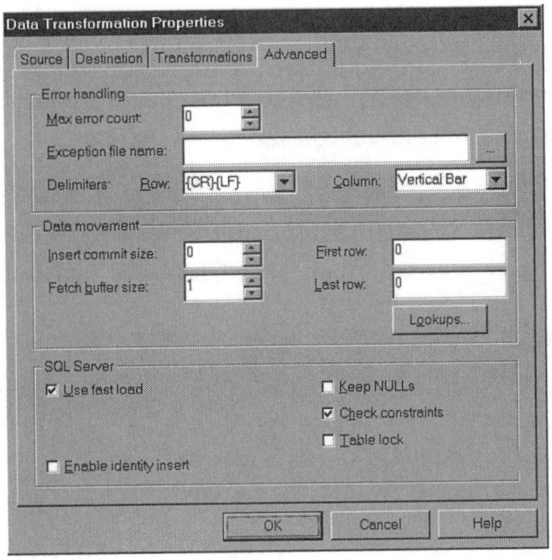

FIGURE 7.14

Error handling and data movement are among the properties set on the Advanced tab of the Data Transformation Properties dialog.

The Advanced Properties include

- Max Error Count: The maximum number of allowed errors before the Transform Data task is terminated. The default is 0, which means that the Transform Data task will fail when the first error is encountered.

- Exception File Name, Exception Row Delimiter, and Exception Column Delimiter: The full path of the error-handling file and the delimiters to be used in that file. The data pump places source records into this file when an error transformation status is returned from the transformation script. The setting of the transformation status is discussed later in this chapter.

- Insert Commit Size: The number of inserts that are allowed to take place before a batch is committed. The default is 1000. Raising this number can improve performance, but also increases the use of the computer's memory resources.

- Fetch Buffer Size: The number of records fetched from the OLE DB provider at a time. The default is 100. Raising this number can improve performance, but also increases the use of the computer's memory resources.

- First Row: The number of the first row that is imported. The default is 1, which means that the copy starts with the first record.

- Last Row: The number of the last row that is imported. The default is 0, which means that all the records are copied.

- Fast Load: Whether or not to use fast load to insert rows. This setting has no effect if the destination provider does not support fast load. If fast load is chosen, then the fast load options can also be selected:

  Keep NULLs: Whether or not null values are kept during a load.

  Check constraints: Whether or not constraints are checked.

  Table Lock: Whether or not a table lock is obtained during the transformation.

- Enable Identity Inserts: Whether identity insert is set on or off during the data transformation. This option only applies to SQL Server data destinations.

Tips for Using COM with DTS

Each of the items in the previous list except for the fast load options is a property of the DataPumpTask object. The exact name of each property is the name that appears in that listing, with all spaces removed. The FastLoad constants are implemented as follows:

Constant	Value
DTSFastLoad_CheckConstraints	2
DTSFastLoad_KeepNulls	1
DTSFastLoad_NoOptions	0
DTSFastLoad_TableLock	4

Mapping Source Fields to Destination Fields

The next chore in setting up the Transform Data task is to map the source fields to the appropriate destination fields.

There are many ways of mapping source fields to destination fields. Each separate mapping is implemented as a Column Copy or an ActiveX script.

The Transformation tab of the Data Transformation Properties dialog (shown in Figure 7.15) is the place where source fields are mapped to destination fields. The tab displays all the fields of the source table and all the fields of the destination table. The data types of the fields and their nullability are displayed as ToolTips to assist you in your mapping.

FIGURE 7.15

Create mappings from Source to Destination in the Transformations tab of Transform Data.

Note

If you enabled the lineage option, you will see the two lineage variables listed as if they were fields in the source table. They can be mapped to destination fields in the same way as destination table fields.

Fields are mapped to each other by selecting them in the listing for each table. More than one field can be selected in a table by holding down the Control key while selecting. A range of fields can be selected by holding down the Shift key while selecting.

Mappings can be removed by selecting the mapping line or by selecting the corresponding fields and pressing the Delete button.

After selecting all the fields you want from both lists, select ActiveX Script or Copy Column in the new transformation list. Click the New button and you will see a black line drawn from the source to the destination, which shows your selection.

Tips for Using COM with DTS

The `DataPumpTask` object has a collection of `Transformation` objects. One `Transformation` object is produced for each set of mappings created on this Transformations tab. These transformation objects have a `SourceColumns` property and a `DestinationColumns` property which specify the collections of columns that have been selected for the particular transformation. Each item in this collection has only the name of the column and its ordinal number. In code, the columns are referred to as members of these collections, as in `DTSDestination("FieldName")`, `DTSSource(FieldName)`, `DTSDestination("Number")`, or `DTSSource(Number)`.

Figure 7.16 shows a one-to-one mapping for all the fields.

Figure 7.17 shows a many-to-many mapping for all the fields. A many-to-many mapping reduces the overhead of a Transform Data task and can significantly improve performance.

FIGURE 7.16

In a one-to-one mapping, each field is connected to one other field.

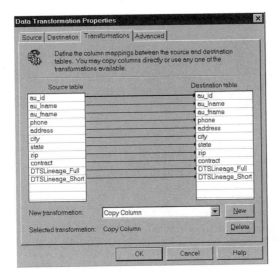

FIGURE 7.17

In a many-to-many mapping, all the fields participate in one transformation with all the other fields.

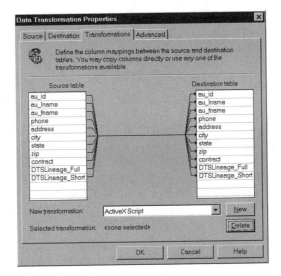

Figure 7.18 shows a combination of mappings.

Figure 7.19 shows how fields in the source table can participate in many transformations. The author ID is being transferred directly to the destination in one transformation. In a second transformation, various coded information in the ID is split into separate fields. In a third transformation, the transformation of the contract information is being handled differently, depending on which author is involved. On the other hand, fields in the destination table can only participate in one transformation.

FIGURE 7.18

One Transform Data Task can include one-to-one, one-to-many, many-to-one, and many-to-many mappings.

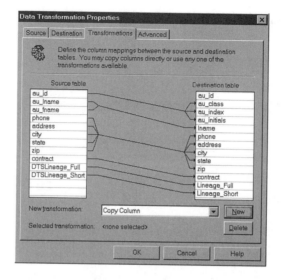

FIGURE 7.19

Many transformations can use the same field from the source table. In this case, three transformations are using au_id.

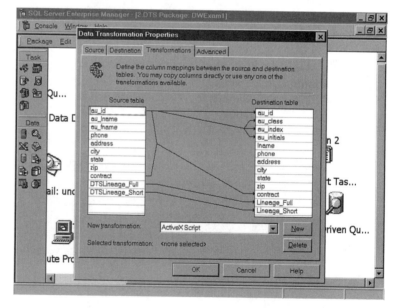

It is also possible to have mappings that include only source fields or only destination fields (see Figure 7.20). This could happen for a destination field if its value is being set by a global variable or a lookup. This could happen for a source field if a field is being used to set a global variable, but the field's value is not being used in the destination table. A transformation script is run for these one-sided cases even though no transformation is actually taking place.

FIGURE 7.20

A transformation that only has a field from the source and another that only has fields from the destination are represented as lines that end somewhere between the two tables.

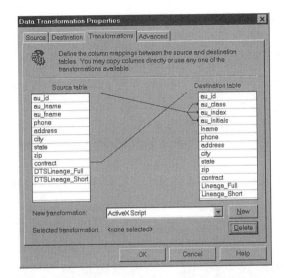

Figure 7.21 shows the Transformation Flags dialog. Choose this dialog by right-clicking a mapping line and selecting the Flags pop-up menu choice. The flags determine how transformations are applied when data types do not match between the source and the destination.

FIGURE 7.21

The Transformation Flags dialog provides data type transformation choices that can be customized for each mapping.

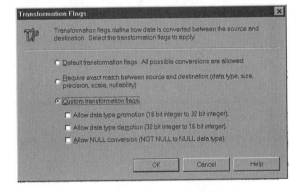

Here are the choices in the Transformation Flags dialog:

- All possible conversions between varying data types are allowed. This is the default choice.

- An exact match of data types is required. This match includes data type, size, precision, scale, and nullability.

- Customized conversion flags can be set to

    Allow data type demotion. A 16-bit integer is allowed to be changed into a 32-bit integer.

    Allow data type demotion. A 32-bit integer is allowed to be changed into a 16-bit integer.

    Allow a NULL conversion, where a NULL data type is allowed to receive data from a NOT NULL data type.

Tips for Using COM with DTS

The Transformation object has a TransformFlags property with a long integer value. There are 12 values for the DTSTransformFlags that can be used individually or in various combinations. The four choices for conversion flags in the interface map to four of these choices. The use of all the flags in code gives much more control over data type conversion issues than what is provided in the interface.

You can also right-click a mapping line and select Test from the pop-up menu to test that particular transformation. Figure 7.22 shows the data generated by a test of one transformation. The results of these tests are written to a text file and do not affect the data in either the source or the destination connection.

There is a dialog for ActiveX script transformations that shows the ActiveX script and its properties. Copy Column Transformations have a separate dialog that shows the column order. Any of the following procedures will call the ActiveX Script Transformation Properties dialog or the Column Order dialog:

- Double-click a mapping line.
- Right-click a mapping line. Choose Properties from the pop-up menu.
- Select a mapping line. Use the Ctrl+P keystroke combination.

The Column Order dialog, shown in Figure 7.23, allows the order of the columns chosen for this transformation to be changed. The order of the columns determines which column from the source will be copied into which column in the destination.

FIGURE 7.22

*An individual
transformation
can be tested by
right-clicking the
mapping line and
selecting Test. The
progress of the
test is shown in
the Testing
Transformation
dialog and the
data produced by
the test is shown
in the Preview
Data dialog.*

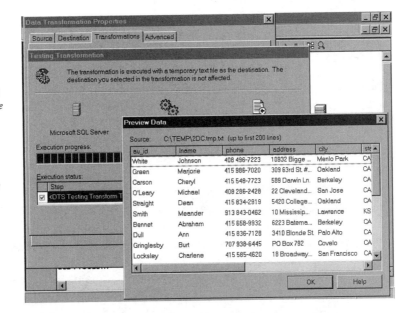

FIGURE 7.23

*The ordering of
the fields in a
Column Copy can
be changed in the
Column Order
dialog.*

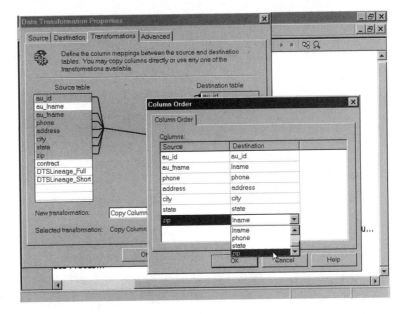

The ActiveX Script Transformation Properties dialog is discussed in the following
section.

Creating ActiveX Scripts for Transformations

The ability to create ActiveX scripts for your transformation is the most powerful tool in DTS, but the power of this tool has a price. If you want the fastest possible speed in a data import, don't use an ActiveX script. A Transform Data task using a column copy is almost as fast as a Bulk Insert task. A transformation using an ActiveX script usually takes two to four times longer than a column copy.

> **Caution**
>
> The 2-fold to 4-fold performance penalty is the minimum cost of using an ActiveX script transformation. Performance can be much worse than that. Don't open connections or call other time-consuming functions inside a transformation ActiveX script. These scripts are executed once for every record in the source data. If there are a million records in the source, this piece of code is going to run a million times.

Using the DTS Designer to Create an ActiveX Script

Figure 7.24 shows the ActiveX Script Transformation Properties dialog. This dialog opens when you create a new ActiveX transformation. You can also open the dialog by double-clicking the transformation's mapping line.

In creating an ActiveX script first select which scripting language you want to use. There are three choices in the Language list:

- Microsoft Visual Basic Scripting Edition
- Microsoft JScript
- PerlScript

> **Caution**
>
> The SQL Server product documentation states that "ActiveX scripts and transformations have been fully tested with the Microsoft-supplied Visual Basic and Jscript scripting engines only." PerlScript is not supplied with SQL Server. It does not appear as a language choice unless you install the PerlScript library.

FIGURE 7.24

The ActiveX Script Transformation Properties dialog provides a simple user interface for creating transformation scripts.

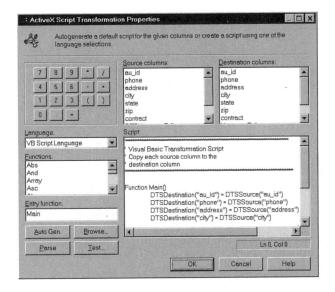

When you first open the ActiveX Script Transformation Properties window, you see that a default script has already been generated.

The default script performs exactly the same action as a column copy transformation. Each field in the source is copied to the same field in the destination, based on the ordinal position of the fields in the two collections. The first field is copied to the first field in the destination, the second field is copied to the second, and so on. The names of the fields are ignored in this mapping process.

Listing 7.1 is an example of a default script. The data source is the authors table from the pubs sample database. The data destination has fields with identical names as the source, except that the first field, au_id, is not included. All nine of the fields in the source have been mapped to all eight of the fields in the destination.

LISTING 7.1 Sample Script Mapping Fields from a Source to a Destination

```
'*************************************************************************
'  Visual Basic Transformation Script
'  Copy each source column to the
'  destination column
'*************************************************************************

Function Main()
    DTSDestination("au_lname") = DTSSource("au_id")
    DTSDestination("au_fname") = DTSSource("au_lname")
```

continues

LISTING 7.1   continued

```
    DTSDestination("phone") = DTSSource("au_fname")
    DTSDestination("address") = DTSSource("phone")
    DTSDestination("city") = DTSSource("address")
    DTSDestination("state") = DTSSource("city")
    DTSDestination("zip") = DTSSource("state")
    DTSDestination("contract") = DTSSource("zip")
    Main = DTSTransformStat_OK
End Function
```

The default script is very useful when the fields have been lined up in the proper order. In a situation like this, it's not very helpful.

There are three ways to modify or create a script for your transformation languages:

- Automatically generate the script. The default script is generated when the ActiveX transformation is first created. If you want, you can regenerate the script in a different scripting language. You may also want to return to the original script after experimenting with some changes. The default script can be re-created by pressing the Auto Gen. button.

- Insert a script from a file. A Browse button is provided to choose the file.

- Write the script in the Script textbox.

There are a variety of tools provided in the dialog to aid in writing and editing scripts. There is a list of the functions available in the scripting language. There are lists for the source columns and the destination columns that have been included in this transformation. Double-clicking an item in any one of these lists will insert that value into the script textbox. There is also a keypad of numbers and symbols that can be inserted into the script.

> **Note**
>
> I can't imagine why I need to click a number rather than typing it on the keyboard, but the column insertion is a very good feature. Not only does it help me get the column names correct, but it also references them as members of the DTSDestination collection or the DTSSource collection. Having this collection reference automatically generated can save a lot of time.

> ### Tip
>
> There can be a performance gain by referring to the columns by their ordinal number rather than by their name, such as `DTSDestination(1)` instead of `DTSDestination("au_lname")`. Unfortunately this is not an option in the automatically generated script. Taking advantage of this gain would certainly add additional time in setting up the transformation and would make maintenance more confusing.

Finally, there is a Parse button to check the script's syntax and a Test button to run the script. This is the same test that can be run from the Transformation tab of the Data Transformation Properties dialog. The results of the script test are both displayed on the screen and saved to a text file.

Writing Transform Data ActiveX Scripts

To write a data transformation ActiveX script you must know one of the scripting languages. You also need to know about the three topics that are going to be covered in this section:

- Setting the DTS Transformation Status for a script.
- Creating and using variables.
- Creating and using lookups.

> ### Note
>
> Basic information about the syntax and use of VBScript can be found in Appendix X. Examples of ActiveX scripts used for various transformation purposes can be found in Chapter 11, "Writing ActiveX Scripts".

Setting the DTS Transformation Status

Set the DTS Transformation Status value in the ActiveX script to tell the data pump what it should do with a particular record. Should the record be inserted into the destination table? Should it be handled as an error? Should the entire Transform Data task be aborted because of what has happened in the processing of this record?

The status value is set as the return value from the Main function in your ActiveX transformation script. The following is the final line of code that appears in the default Transform Data script:

```
Main = DTSTransformStat_OK
```

This value is returned to the Data Pump and tells it that the script has been completed successfully.

The values that are used to return the Transformation Status are defined in the Data Pump library, Dtspump.dll. All the values for this constant that can be used with the Transfer Data transformation scripts are listed next. (There are four additional Transformation Status values that can be used with data-driven Queries. Those values will be described later in this chapter.)

DTSTransformStat_OK

The transformation was successful.

- Value   1
- Write the results of this transformation to the destination table.
- There are no error messages.

DTSTransformStat_SkipRow

Skip all transformations for this row.

- Value   2
- Do not write the results of the current transformation to the destination table.
- Do not continue with any processing of other transformations for this row.
- There are no error messages.

DTSTransformStat_SkipFetch

Skip fetching the next row. This status flag can be used to create more than one record in the destination for one record in the source.

- Value   4
- Write the results of the current transformation to the destination table.
- Continue with any processing of other transformations for this row.
- Re-execute this transformation with the same source row.
- There are no error messages.

DTSTransformStat_SkipInsert

Skip the insert for this transformation.

- Value 8
- Do not write the results of this transformation to the destination table.
- Continue with any processing of other transformations for this row.
- There are no error messages.

DTSTransformStat_Info

The transformation was successful and there are information messages.

- Value 4096
- Write the results of this transformation to the destination table.
- Call the error sink with the additional information.

DTSTransformStat_Error

An error has occurred. This status is normally not used by itself.

- Value 8192
- Call the error sink with the information.

DTSTransformStat_ErrorSkipRow

An error has occurred and the row should be skipped.

- Value 8194 (8192 + 2)
- Do not write the results of this transformation to the destination table.
- Do not continue with any processing of other transformations for this row.
- Call the error sink with the information.
- Do not write this record to the exception file.

DTSTransformStat_ExceptionRow

Handle this row as an exception.

- Value 8448 (8192 + 256)
- Do not write the results of this transformation to the destination table.
- Do not continue with any processing of other transformations for this row.
- Call the error sink with the information.
- Write this record to the exception file.

DTSTransformStat_AbortPump

Abort the Transform Data task. This status is used in combination with other status messages.

- Value 16384
- Do not process any more rows.
- Return the value DTSTransformExec_AbortPump as the result of the Transform Data task.

DTSTransformStat_NoMoreRows

There are no more rows in the data source.

- Value 32768
- Do not process any more rows.

Creating and Using Global Variables

Global variables can be used for communicating throughout a DTS package. Communication can take place between different tasks and also between each execution of a transformation script.

A transformation script is executed separately for each record in the source data. Any local variables that are created within the transformation script are destroyed when the processing of an individual record has been completed. If you need to pass information from one execution of a transformation script to the next, you must use global variables.

Global variables can be used for combining information from several rows in the source data into one row in the destination. If you have three rows that have information that is going to be combined into one row, you could process that information like this:

- Store the information that you want to use from the first two rows in global variables as they are being processed.
- Use DTSTransformStat_SkipInsert to block the insertion of a separate record for those two rows.
- When the third record is being processed, retrieve the data values that you have stored in the global variables. Use that data along with the data values in the third record to assign values to the fields in the data destination.
- Use DTSTransformStat_OK to write this third record to the destination table.

Global variables have a variant data type. They can be used for text, for numbers, and as object variables.

Creating Global Variables in the User Interface

Global variables are created in the DTS Designer with the following steps:

1. Select Properties from the main DTS Designer Package menu. Make sure no objects on the design sheet are selected when you make this selection or the properties of that object will be displayed rather than the properties of the package as a whole.

2. Select the Global Variables tab in the DTS Package Properties dialog.

3. Click the New button.

4. Enter a name and choose a data type for the variable.

5. You may also enter a value for the global variable, which will be the initial value that the global variable holds each time the package is executed.

The Global Variables tab of the DTS Package Properties dialog is shown in Figure 7.25.

FIGURE 7.25

Global variables are created in the DTS Package Properties dialog and can be referenced throughout the package.

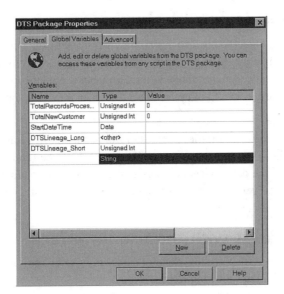

Creating Global Variables in an ActiveX Script

You can also create global variables in ActiveX scripts. These global variables exist only for the duration of the package's execution. Because these variables are not saved after the package is executed, you will not be able to view them in the Package Properties dialog.

Use the AddGlobalVariable method of the GlobalVariables collection to create a global variable. The two parameters for this method are the name of the global variable and its initial value.

```
GlobalVariables.AddGlobalVariable "VarName", "VarValue"
```

Referencing Global Variables in an ActiveX Script

A global variable is always referenced as a member of the GlobalVariables collection.

The following code retrieves a value from the global variable and places it into a local variable within the script:

```
lRecordCount = GlobalVariables("RecordCount")
```

The following code assigns a new value to a global variable:

```
GlobalVariables("RecordCount") = GlobalVariables("RecordCount") + 1
```

Creating and Using Lookups

You can use a Lookup object to retrieve information from a separate data source during a transformation. Lookups are especially useful when inserting records into dimension tables. If your source data contains abbreviations, you can use a lookup to replace those fields with their full text value. Lookups are also useful for checking the validity of your data.

You could open a recordset and retrieve values of fields directly in a transformation script, but this would be too time consuming. That script could be running thousands of times. With a lookup, the data connection only has to be made. Lookup values can be cached as they are retrieved, so if the same value is needed again, it's immediately available. The process is very efficient.

Creating Lookups with the User Interface

Lookup objects are made for a specific data transformation task. You can create them in the DTS Designer with the following steps:

1. Create the connection that the Lookup object is going to use, unless you are going to use an existing connection.
2. Select the Advanced tab in the DTS Package Properties dialog.
3. Click the Lookups button. The Data Transformation Lookups dialog is displayed.
4. Click the Add button.
5. Enter the lookup's name and choose a connection for the lookup from the list.

6. Push the expand button for the lookup's query. The Data Transformation Services Query Designer dialog opens so you can create the query for the lookup. A lookup query usually returns one field, although it can be set up to return multiple fields. One or more parameters are included in the query by using question marks. Here is a typical lookup query that finds the name of the state when given the value of the state abbreviation:

```
Select StateName from tblStateLookup where StateAbbreviation = ?
```

You may enter a value for the cache. This sets the value of the MaxCacheRows property of the Lookup object. If you don't enter a value, the default of 100 rows will be used. If you enter 0, then no rows will be cached for the lookup. The cache will be filled with rows as they are retrieved. When the assigned cache size is reached, each additional retrieval will cause one of the rows to be removed from the cache.

The Data Transformation Lookups dialog is shown in Figure 7.26

7

THE CORE DATA
TRANSFORMATION
TASKS

FIGURE 7.26

You can create lookups to allow your transformation scripts to efficiently access information from other data sources.

Creating Lookup Objects in an ActiveX Script

You can also create Lookup objects in ActiveX scripts. Use the AddLookup method of the Lookups collection. This would normally be done in an ActiveX script task or a Workflow ActiveX script, rather than in a transformation script.

The parameters for the AddLookup method are the Name of the lookup, the query string, the Connection ID, and the MaxCacheRows.

```
Lookups.AddLookup "FindStateName", "Select StateName _

    from tblStateLookup where StateAbbreviation = ?", 3, 50
```

Using a Lookup in an ActiveX Script

You use the `Execute` method of the `Lookup` object to return the value for a lookup. This line of code will use the `Lookup` object to replace the state abbreviation from the source with the state name in the destination:

```
DTSDestination("StateName") = _

    DTSLookups("FindStateName").Execute(DTSSource("StateAbbreviation"))
```

You can also create a `Lookup` object that uses two or more parameters:

```
DTSDestionation("Description") =_

    DTSLookups("FindDescription").Execute_

    (DTSSource("ProdID"), DTSSource("Supplier"))
```

The Data-Driven Query Task

The Data-Driven Query task is a Transform Data task with some special enhancements. Everything you do with a Transform Data task you can also do with a Data-Driven Query task. In addition, you can use data-driven queries to update or delete records in the destination data source.

Don't use a Data-Driven Query task if a regular Transform Data task will get the job done. Data-Driven Query tasks are much slower. Use data-driven queries when you specifically need to update information in existing records, such as when you are changing fields in a dimension table.

> **Note**
>
> A data-driven query gets its name from the parameter query that is used to determine what records should be changed in the data destination. A Transform Data task can only insert rows in the destination. A Data-Driven Query task can update, delete, or insert rows, or call a stored procedure. The parameters in the query are filled with values taken from the destination record that has been created by the current transformation process. The query is data-driven because its effect is determined by the data in the current destination fields.

Source Fields or Destination Fields?

When I first heard about data-driven queries, I somehow got the impression that the data that was used for the query parameters was taken from the source fields. I guess that's just what made sense. You're putting data into a table and you have a data source, so you might as well take the data from the data source.

But I was wrong. You don't use data source fields for your data-driven queries—you take fields from the data destination. You choose specific destination fields to fill the parameters of the data-driven queries.

I'm glad I was wrong, because I can assign whatever values I want to the destination fields that are being used by the data-driven query. I can use values that have come from the data source, values that have come from a global variable, or values that have come from a lookup. But whatever values I use, I have to assign them to destination fields before they can be used by the data-driven query.

--tep

Creating a New Data-Driven Query Task

You begin the process of creating a Data-Driven Query task in the DTS Designer by doing one of these three actions:

- Click the Data-Driven Query task icon on the task palette.
- Select Data-Driven Query task from the Task menu.
- Right-click the design sheet, choose Add Task, and select Data-Driven Query task on the pop-up menu.

The process of setting the properties for a data-driven query is very similar to setting the properties for a Transform Data task. Besides the four tabs found in the Data Transformation Properties dialog, there is an additional Queries tab. The Source, Destination, Transformations, and Options tabs, and the dialog forms that are called from these tabs, are almost identical for the two tasks. Here are the differences:

- On the Source and Destination tabs for the Data-Driven Query Properties dialog there are lists for choosing the source and the destination connections for this task. Both of these tasks need these two connections. The difference is only in the DTS Designer interface. The Designer requires you to select the two connections you are using before you create a Transform Data task; for a Data-Driven Query task you don't have to pick the connections until after you have started the process.

- The Options tab does not include the fast load and identity insert options. The Data-Driven Query task is a specialized data transformation that cannot use these speed optimizations.

- The Test button in the ActiveX Script Transformation Properties dialog has been removed for the Data-Driven Query task. Because the result of a Data-Driven Query task is a change of existing records in the data destination, it would be hard to show the results of a test.

Creating the Parameter Queries for the Data-Driven Query Task

The parameter queries and parameter mappings are created on the Queries tab of the Data-Driven Query Properties dialog, shown in Figure 7.27. You can create one query for each of the four possible query types—insert, update, delete, and user (which is used for calling a stored procedure). The queries can be either typed in the query window or created with the Data Transformation Services Query Designer using the Build button. After you have created the query, check its syntax with the Parse/Show Parameters button.

FIGURE 7.27

You can create queries for four different actions on the Queries tab of the Data-Driven Query Properties dialog.

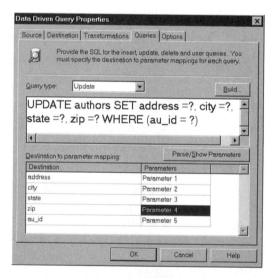

time. The proper query is chosen to run on the basis of the Transformation Status flag that you set in your ActiveX script. I'm not recommending that you set the wrong type of query for the data-driven queries you write. That could become confusing very quickly. But you should be aware that DTS is not enforcing the specification that a particular type of query is being created.

The parameters for the queries are created in the lower box on the Queries tab. The numbered parameters are listed on the right. The numbers represent the order in which the question marks appear in the text of the query. All the available fields from the data destination are in the lists for the Destination column.

Tips for Using COM with DTS

The data-driven queries are set as properties of the `DataDrivenQueryTask` object. The query statements are set as the `DeleteQuery`, `InsertQuery`, `UpdateQuery`, and `UserQuery` properties.

The parameters used for these queries are set in the `DeleteQueryColumns`, `InsertQueryColumns`, `UpdateQueryColumns`, and `UserQueryColumns` properties.

Each of these four properties represents a collection of columns that have two properties—an ordinal position and a column name.

Setting the Transformation Status when Executing a Data-Driven Query

Data-driven queries are run after the transformation script for a particular record has finished executing. The Transformation Status value that is returned from the Main function of the script tells the Data Pump which, if any, data-driven queries should be run.

All the Transformation Status values that are used for the Transform Data task, except for `DTSTransformStat_OK`, can also be used for the Data-Driven Query task. In addition, there are four Transformation Status values that are used to instruct the Data Pump to run each of the four data-driven queries.

You can use conditional logic in your ActiveX transformation script to determine which data-driven query, if any, should be run for each particular record that is being processed. You can only use one of the data-driven queries each time a transformation script is executed. If you want more than one of the queries to be executed for one record, you can do one of these two things:

- Add in the SkipFetch status so that the same script will be executed another time.
- Define an additional transformation for that record to execute another query.

The four Transformation Status values used for the Data-Driven Query task are described here.

- `DTSTransformStat_InsertQuery`

  Execute the Insert Query. This is the status value assigned in the default script for the Data-Driven Query task.

  Value   16

- `DTSTransformStat_UpdateQuery`

  Execute the Update Query.

  Value   32

- `DTSTransformStat_DeleteQuery`

  Execute the Delete Query.

  Value   64

- `DTSTransformStat_UserQuery`

  Execute the User Query.

  Value   8

Summary

The main goal of this chapter has been to present the two core transformation tasks—the Transform Data task and the Data-Driven Query task. Along with that has come a discussion of connections, transformation scripts, Transformation Status constants, global variables, and lookups.

Many of the topics started in this chapter are continued in later chapters:

- Chapter 8, "Using Other DTS Tasks," presents the other six tasks.
- Chapter 9, "DTS Packages," shows how the tasks can be brought together into a logical whole as a DTS Package.
- Chapter 11, "Writing ActiveX Scripts," returns to the topic of ActiveX scripts, with a number of scripting examples.
- Finally, Chapter 12, "Programming with the DTS Object Model," presents a reference for the Data Transformation Services Object model.

Using Other DTS Tasks

by Tim Peterson

CHAPTER 8

The Data Transformation Services (DTS) provides an integrated development environment for transforming data. Chapter 7 presented detailed information about the two tasks that actually do the work of data transformation—the Transform Data task and the Data-Driven Query task. This chapter continues with the details about the other six tasks. Chapter 9 then goes on to explain how all these tasks are used together in a DTS Package.

Here are the six tasks discussed in this chapter:

- The Bulk Insert task provides high-speed import from text files into SQL Server.
- The Active Script task is a tool for programmatic control of a DTS Package.
- The Execute SQL task integrates the DTS Package with the database server, giving the capability to call stored procedures and issue other queries.
- The Transfer SQL Server Objects task can be used to copy database objects from one SQL Server database to another.
- The Send Mail task integrates DTS Packages with the messaging system, allowing the package to email reports on its activities.
- The Execute Process task integrates DTS Packages with the operating system, by starting programs and running batch files.

If additional capabilities are needed, then custom DTS tasks can be created.

> **Note**
>
> A beta version of a new custom task, the OLAP Services Processing Task, was publicly released by Microsoft in May 1999. This task is described in Chapter 16, "Processing and Browsing Cubes."

Setting Up a Task

You begin the process of creating any of the tasks, except for the Transform Data task, by doing one of these three things:

- Click the task's icon on the task palette.
- Select the task on the Task menu
- Right-click the design sheet, choose Add Task, and select the task on the pop-up menu.

Each task has its own specific Properties dialog, which is opened when the task is first created. You can also open the Properties dialog by double-clicking the task's icon in the design sheet.

Right-clicking the task's icon and selecting Workflow and Workflow Properties brings up the Workflow Properties dialog for each task. Chapter 11 discusses how to use this dialog to set precedences and choose Step Properties.

> ## Tips for Using COM with DTS
>
> All the tasks have a Name property that is set automatically when a task is created using the DTS Designer. The Name is used for referring to a task in code. It is never displayed in the interface. When you create a task using code, you can assign whatever Name you want to a task.
>
> If you know the name of the step with which a task is associated, you can retrieve the name of the task by using the step's TaskName property. This can be helpful because the step's name is displayed in the user interface.
>
> All tasks that use a connection have a ConnectionID Property. This is a unique integer value assigned to the particular connection at the time it is created. This value is assigned automatically when you create and use connections in the DTS Designer. When working with these objects in code, the programmer has to keep track of the values used for the ConnectionID.

The Bulk Insert Task

The Bulk Insert task provides the quickest way to import records from a text file into SQL Server. This task is based on the Transact-SQL BULK INSERT statement and is implemented by SQL Server in exactly the same way. You cannot perform data transformations during a Bulk Insert. The main benefit of this task is speed. Figure 8.1 shows the Bulk Insert Properties dialog.

Tip

Don't expect to get the best possible speed from Bulk Insert without becoming familiar with the properties on the Options tab, discussed later. Some of these settings can greatly increase the speed of a Bulk Insert. The most important performance setting is the Lock Entire Table option.

FIGURE 8.1

The Bulk Insert task provides the fastest way of inserting records into SQL Server from a text file.

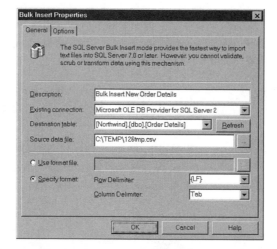

Note

The Bulk Insert task and the Transact-SQL BULK INSERT statement have similar functionality to the bcp utility which was used in previous versions of SQL Server. Before version 7.0, bcp was the primary way many people used to import data into SQL Server. The implementation of the bulk insert in SQL Server 7.0 is between two and four times faster than the old implementation of bcp.

Books On Line states that the BULK INSERT statement is faster than using bcp. While that was true in beta versions of SQL Server 7.0, it is not true in the final version that was released. The bcp utility was changed so that it uses exactly the same functionality as BULK INSERT.

So you really have three options that, underneath the surface, are actually the same thing—the Bulk Insert Task, the BULK INSERT statement, and the bcp utility.

There are two things you can do with bcp that you cannot do with the other bulk insert options.

You can bulk copy records out of SQL Server using bcp, whereas the others only bulk copy in.

If you use bcp interactively, from a command prompt, it will generate a format file for that bulk insert. Format files can be used to control field mappings in all the bulk insert options, but they can't be created with the others.

Tip

If the best import speed is not required, you can use a Transform Data task to import your text files into SQL Server. If you use all column copy transformations, this Transform Data task will also go very quickly. You have the advantage of a much friendlier interface in setting up the file import when you use the Transform Data task. Use the Bulk Insert only when you need the greatest speed.

The Destination for a Bulk Insert

An existing connection must be used for the data destination of a Bulk Insert task. The connection must be to a SQL Server database. The Bulk Insert task cannot be used for any other data destinations. If you don't have an existing connection that will work for this task, you have to close the Bulk Insert Properties dialog, create the connection, and then return to the dialog to select that new connection. You select the table or view used for the destination from the list.

The Source Data File and the Format File

The source for the Bulk Insert task is a data file, which can be selected from a file browsing dialog by clicking the expand button.

If you choose not to use a format file, you can pick the correct row delimiter and column delimiter from the lists. The default values are a tab character and a line feed character. If you are using a format file, you can also use the browsing dialog to select it.

The Transact-SQL Bulk Insert command implements the format file and delimiter choices with these parameters: FORMATFILE, ROWTERMINATOR, and FIELDTERMINATOR.

> **Tip**
>
> The properties discussed in this section are implemented as these properties of the `BulkInsertTask` object: `DataFile`, `FormatFile`, `RowDelimiter`, and `ColumnDelimiter`.

Normally a Bulk Insert takes data from the fields of a source file and puts it into the same number of fields in the data destination, using the same order. If you don't have the same number of fields or if the fields are in different orders, you usually have two options:

- Use a View in place of the destination table, which lines up the fields with the source text file. This is usually the easiest option to implement

- Use a format file. This option is usually harder to implement, but it gives the most flexibility.

These options are discussed in the following sections.

Using a View with a Bulk Insert Task

You can use a view to reconcile differences between the source and destination in all cases, except when the source data file has more fields than the destination table. In that one case, you have to use a format file. In all other case, it's easier to use a view.

For example, you have a destination table, tblDest, with five fields:

- field1
- field2
- field3
- field4
- field5

You have a source text file with three of these fields, but they're in a different order:

- field2
- field5
- field4

You want to use a Bulk Insert task to load the information from field2, field4, and field5 into tblDest. You could use a format file. But you also could create the following view and select this view as the destination for the Bulk Insert:

```
CREATE VIEW vwBulkInsertDest
AS
SELECT field2, field5, field4 from tblDest
```

If you use `vwBulkInsertDest` as the destination for the Bulk Insert, the fields will be lined up correctly. The view matches both the number of the columns and the order of the columns in the source text file.

Using a Format File with a Bulk Insert Task

Using a format file gives you more control over the Bulk Insert task. Listing 8.1 shows a format file created with the fields in the categories table from the Northwind sample database.

LISTING 8.1   The Basic Layout of a Format File Used for a Bulk Insert

```
7.0
6
1       SQLCHAR     0       4       " "       1       stor_id
2       SQLCHAR     0       40      " "       2       stor_name
3       SQLCHAR     0       40      " "       3       stor_address
4       SQLCHAR     0       20      " "       4       city
5       SQLCHAR     0       2       " "       5       state
6       SQLCHAR     0       5       " "       6       zip
```

A format file for a Bulk Insert has the following elements:

- A version number at the top—in this case, 7.0.
- The number of fields in the source data file is on the second line—in this case, 6.
- One row of information for each of the fields in the source data file—in this case, 6 rows.
- The first five columns specify information about the source data file: field order, field data type, prefix length, maximum data length, and delimiter.
- The last two columns specify information about the destination: column order and column name.

You can, of course, create format files by learning the required format and using a word processor. The easy way to create a format file, though, is to use the bcp utility interactively.

Open a Command Prompt and type in a bcp command. The following command could be used to generate the format file in Listing 8.1:

```
bcp pubs.dbo.stores out c:\temp\stores.txt
```

The bcp utility will ask you a number of questions about the fields in this bulk copy. One of the last questions you will be asked is whether or not you want to create a format file. If you give an affirmative response, you will be asked for the host file name, which is used as the name of the format file that will be created.

Extra Fields in the Source Text File

If the text file being used as the source for a Bulk Insert task has more fields than the destination, you must use a format file. This is the one situation when using a View is not an option.

For example, you want to run a Bulk Insert into the stores table from the previous example. Your source text file has the six fields for that table but also has three extra fields—stor_type, stor_descript, and manager_name.

Start by generating the format file in Listing 8.1. Change the number of columns on the second line of the format file to 9. Now add the extra columns in the order they appear in the source text file. Change the numbers in the first column, so they go consecutively from 1 through 9, as shown in Listing 8.2. Set the value to 0 in the column used for the destination column order, for those extra columns that are not in the database.

LISTING 8.2 Adding Additional Fields with a Format File

```
7.0
9
1       SQLCHAR    0    4     " "    1    stor_id
2       SQLCHAR    0    40    " "    0    manager_name
3       SQLCHAR    0    40    " "    2    stor_name
4       SQLCHAR    0    40    " "    3    stor_address
5       SQLCHAR    0    20    " "    4    city
6       SQLCHAR    0    2     " "    5    state
7       SQLCHAR    0    5     " "    6    zip
8       SQLCHAR    0    40    " "    0    stor_type
9       SQLCHAR    0    40    " "    0    stor_descript
```

Extra Fields in the Data Destination Table

If you have more fields in the destination table, you can use a view as the destination or use a format file. In this case, you have to put a zero in the source field length column, an empty string in the delimiter field, and a zero in the column for the destination column order.

Listing 8.3 shows a format file for a source file that has only three of the six fields that are in stores.

LISTING 8.3 "Zeroing Out" Information in the Format File when There Is No Data in the Source for Fields in the Destination

```
7.0
6
1    SQLCHAR    0    4     " "    1    stor_id
2    SQLCHAR    0    40    " "    2    stor_name
3    SQLCHAR    0    0     " "    0    stor_address
4    SQLCHAR    0    20    " "    4    city
5    SQLCHAR    0    0     " "    0    state
6    SQLCHAR    0    0     " "    0    zip
```

Rearranging Fields When Moving from Source to Destination

The other situation where you need either a view or a format file is when you have to change the order of the fields in the Bulk Insert to make the fields line up properly from source to destination.

You have a text file to import into stores that has the correct six fields, but the field order in this text file is stor_name, stor_id, stor_address, city, state, zip.

The rows describing the fields in the format file must be in the order that those rows appear in the source text file. But the numbers in the sixth column must reflect the actual order of those fields in the destination table. Listing 8.4 shows a format file adjusting the order of fields that differ in the source and destination tables.

LISTING 8.4 Switching the Numbering in Column Six Reorders Fields as They Enter the Destination Table

```
7.0
6
1    SQLCHAR    0    40    " "    2    stor_name
2    SQLCHAR    0    4     " "    1    stor_id
3    SQLCHAR    0    40    " "    3    stor_address
4    SQLCHAR    0    20    " "    4    city
5    SQLCHAR    0    2     " "    5    state
6    SQLCHAR    0    5     " "    6    zip
```

Other Properties of the Bulk Insert Task

The Options tab of the Bulk Insert Properties dialog, shown in Figure 8.2, has a number of choices, which are discussed in the following sections.

FIGURE 8.2

*Many settings on
the Options tab of
the Bulk Insert
Properties dialog
greatly affect
performance.*

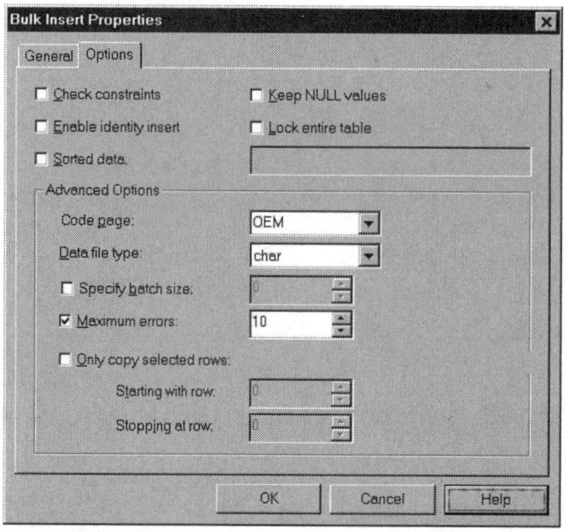

> **Tip**
>
> These properties are implemented in the object model as Properties of the
> `BulkInsertTask`. The exact name used in the model is indicated for each
> property.

Check Constraints

When this option is selected, the data is checked for compliance with all constraints as it
is added to the destination table. By default, constraints are ignored when adding records
with a Bulk Insert.

Default value: `False`

Effect on performance: Improves performance when selected

Object property: `CheckConstraints`

Equivalent parameter of the Bulk Insert command: `CHECK_CONSTRAINTS`

You enable constraints in Transact-SQL code with the `CHECK` parameter in the `ALTER
TABLE` statement. You can disable them with the `NO CHECK` parameter. Selecting or not
selecting this property implements identical behavior for the Bulk Insert task, though
other data modifications taking place at the same time will still have the constraints
enforced.

The Bulk Insert task runs more quickly if the constraints are not checked. You can create
an Execute SQL task that checks for and processes any records that have been entered

into the table that violate the table's constraints. Set this Execute SQL task to take place on the successful completion of the Bulk Insert task.

> **Note**
>
> Triggers are never fired during a Bulk Insert task. If you want to check constraints and fire triggers after a Bulk Insert, you can use the following command:
>
> ```
> Update tblCustomer set PhoneNumber = PhoneNumber
> ```
>
> This command fails if any records in the table violate the constraints.
>
> All the update triggers will be run by this command. If you take all your insert triggers and also make them update triggers, this code activates all the triggers that were missed during the Bulk Insert. If any of the triggers fail to successfully complete, this update command fails.
>
> You need more complex code to clean up the data if it fails this constraint and trigger test.

Keep NULL values

Selecting this option causes null values to be inserted into the destination table wherever there are empty values in the source. The default behavior is to insert the values that have been defined in the destination table as defaults wherever there are empty fields.

Default value: `False`

Effect on performance: Improves performance when selected

Object property: `KeepNulls`

Equivalent parameter of the Bulk Insert command: `KEEPNULLS`

A Bulk Insert task that keeps nulls could run faster. You can create an Execute SQL task after the Bulk Insert that will apply the table's defaults. Here is a SQL statement that puts the default value into all the PhoneNumber fields that have empty values:

```
Update tblCustomer set PhoneNumber = Null where PhoneNumber = Null
```

This strategy assumes that there are no records in the PhoneNumber field where you intentionally want to place a `Null` value.

Enable Identity Insert

This option allows the insertion of values into an Identity column in the destination table.

Default value: `False`

Effect on performance: Negligible

Object property: `KeepIdentity`

Equivalent parameter of the Bulk Insert command: `KEEPIDENTITY`

There are three possible ways to handle a Bulk Insert into a table that has an identity column:

- If you want to ignore the values for the identity column in the source data file, leave the default setting of `False` for this property. The table's identity column will be filled with automatically generated values as in a normal record insert.
- If you want to keep the values for the identity column that are in your source data file, select this option. SQL Server sets the `IDENTITY_INSERT` option on for the Bulk Insert and writes the values from the text file into the table.
- If your text file does not have a field for the identity column, you must use a format file. This format file must indicate that the identity field is to be skipped when importing data. The table's identity column will be filled with the automatically generated values.

Lock Entire Table

SQL Server has a special locking mechanism that is available for Bulk Inserts. This mechanism is enabled either by selecting this property or by using `sp_tableoption` to set the "table lock on bulk load" option to true.

Default value: `False`

Effect on performance: Significantly improves performance when selected

Object property: `TableLock`

Equivalent parameter of the Bulk Insert command: `TABLOCK`

When this special locking mechanism is enabled, a Bulk Insert acquires a bulk update lock. This lock allows other Bulk Inserts to take place at the same time but prevents any other processes from accessing the table.

If this property is not selected and the "table lock on bulk load" option is set to `False`, then the Bulk Insert will acquire individual record locks. This significantly reduces the speed of the Bulk Insert task.

Sorted Data

By default, the Bulk Insert task processes the records in the data file as if they were in no particular order. Setting this property to true improves the performance of a Bulk Insert, if the following three requirements are met:

- A clustered index exists on the table.
- The data file is ordered in the same order as that clustered index.
- The order specified by the SortedData property matches the ordering of the table's clustered index.

Default value: Not selected. Empty string for property value.

Effect on performance: Improves performance when selected, but only if all the requirements for its proper use are met.

Object property: SortedData, which holds the string specifying the sort order.

Equivalent parameter of the Bulk Insert command: ORDER

If the table does not have a clustered index or an ordering other than the clustered index is specified, this property is ignored.

The ordering string is constructed in the same way as the syntax of the ORDER BY clause in a SQL statement. If the ordering of customers is alphabetical by city and oldest to youngest within a city, the ordering string would be:

```
City, Age DESC
```

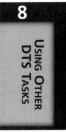

Code Page

This option specifies the code page that has been used for the data in the source file. This property affects the Bulk Insert only in cases where there are characters with values less than 32 or greater than 127.

Default value: OEM

Other possible values: ACP, RAW, Specific code page number

Effect on performance: Usually none

Object property: CodePage

Equivalent parameter of the Bulk Insert command: CODEPAGE

Data File Type

There are two choices made in this property—the choice between char and native data types and the choice between regular character fields and Unicode character fields.

If you have Unicode data in your data, you must use widechar or widenative to Bulk Insert your data.

char and widechar are used for inserting data from a file that has character fields. native and widenative use a variety of data types in their fields. These native files must be created by bulk copying data out of SQL Server with bcp. If you are using text files to transfer data between two SQL Server databases, using native mode improves performance.

Default value: char

Other possible values: native, widechar, widenative

Effect on performance: Using native and widenative improves performance when using a text file to transfer data from one SQL Server to another.

Object property: DataFileType

Equivalent parameter of the Bulk Insert command: DATAFILETYPE

Specify Batch Size

By default, all records are inserted into the destination table as a single transaction. This property allows for fewer records to be included in each transaction. If a failure takes place during the Bulk Insert, all inserts in the current transaction are rolled back. If some batches have already been committed, those records stay in the destination database.

Default value: Not selected. Batch size of 0, indicating that all records are to be inserted in one batch.

Effect on performance: Import speed increases as the batch size is increased, unless there are limiting factors such as inadequate space for the transaction log.

Object property: BatchSize

Equivalent parameter of the Bulk Insert command: BATCHSIZE

This is the one area where the Bulk Insert properties do not exactly match the parameters of the Bulk Insert Transact-SQL command. Two parameters are available in the Transact-SQL command that are not available when doing a Bulk Insert task. The KILOBYTES_PER_BATCH and ROWS_PER_BATCH are both used by SQL Server to perform the Bulk Insert more efficiently.

Maximum Errors

This property specifies the maximum number of allowable errors before the Bulk Insert task is terminated.

Default value: Selected, with value set to 10

Effect on performance: None

Object property: MaximumErrors

Equivalent parameter of the Bulk Insert command: MAXERRORS

Each transaction within the Bulk Insert is always terminated on the first error that occurs within that transaction. If the batch size has not been changed, all the records are included in a single transaction, so the whole Bulk Insert fails on the first error. If you want all acceptable records to be inserted, regardless of how many records are rejected, set the batch size to 1 and Maximum Errors to 0.

Only Copy Selected Rows, Starting with Row, and Stopping at Row

These properties allow you to choose to include only a particular range of records from the source data file in your Bulk Insert.

Default values: Not selected, 1, and 0. All the records in the file are included in the Bulk Insert.

Effect on performance: None

Object Properties: FirstRow and LastRow

Equivalent parameters of the Bulk Insert command: FIRSTROW and LASTROW

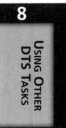

The ActiveX Script Task

ActiveX scripts can be included in your DTS Package in the following three places:

- In the transformation scripts of the Transform Data task and the Data-Driven Query task, as discussed in Chapter 7, "The Core Data Transformation Tasks."
- In the workflow scripts, which can be run before any of the tasks. These scripts have a primary purpose of determining whether the task should be executed. These scripts are discussed in Chapter 9, "DTS Packages."
- As a separate task, which is the topic of discussion here.

The ActiveX Script Task Properties dialog, as shown in Figure 8.3, is almost identical to the ActiveX Script Transformation Properties dialog used for the Transform Data task. This dialog has already been described in Chapter 7.

FIGURE 8.3

The ActiveX Script Task Properties dialog is used to create scripts that execute apart from a particular data transformation task. The default script is shown here.

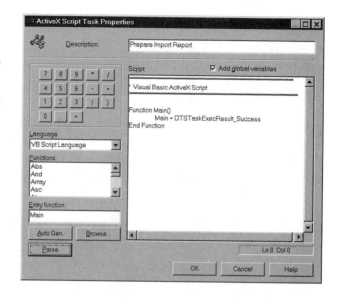

The differences between the ActiveX Script Task Properties dialog and the ActiveX Script Transformation Properties dialog are as follows:

- The Task dialog has a box for entering the task Description.

- The Task dialog has a check box for adding global variables. By default, global variables cannot be referenced in an ActiveX Script task. This check box adds the capability to use global variables.

- The Task dialog has a box for specifying the Entry function, the function in the Script that is called when the Script is executed. The Entry function defaults to Main.

- The Task dialog does not have the lists with the source and the destination fields. ActiveX Script tasks are not associated with connections.

- The Task dialog does not have a button for testing the script.

You can set the return value of the Main function in an ActiveX Script task to one of the two Task Execution Result constants:

- `DTSTaskExecResult_Success`: 0—The task executed successfully.

- `DTSTaskExecResult_Failure`: 0—The task failed.

> **Tip**
>
> It is important to avoid time-consuming commands in transformation scripts because they are executed once for each record in the source data. That concern is not present with the ActiveX Script task. This task would normally be run just once during the execution of a DTS Package.

Here are some of the things you can do with an ActiveX Script task:

- Modify the properties of other DTS objects as the task is running. The most useful example of this is probably changing the data source that a connection is using. That would allow tasks to be coded to use one data connection, although they are actually using many different data sources.

- Implement basic control of flow for the DTS Package. The two Task Execution Results can be used to specify Success or Failure for this task. Control of flow within the package can be set so that the success of this ActiveX script leads to one course of action, and a failure leads to a separate course of action.

- Implement complex control of flow for the DTS Package. The ordering of tasks in a package is normally controlled by the steps and their precedences, as discussed in Chapter 11, "Writing ActiveX Scripts." But if the control of flow is not known in advance, it could be set from within an ActiveX Script. The script can use the execute method to run other tasks in the package, to programmatically control the order of those tasks.

- Execute other DTS Packages.

- Create any COM object. An ActiveX Script task can open up an ADO recordset, read the data, modify the data, and change the flow of the DTS Package based on that knowledge.

- Read from text files and write to text files.

- If this DTS Package is always going to be run interactively, the script could present message boxes and input boxes.

- Execute whatever commands are available in the particular scripting language.

See Chapter 11 for examples of ActiveX scripts.

8

**USING OTHER
DTS TASKS**

> **Tip**
>
> The object name for this task drops the "X" in "ActiveX". It's the
> ActiveScriptTask object. This object has five properties that are set in the
> interface—ActiveXScript for the script's text; AddGlobalVariables;
> Description; ScriptLanguage; which defaults to "VBScript"; and FunctionName
> property for the entry function.

The Execute SQL Task

Figure 8.4 shows the Execute SQL Properties dialog.

FIGURE 8.4

*The Execute SQL
task is used to run
one or more SQL
statements.*

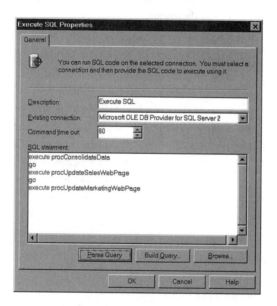

A description for this task can be entered. The task must be associated with a connection,
which determines in which database the SQL script is executed. You pick the connection
from the list of connections that have been created.

The command timeout can be set, which is the length of time in seconds that the task
waits until it reports that the command has failed. The default for the timeout is 0, which
causes the task to wait indefinitely.

The SQL statement can either be written in the box, created using the Data
Transformation Services Query Designer with the Build Query button, or imported from

a file with the Browse button. You can check the syntax of the query with the Parse Query button.

These SQL queries have the following characteristics:

- They can have one or more SQL statements.
- The SQL statements can be submitted or separated into batches with the GO batch terminator.
- The GO command must always be on a line by itself and must begin in the first position of that line.
- GO is the only command that the Execute SQL task recognizes by itself. Everything else is passed through in batches to the OLE DB provider that is being used by the Connection.

> **Tip**
>
> The properties of the ExecuteSQLTask object that can be set from the DTS Designer are Description, CommandTimeout, and SQLStatement. There is, of course, also a ConnectionID property and a Name property. Finally, there is a read-only CommandProperties property, which holds a collection of command properties specific to each OLE DB provider.

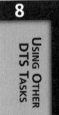

8

USING OTHER
DTS TASKS

The Transfer SQL Server Objects Task

The Transfer SQL Server Objects task can only be used for SQL Server databases. It provides the capability to transfer data and the database objects you choose from one SQL Server to another. Objects you can transfer include:

- Tables, with or without the data in them
- Indexes
- Referential integrity constraints
- Triggers
- Views
- Stored procedures
- Rules
- Defaults

- User-defined data types
- Database users
- SQL Server logins
- Object-level permissions
- Full text indexes

The Transfer SQL Server Objects Properties dialog has tabs for Source, Destination, and Transfer, as shown in Figure 8.5.

FIGURE 8.5

The Transfer SQL Server Objects task is used to move objects and data from one SQL Server to another.

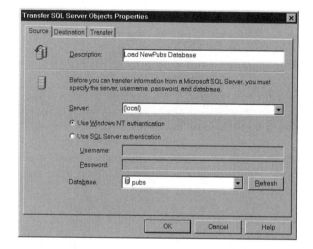

The Source and the Destination

The Source and Destination tabs are identical, except for the box to enter the description of the task on the Source tab.

This task does not use the Connection objects. Instead, you have to enter the entire source and destination connection information specifically for this task. This information includes the SQL Server name, the authentication information, and the database.

Tips for Using COM with DTS

The properties of the `TransferObjectsTask` object that are set on the Source and Destination tabs include: `Description`, `SourceDatabase`, `SourceServer`, `SourceUseTrustedConnection`, `SourceLogin`, `SourcePassword`, `DestinationUseTrustedConnection`, `DestinationServer`, `DestinationDatabase`, `DestinationLogin`, and `DestinationPassword`.

Transfer Choices

You have a detailed level of control over what objects you want to include in your transfer, as well as controlling how that transfer is executed. These choices are made on the Transfer tab of the dialog (see Figure 8.6) and on two additional windows that can be called from this tab.

FIGURE 8.6

The Transfer tab of the dialog and the two dialogs that can be called from this tab give you a high level of control over your object transfer.

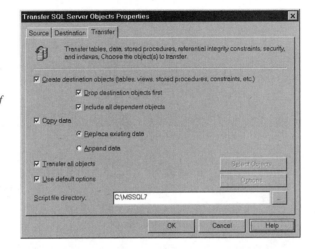

Note

The Transfer SQL Server Objects task has an especially convenient interface. There are intelligent default values chosen and the ability to quickly adjust the object transfer so that it fits particular needs.

You make five main choices when creating a Transfer SQL Server Objects task. These choices and the properties that implement them in the object model are as follows:

1. Do you want to create objects in the destination database? The check box sets the `CopySchema` property to `True`.

   If so, do you want to drop the destination objects? The check box sets the `DropDestinationObjectsFirst` property to `True`.

   Do you want to create (or drop and create) all dependent objects? The check box sets the `DropDestinationObjectsFirst` property to `True`.

   The default choice is to choose all three.

2. Do you want to copy data from the source to the destination? The check box sets the CopyData property to True.

   If so, you can choose to replace existing data or append data. Selecting each option button sets a flag in the ScriptOption property.

   The default choice is to copy data and replace the existing data.

3. Do you want to transfer all objects? The check box sets the CopyAllObjects property to True.

   The default choice is to select all. If you choose to transfer only some objects, the Select Objects button is enabled.

4. Do you want to use the default options? Leaving the box unchecked sets the appropriate flags in ScriptOption and ScriptOptionEx.

   If you don't want the default options, the Options button is enabled to give you access to the Advanced Transfers Option dialog.

5. In what directory do you want to place the scripts generated for this object transfer? Type in a directory path or select the expand button to choose one from the directory picker. The ScriptFileDirectory property will be set to the string value that you select. When the task is executed, a separate script for each kind of object being dropped or created is placed in that directory.

Caution

It's important to use these Object Transfer Options carefully. When you choose to drop destination objects first, you are choosing to completely overwrite those objects. Any modifications that you or any other developer has made to those destination objects will be lost. And if you also choose to include all dependent objects, you will be overwriting objects even when you don't select them individually.

Selecting Objects for the Transfer

Figure 8.7 shows the Select Objects dialog.

You can select the various types of objects you want to consider for transferring with the check boxes at the top of the dialog. The objects in the list can be selected or unselected individually. You can also select all the objects in the list with the Select All button or select a range of objects by pressing the Shift key while you are selecting two objects.

FIGURE 8.7

The Select Objects dialog is where you choose the objects you want to include in the Transfer SQL Server Objects task.

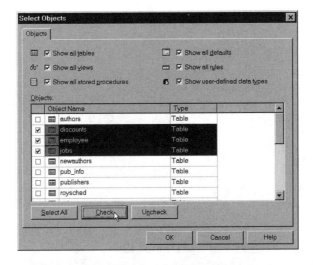

> **Note**
>
> You can't decide whether to include indexes, constraints, triggers, or security objects in this box. Those choices are made by setting options in the Advanced Transfer Options dialog.

> **Tips for Using COM with DTS**
>
> The inclusion or exclusion of objects is implemented in the COM interface with a set of three methods of the `TransferObjectsTask` object.
>
> `AddObjectForTransfer` adds an additional object to the list to be transferred.
>
> `object.AddObjectForTransfer(ObjectName, OwnerName, DTSSQLObjectType)`
>
> The valid constants for `DTSSQLObjectType` are:
>
> `DTSSQLObj_AllDatabaseObjects`
>
> `DTSSQLObj_AllDatabaseUserObjects`
>
> `DTSSQLObj_Default`
>
> `DTSSQLObj_Rule`
>
> `DTSSQLObj_StoredProcedure`
>
> `DTSSQLObj_SystemTable`
>
> `DTSSQLObj_Trigger`
>
> *continues*

```
DTSSQLObj_UserDefinedDatatype

DTSSQLObj_UserTable

DTSSQLObj_View
```

GetObjectForTransfer iterates the objects on the list to be transferred.

```
object.GetObjectForTransfer(Index, ObjectName, OwnerName,_

     DTSSQLObjectType)
```

The Index is a 0-based index used to number the objects being transferred.

ResetObjectsList removes all the objects from the list to be transferred.

```
object.ResetObjectsList
```

Advanced Transfer Options

Figure 8.8 shows the Advanced Transfer Options dialog. You can reach this dialog by pressing the Options button on the Transfer tab of the Transfer SQL Server Objects Properties dialog.

FIGURE 8.8

In the Advanced Transfer Options dialog, you decide some of the details of the Transfer SQL Server Objects task. The default choices are shown here.

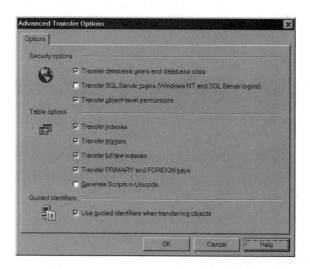

The nine check boxes on the Advanced Transfer Options dialog all set flags for ScriptOption or the ScriptOptionEx properties of the TransferObjectsTask object. Fifty-two constants are listed for these flags in the SQL Server product documentation. You have several choices through the user interface. You gain precise control if you set these properties in code.

The selection of flags that are in effect for the default options is displayed the first time you open the Advanced Transfer Options dialog. The individual choices you have include:

- Transfer database users and database roles. Included in default options.
- Transfer SQL Server logins. Not included in default.
- Transfer object-level permissions. Included in default.
- Transfer indexes. Included in default. The individual flags you can use in code give you the capability to choose individually whether to transfer clustered indexes, nonclustered indexes, and unique indexes.
- Transfer triggers. Included in default.
- Transfer full text indexes. Included in default.
- Transfer PRIMARY and FOREIGN keys. Included in default. When this box is checked, all five types of constraints are transferred—Primary Key Constraint, Unique Constraint, Foreign Key Constraint, Check Constraint, and Default Constraint. When this box is unchecked, none of these five constraints is transferred. In code, you can specify whether to include each of the constraints individually.
- Generate Scripts in Unicode. In the default, Unicode is not used for the scripts.
- Use quoted identifiers when transferring objects. Quoted identifiers are used in the default.

The Send Mail Task

The Send Mail task is used to send an email message from within a DTS Package. It is included as a task in DTS to provide a convenient method for the results of a DTS Package to be communicated to the individuals who need to be informed. The properties of the Send Mail task are the standard elements of an email message, as shown in the Send Mail Properties dialog in Figure 8.9.

The Microsoft Messaging API must be installed for the Send Mail task to work.

The attachments that are sent with the email do not have to exist at the time this task is created. They can be created at the time the DTS Package is run. For example, you could use a set of global variables to track the number of records that have been processed. These global variables could be used in an ActiveX Script task to write a report out to a text file. The Send Mail attachment could be pointed to the name of that file, so that it could be sent to a database administrator as the final action of the DTS Package.

FIGURE 8.9

The Send Mail task gives you a convenient method to inform people of the results of a DTS Package.

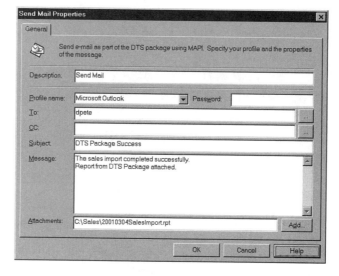

You can also change the various properties of the Send Mail task dynamically using ActiveX scripts, as the DTS Package is being run. A message could be dynamically constructed, the subject could be changed, and the email could be sent to different groups of people. All these decisions could be determined programmatically, by what happens in the package.

Tip

The properties of the `SendMailTask` object that you would most likely change dynamically during a package are: `ToLine`, `CCLine`, `Subject`, `MessageText`, and `FileAttachments`.

Other properties of this object include `IsNTService`, `Password`, and `SaveMailInSentItemsFolder`.

The methods of this object are `Execute`, `GetDefaultProfileName`, `InitializeMAPI`, `Logoff`, `Logon`, `ResolveName`, `ShowAddressBook`, and `UninitializeMAPI`.

The Execute Process Task

The Execute Process task runs an operating system program. This is the simplest of all the tasks, but it can be very useful. Many organizations have existing programs or batch processes for transferring data. These existing programs can be incorporated into a DTS

Package, by using this Execute Process task. These existing programs and new transformation tasks can all be integrated together, with each part set to run in the proper sequence.

Figure 8.10 shows the Execute Process Properties dialog.

FIGURE 8.10

The Execute Process task can be used to start programs of batch processes.

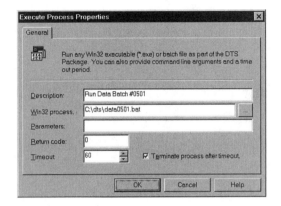

You can select an executable program or batch process with a file dialog. There is a box to enter any parameters.

The Execute Process task expects to receive a return code from the executable program. The default for the return code is 0. If the task does not receive the correct return code, the task reports back to the package that it has failed.

A timeout in number of seconds can also be set. The default for the timeout is 0. This default means that the task waits indefinitely for the return code. If the timeout is set to a different value and the task does not receive the return code, the task reports that it has failed.

If the timeout is set to a nonzero value, then the Terminate Process After Timeout check box is enabled. If this check box is selected, the process is terminated when the timeout is reached.

Tip

The properties of the `CreateProcessTask` object are `Description`, `ProcessCommandLine` (containing the executable path and the parameters), `SuccessReturnCode`, `Timeout`, `TerminateProcessAfterTimeOut`, and `FailPackageOnTimeout`.

continues

The `FailPackageOnTimeout` cannot be set in the DTS Designer. If set to `True`, the entire package is terminated when the timeout set in the Execute Process task expires.

Creating Custom Tasks

You can create your own custom tasks to extend the capabilities of DTS Packages. These custom tasks are created as .dll files with C++ or Visual Basic. They can be given an icon and included with the eight built-in tasks.

A sample C++ project named dtstask shows how to create custom tasks. This project is installed as a part of SQL Server setup, if the development tools and samples are selected in the installation. These files are installed in MSSQL7\DevTools\Samples\dts\dtstask project.

Custom tasks are registered by selecting Task, Register Custom Task from the menu. Figure 8.11 shows the dialog for registering a custom task.

FIGURE 8.11

Custom tasks can be created with Visual Basic or C++. After being registered in the DTS Designer, they operate in the same manner as the built-in tasks.

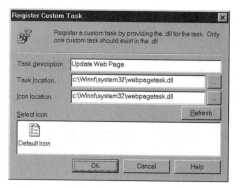

Summary

All DTS tasks are useful in the preparation of data for OLAP. Some tasks are more important than others, but each has its place.

The main work of adding new data into the Fact Table is done by the Transform Data task. Transform scripts are used to cleanse the data. Lookups are used to expand abbreviations and codes. Data-Driven Query tasks can be used to update the dimension tables.

Bulk Insert tasks are used to rapidly import data from text files into SQL Server. A Bulk Insert can be used to load data into SQL Server as a preliminary step to the data transformation. Execute Process tasks execute batch files and other processes. They can be used to run programs that extract data from other systems so that it can be loaded into the data mart.

ActiveX Script tasks can be used to monitor what is happening in the other tasks. They can prepare email messages to be sent by the Send Mail task so that the DTS Package can report what it is doing.

The Execute SQL task can be used to execute stored procedures that are carrying out further data processing or analysis within the database engine. The Transfer SQL Server Objects task is used to move objects from one SQL Server to another.

The tasks are the building blocks of the Data Transformation Services. In Chapter 11, you will learn how these pieces are put together with the workflow objects, steps, precedences, workflow scripts, Repository, and package properties to construct a complete data transformation package.

8

USING OTHER
DTS TASKS

DTS Packages

by Tim Peterson

CHAPTER 9

The previous two chapters described the various tasks available in the Data Transformation Services(DTS). Now you will learn how all those tasks fit together into the executable programming unit called a DTS Package.

The Steps Objects Collection

The DTS Package is the highest level object in the DTS Object Model. A package has four collections of objects. Three of them have already been discussed:

- Connections (covered in Chapter 7)
- Global variables(covered in Chapter 7)
- Tasks (covered in Chapters 7 and 8)

The fourth object collection is the collection of Steps.

Steps control the flow of execution of the tasks in a DTS Package. Tasks do the work. Steps keep the tasks in the right order. Every task object must be associated with one and only one step.

A Step object is created for you whenever a task is created in the DTS Package Designer. If you create a task using code, the Step object will not be automatically created. You have to create it explicitly in the code. How to write this code is described in Chapter 12.

> **Note**
>
> Tasks and steps are on an equal level in the DTS object hierarchy, but in their relationship, the task appears to be contained within a step. The task isn't executed until the step allows it to be executed. The two objects are so closely connected that it's hard to talk about one without talking about the other.

A Step object has a variety of properties associated with it. Many of these properties can be set on the Options tab of the Workflow Properties dialog, shown in Figure 9.1. Open the Workflow Properties dialog by right-clicking any task icon and selecting Workflow, Workflow Properties. For a Data Transformation task, you click the black arrow and pick Workflow Properties.

FIGURE 9.1

You can set many of the properties of a Step object on the Options tab of the Workflow Properties dialog.

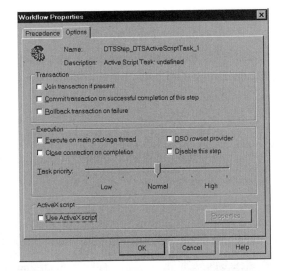

> ## Note
>
> Remember, as discussed in Chapter 6, there is a big difference between the black arrow used to symbolize a Transform Data task and the three colorful Workflow arrows—On Completion, On Success, or On Failure. The Transform Data task is drawn between two connections, while the Workflow arrows are drawn between two tasks.
>
> You can open the Workflow Properties dialog by double-clicking one of the Workflow arrows. But opened in this way, the Options tab is not available. Most of the properties of the Step object are associated with one particular task and it would be confusing to set those properties when clicking an arrow that connects two different tasks.

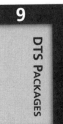

There are separate sections later in this chapter that discuss several of the properties set on the Options tab:

- Workflow ActiveX scripts
- Transactions in DTS Packages
- Threads and priority of execution
- DTS Packages as data sources

A Step object has a Name property, which is created automatically by the DTS Designer. The Name of the step is displayed on the Options tab.

A Step object also has a TaskName property, which is not displayed. The TaskName is the name of the task with which this particular step is associated.

Steps have an Execute method, but this method is not usually used in code. When the DTS Package is executed, the Execute method of each of the steps is called automatically. When and if the task associated with a step is actually executed is determined by the precedence constraints, which is the topic of the next section.

Precedence Constraints

The Step object has a property called PrecedenceConstraints, which contains the PrecedenceConstraints collection for that particular step.

The precedence constraints in a DTS Package determine the order for the various tasks. They also can make the execution of one task dependent on the outcome of another task.

When I describe the precedence constraints, I will be talking about how they control the order of the steps in a DTS Package. But remember, each step is associated with one and only one task. Any time I say that a step is controlling another step, you can think of one task controlling another task.

There are three significant factors in a precedence constraint:

- The step that is being controlled by the constraint. This is called the Destination Step.
- The step that is doing the controlling. This is called the Source Step.
- The type of precedence. There are six types, three of which are available in the DTS Package Designer—On Success, On Failure, and On Completion. The other three can only be manipulated in code—If Inactive, When In Progress, and When Waiting.

Each precedence constraint can only have one Destination Step and one Source Step, but each step can participate in many different precedence constraints. If you want to make one step dependent on 50 other steps, you can do that by creating 50 precedence constraints. Similarly, you can make one step the Source Step for as many different precedence constraints as you like.

> **Note**
>
> The whole topic of precedence constraints can seem somewhat confusing, because there are so many details. As they are displayed in the DTS Package Designer, though, precedence constraints are very easy to understand. If you see

a colored arrow pointing from TaskA to TaskB, that's a precedence constraint. TaskB will not be executed until TaskA has completed. TaskB will not be executed at all, unless the result of TaskA matches the result specified in the precedence constraint.

Creating Precedence Constraints in the DTS Package Designer

You can create precedence constraints in a variety of ways using the DTS Package Designer. The most obvious way, shown in Figure 9.2, is

1. Select the icon for the task associated with the Source Step.

2. Hold down the shift key and select the icon for the task that is associated with the Destination Step.

3. Select one of the three types of precedence from the Workflow menu: On Completion, On Success, or On Failure.

FIGURE 9.2

Create a precedence constraint by selecting the two tasks involved and choosing the appropriate type of precedence from the Workflow menu.

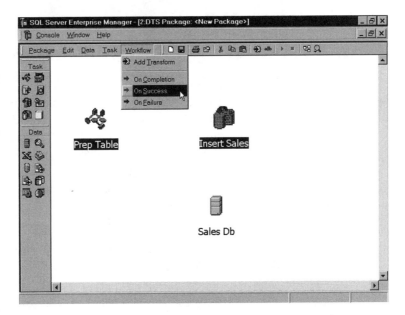

Precedence constraints can also be created on the Precedence tab of the Workflow Properties dialog, as shown in Figure 9.3. You have the advantage of being able to create many precedence constraints at the same time with this method. You can use any of the three precedence types, but all the constraints you create in this dialog will have the same destination step—the step associated with the task you right-clicked when opening the dialog.

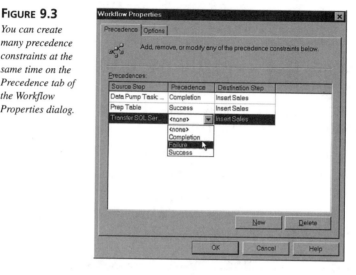

Creating Precedence Constraints in Code

The characteristics of a precedence constraint are set as follows using code:

- Each step has a `PrecedenceConstraints` property that contains the `PrecedenceConstraints` collection for that step. This step appears in the user interface as the Destination Step for all the steps in its collection. For a particular `PrecedenceConstraint` object, the Destination Step's name can be obtained by requesting the parent's parent's name. The parent of the `PrecedenceConstraint` object is the `PrecedenceConstraints` collection and the parent of that collection is the Destination Step:

  ```
  msgbox "The Destination Step Name - " & oPrecedence.Parent.Parent.Name
  ```

- Each `PrecedenceConstraint` object has a `StepName` property, which is the Source Step for the precedence constraint.

- There are two properties of the `PrecedenceConstraint` object which together determine the type of precedence—the `PrecedenceBasis` property and the `Value` property. These properties are described shortly.

The precedence constraint is based on one of two types of information:

- The Execution Result—Whether a step's execution resulted in Success or Failure.
- The Execution Status—Whether a step's execution status is Completed, Inactive, In Progress, or Waiting.

The `PrecedenceBasis` property indicates which of these types of information should be used in determining the precedence. The two `DTSStepPrecedenceBasis` constants used for this property are shown in Table 9.1.

TABLE 9.1 Constants Used for the `PrecedenceBasis` Property of the `PrecedenceConstraint` Object

Constant	Value
DTSStepPrecedenceBasis_ExecResult	1
DTSStepPrecedenceBasis_ExecStatus	0

The `Value` property indicates which of the specific Execution Results or Execution Status values are going to determine the precedence. The `Value` property uses either the DTSStepExecResult constants or the DTSStepExecStatus constants, depending on what has been chosen for the `PrecedenceBasis` property. The values for these two types of constants are shown in Table 9.2 and Table 9.3. These same constants are used as the values for the `ExecutionResult` and the `ExecutionStatus` properties of the `Step` object.

TABLE 9.2 Constants Used for the `Value` Property of the `PrecedenceConstraint` Object when `PrecedenceBasis` Is Set to `Result`. These Constants Are Also the Values of the `ExecutionResult` Property of the `Step` Object.

Constant	Value	DTS Designer Implementation
DTSStepExecResult_Failure	1	On Failure Precedence
DTSStepExecResult_Success	0	On Success Precedence

TABLE 9.3 Constants Used for the `Value` Property of the `PrecedenceConstraint` Object when `PrecedenceBasis` Is Set to `Status`. These Constants Are Also the Values of the `ExecutionStatus` Property of the `Step` Object.

Constant	Value	DTS Designer Implementation
DTSStepExecStat_Completed	4	On Completion Precedence
DTSStepExecStat_Inactive	3	Not Implemented in DTS Designer
DTSStepExecStat_InProgress	2	Not Implemented in DTS Designer
DTSStepExecStat_Waiting	1	Not Implemented in DTS Designer

The Six Types of Precedence

Three types of precedence can be chosen in the DTS Designer. The other three can be set in code, by using the `PrecedenceBasis` and `Value` properties.

On Success

The Destination Step will not be executed until the Source Step has successfully completed. If the Source Step fails or is never executed, the Destination Step will not be executed.

You can serialize the flow of the tasks in your DTS Package by using On Success precedence. Each step waits for the successful completion of the previous step before starting its execution.

On Failure

The Destination Step will not be executed until the Source Step has failed. If the Source Step succeeds or is never executed, the Destination Step will not be executed.

Use On Failure to trigger events that are to happen when tasks fail. Perhaps you want to take some corrective action and then try the task again. You could also use On Failure to call a Send Mail task to inform an administrator of the problem.

On Completion

The Destination Step will not be executed until the Source Step has been completed, either successfully or with a failure. If the Source Step is never executed, the Destination Step will not be executed.

There are some tasks that need to be done whether or not the previous tasks have been successful. An Execute SQL task that creates a table is a good example. If the table creation task is successful, the processing can continue. If the table creation fails, that's probably because the table already exists, so the processing can continue, anyway. On Completion could also be used to create a report, if that report should be created no matter what else happened.

If Inactive

The Destination Step will not be executed unless the `DisableStep` Property of the `Step` Object is set to `True`.

There may be some alternative processing that needs to be done at the times when a task is disabled. You can use this precedence constraint to automatically send the flow of operation to that alternative track.

When In Progress

The Destination Step will not be executed until the Source Step is in the process of being executed. If the Source step is never executed, the Destination Step will not be executed. If the Source Step completes execution before the Destination Step has a chance to start executing, the Destination Step will not be executed.

This precedence constraint can be used in a SendMail task to inform an administrator that a task has begun.

When Waiting

The Destination Step will not be executed unless the Source Step is waiting to be executed. If the Source step starts its execution before the Destination Step has a chance to start, the Destination Step will not be executed.

> **Note**
>
> The only documentation I have found for these last three precedence constraint types is in the list of available constants for these properties. I have never seen them mentioned in other Microsoft literature. They all work, but the logic of the program flow is harder to understand, especially using When Waiting.

Setting the Execution Status in Code

You can change the execution of a step by setting the ExecutionStatus property of the Step object in code.

- If a step has already been executed and you then set the ExecutionStatus property to DTSStepExecStat_Waiting, the step will be executed again.
- If a step is waiting to be executed and you set the ExecutionStatus to any of the constants listed in Table 9.3 besides DTSStepExecStat_Waiting, the step will not be executed.

9

DTS PACKAGES

> **Note**
>
> The ExecutionStatus property of the Step object is listed in the DTS Reference in Books On Line as a read-only property. But there is a sample ActiveX script in Books On Line that sets the property to DTSStepExecStat_Waiting for the purpose of executing a task in a loop.

Other Factors That Determine When a Step Will Execute

Steps don't execute immediately when all the precedence constraints have been satisfied. There are several other factors that affect the control of flow of the various steps and tasks, all of which are discussed later in this chapter:

- The number of threads that are available to the package. If a thread is not available, a step will not be run, even if all its precedence constraints have been satisfied.
- The thread priority assigned to each step.
- The Workflow ActiveX scripts. These scripts provide an additional opportunity to change the control of flow of the application, by executing or not executing a particular task.

Threads and Priority of Execution

DTS is a multithreaded application. Many tasks can be executed simultaneously, each one with its own separate thread.

Package-Level Thread Execution Parameters

There are two thread execution properties for the DTS Package as a whole. These properties can be set on the General tab of the DTS Package Properties dialog, as shown in Figure 9.4. To open the dialog, make sure no objects are selected in the Design Sheet, and then choose Properties from the Package menu.

The Priority Class

This setting determines the Microsoft Win32 process priority class for the DTS Package when it is executed. The possible values are Low, Normal, and High.

In the object model, this setting is the `PackagePriorityClass` property of the `Package` object. The three allowed settings for this property are displayed in Table 9.4

TABLE 9.4   Constants for the `PackagePriorityClass` of the `Package` Object

Constant	*Value*
`DTSPackagePriorityClass_Low`	1
`DTSPackagePriorityClass_Normal`	2
`DTSPackagePriorityClass_High`	3

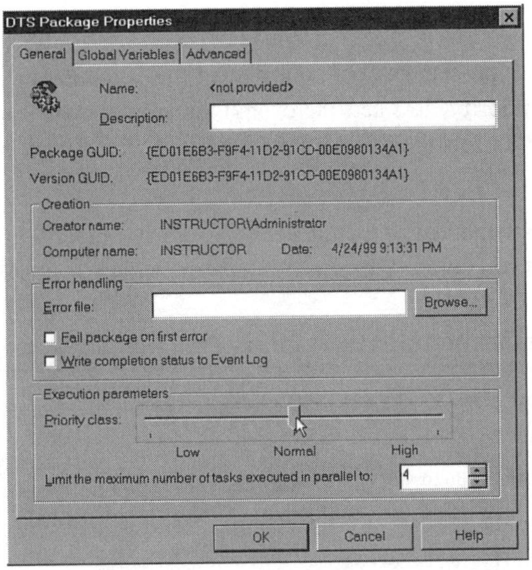

FIGURE 9.4

The priority class and the maximum number of parallel tasks are the two thread execution parameters that can be set for the DTS Package as a whole.

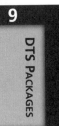

> **Note**
>
> The help file for the DTS Designer incorrectly states that there are five possible values for PackagePriorityClass. Somebody may have confused this setting with the task priority for an individual step, where there are five choices.

The Number of Tasks Executed in Parallel

This choice limits the number of steps that are allowed to execute concurrently on separate threads. The default value is 4.

This setting can affect the performance of a DTS Package. Raising this value, especially in situations when multiple processors are available, can increase the speed of a package's execution. More steps can be executed simultaneously, as long as each step has had its precedence constraints satisfied. But if this value is set too high, package execution can be slowed because of excessive switching between threads.

In code, this is the `MaxConcurrentSteps` property of the `Package` object.

Step-Level Thread Execution Parameters

There are five settings in the Execution group on the Options tab of the Workflow Properties dialog (refer to Figure 9.1).

9

DTS PACKAGES

Task Priority

The task priority gives a precise level of control over the execution priority of an individual task. The PackagePriorityClass sets the overall thread priority class to Low, Normal, or High. The task priority sets the relative thread priority within each of the three priority classes.

The task priority is implemented as the RelativePriority property of the Step object. The five constants that can be used for this property are shown in Table 9.5.

TABLE 9.5 Constants for the RelativePriority Property of the Step Object

Constant	Value
DTSStepRelativePriority_Lowest	1
DTSStepRelativePriority_BelowNormal	2
DTSStepRelativePriority_Normal	3
DTSStepRelativePriority_AboveNormal	4
DTSStepRelativePriority_Highest	5

Execute on Main Package Thread

DTS normally spawns separate threads to execute different steps of the package. This setting changes that behavior for one particular step by forcing that step to be executed on the main package thread.

These are the situations where it is necessary to execute a process on the main package thread:

- The data provider is not free-threaded and does not support parallel execution of tasks. This is true for the Microsoft Jet OLE DB Provider, as well as the providers for Excel, dBase, Paradox, and HTML files. If more than one task is being executed with one of these providers at the same time, they should all be executed on the main package thread.
- You want to debug multiple ActiveX scripts with the script debugger provided with Microsoft Visual InterDev 6.0 or the Microsoft Windows NT 4.0 Option Pack.

> **Caution**
>
> The DTS Designer Help File warns that there can be serious errors if several tasks are being executed simultaneously using data sources that do not support parallel execution. Use the Execute on Main Thread option to avoid those problems.

The `ExecuteInMainThread` property of the `Step` object implements this option. It is a Boolean property, with a default value of `False`.

Close Connection on Completion

The default behavior for opening and closing data connections is as follows:

- Do not open a connection until it is needed by a task.
- Do not close an open connection until the package completes its execution.

This default behavior is usually the most efficient, because it minimizes the number of times that data connections have to be established.

The Close connection on completion option allows you to override the default behavior for a particular step by closing all of the step's connections when the step is finished.

There are two reasons why you would consider using this option:

- Some data providers have better performance if connections are not left open.
- If there are many connections in a package and inadequate memory resources, closing the connections could conserve memory and improve overall performance.

You can set this option in code with the `CloseConnection` property of the `Step` object. This is a Boolean property with a default value of `False`.

DSO Rowset Provider

When you select this option you can return a rowset that contains the destination records generated by this step. This rowset is provided through an OLE DB data provider called DTSPackageDSO (PDSO). When the PDSO is called by an application, the PDSO executes the requested DTS Package and returns the resulting rowset to the client.

This option is the `Step` object's `IsPackageDSORowset` property, a Boolean value with a default value of `False`.

It is discussed in the "DTS Packages as Data Sources" section later in this chapter.

Disable This Step

Choose this option to block the execution of this step when the package is executed. As discussed previously, you can specify another task to run if and only if a particular task is disabled. Do this by using the `DTSStepExecStat_Inactive` constant for the `Value` property and the `DTSStepPrecedenceBasis_ExecStatus` constant for the `PrecedenceBasis` property. Both of these are properties of the `PrecedenceConstraint` object.

This option is implemented with the `DisableStep` property of the `Step` object.

9

DTS PACKAGES

Workflow ActiveX Scripts

There are three places where ActiveX scripts are used in a DTS Package—in Transformations, in ActiveX script tasks, and in Workflow control.

A Workflow ActiveX script is run at the beginning of a step's execution, before the task associated with that step is executed. The main purpose for the Workflow script is to specify if the task should be executed now, executed later, or not executed at all. You make this decision by setting the appropriate return value for the entry function of the script. The three return values are documented in the following sections.

You choose to use a Workflow ActiveX script by selecting the Use ActiveX Script box at the bottom of the Options tab of the Workflow Properties dialog (shown in Figure 9.1). To write the script, select the Properties button located beside that check box. The Workflow ActiveX Script Properties dialog, shown in Figure 9.5, opens.

FIGURE 9.5

The scripts created in the Workflow ActiveX Script Properties dialog determine whether or not a task is executed.

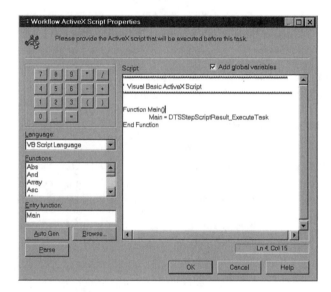

The Workflow ActiveX Script Properties dialog is identical to the ActiveX Script Task Properties dialog described in Chapter 8, except for not having a box to enter a Description for the task.

Script Result Constants

The following are the three script results you can use with Workflow ActiveX scripts. These values are assigned as the return value of the entry function. All three use the following syntax:

```
Main = DTSStepScriptResult_ExecuteTask
```

- `DTSStepScriptResult_ExecuteTask` — Execute the task associated with this step immediately upon completion of the Workflow script. This is the default return value for a Workflow script. It is also the return value when the Auto Generate script button is chosen.

  Value 0

- `DTSStepScriptResult_DontExecuteTask` — The task associated with this step is not performed during the execution of the package.

  Value 1

- `DTSStepScriptResult_RetryLater` — The task associated with this step is not executed when the Workflow script completes. The execution method of the task is called again later in the execution of the package. When the step is retried, the Workflow script is again executed before the task.

  Value 2

Using the Script Results for Looping

You can use the Retry Later script result to create a loop in the flow of the DTS Package.

- The Workflow script checks for the existence of a file or opens a recordset to check the state of data in a table.
- Create a global variable to serve as a counter. Increment the global variable each time the Workflow script is run.
- If the file is not found or the data is not in the proper state, the Workflow script returns the Retry Later script result.
- If everything is ready for the task to be run, the script returns the Execute Task script result.
- If the global variable reaches a certain value without the specifications being met, the loop is terminated with a return of the Don't Execute Task script result.

You can find examples of this and other Workflow scripts in Chapter 11, "Writing ActiveX Scripts."

Properties of the Workflow Script

Workflow scripts are implemented with the following properties of the `Step` object:

- The `FunctionName` property specifies the entry function of the script. The default function name is `Main`.

- The `ActiveXScript` property is the text of the Workflow ActiveX script.
- The `ScriptLanguage` is the scripting language used for the script.
- The `AddGlobalVariables` property determines whether or not global variables can be used in this workflow script. The default value is `True`.

Transactions in DTS Packages

Some or all of the tasks in a DTS Package can be joined together into transactions. If you use a transaction in a package, an error in one task will cause all the data changes made by other tasks in the transaction to be rolled back. If you do not use transactions, data modifications already completed will remain even if an error occurs that causes a task or the entire package to terminate with an error.

A package can have many transactions, but only one of them can be in effect at a time. Whether or not data modifications are successfully rolled back when a transaction fails depends on the transactional support of the OLE DB provider.

The transaction properties are set in two places—for the package as a whole and for each task.

Transaction Properties Set at the Package Level

Set the three package transaction properties on the Advanced tab of the DTS Package Properties dialog, shown in Figure 9.6.

FIGURE 9.6

Transaction properties for the package as a whole can be set on the Advanced tab of the DTS Package Properties dialog.

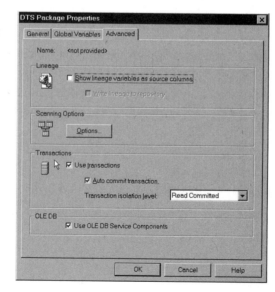

Use Transactions

The Use Transactions option determines whether or not the DTS Package will support a transaction. You can choose to include a particular step in the transaction by selecting Join Transaction if Present in the Step Properties dialog. If you don't include any steps in the transaction, your selection of Use Transactions will have no effect on the Package.

This option is the UseTransaction property of the Transaction object. It is a Boolean property with a default value of True.

Auto Commit Transaction

If Auto Commit Transaction is selected and a transaction is in effect, that transaction will be automatically committed when the execution of the package is completed.

If this option is set to False, then a transaction that is in progress when the package completes its execution will be rolled back.

The AutoCommitTransaction property of the Package object sets this option. This is a Boolean property with a default value of True.

> **Note**
>
> The help file for the DTS Designer incorrectly states that setting the Auto Commit Transaction option to False will implement the Implicit Transaction mode for all the connections in the DTS Package. This behavior can be set in SQL Server with the SET IMPLICIT_TRANSACTIONS ON command. In implicit trans-actions mode, each data modification statement must be explicitly committed. My testing indicates that Auto Commit Transaction does not implement Implicit Transaction mode. It sets the behavior as described in the DTS Object Model Reference in the Books On Line—causing a commit or a rollback of outstanding transactions when the package finishes its execution. If a task is not participat-ing in a transaction, its data modification statements commit normally, regard-less of how this property is set.

9

DTS PACKAGES

Transaction Isolation Level

The Transaction Isolation Level can be set to one of five levels in the DTS Designer. These five levels are assigned using eight constants for the corresponding property, the TransactionIsolationLevel property of the Package object.

Here are some definitions of terms used in defining Transaction Isolation Levels:

Dirty read—Reading data that has been changed by another user, even though that change hasn't been committed and might still be rolled back.

Non-repeatable read—Reading data that might have committed updates by another user before you read it again.

Phantom read—You read a set of data and then another user adds data to that set. When you read it again, you see the phantoms, the new records that have been added. Phantom reads always involved committed inserts to a table.

DTSIsoLevel_Chaos

Chaos is not implemented in SQL Server.

- Value: 16
- ANSI SQL-92 Isolation Level 0

At this isolation level, the same data can be updated by two different users at the same time. (That's why it's called chaos.)

> **Note**
>
> When would you use chaos for a transaction? Hopefully, only when your database is in single-user mode.
>
> Transact-SQL does not allow you to set this level of transaction isolation. But when a database is set to single-user mode, no locks are taken and no locks are checked. Locks aren't needed because there aren't any other users that can interfere with what you're doing.
>
> That's what happens with chaos. It's all right to ignore locks when there's only one user. In fact, it can significantly speed up processing, because the locking procedures take time.

DTSIsoLevel_ReadUncommitted

This is the equivalent to Transact-SQL's SET TRANSACTION ISOLATION LEVEL READ UNCOMMITTED.

- Value: 256
- ANSI SQL-92 Isolation Level 1
- Equivalent to constant DTSIsoLevel_Browse
- Allows dirty reads, non-repeatable reads, and phantom reads

This isolation level is useful for running complex decision support queries on data that is being updated. No locks are taken and no locks are honored when reading data at this level.

DTSIsoLevel_ReadCommitted

This level is the equivalent of Transact-SQL's SET TRANSACTION ISOLATION LEVEL READ COMMITTED.

- Value: 4096
- ANSI SQL-92 Isolation Level 2
- Equivalent to constant DTSIsolevel_CursorStability
- Does not allow dirty reads
- Allows non-repeatable reads and phantom reads

This is the default transaction isolation level in SQL Server and in DTS. You are not allowed to read data modifications that have not been committed at this level.

DTSIsoLevel_RepeatableRead

DTSIsoLevel_RepeatableRead is equivalent to Transact-SQL's SET TRANSACTION ISOLATION LEVEL REPEATABLE READ.

- Value: 65536
- ANSI SQL-92 Isolation Level 3
- Does not allow dirty reads or non-repeatable reads
- Allows phantom reads

If you start a transaction in this isolation level and you read some data, you are guaranteed that the data you have read will not be changed until your transaction ends.

DTSIsoLevel_Serializable

This is the equivalent of Transact-SQL's SET TRANSACTION ISOLATION LEVEL SERIALIZABLE.

- Value: 1048576
- ANSI SQL-92 Isolation Level 4
- Equivalent to constant DTSIsoLevel_Isolated
- Does not allow dirty reads, non-repeatable reads, or phantom reads

This level provides total isolation for the data being used in the transaction. You cannot read any data that other users have locked. No other users can change or update the data

9

DTS PACKAGES

or put any locks on the data, including shared locks. Other users are not permitted to add new records to recordsets that have been viewed by any queries in your transaction.

Transaction Settings for the Steps

You configure a step's participation in a transaction on the Options tab of the Workflow Properties dialog (shown in Figure 9.1).

Join Transaction if Present

When you select this option, the step participates in the current transaction.

There can be only one transaction active in a package at a time. If one is currently active, this step joins it. If a transaction is not active, this step starts a new one.

In code, this option is implemented as the `JoinTransactionIfPresent` property of the `Step` object. This is a Boolean property with a default value of `False`.

Commit Transaction on Successful Completion of This Step

When this option is selected, the current transaction is committed if this step completes successfully. All the data modifications made in the step and in previous steps included in the transaction are committed.

After the step completes and the transaction is committed, the next step that is set to join a transaction starts a new transaction.

This option is the `CommitSuccess` property of the `Step` object.

> **Note**
>
> The documentation on the `CommitSuccess` property in Books On Line incorrectly states that this property specifies whether a step is committed on successful completion. The whole transaction is committed, not just this particular step.

Rollback Transaction on Failure

If this option is selected, the current transaction rolls back if the step fails. All the data modifications made in this step and in previous steps included in the transaction are rolled back.

If the step fails and the transaction is rolled back, the next step that is set to join a transaction starts a new transaction.

If the option is not selected, this step is included in a transaction, and the step fails, the transaction continues without being committed or rolled back.

This option is the RollbackFailure property of the Step object.

> **Note**
>
> The documentation in Books On Line is also incorrect for this property. The whole transaction is rolled back, not just this particular step.

Implementation of Transactions by OLE DB Providers

Not all OLE DB providers implement transactions. Check the product documentation for the provider. It must support the ITransactionJoin interface, or that provider cannot be used for transactions.

DTS Packages as Data Sources

A DTS Package can be used as a data source. When it is, it returns records to the application that is calling the package, rather than sending data to a data destination.

You can use the Transact-SQL OPENROWSET statement to query a DTS Package. You can also register a DTS Package as a linked server. A DTS Package can be set up to retrieve data from another DTS Package. Within one package, you can use the results from one Transform Data task as the data source for another Transform Data task. All these topics will be discussed in this section.

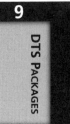

> **Note**
>
> One place where I find this capability to be useful is in testing. As new data transformations are being written, the results from those transformations can be viewed by using an OPENROWSET query. This is often easier than executing the data transformation and querying the results in the data destination.

The Data Provider DTSPackageDSO

A DTS Package is used as a data source through an OLE DB data provider called the DTSPackageDSO (PDSO). When the PDSO is called by a client application, the PDSO executes the requested DTS Package and returns the resulting rowset to the client.

Setting Up a DTS Package to Be a Data Source

Only the results of a Transform Data task can be used as a data source. You make a DTS Package into a data source by selecting the DSO Rowset Provider box on the Options tab of the Workflow properties dialog (shown in Figure 9.1) for a particular Transform Data task.

In code you set this option with the IsPackageDSORowset property of the Step object. It is a Boolean property with a default value of False.

This selection has the following results when the DTS Package is called through the data provider, PDSO:

- No records are added to the data destination.
- The records that would normally have been added to the data destination are now returned as the result set to the application that called the DTS Package.
- The Transform Data task that is providing the result set finishes execution successfully, but no tasks that have precedence constraints on that task are executed. That's true whether the precedence constraints are On Success, On Failure, or On Completion. The DTS Package will execute all other tasks, as long as they don't have precedence constraints that depend on the Transform Data task that is returning the rowset.

Caution

I have not been able to successfully return a rowset from a Transform Data task that has a text file as the data destination.

To use a DTS Package as a data source, it must be called through the PDSO. If you have a Transform Data task marked as a row source, you can still execute the package in other ways, without using the PDSO, but it will behave differently. Here is what will happen:

- No records are added to the data destination for the task that is marked as a row source. The DTS Package reports that 0 records are affected by that Transform Data task.
- Nothing is done with the records that would have been sent to the destination for that task.
- The same behavior occurs for precedence constraints as would have occurred if the package were called through the PDSO. No tasks will be executed that have

precedence constraints referring to the Transform Data task marked as the row source. All other tasks will be executed normally.

Note

The DSO Rowset Provider option only makes sense with the Transform Data task. It can be selected on the Workflow Properties dialog for the other types of tasks. However, if it is selected for another kind of task, that task will complete successfully but will block the execution of any tasks dependent on it. If the package is called with the PDSO and the DSO Rowset Provider box is checked on one of the other tasks, an error is returned by PDSO to the client application.

Getting Rid of the Message Boxes

It's not a good idea to use message boxes in scripts used in DTS Packages, because DTS Packages are normally scheduled to run without user intervention. I do, however, have the habit of using message boxes as part of the process of writing and testing DTS scripts.

As I mentioned previously, I also like using packages as rowset providers when I'm testing a DTS Package.

I discovered that these two strategies don't fit together very well.

I already was using a message box in one of the scripts in my package when I decided to call the package through the PDSO. I set the DSO Rowset Provider option for the Transform Data task that I wanted to query. Then I used an OPENRECORDSET command in the Query Analyzer. Right away I realized I had a problem.

The message box did not appear, the query never completed, I couldn't cancel the query, and I couldn't close the Query Analyzer. I tried using sp_who and KILL to get rid of the offending connection. Even that didn't work.

Finally, I had to stop and restart SQL Server.

I'd like to say that this only happened to me once, but that wouldn't be quite true. I still like using message boxes. But I've been learning to get rid of them before using the PDSO.

--tep

9

DTS PACKAGES

Querying a DTS Package with OPENROWSET

A recordset can be returned from a DTS Package by using the Transact-SQL statement
OPENROWSET. This command can be used to link to any data source for which an OLE DB
provider is available.

The following three parameters are used with OPENROWSET when it is used to return a
recordset from a DTS Package:

- Provider name—This is always 'DTSPackageDSO' when querying DTS Packages.
- Provider string—Any combination of the switches that are used with dtsrun can
  also be used with OPENROWSET. The use of dtsrun is documented toward the end of
  Chapter 6. Various forms of this string, used to retrieve packages from different
  modes of storage, are shown later in this section.
- Query—The query that is to be executed.

The query that is used in the OPENROWSET statement has four forms. The first three are
equivalent. You must use the fourth when you are using OPENROWSET with a DTS Package
that has more than one Transform Data task marked as a DSO rowset source.

- 'SELECT *'
- 'SELECT * FROM ALL'
- 'SELECT * FROM *Package Name*'
- 'SELECT * FROM *Step Name*'

This is an example of an OPENROWSET statement used to return a rowset from a DTS
Package stored in the file c:\MSSQL7\dts\salesimport.dts.

```
SELECT * FROM OPENROWSET(
    'DTSPackageDSO',
    '/FC:\MSSQL7\dts\salesimport.dts',
    'Select *')
```

If that package had more than one Transform Data task marked with the DSO rowset
provider option, than the query parameter would have to be changed to explicitly reference the step related to the task that has the desired rowset.

```
SELECT * FROM OPENROWSET(
    'DTSpackageDSO',
    '/FC:\MSSQL7\dts\salesimport.dts',
    'Select * FROM DTSStep_DTSDataPumpTask_5')
```

The next example shows OPENROWSET being used to return a rowset from a DTS Package
stored in SQL Server. A trusted connection (/E) is being used.

```
SELECT * FROM OPENROWSET(
    'DTSpackageDSO',
    '/E /Sserver1 /NSalesImport',
    'Select *')
```

The last example shows OPENROWSET used to return a rowset from a DTS Package stored in the repository. The user ID and password are being supplied (/Usa /P). Both a package (/G) and a version (/V) are specified. If the version is omitted, the most recent version is returned.

```
SELECT * FROM OPENROWSET(
    'DTSpackageDSO',
    '/Usa /P /Sserver1 /E /Rmsdb
    /G{9F99EE87-FE2F-11D2-91A8-00E0980134A1} /V943767260,
    'SELECT * FROM ALL'
```

Registering a DTS Package as a Linked Server

If a rowset is going to be returned from a DTS Package on an occasional basis, using the OPENROWSET statement is the easiest method. But if you are frequently querying a DTS Package, it would be easier to register the package as a linked server. After it is registered, it can be referenced in queries as easily as if it were another table in your database.

Linked servers are registered using the system stored procedure sp_addlinkedserver. This procedure requires four parameters:

- The linked server name—This is the name you want to use when you refer to the linked server in SQL statements. You can set this to any string, as long as it is different from all the linked servers that have been previously registered.

- The product name—This parameter must be included in the procedure call, but the content does not affect the result. It is being used as a placeholder. You can use any string value.

- The provider name—For DTS Packages this must be 'DTSPackageDSO'.

- The location—Use the same string as you would for the OPENROWSET provider string, as described previously.

Here is an example of the use of sp_addlinkedserver, registering the same package as was accessed by the first OPENROWSET statement:

```
sp_addlinkedserver
    'SalesDTSLinkedServer',
    'xxx' ,
    'DTSpackageDSO',
    '/FC:\MSSQL7\dts\salesimport.dts'
```

9

DTS PACKAGES

After the DTS Package is registered as a linked server, you can reference it in SQL statements as if it were any other server. Either the package name or the step name can be used for the table name in the SQL statement. The name of the database and the name of the object owner are omitted, for a *Linked Server name...Package or Step Name* syntax.

```
SELECT * FROM SalesDTSLinkedServer...DTSStep_DTSDataPumpTask_5
```

Step-Chaining

It is possible to use the results from one Transform Data task as the data source for another Transform Data task. This can be done within a package or between separate packages. Microsoft refers to this DTS feature as *step-chaining*.

To set up step-chaining, use an OPENROWSET query as the source query for the data transformation, as shown in Figure 9.7.

FIGURE 9.7

In step-chaining, the data source for a Data Transform task is set to the results from a different Data Transform task, using an OPENROWSET query.

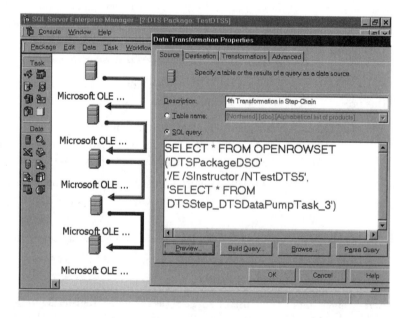

All the previous rules for using DTS as a data source apply:

- Check the DSO Rowset Provider box in the Workflow options of the step that is going to be the source of the recordset.
- If more than one Transform Data task has the rowset provider property set, the query in the OPENROWSET command must explicitly name the correct step.

- Make sure there are no precedence constraints based on the tasks that are rowset providers, because those constraints would prevent the other tasks from being executed.

> **Tip**
>
> Here is an example of where step-chaining could be valuable.
>
> Your goal is to create a DTS Package to be used by many different users, with many different data sources. You create the basic functionality of this package just one time. As you adapt the package, you create a separate, customized Transform Data task for each new source. Using step-chaining, you make each customized transformation the source data for your generic transformation.
>
> You could include these customized tasks in a multiuse DTS Package. For more convenient maintenance, though, I think it is best to leave each customized task in its own separate DTS Package.

Package Error Handling

There are three error-handling properties that can be set for a DTS Package. They are all located on the General tab of the DTS Package Properties dialog (shown in Figure 9.4).

Error File

Step and package error information is written to a file if a file path and name are provided in this box.

Information about the execution of a package is not be written if the package and all its tasks complete successfully. If either the package fails or any one of the tasks fails, all the information is appended to the end of this text file.

The error file is set with the LogFileName property of the Package object. The default setting is to not have an error file.

Here is a sample entry in the error file for the execution of a package that was successful, but had one failed task:

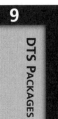

```
*********************************************************************
The execution of the following DTS Package succeeded:
Package Name: SalesUpdateAnalysis
Package Description: (null)
Package ID: {EF458B3B-F5CD-11D2-91C2-00E0980134A1}
Package Version: {EF458B3C-F5CD-11D2-91C2-00E0980134A1}
```

```
Package Execution Lineage: {EED6D7E0-F6B7-11D2-91C7-00E0980134A1}
Executed On: SERVER1
Executed By: Administrator
Execution Started: 4/19/99 7:58:20 PM
Execution Completed: 4/19/99 7:58:20 PM
Package Steps execution information:
Step 'DTSStep_DTSExecuteSQLTask_1' failed
Step 'DTSStep_DTSExecuteSQLTask_2' succeeded
***********************************************************************
```

Fail Package on First Error

If this option is chosen, the first step that reports an error will cause the package execution to be terminated with an error message. If this option is not chosen, all the tasks in a package can fail and the package will still report that it has been successful.

If a transaction is in process when the package execution is terminated by this option, all the data modifications in that transaction will be rolled back, regardless of the AutoCommitTransaction property.

This option is implemented with the FailOnError property of the Package object. This is a Boolean property with a default value of False.

Write Completion Status to Event Log

Using this option causes an entry to be made in the Windows NT Application Event Log for every execution of the DTS Package. The same kind of information included in the Error Log file is written, except that an entry is also made for successful completion.

This is the WriteCompletionStatusToNTEventLog Property of the Package object. It is a Boolean property with a default value of True. The default value is in effect when you create a new package in code, and do not specify a value for WriteCompletionStatusToNTEventLog. When you create a new package using the Package Designer, the initial value for this option is False.

Versioning DTS Packages

Every time a DTS Package is saved, a new version of the package is created. You can view the version history of a package stored in the Repository or in SQL Server by right-clicking the name of the package in the Enterprise Manager and selecting Versions. The DTS Package Versions dialog, shown in Figure 9.8, appears. The dialog gives you the option of opening any version of the package for editing.

FIGURE 9.8

The DTS Package Versions dialog shows all the versions that have been created for a particular package.

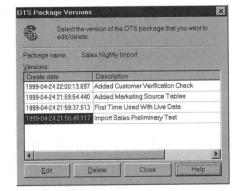

Note

When you choose a particular version of a DTS Package for editing and then save your changes, you don't overwrite the previous version. Instead, a new version is saved. The only way you can get rid of previous versions is by explicitly deleting them.

For packages saved in SQL Server, you have the option of deleting any of the versions in the DTS Package Versions dialog.

You can remove any particular version of a package from either the Repository or SQL server by using one of these two package methods: RemoveFromRepository or RemoveFromSQLServer. Both methods remove only one version of a package. If the version is not specified, the most recent one is removed.

The versions of a DTS Package saved in the same file can be viewed in a Select Package dialog, as shown in Figure 9.9. You receive this dialog when you choose Open Package from the All Tasks menu choice on the Data Transformation Services popup menu.

FIGURE 9.9

The Select Package dialog shows all the versions of all the packages saved in one particular file.

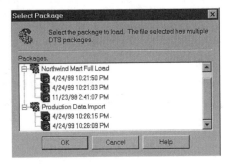

9

DTS PACKAGES

The Package GUID and the Version GUID

The Package GUID and Version GUID are displayed on the General tab of the DTS Package Properties dialog (shown in Figure 9.4). These two values are 8-byte Globally Unique Identifiers.

The Package GUID uniquely identifies a package. A Version GUID uniquely identifies a specific version of a package.

When a package is first created, the two GUID values will be the same. When later versions are created, the Package GUID remains the same and the Version GUID changes.

The Version GUID is used for one of the lineage variables, DTSLineage_Full, to mark records with the package in which they were transformed. The other lineage variable, DTSLineage_Short, identifies the particular time this package was executed.

Either the Package GUID or the Version GUID can be used to identify a package for retrieval or for deletion. When the Package GUID is used by itself, only the most recent version of the package is referenced. Reference any of the package's versions by using the Version GUID.

These values are implemented as the PackageID and the VersionID properties of the Package object. These are read-only properties that use the 128-bit uniqueidentifier data type, which is new in SQL Server 7.0.

Encrypting DTS Packages

DTS Package security differs depending on the package storage location. Those differences are discussed in the next section, "Storing DTS Packages."

A DTS Package saved to SQL Server or to a file can be given an Owner password, a User password, or both passwords. If one or both of the passwords is assigned, the package is encrypted. The encryption includes all the objects, collections, and properties in the packages except for Name, Description, PackageID, VersionID, and CreationDate, which are used to identify packages for retrieval.

Anyone attempting to retrieve an encrypted package must supply the passwords. The two passwords give the following permissions:

- The Owner password gives the right to edit or execute the package.
- The User password gives the right to execute but not edit the package.

Storing DTS Packages

DTS Packages can be saved in three different places, each of which has advantages:

- The Repository is the preferred location for data warehousing because the lineage of the source data can be traced.
- SQL Server storage in the msdb database, but not in the Repository, provides the fastest retrieval.
- File system storage allows DTS Packages to be easily shared among users.

The Save DTS Package dialog has a list box with the three storage options. The other choices you make in this dialog change as you choose a different storage location. Figure 9.10 shows the dialog as it appears when you are saving to the SQL Server Repository.

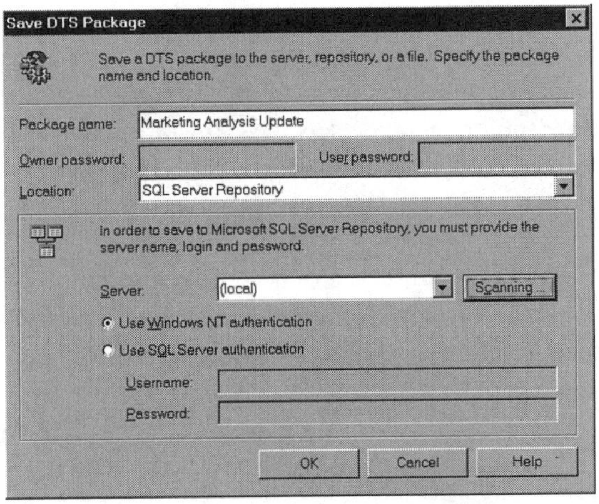

FIGURE 9.10

The Save DTS Package dialog presents choices to the user that differ depending on which storage method is selected.

9

DTS PACKAGES

Note

Which of the three package storage choices will you use most often? I prefer SQL Server storage. It's more convenient than using File Storage and it's much quicker than saving to the Repository.

I like to save packages frequently while I'm working on them. When I'm creating a complex package, the time it takes to save to the Repository can become a nuisance. It also takes significantly longer to retrieve a package from the Repository.

continues

Even so, I save more packages to the Repository than to SQL Server, because more than half of my packages use lineage variables. You can't save a package in SQL Server storage if it uses lineage variables.

I use the file storage method to archive my packages. I like having extra copies of my important packages stored in the file system. It's a convenient way to organize packages for long-term storage. And the copy stored in a file gives me a convenient package backup, in case something happens to the copy stored in the Repository or in SQL Server.

Storing DTS Packages in the SQL Server Repository

The Microsoft Repository provides a standard method for different products to share information. A DTS Package saved to the Repository is physically located in the msdb database. The package's characteristics are available through the various interfaces provided by the repository's information models. The structure and use of the repository are discussed in Chapter 13.

Here are the details on saving and retrieving packages when using the Repository:

- Packages stored in the Repository must have unique names. If SQL Server is installed with a case-insensitive sort order, names with letters of different case are considered the same. If the case-sensitive sort order is used, names with different case are considered to be unique.

- When saving to the Repository, there is a button on the Save DTS Package dialog to bring up the Scanning Options dialog. These options are also discussed in Chapter 13.

- DTS Package encryption is not available for packages saved to the Repository, so you are not allowed to provide an Owner password or a User Password.

- Windows NT security information is required.

- To use a package in the Repository, a user must have permission to use the msdb database.

DTS Packages are saved to the Repository with the SaveToRepository method of the Package object. SaveToRepository has the following parameters:

- Repository Server Name.
- Repository Database Name—Usually msdb.

- Repository User Name.
- Repository User Password.
- Repository Storage Flags—Optional parameter. Described following this list.
- CategoryID—(Optional parameter. Not currently being used.)
- Variable used as a pointer to the screen layout information for the package.

The Repository Storage Flags are a combination of the `DTSRepositoryMetadataOptions` and the `DTSRepositoryStorageFlags`. The Repository Metadata Options contain the scanning choices and are discussed in Chapter 13.

There are two storage flags, which present the choice between using SQL Server authentication (the default) or a Windows NT trusted connection, as listed in Table 9.6.

TABLE 9.6 The `Step` Object's `RelativePriority` Property Constants

Constant	Value	Meaning
DTSReposFlag_Default	0	Use SQL Server Security
DTSReposFlag_UseTrustedConnection	256	Use Windows NT Trusted Connection

The following are two examples of using the `SaveToRepository` method in Visual Basic. The first saves a package using SQL Server security. The second shows Windows NT security.

```
oPkg.SaveToRepository "Server1", "msdb", "User1", "Password1", _
    DTSReposFlag_Default

oPkg.SaveToRepository "Server1", "msdb",,, _
    DTSreposFlag_UseTrustedConnection
```

The `LoadFromRepository` method is used to retrieve a package that is stored in the Repository. The `RemoveFromRepository` method is used to delete a package from the Repository.

Both of these are `Package` object methods. Their parameters are identical, except the last one is not included with `RemoveFromRepository`.

- Repository Server Name.
- Repository Database Name—Usually msdb.
- Repository User Name.
- Repository User Password.
- Package GUID.

- Version GUID—Optional. If the Version GUID is not provided the most recent version of the package is loaded or removed.
- Package name—Optional parameter.
- Flags—Optional parameter. Uses the constants in Table 9.6.
- Variable used as a pointer to the screen layout information for the package—Not used for RemoveFromRepository.

Storing DTS Packages in SQL Server, Outside the Repository

DTS Packages saved in the repository are physically located in the msdb database. Packages saved in SQL Server, outside the Repository, are also saved in the msdb database—in the sysdtspackages table using the image data type.

Here are the details on saving and retrieving packages when using SQL Server, outside the Repository:

- The naming rules are the same as for saving packages to the Repository. Packages stored in the Repository must have unique names. Be sure to keep in mind the case-sensitivity configurations from your SQL Server install.
- If you want the package to be encrypted, you can provide an Owner password, a User Password, or both.
- Windows NT security information is required.
- To use a package in the Repository, a user must have permission to use the msdb database.

DTS Packages are saved to SQL Server with the SaveToSQLServer method of the Package object. SaveToSQLServer has the following parameters:

- Server Name.
- Server User Name.
- Server User Password.
- Whether to use a trusted connection—True or False.
- Package Owner Password—Optional parameter.
- Package User Password—Optional parameter.
- Package CategoryID—(Optional parameter. Not currently being used.)
- Variable used as a pointer to the screen layout information for the package.
- Reuse passwords—Optional parameter; True or False.

As with the Repository, there are also methods for loading the package and deleting the package—`LoadFromSQLServer` and `RemoveFromSQLServer`. Their usage is very similar to the methods for the Repository.

Storing DTS Packages in the File System

DTS can save one or more packages in a single COM-structured storage file. Each saved package can have one or more versions, all stored in the same file.

Packages stored in files are not displayed in the Enterprise Manager, as are the packages stored in the Repository or in SQL Server. To retrieve a package from a file, right-click Data Transformation Services in the Console Tree, choose All Tasks, and then choose Open Package. A Select File dialog appears. After you have selected a *.dts file, the packages and versions in that particular file are displayed in the Select Package dialog, as shown in Figure 9.11.

FIGURE 9.11

The Select Package dialog shows the packages and their versions.

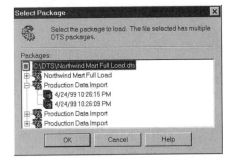

Here are the details on saving and retrieving packages when using SQL Server, outside the Repository:

- The naming rules are different for DTS Packages stored in files. As Figure 9.11 shows, you can have many packages with the exact same name in one file. This, of course, is in addition to having different versions of one package. The different packages are distinguished by their Package GUIDs.
- If you want the package to be encrypted, you can provide an Owner password, a User Password, or both.
- To use a package stored in a file, a user must have the appropriate file system permissions.

DTS Packages are saved to a file with the `SaveToStorageFile` method of the `Package` object. `SaveToStorageFile` has fewer parameters than the comparable methods for the other storage types.

- Filename.
- Package Owner Password—Optional parameter.
- Package User Password—Optional parameter.
- Pointer to the screen layout information for the package.
- Reuse passwords—Optional parameter; True or False.

There is no method to delete a package or a version of a package from a file. The method for retrieving a package from a file is called LoadFromStorageFile. It has the following parameters:

- File Name.
- Password—Either the Owner or the User password, if the file is encrypted.
- Package GUID.
- Version GUID—Optional. If the Version GUID is not provided, the most recent version of the package is loaded.
- Package name—Optional Parameter.
- Pointer to the screen layout information for the package.

Scheduling DTS Packages

You can schedule a DTS Package saved in SQL Server or the Repository by right-clicking that particular package in the Enterprise Manager and selecting Schedule Package. The Edit Recurring Job Schedule dialog (shown in Figure 9.12) appears and gives you the scheduling choices.

FIGURE 9.12

You can schedule packages to be executed by the SQL Server Agent as recurring jobs.

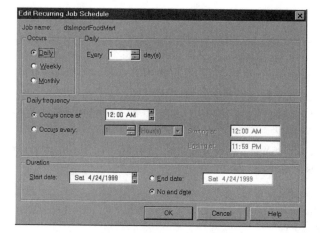

You can view the details of the scheduling and modify them by selecting Management, SQL Server Agent, and Jobs in the Console Tree of the Enterprise Manager.

Other DTS Package Object Properties

The DTS Package properties are presented in a variety of different places in this book:

- AutoCommitTransaction, TransactionIsolationLevel, and UseTransaction are covered in the section on transactions in this chapter.
- MaxConcurrentSteps and PackagePriorityClass are covered in the section on threads and priority of execution in this chapter.
- LineageOptions property is covered in Chapter 13, "Using the Repository in Data Transformations."
- FailOnError, LogFileName, and WriteCompletionStatusToNTEventLog are covered in the section on error handling in this chapter.
- PackageID and VersionID are covered in the section on DTS Package versions in this chapter.

The remaining package properties are covered in this section. Many of these properties are read-only.

All the methods and the events of the Package object are covered in Chapter 12.

CreationDate, CreatorComputerName, and CreatorName

These three read-only properties provide information about the creation of the package. The CreatorName uses the Windows NT formatting that combines the Domain Name and the User Name: Domain/Username. This property will not have a value if the package is created on a computer running Microsoft Windows 95.

These three values are all displayed in the Creation box on the General tab of the DTS Package Properties dialog.

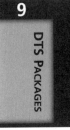

9

DTS PACKAGES

Name and Description

Name and Description are also displayed on the General tab of the DTS Package Properties dialog.

You choose the Name when you first create the package, and it cannot be changed. You can set or modify the Description at any time in the dialog.

> **Tip**
>
> Description is a convenient property to use for identifying different versions of the same package. When you are choosing which version of a package to view, the Description property is shown for each version. See the "Versioning DTS Packages" section earlier in this chapter.

Parent

All the objects in the DTS hierarchy have a Parent property. For members of a collection, the parent is the Collection object. For collections, the parent is the object that contains that collection. For the package, the highest object in the hierarchy, the parent is itself.

PrecedenceBasis

This property is listed in the DTS Reference in Books On line as a property both of the PrecedenceConstraint object and the Package object.

> **Note**
>
> The PrecedenceBasis Property works fine as a property of a PrecedenceConstraint, but when I have tried to reference it as a Package property, I get the error: "Object doesn't support this property or method."
>
> I don't know what this property would mean as a package property, unless it would be to set a default for all the precedence constraints within a particular package.
>
> My conclusion is that Books On Line listed PrecedenceBasis incorrectly as a property of the Package object.

UseOLEDBServiceComponents

This Boolean property is set on the Advanced tab of the DTS Package Property dialog. The default value is True.

When this property is selected, the OLE DB components are instantiated using the OLE DB Service Components. When this property is set to `False`, the data source objects are instantiated directly. This setting is ignored for the Data Transformation Services providers and for the SQL Server OLE DB Provider.

Other `Step` Object Properties

The following `Step` Object properties have already been discussed in this chapter:

- `AddGlobalVariables`, `ActiveXScript`, `ScriptLanguage`, and `FunctionName` are covered in the "Workflow ActiveX Scripts" section.
- `CloseConnection`, `DisableStep`, `ExecuteInMainThread`, and `RelativePriority` are covered in the section "Threads and Priority of Execution."
- `IsPackageDSORowset` is covered in "DTS Packages as Data Sources."
- `JoinTransactionIfPresent`, `CommitSuccess`, and `RollbackFailure` are covered in the section "Transactions in DTS Packages."
- `Name` and `TaskName` are covered in "The Steps Objects Collection."
- `PrecedenceConstraints`, `ExecutionResult`, and `ExecutionStatus` are covered in the "Precedence Constraints" section.

The remaining step properties are discussed in this section.

`StartTime`, `FinishTime`, and `ExecutionTime`

`StartTime` and `FinishTime` are read-only properties with a date data type. `ExecutionTime` is a read-only integer, giving the duration of the task in seconds.

`Description`

The `Description` property on the `Step` object cannot be set in the DTS Designer, but it can be set in code. The `Description` appears on the Options tab of the Workflow Properties dialog.

`Parent`

The `Parent` property of the `Step` object returns the Steps collection.

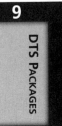

9

DTS PACKAGES

Summary

You have seen all the pieces of DTS in Chapters 7 through 9:

- The two data transformation tasks, the connections and the global variables in Chapter 7.
- The Bulk Insert task, the Execute SQL task, and all the other tasks in Chapter 8.
- The steps, the precedence constraints, thread handling, Workflow scripts, transactions, using packages as data sources, versioning packages, encrypting packages, and storing packages in Chapter 9.

The pieces of DTS fit together to create a programming environment designed for the transformation of data.

The goal of DTS is to take data from anywhere, transform that data with whatever process is needed, put that data wherever it needs to go, and keep everything that is happening within a well-controlled, well-documented, easily manipulated environment.

There are five more chapters on data transformation, each presenting a specialized topic:

- Chapter 10, "Using the DTS Import and Export Wizards," presents two excellent tools that provide a subset of the DTS functionality in a very user-friendly format.
- Chapter 11 offers examples of the various kinds of ActiveX scripts used in DTS—script transformations, script tasks, and scripts in Workflow steps.
- Chapter 12, "Programming with the DTS Object Model," presents examples of using the DTS Component Object Model to programmatically control DTS from Visual Basic.
- Chapter 13 shows the use of the Repository in transforming data.
- Chapter 14 discusses transformation tools that are available from other companies.

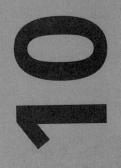

CHAPTER 10

Using the DTS Import and Export Wizards

by Tim Peterson

IN THIS CHAPTER

Wizards have two primary functions in a user interface:

- Organize complex jobs into an orderly sequence of events so that a person just starting to become familiar with a piece of software can make all the necessary choices.

- Automate repetitive jobs so that they can be accomplished more quickly.

The two Data Transformation Services (DTS) Wizards accomplish both of these goals. They provide an excellent learning tool for a person who is first learning about DTS. They also can provide a significant time savings for an experienced user in certain situations.

> **Note**
>
> It's difficult to tell the difference between the DTS Import Wizard and the DTS Export Wizard. They do exactly the same things. They even look the same, except for the name in the title bar.

Figure 10.1 shows the opening screen of the DTS Import Wizard.

FIGURE 10.1

The opening screen of the DTS Import Wizard. Whether this wizard is called the DTS Import Wizard, the DTS Export Wizard, or just the DTS Wizard, it does the same things.

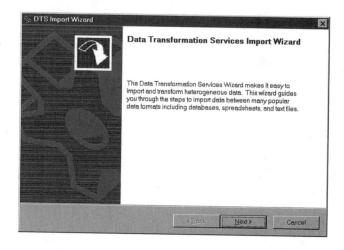

When to Use the DTS Import and Export Wizards

The primary reason for an experienced user to use the DTS Import Wizard or the DTS Export Wizard is for automating the transfer of multiple tables from a data source to a data destination.

The wizards provide the following assistance that is unavailable using the DTS Designer:

- You can pick the tables to transfer from a list of all the tables available in the data source. You can select many or all of them, and the wizard sets up all the data sources at one time. In the DTS Designer, each data transformation must be set up individually.
- The capability to pick many or all of the tables is especially useful in situations where the data destination has tables with the same names and field names. The wizard sets up all the data transformations automatically.
- If new tables need to be created in the data destination, an Execute SQL task is created automatically with the code to create each of the new tables.
- If tables in the destination are to be dropped and recreated, the wizard creates two Execute SQL tasks for each table being transferred.
- The wizard creates an Execute SQL task for each table to delete records in the destination tables, if that is requested.

The wizards are most helpful when the transformations are simple. But even in complex situations, the wizards can be a good place to start setting up a data transformation.

The wizards include the capability to implement the following DTS functionality:

- Connections to a data source and a data destination
- Transform Data tasks
- Copying fields in Transform Data tasks
- ActiveX Script transformations in Transform Data tasks
- Transfer SQL Server Objects tasks
- Executing a package
- Saving a package with any of the three types of storage
- Scheduling a package

10

USING THE DTS
IMPORT AND
EXPORT WIZARDS

The following section discusses the functionality that is not available through the wizards. You can implement any of the missing functionality by creating a package with the wizard, saving it, and then opening up the package with the DTS Designer.

What You Cannot Do with the Import and Export Wizards

Here are the main things you cannot do with the DTS Wizards:

- Create or use Lookups.
- Create or use global variables.
- Create more than one transformation script for a Transform Data task.
- Choose Registry options, except for saving to the Registry.
- Use the lineage variables.
- Create a Data-Driven Query task.
- Create a Bulk Insert task.

  All transformations from text files into SQL Server that are set up with the DTS Import Wizard are implemented using the Transform Data task.

- Create an ActiveX Script task.
- Create a Send Mail task.
- Create an Execute Process task.
- Create a custom task.
- Manipulate Execute SQL tasks.

  Execute SQL tasks are created by the wizards for dropping, creating, or deleting from tables, but you can't create an Execute SQL task for any other purpose, or use the wizard to modify the ones that are automatically created.

- Set precedence constraints.

  Some precedence constraints automatically are created to coordinate dropping tables, creating tables, and deleting records from tables.

- Use workflow scripts.
- Set execution and thread properties.
- Use the package as a rowset provider.
- Use transactions.
- Set package error handling options.

Starting the Wizards

The DTS Wizards are made available in a variety of ways, both inside and outside SQL Server's Enterprise Manager. The wizards are much more prominent than the DTS Designer.

Here are the ways you can run the wizards from inside the Enterprise Manager:

- Right-click the Data Transformation Services folder in the Console Tree. Select All Tasks. Select either Import Data or Export Data.
- Right-click the name of the server, on Databases, on any database, on Tables, or on any individual table. Select All Tasks. Select either Import Data or Export Data.
- Select any of the objects previously listed. Select Action, All Tasks from the menu. Select either Import Data or Export Data.
- Select Tools, Data Transformation Services from the menu. Select either Import Data or Export Data.
- Select Tools, Wizards from the menu. Expand the listing for Data Transformation Services. Select either Import Data or Export Data.

Whenever you run the wizards from within the Enterprise Manager, you start either the DTS Import Wizard or the DTS Export Wizard. When you're outside the Enterprise Manager, the two wizards become one. They are known simply as the DTS Wizard.

Here are the ways you can run the wizards from outside the Enterprise Manager:

- From the Start button, select Programs, Microsoft SQL Server 7.0, and Import and Export Data.
- Using the dtswiz utility from the command line. The parameters for dtswiz are described later.
- Using the new SQL Namespace object model (SQL-NS). This is described in the last section of this chapter, "Integrating the DTS Wizards With Other Applications."

The dtswiz utility has the following parameters. None of these parameters is required.

- /n   Use Windows NT authentication. This parameter is not normally needed because Windows NT authentication will be used anyway if it's not specified and no username and password are supplied.
- /u   SQL Server login ID.
- /p   Password for the SQL Server login ID.
- /f   Name of the file to which the package will be saved.

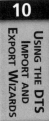

10

USING THE DTS
IMPORT AND
EXPORT WIZARDS

- /I   Call the DTS Import Wizard.

- /x   Call the DTS Export Wizard. If neither the import nor export is specified, the wizard is opened as the DTS Wizard.

- /r   The name of the data provider used for the import, such as MSDASQL for the Microsoft OLE DB Provider for ODBC.

- /s   The name of the SQL Server.

- /d   The name of the SQL Server database used in the import or export.

- /y   Prevents the SQL Server databases from being seen in the lists of source and destination databases.

Choosing a Data Source and a Data Destination

All the functionality for setting up connections in the DTS Designer, presented in Chapter 7, "The Core Data Transformation Tasks" is available in the DTS Wizards. The screens are almost identical with the ones that are presented in the DTS Designer, except that many of them are presented sequentially, as the user moves through the wizard.

The wizard always requires you to set up two, and only two, data connections. One of the connections is used as the data source, and the other is used as the data destination.

Figure 10.2 shows the Data Source tab of the wizard, with the choices presented for the Microsoft OLE DB Provider for SQL Server. Note, as in the Designer, there is a button for setting Advanced Properties of the OLE DB driver.

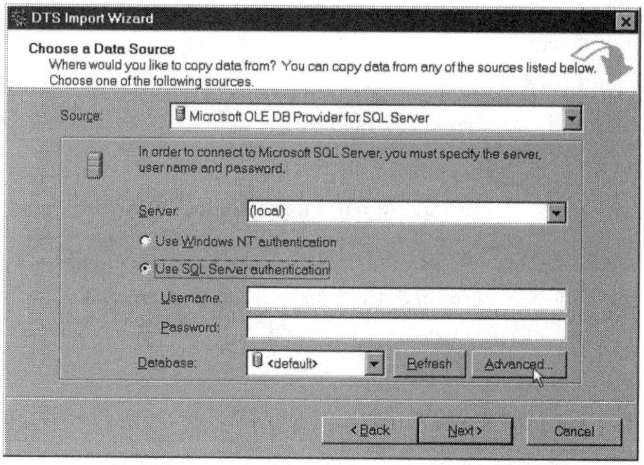

FIGURE 10.2

Choosing a data source with the DTS Wizards is the same as setting up a data connection in the DTS Designer.

If a text file is chosen as the data source, the same screens that are presented in the DTS Designer for specifying text files are now presented as the next tabs in the wizard, as shown in Figure 10.3.

FIGURE **10.3**

The wizard pre-sents tabs for specifying the for-mat for a text file.

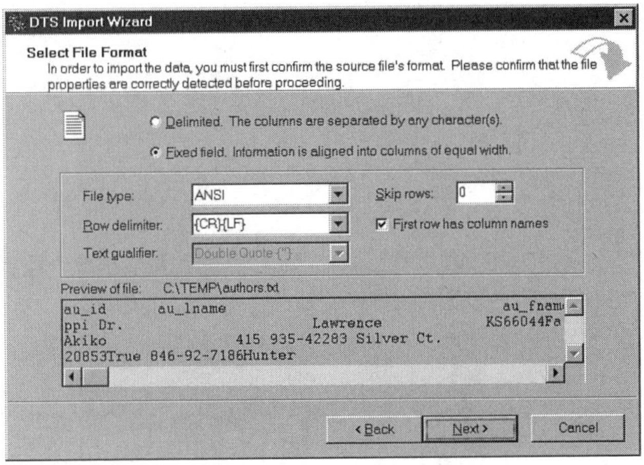

The tab for choosing a destination is identical to the tab for choosing the source. Figure 10.4 shows this screen, now with the ODBC Data Source selected.

FIGURE **10.4**

The data destina-tion is selected in the same way as the data source.

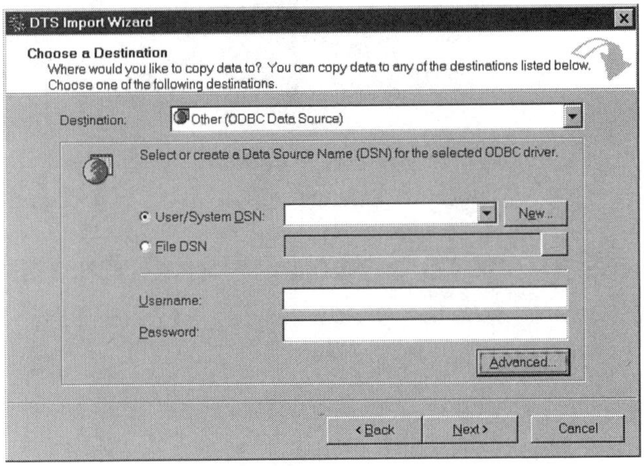

10

USING THE DTS
IMPORT AND
EXPORT WIZARDS

Setting Up the Data Transformation

After choosing the data source and the data destination, the next screen, Figure 10.5, presents three options:

- Copy table(s) from the source database
- Use a query to specify the data to transfer
- Transfer objects and data between SQL Server 7.0 databases

FIGURE 10.5

The wizard presents these three options after the data source and the data destination have been chosen.

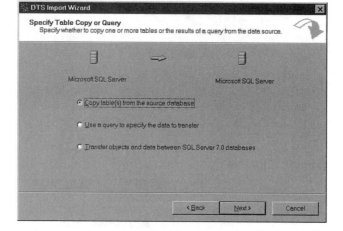

If the third option is picked, the wizard continues with setting up a Transfer SQL Objects task, which is described later in this chapter.

Using a Query to Specify the Data to Transfer

If the second option is used, the wizard presents a tab for creating the SQL statement to be used as the data source, as shown in Figure 10.6.

The Browse button provides an Open File dialog. The Parse button checks the syntax of the query. The Query Builder button directs the wizard on a path of three extra tabs that provide a simple format for creating a query.

The Select Columns tab gives an opportunity to choose any field from any of the tables in the data source. The Specify Sort Order tab gives the opportunity to choose fields to be sorted. The Specify Query Criteria tab gives the capability to specify criteria to limit the rows returned. There are expand buttons for each line on this third tab, which open the Select a Value dialog. This dialog presents the actual data from the fields in the data source so that you can pick one to use as a limiting criterion in the query. Figure 10.7 shows the Specify Query Criteria tab and the Select a Value dialog.

FIGURE 10.6

The Type SQL Statement tab. Note the lack of a join clause in this generated query.

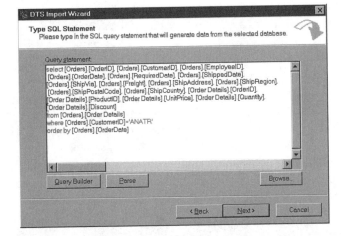

FIGURE 10.7

You can choose criteria to limit the query on the third tab of the Query Builder. Click the expand button and you get to pick from actual source data values.

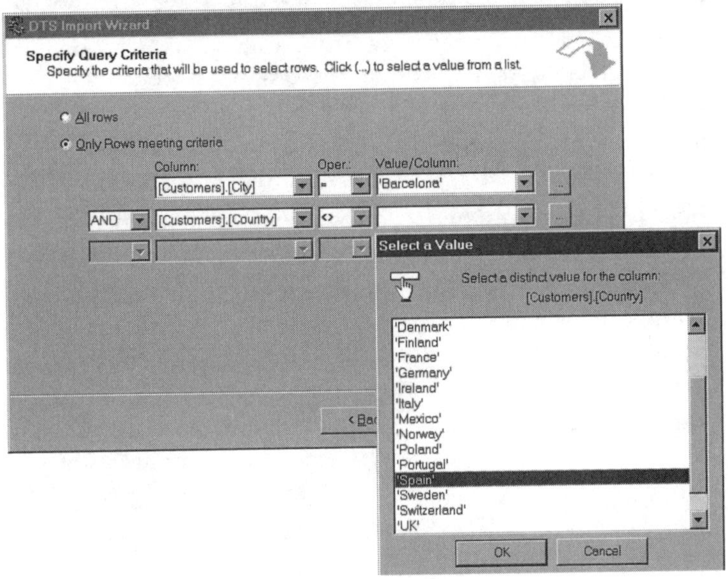

Note

The Query Builder in the DTS Wizard could be useful, but it doesn't provide any opportunity to specify joins, except as criteria expressions on the third tab. If you include more than one table and you don't specify a join on the third tab, the query is written as a cross-join, without giving any warning to the user.

At first glance, this Query Builder looks like it could be useful to a person without much experience in the world of SQL. It is easy to use—except for not providing much help with the joins.

If you do specify joins between tables on the criteria tab, they are written with the non-ANSI standard join syntax in the WHERE clause of the SQL statement. When you're done with the Query Builder, you are returned to the Type SQL Statement tab and can edit the generated query in any way that you choose.

The DTS Query Designer that's available in many different places in the DTS Designer is a far more convenient and sophisticated tool for building queries.

A Four Table Cross-Join

I've never seen anyone actually create a cross-join by accident using the DTS Wizards. I had to try it, just to make sure that it would really work. Well, it does.

It did take me four attempts, though. The first three times, I ended up with name conflicts between the columns of the different tables I included.

Finally, I just included one field each from the following four tables in Northwind: Categories, Customers, Order Details, and Products.

How many records will that be? I forgot to figure it out before I executed the package. It's still running, while I'm writing this. It just passed ~~four six ten~~ twenty-nine million records transferred and still going strong. I'm glad those weren't four really big tables!

Well, I finally gave up, after 1 hour, 45,000,000 records, and 5.5 GB of disk space consumed. My hard drive wasn't going to have room for the job to complete.

How many records would it have been? 2155 X 91 X 77 X 8 = 120,800,680!

--tep

Copy Table(s) from the Source Database

If the first of the three basic options is picked, the wizard presents a list of all the available tables in the data source, as shown in Figure 10.8. The capability to set up transformations for many tables at the same time is the greatest advantage the DTS Wizards have over the DTS Designer.

FIGURE 10.8

You can create transformations for one, many, or all of the tables in the data source.

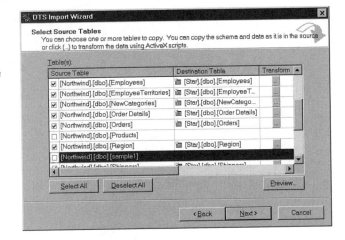

The Destination Tables

For each table you select, the wizard automatically adds a destination table with the same name, whether or not that table actually exists. You can change the selection of the destination table by picking from a list of all the tables that exist in the data destination. You can also type a name in the destination table column for a new table that you want to be created for this transformation.

A Preview button at the bottom of the Select Source Tables tab displays the Data box, as shown in Figure 10.9.

FIGURE 10.9

The Data box displays up to 100 records from the data destination.

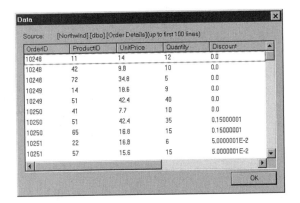

The expand button in the Transform column opens up the Column Mappings and Transformations dialog, shown in Figure 10.10.

FIGURE **10.10**

You can open the column Mappings and Transformations dialog with the expand button in the Transform column of the Select Source Tables tab.

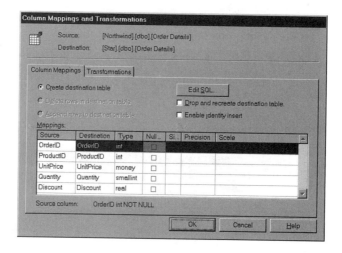

The Mappings and Transformations dialog has three primary choices on the Column Mappings tab:

- Create destination table
- Delete rows in destination table
- Append rows to destination table

If you have chosen a destination table that does not now exist, the choice for creating a destination table is the only one available. If you have chosen a destination table that does exist, the append rows choice is selected, but you can change to either of the other two.

When the option for creating a destination table is selected, the Edit SQL button is enabled. This button opens the Create Table SQL Statement dialog, shown in Figure 10.11. This dialog opens with a SQL statement that creates a destination table that is identical in structure to the source table that has been selected. You can edit the SQL statement. While editing, you can return to the automatically generated statement by selecting the Auto Generate button.

FIGURE 10.11

The Create Table SQL Statement dialog is used to write the SQL statement for creating a new table in the data destination.

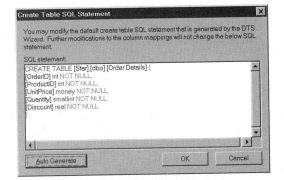

> **Note**
>
> In the Data Designer, if you are setting up a transformation into a new table, that table is actually created in the data destination at the time you design it. That's not true with the wizard. No new tables are created until the package is actually run. The text that is written in the Create Table SQL statement is used in an Execute SQL task in the DTS Package that the wizard creates.

When you choose the Create Destination Table option, you also have the choice of dropping and re-creating the destination table. When this option is selected, the wizard creates an additional Execute SQL task to drop the table. The DTS Package runs successfully whether or not the table exists at the time the package is executed. An On Completion precedence constraint is set between the two Execute SQL statements. If the table doesn't exist, the Drop Table task fails. If the table does exist, the Drop Table task is successful. Either way, the workflow goes on to the Create Table task. Figure 10.12 shows the DTS Designer view of a transformation where the choice has been made to drop and re-create the destination table.

The option for deleting rows in the destination table sets up an Execute SQL task that deletes all the rows before the Transform Data task is run.

For all three options, there is the additional possibility of selecting the Enable Identity Insert box, so that the `identity_insert` property is on while the transformation is being run. This property allows values to be inserted into the normally auto-generated `Identity` field.

10

USING THE DTS IMPORT AND EXPORT WIZARDS

FIGURE 10.12

Two Execute SQL tasks are created to carry out the Drop Table and Create Table actions.

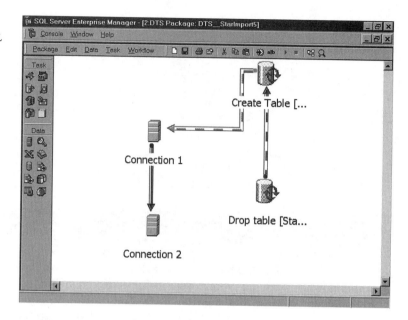

The Data Transformations

The bottom of the Column Mappings tab shows the actual mappings of the columns from the source to the destination. The default mapping that is prepared simply matches the first field in the source with the field in the destination, in the same way as is done in the DTS Designer. The Source columns in this box can be changed, so that a different column is used for a particular destination column. You can also choose to ignore a particular column in the destination. That column then does not appear in the list of fields being copied or transformed.

Figure 10.13 shows the Transformations tab of the Column Mappings and Transformations dialog.

The Transformations tab presents the same two choices for creating transformations that are available in the DTS Designer:

- Copy the source columns directly to the destination columns
- Transform information as it is copied to the destination

FIGURE 10.13

You can choose to copy columns or write an ActiveX transformation script on the Transformations tab of the Column Mappings and Transformations dialog.

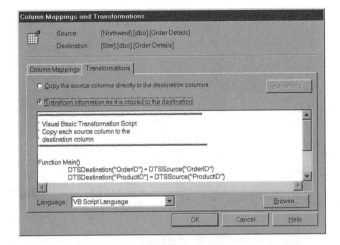

Note

With both choices, you can only have one copy or one transformation for a Transform Data task. You can't make separate mappings for different sets of fields, as you can with the DTS Designer.

When you select the option for copying columns, the Advanced button is enabled. This button calls the same Advanced Transformation Properties dialog as the one that is used in the DTS Designer, as shown in Figure 10.14.

FIGURE 10.14

Use the Advanced Transformation Properties dialog for specifying details on how much data type flexibility there should be as columns are copied from the source to the destination.

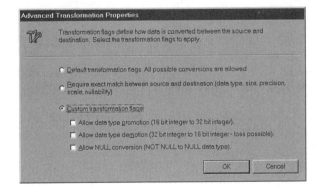

10

USING THE DTS IMPORT AND EXPORT WIZARDS

When the Transform Information option is selected, you are given three options:

- Writing or editing the ActiveX script used for the transformation
- Browsing to find a file that contains an ActiveX script to use
- Choosing a different scripting language

A default script is generated when first opening the dialog. This script implements a simple copy of each field from the source table to the destination table, based on the mappings that have been selected on the Column Mappings tab.

If the column mappings are changed, the wizard asks whether a new default script should be generated that uses the changed mappings. In the same way, if the scripting language is changed, the wizard asks whether a new script should be generated using the new language. You can choose to accept the new script or leave the current script unchanged.

Setting Up a Transfer of SQL Server Objects

The DTS Wizard provides the functionality of the Transform Data task. The other task that the wizard provides is the Transfer SQL Server Objects task.

The Transfer SQL Server Objects option can only be used between two SQL Server databases. If you are using connections to other data sources, you can transfer data, and you can create tables in the destination that match the source. You can't transfer any other kinds of objects.

You choose this task by selecting the Transfer Objects and Data Between SQL Server 7.0 Databases option on the Specify Table Copy or Query tab of the wizard. After making this selection, the Select Objects to Transfer tab, shown in Figure 10.15, appears. This tab has exactly the same choices as the Transfer SQL Server Objects Properties dialog. The three buttons on this tab, Select Objects, Options, and the expand button, bring you to the same dialogs that you would receive if you were using the DTS Designer.

Refer to Chapter 8, "Using Other DTS Tasks," for more information about setting up the Transfer SQL Server Objects task. You make the same choices with the DTS Wizard as you make with the DTS Designer.

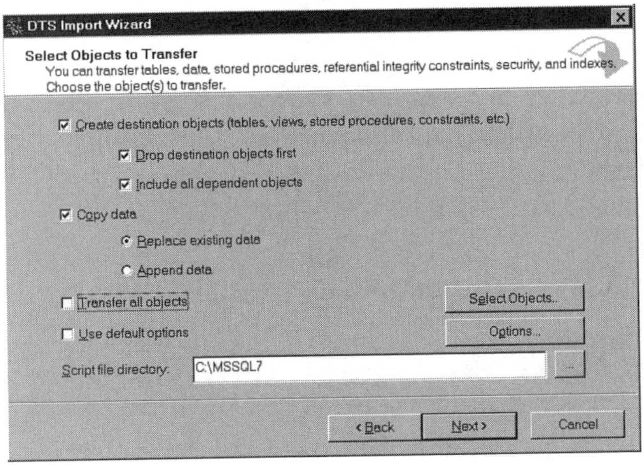

FIGURE 10.15

This is the tab in the DTS wizard where you choose options for transferring objects between SQL Server databases.

Executing, Scheduling, Saving, and Replicating the Package

The last step in using the DTS Wizard is to decide what you want to do with your new package. The Save, Schedule and Replicate Package tab, shown in Figure 10.16, gives you all these choices.

FIGURE 10.16

You can run, save, schedule, and replicate your new DTS Package.

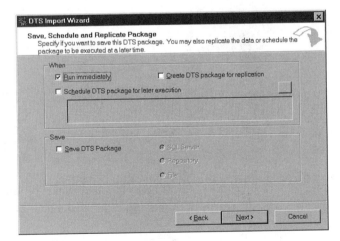

You can do four things with your new package, in various combinations:

- Run Immediately   This is the only choice selected by default. No matter what else you choose to do with the package, you can still make this choice.

- Create DTS Package for Replication   This choice is not available unless you also choose to run the package immediately.
- Schedule DTS Package for Later Execution   You can schedule the package to run a single time in the future or on a regular schedule.
- Save DTS Package   This option can be chosen by itself and it is also chosen automatically when Schedule DTS Package is chosen.

Create DTS Package for Replication

You choose this option if you want to use the data destination as a replication publication. This can be a convenient way to set up replication from non-SQL Server data sources. Replication normally requires a SQL Server data source. When you use DTS with this replication option, you can work around this limitation. The DTS package creates the data for the replication publication, which can then be replicated like any other publication.

The Create Publication Wizard, shown in Figure 10.17, opens automatically after the DTS Wizard is finished, to allow you to set up all the choices for replication.

FIGURE 10.17

If you choose to create the DTS Package for replication, the Create Publication Wizard opens when the DTS Wizard is done.

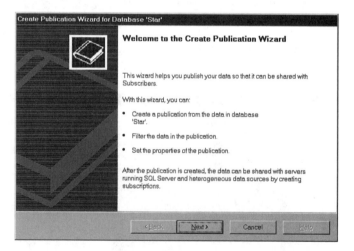

If you don't save the package, this can only be a one-time snapshot publication. If you do save it, then you can set up a publication that is periodically refreshed.

Schedule DTS Package for Later Execution

When you choose to schedule the DTS Package, the expand button is enabled, which brings you to the Edit Recurring Job Schedule dialog, shown in Figure 10.18.

If you choose to schedule the package, but you don't select any particular form of scheduling, the wizard schedules the package to be executed once a day at midnight. You can change or delete this scheduled package execution at any time in the Jobs section of the SQL Server Agent.

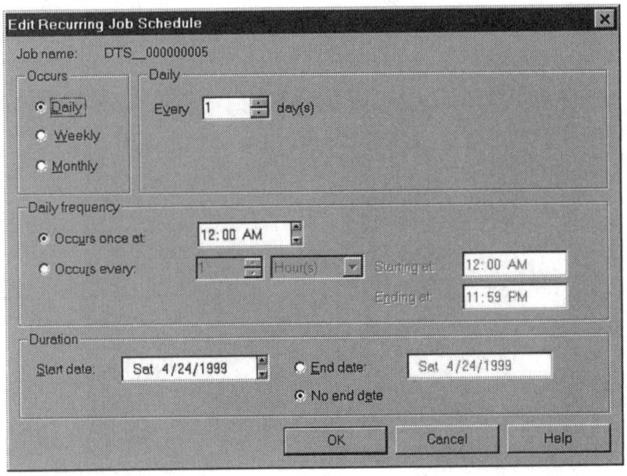

FIGURE 10.18

The wizard provides all the options for choices in scheduling a DTS Package.

Save DTS Package

If you choose to save the DTS Package, the three package storage options appear: SQL Server, Repository, and File.

The next tab in the wizard presents the additional choices that are needed to successfully save a DTS Package, as shown in Figure 10.19. These choices are identical to the choices presented when you save a package in the DTS Designer, except that if you change your mind about which storage method you want to use, you can't change it on this tab—you have to back up to the previous tab.

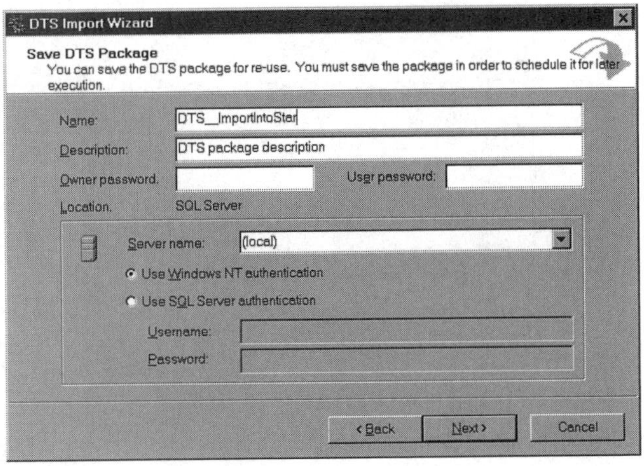

FIGURE 10.19

The wizard presents this tab when you choose to save the DTS Package.

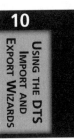

10

USING THE DTS IMPORT AND EXPORT WIZARDS

Completing the Wizard

Figure 10.20 shows the last screen of the DTS Wizard. Here you can review the choices you have made, and you still have the opportunity to go back and change any of them.

FIGURE 10.20

The DTS Wizard ends with a screen that lets you review your choices before you commit them.

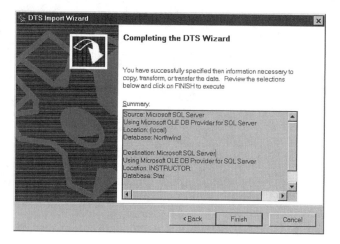

When you click Finish on this screen, the transferring data box appears, displaying a progress report as your package is executed, scheduled, and/or saved. If any errors occur, you can click the line with the error and receive a description of the error message. Figure 10.21 shows a sample error message.

FIGURE 10.21

You can receive an error report by clicking on any errors that appear in the Transferring Data box.

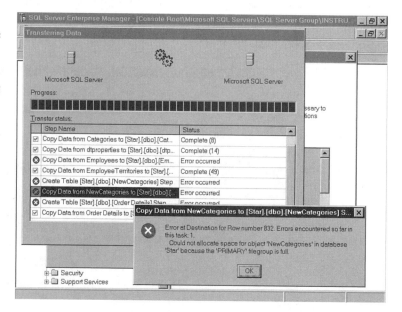

Integrating the DTS Wizards with Other Applications

The SQL Namespace (SQL-NS) object model is a new feature in SQL Server 7.0 that gives programs the capability to call Enterprise Manager interface components.

 I have included a sample Visual Basic program for calling the DTS Wizards. Only two objects and four methods from SQL-NS are needed in this program:

- The SQLNamespace object is the highest level object in the SQL-NS object hierarchy.

- The Initialize method of the SQLNamespace object is used to connect to a particular SQL Server.

- The SQLNamespaceObject object can be used to execute commands that call various objects in the Enterprise Manager.

- The GetRootItem method of the SQLNamespace object returns a handle to the root object of the hierarchy. In this case, the root object is the SQL Server.

- The GetSQLNamespaceObject of the SQLNamespace object is used to create a SQLNamespaceObject. This method has one parameter—the level of the Enterprise Manager Console Tree at which the SQLNamespaceObject is being created. For calling the DTS Wizards, the SQLNamespaceObject should be created at the SQL Server level of the hierarchy.

- The ExecuteCommandByID method of the SQLNamespaceObject calls one of the Enterprise Manager's interface components. This method has three parameters: a command ID constant, a handle to the application window, and a constant that determines whether the called object will be modal. The command ID constants for calling the DTS Wizards are SQLNS_CmdID_DTS_Import and SQLNS_CmdID_DTS_Export.

Listing 10.1 is the code for the Run DTS Wizards application.

LISTING 10.1 A VB Program for Calling the DTS Wizards

```
Option Explicit

'Project must include the Microsoft SQLNamespace Object Library
'This Object Library implemented in Mssql7\Binn\Sqlns.dll
Dim oSQLNS As SQLNamespace
```

continues

10

USING THE DTS
IMPORT AND
EXPORT WIZARDS

LISTING 10.1   continued

```
Dim hServer As Long

Private Sub Form_Load()
On Error GoTo ErrHandler

  Dim oSQLNSObject As SQLNamespaceObject
  Dim sAppName As String

  'Create the SQL Namespace object
  Set oSQLNS = New SQLNamespace

  'Initialize the SQLNameSpace object
  'Change Connection String as needed
  'For Trusted Connection, use "Server=.;Trusted_Connection=Yes;"
  oSQLNS.Initialize "RunDTSWiz", SQLNSRootType_Server, _
      "Server=.;UID=sa;pwd=;", hWnd

  'Get root object of type Server
  hServer = oSQLNS.GetRootItem

Exit Sub
ErrHandler:
  MsgBox Err.Description & " " & Err.Number, vbOKOnly, "Error"
End Sub

Private Sub Command1_Click()
    On Error GoTo ErrHandler

  'Create a SQLNamespaceObject object
  'SQLNamespaceObject objects are used for executing Namespace commands
  Dim oSQLNSObject As SQLNS.SQLNamespaceObject
  Set oSQLNSObject = oSQLNS.GetSQLNamespaceObject(hServer)

  'Call the DTS Import wizard
  oSQLNSObject.ExecuteCommandByID SQLNS_CmdID_WIZARD_DTSIMPORT, _
      hWnd, SQLNamespace_PreferModal

  'Or call the DTS Export wizard
  'oSQLNSObject.ExecuteCommandByID SQLNS_CmdID_WIZARD_DTSEXPORT,
      hWnd, SQLNamespace_PreferModal

Exit Sub

ErrHandler:
  MsgBox Err.Description & " " & Err.Number, vbOKOnly, "Error"
End Sub
```

Summary

Don't forget to use the DTS Wizards. The wizards won't give you the whole DTS programming environment, but they can make your job easier.

If you are transferring a lot of tables, you might as well start your data transformations with the wizards. You can always finish the job with the DTS Designer.

Writing ActiveX Scripts

by Tim Peterson

IN THIS CHAPTER

This chapter and the next show you some of the ways you can use ActiveX scripts in DTS packages. This chapter focuses on using scripts for Data Transformations. Chapter 12, "Programming with the DTS Object Model," shows how to use the objects, properties, and methods of the DTS Object Model in scripts. The code samples for each chapter can be found in the \Samples directory on the CD-ROM that comes with this book.

Most of these code samples are included in a set of three DTS Packages, which are based on the following scenario:

You are building a star schema from the sales data of your company, Northwind, so that you can provide your managers with the wonders of OLAP. You want to import data into your star schema on a periodic basis. To begin with, you will be setting up monthly imports. Because your company has been acquiring other businesses recently, you want to design a schema that can receive data from a variety of sources. Your supervisor has decided that your new star schema database will be called OLAPUnleashed.

Three DTS packages have been created for this data transformation:

- OLAPUnleashedCreateDatabase—Drops and re-creates the OLAPUnleashed database. It creates the tables, but does not fill them with data, except for the Time dimension, which contains six years of days.

- OLAPUnleashedInitialLoad—Transforms the Northwind data and loads it into OLAPUnleashed. This package executes the OLAPUnleashedCreateDatabase package if the OLAPUnleashed database has not yet been created. The code assumes that the OLAPUnleashedCreateDatabase package has been saved in SQL Server storage on the local server.

- OLAPUnleashedDTSTools—Contains some tools that help control the flow of a package while it is being designed.

You can find these three DTS packages in a separate directory on the CD at Samples\DTS. You will also find separate files for each script and query that are used in each of the packages.

The OLAPUnleashedInitialLoad Package, shown in Figure 11.1, provides most of the code samples for this chapter.

> **Note**
>
> The examples in this chapter are written in VBScript. You can also, of course, use JScript and PerlScript for your scripts.

WRITING ACTIVEX
SCRIPTS

FIGURE 11.1

The OLAPUnleashed InitialLoad Package moves data from the Northwind database to the OLAPUnleashed database.

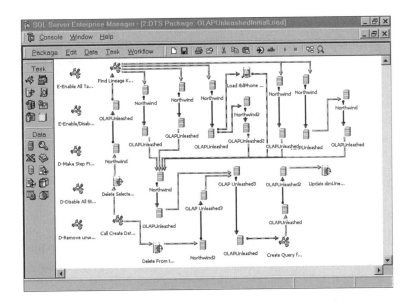

The Three Kinds of Scripts

There are three kinds of scripts used in DTS. They differ from one another in the purpose for which they are used. The three kinds of scripts are:

- Transformation scripts—Used in Transform Data and Data-Driven Query tasks.
- Workflow scripts—Can be used in the steps associated with any task.
- Scripts in an ActiveX Script task.

Transformation Scripts

A transformation script is executed as a part of the transformation of data by a Data Transform task or a Data-Driven Query task. Each column mapping in the task can have its own script. If you don't need a script for a particular set of column mappings, a copy column can be selected instead.

Transformation scripts are executed one time for every record in the data source. Therefore it is important that you not include code that is going to take a significant amount of time to execute.

The return value from the script's entry procedure instructs the data pump what to do with the particular record. These return values are documented in Chapter 7, "The Core Data Transformation Tasks." The most commonly used ones are:

- `DTSTransformStat_OK`—All is well. Insert the record into the destination table.

- `DTSTransformStat_SkipRow`—You are rejecting this record or you want to gather information from several rows to insert into one row. Don't insert this record into the destination.

- `DTSTransformStat_SkipRow` or `DTSTransformStat_SkipInsert`—You want to skip inserting one particular row in the destination table. Skip Row skips one row in the source table, while Skip Insert skips one row in the destination table—and that can make a difference if you're going from one to many records, or the other way around.

- `DTSTransformStat_SkipFetch`—You want to insert an extra record into the destination.

- `DTSTransformStat_Info`, `DTSTransformStat_ExceptionRow`, or `DTSTransformStat_Error`—You want to send this record to the error file.

- `DTSTransformStat_AbortPump`—You want to abort the whole task with an error message.

Additional return values that you can use in data-driven queries are:

- `DTSTransformStat_InsertQuery`—Execute the insert query.

- `DTSTransformStat_UpdateQuery`—Execute the update query.

- `DTSTransformStat_DeleteQuery`—Execute the delete query.

- `DTSTransformStat_UserQuery`—Execute the user query; typically used for stored procedures.

Workflow Scripts

You can create one Workflow script for each task in your DTS package. Workflow scripts are executed by a step before the task associated with that step is run.

A Workflow script is most often used for checking whether or not a task should be run. There are three return values from these scripts:

- `DTSStepScriptResult_ExecuteTask`—Run the task now.

- `DTSStepScriptResult_RetryLater`—Run the task later.

- `DTSStepScriptResult_DontExecuteTask`—Don't run the task now or later.

Workflow scripts can also be used to set up looping in a DTS package.

Because these scripts are only executed once each time a step is run, it's generally fine to put more time-consuming procedures in them. One long Workflow script won't be noticed in the length of time it takes to run a DTS package.

Scripts in ActiveX Script Tasks

Executing a script is the entire purpose of an ActiveX Script task. Like a Workflow script, it is fine to put more time-consuming code into an ActiveX Script task because it's normally only run once.

Some of the things you could do in an ActiveX script are:

- Open a connection to a data source.
- Retrieve a recordset and manipulate the data in it.
- Read from a file or write to a file.
- Write out a report to a file.
- Modify DTS object properties.

The return values from a script used in an ActiveX Script task determine whether the task is marked as a success or a failure:

- `DTSTaskExecResult_Success`—The task is a success.
- `DTSTaskExecResult_Failure`—The task is a failure.

Basic Data Cleansing in Transformations

The code in the following sections illustrates a variety of basic data cleansing situations. These examples are all taken from the DTS Package OLAPUnleashedInitialLoad. The particular tasks are identified by the task Description field.

> **Note**
>
> When referring to tasks, it is easier to use the Task Description than the Task Name. The Name can neither be assigned nor viewed by the user in the DTS Designer. The Task Description can be assigned and viewed, it is displayed underneath the task's icon in the Designer interface, and it appears as the ToolTip for the task's icon.

Copying Fields and Replacing Nulls with a Transformation Script

The fields in a data transformation script are always referenced as members of the DTSDestination collection or the DTSSource collection. The reference can use either the name of the field or the number that represents the field's place in the collection. The following two blocks of code are equivalent. This sample is taken from the Load dimEmployee task in the DTS Package OLAPUnleashedInitialLoad.

```
'Copy the other fields, replacing nulls as necessary
DTSDestination("NorthwindEmployeeID") = _
    ReplaceNull(DTSSource("EmployeeID"),0)
DTSDestination("Address") = ReplaceNull(DTSSource("Address"),"Unknown")
DTSDestination("City") = ReplaceNull(DTSSource("City"),"Unknown")
DTSDestination("Region") = ReplaceNull( DTSSource("Region"),"Unknown")
DTSDestination("PostalCode") = _
    ReplaceNull(DTSSource("PostalCode"),"Unknown")
DTSDestination("Country") = ReplaceNull(DTSSource("Country"),"Unknown")
'Copy the other fields, replacing nulls as necessary,
'    using the field index rather than the field name
DTSDestination(1) = ReplaceNull(DTSSource(1),0)
DTSDestination(7) = ReplaceNull(DTSSource(6),"Unknown")
DTSDestination(8) = ReplaceNull(DTSSource(7),"Unknown")
DTSDestination(9) =ReplaceNull( DTSSource(8),"Unknown")
DTSDestination(10) = ReplaceNull(DTSSource(9),"Unknown")
DTSDestination(11) = ReplaceNull(DTSSource(10),"Unknown")
```

There can be a performance gain when using the index values rather than the field names, but the code is also harder to read and write.

 This code sample uses a simple function called `ReplaceNull` to fill in a value for all the null values in the source data. The first parameter for `ReplaceNull` is the field that is being checked. The second parameter is the value that is used in place of the null value. Here is the code for the `ReplaceNull` function:

```
Function ReplaceNull (str, rtn)
IF ISNULL(str) THEN
    ReplaceNull = rtn
ELSE
    ReplaceNull = str
END IF
End Function
```

Note

ReplaceNull is the equivalent of the Transact-SQL function ISNULL. The following T-SQL statement will return "None" if this particular customer doesn't have a fax number. If the customer does have a fax number, the statement will return the number itself:

```
SELECT ISNULL([FaxNumber], "None")

    FROM tblCustomer

    WHERE CustomerPK = 15982
```

VBScript also has an ISNULL function that's very different from the Transact-SQL ISNULL. The VBScript ISNULL can only be used to check to see if a value is null. It can't be used to replace that null value with anything else. `ISNULL(DTSSource("FaxNumber"))` will return `TRUE` if this customer doesn't have a fax number and `FALSE` if the customer has a number.

You can use the `ReplaceNull` function in VBScript in the same way as you would use the ISNULL function in Transact-SQL. `ReplaceNull(DTSSource ("FaxNumber"),"None")` will return "None" or the number itself.

Tip

If you want the fastest speed in a data transformation, you won't do any data checking or data modification. You shouldn't even use a function like `ReplaceNull`. And, if the only thing you want to do is copy data from a source to a destination, you don't need a transformation script at all. You can use the Copy Column transformation choice instead of the ActiveX script transformation.

Combining Fields and Dividing Fields

You can use a script to join two fields from one record into one field or to split one field into two.

It's easy to combine two separate names into a full name. Here's an example from the Load dimEmployee task.

```
'Concatenate Last and First Name
DTSDestination("EmployeeName") = _
    DTSSource("LastName") + ", " + DTSSource("FirstName")
```

 It's harder to split names apart. Here's code that will do it, but doesn't come close to handling all the possibilities. You can find this code in the Load dimSupplier task.

```
'Split ContactName into first and last names
'This code expects to find a first name and a last name
'    divided by one space.
'If it finds no spaces or more than one space,
'    the record is added to the error file.
'The record is also still added to the database.
DTSDestination("ContactName") =_
    ReplaceNull(DTSSource("ContactName"),"None")
bNameError = CBOOL(FALSE)
```

```
IF DTSDestination("ContactName") = "None" THEN
    DTSDestination("ContactFirstName") = "None"
    DTSDestination("ContactLastName") = "None"
ELSE
    lFirstSpace = INSTR(DTSDestination(1, "ContactName"), " ")
    IF lFirstSpace = 0 THEN
        bNameError = CBOOL(TRUE)
    ELSE
        lSecondSpace =  INSTR(lFirstSpace + 1, _
            (DTSDestination("ContactName")), " ")
        IF lSecondSpace> 0 THEN
            bNameError = CBOOL(TRUE)
        END IF
    END IF

    IF bNameError = FALSE THEN
        DTSDestination("ContactFirstName") = _
            LEFT(DTSSource("ContactName"), lFirstSpace-1)
        DTSDestination("ContactLastName") = _
            MID(DTSSource("ContactName"), lFirstSpace+1)
    ELSE
        DTSDestination("ContactFirstName") = "Error"
        DTSDestination("ContactLastName") ="Error"
        Main = Main + DTSTransformStat_Info
    END IF
END IF
```

> **Note**
>
> The "Error Handling in Transformation Scripts" section later in this chapter discusses setting the entry function return status so that a record is added to the error file.
>
> There is one record in Northwind that fails the preceding test because it has extra spaces in the name. The DTS Package writes this error to the SupplierError.txt file, which by default is installed in the c:\dts\Error directory.

Data Verification

You can use scripts to check for conformity to business rules that define the appropriate range of values for a particular field or check to see if the value in one field is consistent with values in other fields.

 The Load dimEmployee script, for example, checks to see if an employee is at least 16 years old.

```
'Verify the dates
'If it's not a date or if the date is outside the acceptable range,
'    set the destination field to NULL
'Set the return value for the Entry function Main,
'    so this record will be entered into the error file.
IF ISDATE(DTSSource("BirthDate")) AND _
'Check to see if Employee is over 16
    DateDiff("yyyy", DTSSource("BirthDate"), Now())>= 16 THEN
    DTSDestination("BirthDate") = DTSSource("BirthDate")
ELSE
    DTSDestination("BirthDate") = NULL
    Main = Main + DTSTransformStat_Info
END IF
```

> **Note**
>
> I modified the source query for the Load dimEmployee task so that some of the employee records would fail this age-limit business rule. The code adds 25 years to each employee's birth date.
>
> ```
> SELECT [EmployeeID], [LastName],
>     [FirstName], DATEADD(yy, 25, [BirthDate]) AS BirthDate,
>     [HireDate], [Address],
>     [City], [Region],
>     [PostalCode],        [Country],
>     [ReportsTo]
> FROM [Northwind].[dbo].[Employees]
> ```
>
> The error file for this transformation is EmployeeError.txt.

Data Formatting

You can apply formatting to data in a transformation script. The Load tblPhone task includes a function that formats a phone number. The function has two parameters—the phone number that is to be formatted and the particular style of formatting that is to be applied. The formatting style is determined by looking at which country the record is from.

```
Function fctFormatPhone(sPhone, sFormat)
Dim sPhoneDigits, sChar, sFormatted, lChar

SELECT CASE sFormat

  CASE "3.3.4"
```

```
'First strip out all but the digits
  FOR lChar = 1 TO LEN(sPhone)

      sChar = MID(sPhone, lChar, 1)

      IF sChar>= "0" AND sChar <= "9" THEN
          sPhoneDigits = sPhoneDigits & sChar
      END IF

  NEXT

  'Return ERROR if we don't have the right number of digits
  IF LEN(sPhoneDigits) <> 10 THEN
      fctFormatPhone = "ERROR"
  ELSE
      sFormatted = LEFT(sPhoneDigits, 3) & "."
      sFormatted = sFormatted & MID(sPhoneDigits,4,3) & "."
      sFormatted = sFormatted & RIGHT(sPhoneDigits,4)
      fctFormatPhone = sFormatted
  END IF

CASE "None"
    'Apply no formatting
    fctFormatPhone = sPhone

CASE ELSE
    'Apply no formatting
    fctFormatPhone = sPhone

END SELECT
End Function
```

Using Lookups for More Complex Data Cleansing

A Lookup provides a connection to another table from inside a data transformation script. Lookups can help make data transformation code simpler and more flexible.

Using a Lookup to Determine the Proper Format

In the phone formatting example in the last section, the particular format is determined by using a lookup called PhoneFormat. The text of the query for this lookup is:

```
SELECT FormatName
FROM lkpPhoneFormat
WHERE Country = ?
```

The lkpPhoneFormat table is shown in Table 11.1.

TABLE 11.1   The Phone Format Lookup Table

PhoneFormatPK	Country	FormatName
1	USA	3.3.4
2	Canada	3.3.4
3	Germany	German
4	Norway	Scandinavian

The lookup is used in the script of the Load tblPhone task to find which format, if any, to apply to the phone number. The lookup takes the name of the country from the data source, replaces the "?" in the lookup query with that name, runs the lookup query, and returns the appropriate FormatName.

 Here is the code from the Load tblPhone transformation script, which executes the lookup and uses the returned value to call the fctFormatPhone function:

```
'Look up the Phone Format, based on the country of the customer
sFormat = DTSLookups("PhoneFormat").Execute(DTSSource("Country"))

If ISNULL(sFormat) OR sFormat = "" THEN
    sFormat = "None"
END IF

DTSDestination("PhoneFormat") = sFormat
sPhone = fctFormatPhone(sPhone, sFormat)
DTSDestination("PhoneNumber") = sPhone
```

Using a Lookup to Homogenize Data

Data is often inconsistent, either because data consistency rules were not being enforced when the data was entered or because the data is being combined from different sources. A lookup table can homogenize the data so that no matter what its original form, it is made consistent as it is brought into the data warehouse.

You can use a lookup table with these fields to homogenize Country information:

- PK—A primary key identity field.
- CountrySource—All the possible forms of state names and abbreviations from the various data sources.
- CountryAbbreviation—The abbreviation used for the country name in mailing.
- CountryName—The name of the country.

A sample of the data in `lkpCountry` is shown in Table 11.2, showing how the various ways of referring to the United States can be homogenized.

TABLE 11.2   The Country Lookup Table

CountryPK	CountrySource	CountryAbbreviation	CountryName
1	United States	USA	United States of America
2	U.S.A.	USA	United States of America
3	US	USA	United States of America
4	United States of America	USA	United States of America
5	U.S.	USA	United States of America

You can write a lookup query to replace the source data with the `CountryAbbreviation` like this:

```
SELECT CountryAbbreviation FROM lkpPhoneFormat WHERE CountrySource = ?
```

If you named this lookup query `FindCountryAbbreviation`, the code you would use in the transformation script would be:

```
DTSDestination("Country") = DTSLookups("FindCountryAbbreviation")._
    Execute(DTSSource("Country"))
```

Using a Lookup to Fill in Missing Data

When data is missing from a record, it is sometimes possible to determine the absent information from the data that is available.

 In the Load dimCustomer task, the available geographical information is used to try to fill in the information that is missing. First, an attempt is made to look up the Country, using the City and Region data. If City and Country are available, but not region, an attempt is made to determine the Region. Finally the appropriate lookups are made to find the SalesDistrict and the SalesRegion.

```
'Address and Sales District/Region assignment
Dim sCountry, sRegion, sCity, sPostalCode, sAddress
Dim  sSalesRegion, sSalesDistrict

sAddress = ReplaceNull(DTSSource("Address"),"Unknown")
sCity =  ReplaceNull(DTSSource("City"),"Unknown")
sRegion =  ReplaceNull(DTSSource("Region"),"Unknown")
sPostalCode =  ReplaceNull(DTSSource("PostalCode"),"Unknown")
sCountry =  ReplaceNull(DTSSource("Country"),"Unknown")
```

```
IF sCountry = "Unknown" THEN
    sCountry = DTSLookups("Country").Execute(sRegion, sCity)
    sCountry = ReplaceNull(sCountry, "Unknown")
END IF

IF sRegion = "Unknown" THEN
    sRegion = DTSLookups("Region").Execute(sCountry,sCity)
    sRegion = ReplaceNull(sRegion, "Unknown")
END IF

sSalesDistrict =_
    DTSLookups("SalesDistrict").Execute(sCity, sRegion, sCountry)
sSalesDistrict = ReplaceNull(sSalesDistrict, "Unknown")

sSalesRegion = DTSLookups("SalesRegion").Execute(sSalesDistrict)

DTSDestination("SalesDistrict") = sSalesDistrict
DTSDestination("SalesRegion") = sSalesRegion
DTSDestination("Address") = sAddress
DTSDestination("City") = sCity
DTSDestination("Region") = sRegion
DTSDestination("PostalCode") = sPostalCode
DTSDestination("Country") = sCountry
```

When you use more than one parameter in a lookup query, the parameters are placed in the query in the same order they are used in the execute statement. You must always include all the parameters that have been defined for a lookup query.

The queries for determining Region and Country must handle the possible duplication of names. The query for SalesDistrict must handle situations where a District includes all of a Region or a country.

Here are the four lookup queries used with this code:

```
--Country
SELECT Country Lookup Query
FROM lkpSalesDistrictRegion
WHERE City = ? AND Region = ? AND DuplicateRegionAndCity = 0

--Region
SELECT Region Lookup Query
FROM lkpSalesDistrictRegion
WHERE (City = ?) AND (Country = ?) AND
    DuplicateCountryAndCity = 0

--SalesRegion Lookup Query
SELECT MAX(SalesDistrict)
FROM lkpSalesDistrictRegion
WHERE city IN (?, 'ALL', 'None') AND Region IN (?, 'ALL', 'None') AND
    Country = ?
```

```
--SalesDistrict Lookup Query
SELECT SalesRegion
FROM lkpSalesDistrictRegion
WHERE SalesDistrict = ?
```

The Amazing Variety of Driver's License Numbers

There are a lot of horror stories around about dirty data. I found out about dirty data with my first data warehousing project.

I was importing daily rental records into a centralized SQL Server database for an international car rental company. The records were downloaded from a production system each night, and I received them as tilde-delimited text files. The company was organized around franchises and had never before built a corporate-wide list of customers. One of the driving forces for this project was to build that list so that it could be used for marketing—both in promotional programs and in repeat-customer award programs.

Customers could not be positively identified by name and address. Name spelling was very inconsistent and the company wanted to maintain a person's identity even when that customer moved.

Frequent Flyer numbers could identify customers, but only about 20% of the customers participated in the Frequent Flyer promotional program and, for the records from those customers, at least 10% were missing the numbers.

I was told that a combination of the number in the Driver's License field and the State field would give a positive identification of a unique individual. Frequent Flyer numbers and names could be used to try to identify an individual who had moved between states.

I started working on setting up the data transformation. The initial import was going to include about one million rental records representing about six months of history.

As I was looking at some preliminary runs, it appeared that there were some individuals showing up with too many rentals. I started looking at the driver's license numbers for those individuals, and I found some amazing patterns:

11111111111—300 rentals

1111111111—85 rentals

111111111—125 rentals

11111111—48 rentals

On and on it went—every possible number of repeated 1s, every possible number of repeated 2s, and every possible number of every other repeated digit was appearing an unusual number of times.

Besides that, there were 85 people who had a Driver's License number of "Not Allowed To Drive" and another 45 that had the same phrase in French. Looking more carefully, I discovered that the Driver's License field had been used for all kinds of comments. (And, of course, there was a rigid corporate policy of not allowing anyone without a driver's license to rent a car.)

What did I do? Despite all the bad data, the Driver's License field was still our best hope for identifying the renters. I built a table that contained all the duplicate driver's license numbers and the number of times each one occurred. The obviously bad license numbers were flagged and removed from the data in a first round of processing. We developed an algorithm to judge what constituted a positive identification of a person, starting with Frequent Flyer numbers, looking at driver's license numbers and states, considering a SOUNDEX on last name and first name, and finally looking at phone numbers and addresses.

In the end I estimated that the algorithm correctly identified 95% of the duplicate customer names. I knew I could get the identification to 99%, but the company decided I had spent too much time and money already.

Companies are always too optimistic about the condition of their data. Data warehousing and other OLAP projects become the occasion for companies to discover how bad their data really is. Bad data doesn't come as a result of OLAP projects, but the OLAP developers often become the messengers who bring the bad news.

--tep

Finding the Values for the Keys in the Fact Table

If you are using generated key values for your star schema, you will have to find a way to retrieve those values when you are filling the fact table. There are three general strategies for doing this, each of which can be advantageous in certain situations:

- Use a SQL query as the source for the data transformation that fills the fact table. Use a join in this query between the tables in the source database and the dimension tables in the destination database to retrieve the keys for the fact table. This strategy provides the best performance if SQL Server is able to create an efficient join between its tables and the tables in the other database.

- Import the source tables for the fact table into SQL Server. Then create a SQL query as in the first example. This strategy could provide better performance than the first strategy, depending on the particular types of databases involved in the join.

- Use lookups in the data transformation script to retrieve the appropriate key values. This would most likely give the worst performance, but it could be the easiest to create. This strategy separates out the finding of each key value into a separate piece of code, rather than finding them all at once, as in strategies 1 and 2.

The OLAPUnleashedInitialLoad package uses a combination of the second and third strategies with the following tasks to fill the Order Detail fact table:

1. An Execute SQL task deletes all the records from the OLAPUnleashed table tmpOrderDetailLoad.

2. A data transformation using all column copies loads the records from the Northwind table Order Details into tmpOrderDetailLoad.

3. Many of the key values needed for the Order Detail fact table are also stored in the Order dimension table. These key values are found using lookups in the Load dimOrder task.

4. The Order Detail fact table is loaded by a task called Load factOrderDetail. This task is not allowed to run until all the dimension tables are loaded and tmpOrderDetailLoad has been loaded.

 The source SQL query for Load factOrderDetail gets most of the key values for the fact table by joining dimOrder and tmpOrderDetailLoad.

```
SELECT
    o.OrderPK, o.EmployeeFK, o.ShipperFK,
    o.CustomerFK, o.OrderTimeFK, o.RequiredTimeFK,
    o.ShippedTimeFK,od.OrderID, od.ProductID, od.Quantity,
    CONVERT(numeric(3, 3), od.Discount) AS Discount,
    CONVERT(numeric(10, 2), od.UnitPrice) AS UnitPrice,
    CONVERT(numeric(10, 2), od.UnitPrice * od.Quantity) AS Price,
    CONVERT(numeric(10, 2), od.UnitPrice * od.Quantity *
        (1 - od.Discount)) AS NetPrice
FROM tmpOrderDetailLoad od LEFT OUTER JOIN dimOrder o
    ON od.OrderID = o.NorthwindOrderID
```

The remaining key values for factOrderDetail are obtained by using lookups in the transformation scripts.

```
'Lookup Foreign Key values
DTSDestination("ProductFK") = _
    DTSLookups("ProductFK").Execute(DTSSource("ProductID"))
DTSDestination("SupplierFK") = _
    DTSLookups("SupplierFK").Execute(DTSSource("ProductID"))
```

Error Handling in Transformation Scripts

Errors are handled in a transformation script by setting the entry function to different transformation status codes. These codes can be used by themselves or in combination with other status codes. You can handle situations with a whole range of options:

- You can write the error record to the error log that you have set for the particular task, but have the task continue as if no error had occurred. Do this by adding the DTSTransformStat_Info constant into the return value for the entry function. When you execute the DTS Package, the report onscreen (see Figure 11.2) shows that errors have occurred for this task. But the package will continue to execute even if you have set the precedence to be contingent on the success of this task. You can choose whether or not to write the records with the errors to the destination table, by adding in other status constants.

  To write the record to the error log but still include the record in the destination table:

  ```
  Main = DTSTransformStat_Info + DTSTransformStat_OK
  ```

  To write the record to the error log and not include the record in the destination table:

  ```
  Main = DTSTransformStat_Info + DTSTransformStat_SkipInsert
  ```

  To skip all additional transformation scripts that would be executed for this row of data:

  ```
  Main = DTSTransformStat_Info + DTSTransformStat_SkipRow
  ```

- You can tell the system to treat this problem as an error by using the DTSTransformStat_Error constant. These errors are counted, and when the count exceeds the Max error count property, the execution of the task is terminated, all the task's data modifications are rolled back, and any tasks that have On Success precedence set for this task are not executed. If the Max error count threshold is not exceeded, the contingent tasks will still be executed even if some errors have occurred. The non-error records entered by this task will remain in the table, but all records with an error will not be included—they will be written to the error log.

  ```
  Main = DTSTransformStat_Error
  ```

- If you want to handle a particular error in the most serious way, you can set the return value of the entry function to DTSTransformStat_AbortPump, which will immediately terminate the transformation task. The effect of setting this constant is the same as if the Max error count had been exceeded.

  ```
  Main = DTSTransformStat_AbortPump
  ```

FIGURE **11.2**

A task shows errors when DTSTransformStat_Info *is set, but those errors do not stop contingent tasks from executing.*

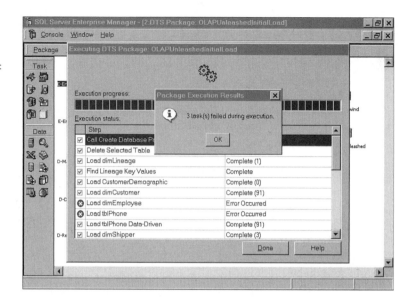

Dividing One Record into Several Records

The Load tblPhone task has an example of dividing one record into several records. The Customers table in Northwind has a Fax Number field and a Phone Number field. These fields are separated out into separate records in OLAPUnleashed. A third type of phone number, Alternate Phone, is added so that the code can illustrate going from one record to three. A value of "123" is used for all Alternate Phone numbers. This value will fail some of the phone number formatting checks. This failure will trigger the task's error handling capability.

The following SQL query is the source for Load tblPhone:

```
SELECT
    c.Phone,
    c.Fax,
    '123' AS "AlternatePhone",
    c.Country,
    d.CustomerPK
FROM Customers c INNER JOIN OLAPUnleashed..dimCustomer d
    ON c.CustomerID = d.NorthwindCustomerID
```

Table 11.3 shows the result of this source query.

TABLE 11.3 The Result of the Source Query for Load tblPhone

Phone	Fax	AlternatePhone	Country	CustomerPK
00-0074321	030-0076545	123	Germany	9739
(5)555-4729	(5)555-3745	123	Mexico	9740
(5)555-3932	NULL	123	Mexico	9741

The goal is to have one record in tblPhone for each separate non-null phone number, as shown in Table 11.4.

TABLE 11.4 The Normalized Phone Numbers in tblPhone

Phone	Fax	AlternatePhone	Country	CustomerPK
1	9739	Phone	German	00-0074321
2	9739	Fax	German	030-0076545
3	9739	AlternatePhone	German	123
4	9740	Phone	None	(5)555-4729
5	9740	Fax	None	(5)555-3745
6	9740	AlternatePhone	None	123
7	9741	Phone	None	(5)555-3932
8	9741	AlternatePhone	None	123

A global variable named PhoneType is used for this transformation. It keeps track of which type of phone number is currently being processed. When the value of PhoneType is 1, the first field that holds a phone number, Phone, is checked. When PhoneType is 2, Fax is checked. When it's 3, AlternatePhone is checked.

 The following code looks for a non-null value in each of the phone number fields. When a record is first being processed, the global variable PhoneType is set to 1, so that the Phone field will be examined. If the value of any of the fields is NULL, the global variable is incremented and the next field is checked. As soon as a non-NULL record is found, processing is allowed to continue, so that phone number can be added to the destination. You can easily extend this strategy to create any number of records from one record.

```
'Initialize the PhoneType Global Variable
'    if this is the first time through.
IF DTSGlobalVariables("PhoneType").Value = "" THEN
    DTSGlobalVariables("PhoneType").Value = 1
END IF
```

```
'Initialize bAddRecord, assuming success
bAddRecord = CBOOL(TRUE)

'Check for Phone
IF DTSGlobalVariables("PhoneType").Value = 1 THEN
    IF  ISNULL(DTSSource("Phone")) OR DTSSource("Phone") = "" THEN
        DTSGlobalVariables("PhoneType").Value = 2
    END IF
END IF

'Check for Fax
IF DTSGlobalVariables("PhoneType").Value = 2 THEN
    IF ISNULL(DTSSource("Fax"))  OR DTSSource("Fax") = "" THEN
        DTSGlobalVariables("PhoneType").Value = 3
    END IF
END IF

'Check for AlternatePhone
IF DTSGlobalVariables("PhoneType").Value = 3 THEN
    IF ISNULL(DTSSource("AlternatePhone"))  OR _
            DTSSource("AlternatePhone") = "" THEN
        bAddRecord = CBOOL(FALSE)
    END IF
END IF
```

If a record is found that should be added, that record is processed. The following code shows that processing. First, the PhoneType field is given the proper value. Second, the phone number is formatted. Some of the code was shown earlier in the section that discussed the use of lookups for formatting.

```
IF bAddRecord = TRUE THEN

    SELECT CASE DTSGlobalVariables("PhoneType").Value

        CASE 1
            DTSDestination("PhoneType") = "Phone"
            sPhone = DTSSource("Phone")

        CASE 2
            DTSDestination("PhoneType") = "Fax"
            sPhone = DTSSource("Fax")

        CASE 3
            DTSDestination("PhoneType") = "AlternatePhone"
            sPhone = DTSSource("AlternatePhone")

    END SELECT

    'Look up the Phone Format, based on the country of the customer
    sFormat = DTSLookups("PhoneFormat").Execute(DTSSource("Country"))
```

```
    If ISNULL(sFormat) OR sFormat = "" THEN
        sFormat = "None"
    END IF

    DTSDestination("PhoneFormat") = sFormat
    sPhone = fctFormatPhone(sPhone, sFormat)
    DTSDestination("PhoneNumber") = sPhone
END IF
```

The code continues, setting the status value and incrementing the global variable that is controlling which phone number is currently being considered.

The error handling status is set first, as the following code shows. If the phone number is invalid, the Boolean bAddRecord variable is set to FALSE.

```
'Handle the error
IF sPhone = "ERROR" THEN
    'Write the record in the error file
    Main = DTSTransformStat_Info
    'Skip the insert because of the error
    bAddRecord = CBOOL(FALSE)
END IF
```

The record should not be added if bAddRecord has been set to FALSE, either because there was an error or because the code has arrived at the last of the phone types and it is null. The Skip Insert status is added to any previously assigned status value.

```
IF bAddRecord = FALSE THEN
    'Skip the insert
    Main = Main + DTSTransformStat_SkipInsert
```

The package keeps track of how many records are added to each table. If a record is added to tblPhone, the following code counts it.

```
ELSE
    'Increment the record counter
    IF ISNULL(DTSGlobalVariables("tblPhoneInsertedCount").Value) THEN
        DTSGlobalVariables("tblPhoneInsertedCount").Value = 1
    ELSE
        DTSGlobalVariables("tblPhoneInsertedCount").Value = _
        CLng(DTSGlobalVariables("tblPhoneInsertedCount").Value + 1)
    END IF
END IF
```

Now the PhoneType global variable is incremented, or returned to 1 if it has exceeded the number of types that are being checked.

```
'Increment the PhoneType Global Variable
DTSGlobalVariables("PhoneType").Value = _
        DTSGlobalVariables("PhoneType").Value + 1
```

```
'Roll back to 1, if we've made it to 4
IF DTSGlobalVariables("PhoneType").Value> 3 THEN
    DTSGlobalVariables("PhoneType").Value = 1
END IF
```

If it's not time to look at a new record, the code has to stay on the same source record. That is done by adding in the Skip Fetch status. Again, note that this status is being used in combination with the previous statuses that have been assigned.

```
'Stay on this record, unless we're starting over with PhoneType 1
IF DTSGlobalVariables("PhoneType")> 1 THEN
    Main = Main + DTSTransformStat_SkipFetch
END IF
Finally, the OK status is assigned, if needed, and the script ends.
'Assign a status of OK, if no status has yet been assigned.
IF Main = 0 THEN
    Main = DTSTransformStat_OK
END IF
End Function
```

> **Note**
>
> The Skip Fetch status keeps the processing on the same source record. The Skip Insert status prevents the record from being inserted, keeping the processing on the same destination record. In the previous code sample, these statuses can occur together. If a fax number is being processed and it turns out to be invalid, the script will be called again to process a potential AlternatePhone number so both the source and the destination record will remain the same.

> **Note**
>
> Skip Insert is also used when you want to move from many records to one—to undo the normalization of the phone records, for example. The values that are to be inserted are collected into a set of global variables until the whole set has been retrieved.

Using Data-Driven Queries for a Data Transformation

Data-driven queries provide additional control over the data transformation process.

The OLAPUnleashed Initial Load package has a data-driven query task called Load tblPhone Data Driven, which could be used instead of the Transform Data task Load tblPhone. The data-driven version loads a table tblPhoneDDQ with the same data that is loaded into tblPhone. The data-driven task uses an error table, tblPhoneNumberErr, rather than an error file to record incorrect phone numbers.

The Load tblPhone Data Driven task runs four separate queries, depending on the particular data:

- A User query is run when a formatting error occurs. Phone numbers with formatting errors are placed in an error table, rather than being written to the error file.

  ```
  INSERT INTO tblPhoneNumberErr (CustomerFK, PhoneType, PhoneFormat,
  PhoneNumber)
  VALUES (?,?,?,?)
  ```

- A Delete query runs when a number for a particular customer and phone type is NULL, but a matching record already exists in tblPhone.

  ```
  DELETE FROM tblPhone
  WHERE PHONEPK = ?
  ```

- An Update query is run when a record matches the customer and phone type but has a different number in the new data.

  ```
  UPDATE tblPhone SET PhoneNumber =?, LineageFK = ?
  WHERE CustomerFK = ? AND PhoneType = ?
  ```

- An Insert query runs when none of the previous situations occurs.

  ```
  INSERT INTO tblPhone(CustomerFK, PhoneType, PhoneFormat, PhoneNumber)
  VALUES (?,?,?,?)
  ```

 The VBScript in the Load tblPhone Data Driven task and the VBScript in the Load tblPhone task use different logic in processing the various phone types. The Load tblPhone's VBScript ignores a NULL value and goes on to the next phone type. The Load tblPhone Data Driven task's VBScript calls the Delete query when it encounters a NULL value.

```
'Call the right Query

IF ISNULL(sPhone) THEN
    'If Null, delete the existing phone number
    '    of that type for that customer
    Main = DTSTransformStat_DeleteQuery
END IF
```

```
IF sPhoneFormatted = "ERROR" THEN
    'Write record in error table instead of destination table
    'Assign the destination as the original source number
    DTSDestination("PhoneNumber") = sPhone
    Main = DTSTransformStat_UserQuery
END IF

lPhonePK =  DTSLookups("CheckForNumberChange").Execute(_
        DTSDestination("CustomerFK"),_
        DTSDestination("PhoneType"))
IF NOT ISNULL(lPhonePK ) AND lPhonePK <> "" AND lPhonePK <> 0 THEN
    Main = DTSTransformStat_UpdateQuery
END IF

'Assign a status of InsertQuery, if no status has yet been assigned.
IF Main = 0 THEN
    Main = DTSTransformStat_InsertQuery
END IF
```

The benefit of using a data-driven query is a higher level of control over what happens to your data. The main drawback is that it can take longer to execute.

Summary

I hope you have some new ideas about how you can use transformation scripts to accomplish your data transformations. The next chapter shows you how to gain control over the DTS environment by using ActiveX tasks, Workflow scripts, and the DTS Object hierarchy.

Programming with the DTS Object Model

by Tim Peterson

IN THIS CHAPTER

Most of the DTS collections, objects, and properties have already been discussed in Chapter 7, "The Core Data Transformation Tasks," Chapter 8, "Using Other DTS Tasks," and Chapter 9, "DTS Packages." This chapter pulls the DTS programming information together. The code examples show how these objects can be used from Visual Basic and also how to use them in the scripts inside a DTS Package.

The DTS COM Interfaces

The DTS object model conforms to the 32-bit Component Object Model (COM). The model is implemented with three interfaces, which are contained in two *.dll files:

- The Microsoft DTS Package Object Library is implemented in dtspkg.dll. Visual Basic and other applications that support OLE Automation can use this library.
- The Microsoft DTSDataPump Scripting Object Library is also called DTSPump. It is implemented in dtspump.dll. This interface is used by ActiveX scripting tasks.
- The third interface, the data pump, is also implemented in dtspump.dll. This library uses a COM interface without OLE automation, so it cannot be used by Visual Basic. The data pump allows C++ programmers to create custom transformations.

The effect of these three libraries is to create three different levels of DTS control:

- You get the most control using C++.
- You can't do quite as much with Visual Basic. Specifically, you can't create new types of custom transformations. You can, however, create and modify packages and use all the DTS object model's properties and methods.
- Your lowest level of control is when you are using the ActiveX scripts inside a package. You can still do most things—creating objects, modifying properties, and calling methods. But you can't view or modify some of the properties of the data pump.

> **Caution**
>
> There are some things you can do with DTS objects in the package's scripts that you maybe shouldn't do. You can create other tasks in the same package from inside a script, but if you do, that task will not be visible from within the DTS Designer. It will be fully functional, and it will be saved when the package is saved. You can assign whatever properties you want to it. But you will never see it in the Designer interface, even after you close and reopen the package.

The DTS Object Hierarchy

The package is the highest object in the DTS object model. The package contains four collections:

- Tasks
- Connections
- Steps
- Global Variables

The Package and each of these four types of objects is described in a section later in this chapter. Figure 12.1 shows the highest level of the DTS object diagram.

FIGURE 12.1

The highest levels of the DTS object hierarchy.

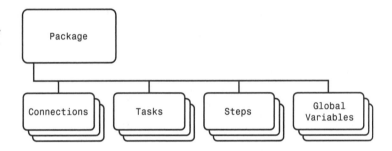

Using the DTS Package Object

This section shows you how to obtain a reference a DTS Package and how to use its properties, methods, and events. The following sections tell about the collections of the DTS Package object.

Referencing a DTS Package

You can create a new DTS Package in Visual Basic by declaring a New object variable of type DTS.Package.

```
Dim pkg As New DTS.Package
```

If you want to open an existing package, you declare the object variable without using the New keyword and then use one of the three Load methods described in Chapter 9:

- LoadFromRepository
- LoadFromSQLServer
- LoadFromStorageFile

```
Dim pkg As DTS.Package
pkg.LoadFromRepository "Server1", "msdb",, _
    "OLAPUnleashedInitialLoad", DTSreposFlag_UseTrustedConnection
```

When you want to reference the Package object from within an ActiveX script, you have to use the Parent property of one of the Package's collections.

```
Dim pkg
Set pkg = DTSGlobalVariables.Parent
```

Package Properties

The DTS Package object properties were all described in Chapter 9. Listing 12.1 sets the Read/Write properties for the OLAPUnleashedInitialLoad package.

LISTING 12.1   Visual Basic Code That Sets the Read/Write Properties of the Package Object

```
Dim pkg As New DTS.Package
pkg.Name = "OLAPUnleashedInitialLoad"
pkg.Description = "Load OLAP Unleashed Database - Preliminary Version"
pkg.WriteCompletionStatusToNTEventLog = False
pkg.LogFileName = "C:\DTS\Error\NorthwindToOLAPUnleashed.txt"
pkg.FailOnError = False
pkg.PackagePriorityClass = DTSPackagePriorityClass_Normal
pkg.MaxConcurrentSteps = 8
pkg.LineageOptions = DTSLineage_AddLineageVariables + _
    DTSLineage_WriteToReposIfAvailable
pkg.UseTransaction = True
pkg.TransactionIsolationLevel = DTSIsoLevel_ReadCommitted
pkg.AutoCommitTransaction = True
pkg.RepositoryMetadataOptions = DTSReposMetadata_ScanCatalogIfNotFound + _
    DTSReposMetadata_UseScannedCatalogIfPresent
pkg.UseOLEDBServiceComponents = True
```

The read-only properties for a package and typical values would be:

```
Msgbox CSTR(pkg.PackageID)

        {FFE772C1-1AA8-11D3-8B8A-0090277A4420}

Msgbox CSTR(pkg.VersionID)

        {FFE772C2-1AA8-11D3-8B8A-0090277A4420}

Msgbox pkg.CreatorName

        SQLServerUsers\timpete

Msgbox pkg.CreatorComputerName
```

```
        SQLServer4
Msgbox CSTR(pkg.CreationDate)

        6/4/99 2:21:11 PM
```

The Parent property always returns a reference to an object. For the package, the parent is the package itself. The following two code samples accomplish the same thing.

```
Set pkgNew = pkg.Parent
```

```
Set pkgNew = pkg
```

Package Methods

The following Save, Load, and Remove methods of the Package object were all discussed in Chapter 9:

- SaveToRepository
- SaveToSQLServer
- SaveToStorageFile
- LoadFromRepository
- LoadFromSQLServer
- LoadFromStorageFile
- RemoveFromRepository
- RemoveFromSQLServer

Here are the other methods of the Package object:

- Execute — This method runs the package.
- GetDTSVersionInfo — This method is used to get information about the version of the DTS Package.
- GetLastExecutionLineage — This method retrieves the Lineage variables from the last execution of the package.
- GetSavedPackageInfos — This method returns a list of versions that have been stored in a particular storage file.
- SaveAs — This method saves the package as a different package, having a new package ID.
- StartPreparationForStepsExecutingOnMainThread — This method is reserved for internal use.
- Uninitialize — This method clears the package and allows the Package object to be reused. It is used for creating new custom tasks.

Listing 12.2 executes one DTS Package from another package. This code is from the Call Create Database Package task of the OLAPUnleashedInitialLoad package. It checks to see whether the OLAPUnleashed database exists, and if it does not, executes the OLAPUnleashedCreateDatabase package. This code also shows how an ADO recordset can be called from a DTS script.

LISTING 12.2   ActiveX Script Code for Call Create Database Package Task

```
'Call Create Database Package
Option Explicit

Function Main()
Dim pkg, con, rst, sql
Dim pkgExecute 'Package that is executed

Set pkg = DTSGlobalVariables.Parent
Set con =  CreateObject("ADODB.Connection")
Set rst = CreateObject("ADODB.Recordset")

con.Provider = "sqloledb"
con.Properties("Data Source").Value = "."
con.Properties("Initial Catalog").Value = "master"
con.Properties("Integrated Security").Value = "SSPI"
con.Open

sql = "Select name from master..sysdatabases "
sql = sql & " where name = 'OLAPUnleashed'"
rst.Open sql, con

IF rst.EOF THEN
    Set pkgExecute = CreateObject("DTS.Package")
    pkgExecute.LoadFromSQLServer "(local)", "sa", "",,,,,_
        "OLAPUnleashedCreateDatabase"

    pkgExecute.Execute

END IF

    Main = DTSTaskExecResult_Success
End Function
```

Package Events

The following events return information to an application that calls a DTS Package. Each of these events is raised on the task level within the application. In other words, the OnStart event occurs once each time a task is started. All the events have a parameter that indicates which task has triggered the event.

- OnError—The OnError event returns all the available error information. The Cancel argument can be used to terminate execution of the package as a result of the error having occurred.

- OnFinish—A task or step has completed.

- OnProgress—Custom tasks can, but don't have to, report on what percent of the task has been accomplished or on the number of rows that have been processed. If the custom task is not able to report a percent, a value of 0 percent is returned.

- OnQueryCancel—This event is raised when a package cancels the execution of a task.

- OnStart—A task or step has started execution.

Properties and Methods of the Package's Collections

The four collections of the Package object have almost identical properties and methods.

The properties of these collections are

- Count—The number of members in the collection. The following code displays the number of Steps in a Package.

  ```
  Msgbox CSTR(pkg.Steps.Count)
  ```

- Parent—The Parent object. For these four collections, the parent is the Package object.

The methods common to all the collections are

- Add—Adds an object to a collection. You must have already created the object before adding it.

  ```
  Dim con As DTS.Connection
  Set con = Pkg.Connections.New("SQLOLEDB.1")
  Con.ID = 12 'Must set the ID property for the connection
  'Set other properties here
  pkg.Connections.Add con
  ```

- Insert—Places an object in a collection at a particular ordinal position.

  ```
  Pkg.Connections.Insert 5, con
  ```

- Item—Retrieves an object from a collection.

  ```
  Set con = pkg.Connections(5)
  ```

- New—Creates a new object for the collection. When a connection is being created, the name of the OLE DB provider must be included. When a task is being created, the particular type of custom task needs to be specified.

```
Dim tsk As DTS.Task
Set tsk = pkg.Tasks.New("DTSDataPumpTask")
```

- Remove—Removes an object from the collection, either by specifying an ordinal position or an object name.

```
Pkg.Connections.Remove(5)
Pkg.Tasks.Remove("DTSTask_DTSActiveScriptTask_1")
```

In addition to these common methods, the collections have these methods, which are specific to one of the collections:

- The Connections collection has a BeginAcquireMultipleConnections method and an EndAcquireMultipleConnections method. These methods are only used when creating custom tasks.
- The GlobalVariables collection has an AddGlobalVariable method, which adds a global variable with a single command. Its effect is the same as using the New and then the Add method.

```
pkg.GlobalVariables.AddGlobalVariable "VarName", "VarValue"
```

Using Global Variable Objects

Global Variable object has no methods and only three properties:

- Name—Used to identify which global variable is being referenced.
- Value—The content of the global variable. The following code displays a message box with the value in a global variable.

```
Msgbox pkg.GlobalVariables("VarName").Value
```

- Parent—The GlobalVariables collection.

From inside a script in a package, you can refer to a global variable either as a member of the GlobalVariables collection, which requires a reference to the package, or more directly as a part of the DTSGlobalVariables collection. The following two references inside a script are identical:

```
pkg.GlobalVariables("ProductID").Value
```

```
DTSGlobalVariables("ProductID").Value
```

You can create new global variables with either the New and Add methods or by using the AddGlobalVariable method. When using either one of these from Visual Basic, you create a global variable that is persistent in between the times the package is executed. You can see your global variable in the DTS Package Properties dialog.

You can also create global variables in either of these ways from inside of scripts. When you do, though, the global variables are not persistent. They disappear after the package has finished executing.

Normally, inside a script, you would create a global variable simply by referencing it. Global variables created in this way can be used throughout the execution of a package. They function the same as if they had been created with one of the methods of the `GlobalVariables` collection.

```
DTSGlobalVariables("NewVariable") = 10
```

> **Note**
>
> I don't believe there's any way to force the explicit declaration of global variables. I wish there were. More than once, I have tried to use a global variable, only to discover that I have misspelled it. DTS assumes that I want a new global variable, so it creates one, and the value that I thought I had put in that global variable then disappears.

> **Caution**
>
> Global variables have a variant data type. You can use them for strings, numbers, and even object variables. But I have experienced significant problems when DTS has become confused about the data type I am using in a global variable. I have had access violations, with the Enterprise Manager being shut down, and all the work on my DTS Package from the last hour unsaved. Occasionally, I've even had DTS Packages corrupted, so that I can't open up the most recent saved version after an access violation has occurred.
>
> I've found a way to avoid these problems. That is to always explicitly assign data types when using global variables inside scripts, using syntax like this:
>
> ```
> DTSGlobalVariables("StringVariable") = CSTR(pkg.Name)
> ```
> ```
> DTSGlobalVariables("IntegerVariable") = CLNG(con.ID)
> ```
>
> The lineage variable, `DTSLineage_Long`, has a uniqueidentifier data type. I have found that the easiest way to work with this variable in code is to change it to a string.

Using Connection Objects

Figure 12.2 shows the place of `Connections` in the DTS object hierarchy.

FIGURE 12.2

Connections *is one of the collections of the* Package *object, and each connection has an* OLEDBProperties *collection.*

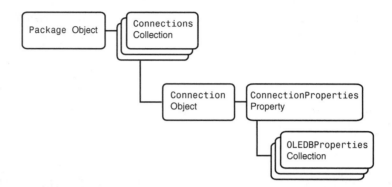

There is one required property for the Connection object—the ID. This property must be set before the Connection object is added to the Connection collection.

Methods of the Connection Object

The Connection object has just two methods, AcquireConnection and ReleaseConnection. You only use the AcquireConnection method when creating a custom task. The ReleaseConnection method is needed to free a connection so that you could change its properties dynamically in code.

 Listing 12.3 waits until a Connection is not being used. The connection is dropped, and the database name for the connection is changed.

LISTING 12.3   ActiveX Script That Changes the Name of a Database

```
'ChangeDatabase script

Option Explicit

Function Main()

Dim pkg, con
Set pkg = DTSGlobalVariables.Parent
Set con = pkg.Connections(1)

Do Until con.InUse = False 'Loop until connection is free.
    DoEvents
Loop

con.Releaseconnection    'Drop the connection
con.Catalog = "Northwind" 'Change the database

Main = DTSTaskExecResult_Success

End Function
```

> **Tip**
>
> Listing 12.3 checks to see whether the connection is not being used before releasing the connection. Remember that DTS Packages are multithreaded. Connections can be used by more than one task, and those tasks can be run simultaneously. Make sure that you're not trying to modify a connection while it's in use elsewhere.

The Properties of the `Collection` Object

Listing 12.4 creates a new connection, sets all the `Connection` object's read/write properties, and reads all the connection's read-only properties.

LISTING 12.4   VBScript That Sets and Reads Connection Properties

```vbscript
'ConnectionProperties script

Option Explicit

'Display the properties of the OLEDBProperties collection
Function Main

Dim pkg, con
Dim idx, msg

Set pkg = DTSGlobalVariables.Parent

'SQLOLEDB.1 is the name of the OLEDB provider for SQL Server
Set con = pkg.Connections.New("SQLOLEDB.1")

    'Set the read/write properties of the connection object
con.Name = "NorthwindConnection"
con.ID = 1
con.DataSource = "Marketing1"
con.Catalog = "Northwind"
con.Description = "Marketing1 Connection"
con.UseTrustedConnection = True
'con.UserID = "user1" 'Not needed with trusted connection.
'con.Password = "abc" 'Not needed with trusted connection.
con.Reusable = True
con.ConnectImmediate = False
con.ConnectionTimeout = 15    'In seconds.

'Add the new connection to the connections collection
pkg.Connections.Add con
```

continues

LISTING 12.4   continued

```
'Display the read-only connection properties
Msgbox "Connected Property Value - " & cstr(con.Connected)
Msgbox "InTransaction Property Value - " & cstr(con.InTransaction)
Msgbox "InUse Property Value - " & cstr(con.InUse)
Msgbox "LastOwnerTaskName Property Value - " & con.LastOwnerTaskName
Msgbox "Parent's Parent's Name Property Value - " _
    & con.Parent.Parent.Name
Msgbox "ProviderID Property Value - " & con.ProviderID

Main = DTSTaskExecResult_Success

End Function
```

The `OLEDBProperties` Collection

Each connection object has a property called `ConnectionProperties`, which contains a collection called `OLEDBProperties`. This collection contains values that are different for each OLE DB provider. You can set some of these values in the DTS Designer user interface as properties or advanced properties of the connection. Many of these properties can only be set in code.

The `OLEDBProperties` collection has only one method—`Item`. The collection has two properties—`Count` and `Parent`.

 Listing 12.5 sets up a loop to display all the properties in the `OLEDBProperties` collection for the connection.

LISTING 12.5   ActiveX Script That Displays the OLEDBProperties

```
'OLEDBProperties Script

Option Explicit

'Display the properties of the OLEDBProperties collection
Function Main

Dim pkg, con
Dim idx, msg

Set pkg = DTSGlobalVariables.Parent
Set con = pkg.Connections(1)

For idx = 1 to con .ConnectionProperties.Count - 1
    msg = "OLEDBPropery Index - " & cstr(idx)
```

```
    msg = msg & vbCrLf & vbCrLf
    msg = msg & "Name - " & con .ConnectionProperties.Item(idx).Name
    msg = msg & vbCrLf & vbCrLf
    msg = msg & "PropertyID - "
    msg = msg & cstr(con.ConnectionProperties.Item(idx).PropertyID)
    msg = msg & vbCrLf & vbCrLf
    msg = msg & "PropertySet - "
    msg = msg &  cstr(con.ConnectionProperties.Item(idx).PropertySet)
    msg = msg & vbCrLf & vbCrLf
    msg = msg & "Value - "
    msg = msg &  cstr(con.ConnectionProperties.Item(idx).Value)
    Msgbox msg
Next

Main = DTSTaskExecResult_Success

End Function
```

There can be a lot of properties in the `OLEDBProperties` collection. Here's an example for the OLE DB Provider for SQL Server:

```
con.ConnectionProperties("Active Sessions") = 0
con.ConnectionProperties("Application Name") = "DTS Designer"
con.ConnectionProperties("Asynchable Abort") = False
con.ConnectionProperties("Asynchable Commit") = False
con.ConnectionProperties("Auto Translate") = True
con.ConnectionProperties("Catalog Location") = 1
con.ConnectionProperties("Catalog Term") = "database"
con.ConnectionProperties("Catalog Usage") = 15
con.ConnectionProperties("Column Definition") = 1
con.ConnectionProperties("Connection Status") = 1
con.ConnectionProperties("Current Catalog") = "OLAPUnleashed"
con.ConnectionProperties("Data Source") = "(local)"
con.ConnectionProperties("Data Source Name") = "(local)"
con.ConnectionProperties("Data Source Object Threading Model") = 1
con.ConnectionProperties("DBMS Name") = "Microsoft SQL Server"
con.ConnectionProperties("DBMS Version") = "07.00.0623"
con.ConnectionProperties("Enable Fastload") = False
con.ConnectionProperties("GROUP BY Support") = 4
con.ConnectionProperties("Heterogeneous Table Support") = 3
con.ConnectionProperties("Identifier Case Sensitivity") = 8
con.ConnectionProperties("Initial Catalog") = "OLAPUnleashed"
con.ConnectionProperties("Integrated Security") = "SSPI"
con.ConnectionProperties("Isolation Levels") = 1118464
con.ConnectionProperties("Isolation Retention") = 0
con.ConnectionProperties("Locale Identifier") = 1033
con.ConnectionProperties("Maximum Index Size") = 900
con.ConnectionProperties("Maximum Open Chapters") = 0
con.ConnectionProperties("Maximum Row Size") = 8060
```

12

PROGRAMMING
WITH THE DTS
OBJECT MODEL

```
con.ConnectionProperties("Maximum Row Size Includes BLOB") = False
con.ConnectionProperties("Maximum Tables in SELECT") = 256
con.ConnectionProperties("Multiple Connections") = True
con.ConnectionProperties("Multiple Parameter Sets") = True
con.ConnectionProperties("Multiple Results") = 1
con.ConnectionProperties("Multiple Storage Objects") = False
con.ConnectionProperties("Multi-Table Update") = False
con.ConnectionProperties("NULL Collation Order") = 4
con.ConnectionProperties("NULL Concatenation Behavior") = 1
con.ConnectionProperties("OLE DB Version") = "02.00"
con.ConnectionProperties("OLE Object Support") = 1
con.ConnectionProperties("Open Rowset Support") = 0
con.ConnectionProperties("ORDER BY Columns in Select List") = False
con.ConnectionProperties("Output Parameter Availability") = 4
con.ConnectionProperties("Packet Size") = 4096
con.ConnectionProperties("Pass By Ref Accessors") = True
con.ConnectionProperties("Persist Security Info") = True
con.ConnectionProperties("Persistent ID Type") = 4
con.ConnectionProperties("Prepare Abort Behavior") = 2
con.ConnectionProperties("Prepare Commit Behavior") = 2
con.ConnectionProperties("Procedure Term") = "stored procedure"
con.ConnectionProperties("Prompt") = 4
con.ConnectionProperties("Provider Friendly Name") = "Microsoft OLE DB Provider
for SQL Server"
con.ConnectionProperties("Provider Name") = "sqloledb.dll"
con.ConnectionProperties("Provider Version") = "07.01.0623"
con.ConnectionProperties("Quoted Identifier Sensitivity") = 8
con.ConnectionProperties("Read-Only Data Source") = False
con.ConnectionProperties("Rowset Conversions on Command") = True
con.ConnectionProperties("Schema Term") = "owner"
con.ConnectionProperties("Schema Usage") = 15
con.ConnectionProperties("Server Name") = "INSTRUCTOR"
con.ConnectionProperties("SQL Support") = 283
con.ConnectionProperties("Structured Storage") = 1
con.ConnectionProperties("Subquery Support") = 31
con.ConnectionProperties("Table Term") = "table"
con.ConnectionProperties("Transaction DDL") = 8
con.ConnectionProperties("Unicode Comparison Style") = 196609
con.ConnectionProperties("Unicode Locale Id") = 1033
con.ConnectionProperties("Use Procedure for Prepare") = 1
con.ConnectionProperties("User Name") = "dbo"
con.ConnectionProperties("Workstation ID") = "SQLServer9"
```

Using Step Objects

The Step object is a part of the Step collection, and it has one collection itself: the collection of PrecedenceConstraints, as shown in Figure 12.3.

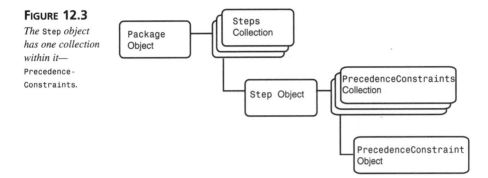

FIGURE 12.3
The Step *object has one collection within it—*
Precedence-
Constraints.

Methods of the Step Object

The Step object has two methods, both of which are used internally by the package and would not normally be used in code except when creating a new custom task. These two methods are

- Execute—This method is normally called by the package. Each step is executed in the process of the package being executed.
- GetExecutionErrorInfo—This is error information that is in addition to the package error information. Step error information is not available to applications that have executed a package, unless that step error information is passed on to the package error handler.

Properties of the Step Object

The properties of the Step object were all discussed in Chapter 9.

There are two required properties—Name and TaskName. These both have to be specified before the Step can be added to the Step collection. The Task object that is named doesn't have to exist, but a valid name has to be supplied to create the Step object.

Listing 12.6 creates a new step and assigns all the Read/Write properties. This is a portion of code generated by the ScriptPkg application, which is described in the section "The DTS Package Scripting Tool."

LISTING 12.6 Visual Basic Code That Creates a New Step

```
dim oStep as DTS.Step
Set oStep = goPackage.Steps.New
oStep.Name = "Copy Data from_
```

continues

LISTING 12.6   continued

```
CustomerDemographics to_
    [OLAPUnleashed].[dbo].[dimCustomerDemographic]_
    Step"
oStep.Description = "Load CustomerDemographic"
oStep.TaskName = "Copy Data from_
    CustomerDemographics to_
    [OLAPUnleashed].[dbo].[dimCustomerDemographic]_
    Task"
oStep.ExecutionStatus = DTSStepExecStat_Waiting.

oStep.CommitSuccess = False
oStep.RollbackFailure = False
oStep.ScriptLanguage = "VBScript"
oStep.AddGlobalVariables = True oStep.FunctionName = "Main" oStep.ActiveXScript
= "Function Main()" & vbCrLf
oStep.ActiveXScript = oStep.ActiveXScript &_
    "Main = DTSStepScriptResult_ExecuteTask" &_
    vbCrLf
oStep.ActiveXScript = oStep.ActiveXScript &_
    "End Function"
oStep.RelativePriority =_
    DTSStepRelativePriority_Normal
oStep.CloseConnection = False
oStep.ExecuteInMainThread = False
oStep.IsPackageDSORowset = False
oStep.JoinTransactionIfPresent = False
oStep.DisableStep = False
pkg.Steps.Add oStep
set oStep = Nothing
```

> **Note**
>
> The Name property and the TaskName property in Listing 12.6 show a Step name and an Object name that have been assigned by using the DTS Import Wizard. If a task is created in the DTS Designer, the Task Name takes the form of DTSTask_DTSActiveScriptTask_6, and the name of the corresponding step will be DTSStep_DTSActiveScriptTask_6. Each type of custom task is numbered separately in this naming convention.
>
> If you create your own steps and tasks in code, you can name them however you want. But if you use the wizard or the Designer, you have to use the names that are assigned.

Here are the read-only properties of the Step object:

```
Dim pkg, stp
Set pkg = GlobalVariables.Parent
Set stp = pkg.Step(1)

SELECT CASE stp.ExecutionResult
    CASE DTSStepExecResult_Failure '1
        Msgbox "Failure!"
    CASE DTSStepExecResult_Success '0
        Msgbox "Success!"
END SELECT
MSGBOX CSTR(stp.StartTime) 'The time the step started executing.
MSGBOX CSTR(stp.FinishTime) 'The time the step completed.
MSGBOX CSTR(stp.ExecutionTime) 'Execution time in seconds.
```

The `PrecedenceConstraints` Collection of the Step Object

The Step object has a property called PrecedenceConstraints, which contains the PrecedenceConstraints collection. These objects determine the workflow of the package.

The PrecedenceConstraints collection has methods and properties almost identical to the four collections of the Package object:

- Count and Parent properties
- The Add, Insert, Item, New, and Remove methods
- A special method, AddConstraint, that adds a constraint using just this one method

The PrecedenceConstraint objects have four properties:

- Parent — The PrecedenceConstraints collection. If you want to retrieve the name of the step that contains this PrecedenceConstraint, you can retrieve the name of the parent's parent.
  ```
  Dim prc As DTS.PrecedenceConstraint
  Msgbox prc.Parent.Parent.Name
  ```
- StepName — The name of the step that is being given precedence. The StepName is the name of the controlling step for this precedence constraint. The dependent step, the step that is being controlled, is the step that contains this precedence constraint.
- PrecedenceBasis — Whether the precedence is going to be controlled by the Execution Status or the Execution Result.
- Value — The constants that are used for the various Statuses and Results.

The use of the `PrecedenceBasis` and the `Value` properties are fully described in Chapter 9.

Listing 12.7 creates a new precedence constraint.

LISTING 12.7   ActiveX Script That Creates a Precedence Constraint.

```
Dim pkg, stp, prc
Set pkg = DTSGlobalVariables.Parent

'The dependent task.
set stp = pkg.Steps("DTSStep_DTSExecuteSQLTask_1")

'The controlling task.
Set prc = stp.PrecedenceConstraints.New("DTSStep_DTSDataPumpTask_4")

'The controlling task must be mentioned again.
prc.StepName = "DTSStep_DTSDataPumpTask_4"

'Set the PrecedenceBasis and the Value
prc.PrecedenceBasis = DTSStepPrecedenceBasis_ExecResult =
DTSStepExecResult_Success

'Add the precedence constraint
stp.PrecedenceConstraints.Add prc
```

Using Task Objects

Task objects are always created as an instance of a particular custom task. Figure 12.4 shows the object hierarchy of the task objects.

FIGURE 12.4

Each Task object is implemented as a particular custom task.

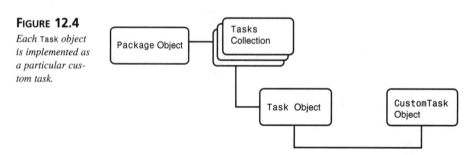

The particular custom task that is created determines the particular methods and properties available to the task. The Data Pump task and the Data-Driven Query task are the most complex and are discussed in greater detail later in this chapter, in the section "Using the Data Pump and the Data Driven Query Custom Task Objects."

Referencing Task and CustomTask Objects

Tasks and custom tasks are usually referenced together. For example, when you create a new task, you declare both a Task object variable and a CustomTask object variable. The CustomTask object variable is declared for whatever specific custom task is being used. The CustomTask variable is then set equal to the CustomTask property of the Task object. All the properties of the task can then be assigned through the CustomTask object variable.

> **Note**
>
> The Task is a general type of object. The CustomTask is a more specific object. There is one property you have to assign with the Task object—the CustomTask property. There are two more properties, Description and Name, that you can assign with either object because these properties are common to all types of tasks. All the other properties of a Task must be assigned through the CustomTask object that is paired with the Task.

Listing 12.8 creates an Execute SQL task and assigns its properties.

LISTING 12.8 Visual Basic Code That Creates a Task Called DTSTask_DTSExecuteSQLTask_3

```
Dim tsk as DTS.Task
Dim cus as DTS.ExecuteSQLTask
Set tsk = pkg.Tasks.New("DTSExecuteSQLTask")
Set cus = tsk.CustomTask
cus.Name = "DTSTask_DTSExecuteSQLTask_3"
cus.Description = "Delete From tmpOrderDetailLoad"
cus.SQLStatement = "Delete tmpOrderDetailLoad"
cus.ConnectionID = 13
cus.CommandTimeout = 0
pkg.Tasks.Add tsk
set cus = Nothing
Set tsk = Nothing
```

Retrieving a property also requires the use of both the Task object and the CustomTask object. The following VBScript code sample shows how to get a reference to a property of the CustomTask, when all you know is the name of the Step associated with that Task:

```
Dim pkg, stp, tsk, cus
Set pkg = DTSGlobalVariables.Parent
Set stp = pkg.Steps("DTSStep_DTSActiveScriptTask_3")
Set tsk = stp.TaskName
```

```
Set cus = tsk.CustomTask
Msgbox cus.SQLStatement
```

Properties of the Task Object

The generic Task object has one method—Execute, no collections, and five properties. These properties are

- CustomTask—The Custom Task object that is paired with this Task object.
- CustomTaskID—The type of Custom Task. Table 12.1 lists the choices for CustomTaskId.
- Description—The description of the task.
- Name—The name of the task.
- Parent—The parent, which is the Tasks collection.

The CustomTaskID property specifies which type of Custom Task is being used for this Task. This CustomTaskID property is also used in the New method of the Tasks collection, when a Task object is first created:

```
Set tsk = pkg.Tasks.New("DTSActiveScriptTask")
```

Table 12.1 shows the CustomTaskID values.

TABLE 12.1 The CustomTaskId's for the Custom Tasks

Custom Task	CustomTaskID *Property*
Active Script task	DTSActiveScriptTask
Create Process task	DTSCreateProcessTask
Execute SQL task	DTSExecuteSQLTask
Data-Driven Query task	DTSDataDrivenQueryTask
Transfer Objects task	DTSTransferObjectsTask
Send Mail task	DTSSendMailTask
Bulk Insert task	DTSBulkInsertTask
Data Transformation task	DTSDataPumpTask
OLAP Process task	DTSOlapProcess.Task

Note

The OLAP Process task was not included in the initial release of SQL Server 7.0. It's available in the Data Transformation Services Task Kit 1. This task is discussed in Chapter 16, "Processing and Browsing Cubes."

Properties of the `CustomTask` Object

The `CustomTask` object also has one method—`Execute`. Only two properties are common to all custom tasks. These two properties, `Name` and `Description`, are shared between the `CustomTask` and the `Task` object. They can be assigned with either object and always contain the same value for both.

Properties of the Various Types of Custom Tasks

The Data Transformation task and the Data-Driven Query task are discussed in more detail in the following section. The specific properties for each of the other custom tasks were discussed in Chapter 8.

Using the `Data Pump` and the `Data Driven Query Custom Task` Objects

The two transformation tasks—the Transform Data task and the Data-Driven Query task—have a more complex structure than the other tasks. Figures 12.5 and 12.6 show the object models for these tasks.

FIGURE 12.5
The Transform Data task (`DataPumpTask`) object model.

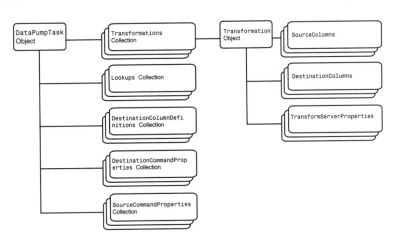

FIGURE 12.6

The Data-Driven Query task object model.

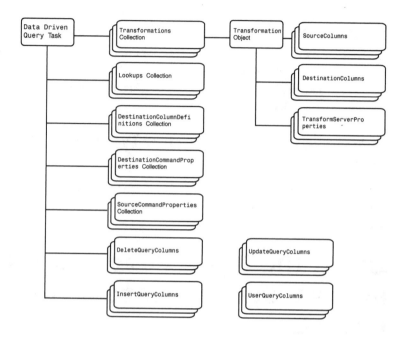

Collections for the Transform Data and the Data-Driven Query Tasks

The two transformation tasks both have five collections:

- SourceCommandProperties
- DestinationCommandProperties
- DestinationColumnDefinitions
- Lookups
- Transformations

The SourceCommandProperties and the DestinationCommandProperties collections both contain OLEDBProperties collections, specifying information about the particular OLE DB service provider.

The DestinationColumnDefinitions collection is a group of column definitions for the destination of the transformation task.

The Lookups Collection

The Lookups collection has properties and methods similar to those of the Global Variables collection and the PrecedenceConstraints collection:

- Count and Parent properties
- The Add, Insert, Item, New, and Remove methods
- A special method, AddLookup, that adds a Lookup using just this one method

A Lookup object has no methods and five properties:

- ConnectionID—A Lookup must refer to an existing Connection object in the package. This property of the Lookup connects the Lookup to the ID property of that Connection object.
- MaxCacheRows—The number of the rows that are cached by the Lookup.
- Name—The name of the Lookup. The Name property is used in the script to execute the Lookup.
- Parent—The Lookups collection of this particular transformation task.
- Query—The text of the parameterized query that is used to Lookup the required data.

Listing 12.9 creates a Lookup. This code requires that "cus" already be declared and set as a Custom Task object variable for a Transform Data or a Data-Driven Query task.

LISTING 12.9 Visual Basic Code That Creates a Lookup.Dim lkp As DTS.Lookup

```
Set lkp = cus.Lookups.New ("Country")
lkp.Name = "Country"
lkp.ConnectionID = 10
lkp.Query = "SELECT Country FROM lkpSalesDistrictRegion " & vbCRLF
lkp.Query = lkp.Query & "WHERE City = ? AND Region = ? AND
DuplicateRegionAndCity = 0"
lkp.MaxCacheRows = 0
cus.Lookups.Add lkp
Set lkp = Nothing
```

The Transformations Collection

The Transformations collection has the typical two properties and five methods:

- Count and Parent properties
- The Add, Insert, Item, New, and Remove methods

Each Transformation object has three properties, which themselves contain collections:

- DestinationColumns
- SourceColumns
- TransformServerProperties

The `DestinationColumns` and the `SourceColumns` properties define collections of columns. Each column in the collection can be referenced by its name or by its ordinal number. The columns have other properties, which vary depending on the OLE DB provider.

Listing 12.10 creates a new member of the `SourceColumns` collection. This sample assumes that a `Transformation` object variable "trn" has already been created and set.

Listing 12.10   Visual Basic Code That Creates a New Source Column

```
Dim clm As DTS.Column
Set clm = trn.SourceColumns.New("LastName",2)
clm.Name = "LastName"
clm.Ordinal = 2
clm.Flags = 0
clm.Size = 0
clm.DataType = 0
clm.Precision = 0
clm.NumericScale = 0
clm.Nullable = True
trn.SourceColumns.Add clm
clm = Nothing
```

The `TransformServerProperties` collection has three properties defined for both the Transform Data task and the Data-Driven Query task. These three properties are not required by the DTS object model. They are the three properties that are set by these two custom tasks. Future custom tasks could implement a different set of `TransformServerProperties`.

- Text — The text of the ActiveX Script.
- Language — The scripting language—VBScript, Jscript, or PerlScript.
- FunctionEntry — The function in the script that is initially called. `Main` is the default name for `FunctionEntry`.

Listing 12.11 sets the `TransformServerProperties`. This sample assumes that a `Transformation` object variable "trn" has already been created and set.

Listing 12.11   Visual Basic Code That Sets the TransformServerProperties

```
Dim trnProps as DTS.Properties
Set trnProps = trn.TransformServerProperties
trnProps("Text") = "'Load dimProduct" & vbCRLF
trnProps("Text") = trnProps("Text") & "Option Explicit" & vbCRLF
trnProps("Text") = trnProps("Text") & "" & vbCRLF
```

continues

LISTING **12.11** continued

```
trnProps("Text") = trnProps("Text") & "Function Main()" & vbCRLFvbCRLF
trnProps("Text") = trnProps("Text") & "'Lookup value for LineageFK in ""
trnProps("Text") = trnProps("Text") & "the Global Variable" & vbCRLF
trnProps("Text") = trnProps("Text") & "DTSDestination(""LineageFK"") = "
trnProps("Text") = trnProps("Text") & "DTSGlobalVariables"
trnProps("Text") = trnProps("Text") & "(""dimProduct"").Value"
trnProps("Text") = trnProps("Text") & vbCRLF
...............
   .
   .
   .
trnProps("Text") = trnProps("Text") & "    ReplaceNull = str" & vbCRLF
trnProps("Text") = trnProps("Text") & "END IF" & vbCRLF
trnProps("Text") = trnProps("Text") & "" & vbCRLF
trnProps("Text") = trnProps("Text") & "End Function" & vbCRLF
trnProps("Language") = "VBScript"
trnProps("FunctionEntry") = "Main"
Set trnProps = Nothing
```

12

PROGRAMMING
WITH THE DTS
OBJECT MODEL

The other properties of the Transformation object include

- ForceBlobsInMemory — Whether or not to force DTS to store each BLOB column in a single memory allocation.

- ForceSourceBlobsBuffered — Whether or not to always buffer BLOB columns.

- InMemoryBlobSize — The amount of storage in bytes allocated for each BLOB column.

- Name — The name of the transformation.

- Parent — The Transformations collection.

- TransformFlags — Which of the twelve DTSTransformFlags constants have been chosen, which determines how data type variations are going to be handled in the transformation.

- TransformServer — Specifies the dispatch interface of the COM server object.

- TransformServerID — The Class Identifier of the Transformation object. For a Transform Data task, this is "DTS.DataPumpTransformScript.1".

- TransformServerParameter — Used for an initialization parameter if the transform server requires it.

- FunctionEntry — The function in the script that is initially called. Main is the default name for FunctionEntry.

Listing 12.12 creates a Transformation object and sets its properties. This sample assumes that a CustomTask object variable "cus" has already been created and set.

LISTING 12.12   Visual Basic Code That Creates a New Transformation

```
Dim trn as DTS.Transformation
Sim clm as DTS.Column
Set trn = cus.Transformations.New("DTS.DataPumpTransformScript.1")
trn.Name = "DTSTransformation__1"
trn.TransformFlags = 63
trn.ForceSourceBlobsBuffered = 0
trn.ForceBlobsInMemory = False
trn.InMemoryBlobSize = 1048576

Set clm = trn.SourceColumns.New("CustomerTypeID",1)
clm.Name = "CustomerTypeID"
clm.Ordinal = 1
clm.Flags = 0
clm.Size = 0
clm.DataType = 0
clm.Precision = 0
clm.NumericScale = 0
clm.Nullable = True
trn.SourceColumns.Add clm
Set clm = Nothing

Set clm = trn.SourceColumns.New("CustomerDesc",2)
clm.Name = "CustomerDesc"
clm.Ordinal = 2
clm.Flags = 0
clm.Size = 0
clm.DataType = 0
clm.Precision = 0
clm.NumericScale = 0
clm.Nullable = True
trn.SourceColumns.Add clm
Set clm = Nothing

Set clm = trn.DestinationColumns.New("LineageFK",2)
clm.Name = "LineageFK"
clm.Ordinal = 2
clm.Flags = 0
clm.Size = 0
clm.DataType = 0
clm.Precision = 0
clm.NumericScale = 0
clm.Nullable = True
trn.DestinationColumns.Add clm
Set clm = Nothing

Set clm = trn.DestinationColumns.New("NorthwindCustomerTypeID",2)
clm.Name = "NorthwindCustomerTypeID"
```

```
clm.Ordinal = 2
clm.Flags = 0
clm.Size = 0
clm.DataType = 0
clm.Precision = 0
clm.NumericScale = 0
clm.Nullable = True
trn.DestinationColumns.Add clm
Set clm = Nothing

Set clm = trn.DestinationColumns.New("CustomerDesc",4)
clm.Name = "CustomerDesc"
clm.Ordinal = 4
clm.Flags = 0
clm.Size = 0
clm.DataType = 0
clm.Precision = 0
clm.NumericScale = 0
clm.Nullable = True
trn.DestinationColumns.Add clm
Set clm = Nothing

Set trnProps = trn.TransformServerProperties
trnProps("Text") = "'Load dimCustomerDemographic" & vbCRLF
trnProps("Text") = trnProps("Text") & "Option Explicit" & vbCRLF
trnProps("Text") = trnProps("Text") & "" & vbCRLF
trnProps("Text") = trnProps("Text") & "Function Main()" & vbCRLF
trnProps("Text") = trnProps("Text") & "DTSDestination(""CustomerDesc"") "
trnProps("Text") = trnProps("Text") & "= DTSSource(""CustomerDesc"")"
trnProps("Text") = trnProps("Text") & vbCRLF
trnProps("Text") = trnProps("Text") & "" & vbCRLF
trnProps("Text") = trnProps("Text") & "Main = DTSTransformStat_OK"
trnProps("Text") = trnProps("Text") & vbCRLF
trnProps("Text") = trnProps("Text") & "" & vbCRLF
trnProps("Text") = trnProps("Text") & "End Function" & vbCRLF
trnProps("Language") = "VBScript"
trnProps("FunctionEntry") = "Main"
Set trnProps = Nothing

cus.Transformations.Add trn
set trn = Nothing
```

Additional Properties for the Data-Driven Query Task

The Data-Driven Query task includes all the collections and most of the properties of the Transform Data task. In addition, the Data-Driven Query task has a set of properties that define the parameterized queries. Each of the four queries has a query property and a collection of columns that contain the parameters, in order, that are used for the parameters in the query. These properties are

- `DeleteQuery` and `DeleteQueryColumns`
- `InsertQuery` and `InsertQueryColumns`
- `UpdateQuery` and `UpdateQueryColumns`
- `UserQuery` and `UserQueryColumns`

The DTS Package Scripting Tool

One of the most helpful tools for using and learning how to use the DTS object model is a Visual Basic tool called ScriptPkg. The code for ScriptPkg is distributed on the SQL Server 7.0 installation CD in a self-extracting file at devtools\samples\dts\dtsdem.exe.

When you run ScriptPkg, you can choose to script any DTS Package that has been stored in SQL Server. This utility opens the package, reads the definition of all the package objects, and creates a script of the object definition. The script is in a format that can be executed with Visual Basic to re-create the entire package. Scripts created by ScriptPkg for the DTS Packages included with this book are all on the CD.

The code in ScriptPkg is a great learning tool. It provides a working example of how to read the definition of DTS objects. And the scripts produced by ScriptPkg show how to write code for creating or modifying DTS objects.

Being able to script a package provides the opportunity to make naming changes that apply to all the objects in a package.

One thing that ScriptPkg does not save is the visual representation of the package that you create with the DTS Designer. When a script produced by ScriptPkg is executed to re-create a package, a new visual display is created.

When ScriptPkg is used on large packages, it is necessary to split the script into smaller pieces before they can be executed with Visual Basic.

 The full script of OLAPUnleashedInitialLoad is on the CD, as it was created by ScriptPkg. You can find it with the other samples from this chapter. It is in a file called `OLAPUnleashedInitialLoad.txt`.

The DTS Designer Control of Flow Tools

I have written five ActiveX Script tasks to help control the flow of DTS tasks during the design of a DTS Package, which I have put into a DTS Package called Unleashed DTS Tool Collection. Three of these tools are used together to automate the enabling and disabling of tasks, one of the tools sets and removes precedence constraints, and the other removes unwanted connections from the package. This DTS Package is on the CD in the \Samples\DTS directory. The code samples are also listed with the code from this chapter. Figure 12.7 shows this package.

FIGURE 12.7

The Unleashed DTS Tool Collection provides five tools that assist in the development of a DTS Package.

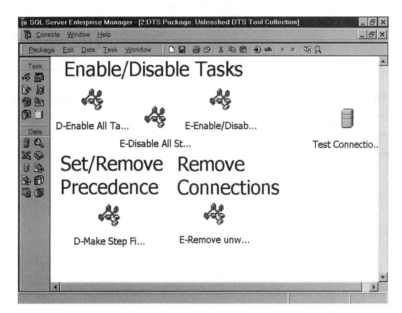

The Enable/Disable Task Tools

One of the complaints that people have about the DTS Designer is that you can't execute one task by itself. You can, of course, go to the workflow properties of each task and disable the step, but then you have to go and enable them all again. This set of three tools automates that process.

All DTS tasks, except for the Data Transform tasks, can be copied in one DTS Package and pasted into another. You can copy and paste these tools into the DTS Packages you are developing and delete them when the development process is complete.

The three tools provide complementary choices for enabling and disabling tasks:

- The Disable All Tasks Except E tool allows you to disable all except a few tasks.
- The Enable All Tasks Except D tool allows you to enable all except a few tasks.
- The Enable/Disable As Marked D And E tool both disables and enables tasks but only affects the ones you have specifically selected.

You mark tasks for disabling and enabling by placing an "E-" or "D-" prefix on the description of each task.

Here's how these tools are used. If you have a package that has 40 different tasks and you are developing a new task, you maybe want to run that one new task repeatedly, without running the other 40. You would use the Disable All Tasks Except E tool and put the prefix "E-" on the description of your new task. If you need any other tasks to run before your new task, you can mark them with an "E-" prefix tool. All the other tasks will be automatically disabled. When you are through testing the new task and want all the tasks to be enabled again, you can use the Enable All Tasks Except D tool.

The Enable/Disable tools can themselves be enabled and disabled by marking them with the "E-" and "D-" prefix. Note that, unless precedence is assigned to these tools, the enabling and disabling of particular tasks might occur for the current execution of the package, or it might not go into effect until the following execution.

The code for all three tools is similar. Listing 12.13 shows the code for the Disable All Tasks Except E tool.

LISTING 12.13 ActiveX Script That Disables All Tasks, Except Those That Have Been Marked with an "E"

```
'Disable All Steps Except E
Option Explicit
Function Main()
DIM pkg, stp, tsk, cus
SET pkg = DTSGlobalVariables.Parent

FOR EACH stp IN pkg.Steps
    Set tsk = pkg.Tasks(stp.TaskName)
    Set cus = tsk.CustomTask
    IF LEFT(cus.Description,2) <> "E-" THEN
        stp.DisableStep = True
    END IF
NEXT

Main = DTSTaskExecResult_Success
End Function
```

The Tool for Setting and Removing Precedence Constraints

I have found that there are times in the development process when I want a particular task to execute before all other tasks, and there are other times I want a particular task to execute after all other tasks. I created the Make Step First or Last tool to automate that process for me.

This tool presents three input boxes to make the following choices:

- The name of the step you want to make first or last
- Whether you want the step to be first or last or whether you want to remove the step from being first or last
- Whether you want to use On Success, On Failure, or On Complete precedence

Listing 12.14 shows the code for the Make Step First or Last tool.

12

PROGRAMMING
WITH THE DTS
OBJECT MODEL

LISTING 12.14 ActiveX Script That Sets Precedence Constraints to Make One Task Either First or Last

```
'Make Step First or Last
Option Explicit

Function Main()

DIM pkg, stp, tsk, cus, prc
Dim stpSel
Dim msg, ttl, sErrMsg
Dim sSelectedStep, sFirstOrLast, sAddOrRemove, sPrecType
Dim lBasis, lValue

sErrMsg = ""

set pkg = dTSGlobalVariables.Parent

msg = "Enter the name of the step you want to be first or last."
msg = msg & vbCrLf & "Enter nothing if you don't want to change any precedence."
ttl = "Enter Name of Step"
sSelectedStep = INPUTBOX(msg, ttl)

IF sSelectedStep <> "" THEN
        Set stpSel = pkg.Steps(CSTR(sSelectedStep))

        msg = "Enter 'F' to make this step first."
        msg = msg & vbCrLf & "Enter 'L' to make this step last."
        msg = msg & vbCrLf & "Enter 'RL' to remove all constraints "
```

continues

LISTING 12.14   continued

```
          msg = msg & "from this step."
          msg = msg & vbCrLf & "Enter 'RF ' to remove all constraints "
          msg = msg & "that reference this step."
          ttl = "Choose What Constraints to use"
          sFirstOrLast =INPUTBOX(msg, ttl)
ELSE
          sErrMsg = "No step was selected."
END IF

sFirstOrLast = UCASE(sFirstOrLast)


SELECT CASE sFirstOrLast

          CASE "L", "F"
                  sAddOrRemove = "Add"
          CASE    "RL", "RF"
                  sAddOrRemove = "Remove"
          CASE ELSE
                  sErrMsg = "No precedence was set because first "
                  sErrMsg = sErrMsg & "or last was not picked."
END SELECT

IF sErrMsg = "" AND sAddOrRemove = "Add" THEN
          msg = "Enter 'C' for On Complete Precedence"
          msg = msg & vbCrLf &  "Enter 'F' for On Failure Precedence"
          msg = msg & vbCrLf &  "Enter 'S' for On Success Precedence"

          sPrecType =INPUTBOX(msg,  ttl)
          sPrecType = UCASE(sPrecType)

          IF sPrecType ="C" THEN
                  lBasis = DTSStepPrecedenceBasis_ExecStatus
                  lValue = DTSStepExecStat_Completed
          ELSEIF sPrecType = "F" THEN
                  lBasis = DTSStepPrecedenceBasis_ExecResult
                  lValue = DTSStepExecResult_Failure
          ELSEIF sPrecType = "S" THEN
                  lBasis = DTSStepPrecedenceBasis_ExecResult
                  lValue = DTSStepExecResult_Success
          ELSE
                  sErrMsg = "No precedence was set because the type of  "
                  sErrMsg = sErrMsg & "precedence was not selected."
          END IF
END IF

If sErrMsg = "" THEN

    For each stp in pkg.Steps
```

```
'Enable this code to pick only a specific type of task:
'        Set tsk = pkg.Tasks(stp.Taskname)
'        IF tsk.CustomTaskID = "DTSExecuteSQLTask" THEN
'Also enable END IF below

        IF stp.Name <> sSelectedStep THEN

            IF sFirstOrLast = "F" THEN

                For Each prc in stp.PrecedenceConstraints
                    If prc.StepName = CSTR(sSelectedStep) Then
                        stp.PrecedenceConstraints.Remove(prc.StepName)
                    End If
                NEXT

                Set prc = stp.PrecedenceConstraints.New(sSelectedStep)
                prc.StepName =sSelectedStep
                prc.PrecedenceBasis = lBasis
                prc.Value = lValue
                stp.PrecedenceConstraints.Add prc
            ELSEIF sFirstOrLast = "L" THEN

                For Each prc in stpSel.PrecedenceConstraints
                    If prc.StepName = stp.Name Then
                        stpSel.PrecedenceConstraints.Remove(prc.StepName)
                    End If
                NEXT
                Set prc = stpSel.PrecedenceConstraints.New(stp.Name)
                prc.StepName =stp.Name
                prc.PrecedenceBasis = lBasis
                prc.Value = lValue
                stpSel.PrecedenceConstraints.Add prc

            ELSEIF sFirstOrLast = "RL" THEN

                For Each prc in stpSel.PrecedenceConstraints
                    stpSel.PrecedenceConstraints.Remove(prc.StepName)
                NEXT

                EXIT FOR   'Only need to do this once

            ELSEIF sFirstOrLast = "RF" THEN

                For Each prc in stp.PrecedenceConstraints
                    If prc.StepName = CSTR(sSelectedStep) Then
                        stp.PrecedenceConstraints.Remove(prc.StepName)
                    End If
                NEXT

            END IF
```

continues

12

PROGRAMMING
WITH THE DTS
OBJECT MODEL

LISTING 12.14   continued

```
                set prc = Nothing
        END IF

        'Enable the following END IF when selecting
        '    specific types of custom tasks
        'END IF

    NEXT
END IF

IF sErrMsg <> "" THEN
    msg = sErrMsg
    ttl = "Setting Precedence Canceled"
    MSGBOX msg, vbOK, ttl
END IF

Main = DTSTaskExecResult_Success

End Function
```

> **Note**
>
> When this tool is used, the visual display of the precedence constraints in the DTS Designer is not immediately updated. The display is updated when you close and reopen the package or when you open the Workflow Properties dialog for any of the steps in the package.

The Remove Unwanted Connections Tool

When connection objects are deleted from the Package Designer, those connections are not actually removed from the package. Listing 12.15 shows the code for the Remove Unwanted Connections tool, which removes those unwanted connections. Because of the danger of deleting connections that are needed, the code in this tool is not active until the script is edited to set the bCodeEnabled variable to TRUE. Specific connections are chosen for removal or for saving by editing the SELECT CASE structure in the script.

LISTING 12.15   ActiveX Script That Removes Unwanted Connections

```
'Remove unwanted connections
Option Explicit

Function Main()
```

```
DIM pkg, stp, tsk, cus, con
DIM msg, ttl
Dim bCodeEnabled

SET pkg = DTSGlobalVariables.Parent

'IMPORTANT
'Removal Code is disabled or enabled with the following variable
bCodeEnabled =0  '0 for Disabled, 1 for Enabled

FOR EACH con IN pkg.connections

    SELECT CASE con.Name

        'List all the connections you want to save
        CASE "Northwind", "OLAPUnleashed"
            msgbox "Keeping - " & con.Name

        'Use this case for removing a few connections
        CASE "Whatever"
            msgbox "Removing - " & con.Name
            pkg.connections.Remove(con.Name)

         case else for removing most of the connections
        CASE ELSE

            IF bCodeEnabled = 0 THEN
                msg =   "Code is disabled. No connections will be "
                msg = msg & "removed." & vbCrLf & vbCrLf
                msg = msg & "To enable code, change the value of "
                msg = msg & "bCodeEnabled at the top of this "
                msg = msg & "function." & vbCrLf & vbCrLf
                msg = msg & "If the code had been enabled, the "
                msg = msg & "following connection would have been "
                msg = msg & "removed - " & vbCrLf & vbCrLf
                msg = msg & con.Name
                ttl = "Code is disabled."
                msgbox msg,, ttl
            ELSE
                msg = "Do you want to remove this connection? "
                msg = msg & vbCrLf & vbCrLf & con.Name
                ttl = "Removing Connection"
                IF msgbox(msg, vbYesNo, ttl) = vbYes THEN
                    pkg.connections.Remove(con.Name)
                END IF
            END IF
    END SELECT
NEXT

Main = DTSTaskExecResult_Success
End Function
```

Summary

You saw quite a bit of code in Chapter 11 and now again in this chapter. You'll see some more code in Chapter 13, "Using the Repository in Data Transformations."

CHAPTER 13

Using the Repository in Data Transformations

by Tim Peterson

IN THIS CHAPTER

The Microsoft Repository ships with both SQL Server 7.0 and Visual Studio. Its purpose is to provide a centralized location for an organization's metadata.

This chapter examines how the Repository is used with the Data Transformation Services to record metadata and make that metadata available to the people using an OLAP system.

Metadata in an OLAP System

Metadata is the description of data. Here are some of the reasons metadata is needed in an OLAP system:

- There can be many types of data sources, each of which defines data in a different way. Metadata provides a consistent way to describe data structures, no matter what the data source happens to be.

- It's important to be able to describe the changes that are made to data as it is being transformed, so that an organization's people can be confident that the data they are viewing in their OLAP browsing accurately represent the organization's data.

- People who are using an OLAP system need to have a clear explanation of the meaning of the different fields, measures, levels, and dimensions. One of the important parts of metadata is a user-friendly description of the data.

Analysts often talk about two types of metadata in an OLAP system—technical and business.

Technical metadata describes data in a way that is clear and unambiguous. It is the kind of information that a computer program needs to process data correctly, such as

- Names of fields, tables, and databases
- Names of levels, hierarchies, dimensions, cubes, and OLAP databases
- Data types
- Field lengths
- Field nullability
- Default values
- Indexes
- Primary keys and foreign keys
- Relationships
- Rules and check constraints
- Transformations and mappings

- Data cleansing procedures
- Security information
- History of data structure creation and modification
- History of data transformations
- Data lineage of individual records

Business metadata describes data to nontechnical users so that they can understand the information they are viewing. It includes

- Descriptions of fields, tables, and databases
- Descriptions of levels, hierarchies, dimensions, cubes, and OLAP databases
- Descriptions of transformations and mappings
- Descriptions of data cleansing procedures
- Reports
- References to the technical metadata

The Structure of the Microsoft Repository

The Microsoft Repository is organized around a set of objects called information models. An *information model* is a template for a particular kind of data. The information models have a hierarchical relationship, with the more specific models inheriting characteristics from their parent models.

The root model, from which all other information models are derived, is the Unified Modeling Language (UML) Model. There is an information model for COM and another one for data types. A generic model specifies the relationships between models. The information models that relate to databases, data transformations, and OLAP are shown in Figure 13.1.

Here's a description of each of the models that hold database information:

- The Database Information Model is the basic model used to store database information. It stores the metadata about the data sources and data destinations. This model is derived from the Unified Modeling Language Information Model.
- The SQL Server Information Model, the Oracle Information Model, and the DB2 Information Model are used to store information that is specific to each database system. These models are derived from the Database Information Model.

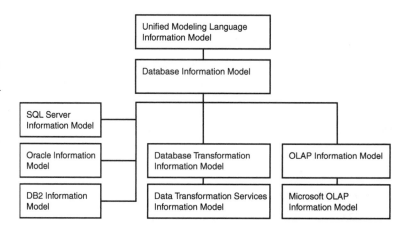

FIGURE **13.1**

The Microsoft Repository has many information models that hold database information. All information models are derived from the Unified Modeling Language model.

- The Database Transformation Information Model is the basic model used to store information about data transformations. This model is also derived from the Database Information Model.

- The Data Transformation Services Information Model stores data transformation information that is specific to Microsoft's Data Transformation Services. This model is derived from the Database Transformation Information Model. This model is derived from the Database Information Model.

- The OLAP Information Model is the basic model for multidimensional data structures. This model is also derived from the Database Transformation Information Model.

- The Microsoft OLAP Information Model stores multidimensional data information that is specific to Microsoft OLAP Services. This model is also derived from the OLAP Information Model.

The Repository is physically located in a set of tables in a database. The default location of the Repository, as it is shipped with SQL Server 7.0, is the msdb database.

DTS Packages and the Repository

There are three choices that determine the relationship between a DTS Package and the Repository:

- Storage—If the DTS Package is stored in a file or in SQL Server outside the Repository, there is no connection between the package and the Repository.

- Lineage—If you are storing the DTS Package in the Repository, you can use the lineage variables to identify which records were created with a particular execution of a particular version of a DTS Package.

• Scanning—If you are storing the DTS Package in the Repository, you can choose whether or not to scan the metadata of data sources and data destinations into the Repository.

The Storage Choice

You can choose to save a DTS Package to the Repository, to SQL Server outside the Repository, or to a file. If you don't save the package in the Repository, your package will have no connection to the Repository. Specifically, this means the following:

• You will not be able to query the Repository for information about the package.

• You will not be able to use lineage variables to record the history of your records.

• You will not be able to use the database scanning options to save data source and data destination metadata.

When you are using the DTS Package Designer or the DTS Wizard, you are given the storage location choice whenever you save a package for the first time. You make this choice again whenever you pick Save As from the Package menu in the DTS Package Designer.

When you save a package using code, you choose the storage form by using different methods of the package object. These methods are described in Chapter 9, "DTS Packages."

13

DATA
TRANSFORMATION
REPOSITORY

Saving an Extra Copy of a DTS Package in a Different Storage Format

Because of the importance of metadata in an OLAP system, I nearly always use the Repository as the storage for my DTS packages. I still, though, save copies of my packages in file format. I do this to archive my packages and also to transfer the packages to different computers.

I like using SQL Server storage for DTS packages. Opening and saving packages when using SQL Server storage is much quicker than when using the Repository. But if you have enabled the lineage variables in the package, you will not be able to save the package to SQL Server. That generates an error, while saving the package to a file does not.

There have been times (not lately, fortunately!) when database packages that I have saved to the Repository became corrupted. I had this problem particularly when I was learning that I needed to be very specific about data types when using global variables. I have experienced package corruption only when I saved a package to the Repository—never when using the other storage options.

continues

My first experience with package corruption came one holiday weekend, when the family went to the lake and I stayed home to create DTS packages so that I could meet a deadline. On Saturday evening, I experienced an Access Violation, which shut down the Enterprise Manager. When I started the Enterprise Manager again, I tried to open the DTS Package I was designing, but I received an error message. Not only was the current version corrupted, but also the previous three versions I had saved. I lost all the work I had done that day! I guess I should have gone to the lake.

After a few of these unfortunate experiences, I started the practice of saving extra copies of my DTS packages to file storage, so I have an archive of package versions that I can use in an emergency. I can't usually save my packages to SQL Server because I'm nearly always using the lineage variables. So I save a copy of each version of my packages in file storage.

By the way, I haven't had the package corruption problem lately. Either the product is more stable or I've learned to avoid the problem areas. But for now, at least, I'm going to continue keeping extra copies of my packages saved as files.

--tep

The Lineage Options

Lineage is the history of a particular record of data. Lineage includes both a description of the source of the record and a description of how that record has been transformed to reach its present state. You save the lineage of a record by adding fields that identify its lineage to that record.

There are two lineage variables used in DTS and the Repository. One of them records the version of the package that was used to create each record. The other variable identifies the particular execution of the package that created the record.

Here are the two lineage variables:

Variable	Data Type	Description
DTSLineage_Full	uniqueidentifier	Uniquely identifies the DTS Package version used for the transformation
DTSLineage_Short	integer (4-byte)	Uniquely identifies the date and time a DTS Package was executed

The lineage variables are enabled in the Package Designer with two check boxes on the Advanced tab of the DTS Package Properties dialog (shown in Figure 13.2):

- Show lineage variables as source columns. If you select this option, these two lineage variables will be included as if they were source columns for every transformation in your package. By default this option is not selected.

- Write lineage to repository. This option is available only if the other option has been selected.

  The DTSLineage_Full variable is always written to the repository. If this option is not selected, the DTSLineage_Short variable is not written to the repository. Therefore, no record of the package execution is saved. The lineage variables still both appear as source columns.

FIGURE 13.2

You can set lineage options for a package by selecting none, one, or both of the Lineage check boxes.

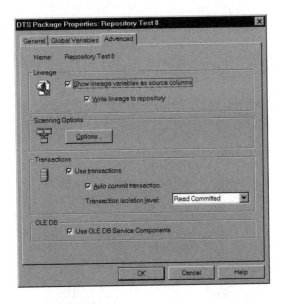

13

DATA
TRANSFORMATION
REPOSITORY

When you select the first check box, you will see the lineage variables appear as columns in the source table on the Transformations tab of the Data Transformation Properties dialog, as shown in Figure 13.3.

These lineage variables are not automatically entered into the destination records. You have to create columns to receive them and create the mappings to those columns, as with any other destination field. These mappings are shown in Figure 13.4. A space-efficient strategy for saving the lineage variables is discussed in the section "Creating a Lineage Dimension."

FIGURE 13.3

The lineage variables won't be saved unless they're mapped to destination fields.

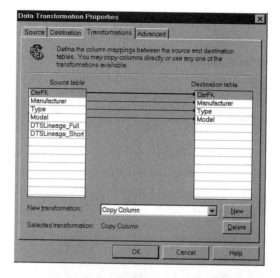

FIGURE 13.4

When the lineage variables are saved, the history of the record is preserved.

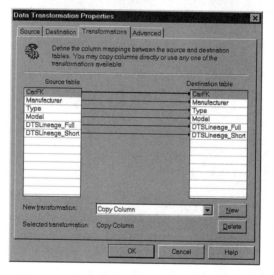

In the DTS Object Model, LineageOptions is a property of the Package object. This property must contain one of the values shown in Table 13.1.

TABLE 13.1 The DTSLineageOptions Constants

Constant	Value	Choose by Selecting
DTSLineage_None	0	Neither check box
DTSLineage_AddLineageVariables	1	First check box

Constant	Value	Choose by Selecting
DTSLineage_WriteToReposIfAvailable	2	Not available in interface
DTSLineage_WriteToReposRequired	3	Both check boxes

> **Note**
>
> The DTSLineage_WriteToReposIfAvailable is not described in detail in the product documentation. It appears to have the same behavior as DTSLineage_WriteToReposRequired.

The Scanning Options

The definition of a DTS Package is not complete without a full definition of the data sources and the data destinations. There is a potential for confusion because these sources and destinations can be a variety of relational database systems and non-relational data stores.

The Repository provides a format for systematically describing and cataloging metadata, no matter what databases or other data stores are being used. The scanning options determine how the package relates to the metadata definitions stored in the Repository and how often that metadata is refreshed.

Scanning is set on the Scanning Options dialog, shown in Figure 13.5. This dialog is called from the Options button on the Advanced tab of the DTS Package Properties dialog.

FIGURE 13.5

You can choose from among several possibilities for scanning tables into the Repository.

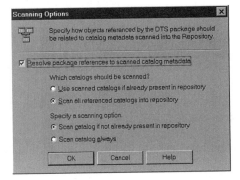

13

DATA TRANSFORMATION REPOSITORY

Here are the choices in the Scanning Options dialog:

- Resolve Package References to Scanned Catalog Metadata check box—If you do not select this check box, the other options are not available. The default is for this check box to not be selected.
- An option group with two choices for which catalogs should be scanned:

  Use Scanned Catalogs if Already Present in Repository. This is the default choice, if the scanning resolution check box has been selected.

  Scan All Referenced Catalogs into Repository.
- An option group of two choices for specifying a scanning option

  Scan Catalog If Not Already Present in Repository. This is the default choice, if the scanning resolution checkbox has been selected.

  Scan Catalog Always.

The DTS Object Model implements all the scanning options with a property of the Package object called `RepositoryMetadataOptions`. The values for this property are shown in Table 13.2. I have listed the five options in this table in an order that corresponds to the way these choices appear in the Scanning Options dialog. The second and third options in the list are made in the first option group. The fourth and fifth options are made in the second option group.

TABLE 13.2   The `DTSRepositoryMetadata` Constants

Constant	Value	Description
`DTSReposMetadata_`	0	Does no scanner resolution. This is the default choice.
`DTSReposMetadata_` `UseScannedCatalogIfPresent`	2	Will use any scanned objects found; nonscanned references will create local objects.
`DTSReposMetadata_` `RequireScannedCatalog`	1	Requires that any database objects must have been scanned into repository.
`DTSReposMetadata_` `ScanCatalogIfNotFound`	4	Package will issue a scan on all catalogs that are not found already scanned.
`DTSReposMetadata_` `ScanCatalogAlways`	8	The package will scan all catalogs referenced, rescanning if already scanned.

The DTS Package Designer interface requires you to do one of the following:

- Choose a value of 0 for the `RepositoryMetadataOptions` by leaving the checkbox unchecked, OR
- Choose two of the options for `RepositoryMetadataOptions`, with one choice from each of the two option groups.

If you leave the checkbox unchecked, the metadata for all the databases and data stores in your DTS Package will not be scanned into the repository. If you choose scanning, with any combination of the other options, the metadata for those databases and data stores will be written to the repository when the package is executed, if it's not already there.

The Repository Viewer

The SQL Server 7.0 Enterprise Manager provides a Repository Viewer for browsing the metadata that has been stored in the Repository. You can use the viewer to update some of the business metadata contained in the Repository, but none of the technical metadata. The viewer is found under Data Transformation Services in the console tree, in the Metadata node.

The Repository Viewer consists of three separate tools:

- A database metadata browser
- A Repository lineage lookup
- A DTS Package browser

The Database Metadata Browser

The database metadata browser (shown in Figure 13.6) provides a hierarchical view of all the databases that have been scanned into the database.

Databases can be scanned into the repository in two ways:

- Through the scanning options of the DTS Package.
- By highlighting the Metadata node in the Enterprise Manager console and selecting Import Metadata from the Action menu (or by right-clicking the Metadata node and choosing Import Metadata from the pop-up menu). This selection calls the Connection Properties dialog (shown in Figure 13.7), which is used to select a database to be scanned into the repository.

FIGURE 13.6

You can view both business and technical metadata with the database metadata browser.

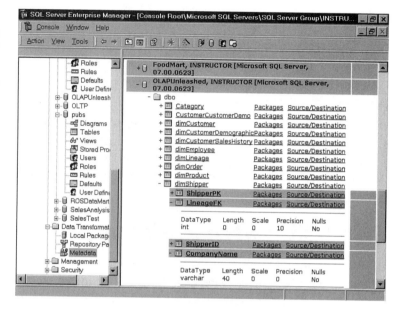

FIGURE 13.7

You can scan a database into the Repository if you have an OLE DB driver for that particular data source.

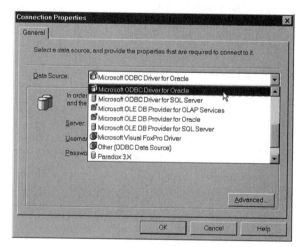

The database metadata browser provides a view of the following technical metadata:

- Name and version of the database system containing the database
- Names of fields, tables, and databases
- Data types
- Field lengths, precision, and scale

- Field nullability
- Information about the DTS packages that use each table and each field, including lineage information and the design of each package
- DTS Package Source and Destination fields for each field in the database. If a particular field is used as a source column in a DTS transformation, the browser displays information about the destination column. If a field is used as the destination column, the browser displays information about the source.
- Object owners

When you click on the table or field hyperlink in the browser, a separate page opens that displays business metadata, as shown in Figure 13.8. The browser provides read/write access to the following business metadata:

- Descriptions of fields, tables, and databases
- Comments about fields, tables, and databases

FIGURE 13.8

You can view and edit the descriptions and the comments that are stored in the repository.

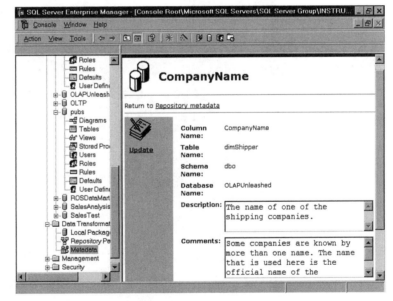

A Repository Lineage Lookup

The repository lineage lookup is a simple tool for finding the version of the DTS Package and the execution time for the transformation that created a particular record. The entry form for the lookup is shown in Figure 13.9. The results are displayed in Figure 13.10.

FIGURE **13.9**

You can retrieve the package information by entering the long and short lineage variables.

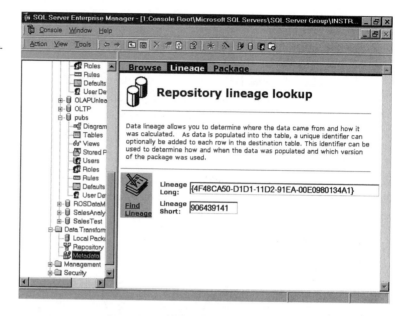

FIGURE **13.10**

This is the information you receive when you use the Repository lineage lookup tool.

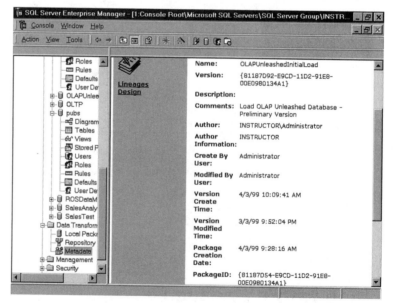

A DTS Package Browser

Information about DTS packages, package versions, and package executions is available in a hierarchical format in the DTS Package browsing tool, shown in Figure 13.11. For each package, version, and execution, you have the option of viewing the package design. When you pick that option, the DTS Package Designer opens with the selected version of the package displayed.

FIGURE **13.11**

The DTS Package browser allows you to view information about all the packages that have been saved to the Repository.

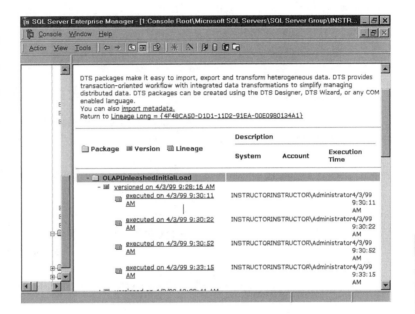

Accessing Repository Metadata with Code

You can download the Repository Software Development Kit (SDK) from Microsoft's Web site. This SDK includes code for several sample Visual Basic programs that access and use repository metadata, including:

- Importing an Access Database—Enters metadata from a Microsoft Access database into the Repository.
- Creating Databases from Repository using ADO—Creates a SQL Server database from Repository metadata.
- Simple Transformation—Populates the Data Transformation Information Model with transformations that create a simple data warehouse.
- Data Transformation Services—Retrieves transformation metadata from a DTS package stored in the Repository.
- On-Line Analytical Processing (OLAP)—Populates the OLAP Information Model.

- OLE DB Scanner Client—Retrieves data from a database using the OLE DB Scanner Client tool and stores that data in the Repository.
- Repository Type Information Model Navigation—Builds a tree structure to browse Repository type information models.

The SDK also includes a Repository Browser which provides a hierarchical view of the contents of a Repository database.

Creating a Lineage Dimension

You can use a lineage dimension for efficient storage of the lineage variables and other data describing the execution of a DTS package.

Saving Lineage Variables with Each Record

The alternative to creating a lineage dimension is to use the built-in DTS capability that adds the lineage variables to each record created by a transformation. This is a simple way to positively identify the record's history. If there is any question about the accuracy of the data in a record, the particular version of the DTS Package that created it can be examined. If there is a problem with a particular version of a package or even with a particular execution of a package, all the records affected can be identified by their lineage variables.

There is one drawback in using the lineage variables—they can significantly increase the size of a typical data mart. Take a look at the lineage variable math for a typical fact table:

1. The star schema has 8 dimensions, each of which has a 4-byte integer key in the fact table, for a total of 32 bytes of storage per fact table record.
2. The fact table has 6 measures. Two of them are 4-byte integers, two of them have the money data type, and two of them have a datetime data type, for a total of 40 bytes per fact table record.
3. The lineage variables are a 16-byte unique identifier and a 4-byte integer, for a total of 20 bytes per record.
4. Without the lineage variables each fact table record is 72 bytes. With the lineage variable each fact table record is 92 bytes, an increase of 28%.

Fields for a Lineage Dimension

Most large data marts would benefit by replacing the lineage variables with a lineage dimension. This dimension would have a 4-byte key in the fact table instead of the 20 bytes of space taken by the two lineage variables. A lineage dimension can also provide ready access to more detailed information about the transformations, including the individual tasks that created the records, the number of records processed by a task, and key values of the records that were processed.

A lineage transformation is implemented as the dimLineage table in the OLAPUnleashed sample database included with this book. The fields in this dimension table are shown in Table 13.3. One record is entered into this table for each Transform Data Task and each Data-Driven Query Task in a transformation.

TABLE 13.3 The Fields for a Sample Lineage Dimension

Field Name	Description
LineagePK	Primary key
Lineage_Full	Long lineage variable
Lineage_Short	Short lineage variable
PackageName	Name of the DTS Package
PackageDescription	Description of the package
StepName	Name of the step
StepIndex	Index number of the step
DataSource	Name of data source
DataDestination	Name of data destination
TableDestination	Name of destination table
TaskName	Name of the task
TaskDescription	Description of the task
InsertedCount	Number of records inserted
UpdatedCount	Number of records updated
StepStartTime	Time the step execution started
StepExecutionTime	Length of time for step execution

Processing for a Lineage Dimension

The processing strategy for a lineage dimension has the following steps:

1. At the beginning of the package, insert a record into dimLineage for each Transform Data Task and each Data-Driven Query Task.

2. Put the primary key values from dimLineage for each task in this package into global variables.

3. As each Transform Data task and Data-Driven Query task is executed, read the corresponding global variable for the dimLineage primary key and put that value in all the destination records.

4. As each task is processed, increment the global variables that are counting the number of records inserted or updated for that task.

5. At the end of the package, update all the records in dimLineage, with the information regarding numbers of records.

 Listing 13.1 shows the code for inserting the records into dimLineage for this package. This code is used in the first Transform Data task that is executed in the OLAPUnleashedInitialLoad package.

The code looks at each task, by examining each step index number. It checks to see if the task is a Transform Data Task or a Data-Driven Query Task. If it is, a record for that task is added into dimLineage.

The script returns DTSTransformStat_SkipFetch until the last task has been examined, so that it will be run again. The step index number is placed in a global variable, DTSGlobalVariables("StepIndex").Value, so the next time the script is run, it will start by examining the following step in the steps collection.

When the end of the collection is reached without finding any more tasks to add to dimLineage, then DTSTransformStat_SkipInsert is returned and the task is finished.

LISTING 13.1   Script for Inserting Records into dimLineage

```
'Load dimLineage

Option Explicit

Function Main()

Dim pkg, stp, tsk, cus
Dim idx
Dim bAddTask

SET pkg = DTSGlobalVariables.Parent

'Put the lineage variables into global variables
DTSGlobalVariables("Lineage_Full").Value = _
    CSTR(DTSSource("DTSLineage_Full"))
DTSGlobalVariables("Lineage_Short").Value = _
    CSTR(DTSSource("DTSLineage_Short"))

'Assign the values for the Destination fields that
'    are the same for all records in this package
```

```
DTSDestination("Lineage_Full") = DTSSource("DTSLineage_Full")
DTSDestination("Lineage_Short") = DTSSource("DTSLineage_Short")
DTSDestination("PackageName") = pkg.Name
DTSDestination("PackageDescription") = pkg.Description

If DTSGlobalVariables("StepIndex").Value = "" Then
    DTSGlobalVariables("StepIndex").Value = 0
END IF

idx = cstr(DTSGlobalVariables("StepIndex").Value )
DO UNTIL CLng( idx) = pkg.Steps.Count

    idx = idx + 1

    'Initialize bAddTask
    bAddTask = CBool(FALSE )

    Set stp = pkg.Steps(idx)
    Set tsk = pkg.Tasks(stp.TaskName)

    IF tsk.CustomTaskID = "DTSDataPumpTask" OR tsk.CustomTaskID = _
        "DataDrivenQueryTask" THEN
        'We found a task to add to dimLineage. Exit Loop and process.
        bAddTask = CBool(TRUE )
        EXIT DO
    END IF

LOOP

IF bAddTask = TRUE THEN

    'Increment the global variable that's counting the records
    IF ISNULL(DTSGlobalVariables("dimLineageInsertedCount").Value) THEN
        DTSGlobalVariables("dimLineageInsertedCount").Value = 1
    ELSE
        DTSGlobalVariables("dimLineageInsertedCount").Value = _
        CLng(DTSGlobalVariables("dimLineageInsertedCount").Value + 1)
    END IF


    Set cus = tsk.CustomTask
    DTSDestination("StepName") = stp.Name
    DTSDestination("StepIndex") = idx
    DTSDestination("DataSource") = "Northwind"
    DTSDestination("DataDestination") = "OLAPUnleashed"
    DTSDestination("TaskName") = cus.Name
    DTSDestination("TaskDescription") = cus.Description
    DTSDestination("TableDestination") = _
        fctTableOnly(cus.DestinationObjectName)
END IF
```

13

DATA
TRANSFORMATION
REPOSITORY

continues

LISTING 13.1 continued

```
IF  idx> pkg.Steps.Count OR  bAddTask = FALSE THEN
    'We're done - No more records to add

    'Re-initialize the global variable
    DTSGlobalVariables("StepIndex").Value = 0

    'And exit without inserting this last non-record
    Main = DTSTransformStat_SkipInsert
ELSE
    'We're going to add a record and see if there are more

    'Increment the step counter
    DTSGlobalVariables("StepIndex").Value = idx

    'Call the transformation again
    Main = DTSTransformStat_SkipFetch
END IF

End Function


Function fctTableOnly(sTableName)
'This function strips the database and object owner identifiers
'    off the table name
Dim lStart

lStart = InStr(2, sTableName, "[") + 1
lStart = InStr(lStart, sTableName, "[") + 1
sTableName = MID(sTableName, lStart)
sTableName = LEFT(sTableName, LEN(sTableName)-1)

fctTableOnly = sTableName

End Function
```

Listing 13.2 shows the code that retrieves the primary key values from the new records
and enters those values into a set of global variables. This script is in an ActiveX Script
task in the OLAPUnleashedInitialLoad package, with a description of "Find Lineage Key
Values."

The name of the destination table is used as the name for the global variable. This name
is itself assigned with a global variable:

```
DTSGlobalVariables("gv").Value = CSTR(rst.Fields("TableDestination"))
DTSGlobalVariables(DTSGlobalVariables("gv").Value).Value = _
    CLNG(rst.Fields("LineagePK"))
```

This convention makes it easy to remember how to refer to each of the global variables
in the individual tasks.

The example code also illustrates how to open and read an ADO recordset in a script.

LISTING 13.2 Code for "Find Lineage Key Values"

```
'Find Lineage Key Values

Option Explicit

Function Main()

Dim con, rst, sql
Dim sLineageFull, sLineageShort

Set con = CreateObject("ADODB.Connection")
Set rst = CreateObject("ADODB.Recordset")

con.Provider = "sqloledb"
con.Properties("Data Source").Value = "."
con.Properties("Initial Catalog").Value = "OLAPUnleashed"
con.Properties("Integrated Security").Value = "SSPI"
con.Open

sLineageFull = DTSGlobalVariables("Lineage_Full").Value
sLineageShort = DTSGlobalVariables("Lineage_Short").Value

sql = "SELECT * FROM dimLineage "
sql = sql & " WHERE Lineage_Full = '" & sLineageFull & "'"
sql = sql &  " AND Lineage_Short = " & sLineageShort
'msgbox sql
rst.Open sql, con

IF NOT rst.EOF THEN
    rst.MoveFirst
END IF

DO UNTIL rst.EOF

    DTSGlobalVariables("gv").Value = CSTR(rst.Fields("TableDestination"))
    DTSGlobalVariables(DTSGlobalVariables("gv").Value).Value = _
        CLNG(rst.Fields("LineagePK"))

    rst.MoveNext
LOOP

Main = DTSTaskExecResult_Success

End Function
```

It's easy for each task to take the value from the global variable and put it into the appropriate destination field:

```
'Find value for LineageFK in the Global Variable
DTSDestination("LineageFK") = DTSGlobalVariables("dimCustomer").Value
```

Each task also contains the code that counts the number of records that are being processed. The code checks to see if it's the first record, and if it is, initializes the global variable to 1. If it's not the first record, it increments the previous value by 1.

```
'Increment the global variable that's counting the records
IF ISNULL(DTSGlobalVariables("dimCustomerInsertedCount").Value) THEN
    DTSGlobalVariables("dimCustomerInsertedCount").Value = 1
ELSE
    DTSGlobalVariables("dimCustomerInsertedCount").Value = _
        CLng(DTSGlobalVariables("dimCustomerInsertedCount").Value + 1)
END IF
```

When all the Transform Data and Data-Driven Query tasks have finished, dimLineage needs to be updated with all the additional information that has been obtained as the tasks have been executed. The update is accomplished with three tasks:

- An ActiveX Script task, "Create Query for Lineage Report," which creates the source query for the following task.

- A Data Transformation task, "Create Lineage Report," which transforms each of the new records from dimLineage, adds all the additional information to them, and loads them into a table called tblImportReport.

- An Execute SQL task, which updates the records in dimLineage from the records that have just been created for tblImportReport.

The code that creates the source query is shown in Listing 13.3. The query selects all the records from dimLineage that have the lineage variables for this package. That query is then assigned as the SourceSQLStatement property of the next task.

LISTING 13.3   Code for the ActiveX Script Task "Create Query for Lineage Report"

```
'Create Query for Lineage Report

Option Explicit

Function Main()

Dim pkg, stp, tsk, cus
Dim sql
Dim sLineageFull, sLineageShort

Set pkg = DTSGlobalVariables.Parent
Set stp = pkg.Steps("DTSStep_DTSDataPumpTask_4")
Set tsk = pkg.Tasks(stp.TaskName)
Set cus = tsk.CustomTask
```

```
sLineageFull = RemoveNull(DTSGlobalVariables("Lineage_Full"), "1")
sLineageShort = RemoveNull(DTSGlobalVariables("Lineage_Short"), "1")

sql = "SELECT * FROM dimLineage WHERE   "
sql = sql & "Lineage_Full = '" & sLineageFull & "' AND "
sql = sql & "Lineage_Short = " & sLineageShort & " "
sql = sql & "ORDER BY LineagePK"
cus.SourceSQLStatement = sql

Main = DTSTaskExecResult_Success
End Function


Function RemoveNull (str, rtn)

IF ISNULL(str) THEN
    RemoveNull = rtn
ELSE
    RemoveNull = str
END IF

End Function
```

Listing 13.4 contains the code that is used by the Transform Data task that fills the tblImportReport table. Many of the values for this table are taken directly from the source query. Other values are filled in from the appropriate global variables and by reading the properties of the steps.

LISTING 13.4   Code for the Transform Data Task That Creates the Lineage Report

```
'Create Lineage Report

Option Explicit

Function Main()

Dim pkg, stp
Dim lStepIndex

Set pkg = DTSGlobalVariables.Parent
DTSGlobalVariables("StepIndex").Value  = CLng(DTSSource("StepIndex"))
Set stp = pkg.Steps(DTSGlobalVariables("StepIndex").Value)

'Assign values that are going to be the same
DTSDestination("LineagePK") = DTSSource("LineagePK")
DTSDestination("Lineage_Full") = DTSSource("Lineage_Full")
DTSDestination("Lineage_Short") = DTSSource("Lineage_Short")
```

continues

LISTING 13.4   continued

```
DTSDestination("PackageName") = DTSSource("PackageName")
DTSDestination("PackageDescription") = DTSSource("PackageDescription")
DTSDestination("StepName") = DTSSource("StepName")
DTSDestination("StepIndex") = DTSSource("StepIndex")
DTSDestination("DataSource") = DTSSource("DataSource")
DTSDestination("DataDestination") = DTSSource("DataDestination")
DTSDestination("TaskName") = DTSSource("TaskName")
DTSDestination("TaskDescription") = DTSSource("TaskDescription")
DTSDestination("TableDestination") = DTSSource("TableDestination")

'Fill in values that have been stored in global variables

'First create the global variable names, storing them in global variables
DTSGlobalVariables("InsCnt").Value = _
    DTSSource("TableDestination") & "InsertedCount"


DTSGlobalVariables("UpdCnt").Value = _
    DTSSource("TableDestination") & "UpdatedCount"


'Then retrieve the values from the global variables
DTSDestination("InsertedCount") = _
    DTSGlobalVariables(DTSGlobalVariables("InsCnt").Value).Value

DTSDestination("UpdatedCount") = _
    DTSGlobalVariables(DTSGlobalVariables("UpdCnt").Value).Value


'Fill in times
DTSDestination("StepStartTime") = stp.StartTime
DTSDestination("StepExecutionTime") = stp.ExecutionTime

Main = DTSTransformStat_OK

End Function
```

The last step of the process is to update dimLineage with the information that has now
been assembled in tblImportReport. The SQL statement that updates the information is

```
UPDATE dimLineage SET
    InsertedCount = r.InsertedCount,

    UpdatedCount = r.UpdatedCount,

    StepStartTime = r.StepStartTime,
    StepExecutionTime = r.StepExecutionTime
FROM dimLineage l INNER JOIN tblImportReport r
```

Summary

The Repository is a powerful tool for organizing all the diverse information that is a part of an OLAP system. Database administrators need to have access to all the detailed information about the various databases and transformations. Programs that use the data need to be able to access that same metadata programmatically. There needs to be a way to store all the information needed by business analysts, so that they can understand the information they are viewing.

The Repository provides a place for all the technical and business metadata. Metadata can be loaded automatically and it can be accessed programmatically.

Chapter 14, "Third-Party Data Transformation and Repository Tools," presents a third-party tool that helps users programmatically access the Repository. Chapter 34, "Metadata," discusses the use of metadata in managing a data warehousing system.

CHAPTER 14

Third-Party Data Transformation and Repository Tools

by Tim Peterson

IN THIS CHAPTER

There are more than 100 data transformation tools on the market today, with costs ranging from less than $100 to more $100,000. Many of these tools integrate data transformation with data mart or OLAP cube design. This chapter looks at some of these data transformation tools, and a tool that simplifies access to Microsoft's Repository. The greatest emphasis is placed on two products that you can use to extend the capabilities of the SQL Server 7.0 tools—AppsMart from AppsCo and DWGuide from DWSoft.

The Microsoft Data Warehousing Framework and the Microsoft Data Warehousing Alliance

Microsoft has created an environment for data warehousing called the Microsoft Data Warehousing Framework, which includes the following functions:

- Providing access to data from a variety of sources
- Building data warehouses and data marts
- Transforming data and populating data warehouses and data marts
- Creating cubes and storing cube data in a relational or multidimensional format.
- Providing access to OLAP cubes for client applications
- Providing natural language access to data
- Providing tools to manage the data warehouse
- Storing and providing access to metadata

Microsoft provides tools to do all of these things. The following tools are included with the purchase of SQL Server 7.0:

- OLE DB for access to data from a variety of sources
- The Enterprise Manager for building data warehouses and data marts
- DTS for transforming data and populating data warehouses and data marts
- OLAP Services for creating cubes and storing cube data in a relational or multidimensional format
- The PivotTable Services for client access to cube data
- English Query for natural language access to data
- The SQL Server 7.0 database management tools provided with the SQL Server Agent, including scheduling, alerting, and operator notification
- The Repository for storing metadata

Note

There is one important Microsoft OLAP tool that is not included with SQL Server 7.0. Excel 2000, sold separately or as a part of Office 2000, is a client OLAP tool that implements a good deal of the functionality of the PivotTable Services. See Chapter 23, "Implementing Microsoft Excel as an OLAP Client."

The Microsoft Data Warehousing Framework is shown in Figure 14.1.

FIGURE 14.1

The Microsoft Data Warehousing Framework provides a comprehensive set of tools for data warehousing.

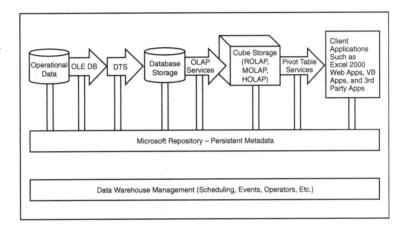

The Microsoft Data Warehousing Alliance is a group of companies that have joined with Microsoft in supporting this framework for data warehousing. These companies provide tools that work together with the Microsoft data warehousing tools. Chapter 21, "Other OLE DB for OLAP Servers," and Chapter 26, "Third-Party OLAP Clients," discuss some of these tools. This chapter discusses tools from Microsoft Data Warehousing Alliance partners that can be used for data transformation and for accessing Repository metadata.

AppsCo's AppsMart—Automating the Creation of Data Marts

AppsCo Software Limited has developed a tool named AppsMart that automates the process of creating data marts. This tool is closely integrated with DTS and OLAP Services in SQL Server 7.0. AppsMart can help you create an OLAP system more quickly and also provides you with the opportunity to create reusable OLAP system templates.

What is referred to as an OLAP system in this book is called a data mart application in the AppsMart documentation. Creating a data mart application involves the following tasks:

- Designing the logical model of the cubes
- Building the star schema in SQL Server for the data mart
- Creating the DTS Package to populate that star schema
- Creating the cubes from the tables in that star schema
- Connecting client applications to those cubes

AppsMart automates all of these tasks. The AppsMart application consists of three modules:

- Scratchpad—Rapid modeling of data marts
- Studio—Managing and tuning data marts
- Template Designer—Creating data mart models for repeated use

Business Templates and the Design Process

You start the process of creating a new data mart application with the Scratchpad module. Within the Scratchpad you have the choice of starting truly from scratch or using the Application Wizard.

When you use the Application Wizard, you choose a predefined template, which provides a model for your data mart. This is the most efficient way to begin the design of a new data mart. You have the capability of creating your own templates with the Template Designer. AppsMart comes with several predefined templates:

- Credit Card Transaction Analysis
- Direct Finance Sales
- Insurance Profitability Analysis
- Purchasing
- Supply Value Chain Analysis

A template consists of a set of business processes. A business process is a subject area of concern to the business, such as Inventory, Manufacturing, or Bill of Materials. When you use a template, you first decide what processes you want to include in your design, as shown in Figure 14.2. Each business process will be created as a separate OLAP cube.

Dimensions and measures are defined in the template for each business process. The dimensions have levels, and a particular level has been chosen as the default lowest level of granularity. You can change this level of granularity as you use the template to design your data mart application (see Figure 14.3). You also can choose which of the template's dimensions and measures to include in your application.

FIGURE 14.2

An AppsMart business template enables you to select processes to include in your data mart.

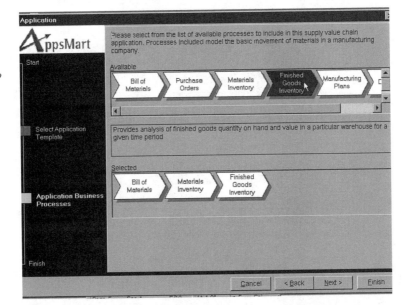

FIGURE 14.3

A business template provides dimensions and measures for you to choose from when you're creating a data mart application.

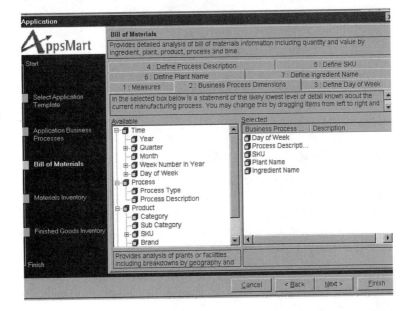

When the wizard is finished, you continue designing the data mart application in the Scratchpad window (shown in Figure 14.4). This is where you start a new application if you're not basing it on a template. You can create new measures, new dimensions, and new cubes with this tool. You can modify or delete any of the structures you have already created.

FIGURE 14.4

The Scratchpad gives you full control of adding or removing data structures in your data mart application.

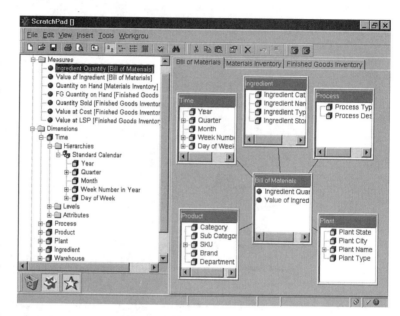

The Scratchpad provides functionality similar to the Cube Editor in the OLAP Manager (described in Chapter 15, "Creating Cubes"). The most significant difference is that the Cube Editor can only be used to create cube structures, but the structures you create with the Scratchpad are used to create the whole data mart application, as described in the following section.

Automatic Generation of Data Structures

When you have finished modifying the data mart application with the Scratchpad, you check the application into the AppsMart Repository. This Repository is a database used to store information generated by the AppsMart application. After checking in the application, you can open it in the Studio module, choose the appropriate version, and deploy the data mart application.

The Deployment Wizard allows you to choose which tools you want to use in the deployment of the application. You can integrate your deployment with the following SQL Server 7.0 tools:

- DTS—A set of DTS packages will be created that will load the data mart. AppsMart sets a few of the needed DTS properties automatically, but you need to check the packages after they are created to see if they will meet your requirements. Most importantly, you have to manually add the appropriate connections to the source data after the packages are generated.
- OLAP Services—Cube structures are generated for the data mart.
- Repository DBM Interface—The data mart metadata is stored in the Repository.

You also have a number of choices regarding the generation of database objects for the data mart.

- Create dimension tables.
- Create fact tables.
- Create sample data.
- Create dimension indexes.
- Create fact indexes.
- Create dimension constraints.
- Create fact constraints.
- Create interfaces.

AppsCo Software's Web address is www.appsco.com.

Updating with Version Control

AppsMart includes a system of version control for the data mart applications. When you want to modify the application, you check it out of the AppsMart Repository, make the changes, and check it back in as a different version. When you generate a new version of your application, the changes are made to every component.

Creating New Templates

New templates are created with the Template Designer. This module, shown in Figure 14.5, is almost identical in appearance and function to the Scratchpad. The process of making a new template is just like the process of making an application. As with a new application, you have the option of basing your template on a previously created template. The only difference between the Template Designer and the Scratchpad is the end result. When you use the Scratchpad, you are creating a new application. When you use the Template Designer, the end result is a template, which itself can be used to create new data mart applications.

FIGURE 14.5

The Template Designer can help you make original templates or templates based on previously created ones.

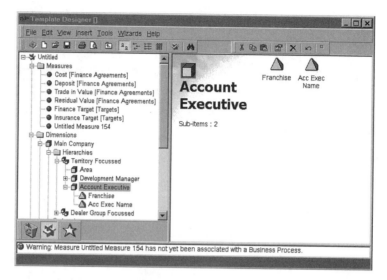

The Value of AppsMart

There are two factors that make AppsMart a valuable tool—the automatic generation of the data mart application and the use of predefined business templates.

SQL Server 7.0 comes with excellent tools that are easy to use. Even so, there's too much repetitive work in setting up a star schema database and then designing the OLAP cubes that are based on a star schema. AppsMart takes these two processes and combines them into one. The total time to set up the schema is cut in half.

Model data marts have been available for several years, but it takes some effort to build an OLAP system in SQL Server 7.0 from a generic model. The ability to create data mart application templates in AppsMart for particular business situations leverages the talents of experienced data mart designers.

In my opinion, AppsMart provides a very convenient interface for setting up data marts and does an excellent job of translating the choices made into database structures and cube structures. The DTS packages that are automatically generated do not appear to me to be as helpful. They require significant additional work after they are created. The generated packages use the relatively inefficient Data-Driven Query Task too often. Still, productivity is gained by the automatic generation of DTS packages from the schema. I expect this aspect of the AppsMart process to improve with time.

AppsMart's literature talks about the need to "de-skill" the process of data mart application development. I think it has been successful in extending SQL Server 7.0's tools so that the whole process is easier to learn. By using the business templates, a less-experienced developer can learn and be assisted by the efforts of more-experienced developers. And even experienced developers will find that AppsMart can significantly shorten development time. This tool does a great job of lessening the unnecessary repetition in the data mart design process.

--tep

DWSoft's DWGuide—Providing Access to Repository Metadata

DWGuide from DWSoft is a tool that provides a user-friendly way to access the Microsoft Repository. SQL Server 7.0 has the built-in Repository browser, but that browser is not a tool designed for the end-users of an OLAP system. The Repository SDK gives you the tools you need to design your own application to provide access to Repository metadata. DWGuide does this work for you. It provides access to metadata stored in the repository in a way that allows you to customize metadata access for your end-users.

There are seven modules in the DWGuide tool:

- Navigator—This is the primary tool in DWGuide. The Navigator provides a simplified view of the metadata in the Repository. This view can be customized for different kinds of users.

- Administrator—This tool allows the Navigator to be used to its full potential. The Administrator is used to set up the metadata relationships that are viewed in the Navigator. You can hide some of the complexity of the metadata that is actually stored in the Repository. You can create virtual relationships between objects— relationships that are not actually in the Repository. These virtual relationships can be used to provide extra non-Repository information to the users. Different types of users can be given views of the metadata tailored to their needs, their level of interest, and their understanding of data structures.

- Browser—The Browser is a replacement for the metadata browser that is included in the Enterprise Manager. It includes additional functionality, especially in being able to make more modifications to the data in the Repository. This tool is intended to be used by administrators.

- DWManager—This tool is used to document the data transformation process. It can be used both to document the transformations in custom programs and to add additional information to the data transformation metadata created by DTS.

- Reporter—The Reporter provides documentation about the information in the Repository.

- Metadata Miner—You can use the Metadata Miner to examine the information in the Repository and find relationships between objects.

- Import—DWGuide provides an Import module to bring data into the Repository from other systems. Currently supported systems include Business Objects, PowerDesigner, WarehouseArchitect, Informatica, and Cognos.

A demo of the DWGuide Navigator is available on DWSoft's Web site (www.dwsoft.com). Figure 14.6 shows the opening screen of the Navigator, where you can choose the type of user you want to be when browsing the metadata. The view of the metadata presented to a Business Apps User is very different from the view presented to the Repository Administrator.

FIGURE 14.6

The first screen of the DWGuide Navigator demo lets you choose which kind of user you want to be.

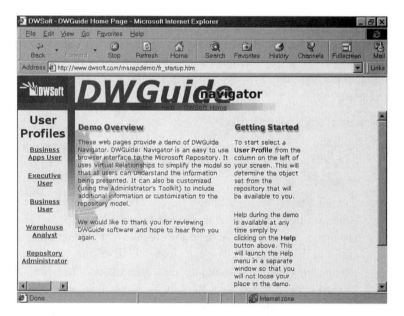

If you elect to use the Navigator as the Repository Administrator, you can view and edit a wide variety of information. As shown in Figure 14.7, you can use a filter to limit fields that are being displayed.

When looking at the information about an individual field in a table, you can view the DTS transformation script that was used to load the data into that field. The view of the script is shown in Figure 14.8. You cannot see this kind of detail about DTS packages in the Enterprise Manager's Metadata Browser without opening up the DTS package in the DTS Designer. The Navigator provides a much more direct connection between a field in a table and the transformation script that was used to generate the data for that field.

FIGURE 14.7

The Navigator can filter field names based on a variety of different criteria.

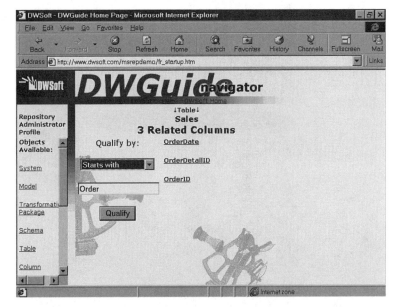

FIGURE 14.8

The Navigator enables you to see the DTS transformation script that was used for a particular field.

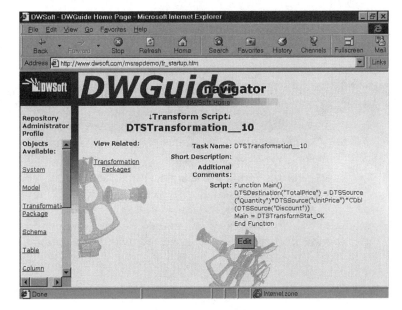

14

THIRD-PARTY AND
REPOSITORY
TOOLS

You can edit the transformation script from within the Navigator, as is shown in Figure 14.9. You can also modify the descriptions of the script. The descriptions of objects and the comments about those objects give the opportunity to provide business users with intelligible descriptions of database objects and transformations.

FIGURE 14.9

You can edit transformation scripts and descriptions of those scripts in the Navigator.

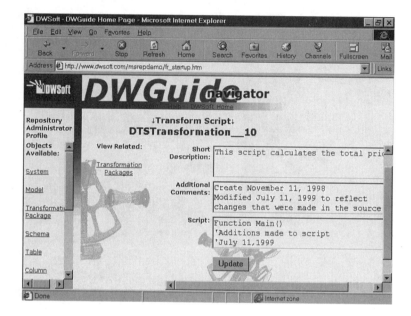

You can also browse for information about a DTS Package. You can look at the description of all the package's tasks and modify many of the properties of the tasks, including the source query, as shown in Figure 14.10.

What DWGuide Adds to Your OLAP System

Metadata is the place that many data warehouses, data marts, and OLAP systems fall short. Metadata is often incomplete. It can be hard to understand. It is sometimes not available at all.

The metadata browsing tools that are available in the SQL Server 7.0 Enterprise Manager can be useful to you as a database administrator, but they do not give you a convenient way to present metadata to the end-user. DWGuide gives the administrator more convenient metadata tools. More importantly, DWGuide gives you the ability to provide the end-user with a customizable view of the metadata.

The DWGuide tools can add significant value to your OLAP system. This is a tool that can help you provide quality business metadata to your end-users.

--tep

FIGURE 14.10

You can choose to edit the source query for a Transform Data task.

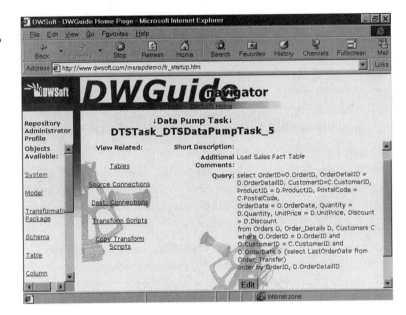

Data Junction's Universal Transformation Suite—Powerful Data Transformation at a Reasonable Price

Data Junction has created some of the most widely used data transformation tools. These tools have a relatively low cost and provide a great deal of functionality. They can also be embedded into other software products.

The newest versions of Data Junction's tools have been combined into a package called the Universal Transformation Suite. This package consists of the following:

- Data Junction 7.0—The newest version of Data Junction's primary data transformation tool.

- Cambrio—A tool used to extract nonstructured data from text files and other sources.

- DJEngine—A programmable, executable data transformation engine that can be embedded in other applications. The DJEngine takes data transformations that have been created with Data Junction or Cambrio and executes them from within an application.

- Custom Database Interface SDK—A Software Development Kit that gives programmers the tools to extend Data Junction's tools to access other data sources.

- Streaming Data SDK—Provides programmers with the ability to configure the DJEngine to read real-time data feeds.

- Data Junction Extraction Language (DJXL)—This language is used to extract data in situations where Cambrio's user interface is inadequate.

Data Junction uses a hub and spoke architecture, where the transformation engine is at the hub or the junction of all the different data formats. Access to a wide variety of data sources is provided, including those that can be accessed through an ODBC driver or an OLE DB provider, flat files, ASCII files, standard database applications, spreadsheet formats, and standard accounting applications.

The basic Data Junction tool for creating data transformations is the Conversion Designer. The Conversion Designer has three tabs—Source (Step 1), Target (Step 2), and Map (Step 3). A convenient interface is provided for mapping transformations, as shown in Figure 14.11.

FIGURE 14.11

You map transformations on the Map (Step 3) tab of the Data Junction Conversion Designer.

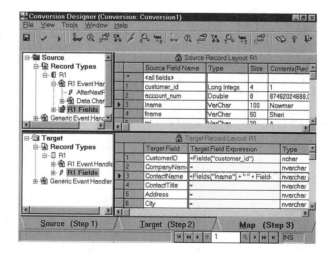

You can call the Target Keys, Indexes, and Options dialog from a toolbar button in the Conversion Designer. The Update/Delete tab of this dialog gives you the opportunity to update or delete records in the target data, as shown in Figure 14.12. This provides you with similar functionality to what you have with the DTS Data-Driven Query task.

FIGURE 14.12

You can update or delete target records with Data Junction.

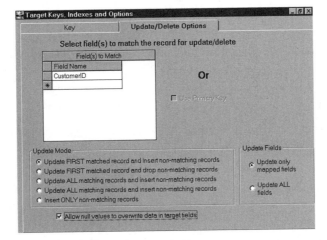

Version 7.0 includes a new tool called the Visual Project Designer that is similar to the DTS Designer. The Visual Project Designer has steps that control the progress of a data transformation. This tool is shown in Figure 14.13. I tested the Beta 3 release of Data Junction Version 7.0.

FIGURE 14.13

Use Data Junction's Visual Project Designer to create a data transformation Project.

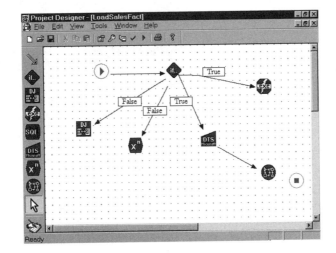

14

THIRD-PARTY AND
REPOSITORY
TOOLS

You can use the following different kinds of steps in the Visual Project Designer:

- Start—The beginning point of a Project, where global variables can be created and set.
- Data Junction Conversion Designer—Executes a data conversion. This step is similar to the Transform Data task in DTS.
- Decision—Allows for conditional branching within the Project.
- Expression—Executes Visual Basic code. This step is similar to the DTS ActiveX Script task.
- Application—Starts an external process. This step is similar to the DTS Execute Process task.
- SQL Statement—Executes a SQL statement. This step is similar to the DTS Execute SQL task.
- Sub-Project—Executes another Project from within this Project.
- DTS—Executes a DTS package.
- Stop—The last step in a Project, where any final actions can be taken.the

Choosing Data Junction

Data Junction provides an excellent set of data transformation tools for a fairly low price. The Visual Project Designer is similar to the DTS Designer, but adds additional functionality with the sub-project step, the special step for executing a DTS package, and the steps for starting and ending a project. On the down side, the Visual Project Designer user interface does not seem as polished as the DTS user interface.

Data Junction's data interface for mapping transformations (Figure 14.11) has an advantage over DTS in that more information can be viewed at the same time. The DTS Data Transformation Properties dialog uses three tabs to present similar information.

Data Junction also includes specialized functions such as address formatting and Year 2000 conversion, which are not included with DTS.

Cambrio provides a visual interface to set up access to diverse data. This capability goes significantly beyond what is provided by DTS.

DTS and Data Junction are similar tools. Data Junction has an edge over DTS with some of its functionality. DTS has the advantage of being integrated into SQL Server 7.0. If you feel DTS does not meet your data transformation needs, Data Junction provides an attractive alternative. These two tools also work well together. You can easily include your DTS Packages in your Data Junction

> Projects. You can execute your DJEngine applications with the Execute Process task in your DTS Packages.
>
> *--tep*

Data Junction's web address is www.datajunction.com.

Informatica's Tools—Data Transformation with all the Features

Informatica has produced a set of data transformation tools that provides benefits in rapid development, high-speed data transformations, and the use of standard interfaces. These tools provide the same functionality as Microsoft's DTS, but include many more features. The data mart templates in Informatica provide similar functionality to the templates in AppsMart. Informatica's tools include

- PowerCenter—An enterprise data integration hub. It is a tool for organizations that are managing data transformations from a number of sources and are supporting a complex data warehouse environment.

- PowerMart—A suite of tools for building and managing data marts. PowerMart can be used apart from PowerCenter in smaller organizations or for separate departments. It can also be used together with PowerCenter to manage full enterprise data warehouses and their data marts.

- Business Components—Application templates that are used for building and populating data marts. Source Business Components are templates that provide a model for data extraction. Analytic Business Components are models that assist in designing decision-support applications.

- PowerConnect—A family of products that can access data and metadata from specialized applications. There are currently three PowerConnect products—for SAP R/3, PeopleSoft, and IBM DB2.

- PowerPlugs—Third-party software programs that work with Informatica's tools by using the same APIs.

Informatica has emphasized its use of an open metadata standard in its products. The standard it has developed with a number of other companies is called the Metadata Exchange Architecture (MX) initiative. This standard is currently in its second iteration, which includes a definition of multidimensional structures for OLAP applications. The updated version of this standard is called MX2.

Choosing the Informatica Tools

Informatica provides a level of sophistication in data transformation tools that is far beyond DTS or Data Junction. This sophistication comes with a price—organizations pay a lot of money for Informatica's tools. As with any tool, there is also a significant expense in training users.

Informatica's tools have well-developed user interfaces. In some cases, there are different options for beginning and advanced users. The user interface for data cleansing is very well developed, especially when compared to cleansing data with ActiveX scripts in DTS.

Informatica's commitment to standard interfaces, its participation in Microsoft's Data Warehousing Alliance, and its support of the Microsoft Repository standard are all positive factors. You should be able to use Informatica's tools together with Microsoft's current and future products, as well as with the products from the other companies that support these common standards.

You would certainly want to consider the Informatica tools or other specialized tools if you needed to access data in the SAP R/3 or PeopleSoft systems. A lot of work has gone into providing an interface to these systems and most organizations would benefit from having somebody else do this preliminary work.

The main issue, though, in considering the possibility of using Informatica, is price. Data cleansing and data transformation are often the most expensive and time-consuming part of a data warehousing project. You can do a lot with DTS. But if you need the highest performance and the quickest development, and you are planning to spend a lot of money on data transformation, you should consider additional tools to enhance DTS or specialized tools like Informatica's that replace DTS.

--tep

Informatica's Web address is www.informatica.com.

Tools from Other Companies

Here's a quick view of some other companies that provide data transformation or repository tools:

- Computer Associates acquired Platinum Technologies at the time this book was being written. Platinum collaborated with Microsoft in the development of the

Repository. The data warehousing tools of the companies are being combined into a comprehensive suite called DecisionBase TND.

The Web address for Computer Associates is `www.cai.com`.

- Information Builders provides SmartMart, an integrated suite of data mart tools. The data transformation tool in this suite is called Copy Manager.

  The Web address for Information Builders in `www.ibi.com`.

- Sagent Technology has bundled its data mart server, Sagent Solution Version 4.0, with SQL Server 7.0. Sagent markets a full line of data transformation and data mart tools, with a primary focus of providing Web access to data.

  The Web address for Sagent Technology is `www.sagent.com`.

- Evolutionary Technologies International's data transformation tool is called ETI*Extract. This tool automates the process of creating separate executable programs that import, transform, and cleanse data. Because these executable programs can be run on separate processors, ETI*Extract is a highly scalable data transformation solution.

  I like the way that ETI*Extract creates an English description of each data transformation as the transformation is being designed, as shown in Figure 14.14. This description automatically becomes part of the business metadata, whereas in DTS, the business description of each transformation must be created manually.

  The Web address for Evolutionary Technologies International is `www.eti.com`.

FIGURE 14.14

*ETI*Extract creates an English description of the transformation and the data transformation code at the same time.*

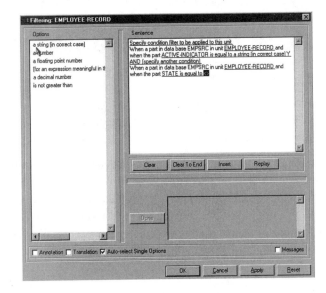

14

THIRD-PARTY AND
REPOSITORY
TOOLS

Choosing Among All the Possible Data Transformation Tools

What factors should you consider when reviewing all these data transformation tools?

- Access to the data sources where you need to extract data.
- Access to a wide variety of other data sources, so that you have the flexibility to add new transformations in the future.
- Ability to efficiently set up data cleansing.
- Use of a standard repository and the ready availability of both business and technical metadata.
- Use of standard interfaces and embedded programming languages.
- Performance and scalability.
- Ease of use.
- Price.

It's important to consider the capabilities of the version of the software that is currently available as well as the plans the company has for extending the software's capabilities in the future. With the rapid consolidation in the industry, it's necessary to consider the long-term prospects of the company that is producing the software. You want to avoid purchasing a data transformation tool from a company that is going out of business next year.

--tep

The Future of Data Transformation Tools

The release of DTS as a component of SQL Server 7.0 has changed the market for data transformation tools. There already was a lot of competition in the field. Microsoft has added to the competitive pressure with the release of DTS as a part of SQL Server.

DTS will be changing with future releases. Other companies will be modifying their offerings to compete with DTS. I expect that there will be a growing number of add-on tools that extend the functionality of DTS. Some of these add-on tools will take the form of additional custom tasks. Others, like AppsMart and DWGuide, will provide more integration of the data transformation process with the rest of the data mart development process.

The data transformation tool vendors will likely continue the growing emphasis on standardization. Metadata, the Repository, and the specification of data transformations will all be standardized so that transformation tools can be used more interchangeably.

Summary

You have a lot of choices in the market place for purchasing data transformation tools. AppsMart and DWGuide have been specifically designed to work with the SQL Server 7.0 tools. They extend rather than replace the functionality of SQL Server. The other data transformation tools described in this chapter can be used with SQL Server 7.0 but, for the most part, they replace the functionality that is available with DTS.

Creating OLAP Cubes

PART
III

Creating Cubes

by Tim Peterson

This chapter shows you how to get started with SQL Server 7.0''s OLAP Manager, the built-in user interface for OLAP Services. You will learn how to install OLAP Services, register OLAP servers, create OLAP databases, and work with OLAP cubes. Most of the power of OLAP Services is available through the OLAP Manager.

This chapter starts the four parts of this book that present Microsoft's OLAP Services:

- Part III, "Creating OLAP Cubes," introduces the OLAP Manager, with chapters on creating cubes, processing cubes, and partitioning cubes.

- Part IV, "Programming the OLAP Server," presents the opportunities to program the OLAP Server, with chapters on the Decision Support Objects, creating Add-In Programs, and programming the PivotTable Service. Part 4 concludes with a chapter on OLE DB for OLAP Servers from other vendors.

- Part V, "Programming the OLAP Client," looks at programming the OLAP Client. This part begins with a chapter on using ADO MD to set up the OLAP data source. Then there are chapters that present four different types of OLAP clients—Excel clients, Web clients, Visual Basic clients, and clients available from other vendors.

- Part VI, "Querying with Multidimensional Expressions (MDX)," presents the MDX language, the Multidimensional Expressions that can be used to query an OLAP cube. There are chapters on building an MDX query, advanced MDX, and on using SQL queries on the OLAP Server. Part 6 concludes with an MDX reference chapter.

This chapter has a series of term sidebars that define the multidimensional terminology used by the OLAP Manager.

Term: OLAP Manager

The OLAP Manager is the graphical user interface shipped with SQL Server 7.0 for creating, editing, processing, and viewing OLAP cubes.

Note

There are many concepts, objects, and structures in the OLAP world that have some correspondence to objects in the relational database world. Here's a chart that shows some of the connections between the two versions of reality. Some of the concepts are more synonymous than others. Multidimensional reality is different, so not everything lines up quite right. But, I think this approximate mapping is helpful.

Relational World	Multidimensional World
SQL Server	OLAP Server
Enterprise Manager	OLAP Manager
Registering a Server	Registering an OLAP Server
Database	OLAP Database
Table	Cube
Rows and Columns	Dimensions
Fields	Measures
Views	Virtual Cubes
File groups	Partitions
Roles	Roles
Indexes	Aggregations
Rebuild Indexes	Process Aggregations
Index Tuning Wizard	Usage-Based Optimization Wizard
SQL	MDX
Query Analyzer	MDX Sample Application
Recordset	Cubeset
Filtering records	Slicing a cube

Installing OLAP Services

The requirements for installation of OLAP Services include:

- An Intel-compatible processor equivalent to at least a Pentium 133Mhz or a processor compatible with a DEC Alpha AXP.
- 32MB minimum RAM, with a recommended level of 64MB.
- 35-85MB of hard disk space for the files.
- Microsoft Windows 2000, Microsoft Windows NT Server with Service Pack 4, or Microsoft Workstation 4.0, with Service Pack 4. The Service Pack is included with the SQL Server 7.0 installation disk.
- TCP/IP must be installed, although the computer does not have to be hooked up to a network.
- Microsoft Internet Explorer 4.01 or later with Service Pack 1. This software is also included with the SQL Server 7.0 installation disk.

15

CREATING CUBES

The client, but not the server components, can be installed on Microsoft Windows 95 with DCOM95 or on Windows 98. Additionally, OLAP Services installation requires the user to log on to the server as a user with Administrator privileges.

> **Note**
>
> I have run OLAP Services on a computer with 64MB of RAM, but the calculation of aggregations was very slow, even when processing a small database. OLAP Services is more effective with faster processors, more RAM, and more disk storage so that more aggregations can be created and stored.

OLAP Services is part of the SQL Server 7.0 software package. It has a separate installation program that you can run from the SQL Server 7.0 installation CD-ROM. When you start installing SQL Server 7.0, you are given the choice to install SQL Server 7.0, OLAP Services, and English Query, which are all run as separate installation programs. Figure 15.1 shows the screen in which you make these choices.

FIGURE 15.1
You can choose to install these services from the SQL Server 7.0 installation program.

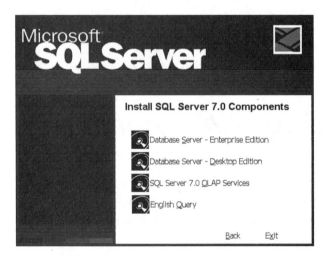

The OLAP Server and client components are required parts of the OLAP Services installation. The OLAP Manager and sample applications are optional parts.

The installation program creates a new item called OLAP Services in the SQL Server 7.0 program group on the Start menu. This item has four shortcuts:

- The MDX Sample Application—A program that looks like the Query Analyzer (isql/w in SQL Server 6.5) that can be used to test MDX queries. The MDX Sample Application is shown in Figure 15.2.

- The OLAP Manager.

- Product Documentation—The subset of SQL Server Books-On-Line that deals with OLAP Services.

- A Readme file.

FIGURE 15.2

The MDX Sample Application provides an interface for testing MDX queries.

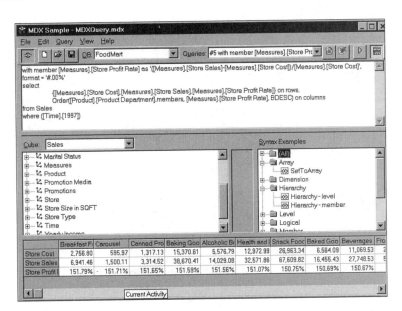

The files installed with OLAP Services are placed in an OLAP Services subdirectory under Program Files, not in the SQL Server installation tree.

The sample database that is installed with OLAP Services is called FoodMart. This database is organized as a star schema. FoodMart has fact tables for inventory and sales and has dimension tables for customer, product, promotion, store, warehouse, days, time_by_day, region, and warehouse_class.

FoodMart is a Microsoft Access 97 database and contains about 23MB of data. Its default path is C:/Program Files/OLAP Services/Samples/FoodMart.mdb.

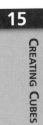

15

CREATING CUBES

OLAP Services runs as a Windows NT service called MSSQLServerOLAPService. It can be set to start automatically when the system is started.

Troubleshooting Installation

There are three things I've seen people have trouble with in the OLAP Services installation:

1. They haven't met the requirement for Microsoft Internet Explorer 4.01 with Service Pack 1. The installation will appear to complete successfully, but the OLAP Manager (and the Enterprise Manager) will not work properly.

2. They haven't met the requirement for TCP/IP being installed. The OLAP Services will not start and the only message that shows up in the error log is "Internal Windows NT Error." You must have TCP/IP installed for the OLAP Services to start.

3. The OLAP Services are installed successfully, but the MSSQLServerOLAPService has not been started. Just go to Service in the Control Panel, start OLAP Services, and, if you want it to always be started when the system is rebooted, change the Startup choice to Automatic.

The OLAP Manager Interface

The OLAP Manager Interface is integrated into the Microsoft Management Console (MMC). The MMC provides a uniform interface for all of Microsoft's new BackOffice products. The interface for each particular product that uses the MMC is called a *snap-in*.

Term: Microsoft Management Console

The Microsoft Management Console (MMC) is a common framework that holds the snap-ins for individual server applications like the OLAP Manager.

The Microsoft Management Console with the OLAP Manager snap-in is shown in Figure 15.3. The console's left panel has the tree view, which provides access to the various levels of the OLAP Manager hierarchy. The right panel in the MMC usually provides more information about the item that's selected in the tree. That is not the case with the OLAP Manager snap-in—the right panel only provides convenient access to Help resources. I expect the OLAP Manager will receive a more interactive interface in the future.

FIGURE 15.3

In the right pane of the Microsoft Management Console, the OLAP Manager snap-in gives quick Help access.

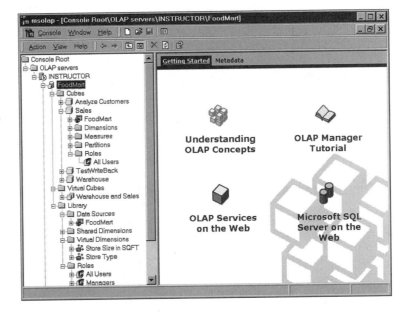

The higher levels of the OLAP Manager hierarchy include:

- Console Root—The starting point
- OLAP Servers
- Individual OLAP Servers that have been registered
- Individual OLAP databases that have been created
- Cubes, Virtual Cubes, and the library—The three components of an OLAP database

The names of the individual cubes that have been created are shown under the Cubes node. Under the name of each cube, the following items are displayed:

- The name(s) of the connection(s) used by the cube
- Dimensions
- Measures
- Partitions
- Roles

The names of the individual virtual cubes that have been defined are shown under the Virtual Cubes node. Each virtual cube has three of the parts that appear for regular cubes:

- Measures
- Dimensions
- Roles

Finally, the library has the following elements:

- Data Sources
- Shared Dimensions
- Virtual Dimensions
- Roles

The Action menu for the Enterprise Manager changes dynamically, depending on which element in the OLAP Manager tree is highlighted.

Registering OLAP Servers

You register OLAP Servers so that you can administer them from the OLAP Manager. The registration of an OLAP Server is similar to registering a SQL Server in the Enterprise Manager.

Term: OLAP Server Registration

An OLAP Server is registered so that the OLAP Manager can administer it.

You can register an OLAP server by right-clicking the OLAP Servers node in the console tree. The Register OLAP Server dialog gives you a box to type in the name of the Server. If the OLAP Manager cannot find the OLAP Server you have named, it tells you and then asks if you want to register the OLAP Server anyway.

Note

If the OLAP Server exists but is not running, you will also be told that you cannot connect and asked if you want to register the Server anyway. Unlike the Enterprise Manager with SQL Server, you cannot stop and start the OLAP Server from the OLAP Manager. You must go to the Services dialog in the Control Panel.

OLAP Databases

An OLAP database is a structure that is used to store a set of related cubes. You should consider putting cubes in the same OLAP database if they have some common data sources, dimensions, virtual dimensions, and roles.

Term: OLAP Database

An OLAP Database is a structure that is used to store a set of related cubes.

There are three main types of structures within an OLAP database:

- Cubes
- Virtual Cubes
- The library

Cubes

Cubes are the fundamental unit for data storage and retrieval in an OLAP system. The cube is roughly equivalent to a table in a Relational Database System. Cubes are made up of measures and dimensions.

Term: Cubes

The fundamental unit for data storage and retrieval in an OLAP system is the cube.

The dimensions of a cube are the perspectives from which the data can be viewed and analyzed. It's easy to visualize the two dimensions of a relational system—rows and columns. But a Microsoft OLAP cube can have up to 64 dimensions. The MDX syntax uses the following syntax to refer to the first five dimensions:

- Columns
- Rows
- Pages
- Sections
- Chapters

Term: Dimensions

The dimensions of a cube are the perspectives from which the data can be viewed and analyzed.

The intersection points of a cube's dimensions are called cells. Consider, for example, a cube with five dimensions—time, product, customer, store, and promotion. You would define a cell in this cube by specifying one specific point along each of the dimensions:

- The 68th column in the time dimension
- The 1056th row in the product dimension
- The 10768th page in the customer dimension
- The 15th section in the store dimension
- The 115th chapter in the promotion dimension

You can store and retrieve multiple values in each cell. Each value stored in a cell is called a measure. If a cube has three measures, then each cell would store a value for those three measures.

All the data in a cube can be represented by a star schema. The measures are stored in the measure fields in the fact table. The location of the cell in the cube structure is stored in the key values of the fact table. Each record of a fact table fully defines a cell and the values of the measures within it. In the previous example the fact table record would look like this:

Field Name	Value
TimeFK	68
ProductFK	1056
CustomerFK	10768
StoreFK	15
PromotionFK	115
SaleCount	3
CostAmount	9.57
SaleAmount	11.13

> **Term: Cells and Measures**
>
> A cell is defined by the intersection of all the dimensions of a cube. Measures are the values that are stored in each cell.

Later sections in this chapter discuss creating and editing cubes, dimensions, and measures.

Virtual Cubes

You can browse two or more cubes at the same time in a combined structure called a virtual cube. You can also use a virtual cube to present a subset of the data available in a single cube. A virtual cube is very similar to a view in SQL Server. A virtual cube is defined by selecting the measures, dimensions, and roles from the cubes that are being included in the virtual cube.

> **Term: Virtual Cube**
>
> A virtual cube is a cube that is derived from one or more other cubes.

> **Note**
>
> You should consider what virtual cubes you are planning to define when you decide how to divide your cubes into OLAP databases. You can only join cubes into virtual cubes that are stored in the same OLAP database.

The "Virtual Cubes" section toward the end of this chapter explains how to create and edit virtual cubes.

The Library

In an OLAP database, some of objects are created for one specific cube. Other objects can be used by all the cubes in the database. Each OLAP database has a library which holds components that can be used in one or more of the cubes. Each of the four parts in the library—data sources, shared dimensions, virtual dimensions, and roles—is discussed later in this chapter.

15

CREATING CUBES

> **Term: Library**
>
> The library is the section of the OLAP database that holds components that can be used in all of the database's cubes.

Data Sources

You designate the source for the data in your cubes by setting up one or more data sources.

A new data source can be specified when you build a cube with the Cube Wizard (discussed in "Creating OLAP Cubes with the Cube Wizard" later in this chapter). Data sources can also be set up in the OLAP database library. Either way, the new data source is automatically added to the library and can be used by other cubes in the future.

> **Term: Data Source**
>
> A data source specifies the source of data for an OLAP cube.

You set up a new data source using the Data Link Properties dialog, shown in Figure 15.4. You access this dialog either by right-clicking the Data Sources Library or by selecting the New Data Source button in the Cube Wizard.

FIGURE 15.4

The Data Link Properties dialog is used to specify a new data source.

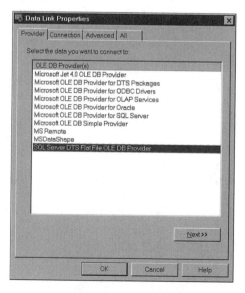

The choices that are on the Connection, Advanced, and All tabs vary depending on which provider is chosen on the first tab. If you want to use an ODBC data source in your cubes, you have to first define that source with the ODBC Administrator. Then you can choose the Microsoft OLE DB for ODBC Driver and specify the ODBC data source you have created.

Shared Dimensions

There are two types of dimensions in an OLAP database, shared and private. Shared dimensions are defined as objects in the library, while private dimensions are defined as objects within a cube.

Shared dimensions and private dimensions are the same, except that private dimensions are only used in the cube in which they are defined, while shared dimensions can be used in any cube in the OLAP database.

> **Term: Shared Dimensions**
>
> A shared dimension is a dimension that is stored in the library and can be used in any cube in the OLAP database.

It's good to use shared dimensions for several reasons:

- Shared dimensions save time in development because a dimension can be created once and used many times.
- Cubes with common shared dimensions can be joined together for viewing in a virtual cube.
- You simplify the overall structure of your OLAP schema when you use shared dimensions. Having fewer dimensions reduces the effort needed for loading data, keeping metadata current, and making modifications to the schema.
- Fewer dimensions can make it easier for users to understand the cubes that they are browsing.

The only place you can create or edit a shared dimension is in the library. There are two tools to work with shared dimensions:

- The Dimension Wizard can only be used to create a new shared dimension.
- The Dimension Editor can be used to create a new shared dimension or edit an existing shared dimension.

> **Note**
>
> The same two tools are used when creating and editing private dimensions within a cube. The tools function in exactly the same way, except that you are working with private dimensions instead of shared dimensions.

Using the Dimension Wizard

Access the Dimension Wizard by right clicking on the Shared Dimensions folder, selecting New Dimension and Wizard. The first screen (shown in Figure 15.5) gives a little instruction about the significance of dimensions and offers a choice between creating a dimension from one or many tables.

FIGURE 15.5

Choose between using one table or multiple tables for a new dimension on the first screen of the Dimension Wizard.

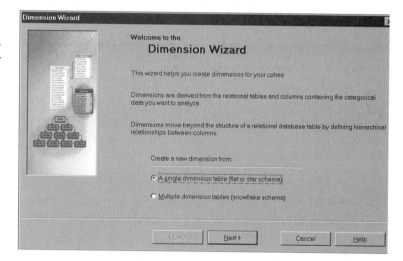

Choosing the Table(s) for the Dimension

If you chose to use many tables, the next two screens enable you to choose the tables and define the appropriate joins in those tables. Figure 15.6 shows the screen for selecting tables. You can have more than one data source for a cube, but when you are creating a dimension, all the tables have to be from the same data source. You can call the Data Link Properties dialog to create a new data source by clicking the New Data Source button. You can also browse the data in your selected tables.

FIGURE 15.6

Select the multiple tables you want on this screen of the Dimension Wizard.

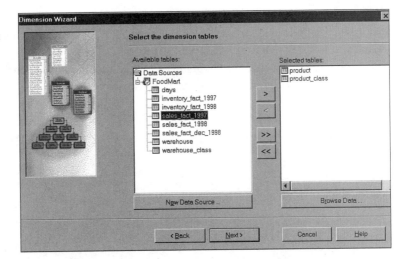

The next screen, shown in Figure 15.7, provides the opportunity to create and edit the joins between the tables you have chosen.

FIGURE 15.7

The Dimension Wizard provides the opportunity to create and edit joins.

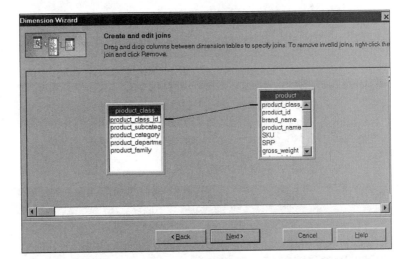

Note

This is the screen that is missing in the DTS Import Wizard! Maybe it can find its way there in the near future.

If you chose to use only one table on the first screen, the next screen enables you to pick that table. The following screen, shown in Figure 15.8, gives you the choice of creating a standard dimension or a time dimension. If you pick a time dimension, you are asked to select the column that contains the field that will be used for this dimension. This column must be selected from the columns in the chosen table that have a datetime data type.

FIGURE 15.8

You can choose the type of dimension for your single-dimension table.

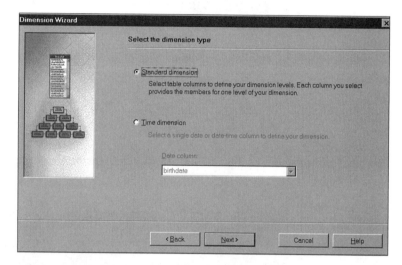

Term: Standard Dimensions and Time Dimensions

A time dimension is a specialized dimension used to represent standard time periods. All other dimensions are referred to as standard dimensions.

Note

You're not given the choice of using a time dimension when you elect to use multiple tables because a time dimension is always based on just one field, so you never would need to include more than one table.

If you are creating a standard dimension, the remaining screens of the wizard are the same whether you are using one table or multiple tables for that dimension. The wizard continues with a screen for choosing the levels of the standard dimension.

Choosing the Levels of a Standard Dimension

A dimension usually has a hierarchy with several levels that are used to drill-up or drill-down through the data. Here are some examples of levels in a hierarchy of a dimension:

- A product dimension could have Product Family, Product Category, Product Subcategory, and Product Name.
- A time dimension could have Year, Quarter, Month, Week, and Day.
- A store hierarchy could have Country, State, City, and Store.
- An employee hierarchy could have Department, Manager, and Employee Name.

The broader categories, like Product Family or Year, are referred to as the higher levels of the hierarchy. In these examples, Product Name and Day would be the lowest levels of their hierarchies.

> **Note**
>
> Using MDX code, you can create more than one hierarchy for a single dimension. One dimension can have many hierarchies but in the OLAP Manager you can only create one hierarchy for a dimension. If you have a dimension table in your underlying schema that contains more than one hierarchy, you have to create two separate dimensions in the OLAP Manager to use those two hierarchies.
>
> Because there's a one-to-one relationship between dimensions and hierarchies in the OLAP Manager, the User Interface normally doesn't refer to the hierarchies at all. The wizard refers to the "levels for your dimension" rather than what would more accurately be the "levels for the hierarchy of your dimension."

Members are the individual values that make up a particular level:

- March, April, and May are three of the members of the Month level of the time dimension's hierarchy.
- Alabama and Hawaii are two of the members of the State level of the store hierarchy.

> **Term: Levels and Their Members**
>
> Dimensions usually have levels that are organized into a hierarchy. The values at each level are referred to as the members of that level.

Figure 15.9 shows the screen where you select the levels of the hierarchy for your dimension. Available columns can be selected by moving them to the Dimension levels listbox. The four top buttons are used for including or excluding fields. The levels are displayed with dots beside them. Fewer dots signify a higher level, while more dots signify a lower level. It works best if you select the higher levels of the hierarchy first. If you change your mind, though, you can move a level up or down with the two lowest buttons that are between the list boxes.

FIGURE 15.9

This is the tab in the Dimension Wizard where you select the levels of a standard dimension

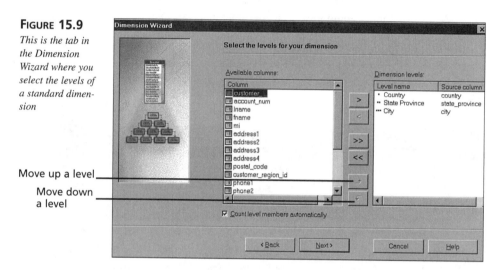

If you check the Count Level Members Automatically check box below the Available Columns list, the OLAP Manager will count and compare the number of members in each level as you add them to the list of selected levels or as you move levels up or down in that list. Normally, there are more and more members as you move down a hierarchy. If you put your levels in such an order that a lower level has fewer members than a higher level, a message box will appear informing you of the potential problem. You have the option to heed the warning or ignore it. If you uncheck the check box, you won't be bothered with the message. You will also be able to create your levels more quickly, because the counting and comparing can take some time.

Choosing the Levels of a Time Dimension

If you chose to create a time dimension, the wizard continues with a specialized screen (shown in Figure 15.10) to create the levels for that dimension. You start by selecting from a list of possible time levels to include in your dimension. You are also given the opportunity to select a specific month and date for the start of the year in your time dimension.

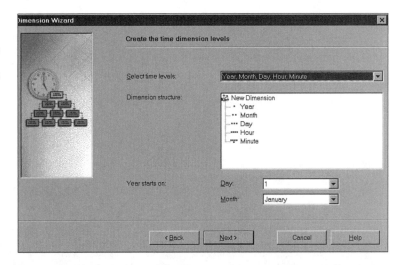

Note

The specialized time dimension included with OLAP Services provides a convenient shortcut for setting up a time dimension. This specialized time dimension has its limitations and is not nearly as flexible as a standard dimension. If you have some special needs for a time dimension that don't fit the specialized time dimension mold, you can always create your time dimension as a standard dimension.

Finishing the Dimension

The final screen of the Dimension Wizard (shown in Figure 15.11) gives you a preview of the levels in your dimension. All the members at each level are displayed. The names of the levels are not shown. You must name your dimension in the box provided on this screen or you cannot click the Finish button.

Using the Dimension Editor

You have more control when creating a dimension with the Dimension Editor than with the Dimension Wizard. You can also use the Dimension Editor to change the properties of a dimension you have already created.

15

CREATING CUBES

FIGURE 15.11

*View your new
dimension and
name it on the last
screen of the
Dimension
Wizard.*

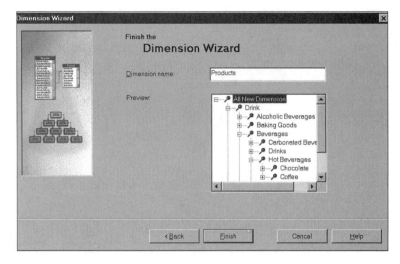

The Dimension Editor is shown in Figure 15.12.

FIGURE 15.12

*The Dimension
Editor provides an
interface for cre-
ating or modifying
dimensions.*

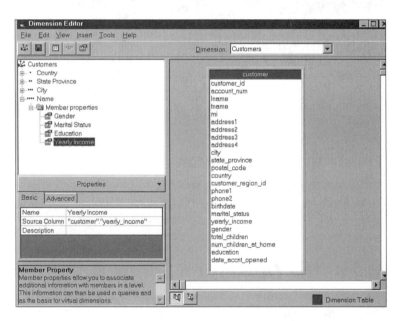

The Dimension Editor Interface

The Dimension Editor interface has three main sections:

- A tree in the upper-left pane displays the various elements in the dimension.

- A Properties box shows Basic and Advanced properties for the item that's selected in the tree. The Properties box can be minimized by clicking the box's heading. The heading still appears at the bottom of the window after it is minimized, so you can click the heading to restore the box. The Properties box can also be shown and hidden by selecting it on the View menu.

- The right side of the window can be switched between a display of the underlying table schema (as shown above in Figure 15.12) and a display of the data (see Figure 15.13). These two displays can be switched back and forth by selecting the one you want on the View menu or by using the two buttons on the lower left corner of this pane.

15.13

The Dimension Editor can display data, too.

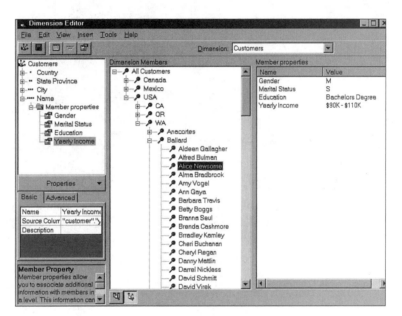

Adding and Editing Tables and Relationships

When the table schema view is selected, tables can be added and removed from the schema pane. A toolbar button calls the Select table dialog, shown in Figure 15.14. This dialog can also be reached by right-clicking in the schema pane. Relationships between tables can also be added and removed.

The Insert Table button

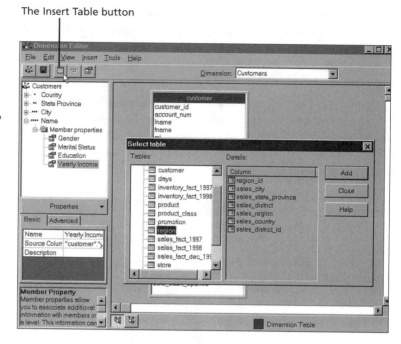

FIGURE 15.14

A toolbar button opens the Select Table dialog, which is used to add a new table to the dimension's schema.

Adding and Moving Levels of the Dimension

To the right of the Select Table toolbar button is a button to call the Select Column dialog for adding a new level. You can create a new level by dragging a field from one of the tables in the schema pane and dropping it onto one of the existing levels. The new level is created directly above the level it is dropped on.

You can raise or lower levels in the hierarchy by selecting them and dragging them to a new position.

Creating Member Properties

The Dimension Editor (but not the Dimension Wizard) enables you to create member properties. Member properties are defined as additional attributes of a particular level of a dimension. The most common level for a member property is the lowest level of the dimension, but the property can be created at any level.

Some potential member properties include:

- The number of square feet declared as a member property at the Store level of the Store dimension.

- Age declared as a member property at the Customer Name level of the Customer dimension.
- The number of days in the month declared as a member property of the Month level of the Time dimension.
- Color declared as a member property at the Product Name level of the Product dimension.

Term: Member Properties

A member property associates additional information with the members in one of the levels of the dimension.

Member properties provide a way for you to include more possibilities for OLAP browsing, without creating additional dimensions. You can use member properties for OLAP browsing in two ways:

- You can reference member properties directly in MDX queries.
- You can use member properties to create virtual dimensions, which you can then use in browsing as if they were regular dimensions. Virtual dimensions are described later in this chapter.

Member properties are created by right-clicking the Member Properties heading that appears under the name of each level in the dimension tree. You then pick the field that you want to use as the basis for the member property from the Select Columns dialog, as shown in Figure 15.15. The right-most button on the toolbar can also be used to call the Select Columns dialog and create a member property.

Note

One last thought about member properties—I think the name for this object is a poor choice because a property is such a clearly defined term in the object programming world. A member property is not a property—it's an object! I don't know if this is a stumbling block for anyone else, but I know I had trouble understanding this strange property when I was first learning Microsoft OLAP Services.

In the general OLAP/data warehousing literature, a member property is usually referred to as an attribute of a level of a dimension.

15

The Insert Member Property button

FIGURE 15.15

A member property can be created for any level of a dimension.

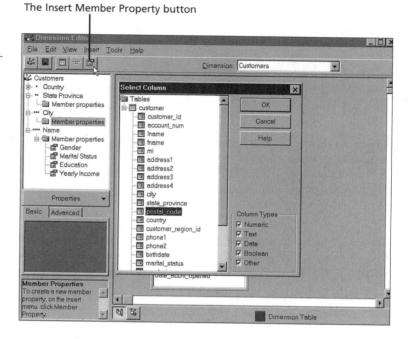

Properties of the Dimension's Objects

When you move from the Dimension Wizard to the Dimension Editor you gain not only the ability to create member properties but also the ability to modify the properties of all the dimension's objects. There are different properties for different types of objects.

The properties are listed in the Properties box on two tabs—Basic and Advanced. You can set the name and the description of the object on the Basic tab. You also set the source of data for that object, which is different for each type of object:

- For the dimension as a whole, it's the Data Source. This property cannot be edited.
- For a level of the dimension, it's the Member Key Column. This property contains a reference to the table and to the field that contains the key values for this level.
- For a member property, it's the Source Column, which also contains a reference to a table and field.

The following are the properties on the Advanced tab for the dimension object:

- All Level—Whether or not the dimension contains an (All) level, which is a top level aggregation for the whole dimension.

- All Caption—The name for the (All) level.
- The Type of dimension—The two choices are Standard and Time. These options were discussed in the "Using the Dimension Wizard" section earlier in this chapter.

The Advanced properties for a level of the dimension are

- Member Name Column—The table and column that contains the values for the names of the members of this level.
- Member Count—The estimated number of members for this level. By default, the OLAP Manager calculates a value for the Member Count. You can use the expand button on this line to recalculate the member count. You can also insert a value into this field.
- Unique Members—Whether or not the members at this level are unique.
- Level Type—If this is a standard dimension, the level type will be Standard. If this is a time dimension, the level type will indicate the particular type of Time that is represented by this level—Years, Half Years, Quarters, Months, Weeks, Days, Hours, Minutes, or Seconds.
- Key Data Size—The size of the key data field.
- Key Data Type—The data type of the key data field. The choices are VarWChar, Char, Small Integer, or Integer.
- Order By Key—If `true`, the members of the level are ordered by the key value. The default is `false`, which orders the members by the member name column.

There are no Advanced properties for the member properties.

The Tools in the Dimension Editor

The Dimension Editor has a Tools menu with three items:

- Process Dimension—Processes the dimension so that the members of the levels and their member properties can be viewed.
- Count Dimension Members—Before counting, you are given a choice as to whether you want to count the members for all the dimensions or only for those members that are currently showing a count of 0, which indicates a dimension that hasn't previously been counted.
- Validate Dimension Structure—Checks the structure of the dimension to see if there is anything in it that would prevent the dimension from being processed.

15

CREATING CUBES

Virtual Dimensions

The library also has a section for virtual dimensions.

If you have a field in a dimension table that you don't want to use as a level of the dimension hierarchy, but you want to use it for OLAP browsing, you have these three choices:

- Create an additional dimension for that one field. This new dimension would have one level in its hierarchy.
- Create a member property from that field and use that member property in the OLAP browsing.
- Create a member property and use that member property to create a virtual dimension.

A virtual dimension can be browsed just like a normal dimension. It appears the same to the user. The significant difference between a regular dimension and a virtual dimension is that the virtual dimension has no aggregates prepared for it when the cube is processed. You can create additional virtual dimensions without increasing the length of time or the amount of space taken for aggregations. But you also lose out on the performance advantage that you get from aggregation.

How do you choose? If you need the best OLAP performance, create a new regular dimension. If you want to conserve time and disk space, create a virtual dimension. If your client tools are set to use member properties directly for browsing, just create a member property and don't bother with the virtual dimension.

> **Term: Virtual Dimensions**
>
> A virtual dimension is created from a member property. It can be browsed like a regular dimension, but has no aggregations calculated for it.

To create new virtual dimensions, call the Virtual Dimension Wizard by right-clicking Virtual Dimensions in the tree and selecting New Virtual Dimension.

After an introductory screen, the wizard presents a screen for selecting the member property that is going to be used for creating the virtual dimension (see Figure 15.16). Only the member properties that already have been defined with the Shared Dimension Editor will appear in the list. This same screen is also presented when a virtual dimension is being edited.

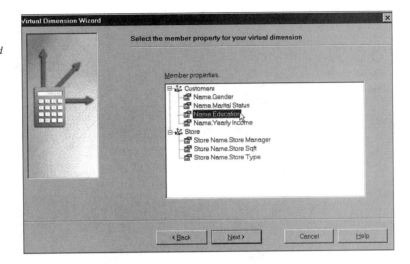

FIGURE 15.16

The Virtual Dimension Wizard enables you to select a member property to be used in a virtual dimension.

Roles

The fourth section in the library is for roles. Roles are used to define the security in the OLAP database. All the roles that have been defined for any of the cubes in the database are displayed in the library. You can use these roles in any of the other cubes in the OLAP database.

You can define new roles in the library, but those roles won't have access to any cube. You have to go to the section on Roles for a particular cube to give a role permission to access that cube.

When you choose to create or edit a role in the library, a dialog appears with the appropriate title. The Create a Database Role dialog is shown in Figure 15.17. You can choose to add either Windows NT users or groups to the particular OLAP database role you are creating.

Term: Roles

OLAP databases use a role-based security. Windows NT users and groups are assigned to roles, which are then given Read or Read/Write access to particular cubes.

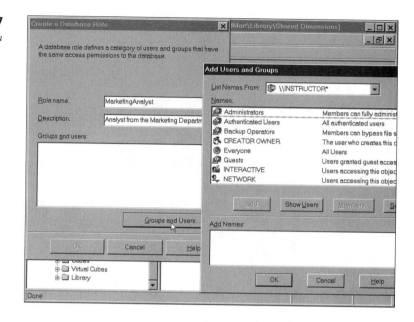

The OLAP database roles are discussed in Chapter 16, "Processing and Browsing
Cubes."

Creating OLAP Cubes with the Cube Wizard

New OLAP cubes can be created with either the Cube Wizard or the Cube Editor. I'll
show you how to use both methods. The Cube Wizard gives fewer choices, but provides
a very convenient, orderly process for creating a cube.

For a full discussion of fact tables, dimensions, and measures, please refer to Chapter 5,
"The Star Schema."

Choosing the Fact Table

After an introductory screen, the Cube Wizard lets you choose a fact table for the cube
(see Figure 15.18). All the tables from all the data sources in the OLAP database are presented as choices. You also have the opportunity to create a new data source, and you can
browse the data in any of the tables.

FIGURE 15.18

Begin creating a new cube by selecting the fact table.

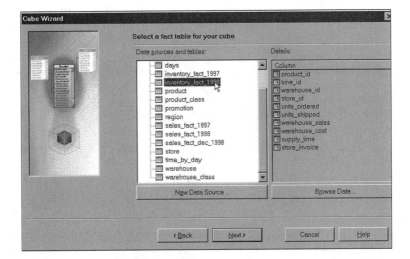

> **Tip**
>
> When you build a dimension you can join tables and select fields from any of the tables that have been joined. You don't have that opportunity when you're selecting a fact table. You can only use one table.
>
> If you need to include fields from more than one source table in your fact table, you have two choices:
>
> 1. Do some additional data transformation to create the single table in your data source.
>
> 2. Create a view in your data source and use that as the basis for the fact table in the cube.
>
> The second option would normally be a lot easier, but could also carry a very significant performance penalty. But if you have reasonably sized tables and a short development time, it's the easy way to create a source for your fact table.

Choosing the Measures

The next screen, shown in Figure 15.19, asks you to choose the measures. Only numeric fields can be selected. You must choose at least one measure before you can continue. The measure is automatically assigned a name, which you can change later with the Cube Editor.

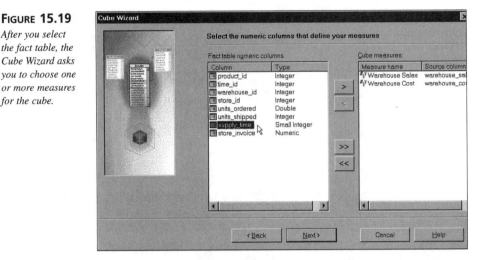

FIGURE 15.19

After you select the fact table, the Cube Wizard asks you to choose one or more measures for the cube.

Note

There are times when you might not have any measures in a fact table. This happens with a fact-less fact table, which was discussed in Chapter 5. In these situations, you can select any of the key values to serve as a measure. Later, with the Cube Editor, you will have to change the Aggregate Function property of the measure to COUNT.

Choosing Dimensions

Dimensions are chosen on the next screen, shown in Figure 15.20. You can include any of the dimensions and virtual dimensions that have been created in the database's library. You can also choose the New Dimension button, which opens the Dimension Wizard to create a new dimension for the cube. The Dimension Wizard is the same as when it is used to create a new shared dimension in the library, with just one difference: On the last screen of the Dimension Wizard you are asked if you want to share this dimension with other cubes. If you leave this box checked, you create a shared dimension. If you uncheck the box, you create a private dimension. If you create a private dimension, you will not be able to create member properties or create a virtual dimension from those member properties.

Different icons are used for shared dimensions, virtual dimensions, and private dimensions in the cube's tree. This makes it easier for you to keep track of the various kinds of dimensions you have included in your cubes.

FIGURE 15.20

*Add existing
shared dimensions
or create new
dimensions on this
screen of the Cube
Wizard.*

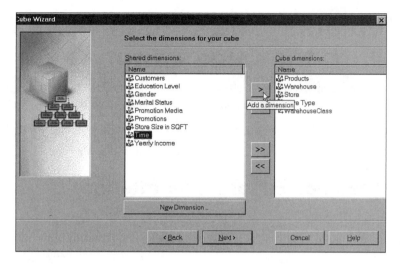

Finishing the Cube

The last screen of the Cube Wizard (see Figure 15.21) displays the cube structure and
enables you to name the cube. You also have the opportunity to browse sample cube data.
Sample data is data that is generated to illustrate what cube browsing would be like without taking the time to process the cube so that real data could be viewed. The sample
data does not reflect the actual data in the data source.

FIGURE 15.21

*Name the new
cube a name on
the last screen of
the Cube Wizard.*

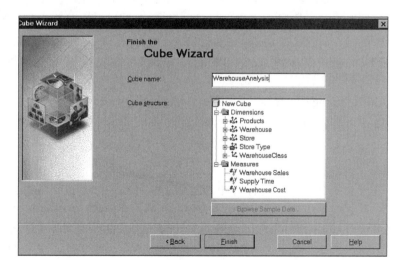

Creating and Editing OLAP Cubes with the Cube Editor

As you might expect, the Cube Editor gives you more flexibility than the Cube Wizard. Two of the most significant additional things you can do with the Cube Editor are:

- Create calculated members.
- View and edit the properties of the objects within the cube.

The Cube Editor's User Interface

The Cube Editor is very similar to the Dimension Editor.

- The tree in the upper left displays the various elements in the cube.
- The Properties box in the lower left shows Basic and Advanced properties for the item that's selected in the tree. The Properties box can be expanded or contracted using the View menu or by clicking the heading on the box.
- The right side of the window can be switched between a display of the underlying table schema (shown in Figure 15.22) and a view that displays sample data that can be browsed (shown in Figure 15.23). These views can be switched from the View menu or by using the two buttons in the lower left-hand corner of the pane.

When you create a cube with the cube editor, you must select a fact table before you do anything else. After that, you can create and edit cube objects in any order you choose.

When the schema is displayed, the dimension tables and the relationships between tables can be added or removed. The fact table cannot be removed, but it can be replaced with a different table.

The following buttons are available on the toolbar:

- New Cube
- Save Changes
- New Table
- New Dimension—Opens the Dimension Manager (as shown in Figure 15.12), which presents the same choices as the Cube Wizard screen for choosing dimensions.
- New Level for a Dimension—This button is only available when a private dimension is highlighted. Shared dimensions can be edited only when they are selected from within the library.
- New Measure
- New Calculated Member
- Manage Cube Roles

New Dimension   New Level

New Table

Save Changes

New Cube

New Measure

New Calculated Member

Manage Cube Roles

FIGURE 15.22

The right pane of the Cube Editor displays the cube's table schema.

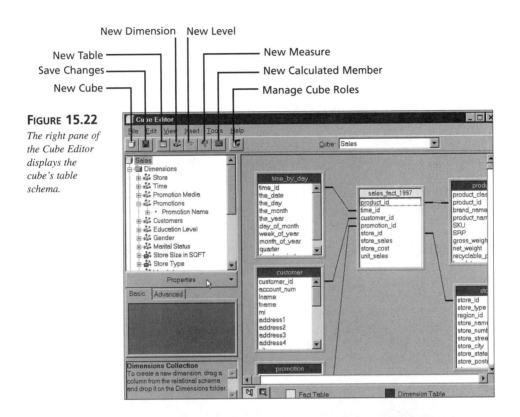

FIGURE 15.23

You can change the Cube Editor's right pane to view sample cube data for browsing.

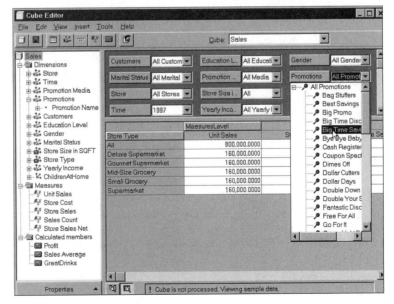

Calculated Members

Calculated members are dimensions or measures that are derived with a formula from other dimensions or measures. They are created with the Calculated Member Builder dialog, which can be called from the Cube Editor by selecting the New Calculated Member toolbar button or by right-clicking Calculated Members in the cube tree. The Calculated Member Builder is shown in Figure 15.24.

FIGURE 15.24

Calculated members can be created in the Calculated Member Builder dialog.

Term: Calculated Members

Calculated members are dimensions or measures that are derived with a formula from other dimensions or measures.

The Calculated Member Builder has a box for writing a Value expression, which is the formula that defines the calculated member. There are two tree structures at the bottom of the dialog which display all the available data and functions. Expressions can be built by highlighting the appropriate function or data member and clicking the Insert button.

> **Note**
>
> Calculated members are roughly equivalent to the With clause in an MDX query. Part VI of this book has a full discussion of MDX query syntax, which is what you use when you create a calculated member.

At the top of the Calculated Member Builder dialog you can enter values for three of the properties of the calculated member—the Parent Dimension, the Parent Member, and the Member Name for the calculated member. The modification of the other calculated member properties is discussed in the section later in this chapter, "Properties of the Cube's Objects."

- The Parent Dimension—There are two kings of calculated members—those that are included as new members in a dimension and those that are used as new measures in the cube. If you are creating the first type, you pick the dimension for your calculated member by specifying the Parent Dimension property. If you are creating a new measure, you have to choose Measures for the Parent Dimension property.

- The Parent Member—Every member of a dimension has a parent member. If, for example, you have a Location dimension, then "St. Paul" and "Minneapolis" would be members at the City level. If the next highest level in the hierarchy is state, then the Parent Member for these two cities would be "Minnesota." If you created a calculated member called "Twin Cities," which provided a combined view of these two cities, the Parent Member property for this calculated member would be "Minnesota." The Parent Member property identifies where the new calculated member fits in the hierarchy, by identifying what member is its parent.

  You don't specify a Parent Member for a calculated member that is used as a measure.

- The Member Name—The name you will use to refer to this calculated member.

Creating a Calculated Member for a Measure

Calculated members can be built for measures for a variety of situations:

- You have a measure for the purchase price and a measure for the sales price, and you want to create a measure for the profit:

```
[Measures].[SalesPrice] - [Measures].[PurchasePrice]
```

- You have a measure for the sum of the selling price of a group of houses and you have a measure for the count of the number of houses sold, and you want to create a measure for the average sales price:

  ```
  [Measures].[SumOfSellingPrice] / [Measures].[CountOfHousesSold]
  ```

- You have a measure for the Store Sales and you want to create a measure that gives the Year To Date Sales Total for each particular period:

  ```
  Sum(YTD(),[Measures].[StoreSales])
  ```

You can also use formulas when you are creating regular measures. If the formula used to create the measure uses only addition or subtraction, as in the previous example for calculating profit, you can use a regular measure instead of a calculated measure. If the formula to create the measure has any multiplication, division, or more complex function, then it will most likely not be additive across the dimensions and cannot be used in a regular measure. It must remain as a calculated measure.

The values used in regular measures that are created with formulas are aggregated when the cube is processed, along with all other measures. Calculated members that are used as measures are not aggregated. The value of a calculated member is calculated as the cube is being browsed. This has the advantage of reducing processing time and disk storage and the disadvantage of slower browsing response speed.

Creating a Calculated Member for a Dimension

Here are some situations where you might want to use a calculated member for a dimension:

- You have a Product Category level in your Product dimension that includes a member called Soft Drinks. The next lower level in your Product Dimension is Product Name. You want to be able to view the Coke, Pepsi, and RC Cola members together as Cola Drinks. You create a calculated member to display this new subcategory.

  Calculated member name—Cola Drinks

  Parent dimension—Product

  Parent member—Soft Drinks

  Value expression:

  ```
  [Product].[Soft Drink].[Pepsi] + [Product].[Soft Drink].[Coke] +
  [Product].[Soft Drink].[RC Cola]
  ```

- You have a Manufacturer level in your Vehicle dimension, which includes members such as Ford, Toyota, Daimler-Chrysler, and Volvo. The next lower level of the Vehicle dimension is called Vehicle Type and has members such as Compact, Sedan, Luxury, Station Wagon, Van, and Pickup. You want to also be able to view all the vans together as one group, regardless of their manufacturer. So you create a calculated member called All Vans which includes all the vans from the different manufacturers.

Calculated member name—All Vans

Parent dimension—Vehicle

Parent member—All Vehicles

Value expression:

```
[Vehicle].[Ford].[Van] + [Vehicle].[Toyota].[Van] + [Vehicle].[Daimler-
Chrysler].[Van] + [Vehicle].[Volvo].[Van]
```

- A small modification was made to a product that caused it to be classified as a new product in your Product dimension. You still want to be able to view the combined sales of the old and new versions of the product. You create a calculated member that provides a combined view of the old and the new version of the product.

Calculated member name—Old And New ProductA

Parent dimension—Product

Parent member—Breakfast Cereal

Value expression:

```
[Product].[Food].[Breakfast Cereal].[Old Cereal A] + [Product].[Food].
➥[Breakfast Cereal].[New Cereal A]
```

Anything that you do with a calculated member for a dimension, you could also accomplish directly by modifying the dimension structure. Here's what you could do with the previous three examples:

- In the Soft Drinks example, add a new level called Subcategory to the Products dimension.

- In the second example, remove Vehicle Type from the product dimension hierarchy and make it into its own separate hierarchy. Then you could browse vehicle type both for a single manufacture and for multiple manufacturers.

- For the last example, add a new level to the Product hierarchy immediately above the individual product level, which would allow previous and current versions of products to be viewed jointly.

How do you decide between using a calculated member for a dimension or changing the dimension's structure? Consider the following factors:

- It's often not practical to change an existing dimension's structure. It's easier to add a calculated member.

- If you change the dimension's structure, the cube must be reprocessed before it can be used. If you add a calculated member, the cube does not have to be reprocessed.

- The new levels in a dimension and the new dimensions would have aggregations created for them when the cube is processed. When you use calculated members, no new aggregations are created. Although you lose some browsing speed, you save processing time and disk space when you use calculated members.

You can use calculated members when you have new OLAP browsing requirements without having to go back and rebuild all your existing dimension structure.

Properties of the Cube's Objects

The properties of the cube's objects can be viewed and edited in the Properties box in the lower left pane of the Cube Editor. The available properties change depending on the type of object that is chosen in the tree.

The properties for the cube object include:

- Name—Cannot be edited
- Description
- Data Source—Cannot be edited
- Fact Table
- Fact Table Size—The estimated number of the rows in the fact table
- Aggregation Prefix—The prefix used in ROLAP aggregations for the aggregation table names

You can set the same properties for shared dimensions and private dimensions. The properties you see in the Cube Editor are the same properties that are displayed in the library's Dimension Editor, with one exception. In the Cube Editor you have one more property—Aggregation Usage.

There is a difference between shared and private dimensions, though, in the ability to edit them. The only property of a shared dimension that can be edited is the Aggregation Usage. The only property of a private dimension that cannot be edited is the Data Source.

Here are the properties for shared and private dimensions:

- Name
- Description

- Data Source—Cannot be edited for any type of dimension
- All Level
- All Caption
- Type
- Aggregation Usage—How the levels of the dimension will be treated when the aggregations are created. You can choose to aggregate only the highest level or the lowest level, you can set a custom aggregation strategy, or you can leave the default choice, which creates aggregations for all levels. This is the only property of a private dimension that can be edited.

None of the properties of the virtual dimensions can be edited in the Cube Editor. The properties for the virtual dimensions include:

- Name
- Source Dimension
- All Level—Always set to `Yes`
- All Caption—Always set to `All`
- Aggregation Usage—Always set to `Top Level Only`

The properties for the measures include:

- Name
- Description
- Source Column
- Aggregation Function—There are four possible types of aggregation for a measure: `SUM`, `COUNT`, `MIN`, and `MAX`.
- Data Type
- Display Format—You can set the formatting for the measure, from a pick list of standard display formats, or you can create your own.
- Is Internal—There are times when you will create a measure only for the purpose of using it in a calculated member. When you do this, you may not want the measure itself to be available for browsing. By setting the Is Internal property to `TRUE`, you prevent this measure from being browsed directly.

> **Note**
>
> I've often heard people ask why they can't choose to use an AVERAGE aggregate for the Aggregation Function for a measure.
>
> There's a fundamental difference between an average value and the four kinds of aggregation that are allowed. Aggregates created by SUM, COUNT, MAX, and MIN can all be aggregated to create new aggregates. If I have five sets of numbers and I have already calculated these four aggregates for each of the five sets, I can easily find the sum of the SUM, the sum of the COUNT, the maximum value of the MAX, and the minimum value of the MIN. I can combine the aggregates to create an overall set of aggregations for the five sets.
>
> Averaging doesn't work like that. If I know the average of each of five sets of numbers, I can't calculate the average for the overall set of numbers. I have to divide the overall sum by the overall count.
>
> Microsoft has been able to achieve a very efficient aggregation strategy for OLAP cubes by building aggregates from other aggregates. It's impossible to do that with averages. They have to be calculated separately at every point, so you don't gain any advantage by calculating some of them. You always have to recalculate the average for every point.
>
> If you have aggregated the SUM of the values and you have aggregated the COUNT of your values, you can create a calculated member for the average and OLAP Services will be able to return that value very quickly. If you only want your users to see the average, you can set the Is Internal property to TRUE for the measures that you have created for the SUM and for the COUNT.

The most important properties for the calculated members were discussed in the previous section on creating calculated members. The full list of properties includes:

- Name
- Parent Dimension
- Parent Member
- Value—What is called the Value expression in the Calculated Member Builder dialog.
- Solve Order—Calculated members can use other calculated members as input. If they do, the calculated members must be solved in the proper order. A number can be entered here to force a particular order for calculation of the members.
- FormatString
- ForeColor, BackColor, FontName, FontSize, FontFlags—Additional options for displaying the calculated members in the OLAP display.

Other Tools Available in the Cube Editor

There are a variety of tools available in the Cube Editor. Choose them from the Tools menu:

- Process Cube—Gets the data from the data source and prepares that data for OLAP browsing. Cube processing is discussed in Chapter 16.

- Design Storage—Design the storage strategy for the data and the aggregations used for the cube. Storage design is discussed in Chapter 16.

- Count Dimension Members—Counts the number of members at each level of each dimension or, only for those dimensions that are currently listed as having no members.

- Validate Cube Structure—Checks to see if the cube structure is valid and can be processed.

- Optimize Schema—Simplifies a cube's schema by removing unnecessary joins.

- Manage Roles—Opens the Manage Roles dialog, as shown in Figure 15.25. This dialog enables you to give additional roles access to this cube. The default access is Read, but you can upgrade the type of access to Read/Write by selecting one of the roles that have been given Cube Access and checking the Grant Read/Write Permission check box.

  You can also open the Manage Roles dialog by clicking the farthest right button on Cube Editor's toolbar.

FIGURE 15.25

You use the Manage Roles dialog to give a role permission to access a particular cube.

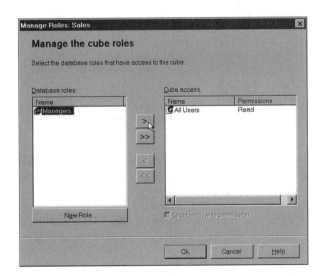

Browsing OLAP Cubes with the Cube Editor

The Data view in the Cube Editor provides the opportunity to browse the OLAP cube you are working on. This browsing is similar to what is available with the Cube Browser, which is discussed in Chapter 16.

Virtual Cubes

Virtual cubes are cubes you create from regular cubes. The first way you can do this is by joining two or more cubes together to create a virtual cube. Or, you can select a portion of a single cube to create a virtual cube.

You could create a virtual cube for the following reasons:

- To combine data that is present in two separate cubes. For example, you might want to combine cubes that contain current data with cubes that contain historical data. Or, you might want to combine cubes used for marketing and for sales, along their shared dimensions.

- To present a subset of the available data so that users are only browsing the data that they want to see.

- To present a subset of the available data for security reasons. You can give users permission to browse a virtual cube, when they don't have permission to browse the underlying cubes. When you use this strategy, you only include the dimensions and measures in the virtual cube that you want users to have permission to browse.

Virtual cubes are very similar to views in a relational database. As with views, virtual cubes do not make a separate copy of data. Rather, they use the data and aggregations that have been created for their constituent cubes.

Virtual cubes appear as one of the four main nodes in the OLAP database tree. You can create a new virtual cube by using the Virtual Cube Wizard. Call this wizard by right-clicking the Virtual Cube node and choosing New Virtual Cube.

The second screen of the wizard, shown in Figure 15.26, is where you choose the cubes that you want to include in your virtual cubes. The following screens show you all the measures and all the dimensions from the cubes you have picked. You can choose any number of them for your new virtual cube.

The last screen of the wizard gives you a box in which to name the virtual cube and a choice as to whether or not you want to process the cube immediately.

FIGURE 15.26

The Virtual Cube Wizard enables you to choose the cubes that will be used in your virtual cube.

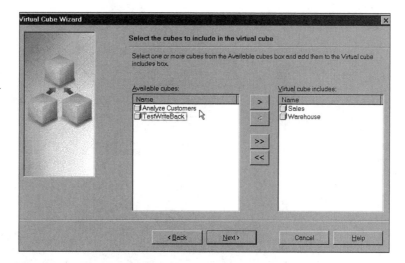

When you choose to edit an existing virtual cube, the same wizard opens and you can choose to change any of the previous cubes, measures, and dimensions that have been included in that virtual cube.

You don't create aggregations for a virtual cube, but you do have to process it. You can browse a virtual cube in the same way you browse a regular cube. You also can manage roles for your virtual cube in the same way you would for a regular cube.

After you have processed your cube, you are allowed to add calculated members to it. Right-click on the virtual cube and choose Manage Calculated Members. Calculated members can be imported from any of the constituent cubes or you can create new calculated members that only exist in the virtual cube. The Calculated Member Manager dialog and the Import Calculated Members dialog are shown in Figure 15.27. Open the Calculated Member dialog by right-clicking a virtual cube in the Cube Manager tree and choosing Manage Calculated Members. The Import Calculated Members dialog is selected from the File menu or by clicking the farthest right toolbar in the Calculated Member dialog.

You can create new calculated members for your virtual cube by selecting the New Calculated Member toolbar button. This button calls the same Calculated Member Builder dialog as is used in the Cube Editor.

15

CREATING CUBES

New Calculated Member

Import Calculated Member

FIGURE 15.27

You can import calculated members or create new calculated members for your virtual cube.

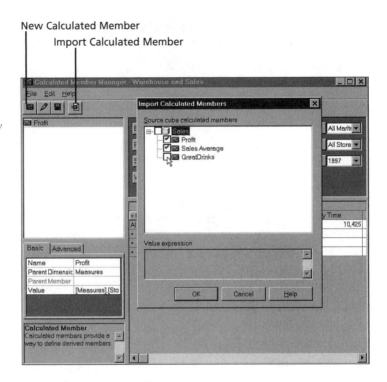

Summary

This chapter has provided an introduction to the use of the OLAP Manager in creating cubes and the objects that go into making cubes. Chapter 16 continues with a discussion of creating cube aggregations, processing cubes, and browsing cubes. Chapter 17 looks at partitioning cubes.

When you have read these three chapters you will be familiar with the OLAP Manager and you'll have a good introduction to the capabilities of the OLAP Services.

Parts IV, V, and VI of this book will show you more of the capabilities of the OLAP Services, both on the client side and the server side. You'll learn how to use Decision Support Objects and the MDX query language to create and browse cubes.

Processing and Browsing Cubes

by Tim Peterson

IN THIS CHAPTER

This chapter shows you how to use the OLAP Manager to do two things—process cubes and browse cubes.

In preparation for processing a cube, you first choose a storage type. OLAP Services provides three distinct ways to store cube data—MOLAP, ROLAP, and HOLAP. After choosing the type of storage, you design the cube aggregations.

When you're ready to process the cube, you have three more choices to make—whether you want to do a full processing, a data refresh, or an incremental update. You can process a cube as a part of a DTS Package.

You have a couple of tools to examine the success of your aggregation strategy. The Usage Analysis Wizard lets you generate a number of reports about browsing performance. The Query-Based Optimization Wizard lets you build your aggregations directly from information about how your cube is actually being used.

The OLAP Manager has a simple cube browser, which is a convenient tool to get a quick view of the cubes you are creating. And if you're not familiar with OLAP browsing, you can use this cube browser to get an introduction to the possibilities of interactive multidimensional analysis.

Selecting the Type of Data Storage—MOLAP, HOLAP, and ROLAP

The OLAP Manager provides a wizard for designing data storage. You can do three things with the Storage Design Wizard:

- Select the type of data storage.
- Design the aggregations.
- Start the processing of the cube.

The Storage Design Wizard can be accessed from a number of different places. Here are three of the most prominent ways to call the wizard:

- Select Design Storage from the Action menu.
- Right-click a cube and select Design Storage from the pop-up menu.
- Select Design Storage from the Tools menu of the cube editor.

The wizard starts with an introductory screen. The second screen, shown in Figure 16.1, gives you the choice of the three types of data storage—MOLAP, ROLAP, and HOLAP.

FIGURE 16.1

Select MOLAP, ROLAP, or HOLAP storage on the screen of the Storage Design Wizard.

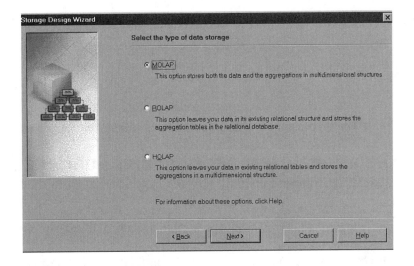

You can create a cube with one of the data storage types and very easily switch to a different storage type. You can create a cube with several partitions that use different storage types.

The fundamental differences between the three types of data storage are in how they store data and how they store the aggregations for that data.

MOLAP—Multidimensional Data Storage

MOLAP uses a type of data storage that was specifically created for multidimensional analysis. MOLAP handles the data and the aggregations like this:

- The data is copied from the data source and stored in the MOLAP cube's specialized multidimensional structure. When the cube is queried, the original data is not needed, because all of that data is available in the cube.

- The aggregations are stored in the specialized multidimensional cube structure.

ROLAP—Relational Data Storage

ROLAP uses the structures of a relational database to store the cube's aggregations. The data and aggregations are handled like this:

- The data is left where it is in the data source. When the cube is queried and the base level of data is needed, that data is retrieved from that original data source.

- The aggregations are stored in the relational database as a set of tables. The information in these tables is retrieved to answer MDX queries that are requesting aggregations.

HOLAP—Hybrid Data Storage

HOLAP is a data storage type that combines features of ROLAP and features of MOLAP. HOLAP handles the data like ROLAP and the aggregations like MOLAP:

- The data is left where it is in the data source. When the cube is queried and the base level of data is needed, that data is retrieved from the original data source.
- The aggregations are stored in the specialized multidimensional cube structure.

Relational Data Storage and Specialized Multidimensional Storage

The relational data storage used by ROLAP is easy to understand. The data, of course, isn't moved at all. The ROLAP aggregations are created as tables in the relational database. Those tables can be viewed and queried using SQL. You can view their structure and browse their data in the Enterprise Manager, just like any other tables. Figure 16.2 shows one of the ROLAP aggregation tables.

FIGURE 16.2

This is one of the tables created by ROLAP aggregation in the FoodMart database.

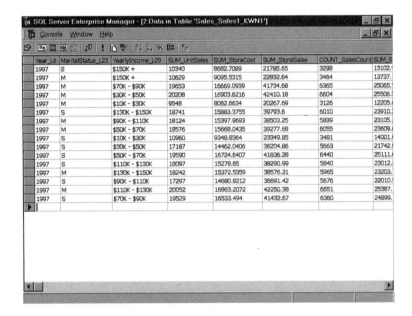

The specialized multidimensional storage that is used in MOLAP and HOLAP cannot be viewed directly, but it's important to understand a little about how it works. When the data is moved from the data source into the MOLAP cube, it goes through a process that is similar to what is called *data tokenization*. In this process, each piece of repeated data in the tables is replaced with a token. This can dramatically reduce the space needed for data storage. The amount of data compression varies greatly, because of differing numbers of repeated fields.

Comparing the Use of MOLAP, HOLAP, and ROLAP

The choice of storage type has a very significant impact on cube processing time, cube storage space, and cube browsing speed. There was not a lot of information about the issues involved in this choice at the time the original product documentation was written. This section can give you a good introduction to these issues, but it is important for you to do your own testing to see how the choices affect your particular situation.

Factors Affecting the Use of MOLAP

Some of the factors affecting the use of MOLAP storage include the following:

- Cube browsing is fastest when using MOLAP, even if no aggregations have been created. The data in the compressed multidimensional format can usually be accessed more quickly than data in a relational database. Table 16.1 compares query processing time among the storage types.

- MOLAP storage always takes more room than HOLAP because the data is copied. At low levels of aggregation, it also takes more room than ROLAP.

- MOLAP cubes can be viewed when the original data source is not available because all the data is stored in the cube. This allows a MOLAP cube to be taken with a user on a laptop, to be copied to a new location, or to be included in an email message.

- MOLAP storage is probably your best choice for data storage, unless you have a lot of data that is not going to be browsed very much. In that case, it does not make sense to use the processing time and disk space that is needed for copying all the data into a multidimensional format.

Table 16.1 shows the approximate time needed to run 38 OLAP queries on a fact table with 15 million rows. The test was run on a 4X400Mhz Xeon Server with 4 GB of RAM. All values are for queries run with no prior caching of data. The information in the table is adapted from the SQL Server 7.0 OLAP Services Performance Tuning and Optimization session at Microsoft's TechEd 99.

TABLE 16.1 Query Performance Comparison

Storage and Aggregation	Processing Time
ROLAP/HOLAP, 0% Aggregation	22 Minutes
ROLAP/HOLAP, 25% Aggregation	17 Minutes
ROLAP/HOLAP, 50% Aggregation	16 Minutes
ROLAP/HOLAP, 75% Aggregation	14 Minutes
HOLAP, 90% Aggregation	10 Minutes
MOLAP, 0% Aggregation	2.5 Minutes
MOLAP, 25% Aggregation	2.0 Minutes
MOLAP, 50% Aggregation	1.9 Minutes
MOLAP, 75% Aggregation	1.6 Minutes
MOLAP, 90% Aggregation	1.5 Minutes

Note

The Pivot Table Services uses a very intelligent caching mechanism for cube browsing. The times listed in Table 16.1 show response times for a cold cache, when no data has been stored. If a query can be fully answered from the cached data, performance times are the same for all storage types and, in this test, were approximately five times better than what was delivered by MOLAP with the cold cache.

How much will the caching help your performance? It depends on how much data your OLAP browsing is accessing. If all or most of the data being used can be cached, you will see consistently good browsing performance. If some of your queries can be answered from the cache while other queries are retrieving data from the server, you will see a significant variation in performance from one query to the next.

Factors Affecting the Use of ROLAP

Some of the factors affecting the use of ROLAP storage include the following:

- Cube browsing is slower than MOLAP and about the same as HOLAP.
- Processing time is much slower, especially at higher levels of aggregation. Table 16.2 compares some processing times among the storage types.
- You cannot browse the cube unless you are connected to the data source.

- If you aren't using many aggregations, ROLAP storage takes almost no space at all.
- ROLAP aggregations take much more space than MOLAP/HOLAP aggregations, especially at higher levels of aggregation.

Table 16.2 shows the approximate time needed to process the cube that was used for the test described in Table 16.1. Note that MOLAP takes more time at 0% aggregation, but ROLAP takes the most time for any other level of aggregation.

TABLE 16.2 Comparison of Processing Speeds

Storage and Aggregation Setting	Processing Time
ROLAP, 0% Aggregation	0 Minutes
ROLAP, 25% Aggregation	2.5 Minutes
ROLAP, 50% Aggregation	9 Minutes
ROLAP, 75% Aggregation	21 Minutes
HOLAP, 0% Aggregation	0 Minutes
HOLAP, 25% Aggregation	0.7 Minute
HOLAP, 50% Aggregation	1 Minute
HOLAP, 75% Aggregation	1.6 Minutes
HOLAP, 90% Aggregation	2.5 Minutes
MOLAP, 0% Aggregation	0.7 Minute
MOLAP, 25% Aggregation	1 Minute
MOLAP, 50% Aggregation	1.3 Minutes
MOLAP, 75% Aggregation	1.9 Minutes
MOLAP, 90% Aggregation	2.8 Minutes

Factors Affecting the Use of HOLAP

Factors that affect the use of HOLAP storage include the following:

- When accessing the lowest level of the data, HOLAP works exactly like ROLAP. When accessing aggregations, HOLAP works exactly like MOLAP.
- You cannot browse the cube unless you are connected to the data source.
- HOLAP is the best data storage choice when you're using a cube that is not accessing the lowest level of the data. If you're just using the aggregations, you get identical speed with MOLAP and HOLAP. And you save time and disk space, when you don't need the copying of data that's provided by MOLAP.

> **Note**
>
> MOLAP is usually the best choice, because it gives the best browsing performance.
>
> HOLAP is the best choice if you don't have the room to store all the data that is copied in MOLAP.
>
> ROLAP is hardly ever the best choice. I think it's good to have ROLAP as an option, but the actual performance of ROLAP in terms of processing time, amount of storage space used, and cube-browsing performance is not very good when compared to the other two options.
>
> It's important to remember how easy it is to switch from one type of data storage to another. You're never locked into one data storage type, unless one of them is required for a particular design goal, such as the need to use cubes when disconnected from the network.

Designing the Cubes' Aggregations

The next screen of the Storage Design Wizard, shown in Figure 16.3, presents the aggregation options.

FIGURE 16.3

The Storage Design Wizard will help you choose aggregation options.

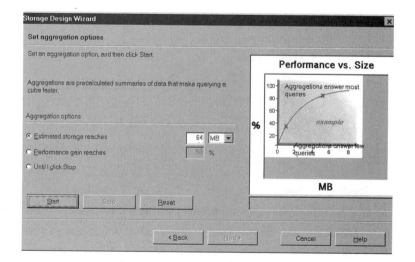

The OLAP Services will design the best possible aggregations for your cube. Your only input is to tell the OLAP Services how much aggregation to do. You have three different ways to make your choice:

- Design aggregations until the estimated storage space for those aggregations reaches a certain size.

- Design aggregations until the estimated average performance gain reaches a particular percentage. This percentage value is supposed to represent the percent of the total possible performance gain.

- Limit the aggregations interactively, by clicking Stop when the aggregations have reached the desired level.

After you make your choice, press the Start button, and the OLAP Manager begins designing aggregations. A graph shows the estimated performance gain and the estimated disk storage space for the aggregates as they are being designed.

Figure 16.4 shows the display as the design process has been completed. An aggregation option of a 100% performance gain was chosen for this example. The shape of the graph can vary, depending on how many levels are in each dimension.

FIGURE 16.4

The aggregation options screen shows a typical curve after aggregations have been designed.

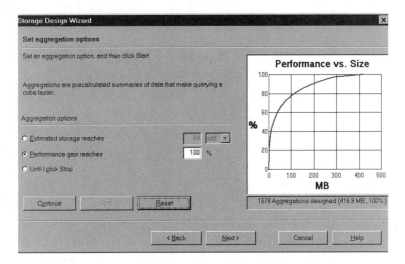

It's usually not best to select 100% of the possible aggregations. Aggregations take processing time and disk space and you achieve much more of the performance gain with the first aggregations created than with the last. Consider the situation in the example shown in Figure 16.4:

- Achieving 100% of the possible performance gain required 1678 aggregations, with an estimated 417MB of storage space.

- 91% of the gain was achieved with 50% of the total storage space—635 aggregations and 208.5MB of storage.
- 80% of the gain was achieved with 25% of the total storage space—473 aggregations and an estimated 114MB of storage.
- 60% of the gain was achieved with 9.2% of the total storage space—301 aggregations and an estimated 38.3MB of storage.
- 40% of the gain was achieved with 2.3% of the total storage space—199 aggregations and an estimated 9.7MB of storage.
- 20% of the gain was achieved with .35% of the total storage space—112 aggregations and an estimated 1.5MB of storage.
- The first 2% of the gain was achieved with .002% of the total storage space—16 aggregations and an estimated .01MB of storage.
- The last 2% of the gain was achieved with 22.7% of the total storage space—290 aggregations and an estimated 94.5MB of storage.

> **Note**
>
> The performance gain information presented here is based on the wizard's estimates. Some users have reported that the portion of the gain returned by the early aggregations is significantly greater than what the wizard reports.

If you don't have disk space and available processing time to do as much aggregation as you would like to do, consider using the Usage-Based Optimization Wizard, described in "Usage-Based Cube Optimization," to create the aggregations that will be used the most frequently.

> **Caution**
>
> The storage estimates made by the Storage Design Wizard are often inaccurate.
>
> 1. The storage space needed for ROLAP is usually quite a bit greater than the estimate provided by the Wizard.
> 2. The storage space for HOLAP is usually much less than the estimate.
> 3. The same storage space estimate is given for MOLAP as for HOLAP. With MOLAP, of course, all the data is copied into the multidimensional storage structure. The space needed for this data is not reflected in the estimate.

You have to add space for the data and space for the aggregates to get the total space needed for MOLAP storage. How much space is the data going to take? MOLAP compresses the data. I've seen situations where it is compressed to 60% of the space taken in SQL Server. I've also seen situations where it is compressed to 10% of the space taken in SQL Server.

In one example I saw documented in a newsgroup, a user chose 100MB of storage with each of the three storage types. The HOLAP cube created the most aggregates and took 9MB of storage. The MOLAP cube created fewer aggregates and took 250MB of storage. The ROLAP cube created the fewest aggregates and took 430MB.

Processing the Cubes

Cubes have to be processed before they can be browsed. Processing loads the data from the data source into the cube structure. Whenever you process the cube, the OLAP Manager displays a detailed report showing what is being done, as shown in Figure 16.5.

FIGURE 16.5

The OLAP Manager shows a detailed report of the progress of the cube processing.

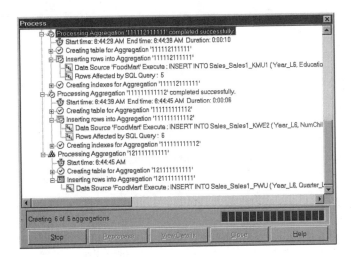

The last screen of the Storage Design Wizard gives you the choice of processing the cube immediately or saving the aggregations for processing later.

The Three Types of Processing

When you choose Process Cube from the Action menu or by right clicking on the cube and selecting Process Cube, the Process a Cube dialog, shown in Figure 16.6, is displayed.

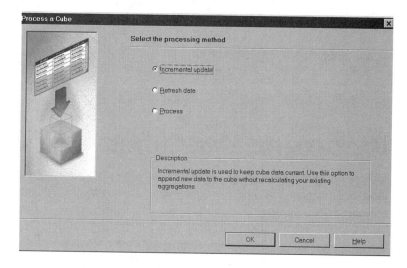

Here's a brief description of the three types of processing:

- Incremental Update—Only new data is processed. Existing data and aggregations are left unchanged. This is the quickest choice.
- Refresh Data—All the data is emptied out of the cube, the cube is loaded with data, and all the aggregates are processed.
- Process—The structure of the cube is validated and built, the cube is loaded with data, and all the aggregates are processed. This is the most time-consuming choice.

The previous cube is still available for OLAP browsing while any of these three types of processing is being carried out. For the incremental update and the refresh data, the new form of the cube will automatically be used by the clients when the processing is finished. For the full cube processing, the clients have to disconnect and reconnect to the cube before they will see the new data.

You have to do a full cube processing if you have changed the structure of the cube or if any of the constituent dimensions have been processed.

You can get by with an incremental update if the structure of the cube hasn't been changed and if you can set a filter that will distinguish between the data that is already in the cube and the new data that is to be included.

Note

None of the three types of cube processing process any of the shared dimensions that are used in the cube. Those shared dimensions must be processed separately, as described later in "Processing Dimensions." The cube processing only updates the fact table and any private dimensions.

The Incremental Update

You have some additional choices to make when you choose an incremental update. An incremental update creates a separate cube partition. You have to use a filter to separate the data that was included in the original cube partition and the data that is included in the incremental update partition. The Incremental Update Wizard guides you through this process.

The Incremental Update Wizard appears when you choose the Incremental Update option in the Process a Cube dialog. On the first screen after the wizard's introduction, you choose the data source and the fact table for the incremental update (see Figure 16.7). The data source and fact table that are currently being used in the cube appear by default. You must choose a fact table that has all the same fields as your current dimension table. You also must choose a data source that has all the dimension tables that are being used in your cube. At the bottom of the screen is a box that contains a list of these required dimension tables.

FIGURE 16.7

The Incremental Update Wizard starts with a screen for choosing the data source and the fact table.

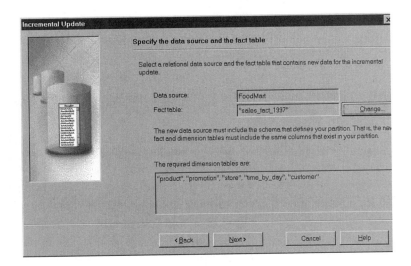

The wizard's next screen, shown in Figure 16.8, provides a box for entering a filtering expression, which is used to identify the records in the fact table that are to be used for the incremental update. The filter takes the form of a SQL WHERE clause, without the word WHERE.

FIGURE 16.8

You specify which records are to be included in the Incremental Update Wizard on the Filter screen.

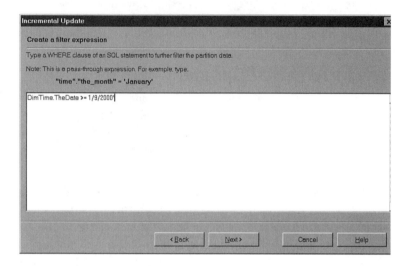

Cubes are often updated on the basis of a date, which would mean using a filter expression like this:

```
DimTime.TheDate>= '1/9/2000'
```

If you are using a lineage dimension, you could use the key value from that dimension to update a cube with records from a particular DTS import:

```
FactSalesDetail.LineageFK = 1893
```

> **Caution**
>
> Make sure that your filter only includes records that have not been previously included in the cube. If you specify a filter that includes records that are already in the cube, those records will be included in all aggregations an additional time, so that your cube will report inflated values. The cube will be incorrect until the next time you do a full process or a data refresh.

When the incremental update is run, the OLAP Manager first creates a new partition and then merges that partition into the existing one, so you still have only a single partition.

Processing Dimensions

Dimensions are processed in a way that's similar to processing cubes. You right click on the dimension in the OLAP Manager tree and select Process. The Process a Dimension dialog appears, which gives you two choices:

- Incremental update—Adds new members to the dimension.
- Rebuild the dimension structure—Used when the structure of the dimension changes or the relationship between dimension members is changed.

If you rebuild the dimension structure, then you have to reprocess all the cubes that use that dimension. You don't have to do anything to the cubes if you just use an incremental update.

You don't have to specify a filter with an incremental update of a dimension. A dimension incremental update process is similar to refreshing the data of the cube. All the members of the dimension are processed. It's more practical to do this with dimension tables, rather than the fact table, because the dimension tables are so much smaller.

> **Caution**
>
> When you modify the structure of a dimension, you are asked if you want to save your changes, but you are not asked if you want to rebuild the dimension structure. The next time any cube using that dimension is processed, the shared dimension will be rebuilt. This will invalidate all other cubes that are based on it.
>
> You must recognize that modifying the structure of a dimension is a major operation. When you do it, you should rebuild the dimension structure immediately and then also process all of the dependent cubes.

The DTS OLAP Services Processing Task

In May 1999, Microsoft publicly posted the Beta 2 version of the Data Transformation Services Task Kit 1, which included one new custom task for DTS—the OLAP Services Processing Task. I don't know how this custom task is going to be distributed in the future, but I expect it will be available in some form.

The OLAP Services Processing Task allows you to process an OLAP cube or a dimension as a part of a DTS Package. The interface for the OLAP Services Processing Task, shown in Figure 16.9, gives you the same options as you have with the Process a Cube dialog and the Incremental Update Wizard.

FIGURE 16.9

You can set up processing for a cube or a dimension with the OLAP Services Processing Task.

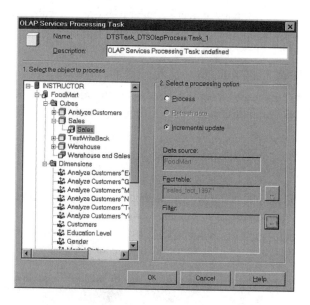

I don't have the full documentation for this custom task and, as I am working with a Beta release, it is subject to change. To display the properties in the version you are working with, you can create a package with one OLAP Services Processing Task and an Active Script Task with this code:

```
Option Explicit

Function Main()
DIM pkg, stp, tsk, cus, prp
DIM msg

SET pkg = DTSGlobalVariables.Parent
SET stp = pkg.Steps("DTSStep_DTSOlapProcess.Task_1")
SET tsk = pkg.Tasks(stp.TaskName)
SET cus = tsk.CustomTask

FOR EACH prp IN cus.Properties
    msg = "Property Name - " & prp.Name & vbCrLf & vbCrLf
    msg = msg & "Value - " & prp.Value
    MSGBOX msg
```

```
NEXT

Main = DTSTaskExecResult_Success
End Function
```

Here are some of the properties in the current version:

- `ProcessOption`—One of the three types of processing. See Table 16.3 for details.
- `DataSource`—The name of the data source as it appears in the OLAP Manager tree. Required for incremental update.
- `FactTable`—The name of the fact table. Required for incremental update.
- `Filter`—The filter used in an incremental update.
- `ItemType`—The type of item being processed. See Table 16.4 for details.
- `TreeKey`—The full tree description of the item being processed, such as

  `SERVER1FoodMart\CubeFolder\Sales\Sales`

TABLE 16.3   `ProcessOption` Options for the OLAP Services Processing Task

`ProcessOption` *Value*	*Type of Processing*
0	Process a cube or rebuild the structure of a dimension
1	Refresh data
2	Incremental update

TABLE 16.4   `ItemType` Options for the OLAP Services Processing Task

`ItemType` *Value*	*Type of Item Selected*
1	An OLAP database
2	A cube or dimension folder
4	A cube
5	A virtual cube
6	A partition
7	A shared dimension
8	A virtual dimension

When an OLAP Database is chosen for processing, all the cubes and dimensions within it are processed. Similarly, when a cube or dimension folder is chosen, all the objects within it are processed.

Usage Analysis

The Usage Analysis Wizard offers six different types of reports on the usage of a cube. It can be called by choosing Usage Analysis from the Action menu or by right-clicking the name of the cube in the OLAP Manager tree and selecting Usage Analysis from the popup menu. The first screen of the wizard is shown in Figure 16.10.

FIGURE 16.10

You choose which report you want to view on the first screen of the Usage Analysis Wizard.

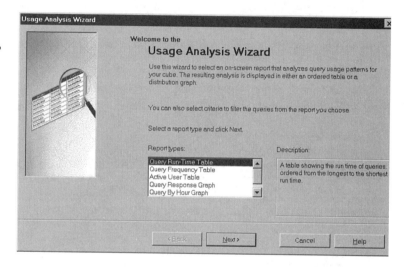

The six reports you can view with the Usage Analysis Wizard are

- Query Run-Time—Shows the longest running queries.
- Query Frequency Table—Shows the queries that are run most frequently.
- Active User Table—Shows the most active users.
- Query Response Graph—Shows the length of response time for the queries.
- Query By Hour Graph—Shows the number of queries issued each hour of the day.
- Query By Date Graph—Shows the number of queries issued each day.

If you want, you can limit the queries included in the report by the following categories:

- Date
- Query response time
- Users
- Number of times a query was run

All these filters are set on the screen shown in Figure 16.11.

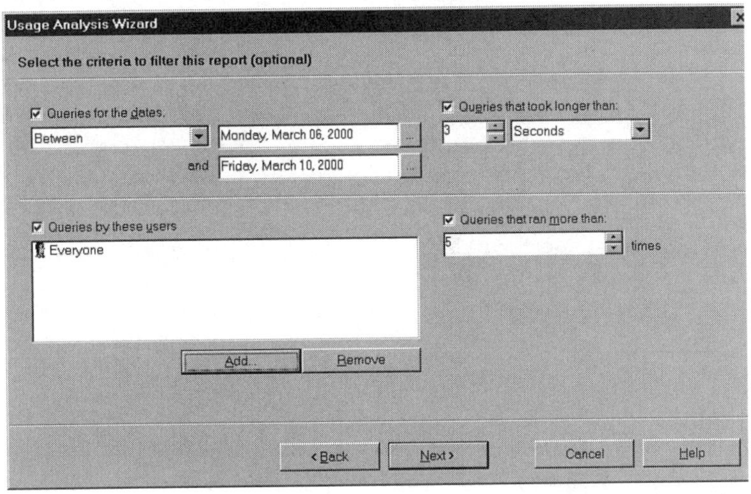

FIGURE 16.11

*You can set filters
on this screen for
the queries that
are included in
the usage report.*

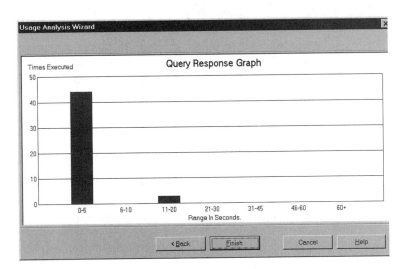

Figure 16.12 shows an example of a Query Response Graph generated by the Usage
Analysis Wizard.

FIGURE 16.12

*The Query
Response Graph
is one of the six
reports available
with the Usage
Analysis Wizard.*

> **Tip**
>
> By default, only 1 out of every 10 queries is stored in the log that is used as the basis for the Usage Analysis Wizard and the Usage-Based Optimization Wizard. If you're going to do usage analysis or usage-based optimization, I think it makes more sense to include all the queries. After all, if you want to look at the longest running queries, you would normally want to see the longest running queries out of all the queries, not just the 1 out of 10 queries that happened to be included in the sampling.
>
> You can change the default setting so that all the queries are logged and are considered in the usage reports and the usage-based optimization. Right-click the OLAP Server in the OLAP Manager tree and select Properties from the popup menu. Select the Query Log tab and change the sample frequency to 1. You can also clear the query log on this tab, if you want to have a fresh start in your query analysis.
>
> One caution, though—the help file indicates that setting this value too low can hurt querying performance. So perhaps you want to set it at 1 only for periods when you are doing intensive analysis.

Usage-Based Cube Optimization

The Usage-Based Optimization Wizard gives you the opportunity to design your aggregations based on the usage pattern for your cube. The wizard considers a particular set of queries that has been issued in cube browsing and then builds aggregates that would help to answer those queries.

Access this wizard by choosing Usage-Based Optimization from the Action menu or by right-clicking the name of a cube in the OLAP Manager tree and selecting Usage-Based Optimization from the Popup menu. The wizard's introductory screen appears. Click Next to see the screen shown in Figure 16.13.

You can choose to base your optimization on all the queries that have been issued. The wizard allows you to filter the queries you are optimizing in several different ways:

- Date
- Query response time
- Users
- Number of times a query was run
- Whether the query was run in a MOLAP cube, a ROLAP table, or the server cache

FIGURE 16.13

The wizard provides several different ways for you to filter the queries you want to optimize.

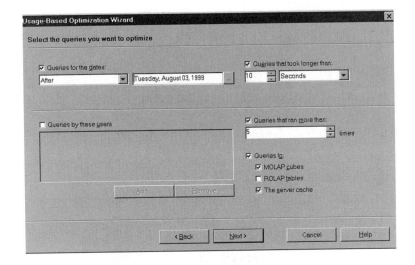

After you have selected the filter, the wizard presents you with a list of the queries that are included within the filtered range. Then the wizard continues on with the same screens that are included in the Storage Design Wizard. You can choose all the things that you always choose when you are designing storage:

- Whether to replace the existing aggregations or add new ones to those that have already been created.
- Whether to use MOLAP, HOLAP, or ROLAP.
- How many aggregations to create; based on estimated storage, performance gain, or an interactive choice.
- Number of times a query is run.
- Whether to process immediately or save for processing later.

Browsing an OLAP Cube

After you have processed a cube, you are able to browse it. Access the Cube Browser by choosing Browse Data from the Action menu or by right-clicking the cube and selecting Browse Data from the pop-up menu. If the cube has not been processed since it was last modified, you receive a message that the cube must be processed before you will be allowed to browse.

The Cube Browser is shown in Figure 16.14. The lower part is called the data grid; the upper part is called the slicer pane.

FIGURE 16.14

The Cube Browser provides OLAP browsing within the OLAP Manager.

Slicer pane

Data grid

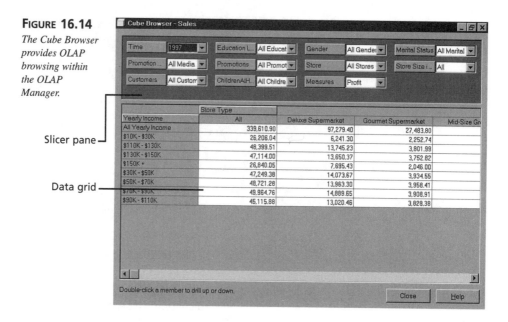

By default, the data grid provides a two-dimensional view of the data in the cube. The members of one dimension appear as the column headings. The members of the second dimension appear as row headings. The name of the dimension is displayed in a single box in a separate row above the names of the dimension's members.

> **Note**
>
> When you're using the Cube Browser, the collection of measures in the cube is treated in the same way as a dimension.

You can easily change the dimensions that are being used in the data grid. Just drag one of the dimensions from the slicer pane and drop it onto the name of one of the dimensions in the data grid. When the dimension is in the proper position for the drop, the pointer becomes a double arrow, indicating that the two dimensions will be exchanged. Figure 16.15 shows a change from the Yearly Income dimension to the Media Type dimension for the rows in the data grid.

You can also add more dimensions to the data grid, either as additional columns or additional rows. Figure 16.16 shows a data grid displaying four dimensions—Media Type and Store Type on the columns, Education Level and Marital Status on the rows.

FIGURE 16.15

You can drag a dimension from the slicer pane and exchange it with one of the dimensions in the data grid.

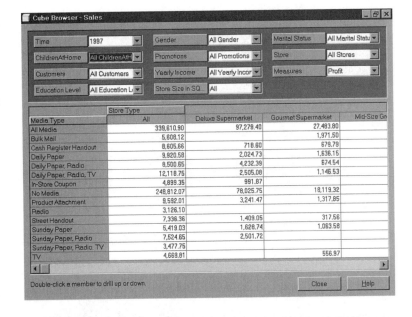

FIGURE 16.16

You can view many dimensions at the same time.

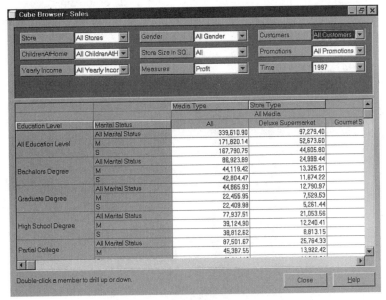

> **Note**
>
> You can use many dimensions in the Cube Browser, but the display of the data grid is not very flexible. The names of the members are always displayed and the width of the columns cannot be modified, so if you add too many dimensions, you can't see any data at all.

> **Note**
>
> You can't remove the last dimension that's being used for rows or columns. If you do, the Cube Browser will automatically replace it with one of the dimensions from the slicer pane.

If you want to change the position of dimensions already being used in the data grid, you can drag one of the dimension names and drop it on another one.

You can drill down to view one of the lower levels of the dimension. For any of the dimensions you are using in the data grid, you can double-click the plus sign that appears beside each member. You can remove the additional detail by clicking the minus sign. Figure 16.17 shows a drill-down on the USA and OR members of the Customer dimension.

FIGURE 16.17

It's easy to drill down into lower levels of a dimension.

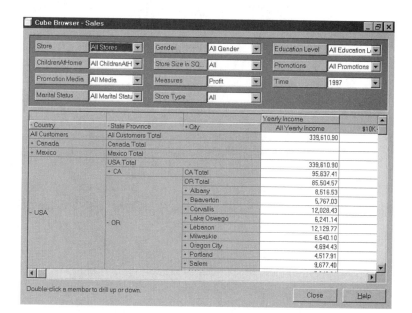

You can also use the dimensions that are in the slicer pane for drilling down. Click the arrow beside a dimension to view all the measures at each of the levels within the dimension. If you select one of these measures, the data in the data grid changes to include only data for that particular member.

> **Note**
>
> In an MDX query, the WHERE clause is known as the slicer clause. It slices the cube, limiting the data to values that are included with a particular member.

Figure 16.18 shows the view of the members of a dimension in the slicer pane, in this case the Store dimension.

FIGURE 16.18

You can look at all the members of all the levels of a dimension in the slicer pane.

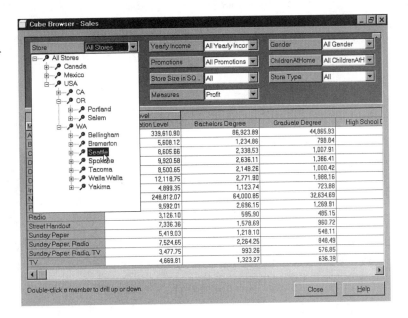

Figure 16.19 shows the view of the cube after it has been sliced by selecting the Seattle member of the Store dimension. Slicing a cube is a process of filtering. All the profit data that is now displayed represents sales only for stores located in Seattle.

The Cube Browser in the OLAP Manager gives you a quick and easy way to browse your cube data. You don't get all the browsing possibilities and you certainly don't get a very flexible display of the cube data. Other cube browsers do a much better job of presenting OLAP results.

FIGURE 16.19

You can drill down into your data by selecting a particular member in one or more of the dimensions displayed in the slicer pane.

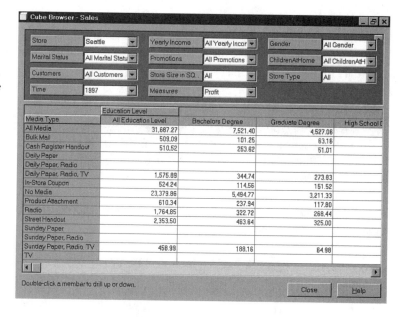

The main advantage of the Cube Browser is that it is available. You can use it to look at your data without having to set up any client applications.

Summary

The OLAP Manager gives you full control of the aggregation and processing options available in the OLAP Services.

The DTS custom task for OLAP Services processing gives you control of cube processing from inside of DTS.

The Cube Browser gives you the basic functionality used in cube browsing.

There's still one more chapter on the OLAP Manager. Chapter 17, "Partitioning Cubes and Administering OLAP Server," examines several additional topics using the OLAP Manager to administer the OLAP Services—managing partitions, implementing security, using OLAP Manager Add-ins, and modifying Server properties.

Partitioning Cubes and Administering OLAP Server

by Tim Peterson

IN THIS CHAPTER

CHAPTER 17

Chapter 17 completes the section on the OLAP Manager with a discussion of topics related to partitioning cubes and administering OLAP Services through the OLAP Manager:

- Creating, merging, and using partitions for improved performance
- Write-enabling a cube to allow interactive analysis
- Managing OLAP Services security
- Adding and using add-ins to the OLAP Manager
- Setting other OLAP Manager Properties

Cube Partitions

A partition is a portion of a cube that is stored in a single file. A single default partition is created for a new cube. There are two primary reasons why you might want to create additional partitions:

- You want to store the cube on more than one logical disk drive, perhaps on multiple machines.
- You want to store different parts of your cube with different storage types. You may, for example, want to store part of your cube with MOLAP storage and part of your cube with HOLAP storage

> **Note**
>
> There is a restriction on the use of user-defined partitions. They are only available in the Enterprise Edition of SQL Server 7.0.

A user-defined partition is also used when you are merging write-back data into a cube. Using a write-back partition is discussed in a section "Write-Enabling a Cube" later in this chapter.

When you use incremental update for a cube, a separate partition is created for the new data, but that partition is not maintained. The OLAP Manager immediately merges it with the default partition, as a part of the incremental update process.

Creating and Editing Cube Partitions

You can find the Partitions folder under the name of the cube in the OLAP Manager tree. All existing partitions, including the default partition, are shown in this folder.

To create a new partition, highlight Partitions and choose New Partition from the Action menu or right-click Partitions and choose New Partition from the popup menu. If you are not using the Enterprise Edition of SQL Server, you receive a message saying that the Enterprise Edition is required for using user-defined partitions.

To edit a partition, you use the Partition Wizard. To open this wizard you highlight one of the existing partitions and choose Edit Partition from the Action menu or right-click the partition and pick Edit Partition from the popup menu.

The Partition Wizard is used both for creating and editing a partition. The first screen of the Partition Wizard, shown in Figure 17.1, is identical to the first screen of the Incremental Update Wizard.

FIGURE 17.1

You choose the data source and the fact table on the first screen of the Partition Wizard.

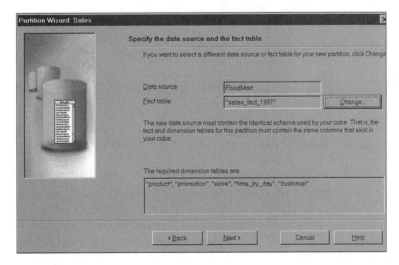

The data source and the fact table from the default partition are set as the default choices for the new partition. If your partition is being built from that same table and data source, you don't have to do anything on the first screen. If you are using a different data source or fact table, you choose them here.

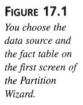

17

PARTITIONS AND
OLAP SERVER

The rules for choosing the data source and the fact table are the same as when you set up an incremental update: You must choose a fact table that has an identical structure to the existing fact table in your cube, and the data source must have all the dimension tables that are listed in the box at the bottom of the screen.

The next screen, shown in Figure 17.2, gives you the option of choosing a particular slice of data for the partition. You can highlight a dimension and pick a member for that dimension in the Members box. Your partition will only contain data from that dimension for that particular member.

FIGURE 17.2

You can select a particular slice of data for your new partition.

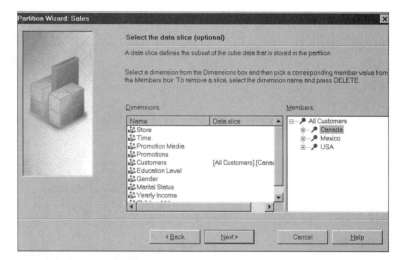

For example, if you wanted to partition the FoodMart cube by the Country level of the Customer dimension, you would create

1. One partition where you choose the USA member in the Customer dimension

2. A second partition where you choose Mexico

3. A third dimension where you choose Canada

You can slice your partition by more than one dimension, but if you do, you have to ensure that all the different combinations of members from dimensions are included in one partition. If you leave out any slices of the data, your cube will not return valid information.

Caution

The Microsoft product documentation is full of warnings when it discusses partitioning. The OLAP Manager is not going to ensure that you have sliced up your cube properly into dimensions. You have to figure that out for yourself. If you include any of the same slices twice, then your cube aggregates are going to be incorrect on the high side. If you leave out any of the slices, then your aggregates will be incorrect on the low side.

It's also possible to create partitions that accurately slice up the data, but then to leave the default partition, which includes all the data. The result is that all the cube values are exactly twice what they should be.

You can run into a similar problem when you use an incremental update. If you use an incremental update without specifying any criteria, all the data that was previously in the cube will be doubled.

The best policy is to keep partition slicing as simple and straightforward as possible. If you have one partition for each of three countries, you won't have a problem when those partitions are viewed together as a cube.

And remember—you are responsible for seeing that all the slices properly fit together. For now, at least, there aren't any warning boxes to tell you there might be a problem.

The final screen of the Partition Wizard, shown in Figure 17.3, allows you to make some aggregation and processing decisions.

FIGURE 17.3

You have a variety of aggregation and processing decisions to make in the Partition Wizard.

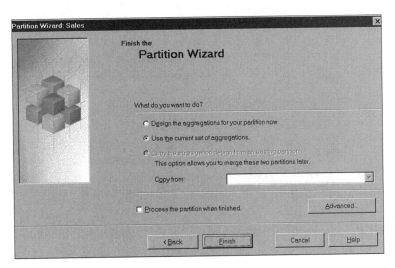

There are three choices you can make for your aggregations:

- Design the aggregations for your partition now. This choice opens the Storage Design Wizard at the conclusion of the Partition Wizard.
- Use the current set of aggregations.
- Copy the aggregations designed for an existing partition. Choose this option if you are planning to merge your partitions back together in the future. Partitions cannot be merged unless they have identical aggregations.

There is a check box for choosing whether or not to process the partition when the wizard is finished. After you make the aggregate decisions, you can proceed to the Advanced Settings by clicking the Advanced button.

The Advanced Settings dialog is shown in Figure 17.4.

FIGURE 17.4

The Partition Wizard's Advanced Settings give you two additional choices for your partitions.

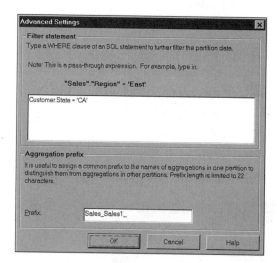

You can make two additional choices for your partition in this dialog:

- A WHERE clause to provide additional partitioning for your data.
- A prefix to be assigned to the aggregations created for this partition.

A reasonable default prefix for the aggregations is provided.

The use of a WHERE clause to partition the data is useful in situations where the desired partitioning cannot be accomplished by choosing members of the various dimensions. Here's an example where you would have to do that: If you had 30 members in the Country level and you wanted to include 10 of them in the first partition, 5 in the second partition, and 15 in the third partition. You can't pick more than one member for a dimension on the wizard's second screen, but you can do it here by writing a set of WHERE clauses for the different partitions. Each one would look like this:

```
Customer.Country IN(""France", "Germany", "Spain", "Portugal", "Italy")
```

> **Note**
>
> You could, in fact, do all of your partition slicing with filters in this Advanced Settings dialog and not use the dimension and member choices on the second screen of the wizard at all. I would not recommend that policy. The slicing on the second tab is more straightforward and less likely to result in partition errors.

Merging Cube Partitions

When you have a cube with more than one partition, you can merge one of the partitions out of existence by right clicking it and selecting Merge. The Merge Partitions dialog will ask you which partition you want to merge into. After choosing the second partition and pushing the Merge button, the newly merged partition is processed. When the processing is completed, you will no longer see the original partition.

> **Note**
>
> You will not be able to merge cube partitions unless they have the same storage type (MOLAP, ROLAP, or HOLAP) and the identical aggregations. If your partitions don't match now, you can edit one of them, choose copy aggregation design on the third tab, and process those aggregations. Then you will be able to merge the two partitions.

Using Partitions to Enhance Performance

You can improve performance by using partitions because they allow you to divide your processing over many machines.

You also improve performance because you are able to make some slices of a cube's data MOLAP, while leaving other portions HOLAP or ROLAP.

MOLAP provides the quickest OLAP browsing response time. The problem with MOLAP is that it also takes up more disk space, because all the data is copied from the source into the multidimensional data structure.

If you have a large cube, but only a portion of the cube is frequently used for browsing, you have a good candidate for partitioning with different storage types. The portion of the cube that is browsed frequently (the current month, perhaps) could be stored with MOLAP, so that browsing would be very quick. The rest of the cube could be stored with HOLAP, so that all the data wouldn't have to be copied and stored on the disk. Queries issued against the lowest level of the older data might not be as fast, but that wouldn't be so important, because the older data is not often used.

You can also create different partitions with different levels of aggregation. You can give the most frequently used data the best possible performance, while not wasting time and disk space to create aggregations that are going to be used only infrequently.

Write-Enabling a Cube

When you write-enable a cube, you are able to change the cube's data. Write-enabled cubes are primarily used for "what if" analysis, in questions like this:

- If sales for this particular product were changed for this particular location, how would that affect the overall sales for the company?

- If we can make 10% of the new residents in the community into customers, how will that affect our total sales?

You write-enable a cube by selecting the cube in the OLAP Manager tree and picking Write-Enable from the Action menu or the popup menu. The Write Enable dialog is shown in Figure 17.5.

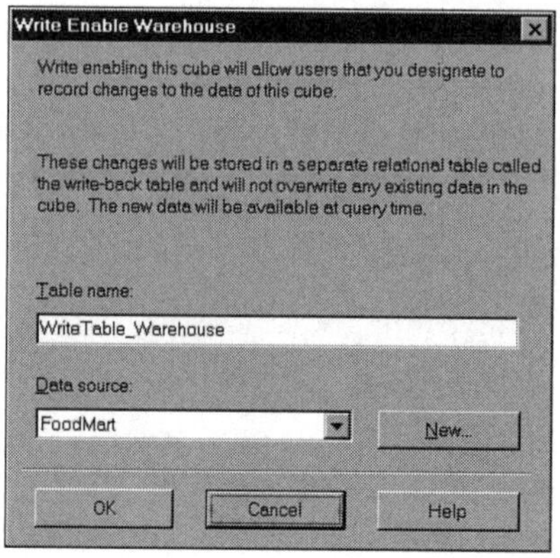

FIGURE 17.5

You specify the name and the location of the write-back table when you write-enable a cube.

Write-enabling is implemented in a cube with a special table called the write-back table, which stores all the differences between the values in the cube and the new data that has been entered. A default name is provided for this table in the dialog, but you can change it. You are also allowed to change the data source, which will be used to store the write-back table.

Here are the rules regarding write-enabled cubes:

- Only users who have been given Read/Write permission in the cube are able to write data (see "Managing OLAP Services Security" later in the chapter).
- Changes can be written to the data only at the lowest level. You can't change aggregated values, because it would be impossible to decide how those changes should be implemented at the non-aggregated level.

You cannot write to a write-enabled cube from within the OLAP Manager. You have to use a client application that supports the write-back capability.

Browsing Write-Back Data

To view the data in the write-back table, select the cube and choose Write-Back Options, Browse Write-Back Data from the Action menu, or right-click the cube and select Write-Back Options, Browse Write-Back Data from the popup menu.

When a write-enabled cube is browsed, the users see the data as it has been modified. OLAP Services combines the data from the cube and the data from the write-back table into a single updated presentation of the data.

Converting Write-Back Data into a Partition

If you have the Enterprise Edition of SQL Server installed, you can convert the information in the write-back into a separate partition which can then be permanently merged with the rest of the cube. The cube that results from this merge is read-only. You do this conversion by choosing the cube and picking the following options from the Action menu or by right clicking on the cube and choosing Write-Back Options, Convert to Partition.

Deleting a Write-Back Partition

You can delete all the changes in the write-back table. If you do that, the results from browsing the cube return to what they were before any data modifications were made. This option is chosen by selecting the cube and picking the following options from the Action menu or by right clicking on the cube and choosing Write-Back Options, Delete Data.

17

PARTITIONS AND OLAP SERVER

Managing OLAP Services Security

You can use three levels of access control when you give users permission to use OLAP database and cube objects—Read, Read/Write, and Admin. You can map Windows NT user accounts and groups to permissions in particular OLAP databases by using Roles. Service Pack 1 for SQL Server 7.0 provides a finer degree of access control with cell-level security.

The Read Level of Access Control

Users with Read access can browse data and data structures. They cannot write to write-enabled cubes, process cubes, or modify the structure of cubes.

Read is the default level of access assigned to a Role in the OLAP Manager.

The Read/Write Level of Access Control

The Read/Write level gives permission to write to write-enabled cubes. Users with Read/Write access cannot process cubes or modify cube structures.

When managing Roles with the OLAP Manager, you have the option of assigning Read/Write access control.

The Admin Level of Access Control

A user with Admin access can use the OLAP Manager interface, process cubes, and modify the structure of cubes.

This level of access cannot be assigned in the OLAP Manager. The OLAP Services installation program creates a Windows NT group called OLAP Administrators which is given this level of access. The user who installed OLAP Services is automatically added to this group. Other users can be added through the Windows NT User Manager.

Roles

Roles are used to connect particular Windows NT users and groups to particular privileges in OLAP Databases. Roles are managed on the OLAP database level. You create a Role in a database and map whatever Windows NT users and groups you want to that Role. Then you assign either Read or Read/Write access to that role for particular cubes within the database.

> **Note**
>
> You cannot use roles to assign the Admin access level. Admin level access is assigned to members of the Windows NT OLAP Administrators group. Being mapped to a particular role has no effect on whether or not a user has Admin access.

Cell-Level Security with SP1

Service Pack 1 (SP1) for SQL Server 7.0, publicly released in June 1999, adds the ability to set up cell-level security for cubes.

In the initial release of SQL Server 7.0, security could only be set on a whole-cube basis. Either a role was given Read or Read/Write access to the whole cube, or it received no access at all. The only way to limit a user's access to specific dimensions of a cube was to create a virtual cube that did not include those particular dimensions. Users could be given access to the virtual cube, but not to the underlying cube. They could not access the prohibited dimensions because those dimensions did not exist in the virtual cube they were using.

With the cell-level security of SP1, you can now use MDX statements to specify which dimensions a particular role can access. It's called cell-level security because you could actually decide to give access to one particular cell and to prevent access to another particular cell. More typically, though, access would be given or withheld for particular dimensions or sets of filtered data.

With SP1, the only way to administer cell-level security is through MDX statements, although Microsoft has suggested that cell-level security is a good candidate for a future OLAP Manager add-in.

Using Add-Ins with the OLAP Manager

Add-ins are additional OLAP Services programs that are integrated into the OLAP Manager. They can be created by Microsoft or by a third-party vendor. Add-ins are managed on the Add-ins tab of the OLAP Server's Properties dialog, as shown in Figure 17.6. Access this dialog by selecting the OLAP Server and choosing Properties from the Action menu or the pop-up menu.

FIGURE 17.6

You can manage add-ins in the OLAP Server's Properties dialog.

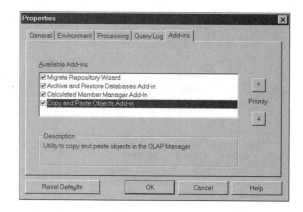

Add-ins are included in the list when their installation programs have registered them. You cannot register an add-in directly from the OLAP Manager.

You choose whether or not to activate an add-in by clicking the check box that appears beside it. A new selection becomes active as soon as the OLAP Manager is stopped and restarted. You can also choose the order in which the add-ins will be loaded by increasing or decreasing their relative priority with the arrows on the right side of the tab.

After add-ins are included, the capabilities they provide are integrated into the existing OLAP Manager menus.

One add-in was shipped with the original release version of SQL Server 7.0. Microsoft made four additional add-ins available on its Web site in May 1999 with the Beta 2 releases of the Add-In Kit for OLAP Manager. These four add-ins are

- Migrate Repository Wizard—The original add-in. It allows you to move the repository used by OLAP to a different server and/or database.

- Archive and Restore Databases Add-In—Allows you to archive and restore OLAP database. Use this utility to transfer an OLAP database from one server to another—saving it on one and restoring it on the other.

- Calculated Member Manager Add-In—Allows you to include calculated members in virtual cubes.

- Copy and Paste Objects Add-In—Allows you to copy and paste cubes, dimensions, and other objects in the OLAP Manager tree.

> **Note**
>
> If you don't have the Archive and Restore Databases Add-In and the Copy and Paste Objects Add-In, take the time to find and install them. They make the task of administering OLAP Services a lot easier.

Other Properties of the OLAP Server

In addition to the Add-ins tab, the OLAP Server Properties dialog has four other tabs to use for viewing and changing properties. Access the dialog by selecting an OLAP Server and choosing Properties from the Action menu, or by right-clicking a server and picking Properties from the popup menu. You can also reset the default property settings by clicking the Reset Defaults button.

The General Tab

Here are the five properties you can set on the General tab (shown in Figure 17.7):

FIGURE 17.7

You can set a variety of miscellaneous properties on the General tab of the Properties dialog.

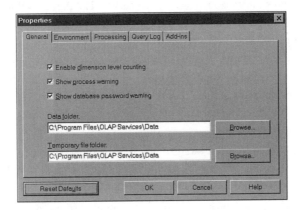

- Enable Dimension Level Counting—Enabled by default. It can be helpful to disable this automatic counting when you are working with dimensions that have a lot of records. The counting process can take a lot of time. If you disable this option, you also disable the warning that a lower level in the hierarchy has fewer members than the higher level.

- Show Process Warning—After a cube is modified, this warning message tells you that you will have to design storage options and process the cube before you can query it. The message is enabled by default, and can be disabled interactively. If you want it to be used again, you can choose it again here in the Properties dialog.

- Show Database Password Warning—Enabled by default. This property enables or disables the message box that warns the user that a password for a data source is being saved in an unencrypted format.

- Data Folder—You can change the folder where OLAP data is saved. If you do, all existing cubes will not be able to access their data unless you move that data to the new folder.

- Temporary File Folder—Changes the folder used by temporary files. If the data folder is changed, the temporary file folder is automatically changed to the same folder. But you can then change the temporary file folder to a different location.

The Environmental Tab

The Environmental tab allows you to set some properties that affect the performance of OLAP Services:

- Maximum Number of Threads—This property sets the number of OLAP Manager threads that can simultaneously access the server. The default value is two times the number of CPUs on the server computer. Valid values are 1 to 1000.

- Large Level Defined As—The number of members that are required before OLAP Services treats a level as a large level. OLAP Services treats small and large levels differently in processing. Small levels are completely sent to the client, even when the client does not request them. Large levels are only sent on request. The default value for the dividing line between small and large levels is 1000 members. Valid values are 1 to 10000.

- Minimum Allocated Memory—The amount of memory allocated exclusively to OLAP Services in megabytes. OLAP Services may use more than this amount of memory. The default is one-half of the server's memory.

- Memory Conservation Threshold—When the amount of memory in megabytes used by OLAP Services approaches this number, memory is conserved and used more efficiently. The default value is all of the server's memory.

The Processing Tab

These properties on the Processing tab also affect OLAP Services performance:

- Read-ahead Buffer Size—The maximum amount of data, in MB, that is placed into the memory each time the database is read. A higher value can improve performance, if the hardware can support it, because the number of times the disk is accessed is reduced. The default value is 4.

- Process Buffer Size—The amount of data, in megabytes, that is processed before an I/O is required. Higher values can improve performance because then there is less disk access. The default value is 4.

- OLE DB Timeout—Whether or not a global data source timeout is used. The default value is False.

- OLE DB Timeout Seconds—A timeout can be set for each data source. If both the global timeout is set and an individual data source timeout is set, the shorter of the two timeouts is used for that data source. The default value for this global timeout is 0, which means that the global timeout is disabled. Valid values are from 0 to 10000 seconds.

The Query Log Tab

The following three properties can be set on the Query Log tab:

- Enable/Disable Query Logging—The check box by the sample frequency enables or disables query logging. By default, query logging is enabled. If you disable query logging, you will not be able to create Usage Analysis reports or optimize aggregations based on usage.

- Sample Frequency—The frequency at which a query is recorded in the log. If this value is set to 1, every query is logged. If this value is set to 100, every 100th query is logged. If the setting is anything greater than 1, you will not get an accurate picture when you analyze usage. If you have one very long-running query, for example, that query might not even show up in the usage reports. If you set the value to a low number, though, you might hurt performance. The default value is 10.

- Clear Entire Log—Clears the entire query log.

Summary

Most of the functionality of OLAP Services is available in the OLAP Manager. And, with the ability to create add-ins, you can extend the OLAP Manager's capabilities.

The following chapters talk about programming the OLAP Server and the OLAP Client. The chapters that provide more information about the OLAP Manager include:

- Chapter 19—Developing an add-in program for OLAP Manager
- Chapters 27–30—Using MDX statements
- Chapters 31–34—Managing a data warehousing system

Programming the OLAP Server

PART
IV

Decision Support Objects

by Tim Peterson

The Decision Support Objects (DSO) object model provides programmatic access to the capabilities of OLAP Services. All of the functionality that is available in the OLAP Manager, except for browsing cube data, is provided through DSO objects. This chapter shows you how to use DSO to read and change that same information in your own programs.

This chapter includes the code for two utilities that partially automate tasks normally done with the OLAP Manager. The OLAPUnleashedAggDesigner automates the process of designing cube aggregations. The OLAPUnleashedStarToCube utility can be used to automatically generate an OLAP cube from a SQL Server 7.0 star schema database. These applications are on the book's CD-ROM.

Most of the shorter code samples in this chapter are included in a Visual Basic project called DSOTesting. This application is also on the book's CD-ROM.

OLAP Server Programming

There are three main tools that you can use for OLAP server programming:

- The Decision Support Objects (DSO) Object Model for controlling multidimensional structures programmatically. DSO does not provide access to the multidimensional data.

- The IOlapAddIn interface for customizing the OLAP Manager user interface, as discussed in Chapter 19, "Developing an Add-In Program for OLAP Services."

- The PivotTable Service, which provides client access to multidimensional data. The PivotTable Service is covered in Chapter 20.

Figure 18.1 shows how these three tools work with the other components of OLAP Services.

Here is how the pieces of OLAP Services fit together:

- The OLAP server creates and manages the multidimensional structures.

- The OLAP server uses a repository to record information about the multidimensional structures that have been created. This repository is stored in a relational database.

- The OLAP Manager uses DSO to present a graphical user interface for viewing and manipulating multidimensional structures.

- You can enhance the OLAP Manager with Custom Add-In programs that implement the IOlapAddIn interface.

- You can replace the OLAP Manager with a custom application written with DSO.

- You have access to multidimensional data through the PivotTable Service. The OLAP Manager uses ADO MD for its access to cube data.

- You can use the OLAP Extensions for OLE DB to access this multidimensional data.

- For easier object-oriented data access you can use ADO with the Multidimensional Extensions, which are built on top of OLE DB.

- The data and aggregations used in OLAP server cubes can be stored in a relational database or in a multidimensional store created by the OLAP server.

- Besides providing access to OLAP server cubes, you can use the PivotTable Service to create and access cubes stored as *.cub files.

FIGURE 18.1

The components of OLAP Services give you access to both the OLAP structures and the OLAP data.

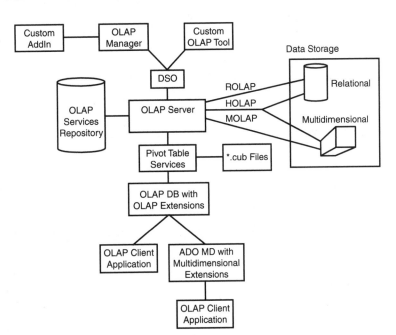

Objects and Interfaces in the DSO Object Model

The OLAP Manager, Figure 18.2, provides a simplified view of the DSO Object Model. Each server has a collection of databases. Each database has collections of cubes, dimensions, data sources, and roles. A virtual cube has a collection of cubes. Cubes have collections of dimensions, data sources, partitions, roles, and measures.

FIGURE 18.2

The OLAP Manager's console tree shows many of the DSO Objects.

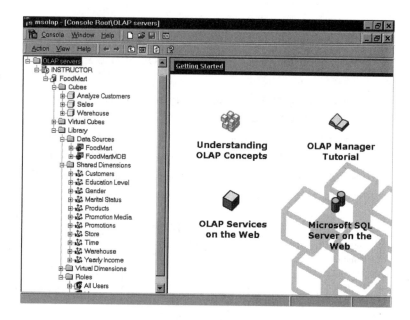

The most important thing to understand in the actual implementation of the DSO Object Model is the distinction between objects that can be referenced directly and those that must be referenced through a DSO Interface. You can use a direct reference when working with these five objects:

- Server—A reference to an OLAP server.
- DataSource—A reference to an external database that is used as the source for the OLAP data
- MemberProperty—An attribute of a level of a dimension, which is used as the basis for a virtual dimension.
- PartitionAnalyzer—A tool for creating aggregations.
- CubeAnalyzer—A tool for analyzing the query log.

Each of these five objects has a section in this chapter.

All other objects, including databases and cubes, must be accessed through one of the six DSO interfaces. When using DSO in Visual Basic programming, these interfaces appear as if they were objects. The six DSO interfaces are

- MDStore—The most important interface, which is implemented by four of the central objects in the DSO hierarchy: Database, Cube, Partition, and Aggregation. Note how the other five interfaces all contain collections of objects that are associated with two or more of these MDStore objects.

- Dimension—Implemented by DatabaseDimension, CubeDimension, PartitionDimension, and AggregationDimension.

- Measure—Implemented by CubeMeasure, PartitionMeasure, and AggregationMeasure.

- Level—Implemented by DatabaseLevel, CubeLevel, PartitionLevel, and AggregationLevel.

- Role—Implemented by DatabaseRole and CubeRole.

- Command—Implemented by DatabaseCommand and CubeCommand.

Each of these interfaces also has a section in this chapter.

> **Caution**
>
> When I first started using the DSO Object Model, I made the mistake of declaring Database and Cube objects directly. It seemed like the obvious thing to do. If you use the Auto List Members option in the VB code editor while you're declaring a DSO variable, both the DSO objects and the DSO interfaces appear in the list of choices. It makes a lot more sense to declare database and cube variables as DSO.Database and DSO.Cube, rather than declaring both as DSO.MDStore.
>
> But the product documentation is correct when it states that you must use the interfaces when programming with these objects. When the Database and Cube objects are referenced directly, they do not have the methods and collections that are needed to build multidimensional structures.
>
> The main problem with this system of using interfaces is that you have to keep track of the different rules that apply to each of the objects that are referenced by the same interface. Different methods, properties, collections, and enumeration values are available to different objects, even though they are all accessed through the same interface. Some of these differences are listed in the product documentation and I have outlined many of the differences in this chapter. I have found, though, that I have to be very careful to check my code to see that it is valid for the particular object I am using.

18

DECISION SUPPORT OBJECTS

The Server Object

The Server is the highest-level object in the DSO hierarchy. You have to use the Server object to establish a connection to an OLAP server. You can also use the Server object to start and stop the OLAP server service, retrieve information about the server, and manage other DSO objects.

Collections of the Server Object

The Server object has two collections—MDStores and CustomProperties. The MDStores collection contains Database objects. The CustomProperties collection contains user-defined properties. The objects used in these two collections are discussed in "The MDStore Interface—Databases, Cubes, Partitions, and Aggregations" and "The Property Object and the CustomProperties Collection" sections later in this chapter.

Connecting to an OLAP Server

You connect to an OLAP server by creating a DSO.Server object variable and using the Server object's Connect method. When you connect to a server, you can refer to the server by name or, if the OLAP server is running on your local machine, you can refer to the OLAP server as "LocalHost".

```
Dim dsoServer As New DSO.Server
dsoServer.Connect ("LocalHost")
```

If you attempt to connect to an OLAP server when the server service is not running, an error will be generated by the Connect method. When this happens you will, though, have a valid reference to the Server object. You can use this reference to start the server.

There are two ways you can disconnect from an OLAP server. You can use the CloseServer method of the Server object or you can set the server's object variable to Nothing.

```
dsoServer.CloseServer
```

or

```
Set dsoServer = Nothing
```

> **Caution**
>
> Use the CloseServer method carefully. I have seen my application immediately terminate without an error being generated when I have used the CloseServer method on a Server object variable that did not have a valid reference.

Starting and Stopping the OLAP Server

The ServiceState property of the Server object can be used to start, stop, and pause the OLAP server service. You can also use this property to query the current state of the server service.

You control the OLAP server by assigning one of the three service control constants. You must add the declaration for these constants to your program.

```
'OLAP server service control Public Constants
Public Const OLAP_SERVICE_RUNNING = &H4
Public Const OLAP_SERVICE_PAUSED = &H7
Public Const OLAP_SERVICE_STOP = &H1

Private Sub cmdStartServer_Click()
  dsoServer.ServiceState = OLAP_SERVICE_RUNNING
End Sub

Private Sub cmdStopServer_Click()
  dsoServer.ServiceState = OLAP_SERVICE_STOP
End Sub

Private Sub cmdPauseServer_Click()
  dsoServer.ServiceState = OLAP_SERVICE_PAUSED
End Sub
```

You use the same property to check the current state of the OLAP server service.

```
'OLAP server status Public Constants
Public Const SERVICE_CONTINUE_PENDING = &H5
Public Const SERVICE_PAUSE_PENDING = &H6
Public Const SERVICE_PAUSED = &H7
Public Const SERVICE_RUNNING = &H4
Public Const SERVICE_START_PENDING = &H2
Public Const SERVICE_STOP_PENDING = &H3
Public Const SERVICE_STOPPED = &H1

Private Sub cmdServiceStateProperty_Click()

Select Case dsoServer.ServiceState
  Case SERVICE_CONTINUE_PENDING
    MsgBox "Service Continue Pending"
  Case SERVICE_PAUSE_PENDING
    MsgBox "Service Pause Pending"
  Case SERVICE_PAUSED
    MsgBox "Service Paused"
  Case SERVICE_RUNNING
    MsgBox "Service Running"
  Case SERVICE_START_PENDING
    MsgBox "Service Start Pending"
  Case SERVICE_STOP_PENDING
    MsgBox "Service Stop Pending"
  Case SERVICE_STOPPED
    MsgBox "Service Stopped"
End Select

End Sub
```

18

DECISION
SUPPORT
OBJECTS

You can use the ServiceState property for a local OLAP server even when you haven't set the server's object variable. Listing 18.1 shows code you would use if you want to be connected to a local server and don't know if you are connected or whether or not the server is running.

 Listing 18.1 is on the CD-ROM for this book. You can find it in the DSOTesting Visual Basic project.

LISTING 18.1   Checking Connection to Server

```
Public Function fctLocalServerConnect(dsoServerToConnect As dso.Server) _
    As Boolean
Dim sTest As String
Dim bReturn As Boolean
Dim dsoServerLocal As New dso.Server
Dim lAttempt As Long

For lAttempt = 1 To 5

  lAttempt = lAttempt + 1
  bReturn = fctCheckStatusAndStart(dsoServerLocal)

  If bReturn = True Then
    Exit For
  End If

Next lAttempt

On Error Resume Next
sTest = dsoServerToConnect.Name
On Error GoTo ProcErr

'If there's no name, there's no connection
If sTest = "" Then
  dsoServerToConnect.Connect ("localhost")
End If

'If the status is unknown, connect without naming
If bReturn = True And dsoServerToConnect.State = stateUnknown Then
  dsoServerToConnect.Connect
End If

fctLocalServerConnect = True

ProcExit:
  Exit Function
ProcErr:
  MsgBox Err.Number & " - " & Err.Description
  fctLocalServerConnect = False
  GoTo ProcExit
```

```
End Function

Private Function fctCheckStatusAndStart( _
    dsoServerLocal As dso.Server) As Boolean

Select Case dsoServerLocal.ServiceState

  Case SERVICE_RUNNING
    fctCheckStatusAndStart = True
  Case SERVICE_CONTINUE_PENDING, SERVICE_START_PENDING
    subWait
    fctCheckStatusAndStart = False
  Case SERVICE_PAUSED, SERVICE_STOPPED
    dsoServerLocal.ServiceState = OLAP_SERVICE_RUNNING
    subWait
    fctCheckStatusAndStart = False
  Case SERVICE_PAUSE_PENDING, SERVICE_STOP_PENDING
    subWait
    fctCheckStatusAndStart = False

End Select

End Function

Private Sub subWait()
Dim dtFinished

dtFinished = DateAdd("s", 1, Now)
Do While dtFinished> Now
  DoEvents
Loop

End Sub
```

Properties of the Server Object

Listing 18.2 displays all the information that can be retrieved by using the Server object's properties.

 Listing 18.2 is on the CD-ROM for this book. You can find it in the DSOTesting Visual Basic project.

LISTING 18.2   Using Server Object Properties to Retrieve Information

```
Dim dsoServer As New DSO.Server
dsoServer.Connect ("LocalHost")

Dim msg As String
```

continues

18

DECISION
SUPPORT
OBJECTS

LISTING 18.2 continued

```
msg = "Property "   & vbTab & vbTab & "Description " & vbTab    & vbTab & _
            "Value"                               & vbCrLf & vbCrLf & _
        "Name "        & vbTab & vbTab & "Name of OLAP Server "   & vbTab & _
            dsoServer.Name                                        & vbCrLf & _
        "Description "          & vbTab & "Server Description "    & vbTab & _
            dsoServer.Description                                 & vbCrLf & _
        "Edition "   & vbTab & vbTab & "OLAP Services Edition "    & vbTab & _
            dsoServer.Edition                                     & vbCrLf & _
        "ClassType " & vbTab & "Should be 1 (clsServer) "         & vbTab & _
            dsoServer.ClassType                                   & vbCrLf & _
        "IsValid "     & vbTab & vbTab & "Server has valid name "  & vbTab & _
            dsoServer.IsValid                                     & vbCrLf & _
        "LockTimeOut "           & vbTab & "Lock request time out " & vbTab & _
            dsoServer.LockTimeout                                 & vbCrLf & _
        "Timeout "     & vbTab & vbTab & "Processing time out     " & vbTab & _
            dsoServer.Timeout                                     & vbCrLf & _
        "State "       & vbTab & vbTab & "State of the connection " & vbTab & _
            dsoServer.State                                       & vbCrLf & _
        "ServiceState "          & vbTab & "State of server service " & vbTab & _
            dsoServer.ServiceState

MsgBox msg, , "Properties of the OLAP Server"
```

Creating Objects with the Server's `CreateObject` Method

You can use the `CreateObject` method to create new instances of any of the objects in the DSO hierarchy. It is usually easier, however, to create DSO objects by using the `AddNew` method of the particular collection in which you want to create the new object. Here's an example of creating two new databases, using each of the methods:

```
Dim dsoDatabase As MDStore

Set dsoDatabase = dsoServer.CreateObject(clsDatabase)
dsoDatabase.Name = "CreateTestDB1"
dsoServer.MDStores.Add dsoDatabase

Set dsoDatabase = dsoServer.MDStores.AddNew("CreateTestDB2")
```

Managing Object Definitions with `Refresh` and `Update`

The `Refresh` method modifies the objects being used by an application to match the current object definitions in the OLAP repository. If any of the objects have been changed by other applications, the `Refresh` method applies those changes to the objects that you are currently using.

The Update method does the opposite of the Refresh method, updating the OLAP repository to reflect any changes that your application has made to OLAP objects. If you modify the properties of an object, but don't use the Update method, your changes will disappear when you close your application. Your changes will never be stored in the repository.

Using the Locking Methods

The LockObject method prevents conflicts between different users who are trying to use or modify the same object. LockObject can use four types of locks, which are listed in the OlapLockTypes enumeration. These lock types, from least restrictive to most restrictive, are

- olapLockRead—No application can change the object's definition until this lock is released. Other applications can read the object's definition and obtain other locks, except for a Write lock.

- olapLockExtendedRead—No application can change or process the object until this lock is released. Other applications can read the object's definition and obtain their own Read or ExtendedRead locks while this lock is in effect.

- olapLockProcess—This lock is used before an object is processed. It prevents all other locks except the Read lock from being obtained.

- olapLockWrite—This lock is used before updating an object's definition in the repository. A Write lock cannot be obtained until all other locks have been released. No other locks can be obtained while a Write lock is in effect.

The product documentation states that you can use the LockObject method with the Server object to lock any of the lockable objects within the server. My experience indicates that is not true. You can only lock the Server object when using the LockObject method. If you want to lock any other specific object, you must use the LockObject method for that particular object.

The product documentation specifies that you use three parameters when you use the Server's LockObject method—the object you are locking, the type of lock, and a string description of the lock. This code, though, does not work:

```
dsoServer.LockObject dsoDatabase, olaplockProcess, "Does Not Work"
```

The following code does work, with the first line locking the server and the second line locking the database:

```
dsoServer.LockObject olaplockProcess, "A Server Lock"
dsoDatabase.LockObject olaplockProcess, "A Database Lock"
```

The UnlockObject method removes a lock that you have applied to one particular object. The UnlockAllObjects method removes all the locks that have been issued by your session. Note that UnlockAllObjects returns a Boolean variable indicating the success or failure of the method.

```
dsoServer.UnlockObject
bReturn = dsoServer.UnlockAllObjects
```

The MDStore Interface— Databases, Cubes, Partitions, and Aggregations

The four objects that store multidimensional data must be referenced through the MDStore interface. These objects are databases, cubes, partitions, and aggregations. Each of these objects is contained in MDStores collections on the next higher level of the hierarchy, as shown in Figure 18.3. The aggregation object does not have an MDStores collection because it is at the bottom of the hierarchy.

FIGURE 18.3

All the objects that store multidimensional data are contained in MDStores *collections.*

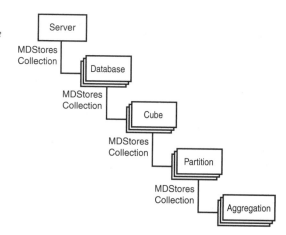

The four MDStore objects have collections, properties, and methods that partially overlap one another. Aggregation objects have the least in common with the others. They are rarely referenced in code and cannot be viewed directly in the OLAP Manager.

Each of the seven collections used by MDStore objects is discussed in its own section in this chapter. Five of these collections—MDStores, Dimensions, Measures, Roles, and Commands—contain objects referenced through one of the interfaces. The other two collections—DataSources and CustomProperties—contain objects that are referenced directly.

Declaring and Setting MDStore Objects

Object variables of the clsDatabase, clsCube, clsPartition, and clsAggregation class type must always be declared as MDStore object variables. These object variables are not assigned to their particular class until they are set to an object that is part of the appropriate collection. In the following example, three MDStore object variables are declared. They are then used to create a new database, cube, and partition on the server. The On Error Resume Next command is used to ignore the error that the AddNew method will generate if these objects already exist. The aggregation object is not included in this example, because aggregations are normally created internally. The creation of aggregations is discussed in "The PartitionAnalyzer Object" section later in this chapter.

```
Dim dsoDatabase As dso.MDStore
Dim dsoCube As dso.MDStore
Dim dsoPartition As dso.MDStore

On Error Resume Next
Set dsoDatabase = dsoServer.MDStores.AddNew("NewDatabase")
Set dsoCube = dsoDatabase.MDStores.AddNew("NewCube")
Set dsoPartition = dsoCube.MDStores.AddNew("NewPartition")
```

If the objects already exist, the object variables can be set to the appropriate member of the collection.

```
Dim dsoDatabase As dso.MDStore
Dim dsoCube As dso.MDStore
Dim dsoPartition As dso.MDStore

Set dsoDatabase = dsoServer.MDStores("NewDatabase")
Set dsoCube = dsoDatabase.MDStores("NewCube")
Set dsoPartition = dsoCube.MDStores("NewPartition")
```

After the objects have been set, the following code can be used to check the class types of the objects. This code calls the fctDSOClassType function, which receives a DSO object variable and returns the appropriate class type. A portion of this function is shown here. You can find the complete function in the Utilities module of the DSOTesting application on the CD-ROM.

```
MsgBox "Class type for dsoDatabase is " & fctDSOClassType(dsoDatabase)
MsgBox "Class type for dsoCube is " & fctDSOClassType(dsoCube)
MsgBox "Class type for dsoPartition is " & fctDSOClassType(dsoPartition)

Public Function fctDSOClassType(obj As Object) As String
Select Case obj.ClassType
  Case clsServer
    fctDSOClassType = "clsServer"
  Case clsDatabase
    fctDSOClassType = "clsDatabase"
```

18

DECISION
SUPPORT
OBJECTS

```
Case clsCube
    fctDSOClassType = "clsCube"
  Case clsPartition
    fctDSOClassType = "clsPartition"
End Select
End Function
```

The Database Object

An OLAP database is a container for multidimensional objects. If you are using common dimensions and common data sources for a set of cubes, it is more efficient to put those objects together into a single database.

The database object contains all the collections in the MDStore interface, except for Measures, which are implemented at the cube level and lower. I usually think of an OLAP database as a collection of cubes but it is also a collection of dimensions, data sources, roles, commands, and properties, as shown in Figure 18.4. The diagram shows both the interface and the class name for each object.

FIGURE 18.4

Collections of the Database object.

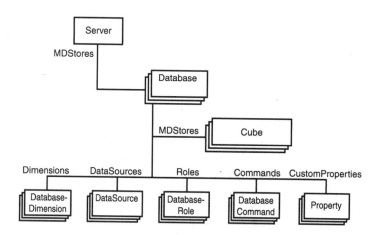

The Cube Object

The Cube object is the second highest level of the MDStore hierarchy. Cubes are at the heart of a multidimensional system. They are the primary objects that people use to view multidimensional data.

There are two types of the Cube object—regular and virtual. These types are distinguished by the SubClassType property of the Cube object. All other MDStore objects have only one value for this property—sbclsRegular. For cube objects, the SubClassType property can be set to either sbclsRegular or sbclsVirtual.

The object hierarchy for a Cube object with a `SubClassType` of Regular is shown in Figure 18.5. Regular cubes have all the collections used in MDStore objects—`MDStores`, `Dimensions`, `Measures`, `DataSources`, `Roles`, `Commands`, and `CustomProperties`.

FIGURE 18.5

Regular cubes contain all the collections of the MDStore interface.

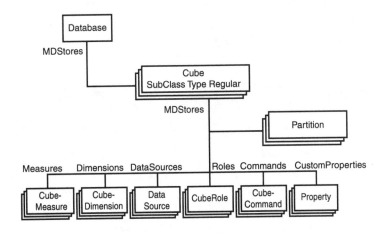

The slightly different hierarchy of virtual cubes is shown in Figure 18.6. Virtual cubes lack the `DataSources` collection of regular cubes. Their `MDStores` collection contains regular cubes instead of partitions.

FIGURE 18.6

When you use virtual cubes, you add an extra level to the MDStore hierarchy.

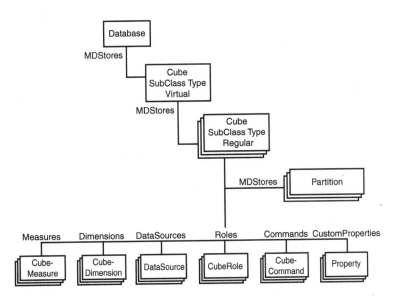

When you create a cube, it is assigned a default SubClassType of `sbclsRegular`. If you want to create a virtual cube, you can specify that subclass when you add the new cube to the database's `MDStores` collection. The following code creates a new virtual cube in the FoodMart sample database. All the dimensions and measures used in a virtual cube must exist in one of the cubes included in the virtual cube's `MDStores` collection.

```
Dim dsoCubeVirtual As DSO.MDStore
Set dsoCubeVirtual = dsoDatabase.MDStores.AddNew("NewVirtualCube", sbclsVirtual)
```

Note

I have not been able to successfully build the `Dimensions`, `Measures`, and `MDStores` collections of a virtual cube using DSO code. I have been able to add dimensions and measures to existing cubes as long as I use objects from cubes that are already included in the virtual cube. The following code adds a new dimension to the virtual cube in the FoodMart sample database:

```
dsoCubVirWarehouseAndSales.Dimensions.AddNew("ChildrenAtHome")
```

I have had a problem adding dimensions and measures from a cube that is not already in the virtual cube's `MDStores` collection. The dimensions and measures have been successfully added to the virtual cube, but I have not been able to add the new cube to the `MDStores` collection. The virtual cube's structure is invalid and it is unusable until edited with the OLAP Manager.

The Partition Object

The `MDStores` collection of a regular Cube object contains Partition objects. Each cube contains a default partition. Multiple partitions are primarily used in situations where a cube has large amounts of data.

The object hierarchy for the Partition object is shown in Figure 18.7. Partitions do not have two of the `MDStores` collections—`Roles` and `Commands`. Two of the other collections, `Measures` and `Dimensions`, are read-only. The Partition object inherits these collections from the Cube object.

The Aggregation Object

The Aggregation object is at the bottom of the MDStore hierarchy. An Aggregation object contains aggregations for a particular set of members of a cube's dimensions. Aggregations are not displayed in the OLAP Manager interface.

FIGURE 18.7
The Partition object is a member of the Cube object's MDStores *collection.*

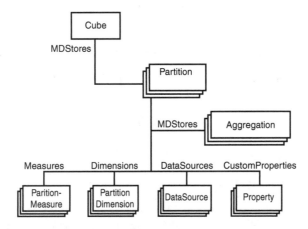

Only one of the MDStore methods is implemented by the Aggregation object—the Clone method. Only the CustomProperties collection is read/write. The Dimensions, Measures, and DataSource collections are inherited from the parent objects and are read-only.

The use of Aggregation objects is discussed in "The PartitionAnalyzer Object" section later in this chapter. The naming of Aggregation objects is discussed in the following section.

The AggregationPrefix Property and the Naming of Aggregation Objects

The AggregationPrefix property values for the Database, Cube, and Partition objects are used in the automatic generation of Aggregation object names. An Aggregation object's name has four parts:

- The Database Prefix—Used only if the Cube Prefix begins with "+".
- The Cube Prefix—Used only if the Partition Prefix begins with "+".
- The Partition Prefix—Always used in the Aggregation object's name.
- The AggregationID—A numeric value that indicates which levels of each dimension are used in this particular Aggregation object. It is always used in naming an Aggregation object.

Here is an example that uses all the prefixes:

| Database Prefix | "FoodMart" |
| Cube Prefix | "+Sales" |

Partition Prefix	"+1997"
AggregationID	214
Generated Aggregation Name	"FoodMart_Sales_1997_214"

With the "+" signs omitted, the database and cube prefixes are ignored:

Database Prefix	"FoodMart"
Cube Prefix	"Sales"
Partition Prefix	"1997"
AggregationID	214
Generated Aggregation Name	"1997_214"

An AggregationID of 214 indicates that the aggregations are being stored for the 2nd level of the first dimension of the cube, the 1st level of the second dimension, and the 4th level of the third dimension.

The Process Method of the MDStore Objects

The Process method populates multidimensional objects with data. The source data is read and aggregations are calculated. The aggregations are stored in the relational database for ROLAP cubes and in a multidimensional format for HOLAP and MOLAP cubes. In MOLAP cubes, the data also is stored in a multidimensional format.

Database, Cube, and Partition objects can all be processed. The Process method is also used for all the objects in the Dimension interface. When you process an object, dependent objects are also processed according to the following rules:

- Processing a database causes all cubes, partitions, and dimensions in the cube to be processed.

- Processing a cube causes all its partitions to be processed. All dimensions used by the cube will also be processed unless their State property is olapStateCurrent.

- Processing a virtual cube causes its constituent cubes to be processed unless their State property is olapStateCurrent.

The six constants in the ProcessType enumeration are used with the Process method. Two of them, processSuspend and processResume, are used to control access to a cube while it's being processed. Another one, processBuildStructure, creates the cube structure without putting any data into it. The other three constants fill the multidimensional objects with data:

- processFull—The object is fully rebuilt. The structure of the object is changed if necessary. All the data is removed and replaced with data from the data sources.

- processRefreshData—The object is not rebuilt. All the data is removed and replaced with new data.

- processDefault—OLAP Services decides which of the two types of processing is necessary. If possible, a data refresh is used. If the structure of the cube has been changed, a full process is done.

The following code fully processes a cube:

```
dsoCube.Process processFull
```

The Clone Method of the MDStore Objects

All of the MDStore objects implement the Clone method, which is used to copy multidimensional objects. This method can be used only between two objects that have the same class type. There are three options used by the Clone method:

- cloneMajorChildren—The default cloning method. This method is also the most comprehensive form of copying, with all properties, major children, and minor children being copied. The children of an object are the members of an object's collections.

- cloneMinorChildren—All properties and the minor children are copied. The minor children include all collections except for the members of the object's MDStores collection.

- cloneObjectProperties—Only the object's properties are copied to the other object.

The following code demonstrates the Clone method. Before the database is cloned, the databases have different descriptions. After the cloning, the descriptions are the same.

```
Dim dsoDatabase As dso.MDStore
Dim dsoDatabaseClone As dso.MDStore
Dim bResult As Boolean

On Error Resume Next
Set dsoDatabase = dsoServer.MDStores.AddNew("NewDatabase")
Set dsoDatabaseClone = dsoServer.MDStores.AddNew("DBClone")
On Error GoTo ProcErr

Set dsoDatabase = dsoServer.MDStores("NewDatabase")
Set dsoDatabaseClone = dsoServer.MDStores("DBClone")

dsoDatabase.Description = "Original Database"
dsoDatabaseClone.Description = "Cloned Database"

MsgBox dsoDatabase.Description & vbCrLf & dsoDatabaseClone.Description
dsoDatabase.Clone dsoDatabaseClone, cloneObjectProperties
MsgBox dsoDatabase.Description & vbCrLf & dsoDatabaseClone.Description
```

18

DECISION
SUPPORT
OBJECTS

The `Merge` Method of the Partition Object

The `Merge` method is used to join two partitions into one partition. This method is used only with the Partition object.

A cube is divided into partitions that contain different slices of data. If you want to merge two partitions, you have to change the target partition's slice so that it will contain all the data of both merging partitions.

For example, you could divide the Sales cube in the FoodMart database into separate partitions for different states. One partition would have the slice [Customers].[All Customers].[USA].[CA], the second would have [Customers].[All Customers].[USA].[WA], and the third would have [Customers].[All Customers].[USA].[OR]. If you wanted to merge two of the partitions you would first have to set the slice for the target partition to [Customers].[All Customers].[USA], so that the data from both of the partitions is allowed in the newly merged partition.

The syntax for the `Merge` method is as follows:

```
dsoPartitionTarget.Merge("NameOfSourcePartition")
```

> **Note**
>
> Creating and merging partitions is possible only if you have the Enterprise Edition of SQL Server installed.

Transaction Methods of the Database Objects

There are three MDStore methods that can be used only with Database objects. The `BeginTrans`, `CommitTrans`, and `Rollback` methods are used to control transactions for processing objects in a database. When these methods are not used, an implicit transaction is used for the processing of an object. By using these methods, you can group the processing of several database objects into a single transaction.

None of these three methods uses any parameters. The following code begins a transaction:

Other MDStore Methods

The `Update`, `LockObject`, and `UnlockObject` methods are implemented for MDStore objects in the same way as they are used with the Server object. They can be used with Database, Cube, and Partition objects. They are covered in "The Server Object" section of this chapter.

MDStore Properties Used for Defining the Data

Some of the most important properties of the MDStore objects are the four that are used to specify the data that is used to populate them:

- SourceTable—The table that is used for the MDStore's fact table. The SourceTable for the Sales Cube in the FoodMart database is "sales_fact_1997"

- SourceTableFilter—A string that specifies the filtering that is to be applied to the SourceTable when creating the fact table. This filter has the form of an SQL WHERE statement, without the word "WHERE". For the Sales Cube in FoodMart, the SourceTableFilter is an empty string. The following filter could be used in FoodMart to restrict the records in the fact table to items where the sales price is more than a dollar:

  "sales_fact_1997"."store_sales"> 1

- FromClause—A string that lists all the tables that are used for the fact table and for the dimension tables. The string is a comma-delimited list, with each table containing the proper string delimiter for the source database. Here is the FromClause in Sales:

  "sales_fact_1997", "product", "promotion", "store",

      "time_by_day", "customer"

- JoinClause—A string that contains all the join conditions for the fact table and dimension tables in an MDStore object. The separate conditions are joined together with AND. Normally, as the sample from Sales shows, the JoinClause specifies the connection between the foreign key values in the fact table and each of the primary keys of the dimension tables.

  ("sales_fact_1997"."product_id"="product"."product_id") AND
  ("sales_fact_1997"."promotion_id"="promotion"."promotion_id") AND
  ("sales_fact_1997"."store_id"="store"."store_id") AND
  ("sales_fact_1997"."time_id"="time_by_day"."time_id") AND
  ("sales_fact_1997"."customer_id"="customer"."customer_id")

The OlapMode Property

The OlapMode property determines whether an object is stored in the ROLAP, HOLAP, or MOLAP storage mode. The setting for this property in the Database object is the default setting for the Cube, the setting for the Cube is the default for the Partition, and the setting for the Partition is the default for the Aggregation.

There are three current settings for the OlapMode property and two more settings reserved for the future, as listed in the OlapStorageModes enumeration:

- olapmodeRolap—ROLAP storage.
- olapmodeHybridIndex—HOLAP storage.
- olapmodeMolapIndex—MOLAP storage.
- olapmodeAggsMolapIndex—Reserved for future use.
- olapmodeAggsRolap—Reserved for future use.

Properties Used in Determining Aggregation Strategy

There are three MDStore properties that are used to help create aggregations. One of these properties, the Analyzer property, specifies a tool that is used for creating aggregates. When used with a cube, the Analyzer property specifies the CubeAnalyzer. When used with a partition, this property specifies the PartitionAnalyzer. These tools are each described in a section later in this chapter.

The other two properties that are used in determining aggregation strategy are EstimatedRows and EstimatedSize. If you can set appropriate values for these properties, the OLAP server can be more effective in creating an aggregation strategy. EstimatedRows is the estimated number of rows in an MDStore object while EstimatedSize is the estimated number of bytes in all the rows of an object.

MDStore Properties for Tracking an Object's State

There are three MDStore properties that give information about an object's state. The LastProcessed property gives the most recent date and time that the MDStore object was processed. The LastUpdated property is never set by OLAP Services. You can use this property to store a date or time that has some use for your application.

The State property is used by OLAP Services to track whether or not an object has been processed since it was last changed. The State property is read-only and contains one of the types of the olapStateType enumeration:

- olapStateCurrent—The object has been processed since it was last changed.
- olapStateMemberPropertiesChanged—Member properties have been changed since the last processing.
- olapStateStructureChanged—The cube's structure has been changed.

- olapStateSourceMappingChanged—The mapping of the cube's structure to the underlying data has been changed.

- olapStateNeverProcessed—The object has not been processed since it was created.

The State property is used internally by OLAP Services when the Process method is used, to determine whether or not related objects are processed.

MDStore Properties That Identify an Object

The other MDStore properties all identify an object in some way:

- Name—A string containing the name of the object. Once an object has been created its name cannot be changed, unless it's a temporary object, as described next.

- IsTemporary—Objects are normally stored in the OLAP Repository as soon as they are created. If you want to create an object that will not be saved, you have to begin its name with a tilde (~). All child objects of a temporary object will also be temporary no matter how they are named.

  Temporary objects cannot be referenced from any other session other than the one in which they were created. Within their own session, temporary objects have the same characteristics as regular objects, except that their names can be changed.

  Temporary objects persist only until the end of the session in which they were created. If you want to save a temporary object, you can change its name, so that it no longer begins with a tilde. It will then become a permanent object and be stored in the Repository.

- Parent—An object variable containing the next highest object in the hierarchy.

- Server—A reference to the Server object.

- Description—A string giving a description of the object. It does not have to be used, but can be useful for providing user-friendly metadata.

- ClassType—One of the following values: clsDatabase, clsCube, clsPartition, or clsAggregation.

- SubClassType—Always sbclsRegular, except for virtual cubes, which have a SubClassType of sbclsVirtual.

- IsDefault—The Default object in a particular collection.

- IsReadWrite—Whether or not the object can be modified.

- IsValid—The structure of the particular object is valid.

The Dimension Interface

Dimensions are the perspectives from which a user can view the data in a cube.

The Dimension Interface is used to provide access to four DSO objects—`DatabaseDimension`, `CubeDimension`, `PartitionDimension`, and `AggregationDimension`. Each of these objects is used in the `Dimensions` collection of the corresponding MDStore object. All the different Dimension objects have two collections—`Levels` and `CustomProperties`. The object model for the `CubeDimension` and the `CubeLevel` objects is shown in Figure 18.8. The model is identical for the other Dimension and Level objects.

FIGURE 18.8

All four Dimension and Level object hierarchies are identical to the one shown here for cubes.

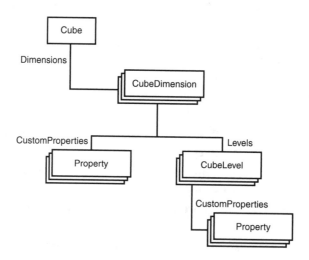

Shared and Private Dimensions

Dimensions can be either shared or private. A shared dimension can be used by all the cubes in a database, while a private dimension can only be used by a single cube. The ability to share dimensions between cubes is an important aspect in building a flexible multidimensional schema. Cubes that share dimensions can be joined together into virtual cubes to view the data from a new perspective.

Both shared and private dimensions are created as DatabaseDimension objects in the Database object's `Dimensions` collection. They are distinguished by a naming convention. Private dimensions have a prefix that contains the name of their cube. The cube name is followed by a carat (^). The "ChildrenAtHome" private dimension in the "Sales" cube is named `"Sales^ChildrenAtHome"`. When a private dimension is displayed in the OLAP Manager, the prefix and carat are removed.

Virtual Dimensions

Virtual dimensions increase the number of dimensions that are available for browsing, without increasing the time it takes to load data into a cube. These dimensions are simpler than normal dimensions. They can contain only two levels, one of which is the "All" level.

A virtual dimension is based on a member property from a separate dimension. Member properties are based on attributed fields in dimension tables. They are discussed in "The MemberProperty Object" section later in this chapter.

OLAP Services does not store aggregations for virtual dimensions. All aggregations are created as the user browses the cube. This, of course, slows down browsing speed. Except for the difference in performance, the client application uses virtual dimensions in the same way as regular dimensions.

You can always create an additional regular dimension from the attribute field that you used for a member property and a virtual dimension. If you create a regular dimension, aggregations will be created and stored for that dimension and browsing speed will be much better. You normally want to use virtual dimensions for dimensions that will be used less frequently.

18

DECISION
SUPPORT
OBJECTS

Multiple Hierarchies Within One Dimension

The DSO object model doesn't allow you to create multiple hierarchies for a dimension. Multiple hierarchies per dimension are used, however, in ADO MD, the Multidimensional Extensions to the ActiveX Data Objects. If you name your dimensions properly with the dimension name and the hierarchy name separated by a dot, client applications using ADO MD will interpret them as multiple hierarchies within one dimension.

If you have a Location dimension that has both a Marketing hierarchy and a Sales hierarchy, you would use DSO to create two separate dimensions and give them the names Location.Marketing and Location.Sales.

Dimension Methods

The Dimension interface has only five methods, all of which are implemented in the same way as they are for the MDStore interface. The Clone method is discussed in the section "The Clone Method of the MDStore Objects." The LockObject and UnLockObject methods are discussed in "Using the Locking Methods." The Update and Refresh methods are discussed in "Managing Object Definitions with Refresh and Update."

The `AggregationUsage` Property

The `AggregationUsage` property allows you to control how aggregations are designed for a particular dimension. The four values for this property are members of the `DimensionAggUsageTypes` enumeration:

- `dimAggUsageStandard`—This is the default value for regular dimensions. The most efficient aggregation design is chosen by OLAP Services, in accordance with the parameters that the users set.

- `dimAggUsageTopOnly`—Only the "All" level of the dimension is used in aggregations, which means that this dimension is really not being used for aggregations at all. This is the default selection for all virtual dimensions.

- `dimAggUsageDetailsOnly`—Only the lowest level of the dimension is used in aggregations.

- `dimAggUsageCustom`—This choice gives you the greatest control over aggregation design. The `EnableAggregations` property of each particular level determines whether or not that level is used in aggregations.

The Dimension Type Property

There are two dimension types that have been implemented in OLAP Services 1.0, with an additional type that is reserved for future use:

- `dimRegular`—For now, all dimensions except for dimensions with the `dimTime` type.

- `dimTime`—A special type of dimension used for time. Only the specific datetime levels specified in the LevelTypes enumeration can be used in this dimension. Those values include `levTimeSeconds`, `levTimeMinutes`, `levTimeHours`, `levTimeDays`, `levTimeWeeks`, `levTimeMonths`, `levTimeQuarters`, `levTimeHalfYears`, and `levTimeYears`. If you want to include any other levels besides these in a time dimension, you must use the `dimRegular` dimension type.

- `dimQuantitative`—Reserved for future use.

Dimension Properties Used for Defining the Data

Two of the three properties used to define the data in a dimension are used in the same way as the MDStore object properties that are discussed in the MDStore section. The `FromClause` contains a comma-separated list of all the tables used in the dimension. The

`JoinClause` contains a list of all the join conditions. The `SourceTable` property is used in a different way. For a dimension, the `SourceTable` property specifies the table that contains the lowest level of the dimension. In the FoodMart sample, for example, the Product dimension's `SourceTable` is Product because the lowest level of the dimension, Product Name, is derived from that table.

Dimension Properties for Tracking an Object's State

These three properties all have the same function as the corresponding properties of the MDStore object—`LastProcessed`, `LastUpdated`, and `State`. `LastProcessed` contains the last time a dimension was processed, `LastUpdated` can be used for any user-defined purpose, and `State` contains one of the five constants in the `olapStateType` enumeration.

Dimension Properties that Identify an Object

Many of these properties also have the same function as the corresponding MDStore object.

- `Name`—Same as MDStore property. A string containing the name of the object.
- `IsTemporary`—Same as MDStore property.
- `Parent`—An object variable containing the MDStore object that has the `Dimensions` collection, which contains this Dimension object.
- `Description`—Same as MDStore property. A string giving a description of the object.
- `ClassType`—One of the following values: `clsDatabaseDimension`, `clsCubeDimension`, `clsPartitionDimension`, or `clsAggregationDimension`.
- `SubClassType`—Always `sbclsRegular` for a Dimension object. Virtual dimensions contain a level that has a `SubClassType` of `sbclsVirtual`, but the `SubClassType` of the virtual dimension itself is `sbclsRegular`.
- `IsValid`—The structure of the particular object is valid.
- `IsShared`—A read-only property that indicates that this is a shared dimension. Shared dimensions are created by using the cube name as a prefix to the dimension name, with the two names separated by a carat (^), as in `Sales^Product`.
- `OrdinalPosition`—The order in which the dimension is added to its parent's collection. The ordinal position is used in setting the order the dimension levels are listed in the AggregationID.

The Level Interface

Levels define the structure of a dimension's hierarchy. As you move up a hierarchy to a higher level, there are fewer members in each level. As you move down a hierarchy to the lower levels, you have more members. If there is an "All" level in a hierarchy, that level is the highest. The lowest level of the hierarchy is referred to as the detail level.

The Level interface is implemented with four separate objects, one for each of the four types of dimensions and MDStores—`DatabaseLevel`, `CubeLevel`, `PartitionLevel`, and `AggregationLevel`.

The Level interface has only two collections—`CustomProperties` and `MemberProperties`. The `Property` and `MemberProperty` objects are each discussed in their own sections later in this chapter.

The Level Interface has no methods.

The `SliceValue` Property of the Level Object

The `SliceValue` property of the Level object is used to define the different slices of a Partition object. When a cube is divided into partitions, the cube data has to be appropriately sliced so that each part of the cube exists in one and only one of the partitions. This slicing is done at a particular level of one or more of the cube's dimensions.

For example, you might want to divide the Sales cube from the FoodMart database into three different partitions each containing data for one of the three countries in the cube. You would slice the cube by setting the `SliceValue` of the Country level of the Customer dimension for each of the three partitions:

```
dsoCountryLevelPart1.SliceValue = "Canada"
dsoCountryLevelPart2.SliceValue = "Mexico"
dsoCountryLevelPart3.SliceValue = "USA"
```

The `SliceValue` property is valid only for `PartitionLevel` objects.

The `EstimatedSize` Property

The OLAP server uses the value of the `EstimatedSize` property when designing aggregations. If you can provide an approximate value, the server will be able to do its job more efficiently.

The `IsDisabled` Property

When the `IsDisabled` property of a Level object is set to `True`, that level is completely ignored in processing and browsing. Disabling a level also automatically disables all subordinate levels.

Properties That Define Aggregations for a Level

Four of the properties of the Level interface relate to the production of aggregations:

- EnableAggregations—This property is used together with the AggregationUsage property of the Dimension object. When custom aggregations are selected for a dimension, only the levels that have EnableAggregations set to True are aggregated.
- LevelType—This property uses the LevelTypes enumerated values. The highest level of each dimension has the value levAll. All other levels of a regular dimension have the value levRegular. Levels of a Time dimension have special values for each level. Those values are listed in "The Dimension Type Property" section earlier in the chapter.
- ColumnSize—For ROLAP cubes. Sets the size of the column used for the storage of the aggregated values.
- ColumnType—Used only for ROLAP cubes. Sets the data type of the column used for the storage of the aggregated values. Use values in the DataTypeEnum enumeration, such as adChar for character fields, adCurrency for money, and adInteger for an integer.

Properties That Define a Level's Data

There are seven properties that are used to define the data used in a Level object:

- FromClause—The content of the SQL FROM clause for the data in this level.
- JoinClause—The content of the SQL JOIN clause for the data in this level.
- MemberNameColumn—The column that contains the names of the members for this level. This property can also be set to a SQL expression that joins data from more than one column.
- MemberKeyColumn—The name of the column or columns that contain the key values used to identify the data in this level.
- Ordering—Use one of the two values in the OrderTypes enumeration. A value of orderKey causes the members of this level to be ordered in the sequence of the member key. A value of orderName orders the values by the member name.
- OrdinalPosition—This property sets the levels of the hierarchy, with 1 being the highest level. The value of the OrdinalPosition property is used when creating the AggregationID.
- IsUnique—If this property is True, then the MemberKeyColumn must contain unique values.

Level Properties That Identify an Object

There are six properties that identify a Level object:

- Name—A string containing the name of the Level object.
- Parent—An object variable containing the Dimension object that has the Levels collection, which contains this Level object.
- Description—A string giving a description of the object.
- ClassType—One of the following values: clsDatabaseLevel, clsCubeLevel, clsPartitionLevel, or clsAggregationLevel.
- SubClassType—The value is sbclsRegular for Level objects that are part of a regular dimension. When a Level object is part of a virtual dimension, the value is sbclsVirtual.
- IsValid—The structure of the particular object is valid.

The Measure Interface

Measures are the values in a fact table that are aggregated and displayed in cube browsing. The Measure interface is implemented for three separate objects—the CubeMeasure, the PartitionMeasure, and the AggregationMeasure.

Measures are not implemented at the database level. In the present edition of OLAP Services you can have shared dimensions but you cannot have shared measures.

The only collection in the Measure interface is the CustomProperties collection.

There are no methods implemented for the Measure interface.

The AggregateFunction Property

The AggregateFunction property sets the function that is used to aggregate the values for a measure. You must use one of the values from the AggregateType enumeration: aggSum, aggCount, aggMin, and aggMax.

If you want to display an average or a more complex function, you have to use a calculated member. That is defined with the Command interface, which is described in its own section later in this chapter.

The `SourceColumn` and `SourceColumnType` Properties

The `SourceColumn` property is a reference to the field in the fact table that contains the data for a measure. The `SourceColumnType` is the datatype of that particular column. The values for `SourceColumnType` are taken from the `DataTypeEnum` enumeration. You must specify a `SourceColumnType` for each measure you create in your cube.

The `FormatString` Property

The `FormatString` is used to format the display of a measure. You can use any valid Visual Basic format string.

The `IsInternal` Property

When you set the `IsInternal` property of a measure to `True`, that measure is not displayed and cannot be queried by client applications. Aggregations are still created for the measure. The `IsInternal` property is usually used for measures that are created solely for the purpose of using them in calculated members. For example, if you are creating an Average Production Time measure, you would need a Total Production Time measure and a Count of Production Units measure. If your analysts are not interested in the Total Production Time measure, you would set its `IsInternal` property to `False`.

Measure Properties That Identify an Object

There are seven properties that identify a `Measure` object:

- `Name`—A string containing the name of the Measure object.
- `Parent`—An object variable containing the MDStore object for the Measure.
- `Description`—A string giving a description of the object.
- `ClassType`—One of the following values: `clsCubeMeasure`, `clsPartitionMeasure`, or `clsAggregationMeasure`.
- `SubClassType`—The value is `sbclsRegular` for Measure objects.
- `IsValid`—The structure of the particular object is valid.
- `OrdinalPosition`—A read-only property that indicates the order in which the measures were added. The first measure is always the default measure of the cube.

The Command Interface

You can execute a series of user-defined commands on an object when that object is accessed. These user-defined commands are controlled through the Command interface.

There are two objects that are accessed through this interface—the `CubeCommand` and the `DatabaseCommand`. The Command interface implements the `CustomProperties` collection.

The interface has four methods implemented for the DatabaseCommand. None of these methods is valid for the CubeCommand. The four methods are `Clone`, `Update`, `LockObject`, and `UnlockObject`, all of which have been discussed in earlier sections.

The `CommandType` Property of the Command Interface

The `CommandType` property is used to distinguish between the different kinds of commands that can be executed. Values from the `CommandTypes` enumeration must be used:

- `cmdCreateMember`—A command that defines calculated members.
- `cmdCreateSet`—A command that is used to define new data sets.
- `cmdCreateLibrary`—A command that registers a DLL so that it can be used in MDX.
- `cmdUnknown`—Any other types of commands.

The `Statement` Property of the Command Interface

The `Statement` property contains the command that is to be executed. Listing 18.3 is a Visual Basic procedure that creates an example for each of the first three CommandTypes—creating a member, creating a set, and creating a library. You have to use the `Update` method of the Cube object to save these new members since the `Update` method cannot be used by a CubeCommand object.

 Listing 18.3 is on the CD-ROM for this book. You can find it in the DSOTesting Visual Basic project.

LISTING 18.3   Creating a Member, Set, and Library

```
Private Sub cmdCreateNewCommnds_Click()
On Error GoTo ProcErr

Dim dsoServer As DSO.Server
Dim dsoDbFoodMart As DSO.MDStore
```

```
    Dim dsoCubWarehouse As DSO.MDStore
    Dim dsoCommand As DSO.Command
    Dim dsoCommandMember As DSO.Command
    Dim dsoCommandSet As DSO.Command
    Dim dsoCommandLibrary As DSO.Command

    Set dsoServer = New DSO.Server
    dsoServer.Connect ("LocalHost")
    Set dsoDbFoodMart = dsoServer.MDStores("FoodMart")
    Set dsoCubWarehouse = dsoDbFoodMart.MDStores("Warehouse")

    'Add the commands to the collection.
    'If they already exist ignore error and go on.
    On Error Resume Next
    Set dsoCommandMember = dsoCubWarehouse.Commands.AddNew("CreatedMember")
    Set dsoCommandSet = dsoCubWarehouse.Commands.AddNew("CreatedSet")
    Set dsoCommandLibrary = dsoCubWarehouse.Commands.AddNew("CreatedLibrary")
    On Error GoTo ProcErr

    'Retrieve the commands from the collection
    'This is needed if the commands already exist.
    Set dsoCommandMember = dsoCubWarehouse.Commands("CreatedMember")
    Set dsoCommandSet = dsoCubWarehouse.Commands("CreatedSet")
    Set dsoCommandLibrary = dsoCubWarehouse.Commands("CreatedLibrary")

    dsoCommandMember.CommandType = cmdCreateMember
    dsoCommandMember.Statement = "CREATE MEMBER Warehouse.Measures.AverageCost " _
        & "As 'Measures.[Warehouse Cost] / Measures.[Units Shipped]'"

    dsoCommandSet.CommandType = cmdCreateSet
    dsoCommandSet.Statement = "CREATE SET Warehouse.USCanada AS '{USA, Canada}'"

    dsoCommandLibrary.CommandType = cmdUseLibrary
    dsoCommandLibrary.Statement = "Use Library ""NewMDXFunction.dll"""

    'The New Library command is removed, because it will generate an error
    dsoCubWarehouse.Commands.Remove ("CreatedLibrary")

    dsoCubWarehouse.Update

    'View all the command names and statements
    For Each dsoCommand In dsoCubWarehouse.Commands
      MsgBox dsoCommand.Name & vbCrLf & dsoCommand.Statement
    Next dsoCommand

    ProcExit:
      Exit Sub
    ProcErr:
      MsgBox Err.Number & " - " & Err.Description
      GoTo ProcExit

    End Sub
```

18

DECISION
SUPPORT
OBJECTS

Command Properties That Identify an Object

The following properties are used to identify a Level object:

- Name—A string containing the name of the Command object.
- Parent—An object variable containing the parent Database or Cube object.
- Description—A string giving a description of the object.
- ClassType—One of the following values: clsDatabaseCommand and clsCubeCommand.
- SubClassType—The value is sbclsRegular for Command objects.
- IsValid—The structure of the particular object is valid. The validity of the Statement property is not checked because there are a lot of different types of valid statements. The Statement property is checked, however, to see that there is some value assigned to it.
- OrdinalPosition—A read-only property that indicates the order in which the commands were added. The order can be significant because the output of one command might be needed to execute one of the other commands.

The Role Interface

Roles are used by OLAP services to control access to DSO objects and data. Like the Command interface, the Role interface is implemented only on the Database and the Cube levels. The only collection in the Role interface is CustomProperties.

> **Note**
>
> Version 1.0 of OLAP Services did not have a very well-developed security system. Service Pack 1 added significant security capabilities. See Chapter 33, "OLAP Security."

Role Interface Methods

The Role interface implements the Clone, LockObject, UnlockObject, and Update methods, which have all been previously discussed.

The one special method used by Role objects is SetPermissions. This method is used to assign access to a particular key. It returns True or False to indicate the result of the permission assignment. SetPermissions requires two parameters. The first parameter, key, is always set with the value "Access". The second parameter, PermissionExpression, can be set to "R" for read-only access or "RW" for read/write access.

```
dsoCubeRole.SetPermissions "Access", "R"
```

The Properties of the Role Interface

There are eight properties of the Role interface:

- Permissions—Valid values are "R" and "RW" for read-only and read/write permission.
- UsersList—A list of users separated by semicolons.
- Name—Name of the Role object.
- Parent—The Cube or the Database object that contains the Role object.
- Description—A description of the Role object.
- ClassType—Either clsDatabaseRole or clsCubeRole.
- SubClassType—The value is sbclsRegular for Role objects.
- IsValid—The Role object is valid.

The DataSource Object

The DataSource object is used to indicate the source of data for a Database, Cube, or Partition object. The DataSource object has only one collection, CustomProperties.

The DataSource has five methods—IsConnected, Clone, LockObject, UnlockObject, and Update. The IsConnected method checks to see if there is a connection to the data source and attempts to connect if not currently connected. The IsConnected method returns a value of True or False, which indicates whether or not the data source is connected.

You don't have to use the IsConnected method to establish connections to your data sources. When information is needed, DSO will automatically make the connection.

Datasource Connection Properties

The ConnectionString property contains the OLE DB initialization parameters that are necessary to access a source database. Valid connection strings are specified by the documentation for individual databases. Here are a couple of samples.

SQL Server ConnectionString:

```
ConnectionString = _
    "Provider=SQLOLEDB.1;Persist Security Info=False;User ID=sa;" & _
    "Initial Catalog=Northwind;Data Source=LocalHost;Connect Timeout=15"
```

18

DECISION
SUPPORT
OBJECTS

OLE DB Provider for ODBC Drivers (Access):

```
ConnectionSTring="Provider=MSDASQL.1;Persist Security Info=False; & _
    "Data Source=FoodMart;Connect Timeout=15"
```

The `Connection` property references an ADO Connection object.

The `OpenQuoteChar` and the `CloseQuoteChar` properties return the values that are used by the particular database for starting and ending string variables. These two properties can be used for constructing strings that can be used no matter what database is used in the connection.

The `SupportedTxnDDL` property returns the connection object's `Transaction DDL` property. This property provides information to the user of a data source about that data source's use of Data Definition Language (DDL).

Properties That Identify a `DataSource`

The following properties identify the `DataSource` object:

- `Name`—Name of the `DataSource` object.
- `Parent`—The object for which this is a `DataSource`.
- `Description`—A description of the `DataSource` object.
- `ClassType`—Always `clsDatasource` for `DataSource` objects.
- `SubClassType`—Always `sbclsRegular` for `DataSource` objects.
- `IsValid`—The `DataSource` object is valid.
- `IsReadOnly`—Whether or not this `DataSource` is read-only.

The `MemberProperty` Object

Source tables that are used to build dimensions have some fields that are used to build the levels of the dimension and many other fields that store additional attribute information. These attribute fields can be used to create member properties, which can then be used to create virtual dimensions. Member properties can also be referenced directly by many OLAP clients.

`MemberProperty` objects have the `CustomProperties` collection. They have no methods. The properties of the `MemberProperty` object include

- `Caption`—The label of the `MemberProperty`, which is displayed to OLAP clients.
- `SourceColumn`—The column used in the `MemberProperty`
- `Name`—The name of the object.

- Description—A description of the object
- Parent—The dimension object that contains the MemberProperty object.
- OrdinalPosition—The position of this MemberProperty in the MemberProperties collection of the parent Dimension object.
- ClassType—Always clsMemberProperty.
- SubClassType—Always sbclsRegular.

The **PartitionAnalyzer** Object

The PartitionAnalyzer object has the properties and the methods that are implemented by the Storage Design Wizard in the OLAP Manager. The wizard provides a very clear picture of the choices that are available when designing aggregations for a partition. It's an excellent tool for beginners who are learning about the options available in OLAP Services.

The problem with the Storage Design Wizard is that it soon becomes very tedious to use. If you are designing or redesigning the storage choices for a number of cubes, it can be quite time-consuming. We have used the PartitionAnalyzer object to create a tool called the OLAPUnleashedAggDesigner to automate the design of cube partitions.

The PartitionAnalyzer object designs aggregations for a partition based on an algorithm that determines which aggregations will add the greatest performance speed to the cube browsing. After each aggregation is created, an estimate of performance gain and storage space is returned, so that the program can decide whether or not to continue creating more aggregations. You can also give the PartitionAnalyzer one or more queries to be used as Goal Queries, so that the aggregations are optimized specifically for them.

Collections of the **PartitionAnalyzer** object

The PartitionAnalyzer object has one collection, DesignedAggregations, which contains the aggregations that have been created. When you are done using the PartitionAnalyzer, you can add or replace the existing aggregations in the Partition's MDStores collection with these newly designed aggregations.

Properties of the `PartitionAnalyzer` Object

The `PartitionAnalyzer` has two properties. The `AggregationAnalysisInitialized` property indicates whether or not the `PartitionAnalyzer` has been initialized. The `Parent` property returns an object reference to the Partition object that contains this `PartitionAnalyzer`. You set a partition's `PartitionAnalyzer` object by using the `Analyzer` property of the Partition object.

Methods to Initialize and Close a `PartitionAnalyzer` Session

You must use the `InitializeDesign` method of the `PartitionAnalyzer` object before you can use any of the other methods. Besides initializing the objects needed for the session, this method makes sure that the partition structure is valid; it returns `True` or `False`.

You should call the `CloseAggregationsAnalysis` method at the conclusion of a `PartitionAnalyzer` session. This method clears the temporary objects that have been used by the `PartitionAnalyzer` and discards all the Aggregation objects that have been created and added to the `DesignedAggregations` collection.

> **Note**
>
> The product documentation refers to the `CloseAggregationsAnalysis` method as the `CloseAggregationAnalysis` method. The singular/plural bug strikes again!

Methods to Add and Analyze Aggregations

There are two methods that can add an aggregation to the `DesignedAggregations` collection. The `AddExistingAggregation` method adds an Aggregation object that already exists. The `NextAnalysisStep` creates a new Aggregation object and adds it to the collection.

Both of these methods analyze the resulting collection of aggregations after the new aggregation has been added. They both return three values:

- `dblPercentageBenefit`—The estimated performance benefit of this set of aggregations.
- `dblAccumulatedSize`—The estimated storage space for this set of aggregations.
- `lngAggregationsCount`—The number of aggregations that are currently in the `DesignedAggregations` collection.

The use of NextAnalysisStep is shown in the section "The OLAPUnleashedAggDesigner."

Methods That Use Goal Queries

There are two PartitionAnalyzer methods that you use when you want your aggregations to be optimized for browsing specific queries. The AddGoalQuery method adds a new Goal Query. The PrepareGoalQueries method must be used after one or more Goal Queries have been added to allow those queries to be used by the PartitionAnalyzer.

The PrepareGoalQueries method has two parameters:

- DatasetName—A numeric string that indicates what combination of levels in the dimensions are to be optimized. The numeric string that is used is the AggregationID, which is used in the automatically generated aggregation name. The AggregationID was discussed in "The Aggregation Object" section earlier in this chapter.

- Frequency—A number indicating the weighting you want to assign to this Goal Query compared to the weightings assigned to other Goal Queries.

The following code adds two Goal Queries. If you want to use Goal Queries, you would use this code before using the NextAnalysisStep method.

```
dsoPartitionAnalyzer.InitializeDesign
dsoPartitionAnalyzer.AddGoalQuery "1322241", 3
dsoPartitionAnalyzer.AddGoalQuery "2322241", 1
dsoPartitionAnalyzer.PrepareGoalQueries
```

The OLAPUnleashedAggDesigner

The OLAPUnleashedAggDesigner utility automates the process of designing aggregations for a set of cubes. Rather than using the OLAP Manager's Storage Design Wizard to set up the aggregation strategy for each cube separately, you can choose any number of cubes, set the aggregation parameters, and process them all in one batch. The code for this utility is included on the CD-ROM with this chapter. In Chapter 19, the same utility is added to the OLAP Manager interface as an add-in.

The user interface for the OLAPUnleashedAggDesigner is shown in Figure 18.9. You type in the name of a server. You then pick one or more cubes from any of the databases in a server. You can choose the ROLAP, HOLAP, or MOLAP storage mode. Limits can be set for one or more of the three analysis parameters. If you leave any of the parameters blank, that value is not checked. The default choice is to process all the selected cubes until a 20% performance gain is reached. You can choose to design aggregations and/or process the selected cubes. You can also interrupt the aggregation design process.

If you try to interrupt the application while a cube is being processed, the processing of that cube will be completed and then the code will stop.

FIGURE 18.9

The OLAPUnleashed-AggDesigner uses the PartitionAnalyzer *object to efficiently design aggregations for multiple cubes.*

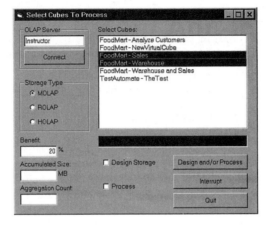

To create the OLAPUnleashedAggDesigner, you need to start a Visual Basic project, add a reference to the Microsoft Decision Support Objects library, and create a form called frmAggDesigner with the controls to make the appropriate selections.

The code for the frmAggDesigner form is shown in Listing 18.4.

 Listing 18.4 is on the CD-ROM for this book.

LISTING 18.4   Code for the OLAPUnleashedAggDesigner Utility

```
Option Explicit

Public dsoServer As DSO.Server
Public gbInterrupt As Boolean

Private Sub cmdConnect_Click()
On Error GoTo ProcErr

Dim dsoDatabase As DSO.MDStore
Dim dsoCube As DSO.MDStore

frmAggDesigner.MousePointer = vbHourglass
txtProcessing.Text = "Connecting to OLAP Server.  Please wait..."
txtProcessing.Refresh

' Set dsoServer to the one typed into the text box.
Set dsoServer = New DSO.Server
dsoServer.Connect (txtDSOServer.Text)
```

```
'Clear cube list.
lstCube.Clear

' Generate the list of databases from the OLAP Server.
For Each dsoDatabase In dsoServer.MDStores
  For Each dsoCube In dsoDatabase.MDStores

    'Only include regular cubes. Do not include virtual cubes.
    If dsoCube.SubClassType = sbclsRegular Then
    lstCube.AddItem dsoDatabase.Name & " - " & dsoCube.Name
    End If
  Next
Next

txtProcessing.Text = "Connected to OLAP Server " & txtDSOServer.Text
txtProcessing.Refresh

ProcExit:
  frmAggDesigner.MousePointer = vbArrow
  Exit Sub
ProcErr:
  subErrHandler "cmdConnect_Click", CStr(Err.Number), Err.Description
  GoTo ProcExit
End Sub

Private Sub cmdDesignProcess_Click()
On Error GoTo ProcErr

Dim idx As Integer

Dim dsoDatabase As DSO.MDStore
Dim dsoCube As DSO.MDStore
Dim dsoPartition As DSO.MDStore
Dim dsoPartitionAnalyzer As DSO.PartitionAnalyzer
Dim dsoAggregation As DSO.MDStore

Dim lDBNameLen As Long
Dim sDBName As String
Dim sCubeName As String
Dim dblPercentage As Double
Dim dblAccumSize As Double
Dim lAggCount As Long
Dim sSelectedCube As String

' Set interrupt variable to false upon starting.
gbInterrupt = False

'Keep user informed
frmAggDesigner.MousePointer = vbArrowHourglass
```

18

DECISION
SUPPORT
OBJECTS

continues

LISTING 18.4   continued

```
' Loop through the list of cubes.
For idx = 0 To lstCube.ListCount - 1

  ' Show progress on screen.
  txtProcessing.Text = "Creating Aggregations for '" & _
    lstCube.List(idx) & "'"
  txtProcessing.Refresh

  ' Create aggregations if this is a selected cube.
  If lstCube.Selected(idx) = True Then

    sSelectedCube = lstCube.List(idx)
    lDBNameLen = InStr(1, sSelectedCube, " - ") - 1
    sDBName = Mid(sSelectedCube, 1, lDBNameLen)
    sCubeName = Mid(sSelectedCube, (lDBNameLen + 4), _
      (Len(sSelectedCube) - lDBNameLen - 3))

    Set dsoDatabase = dsoServer.MDStores(sDBName)
    Set dsoCube = dsoDatabase.MDStores(sCubeName)

    ' Loop through the partitions on this cube.
    For Each dsoPartition In dsoCube.MDStores

      If chkDesignStorage.Value = 1 Then

        ' Remove existing aggregations.
        For Each dsoAggregation In dsoPartition.MDStores
          dsoPartition.MDStores.Remove dsoAggregation.Name
        Next

        ' Set the storage mode
        If optROLAP.Value = True Then
          dsoPartition.OlapMode = olapmodeRolap
        ElseIf optHOLAP.Value = True Then
          dsoPartition.OlapMode = olapmodeHybridIndex
        Else
          dsoPartition.OlapMode = olapmodeMolapIndex
        End If

        ' set the partition analyzer
        Set dsoPartitionAnalyzer = dsoPartition.Analyzer
        dsoPartitionAnalyzer.InitializeDesign

        ' Loop to create aggregations.
        Do While dsoPartitionAnalyzer.NextAnalysisStep( _
            dblPercentage, dblAccumSize, lAggCount)

          If txtBenefit.Text <> "" Then
            If dblPercentage> txtBenefit.Text Then
```

```
            Exit Do
          End If
        End If

        If txtAccumSize.Text <> "" Then
          If dblAccumSize> CDbl(txtAccumSize.Text) * 1024 * 1024 Then
            Exit Do
          End If
        End If

        If txtAggCount.Text <> "" Then
          If lAggCount = txtAggCount.Text Then
            Exit Do
          End If
        End If

        ' Check for an interrupt.
        DoEvents

        If gbInterrupt = True Then
          gbInterrupt = False
          txtProcessing.Text = "Interrupted"
          GoTo ProcExit
        End If

      Loop

      ' Add the aggregations to the partition
      For Each dsoAggregation In dsoPartitionAnalyzer.DesignedAggregations
        dsoPartition.MDStores.Add dsoAggregation
      Next

      dsoPartitionAnalyzer.CloseAggregationsAnalysis
      dsoPartition.Update

    End If
  Next
End If


  ' If cubes are to be processed, call the process procedure
  If chkProcess.Value = 1 Then
    If lstCube.Selected(idx) = True Then
      subProcCube sDBName, sCubeName
    End If
  End If

Next idx
```

18

DECISION SUPPORT OBJECTS

continues

LISTING **18.4** continued

```
    'Inform user.
    txtProcessing.Text = "Finished."

ProcExit:
    frmAggDesigner.MousePointer = vbArrow
    Exit Sub
ProcErr:
    subErrHandler "cmdDesignProcess_Click", CStr(Err.Number), Err.Description
    txtProcessing.Text = "An error occurred."
    GoTo ProcExit
End Sub

Private Sub subProcCube(sDBName As String, sCubeName As String)
On Error GoTo ProcErr

Dim dsoDatabase As DSO.MDStore
Dim dsoCube As DSO.MDStore

'Set up
Set dsoDatabase = dsoServer.MDStores(sDBName)
Set dsoCube = dsoDatabase.MDStores(sCubeName)

'Fill in progress text box
txtProcessing.Text = "Processing " & sDBName & " - " & sCubeName
txtProcessing.Refresh

'Process this cube
dsoCube.Process

'Reset progress text box
txtProcessing.Text = ""

ProcExit:
    Exit Sub
ProcErr:
    subErrHandler "subProcCube", CStr(Err.Number), Err.Description
    GoTo ProcExit
End Sub

Private Sub cmdInterrupt_Click()
On Error GoTo ProcErr

' User has interrupted aggregations, processing.
gbInterrupt = True

ProcExit:
    Exit Sub
ProcErr:
    subErrHandler "cmdInterrupt_Click", CStr(Err.Number), Err.Description
```

```
   GoTo ProcExit
End Sub

Private Sub cmdQuit_Click()
On Error GoTo ProcErr

'Exit the program
frmAggDesigner.Hide
Unload frmAggDesigner

ProcExit:
  Exit Sub
ProcErr:
  subErrHandler "cmdQuit_Click", CStr(Err.Number), Err.Description
  GoTo ProcExit
End Sub

Public Sub subErrHandler(sProcedure As String, sErrNum As String, _
        sErrDesc As String)
On Error Resume Next

Dim msg As String

msg = "Procedure Name - " & sProcedure & vbCrLf & vbCrLf
msg = msg & "Error Number - " & sErrNum & vbCrLf & vbCrLf
msg = msg & "Description - " & sErrDesc

MsgBox msg, , "Error in AggDesigner Utility."

Err.Clear

End Sub
```

18

The OLAPUnleashedAggDesigner shows you how to include the process of designing cube aggregations in your own applications. You can use a simple format for selecting aggregation options, as in the OLAPUnleashedAggDesigner. Or, you automate the process completely, by setting the aggregations parameters at a desired value and running the code in cmdDesignProcess_Click without any user input.

The `CubeAnalyzer` Object

The CubeAnalyzer object contains the properties and the methods that are implemented by the Usage Analysis Wizard in the OLAP Manager. The CubeAnalyzer has no collections or properties; its one method is OpenQueryLogRecordset.

The OpenQueryLogRecordset method returns an ADO recordset that contains detailed information from the Query Log, which stores information about the queries that have been used in cube browsing. This recordset can then be filtered, as in the Usage Analysis Wizard, to view queries that meet one or more particular characteristics.

You must add a reference to the ActiveX Data Objects to your Visual Basic project if you are going to use this method.

The columns that can be returned in the recordset include

- MSOLAP_Database—The name of the OLAP database used in the query.
- MSOLAP_Cube—The name of the cube used in the query.
- MSOLAP_User—The name of the user that ran the query.
- Dataset—A numeric string indicating the levels from each dimension that were used for the query. This string is the same as the AggregationID, discussed in the section "The `AggregationPrefix` Property and the Naming of Aggregation Objects." It is also the same string that is used to add Goal Queries in the `PartitionAnalyzer`. This allows the output from the `CubeAnalyzer` to be easily used as the input to the PartitionAnalyzer.
- StartTime—The date and time the query started.
- Duration—The length of time in seconds that the query ran.
- MOLAPPartitions—The number of MOLAP aggregations that were used to respond to the query.
- ROLAPPartitions—The number of ROLAP aggregations that were used to respond to the query.
- SamplingRate—The sampling rate that was in effect at the time the query was run. The default sampling rate is 10, which means that the data from only 1 out of every 10 queries is recorded. The SamplingRate can be changed in the OLAP Manager by right-clicking a server and selecting Properties.

You would use the following command to return all the information from the query log:

```
Dim dsoCubeAnalyzer As DSO.CubeAnalyzer
Set dsoCubeAnalyzer = dsoCube.Analyzer
Set ADODBQueryLog = dsoCubeAnalyzer.OpenQueryLogRecordset_
    ("SELECT * FROM QueryLog")
```

If you wanted to see only the queries used in the Sales cube of the FoodMart database that were taking more than 5 seconds to process, you would use the following:

```
Set ADODBQueryLog = dsoCubeAnalyzer.OpenQueryLogRecordset( _
    "SELECT Dataset FROM QueryLog " _
    & "WHERE MSOLAP_Database = 'FoodMart' " _
    & "AND MSOLAP_Cube = 'Sales' " _
    & "AND Duration> 5")
```

The Property Object and the CustomProperties Collection

All DSO objects have a `CustomProperties` collection, which allows you to define new properties for those objects. These new properties are defined with the `Property` object and added to the `CustomProperties` collection.

The `Property` object has no methods or collections. It has three properties:

- `Name`—The name you are assigning to the custom property.
- `Value`—The value contained by the custom property.
- `DataType`—The datatype for the values used in this custom property. Acceptable dataypes are those used by Visual Basic and are listed in the vbVarType enumeration.

The `CustomProperties` collection has four methods:

- `Add`—Adds a new `Property` object to the collection.
- `Remove`—Removes one `Property` object from the collection.
- `Clear`—Removes all `Property` objects from the collection.
- `Item`—Retrieves a `Property` object.

If you want to add a custom property to your Cube objects that would indicate who had created a particular cube, you could use the following code:

```
'Add new custom property to the Cube object
Set dsoProperty = dsoCube.CustomProperties.Add(_
    "John Doe", "CubeCreator", vbString)
'Retrieve new property value
MsgBox dsoCube.CustomProperties("CubeCreator").Value
```

18

DECISION SUPPORT OBJECTS

The DSO Repository

A DSO repository is created for each OLAP server to store metadata about that server's objects. This is a special database created specifically to store information about an OLAP server's objects. It is completely separate from the main Repository used by SQL Server for managing metadata about databases and DTS packages.

DSO repository information is not intended to be accessed directly. DSO objects are intended to be viewed and modified only through the use of the OLAP Manager or by using DSO directly.

The DSO repository is stored by default in a Microsoft Access database, with a default path of

..\Program Files\OLAP Services\Bin\msmdrep.mdb

The OLAP Manager provides an option to migrate the DSO repository to a SQL Server database. You can put the DSO repository in any SQL Server you choose. A tool in the OLAP Manager, the Migrate Repository Wizard, is used for this process. Right-click the server in the tree view and select Migrate Repository to see the wizard, shown in Figure 18.10.

FIGURE 18.10

The Migrate Repository Wizard is used to move the DSO repository to a SQL Server database.

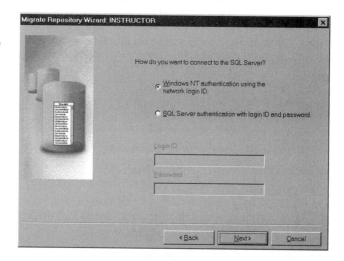

After you have migrated the DSO repository to a SQL Server database, you cannot return it to an Access database. You can, though, move it to a different SQL Server database by again using the Migrate Repository Wizard.

Automatic Cube Creation with the OLAPUnleashedStarToCube Utility

The OLAPUnleashedStarToCube utility illustrates the use of DSO to automatically convert a star schema into an OLAP cube. If the tables and the fields in the star schema follow a set naming convention, all of the dimensions, levels, and measures will be chosen and created automatically. If the utility is used with a star schema that follows the naming convention only partially, the utility will still make the process of creating a cube much more efficient.

 The OLAPUnleashedStarToCube utility is on the CD-ROM for this book. The star schema naming conventions that result in automatic cube generation are as follows:

- There can be no spaces in the names of tables and fields.
- All dimension tables begin with the prefix "dim".
- The first field of the dimension table must be a single field key and must be named with an "ID" or "PK" suffix.
- The fields used for the levels of the dimensions must have a prefix with "lvl" and a single digit number. The field used for the highest level of the hierarchy should have a prefix of "lvl1", the second level "lvl2", and so on.
- The fact table begins with the prefix "fact".
- The foreign keys connecting the fact table to the dimension tables must be named with an "ID" or "FK" suffix. The key fields connecting the fact table to the dimension tables must have identical names (except for the "PK" and the "FK") or the joins creating the cube will not be generated.
- All the fields in the fact table that do not have an "ID" or a "FK" suffix are used as measures.

You can test some of the automatic cube generation capability of the utility by using the OLAPUnleashed database. That database, created by the DTS packages included with the chapters on DTS, follows some but not all of these naming conventions and can be used for testing this utility. Specifically, the levels of the dimensions in the OLAPUnleashed database do not follow the naming conventions. The measures, the dimensions, and the joins will all be chosen automatically, but you will have to select the levels of the dimensions manually in the StarToCube interface.

The user interface for the OLAPUnleashedStarToCube utility is shown in Figure 18.11. When a connection is made to the SQL Server, all the available databases are displayed. When a database is chosen, all the objects named in accordance with the naming convention are entered into the various list boxes. Any of the automatic selections can be changed—for the fact table, the measures, the dimensions, the levels of the dimensions, and the ordering of the levels.

FIGURE 18.11

The OLAPUnleashed-StarToCube utility provides the ability to automatically select or modify the data source objects.

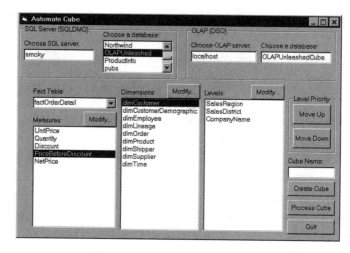

When all the selections have been made, the Create Cube button executes the code that creates the OLAP cube and all its objects. This code is shown in Listing 18.5

LISTING 18.5 Code from OLAPUnleashedStarToCube That Creates the DSO Objects

```
Private Sub cmdCreateCube_Click()
On Error GoTo ProcErr

Dim idx As Integer
Dim dsoDimension As DSO.Dimension
Dim dsoLevel As DSO.Level
Dim dsoMeasure As DSO.Measure

Dim dmoColumn As SQLDMO.Column

Dim col As Collection
Dim sConnect As String

'Inform user of activity
frmMain.MousePointer = vbHourglass

'Various validations
If lstDMODatabase.SelCount = 0 Then
  MsgBox "You must select a SQLDMO database."
  GoTo ProcExit
End If

If txtDSODatabase.Text = "" Then
  MsgBox "You must enter a new DSO database name."
  GoTo ProcExit
End If
```

```
If txtCubeName.Text = "" Then
  MsgBox "You must give this cube a name."
  GoTo ProcExit
End If

'Validate the levels selected
For idx = 0 To lstDimensionTable.ListCount - 1
  Set col = ColOfColDmoColumns.Item(lstDimensionTable.List(idx))
  If col.Count = 0 Then
    MsgBox "You must select at least one level " & vbCrLf & _
      "per selected dimension."
    GoTo ProcExit
  End If
Next idx

'Add the new OLAP database to the Server's MDStores collection
Set dsoDatabase = dsoServer.MDStores.AddNew(txtDSODatabase.Text)
dsoDatabase.Description = ""
dsoDatabase.Update

'Set the connection string for the DMO Source
sConnect = "Provider=SQLOLEDB.1;Persist Security Info=False;" & _
  "Data Source=" & dmoServer.Name & _
  ";Connect Timeout=15;Initial Catalog=" & dmoDatabase.Name & ";" & _
  "Integrated Security=SSPI;"

'Add the new DataSource to the database's DataSources collection
Set dsoDataSource = dsoDatabase.DataSources.AddNew(dmoDatabase.Name)

'Set the DSO data source to be the DMO Database.
dsoDataSource.Name = dmoDatabase.Name
dsoDataSource.ConnectionString = sConnect
dsoDataSource.Update

'Create Shared Dimensions
For idx = 0 To lstDimensionTable.ListCount - 1

  Set dsoDimension = _
    dsoDatabase.Dimensions.AddNew(lstDimensionTable.List(idx))
  Set dsoDimension.DataSource = dsoDataSource
  dsoDimension.FromClause = lstDimensionTable.List(idx)

  Set ColDmoColumns = _
    ColOfColDmoColumns(lstDimensionTable.List(idx))
  For Each dmoColumn In ColDmoColumns
    Set dsoLevel = dsoDimension.Levels.AddNew(dmoColumn.Name)
    dsoLevel.MemberKeyColumn = dsoDimension.Name & _
      "." & dmoColumn.Name
    dsoLevel.ColumnSize = 255 'dmoColumn.Length
    dsoLevel.ColumnType = adChar
```

18

DECISION SUPPORT OBJECTS

continues

LISTING 18.5   continued

```
      dsoLevel.EstimatedSize = 1
   Next

   dsoDimension.Update

Next idx

'Add a new cube to the database's MDStores collection.
Set dsoCube = dsoDatabase.MDStores.AddNew(txtCubeName.Text)

'Add the DataSource to the cube's DataSources collection.
Set dsoDataSource = dsoDatabase.DataSources(1)
dsoCube.DataSources.AddNew (dsoDataSource.Name)

'Set cube properties
dsoCube.SourceTable = QUOTE & cboFactTable.Text & QUOTE
dsoCube.EstimatedRows = 100000

' Add all of the shared dimensions to the cube.
For idx = 0 To lstDimensionTable.ListCount - 1
   dsoCube.Dimensions.AddNew lstDimensionTable.List(idx)
Next idx

'Create the join clause
dsoCube.JoinClause = fctCreateJoinClause

'Inform user if join clause could not be created
If dsoCube.JoinClause = "" Then
   MsgBox "Join clause could not be created. " & vbCrLf & _
          "Create the joins manually with the Cube Editor."
End If

'Define measures for cube
For idx = 0 To lstMeasures.ListCount - 1
   Set dsoMeasure = dsoCube.Measures.AddNew(lstMeasures.List(idx))

   dsoMeasure.SourceColumn = QUOTE & _
     cboFactTable.Text & QUOTE & "." & lstMeasures.List(idx)
   dsoMeasure.SourceColumnType = adSmallInt
   dsoMeasure.AggregateFunction = aggSum
Next idx

'Store the cube dimension in the OLAP Services repository
dsoCube.Update

' Notify user.
MsgBox "Cube " & QUOTE & txtCubeName.Text & _
    QUOTE & " has been created in database " & dsoDatabase.Name & "."
```

```
ProcExit:
  frmMain.MousePointer = vbArrow
  Exit Sub
ProcErr:
  subErrHandler "cmdCreateCube_Click", CStr(Err.Number), Err.Description
  GoTo ProcExit
End Sub

Private Function fctCreateJoinClause() As String
On Error GoTo ProcErr

Dim idx As Long

Dim dmoDimTable As SQLDMO.Table
Dim dmoDimColumn As SQLDMO.Column
Dim sDimTableSuffix As String
Dim sDimKey As String
Dim sDimName As String

'dmoFactTable is declared as a module level variable
Dim dmoFactColumn As SQLDMO.Column
Dim sFactTableSuffix As String
Dim sFactKey As String

Dim sJoinClause As String

'Return empty string on failure
fctCreateJoinClause = ""

'Attempt to create a join for each of the dimensions
For idx = 0 To lstDimensionTable.ListCount - 1

  'Set the object variable for the dimension table
  Set dmoDimTable = dmoDatabase.Tables(lstDimensionTable.List(idx))

  'Assume that the key value will be in the first column
  Set dmoDimColumn = dmoDimTable.Columns(1)

  'Add "And" to the Join string if this is not the first join
  If sJoinClause <> "" Then
    sJoinClause = sJoinClause & " And "
  End If

  'Assign the Dimension Key string to be used in the Join Clause
  sDimKey = QUOTE & dmoDimTable.Name & QUOTE & "." & _
            QUOTE & dmoDimColumn.Name & QUOTE

  'Find the dimension table key suffix
  sDimTableSuffix = Right(dmoDimColumn.Name, 2)
```

continues

18

DECISION
SUPPORT
OBJECTS

LISTING 18.5 continued

```
'Remove the dimension suffix to find the dimension name
sDimName = Mid(dmoDimColumn.Name, 1, Len(dmoDimColumn.Name) - 2)

'Find fact table key suffix, based on naming conventions.
'If none, function returns empty string
Select Case sDimTableSuffix

  Case "ID"
    sFactTableSuffix = "ID"

  Case "PK"
    sFactTableSuffix = "FK"

  Case Else

    'Return empty string on failure
    fctCreateJoinClause = ""
    GoTo ProcExit

End Select

'If this is a time dimension, check for multiple time facts
If InStr(1, dmoDimTable.Name, "time", vbTextCompare) Then

  ' Loop through the fact table columns
  For Each dmoFactColumn In dmoFactTable.Columns

    'Look for "time" in each column name.
    If InStr(1, dmoFactColumn.Name, "time", vbTextCompare) Then

      'Assign the fact table key string for the Join Clause
      sFactKey = QUOTE & dmoFactTable.Name & QUOTE & "." & _
                 QUOTE & dmoFactColumn.Name & QUOTE

      'Add to join clause
      sJoinClause = sJoinClause & sDimKey & " = " & sFactKey

    End If

  Next

Else

  'Not a time dimension.
  'Fact Column name will be Dimension name + fact table suffix
  'Assign the fact table key string for the Join Clause
  sFactKey = QUOTE & dmoFactTable.Name & QUOTE & "." & _
             QUOTE & sDimName & sFactTableSuffix & QUOTE
```

```
      'Add to join clause
      sJoinClause = sJoinClause & sDimKey & " = " & sFactKey

   End If

Next idx

fctCreateJoinClause = sJoinClause

ProcExit:
  Exit Function
ProcErr:
  fctCreateJoinClause = ""
  subErrHandler "fctCreateJoinClause", CStr(Err.Number), Err.Description
  GoTo ProcExit
End Function
```

If all the structures in the cube have been created correctly, you can process the cube by selecting the Process Cube button. If any of the fields that were used to join the tables did not follow the naming convention, the processing will fail. You can edit the cube in the OLAP Manager and add the joins that are needed.

The complete code, the Visual Basic project, and an executable file for the OLAPUnleashedStarToCube utility can be found on the CD-ROM that accompanies this book. If you create the project for yourself, you will need to add the following references to your Visual Basic project:

- Microsoft Decision Support Objects
- Microsoft SQLDMO Object Library
- Microsoft ActiveX Data Objects 2.1 Library
- Microsoft ActiveX Data Objects (Multi-Dimensional) 1.0 Library

Summary

I think the most important thing to remember about DSO is that these are the objects that were used to create the user interface in the OLAP Manager. If you can do something with the OLAP Manager, you should also be able to do it with DSO.

The next chapter, "Developing an Add-In Program for OLAP Services," shows how to extend the functionality of the OLAP Manager. You will see how to take both of the utilities created in this chapter and integrate them into the OLAP Manager's interface.

18

DECISION
SUPPORT
OBJECTS

CHAPTER 19

Developing an Add-In Program for OLAP Services

OLAP Services provides the ability to add new functionality to the OLAP Manager. You can add new nodes to the console tree on the left side of the OLAP Server tree. You can add new menu items and write code that is executed when that menu item is selected.

This chapter shows you how to use the AddInCreator, a utility provided on the book's CD-Rom. The AddInCreator generates a code template that can help you create your own add-ins. You will see how to create several custom add-ins, which will increase your efficiency when using the OLAP Manager:

- The AggDesigner add-in, automating the process of designing cube aggregations. The code for this utility is described in Chapter 18, "Decision Support Objects."
- The StarToCube add-in, automating the process of creating a cube from a star schema. This utility is described in Chapter 18.
- The OLAPUnleashedDocumenter add-in, which outputs information about OLAP objects to a Word document.

The OLAP Add-In Manager

The Microsoft Management Console (MMC) provides a standard interface for Microsoft's BackOffice products. This interface consists of a console tree on the left side of the screen and an HTML display area on the right side. The individual products that use the MMC have snap-in programs. A snap-in displays the product in the MMC interface.

OLAP Services provides a snap-in program for the MMC. This snap-in calls the OLAP Add-In Manager, the tool that controls what is displayed in the OLAP Manager. The OLAP Add-In Manager loads the default OLAP Manager interface, along with any custom add-ins that have been registered and enabled.

There are two add-ins that are shipped with OLAP Services. The Migrate Repository Wizard add-in is discussed in Chapter 18. The DSO Information add-in provides some of the basic operation of the OLAP Manager. Three additional add-ins are available on Microsoft's Web site in the Add-In Kit for OLAP Manager. These add-ins are described in Chapter 17, "Partitioning Cubes and Administering OLAP Services."

Creating a Custom Add-In

You can create a custom add-in as a Microsoft ActiveX DLL project in Visual Basic. Your project must include a reference to the OLAP Add-In Manager, which is installed with OLAP Services. The OLAP Add-In Manager implements the IolapAddIn interface, which includes the following property and methods:

- `IOlapAddIn_Name` Property—The name of this add-in.
- `IOlapAddIn_ProvideChildNodes` Method—Creates new nodes in the OLAP Manager's console tree.
- `IOlapAddIn_ProvideMenuItems` Method—Creates new menu items.
- `IOlapAddIn_ExecuteMenuItem` Method—Code that is to be executed when a menu item is selected.
- `IOlapAddIn_ProvideHTML` Method—Updates the HTML display on the right side of the MMC.
- `IOlapAddIn_ProvideIcon` Method—Sets the icon that is displayed in the console tree.
- `IOlapAddIn_GetObject` Method—Returns a reference to an object associated with the node of the tree.

When you create your add-in, you can also use the standard methods for a class module:

- `Class_Initialize`—Code that should be run when the add-in is first loaded.
- `Class_Terminate`—Code that should be run when the add-is unloaded.

Caution

There are several warnings in Microsoft's Product Documentation regarding the use of custom add-in programs. Do not change any of the existing registry information, do not use undocumented parts of the IOlapAddIn interface, and be aware that mistakes in your add-in program may cause other add-ins and the OLAP Manager itself to function incorrectly.

I have encountered one major problem when creating custom add-ins. Some of the code in the IolapAddIn interface is called repeatedly by the OLAP Add-In Manager. If you have an error in your code, that error can be generated repeatedly, so that the OLAP Manager is disabled and must be terminated with the Windows NT Task Manager. I have seen this problem most often with code in IOlapAddIn_ProvideMenuItems and IOlapAddIn_GetObject.

I handle this problem in my add-in programs by disabling the add-in after the first error takes place. This prevents a repeating error from locking up the OLAP Manager.

Registering a Custom Add-In

You must enter information about your custom add-in into the registry so that the OLAP Add-In Manager will recognize it. The OLAP Manager does not provide a tool to automate this registration. The AddInCreator utility, which is described in this chapter, registers a new add-in automatically. If you are creating an add-in manually, you can register it using the registry editor.

Custom add-ins are registered in the following key:

HKEY_LOCAL_MACHINE\SOFTWARE\Microsoft\OLAP Server\Olap Manager Info\Addins

You have to add the following values:

- A string value for the AddIns key. The value name is the name of the custom add-in. The value data should be True, if you want this add-in to be enabled.
- A new key under the AddIns key. The name of this new key is the name of the custom add-in.
- A string value named "ClassName" for the new key. The value data is the Visual Basic project name, a dot, and the name of the class module, such as "OLAPUnleashedDocumenter.Documenter".
- A string value named "Name" for the new key. The value data is the name of the add-in.
- A string value named "Description" for the new key. The value data is a description of the add-in.
- A string value named "Priority" for the new key. The value data is the relative order in which you want this custom add-in to be loaded. Add-ins with a lower number are loaded before add-ins with a higher number.

Figure 19.1 shows the values for the OLAPUnleashedDocumenter displayed in the registry editor.

You can see the information about all the custom add-ins registered on your computer by right-clicking the server in the OLAP Manager, selecting Properties, and choosing the Add-ins tab. Figure 19.2 shows the registry information about the OLAP Unleashed Documenter.

You can change two of the registry settings in this Properties box. Checking or unchecking the box to the right of the add-in name enables or disables the add-in. Moving the add-in higher or lower in the list changes the numbers in the Priority string. Any changes you make go into effect the next time you open the OLAP Manager, whether you make them with the registry editor or in this dialog box.

FIGURE 19.1

Information about new custom add-ins must be entered into the registry.

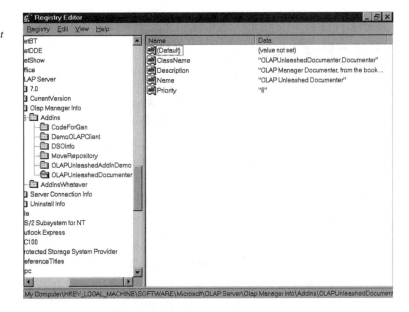

FIGURE 19.2

Information about custom add-ins can be viewed in the Properties dialog.

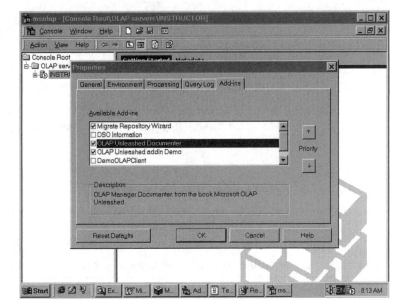

19

DEVELOPING AN
ADD-IN PROGRAM
FOR OLAP

Registering and Using the AddInCreator

 The AddInCreator helps you create new add-ins in two ways. It enters information about the new add-in into the registry and it creates a code template that gives you a starting point for writing the code for your add-in.

The AddInCreator is itself a custom add-in. You will find it on the book's CD-ROM with a filename of AddinCreator.dll. Copy this file into the Windows System directory or to whatever other location you want to keep your add-in files. Register the .dll by selecting Start and Run and executing the following command:

```
regsvr32 AddinCreator.dll
```

If you don't place the file in the Windows System directory or in another location that is on the Windows Path, you must include the full path of the file, as in the following:

```
regsvr32 "c:\Program Files\OLAP Services\Addins\AddinCreator.dll"
```

> **Note**
>
> When you create your own add-in using Visual Basic, you don't have to register the DLL because Visual Basic registers it for you.

Start the Windows NT Registry Editor and find the HKEY_LOCAL_MACHINE\ SOFTWARE\Microsoft\OLAP Server\Olap Manager Info\Addins key. Add the following values:

- A string value, "AddInCreator", for the AddIns key. Set the value data to "True".
- A new key, "AddInCreator", under the AddIns key.
- Four string values under the AddInCreator key, with value names and value data as outlined in Table 19.1.

TABLE 19.1 Registry String Values for AddInCreator Key

Value Name	Value Data
ClassName	AddInCreator.Create
Name	AddInCreator
Priority	3
Description	Automates the creation of OLAP Manager Custom add-ins. From Microsoft OLAP Unleashed.

As you can see, you are following the steps outlined earlier for registering a Custom Add-In. The next time you open the OLAP Manager, the AddInCreator should be available. You can find it by selecting All Tasks and Create AddIn from the Action menu.

The user interface for the AddInCreator is shown in Figure 19.3. You can enter a name and a description for your new add-in. You can also enter the names of new tree nodes and new menu items that you are going to use in your add-in. For the example in this chapter, I have entered the add-in name "TestAddInCreator", tree nodes named "TestTreeNodeMain" and "TestTreeNodeSub", and menu items "TestMenuAction", "TestMenuNew", and "TestMenuSub".

FIGURE 19.3

Enter the basic information for your custom add-in in the AddInCreator.

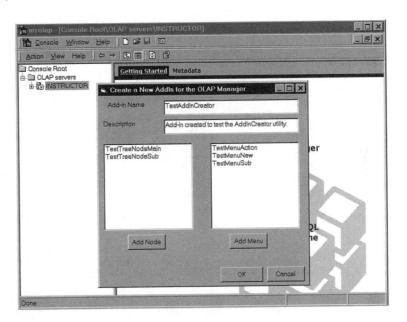

When you select OK, the information about the new add-in is entered into the registry and a code template for the add-in is created in the c:\temp directory.

Now you are ready to start creating the Visual Basic project for your new add-in. Open Visual Basic and start a new Microsoft ActiveX DLL project. Name your project with the same name you gave your new add-in. Do not change the default class module name, "Class1", because it was used by the AddInCreator to register the new add-in.

Select Project and References to register libraries needed for the add-in. You must include a reference to the OLAP Add-In Manager and any other code libraries you will be using.

19

DEVELOPING AN
ADD-IN PROGRAM
FOR OLAP

Find the code template. In this example, it will be c:\temp\TestAddInCreator.txt. Copy the text of the template and paste it into the class module. Select Make TestAddInCreator.dll from the File menu, which will compile and register the new custom add-in. Open the OLAP Manager and examine the list of add-in programs in the server's Property dialog. The new custom add-in, TestAddInCreator, should appear in the list without a check mark, because the AddInCreator disabled it on registration. You can enable it at any point in development to check your work. If you enable it now, close and reopen the OLAP Manager, you will see the two new nodes beneath the list of OLAP Servers. Right-click on any of the new nodes and you will see the three new menu choices, as shown in Figure 19.4.

FIGURE 19.4

The TestAddInCreator creates two new nodes and three new menu choices in the OLAP Manager.

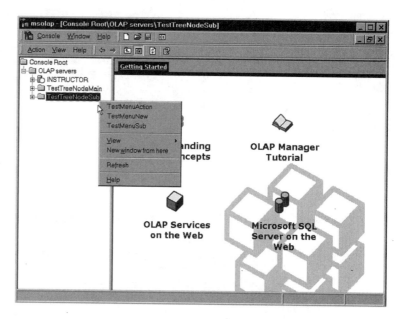

The following sections will show you how to modify the code that is generated by the AddInCreator so that your custom add-in will do something useful.

The Declarations Section

The code that the AddInCreator generates for the declarations section of the class module usually doesn't need to be changed. This code references the IOlapAddIn interface, declares several variables and constants, and declares two enumerations.

The IOlapAddIn interface is implemented by the following line:

```
Implements IolapAddIn
```

When this command is added to the declarations section of a class module, all the methods of the interface are added into the project.

The declarations section of the class module contains a constant with the name of the add-in, because that name is used several other places in the code.

There are two constants and a module-level variable to control the error-handling behavior. If you don't want your add-in to display a message box when an error occurs, change the value of mbDisplayErrMsg to False. By default, the add-in program's functionality is disabled after the first error occurs. This is done to prevent a loop of repeated errors. If you want to change this behavior, change the mbDisableAddInAfterOneError constant to False.

An enumeration called MenuKey is created to hold the key values for all the menu items added by the add-in. These keys are used to coordinate the added menu item with the code that executes when that item is selected.

An enumeration of Icons is also added. The AddInCreator adds only a single value in this enumeration. You can add more icons if you need them for your new tree nodes.

The code for the declarations section of TestAddInCreator is shown in Listing 19.1.

LISTING 19.1 The Declarations Section

```
Option Explicit

Implements IOlapAddIn

Const msAddInName = "TestAddInCreator"
Const mbDisplayErrMsg = True
Const mbDisableAddInAfterOneError = True

Private mbDisableAddIn As Boolean

Private Enum MenuKey
  mnuTestMenuAction = 1
  mnuTestMenuNew
  mnuTestMenuSub
End Enum

Private Enum Icons
  icoForms = 1
End Enum
```

Initialize and Terminate Methods of the Class Module

The generated code for the `Initialize` and `Terminate` methods is shown in Listing 19.2. The only addition the code template makes to these methods is to add error handling and initialize the mbDisableAddIn variable to `False`. This is the variable that is set to `True` after the first error occurs, so that the add-in will be disabled.

LISTING 19.2 The `Initialize` and `Terminate` Methods

```
Private Sub Class_Initialize()
'Add code that is to be run before the rest of the add-in's code
On Error GoTo ProcErr

mbDisableAddIn = False

ProcExit:
  Exit Sub

ProcErr:
  subErrHandler "Class_Initialize", CStr(Err.Number), Err.Description
  GoTo ProcExit


End Sub

Private Sub Class_Terminate()
'Add code that is to be run when the OLAP Manager is being closed
On Error GoTo ProcErr

ProcExit:
  Exit Sub

ProcErr:
  subErrHandler "Class_Terminate", CStr(Err.Number), Err.Description
  GoTo ProcExit

End Sub
```

Assigning the Name Property

The add-in program's name must be assigned for the add-in to function properly. This assignment is made in the IolapAddIn_Name property in the code template and is shown in Listing 19.3. If the name is empty string, the name "UnknownAddIn" is assigned.

LISTING 19.3 Assigning the Name to the Add-In

```
Private Property Get IOlapAddIn_Name() As String
'Assigns the name property of the Add-In
On Error Resume Next

IOlapAddIn_Name = msAddInName

If msAddInName = "" Then
  IOlapAddIn_Name = "UnknownAddIn"
End If

'Clear error without calling error handler
Err.Clear

End Property
```

Adding Tree Nodes

You create new tree nodes in the IolapAddIn_ProvideChildNodes procedure. This procedure has two parameters that can be used in the code to control the placement of the nodes:

- ParentNode—A variable of type DSSAddInsManager.OlapTreeNode which contains a reference to the tree node that is being opened.
- OlapTreeNodes—A reference to the OlapTreeNodes collection, so that you can add new nodes to the collection.

Listing 19.4 shows the template code for creating tree nodes. A Case statement based on the ParentNode's AddInName property lets you add a new tree node only to nodes that have been created by a specific add-in program. A Case statement based on the ParentNode's Caption property allows you to add a node to an existing node with a particular name. Another option, not illustrated in the code, is to query the type of the object associated with the ParentNode. You could, for example, create a new node that would appear only under ParentNodes associated with Cube objects. The AddInCreator creates all the new child nodes under the OLAP Server node. You can cut and paste the statements that create these child nodes and put them in the proper place within the Case statement structure.

LISTING 19.4 Adding Tree Nodes to the Add-In

```
Private Sub IOlapAddIn_ProvideChildNodes( _
    ParentNode As DSSAddInsManager.OlapTreeNode, _
    OlapTreeNodes As DSSAddInsManager.OlapTreeNodes)
```

continues

19

DEVELOPING AN
ADD-IN PROGRAM
FOR OLAP

LISTING 19.4 continued

```
'Adds new nodes to the OLAP Manager console tree
On Error GoTo ProcErr

If mbDisableAddIn = True Then
  GoTo ProcExit
End If

'This code determines where a new node will be added
'  by considering the OwnerAddInName and the Caption of the Parent Node.
'You could also consider the Parent of the ParentNode
'  in making this determination.

If ParentNode.Caption = "OLAP servers" Then
  'The generated code adds all nodes under the OLAP Server node.
  'Move each line of code to the desired location
  OlapTreeNodes.Add "TestTreeNodeMain", icoForms
  OlapTreeNodes.Add "TestTreeNodeSub", icoForms
End If

Select Case ParentNode.OwnerAddInName

  Case msAddInName 'Parent node created by our custom add-in

    Select Case ParentNode.Caption

      Case "TestTreeNodeMain"

      Case "TestTreeNodeSub"

    End Select

  Case "OLAP Manager" 'Parent node created by OLAP Manager

    Select Case ParentNode.Caption

    End Select

  Case Else 'Parent node created by other custom add-in

    'If you use nodes created by other add-ins, you have to assure
    '  that the add-ins are loaded in the proper order.

End Select

ProcExit:
  Exit Sub

ProcErr:
  subErrHandler "IOlapAddIn_ProvideChildNodes", _
```

```
            CStr(Err.Number), Err.Description
    GoTo ProcExit

End Sub
```

The only change to the generated code to make in this section is to move the line adding TestTreeNodeSub so that it becomes a child node of TestTreeNodeMain:

```
    'Move each line of code to the desired location
    OlapTreeNodes.Add "TestTreeNodeMain", icoForms

End If

Select Case ParentNode.OwnerAddInName

  Case msAddInName 'Parent node created by our custom add-in

    Select Case ParentNode.Caption

      Case "TestTreeNodeMain"
        OlapTreeNodes.Add "TestTreeNodeSub", icoForms

      Case "TestTreeNodeSub"
```

Adding Menu Items

The code for creating new menu items is similar to the code for creating new nodes. You are given a reference to the CurrentNode, so that you can control the nodes on which the new menu item will appear. Instead of a reference to the collection of OlapTreeNodes, you are given a reference to the collection of OlapMenuItems, so that you can add your new menu choices.

Menu selections in the OLAP Manager are normally available in two places—on the main menu under Action and on a popup menu. The new menu items you are creating will be available in both places.

An OlapMenuItem property called Key coordinates the individual menu item with the action it is going to carry out. In the sample code, this key is assigned with one of the members of the MenuKey enumeration. When a new menu item is added to the MenuItems collection, you can enter information into five parameters. The first three are required.

- The MenuType. For a regular menu item use mnuStandard. If you were going to add a menu separator, you would use the constant mnuSeparator.

- The Caption property, which is the label displayed on the menu.

- The `Key` property.
- The `ParentKey` property, which is used to indicate the parent menu of a child menu.
- The Flags, which are described next. The menu flags can be added together in a variety of different combinations.

There are three flags that affect the location of the menu item:

- `mnuflagRegular`—Place the menu item on the root of the popup menu and under Action on the application menu.
- `mnuflagTask`—Place the menu as a submenu under All Tasks
- `mnuflagNew`—Place the menu as a submenu under New.

There are three flags that affect the appearance and the operation of the menu item:

- `mnuflagChecked`—Display a check mark by the menu.
- `mnuflagDisabled`—Disable the menu item without changing its appearance.
- `mnuflagGrayed`—Disable the menu item.

There are three other menu flags, one that is used for deleting and two that are used to create parent-child menus:

- `mnuflagDeleteKey`—Enables the Delete menu item, as well as activating Delete on the toolbar and DELETE on the keyboard.
- `mnuflagPopup`—Used to indicate a parent menu item.
- `mnuflagSubmenu`—Used to indicate a child menu item.

There are three menu flags that are reserved for future use—`mnuflagF1`, `mnuflagDoubleClick`, and `mnuflagInsertKey`.

Here is a sample of the code needed to add a new menu item. This item will be placed on the New Task menu and will be disabled.

```
MenuItems.Add mnuStandard, "TestMenuAction", _
        mnuTestMenuAction,,mnuflagTask + mnuflagDisabled
```

Listing 19.5 shows the code generated by the AddInCreator for adding menu items. The default behavior is for all the new menu items to be visible for all nodes added by this new custom add-in. You can move the menu items and add flags to them to control their behavior more precisely.

LISTING 19.5   Code to Add Menu Items

```
Private Sub IOlapAddIn_ProvideMenuItems( _
    CurrentNode As DSSAddInsManager.OlapTreeNode, _
    MenuItems As DSSAddInsManager.OlapMenuItems)
'Adds new menu items
On Error GoTo ProcErr

If mbDisableAddIn = True Then
  GoTo ProcExit
End If

'This code determines where a new menu item will be added
'  by considering the OwnerAddInName, the Caption of the CurrentNode,
'  and, for the OLAP Manager default AddIn, the type of object
'  associated with the node.
'You could also consider the Parent of the CurrentNode
'  in making this determination.
'If you want a new menu item to always be available,
'  place it outside the Select Case block.

Select Case CurrentNode.OwnerAddInName

  Case msAddInName 'Current node created by our custom add-in

    'By default, the menu items are added for all new nodes
    '  created by our new custom add-in.
    'Move each line of code to the appropriate place or places

    MenuItems.Add mnuStandard, "TestMenuAction", mnuTestMenuAction
    MenuItems.Add mnuStandard, "TestMenuNew", mnuTestMenuNew
    MenuItems.Add mnuStandard, "TestMenuSub", mnuTestMenuSub

    Select Case CurrentNode.Caption

      Case "TestTreeNodeMain"

      Case "TestTreeNodeSub"

    End Select

  Case "OLAP Manager" 'Current node created by OLAP Manager

    Select Case CurrentNode.Caption

      Case "OLAP Servers"

    End Select
```

continues

19

DEVELOPING AN
ADD-IN PROGRAM
FOR OLAP

LISTING 19.5 continued

```
      'Make sure the LinkedObject is set
      If CurrentNode.LinkedObject Is Nothing Then

        'No object associated with this node

      Else

        Select Case CurrentNode.LinkedObject.ClassType

          'You must add a reference to the Microsoft Decision Support Objects
          '  in order to use the following ClassType constants
          'Case clsServer

          'Case clsDatabase

          'Case clsCube

        End Select

      End If

    Case Else 'Current node created by other custom add-in

      'If you use nodes created by other add-ins, you have to assure
      '  that the add-ins are loaded in the proper order.

  End Select

ProcExit:
  Exit Sub

ProcErr:
  subErrHandler "IOlapAddIn_ProvideMenuItems", _
        CStr(Err.Number), Err.Description
  GoTo ProcExit

End Sub
```

Add flags to the code adding the menu items, so that the second menu item is placed under the New menu and the first is made the parent menu for the third:

```
MenuItems.Add mnuStandard, "TestMenuAction", _
    mnuTestMenuAction,,mnuflagPopup
MenuItems.Add mnuStandard, "TestMenuNew", _
    mnuTestMenuNew,,mnuflagNew
MenuItems.Add mnuStandard, "TestMenuSub", mnuTestMenuSub, _
    mnuTestMenuAction, mnuflagSubmenu
```

After you have made these changes, select Make TestAddInCreator.dll from the File menu. Open the OLAP Manager and the tree nodes and menus will now appear as in Figure 19.5.

FIGURE 19.5

The TestAddInCreator now has a subordinate node, a subordinate menu, and a New menu.

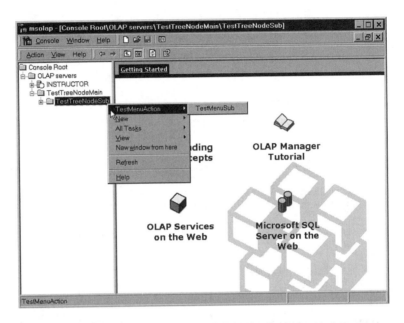

Note

I ran into what appears to be a minor bug while testing this code. When the mnuTestMenuAction item was first in the MenuKey enumeration, it would not work correctly as a parent menu. When I moved the submenu to be first in the enumeration, the code worked fine.

Executing Menu Items

The IolapAddIn_ExecuteMenuItem function has two input parameters and returns one value. The input parameters are CurrentNode and MenuItem, so you know both the MenuItem that was selected and the node that was highlighted at that particular time. You can choose whether or not to consider the CurrentNode when responding to a menu selection. The default code generated by AddInCreator only considers the Key property of the MenuItem.

The return value from this function is one of the constants of the RefreshTreeTypes enumeration. You have four choices regarding the refresh of the console tree after your menu code has been executed:

- `reftreeNoRefresh`
- `reftreeCurrentAndBelow`
- `reftreeParentAndBelow`
- `reftreeAllTree`

The generated code for executing menu items is shown in Listing 19.6. The default behavior of each menu item is to open a message box that announces the menu selection.

LISTING 19.6   The Code to Execute Menu Items

```
Private Function IOlapAddIn_ExecuteMenuItem( _
    CurrentNode As DSSAddInsManager.OlapTreeNode, _
    MenuItem As DSSAddInsManager.OlapMenuItem) _
    As DSSAddInsManager.RefreshTreeTypes
'Code in this function is executed when a menu item is selected
On Error GoTo ProcErr

If mbDisableAddIn = True Then
  GoTo ProcExit
End If

'This code looks only at the menu key when executing menu code.
'You can also consider what node was highlighted when the
'  menu item was selected.

Select Case MenuItem.Key

  Case mnuTestMenuAction
    MsgBox "Menu item selected - TestMenuAction"

  Case mnuTestMenuNew
    MsgBox "Menu item selected - TestMenuNew"

  Case mnuTestMenuSub
    MsgBox "Menu item selected - TestMenuSub"

End Select

ProcExit:
  Exit Function

ProcErr:
  subErrHandler "IOlapAddIn_ExecuteMenuItem", _
      CStr(Err.Number), Err.Description
```

```
    GoTo ProcExit

End Function
```

The Other Methods of the IOLAPAddIn Interface

The `IolapAddIn_ProvideHTML` procedure modifies the HTML display on the right side of the MMC. There is not much sample code generated for this procedure by the AddInCreator. If you want to change the HTML as different nodes are selected, you would use code similar to the code of `ProvideMenuItems`.

The `IOlapAddIn_ProvideIcon` function returns a reference to an icon in a reference file.

The `IOlapAddIn_GetObject` function returns a reference to the object that is associated with a tree node. If you want to associate an object with one of your nodes, you can make that object assignment in this function.

The generated code for these methods is shown in Listing 19.7.

LISTING 19.7   Code to Choose HTML and Icons and to Get the Icon Object

```
Private Sub IOlapAddIn_ProvideHTML( _
    CurrentNode As DSSAddInsManager.OlapTreeNode, _
    CurrentURL As String)
'Selects HTML to be displayed on right hand side of the MMC
On Error GoTo ProcErr

If mbDisableAddIn = True Then
  GoTo ProcExit
End If

'Use code similar to ProvideMenuItems

ProcExit:
  Exit Sub

ProcErr:
  subErrHandler "IOlapAddIn_ProvideHTML", _
       CStr(Err.Number), Err.Description
  GoTo ProcExit

End Sub
```

19

DEVELOPING AN ADD-IN PROGRAM FOR OLAP

continues

LISTING 19.7 continued

```
Private Function IOlapAddIn_ProvideIcon(Index As Integer) _
    As stdole.OLE_HANDLE
'Provides handle to an icon in a resource file
On Error GoTo ProcErr

ProcExit:
  Exit Function

ProcErr:
  subErrHandler "IOlapAddIn_ProvideIcon", _
      CStr(Err.Number), Err.Description
  GoTo ProcExit

End Function

Private Function IOlapAddIn_GetObject( _
    LinkedNode As DSSAddInsManager.OlapTreeNode) As Object
'Provides reference to the object associated with a node.
On Error GoTo ProcErr

'The generated code provides no object references
Select Case LinkedNode.OwnerAddInName

  Case msAddInName

    Select Case LinkedNode.Caption

      Case "TestTreeNodeMain"
        'Set IOlapAddIn_GetObject = objVarTestTreeNodeMain

      Case "TestTreeNodeSub"
        'Set IOlapAddIn_GetObject = objVarTestTreeNodeSub

    End Select

End Select

ProcExit:
  Exit Function

ProcErr:
  subErrHandler "IOlapAddIn_GetObject", _
      CStr(Err.Number), Err.Description
  GoTo ProcExit

End Function
```

Handling Errors

Listing 19.8 contains the error-handling procedure that is generated by the AddInCreator. The procedure handles the error in accordance with the global constants that are set in the declarations section.

LISTING 19.8 The AddInCreator's Error-Handling Procedure

```
Private Sub subErrHandler(sProcedure As String, _
    sErrNum As String, sErrDesc As String)
On Error Resume Next

Dim msg As String

msg = "Add-In Name - " & msAddInName & vbCrLf & vbCrLf
msg = msg & "Procedure Name - " & sProcedure & vbCrLf & vbCrLf
msg = msg & "Error Number - " & sErrNum & vbCrLf & vbCrLf
msg = msg & "Description - " & sErrDesc

If mbDisableAddInAfterOneError Then
  mbDisableAddIn = True
  msg = msg & vbCrLf & vbCrLf & "StarToCube will be disabled."
End If

If mbDisplayErrMsg Then
  MsgBox msg, , "Error in Custom Add-In Program"
End If

Err.Clear

End Sub
```

Sample Custom Add-Ins

There are four sample add-in projects included for this chapter on the book's CD-ROM. Two of the projects use the AddInCreator to turn Visual Basic projects from other chapters into add-in programs. The third project is an additional add-in that documents OLAP objects. The fourth project is the AddInCreator itself, which is discussed in the "Customizing the AddInCreator Utility" section later in this chapter.

The AggDesigner Add-In

The AggDesigner utility was created for Chapter 18. To turn this utility into an add-in program, follow these steps:

1. Select All Tasks, Create AddIn from the Action menu in the OLAP Manager. If this menu item doesn't appear, go back to the "Using the AddInCreator" to register the AddInCreator add-in program.

2. Enter "AggDesigner" as the Add-In Name and "Multiple cube aggregation designer from Microsoft OLAP Unleashed" as the description. Add no tree nodes and one menu item—"Multiple Cube Agg Design."

3. Begin a new Visual Basic ActiveX DLL project. Name the project "AggDesigner." Add references to OLAP Add-In Manager and Microsoft Decision Support Objects.

4. Add the frmAggDesigner.frm to the project. This form was created in the OLAPUnleashedAggDesigner project in Chapter 18.

5. Copy the code from the c:\temp\AggDesigner.txt into the class module.

6. Find the IOlapAddIn_ProvideMenuItems procedure. Move the command that adds the new menu item so that it is available when a server, a database, or a cube object is selected:

```
Select Case CurrentNode.LinkedObject.ClassType

    'You must add a reference to the Microsoft Decision Support Objects
    ' in order to use the following ClassType constants
    Case clsServer
      MenuItems.Add mnuStandard, "Multiple Cube AggDesign", _
          mnuMultipleCubeAggDesign

    Case clsDatabase
      MenuItems.Add mnuStandard, "Multiple Cube AggDesign", _
          mnuMultipleCubeAggDesign

    Case clsCube
      MenuItems.Add mnuStandard, "Multiple Cube AggDesign", _
          mnuMultipleCubeAggDesign


    End Select
```

7. Find the IOlapAddIn_ExecuteMenuItem procedure. Replace the code in the Select box with the following:

```
Case mnuMultipleCubeAggDesign
   frmAggDesigner.Show vbModal
```

You must always use vbModal with forms displayed in an add-in program.

8. Choose Make AggDesigner.dll from the File menu.

9. Open the OLAP Manager. Open the server's Properties dialog and activate the AggDesigner add-in.

10. Close and reopen the OLAP Manager. You should see the Multiple Cube AggDesign on the main menu. Select it and the AggDesigner utility will open. See Chapter 18 for a description of the utility's capabilities.

The AggDesigner add-in is now functional, but it is not integrated very well into the OLAP Manager interface. As a freestanding utility, it was necessary for the AggDesigner to connect to an OLAP server. That's not necessary when it is converted to an add-in. It should display objects from the selected server or from the server in which the selected database or cube is an object.

Replace the IOlapAddIn_ExecuteMenuItem code with the following, which passes a reference of the Server object to the form, adjusts some of the controls on the form, and integrates the form's error handling into the add-in program's error handling.

```
Case mnuMultipleCubeAggDesign

  If CurrentNode.LinkedObject.ClassType = clsServer Then
    Set frmAggDesigner.dsoServer = CurrentNode.LinkedObject
  Else
    Set frmAggDesigner.dsoServer = CurrentNode.LinkedObject.Server
  End If

  frmAggDesigner.txtDSOServer = frmAggDesigner.dsoServer.Name
  frmAggDesigner.txtDSOServer.Locked = True
  frmAggDesigner.txtProcessing.Text = "Cube list not refreshed."
  frmAggDesigner.gsErrDesc = ""

  frmAggDesigner.Show vbModal

  If frmAggDesigner.gsErrDesc <> "" Then
    subErrHandler frmAggDesigner.gsProcedure, frmAggDesigner.gsErrNum, _
        frmAggDesigner.gsErrDesc
  End If
```

It's also necessary to make some modifications to the form. Change the caption on the cmdConnect button to read Refresh Cube List. Replace the messages to the user in cmdConnect_Click with the following:

```
txtProcessing.Text = "Refreshing Cube List - Please Wait"

..

.
txtProcessing.Text = "Cube List Refreshed - Ready"
```

Remove the command that unloads the application in cmdQuit_Click.

Error-handling code in the form needs several modifications. The class module should handle all errors, so that they can be handled in a consistent manner. Here are the necessary error-handling changes for the form:

1. Add the following to the declarations section of the form:

```
Public gsProcedure As String
Public gsErrNum As String
Public gsErrDesc As String
```

2. Replace the form's error handler procedure with the following:

```
Private Sub subErrHandler(sProcedure As String, sErrNum As String, _
        sErrDesc As String)
On Error Resume Next

gsProcedure = "frmAggDesigner - " & sProcedure
gsErrNum = sErrNum
gsErrDesc = sErrDesc

frmMain.Hide

End Sub
```

3. Add code to each procedure in the form to call the Error Handler.

The StarToCube Add-In

The process of creating other add-ins is similar. The StarToCube utility, described in Chapter 18, automates the process of creating a cube from a star schema. It is implemented with a single menu selection called "Convert Star to Cube." Follow the procedure outlined for the AggDesigner, with the following exceptions:

1. The Visual Basic References needed are

    OLAP Add-In Manager

    Microsoft Decision Support Objects

    Microsoft SQLDMO Object Library

    Microsoft ActiveX Data Objects (Multi-Dim) 1.0 Library

    Microsoft ActiveX Data Objects 2.1 Library

2. Use the following code in IOlapAddIn_ExecuteMenuItem:

```
Select Case MenuItem.Key

    Case mnuStarToCube

        If CurrentNode.LinkedObject.ClassType = clsServer Then
```

```
          Set frmMain.dsoServer = CurrentNode.LinkedObject
       Else
          Set frmMain.dsoServer = CurrentNode.LinkedObject.Server
       End If

       frmMain.txtDSOServer = frmMain.dsoServer.Name
       frmMain.txtDSOServer.Locked = True
       frmMain.cmdConnectOLAP.Visible = False

       frmMain.gsErrDesc = ""
       frmMain.Show vbModal
       If frmMain.gsErrDesc <> "" Then
          subErrHandler frmMain.gsProcedure, frmMain.gsErrNum,
    frmMain.gsErrDesc
       End If

    End Select
```

3. Add the same error handling into the forms as you did for the AggDesigner. The global error-handling variables should only be placed in frmMain. There are no other changes needed for the forms.

The Documenter Add-In

The Documenter add-in provides a brief report of objects in an OLAP database. The Visual Basic project for this add-in is included on the book's CD-ROM. Listing 19.9 is taken from the class module for this project. This code illustrates some of the capabilities of IOlapAddIn_ProvideMenuItems. The menu items are disabled if the server is not connected. A main menu and four submenus are created by the code.

LISTING 19.9 Code That Adds a Main Menu with Submenus

```
Private Sub IOlapAddIn_ProvideMenuItems( _
    CurrentNode As DSSAddInsManager.OlapTreeNode, _
    MenuItems As DSSAddInsManager.OlapMenuItems)
On Error GoTo Err

   'Check to see if this node was created by the
   '  OLAP Manager and not by another AddIn
   If CurrentNode.OwnerAddInName = "OLAP Manager" Then

      'Check to see if this node is a server
      If CurrentNode.LinkedObject.ClassType = clsServer Then

        Set dsoServer = CurrentNode.LinkedObject

        'Add a separator
        MenuItems.Add mnuSeparator
```

continues

19

DEVELOPING AN
ADD-IN PROGRAM
FOR OLAP

LISTING 19.9 continued

```
    'Create the main menu.
    '  Disable it if there is no server connected
    If dsoServer.State = stateConnected Then
      MenuItems.Add mnuStandard, "&Document", _
          mnuDocument, , mnuflagRegular + mnuflagPopup
    Else
      MenuItems.Add mnuStandard, "&Document", _
          mnuDocument, , mnuflagGrayed + mnuflagPopup
    End If

    'Create menu items for list
    MenuItems.Add mnuStandard, "Document &Databases", _
        mnuDocDatabase, mnuDocument, mnuflagSubmenu

    MenuItems.Add mnuStandard, "Document &Cubes", _
        mnuDocCube, mnuDocument, mnuflagSubmenu

    MenuItems.Add mnuStandard, "Document &Dimensions", _
        mnuDocDimension, mnuDocument, mnuflagSubmenu

    MenuItems.Add mnuStandard, "Document &Levels", _
        mnuDocLevel, mnuDocument, mnuflagSubmenu

    End If
  End If

ExitProc:
  Exit Sub
Err:
  MsgBox Err.Description & " " & Err.Number
  GoTo ExitProc

End Sub
```

This project must be entered into the registry with a name of
OLAPUnleashedDocumenter and a class name of
OLAPUnleashedDocumenter.Documenter.

Customizing the AddInCreator Utility

The Visual Basic code for the AddInCreator is also included on the CD-ROM. You can
modify the code that generates the code template for the creation of new add-ins so that
it matches your needs. The code that generates the Declarations section is shown in
Listing 19.10. This code is located in the cmdOK_Click procedure on the application's

form. Each `subPrint` command prints one line in the code template, so it's easy to add or remove lines. Quotation marks that need to appear in the template can be entered with the `QUOTE` constant.

LISTING 19.10 AddInCreator Template-Generating Code

```
subPrint "Option Explicit"
subPrint ""
subPrint "Implements IOlapAddIn"
subPrint ""
subPrint "Const msAddInName = " & QUOTE & msAddInName & QUOTE
subPrint "Const mbDisplayErrMsg = True"
subPrint "Const mbDisableAddInAfterOneError = True"
subPrint "Private mbDisableAddIn As Boolean"
subPrint ""

If frmMain.lstMenu.ListCount> 0 Then

  subPrint "Private Enum MenuKey"

  For idx = 0 To frmMain.lstMenu.ListCount - 1
    If idx = 0 Then
      subPrint "  mnu" & fctRemoveSpace(frmMain.lstMenu.List(idx)) & " = 1"
    Else
      subPrint "  mnu" & fctRemoveSpace(frmMain.lstMenu.List(idx))
    End If
  Next idx

  subPrint "End Enum"

  End If

subPrint ""
subPrint "Private Enum Icons"
subPrint "  icoForms = 1"
subPrint "End Enum"
```

If you want to add a new procedure or some new lines of code into an existing procedure, copy that code into the appropriate place in the `cmdOK_Click` procedure. Then paste `subPrint` at the beginning of each line. The Visual Basic code editor will automatically add the closing double quote.

Summary

I expect that there will soon be a number of useful add-ins available for the OLAP Manager. But you don't have to wait for those products. You can create your own customized add-ins now. Many of the tasks that take a significant amount of time to accomplish in the OLAP Manager can be automated with add-in programs.

The PivotTable Service

by Tim Peterson

CHAPTER 20

PivotTable Service is a desktop OLAP server that is provided with OLAP Services. PivotTable Service can be used as a client of OLAP Services, taking cube data from OLAP Services cubes and providing that data to client applications. But PivotTable Service can be used by itself, apart from OLAP Services, to build and manage multidimensional cubes.

Client applications connect to PivotTable Service both to access data from OLAP Services and to access data from local cubes. The interface for client applications is the same in both situations.

The use of PivotTable Service by client applications is discussed in the next part of the book. Chapter 22, "Programming Access to the OLAP Data Sources," discusses how client applications connect to PivotTable Service. Chapters 23 through 26 show how to build OLAP client applications.

This chapter focuses on PivotTable Service as an OLAP server. You will learn how to build and manage local cubes. You will also learn how to use the caching capabilities of PivotTable Service.

The last section of this chapter describes the LocalCube utility, which can be used to create a cube file from a portion of an OLAP Services cube. This utility can also be converted into an OLAP Manager add-in program, so that you can create local cubes directly in the OLAP Manager interface. The LocalCube utility is on the book's CD-ROM.

Creating and Managing Local Cubes

The local cubes created by PivotTable Service are different from the cubes created by OLAP Services in several ways. The most important difference is that PivotTable Service does not provide any capability to create aggregations.

PivotTable Service can create either MOLAP or ROLAP cubes. With MOLAP cubes, the data is stored in a multidimensional format in the .cub file. For ROLAP, the .cub file only stores the dimension members and all the rest of the data remains in its source. The HOLAP choice is not available because HOLAP only varies from ROLAP in the storage of aggregations.

MOLAP cube files are much larger than ROLAP cube files built with the same data. MOLAP cubes take longer to build, but provide faster browsing performance. If you want to use your local cubes when the source data is not available, you must use the MOLAP storage mode.

Other differences with PivotTable Service cubes include the following:

- PivotTable Service does not have a database structure, so each cube is a separate entity.
- You cannot use shared dimensions.
- Cubes do not have partitions.
- You cannot create virtual cubes.
- You cannot use SQL to query local cubes. You must use MDX or ADO MD to access local cube data.
- You cannot define users or restrict access to portions of the cube data.

PivotTable Service is superior to OLAP Services in at least one way. The OLAP Services tools do not let you explicitly declare multiple hierarchies within one dimension. There is a way to work around this limitation, which is described in Chapter 18, "Decision Support Objects." PivotTable Service syntax has the ability to create multiple hierarchies built right into the syntax.

Eight MDX statements are used to create and manage local cubes. All except the first two of these statements can also be used by PivotTable Service to manage a connection to an OLAP Services cube. Each of these statements is discussed in this chapter.

- `CREATE CUBE`—Define the structure of a local cube.
- `INSERT INTO`—Insert data into a local cube from either a relational data source or from an OLAP Services cube.
- `CREATE MEMBER` and `DROP MEMBER`—Create or drop a calculated member.
- `CREATE SET` and `DROP SET`—Create or drop a user-defined set.
- `REFRESH CUBE`—Rebuild the local cube.
- `CREATE CACHE`—Populate the local cache with a portion of the cube data.

The CREATE CUBE Statement

The syntax for `CREATE CUBE` is modeled after the `CREATE TABLE` statement in SQL. It is more complex, of course, because a cube's structure is more complex than a table's.

The shortest possible `CREATE CUBE` statement is shown in Listing 20.1. All the elements in this statement are required. Your cube has to have at least one dimension. You must include at least one level for each dimension. You must have at least one measure and you must specify the function used by that measure. You must give a name to the cube and to all dimensions, hierarchies, levels, and measures that you choose to include.

Commas are used to separate the specification of each dimension, hierarchy, level, and measure. Square braces ([ ]) must be used wherever there is a space in the name of an object.

LISTING 20.1   A Simple CREATE CUBE Statement

```
CREATE CUBE LocalProduct
(
DIMENSION Product,
    LEVEL [Product Name],
MEASURE [Quantity Received] FUNCTION SUM
)
```

A cube with one dimension and one measure isn't very interesting, of course. The CREATE CUBE statement in Listing 20.2 will create a cube similar to, although slightly more complex than, the Warehouse cube in the FoodMart sample database. The example illustrates the following syntactical elements of the CREATE CUBE statement:

- Multiple hierarchies within one dimension.
- Persistent calculated measures with the COMMAND element.
- Dimension types, such as TYPE TIME.
- Level types, such as LEVEL ALL or LEVEL YEAR.
- Sort order for level members with SORTBYKEY or SORTBYNAME
- Uniqueness of members in a level, using UNIQUE.
- Measure formatting.
- Measure datatypes, using the OLEDB numeric types.

LISTING 20.2   Creating the FoodMart Warehouse Cube

```
CREATE CUBE LocalWarehouse
(
DIMENSION Store,
  HIERARCHY [Marketing Location],
    LEVEL [Worldwide] LEVEL ALL,
    LEVEL [Store Country],
    LEVEL [Store Region],
    LEVEL [Store State],
    LEVEL [Store City],
    LEVEL [Store Neighborhood],
    LEVEL [Store Name] SORTBYNAME,
  HIERARCHY [Administration Location],
    LEVEL [Store Country],
    LEVEL [Store State],
    LEVEL [Store City],
```

```
        LEVEL [Store Name],
DIMENSION Time TYPE TIME,
        LEVEL Year TYPE YEAR,
        LEVEL Quarter TYPE QUARTER,
        LEVEL Month TYPE MONTH SORTBYKEY,
DIMENSION [Store Size in SQFT],
        LEVEL [Store Sqft],
DIMENSION [Store Type],
        LEVEL [Store Type],
DIMENSION [Warehouse],
        LEVEL Country,
        LEVEL [State Province],
        LEVEL [City],
        LEVEL [Warehouse Name],
MEASURE [Store Invoice] FUNCTION SUM TYPE DBType_R8,
MEASURE [Supply Time] FUNCTION SUM FORMAT '#,#' TYPE DBTYPE_I4,
MEASURE [Warehouse Cost] FUNCTION SUM TYPE DBType_CY,
MEASURE [Warehouse Sales] FUNCTION SUM TYPE DBType_R8,
MEASURE [Units Shipped] FUNCTION SUM FORMAT '#,#' TYPE DBTYPE_I4,
MEASURE [Units Ordered] FUNCTION SUM FORMAT '#,#' TYPE DBTYPE_I4,
COMMAND [CREATE MEMBER LocalWarehouse.MEASURES.[Warehouse Profit]
        AS 'MEASURES.[Warehouse Sales] - 'MEASURES.[Warehouse Cost]']
)
```

The INSERT INTO Statement

The INSERT INTO statement populates a cube. For ROLAP cubes, only the dimensions are populated. For MOLAP cubes, the dimensions and the data are populated. MOLAP is the default storage mode. Use the OPTIONS DEFER_DATA phrase with the INSERT INTO statement to specify ROLAP storage.

Cubes can be populated with data from any relational source, as well as from OLAP Services cubes. An example of a very simple INSERT INTO statement using a relational source is shown in Listing 20.3. The cube created with the code in Listing 20.1 is populated in the ROLAP mode with this statement. The SELECT clause is a normal SQL SELECT statement. Each level and measure mentioned in the field listing following the name of the cube must be matched by a field in the SELECT list. This example shows data from the relational database underlying FoodMart being inserted into a very simple local cube.

LISTING 20.3 The INSERT INTO Statement Using a Relational Source

```
INSERT INTO WarehouseUnitsOrdered
    (
    [Warehouse Name],
```

continues

20

THE PIVOTTABLE SERVICE

LISTING 20.3   continued

```
    [Units Ordered]
    )
OPTIONS DEFER_DATA
SELECT
    warehouse_name,
    units_Ordered
  FROM  inventory_fact_1998 INNER JOIN warehouse
    ON inventory_fact_1998.warehouse_id = warehouse.warehouse_id
```

Listing 20.4 shows an INSERT INTO statement using data from the Sales cube in the
FoodMart sample database. The local cube being populated in this example has fewer
dimensions and measures than the Sales cube. This INSERT INTO statement creates a
MOLAP cube because the OPTIONS DEFER_DATA clause is not used. All the levels are
qualified with the dimension name in this example. This is not necessary, as long as the
level names are unique in the cube. Measures can also be qualified with the classification
"Measures."

LISTING 20.4   The INSERT INTO Statement Using an OLAP Services Cube Source

```
INSERT INTO SalesByStoreByTime
    (
    Store.[Store Country],
    Store.[Store State],
    Store.[Store City],
    Store.[Store Name],
    Time.Year,
    Time.Quarter,
    Time.Month,

    Measures.[Unit Sales],
    Measures.[Store Cost],
    Measures.[Store Sales]
    )
SELECT
    Sales.[Store:Store Country],
    Sales.[Store:Store State],
    Sales.[Store:Store City],
    Sales.[Store:Store Name],
    Sales.[Time:Year],
    Sales.[Time:Quarter],
    Sales.[Time:Month],

    Sales.[Measures:Unit Sales],
    Sales.[Measures:Store Cost],
    Sales.[Measures:Store Sales]
FROM Sales
```

Some of the additional elements of the INSERT INTO statement include

- OPTIONS PASSTHROUGH—Causes PivotTable Service to skip processing the query. It is sent immediately to the data source. This results in a MOLAP cube being created. PASSTHROUGH processing is often less efficient than regular processing.

- OPTIONS ATTEMPT_DEFER—Attempts to defer processing. If ATTEMPT_DEFER is successful and PASSTHROUGH is not specified, a ROLAP cube is created. If ATTEMPT_DEFER fails, a MOLAP cube is created.

- OPTIONS ATTEMPT_ANALYSIS—Instructs PivotTable Service to attempt to parse the query.

- SKIPONECOLUMN—If one or more columns in the SELECT clause does not have a corresponding element in the INSERT INTO clause, the key word SKIPONECOLUMN can be used in the INSERT INTO clause to ignore the data in that column.

- .NAME and .KEY suffixes—Each level can be based on two columns in the original data, one of the columns being the Name and the other being the Key. Use the .NAME and the .KEY suffixes in the INSERT INTO clause to associate the correct columns with each value.

- DIRECTLYFROMCACHEDROWSET—A local cube can be based on the local cache by using DIRECTLYFROMCACHEDROWSET clause, with a pointer to the rowset, in place of the SELECT clause.

Using CREATE CUBE and INSERT INTO to Create a Local Cube

The following four strings are used together in a ConnectionString to create a local cube with ADO MD:

- The location of the cube file that is to be created.
- The SourceDSN, which specifies the data source.
- A string containing a CREATE CUBE statement.
- A string containing an INSERT INTO statement.

The code in Listing 20.5 creates a simple local cube from an OLAP Services cube. The cube is the same one that was used in Listing 20.3 to illustrate the INSERT INTO statement used with a relational database source. The cube file is actually created with the Open method of the connection object. This code is in the Visual Basic project SimpleCube, which is on the book's CD-ROM.

20

THE PIVOTTABLE SERVICE

LISTING 20.5   Creating a Local Cube

```
Option Explicit

Private Sub Form_Load()

Dim cn As New ADODB.Connection
Dim sLocation As String
Dim sDSN As String
Dim sCreate As String
Dim sInsert As String

sLocation = "LOCATION = c:\temp\WarehouseUnitsOrdered.cub"
sDSN = "Provider=MSOLAP;data source=LocalHost;INITIAL CATALOG=FoodMart"
sDSN = "SOURCE_DSN=""" & sDSN & """"

sCreate = "CREATECUBE=CREATE CUBE WarehouseUnitsOrdered " & _
  "(" & _
  "DIMENSION [Warehouse]," & _
  "    LEVEL [Warehouse Name]," & _
  "MEASURE [Units Ordered] Function SUM" & _
  ")"

sInsert = "INSERTINTO=INSERT INTO WarehouseUnitsOrdered" & _
  "(" & _
  "[Warehouse].[Warehouse Name]," & _
  "[Measures].[Units Ordered]" & _
  ")" & _
" SELECT " & _
  "[Warehouse].[Warehouse:Warehouse Name]," & _
  "[Warehouse].[Measures:Units Ordered]" & _
" FROM [Warehouse]"

cn.ConnectionString = sLocation & ";" & sDSN & ";" & sCreate & ";" & sInsert
cn.Provider = "MSOLAP"
cn.Open ' *.cub File is created right now!

MsgBox "Cube file created -  c:\temp\WarehouseUnitsOrdered.cub"

cn.Close
Unload Form1

End Sub
```

Calculated Members and User-Defined Sets

PivotTable Service provides commands for creating and dropping calculated members and user-defined sets. These commands can be used when working with local cubes, as well as when PivotTable Service is being used to access OLAP Services cubes.

Both calculated members and user-defined sets can be defined with three different scopes:

- Query scope—The member or set is created in the MDX query using a WITH clause.
- Session scope—A CREATE MEMBER or CREATE SET command is used.
- Global scope—The member or set was created using a COMMAND clause in the CREATE CUBE statement.

A global calculated member was created in Listing 20.2. The same member could be created with session scope by issuing the CREATE MEMBER command:

```
CREATE SESSION MEMBER Warehouse.MEASURES.[Warehouse Profit]
    AS 'MEASURES.[Warehouse Sales] - 'MEASURES.[Warehouse Cost]'
```

Creating a user-defined set with session scope is similar. This set creates a combined view of Minneapolis and St. Paul as the Twin Cities:

```
CREATE SESSION SET Warehouse.Store.[Store City].[Twin Cities]
    AS '{Store.[MN].[Minneapolis], Store.[MN].[St. Paul]}'
```

The DROP MEMBER and DROP SET statements can be used to delete the calculated members and user-defined sets:

```
DROP MEMBER Warehouse.MEASURES.[Warehouse Profit]
DROP SET Warehouse.Store.[Store City].[Twin Cities]
```

Refreshing Cubes

The REFRESH CUBE statement causes a different action depending on whether the client is connected to an OLAP Services cube or to a local cube.

- When clients are connected through PivotTable Service to an OLAP Services cube, the command causes the local data cache to be refreshed with the current data from the server's cube.
- When clients are connected to a local cube, the command causes that cube to be rebuilt.

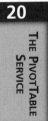

Populating the Data Cache

One of the most important aspects of PivotTable Service is its ability to cache data locally. The data that client applications retrieve from cubes is stored in the local cache. If subsequent queries can be answered completely or partially with information already in the cache, the query response time can be greatly improved.

You also have the ability to preload a subset of the total cube data into the local cache. You can do this for a single query by using the WITH CACHE clause in an MDX query:

```
WITH CACHE AS '({[USA], [Canada]})'
SELECT
    { [Measures].[Units Shipped], [Measures].[Units Ordered] } ON  COLUMNS,
    [Store].[Store Country].members ON ROWS
FROM Warehouse
```

You can preload the cache on the session level by issuing a CREATE CACHE statement:

```
CREATE SESSION CACHE FOR Warehouse AS '({WA, OR})'
```

The LocalCube Utility

The LocalCube utility, shown in Figure 20.1, is a tool that generates a local cube from a subset of an OLAP Services cube. It gives users the ability to pick the dimensions, levels, and measures they want to include in the local cube.

FIGURE 20.1

The LocalCube utility creates a cube file from a subset of an OLAP Services cube.

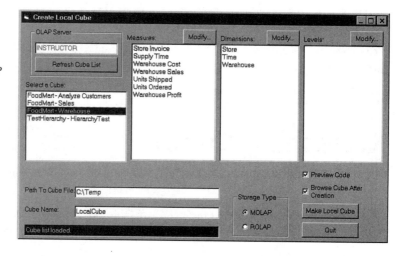

The user can choose to preview and edit the MDX statements that are generated to create the cube. Figure 20.2 shows the Code Editor in the LocalCube utility. The CREATE CUBE statement is shown in one text box. The INSERT INTO and the SELECT clauses of the INSERT INTO statement are shown in separate text boxes. The code is formatted so that the code referencing the same field appears on the same line in all three boxes. Any changes you make in the Code Editor will be incorporated into the local cube that you are creating.

FIGURE 20.2

The Code Editor shows you the MDX code that creates and fills the local cube.

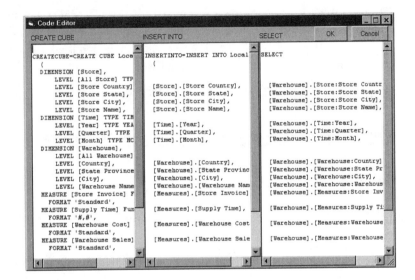

You can also choose to browse the local cube after it is created. Figure 20.3 shows the local cube data displayed in the cube browser.

FIGURE 20.3

You can browse your local cube with the LocalCube utility.

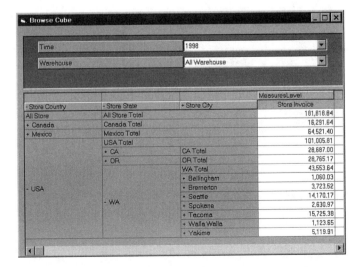

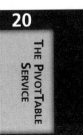

20

THE PIVOTTABLE SERVICE

The Visual Basic project containing the LocalCube utility is on the book's CD-ROM. The following references are needed for the project:

- Microsoft Decision Support Objects
- Microsoft ActiveX Data Objects (Multidimensional) 1.0 Library
- Microsoft ActiveX Data Objects 2.1 Library
- Microsoft Scripting Runtime

The main work of cube creation is accomplished in the cmdCreateCube procedure. This procedure creates the three code strings that are displayed in the Code Editor. The subAddText procedure is called each time more information is added to the three code strings. These two procedures are shown in Listing 20.6.

 Listing 20.6 is on the CD-ROM for this book.

LISTING 20.6 Creating a Local Cube from an OLAP Services Cube

```
Dim QUOTE As String

Dim gsCreateCube As String
Dim gsInsertInto As String
Dim gsSelect As String

Public Enum StringType
  typC 'Part of the CREATE CUBE string
  typI 'Part of the INSERT INTO string
  typS 'Part of the SELECT string
End Enum

Public Enum AddTextLocation
  SAMELINE = -1 'Add text on same line.
  TAB0 = 0 'Add text on next line without any tabs
  TAB1 = 1 'Add text on next line with 1 tab
  TAB2 = 2 'Add text on next line with 2 tabs
  TAB3 = 3 'Add text on next line with 3 tabs
  TAB4 = 4 'Add text on next line with 4 tabs
  TAB5 = 5 'Add text on next line with 5 tabs
End Enum

Private Sub Form_Load()

QUOTE = Chr(&H22)

End Sub

Private Sub cmdMakeCube_Click()
On Error GoTo ProcErr
```

```
Dim idx As Integer
Dim idxDim As Integer
Dim col As Collection

Dim bIsTimeDim As Boolean
Dim bIsPrivateDim As Boolean
Dim bHasHierarchy As Boolean
Dim bNewDimension As Boolean

Dim sSourceCube As String
Dim sDestCube As String
Dim sFullPath As String

Dim sDimension As String
Dim sHierarchy As String
Dim sLevel As String
Dim sMeasure As String
Dim sFormat As String
Dim sDatatype As String

Dim sPreviousDimension As String
Dim lDimLen As Long

Dim cn As ADODB.Connection
Dim cat As New ADOMD.Catalog
Dim sLocation As String
Dim sSourceDSN As String
Dim sConnectionString As String
Dim lFileNum As Long

Dim dsoDimension As DSO.Dimension
Dim dsoLevel As DSO.Level
Dim dsoMeasure As DSO.Measure

Dim msg As String
Dim ttl As String
Dim fso As New Scripting.FileSystemObject

'Initialize global variables used for strings
gsCreateCube = ""
gsInsertInto = ""
gsSelect = ""

'Various Validation Checks

'Validate the measure(s) selected
If lstMeasure.ListCount = 0 Then
  MsgBox "You must select at least one measure."
  GoTo ProcExit
End If
```

continues

LISTING 20.6 continued

```
'Validate the dimensions selected
If lstDimension.ListCount = 0 Then
  MsgBox "You must select at least one dimension."
  GoTo ProcExit
End If

'Validate the cube name
If txtCubeName.Text = "" Then
  MsgBox "You must name this cube."
  GoTo ProcExit
End If

'Validate the levels selected
For idx = 0 To lstDimension.ListCount - 1
  Set col = ColOfColLevels.Item(lstDimension.List(idx))
  If col.Count = 0 Then
    MsgBox "You must select at least one level " & vbCrLf & _
      "per selected dimension."
    GoTo ProcExit
  End If
Next idx

'Create a new ADODBConnection
Set cn = New ADODB.Connection

'Assign Source Cube string
sSourceCube = dsoCubeSelected.Name

'Remove final slash from cube location, if it is there.
If Right(txtLocation.Text, 1) = "\" Then
  txtLocation.Text = Mid(txtLocation.Text, 1, Len(txtLocation.Text) - 1)
End If

'Remove .cub from cube name, if it is there.
If Right(txtCubeName.Text, 4) = ".cub" Then
  txtCubeName.Text = Mid(txtCubeName.Text, 1, Len(txtCubeName.Text) - 4)
End If

'Assign Destination Cube String
sDestCube = txtCubeName.Text

'Create Full Path String
sFullPath = txtLocation.Text & "\" & sDestCube & ".cub"

'Create DSN string
sSourceDSN = "Provider=MSOLAP;Data Source=" & txtDSOServer.Text & _
    ";INITIAL CATALOG=" & dsoDatabaseSelected.Name
sSourceDSN = "SOURCE_DSN=""" & sSourceDSN & """"
```

```
'Start the CREATE CUBE string.
subAddText typC, "CREATECUBE=CREATE CUBE " & sDestCube, TAB0
subAddText typC, "(", TAB1

'Start the INSERT INTO string.
subAddText typI, "INSERTINTO=INSERT INTO " & sDestCube, TAB0
subAddText typI, "(", TAB1

'Start the SELECT string
subAddText typS, "SELECT ", TAB0
subAddText typS, "", TAB1

'Loop through Dimension List box to process each dimension.
For idxDim = 0 To lstDimension.ListCount - 1

  'Assign Dimension name string
  sDimension = lstDimension.List(idxDim)

  'Set the dimension's object variable
  Set dsoDimension = dsoDatabaseSelected.Dimensions(sDimension)

  'Check for hierarchy in the dimension
  If InStr(1, sDimension, ".") = 0 Then
    bHasHierarchy = False
  Else
    bHasHierarchy = True

    'Separate the dimension name and the hierarchy name
    lDimLen = InStr(1, lstDimension.List(idxDim), ".") - 1
    sDimension = Mid(sDimension, 1, lDimLen)
    sHierarchy = Mid(lstDimension.List(idxDim), (lDimLen + 2), _
        (Len(lstDimension.List(idxDim)) - lDimLen))

    'Check to see if this hierarchy is in the same dimension
    '  as the previous one.
    If sDimension = sPreviousDimension Then
      bNewDimension = False
    Else
      bNewDimension = True
    End If

    'Assign the value of of the Previous Dimension
    sPreviousDimension = sDimension

  End If

  'Separate out the dimension name for private dimensions
  If InStr(1, sDimension, "^") <> 0 Then
    lDimLen = InStr(1, sDimension, "^") - 1
```

continues

20

**THE PIVOTTABLE
SERVICE**

LISTING 20.6 continued

```
      sDimension = Mid(sDimension, (lDimLen + 2), _
          (Len(lstDimension.List(idxDim)) - lDimLen))
    End If

    'Check for Time Dimension
    If dsoDimension.DimensionType = dimTime Then
      bIsTimeDim = True
    Else
      bIsTimeDim = False
    End If

    'Add Dimension to the CREATE CUBE string, unless the dimension
    '  has a hierarchy and this is not the first hierarchy
    If bHasHierarchy = True And bNewDimension = False Then

      'Don't add a new dimension

    Else

      'Add the dimension
      subAddText typC, "DIMENSION [" & sDimension & "]", TAB1
      subAddText typI, "", TAB1
      subAddText typS, "", TAB1

      'Add TYPE TIME, if necessary
      If bIsTimeDim Then
        subAddText typC, " TYPE TIME,", SAMELINE
      Else
        subAddText typC, ",", SAMELINE
      End If

    End If

    'Add Hierarchy
    If bHasHierarchy = True Then
      subAddText typC, "HIERARCHY [" & sHierarchy & "], ", TAB2
      subAddText typI, "", TAB1
      subAddText typS, "", TAB1
    End If

    ' Loop through collection of levels
    For Each dsoLevel In ColOfColLevels.Item(lstDimension.List(idxDim))

      'Assign Level name variable
      If dsoLevel.LevelType = levAll Then
        'Create name for ALL dimension, if it is present.
        sLevel = "All " & sDimension
      Else
        sLevel = dsoLevel.Name
```

```
End If

'Add the Level name
subAddText typC, "LEVEL " & "[" & sLevel & "]", TAB3

'Add level type, if necessary
Select Case dsoLevel.LevelType

  Case levAll
    subAddText typC, " TYPE ALL", SAMELINE

  Case levTimeYears
    subAddText typC, " TYPE YEAR", SAMELINE

  Case levTimeHalfYears
    subAddText typC, " TYPE HALFYEAR", SAMELINE

  Case levTimeQuarters
    subAddText typC, " TYPE QUARTER", SAMELINE

  Case levTimeMonths
    subAddText typC, " TYPE MONTH", SAMELINE

  Case levTimeWeeks
    subAddText typC, " TYPE WEEK", SAMELINE

  Case levTimeDays
    subAddText typC, " TYPE DAY", SAMELINE

  Case levTimeHours
    subAddText typC, " TYPE HOUR", SAMELINE

  Case levTimeMinutes
    subAddText typC, " TYPE MINUTE", SAMELINE

  Case levTimeSeconds
    subAddText typC, " TYPE SECOND", SAMELINE

End Select

'Add comma
subAddText typC, ",", SAMELINE

'Create the INSERT INTO and SELECT strings

'First check for a TYPE ALL dimension
If dsoLevel.LevelType = levAll Then

  'Don't add to INSERT INTO and SELECT string for TYPE ALL
  subAddText typI, "", TAB1
```

continues

LISTING 20.6   continued

```
        subAddText typS, "", TAB1

    Else

        'Add Cube name to SELECT string
        subAddText typS, "[" & sSourceCube & "]", TAB1

        'Add Dimension name to INSERT INTO and SELECT string
        subAddText typI, "[" & sDimension & "]", TAB1
        subAddText typS, ".[" & sDimension, SAMELINE

        'Add Hierarchy name to strings, if necessary
        If bHasHierarchy = True Then
          subAddText typI, ".[" & sHierarchy & "]", SAMELINE
          subAddText typS, ":" & sHierarchy, SAMELINE
        End If

        'Add Level name to srings
        subAddText typI, ".[" & dsoLevel.Name & "],", SAMELINE
        subAddText typS, ":" & dsoLevel.Name & "],", SAMELINE

    End If

  Next 'Level in the collection of levels

Next idxDim 'Next dimension

'Measure list box loop
For idx = 0 To lstMeasure.ListCount - 1

  'Assign Measure name
  sMeasure = lstMeasure.List(idx)

  'Set the measure's object variable
  Set dsoMeasure = dsoCubeSelected.Measures(sMeasure)

  'Add measure to CREATE CUBE
  subAddText typC, "MEASURE [" & sMeasure & "]", TAB1

  'Add the aggregate function for the Measure
  Select Case dsoMeasure.AggregateFunction

    Case aggCount
      subAddText typC, " Function COUNT", SAMELINE

    Case aggMax
      subAddText typC, " Function MAX", SAMELINE

    Case aggMin
```

```
      subAddText typC, " Function MIN", SAMELINE

   Case aggSum
      subAddText typC, " Function SUM", SAMELINE

End Select

'Add measure to the INSERT INTO string
subAddText typI, "[Measures].[" & sMeasure & "],", TAB1

'Add measure to the SELECT string
subAddText typS, _
   "[" & sSourceCube & "]." & "[Measures:" & sMeasure & "],", TAB1

'Add FORMAT clause to the CREATE CUBE string
If dsoMeasure.FormatString <> "" Then

   'sFormat = "FORMAT " & QUOTE & dsoMeasure.FormatString & QUOTE
   sFormat = "FORMAT " & "'" & dsoMeasure.FormatString & "'"
   subAddText typC, sFormat & ",", TAB2
   subAddText typI, "", TAB1
   subAddText typS, "", TAB1

Else

   'Add comma to previous line
   subAddText typC, ",", SAMELINE
   subAddText typI, "", TAB1
   subAddText typS, "", TAB1

End If

Next idx

'Remove final commas
gsCreateCube = Mid(gsCreateCube, 1, Len(gsCreateCube) - 1)
gsInsertInto = Mid(gsInsertInto, 1, Len(gsInsertInto) - 5)
gsSelect = Mid(gsSelect, 1, Len(gsSelect) - 5)

'Add closing paranthesis
subAddText typC, ")", TAB1
subAddText typI, ")", TAB1

'Add ROLAP option, if chosen, to the INSERT INTO string
If optROLAP.Value = True Then
   subAddText typI, "OPTIONS DEFER_DATA ", TAB0
End If

'Add FROM clause to SELECT string
subAddText typS, "FROM [" & dsoCubeSelected.Name & "]", TAB0
```

continues

LISTING 20.6 continued

```
'Preview code if checked
If chkPreviewCode.Value = 1 Then

    frmCodeEditor.txtCreateCube = gsCreateCube
    frmCodeEditor.txtInsertInto = gsInsertInto
    frmCodeEditor.txtSelect = gsSelect

    frmCodeEditor.Show vbModal
    frmMain.Refresh

    If gbCreateCube = False Then
      txtProgress.Text = "Create cube canceled."
      GoTo ProcExit
    End If

    'Fill strings from Code Editor
    gsCreateCube = frmCodeEditor.txtCreateCube
    gsInsertInto = frmCodeEditor.txtInsertInto
    gsSelect = frmCodeEditor.txtSelect

End If

'Loop user chooses to overwrite, create a new file, or cancel
Do

  If fso.FileExists(sFullPath) Then

    msg = QUOTE & sFullPath & QUOTE & vbCrLf & _
          "already exists. " & vbCrLf & _
          "Do you want to overwrite this file?"
    ttl = "File Already Exists"
    Select Case MsgBox(msg, vbYesNoCancel, ttl)

      Case vbYes
        'Continue on and overwrite the file
        Exit Do

      Case vbNo
        'Ask for new path
        msg = "Enter file path and name for local cube file:"
        ttl = "File Name"
        sFullPath = InputBox(msg, ttl, sFullPath)

        'User canceled.
        If sFullPath = "" Then
            txtProgress.Text = "Cube Creation Canceled."
            GoTo ProcExit
        End If
```

```
      Case vbCancel
        'Exit the procedure, without doing anything
        txtProgress.Text = "Cube Creation Canceled."
        GoTo ProcExit

    End Select

  Else

    Exit Do 'File does not exist. Continue on

  End If

Loop

frmMain.MousePointer = vbHourglass

'Create location string.
sLocation = "LOCATION= " & sFullPath

'Put everything together
sConnectionString = sLocation & ";" & sSourceDSN & ";" & _
    gsCreateCube & ";" & gsInsertInto & vbCrLf & gsSelect
cn.Provider = "MSOLAP"
cn.ConnectionString = sConnectionString

' Fill in the progress text box.
txtProgress.Text = _
    "Creating " & txtLocation.Text & "\" & txtCubeName & ".cub..."
txtProgress.Refresh

' Create the cube
cn.Open

' Clear progress text box.
txtProgress.Text = ""

' Verify cube creation
If cn Is Nothing Then
    txtProgress.Text = "An Error Occurred: The Cube was NOT Created."
    GoTo ProcExit
Else
    txtProgress.Text = _
        "'" & txtLocation & "\" & txtCubeName & ".cub' Created."
End If

'Browse the cube, if user has chosen to do so.
If chkBrowseCube.Value = 1 Then
```

continues

LISTING 20.6 continued

```
    cat.ActiveConnection = "Data Source=""" & sFullPath & """;" & _
      "Provider=MSOLAP;"
    frmBrowseCube.CubeBrowser1.Connect cat.ActiveConnection, sDestCube
    frmBrowseCube.Show vbModal

End If

cn.Close

ProcExit:
  frmMain.MousePointer = vbArrow
  Exit Sub

ProcErr:
  subErrHandler "cmdMakeCube_Click", _
      CStr(Err.Number), Err.Description
  GoTo ProcExit

End Sub

Public Sub subAddText(strType As StringType, str As String, _
    TextLoc As AddTextLocation)
On Error GoTo ProcErr

Dim idx As Long
Dim bNewLine As Boolean
Dim lNumTab As Long

If TextLoc = SAMELINE Then

  'Don't add a new line or any tabs

Else

  lNumTab = CLng(TextLoc)

  'Add tabs (2 spaces), if necessary
  For idx = 1 To lNumTab
    str = Space(2) & str
  Next idx

  'Add a new line
  str = vbCrLf & str

End If

'Add new text to previous string for cube generating string
Select Case strType
```

```
   Case typC
     gsCreateCube = gsCreateCube & str

   Case typI
     gsInsertInto = gsInsertInto & str

   Case typS
     gsSelect = gsSelect & str

 End Select

 ProcExit:
   Exit Sub

 ProcErr:
   subErrHandler "subAddText", _
       CStr(Err.Number), Err.Description
   GoTo ProcExit

 End Sub
```

The LocalCube utility also makes a good add-in for the OLAP Manager. You can make it into an add-in by following the instructions in the "Sample Custom Add-Ins" section in Chapter 19, "Developing an Add-In Program for OLAP Services." You need to add the following references for this project:

- OLAP Add-In Manager
- Microsoft SQLDMO Object Library
- Microsoft ActiveX Data Objects (Multi-Dim) 1.0 Library
- Microsoft ActiveX Data Objects 2.1 Library

The code that should be used for the menu item that calls the LocalCubeAddIn is shown in Listing 20.7.

LISTING 20.7 Calling the LocalCubeAddIn

```
 Case mnuLocalCube

   If CurrentNode.LinkedObject.ClassType = clsServer Then
     Set frmMain.dsoServer = CurrentNode.LinkedObject
   Else
     Set frmMain.dsoServer = CurrentNode.LinkedObject.Server
   End If

   frmMain.txtDSOServer = frmMain.dsoServer.Name
   frmMain.txtDSOServer.Locked = True
```

continues

20

THE PIVOTTABLE SERVICE

LISTING 20.7   continued

```
    frmMain.txtProgress.Text = "Cube list not refreshed."

    ' Make sure list boxes and text boxes are clean when add-in is called
    frmMain.lstDimension.Clear
    frmMain.lstMeasure.Clear
    frmMain.lstLevel.Clear
    frmMain.txtCubeName = ""

    'Clear out collections of levels
    Set frmMain.ColLevels = Nothing
    Set frmMain.ColOfColLevels = Nothing

    frmMain.gsErrDesc = ""

    frmMain.Show vbModal

    If frmMain.gsErrDesc <> "" Then
      subErrHandler frmMain.gsProcedure, frmMain.gsErrNum, _
          frmMain.gsErrDesc

    End If
```

The easiest way to browse your local cube is with Excel 2000. Chapter 23, "Implementing Microsoft Excel as an OLAP Client," goes more into detail about using Excel with OLAP.

Summary

Microsoft has not given us a convenient interface to design local cubes with PivotTable Service. You can't create aggregations for your local cubes. But once you have a local cube, you can take it with you. Your client applications can interact with that local cube in the same way they work with an OLAP Services cube. The LocalCube utility gives you a start on developing a system to automate the creation of local cubes.

Other OLE DB for OLAP Servers

by Ted Daley

OLE DB provides a flexible and efficient database architecture that offers applications, compilers, and other database components effective access to Microsoft and third-party data stores. OLE DB and third-party development make it easier than ever to implement your OLAP solution. More than 20 companies have pledged to deliver client and/or server products that support Microsoft's OLE DB for OLAP API to provide access to data stored in OLAP data marts.

Since so many choices are possible, choosing the right OLAP Server is not a simple undertaking. This chapter is designed to help you make the best decision possible in your selection of an OLAP Server. Table 21.1 lists 11 OLAP servers now available to leverage Microsoft's OLE DB technology. Brief descriptions of each are presented in the remainder of the chapter.

TABLE 21.1   Servers that Support Microsoft OLE DB for OLAP API

Company	Product	Web Site
Applix, Inc.	Applix Server TM1	www.aplix.com
Cognos Inc.	Cognos PowerPlay Enterprise Server	www.cognos.com
Gentia	GentiaDB	www.gentia.com
Hyperion Solutions CorpHyperion	Essbase OLAP Server	www.hysoft.com
Information Advantage	MYEUREKA!	www.infoadvan.com
MicroStrategy	DSS Server	www.microstrategy.com
NCR Corp	Teradata	www.ncr.com
Pilot Software	Pilot Analysis Server (PAS)	www.pilotsw.com
SAS Institute Inc.	SAS/MDDB Server	www.sas.com
Seagate Software	Seagate Holos	www.seagatesoftware.com
Whitelight Systems Inc.	Analytic Application Server	www.whitelight.com

Applix Server TM1

TM1 Server provides Web access to multidimensional data in two steps. First, it lets users connect to and navigate through data in a TM1 cube via any browser. Second, it allows real-time multidimensional data analysis. TM1 can support both small and large data sets with ease.

Applix TM1 enables a user to review results at a high level and then drill down to find detail level information in real time within seconds. The real power of the system is its ability to immediately consolidate changes in real time all the way up the organizational hierarchy, making it simple to make mission-critical business decisions immediately. Applix TM1 gives users complete and intuitive database functionality without the need for technical expertise. There is support for replication and synchronization; this allows data to be replicated across servers while maintaining security settings. Applix TM1 has an efficient, easy-to-use interface. Administrators and end-users will not require much training.

Cognos PowerPlay Enterprise Server

This product is a good fit for IT sites that want to bring the power of OLAP to Web, Windows, and mobile clients. It is designed for sites that need high-end OLAP performance. PowerPlay Enterprise provides broad server platform support as well as capabilities for multiple client types. PowerPlay Enterprise Server also supports load distribution across multiple servers, which is necessary for sites with heavy data analysis requirements.

Cost of administration is extremely low. Building and deploying data cubes is relatively easy. Also, administrators will not need to spend excessive time training end-users.

The PowerPlay Personal Server, included with PowerPlay Enterprise Server, supports OLAP data analysis for mobile and disconnected users.

GentiaDB

GentiaDB is a multidimensional database server that combines aspects of both OLAP and relational databases. As an OLAP database, it lets you share, access, and analyze data using an unlimited number of dimensions such as time, customer, distribution channel, region, or product. But like a relational database, it offers scalability, support for large data volumes, rapid response times, and data integrity.

Hyperion Essbase OLAP Server

Hyperion Essbase OLAP Server is designed and optimized for information delivery within an enterprise data warehousing strategy. It provides a strategic platform for management reporting, planning, and analysis applications across all business functions.

Hyperion Essbase gives you the flexibility to tailor OLAP applications to the needs and abilities of users without sacrificing power and usability.

The dynamic calculation feature significantly reduces the time to load and calculate large data marts. Partitioning features enable you to separate applications by fiscal years, operating units, and other criteria. The smaller, partitioned cubes streamline production management and make more information available in shorter time frames without degrading performance.

MyEureka!

MyEureka! expands the use of business intelligence by providing all knowledge workers with an easily accessible Web portal to all corporate data and tools. MyEureka! enables users to access and analyze information from multiple business intelligence sources and scales to support large user databases. In addition, MyEureka! makes the securing of reports an easy process. You can restrict the users' view of the data to include only what is pertinent to their role and region.

MyEureka! has two particular strengths: ease of report development and mature server-based architecture. It provides a graphical user interface to make it easy for users to access and analyze information and to create presentation-quality reports using drag-and-drop functionality.

DSS Server

DSS Server is a scalable, relational OLAP server supporting high-performance applications in a wide range of industries. It is a tool that provides a user-friendly and powerful environment for the creation of reports and data marts. The technology is scalable to a large user population, massive databases, large data marts, and a wide range of user skills. DSS Server allows you to use a single integrated architecture to create very large sophisticated data marts directly against your data warehouse using familiar business terminology.

Data mart tables are created via a user-friendly wizard and can be customized using the pre/post-SQL feature. Also, the scheduling capability of DSS Server can be leveraged to automate the creation and updating of the data marts. The use of MicroStrategy's intuitive, reusable and powerful report building objects via a user-friendly wizard greatly simplifies the data mart creation. A whole spectrum of users, from power users to administrators, can now easily create their own customized data marts.

DSS Server also allows for the creation of very large tables in the data mart. This is especially beneficial in applications such as direct-mail campaigns, where mailing lists with 100,000 or more customers are required for effective campaigning. In addition, the entire process of data mart creation and updates can be automated using the scheduling feature of DSS Server.

Teradata

NCR Teradata is an open ANSI-compliant parallel relational database management. Teradata automatically distributes data randomly across all "units of parallelism" and balances and schedules query workloads. The Teradata database uses parallelism to load, process, and back up system and user data.

In a Teradata warehouse, only one or two DBAs are needed because Teradata was designed to let the software manage the system. As a Teradata-based warehouse grows in volume and complexity, the system administrators' responsibilities do not. Teradata provides a number of unique features that reduce many of the time-consuming tasks for the administrator. Teradata has great speed with which it can process and do complex analysis for large volumes of data. Another great feature is scalability. You can start with a small application and scale upward dramatically as your needs inevitably grow.

Pilot Analysis Server (PAS)

Pilot Software's Analysis Server (PAS) holds good value for enterprises that must perform complex data analysis against very large multidimensional data sets. PAS gives the administrator greater control over where the data is stored. In competing products, aggregate data is usually stored in the multidimensional engine while the detail data to support drill-down functions remains in its relational form. Pilot's Analysis Server lets you configure where the different aggregate layers are stored.

For example, more frequently used aggregations would be stored in the multidimensional database, while the administrator might move less-used aggregations into the relational database with the detail data. This makes access more efficient and also allows for analysis of larger data sets.

SAS/MDDB Server

SAS/MDDB Server software makes it easier for business users to derive many views of data quickly, spot trends, and identify possible opportunities or trouble spots, while eliminating the need for IS professionals to create or recreate customized reports to meet business users' changing analysis needs.

SAS Institute's MDDB Server offering includes a fully scalable and portable multidimensional database (MDDB) supporting most hardware platforms and access to internal and external data wherever it resides, including Internet and intranet data. Tightly integrated with the Institute's data warehouse/Web-enabled architecture, the MDDB Server allows unlimited views of data.

Seagate Holos

Holos is an application development tool for a wide range of business intelligence systems incorporating EIS, DSS, and OLAP technology. It enables users to access, analyze, report, and perform multidimensional modeling on data stored in relational data warehouses or legacy systems. It eliminates the need for creating and maintaining a proprietary multidimensional database.

Applications exist in a three-tier client/server architecture. The Seagate Holos system extracts relational data from a data warehouse, converts it to multidimensional OLAP cubes, and then loads Seagate Holos clients with the data for analysis. Its ability to link disparate OLAP data sources, run on cross-platform systems, and create compound OLAP structures make it an appealing choice for deploying enterprise-wide information management applications.

Analytic Application Server

WhiteLight Systems' Analytic Application Server is a powerful engine that can keep up with thousands of users, complex models, and terabytes of data. The server has multidimensional caching (MultiCache), which provides fast query response for frequently requested information by caching information in the Analytic Application Server.

The server's multithreaded architecture shares all server resources across users for scalability. Its query optimizer determines whether to perform analysis on the original database, in the Analytic Application Server, or on the client. This provides high performance and optimizes network and hardware utilization.

Summary

It is imperative for corporate decision-makers to have the best data-analysis tools at their disposal, along with solid methods to share information. In this chapter I have provided a brief description of 11 OLAP server products.

This chapter is not, by any means, a single, definitive source of information on OLAP server vendors. For the most current information on independent OLAP server vendors, go to www.microsoft.com/data/partners/products.htm.

Programming
the OLAP Client

PART

V

Programming Access to the OLAP Data Sources

by Jim Pinkelman

IN THIS CHAPTER

This part of the book is dedicated to the process of developing an application to access data in Microsoft OLAP Services, and OLAP client application.

Microsoft OLAP Services exposes standard Microsoft COM interfaces. As a result, C++, Visual Basic, Java, VB Script, and JScript are among the programming languages which can be used when building applications that interface with OLAP Services. Because the overwhelming majority of Windows programmers is familiar with VB, most of the code in this part of the book is written in VB.

One of the purposes of this part of the book is to give the readers examples containing useful code. Toward this end, most of the examples are in the form of small code segments that can be integrated into more complex, complete applications.

This particular chapter discusses the first functional interface required in building an OLAP client application. This chapter covers the concepts and programming techniques for establishing and using connections to OLAP data sources.

A portion of material contained in this chapter is common to the general Windows programming techniques used when connecting to data sources with Microsoft's data access layers, OLE DB and ADO. However, the primary focus of this chapter is on the specific process and unique characteristics of programming to OLAP data sources, in other words, the use of OLE DB for OLAP and ADOMD.

The Data Connectivity Interface Layers

As Figure 22.1 shows, there are two fundamental data connectivity layers that client applications can use to access data within Microsoft OLAP Services. OLE DB for OLAP extends OLE DB to include objects specific to multidimensional data, and ADOMD extends ADO in the same fashion.

At the lowest level, Microsoft OLE DB and OLE DB for OLAP can be used as the interface. While OLE DB has some performance advantages, this benefit comes at the cost of a complex interface.

Microsoft recommends programming with ActiveX Data Objects (ADO) and ActiveX Data Objects (Multidimensional) (ADOMD). As Figure 22.1 shows, this layer is one level of abstraction above OLE DB. While there is a slight performance penalty that accompanies ADO, the interface is significantly less complex.

For these reasons, the vast majority of connectivity programming to OLAP Services is conducted with ADO and ADOMD, and it is the baseline used for the most of the discussions in the remainder of this chapter.

FIGURE 22.1

Here is the data connectivity architecture for OLAP Services.

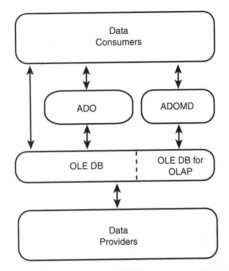

> **Note**
>
> You may recall that it is also possible to connect to an OLAP Server using decision support objects (DSO). However, DSO exists as a tool with which the metadata of a data store can be administered and maintained. It only contains functionality for manipulating the structure of a MD Data provider, and does not provide any functionality for accessing and manipulating the data within the provider.

The ActiveX Data Objects Multidimensional Object Model

Concurrent with the development and release of OLAP Services, Microsoft updated its ADO object model. Specific extensions were added to the model to support the multidimensional data sources that were exposed through OLAP Services.

This ActiveX Data Objects Multidimensional (ADOMD) object model is the key COM interface necessary to create OLAP client applications. Because these automation objects use the standard COM interface, ADOMD can be used with a variety of programming languages including VB, C++, Java, VBScript, and Jscript. To reach to the largest audience, the examples in this chapter use VB.

As of the writing of this book, ADO 2.1 is the latest release of this Data Access object model. However, while it is not important to discuss the latest and greatest characteristics of ADO, it is useful to quickly review the purpose and the structure of some of the more important objects—Connection, Command, and Parameter. Figure 22.2 shows these objects and their important collections.

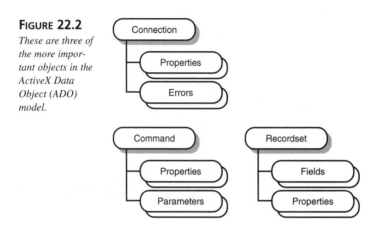

FIGURE 22.2

These are three of the more important objects in the ActiveX Data Object (ADO) model.

The Connection object consists of information about the data provider.

The Command object consists of information about commands to be used on the Connection object.

The Command object has a Parameters collection consisting of Parameter objects that contain information for the Command object.

The Recordset object consists of the records returned from the execution of a query on the data provider. The Recordset object also contains a cursor into the records returned and has two collections, Fields and Properties.

Depending on the programming environment in which you are working, it will be necessary to establish a reference to a type library and/or a dynamic link library to access the ADO objects. Depending on the version of ADO you have installed, the appropriate reference will be similar to MSADO20.tlb or MSADO15.dll. In VB these references will be available in the References selection of the Project menu as something like "Microsoft ActiveX Data Objects 2.1 Library."

Establishing a Data Connection

The basic process of establishing a connection to a data source and retrieving data is demonstrated in the following code:

```
Dim objConn As New ADODB.Connection
Dim objRS As New ADODB.Recordset
Dim objComm As New ADODB.Command

Dim strConnect As String
strConnect = "uid=sa;pwd=;driver={SQL Server};" & _
"server=SERVER;database=pubs;dsn=''"

'Establish Connection
objConn.ConnectionString = strConnect
objConn.Open

'Retrieve Data
objRS.Open "select * from authors", objConn

'Clean up
objRS.Close
objConn.Close
```

Figure 22.3 shows the two objects within the Connection object critical which are the multidimensional extensions to the basic ADO object model. The first object, the Catalog object, translates to a MD database hosted on the server. The Catalog object is primarily used to retrieve metadata. The second object, the Cellset object, contains the results of a query.

FIGURE 22.3

The ADOMD Connection *object has* Catalog *and* Cellset *objects.*

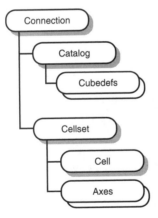

The most significant difference between ADO and ADOMD is the object that contains the results of a query. As discussed previously, when relational data providers are queried, the Recordset object is used to store the results. In contrast, when multidimensional providers are queried, the results are multidimensional in nature and the Cellset object is used to hold the results.

In Microsoft's ADOMD extension, the `Cellset` object was specifically designed to hold data in a multidimensional structure. A subsequent section of this chapter discusses the `Cellset` object in more detail, while the remainder of this chapter is concerned with the connection.

ADOMD.dll is the necessary dynamic link library to access the ADOMD object model. As shown in Figure 22.4, in VB these references will be available in the References selection of the Project menu as something like "Microsoft ActiveX Data Objects 2.0 Library".

FIGURE 22.4

The Microsoft ADOMD objects are available in the Project References list.

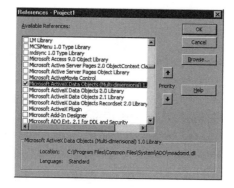

Data Sources

As a multidimensional data provider, Microsoft OLAP Server is usually exposed in one of three ways.

- The OLAP Server itself supports direct connections.
- You can create a standard Data Source Name (DSN)
- A multidimensional data cube file (*.cub) can be accessed.

To open a connection directly to an OLAP Server, the connection string must contain the `DataSource` and the `Provider` parameters. As the "Security" section explains, Windows NT domain security is used for authentication of the user.

The following code shows the process of connecting to an MD data provider:

```
Dim objConn As New ADODB.Connection
Dim objCellset As New ADOMD.Cellset

'Establish Connection
objConn.Open "Data Source=SERVER;Provider=MSOLAP"

'Execute a query
```

```
objCellset.Open "SELECT [Product].[Product Family].Members on Columns _
from Sales", objConn

'Clean up
objCellset.Close
objConn.Close
```

Establishing a connection to an OLAP data provider through a DSN is essentially the same as shown in this code, except that the connection string for `objConn.Open` would just contain the DSN name. Connecting to local cubes, cube files, is discussed later in this chapter.

Security

Security for users of Microsoft OLAP Services is based on the user's access rights to the Windows NT operating system. Therefore, authentication is established when the user logs on to a Windows NT domain.

At the server level, a user of OLAP Services must be in the same domain as the user account used to install the server or in a trusted domain.

At the database and cube levels, user access is based on control rights of the user's NT Account. The OLAP Manager can be used to assign access permissions for database, cubes, and virtual cubes.

> **Note**
>
> Access Control Lists (ACLs) only function when the OLAP Services are installed on an NTFS file system. A FAT file system will not support ACLs.

There are three levels of access control embedded in OLAP Services: Read, Read/Write, and Admin. Each of these levels of access control is established with the OLAP Manager.

As implied by the name, *Read* access provides read-only access to the data and the data structure. *Read/Write* access provides all capabilities in read access plus write access to a cube that is write-enabled. While Read/Write access allows a user to change data, it does not permit a user to change the data structure.

Admin access allows complete control to process and modify the data and the data structure. It is also required for a user to access the OLAP Manager. Admin access controlled by a group named OLAP Administrators that is created when OLAP Services is installed.

> **Caution**
>
> Because Microsoft OLAP Services uses NT-based security, authorization is negotiated outside of the ADOMD connection. If the user specifies a username and password when the connection is established, this information is ignored.

Using roles is an extremely effective method to control end-user cube access. From a broad perspective, implementing roles is a two-step process. While the process of creating roles is briefly presented here, refer to Chapter 15, "Creating Cubes," for more on roles.

First, use the Windows NT User Manger to create the appropriate sets of user accounts and groups. Second, use the OLAP Manager to assign the roles that can access each cube in a database.

The `Catalog` Object

When you are building a client application for OLAP Services, there are two practical uses for the `Catalog` object.

First, in order to execute a query using a connection to the server, it is necessary to set the default database of the connection to the appropriate catalog. Recall that while it is common to have multiple catalogs within an OLAP Server, there is only one "current" or "active" catalog for each connection. If a catalog is not specified within the connection string, the default catalog is used as the active catalog.

Second, access to the `Catalog` object is the primary method of retrieving information about the data structure of the server. Figure 22.3 shows the position of the catalog object in the ADOMD object model.

> **Note**
>
> Unlike many of the objects in the ADOMD object model, there is no `Cellsets` collection that contains `Cellset` objects.

Because there is no `Catalog` collection within the `Connection` object, it is necessary to build a recordset from the collection to obtain a list of the available catalogs from a database.

To use a catalog, it is necessary to specify the name of the catalog in the connection string or to use the `DefaultDatabase` property of the connection.

The following segment of code connects to an OLAP Server, builds a recordset of the catalogs within the server, and iterates through the catalogs making each the default database for the connection:

```
'Initialize ADO Objects
Dim objConn As New ADODB.Connection
Dim objRS As New ADODB.Recordset

'Establish Connection
objConn.Open "Data Source=SERVER;Provider=MSOLAP"

'Build a recordset of catalogs
Set objRS = objConn.OpenSchema(adSchemaCatalogs)

'Iterate through Catalog structure
Do Until objRS.EOF
        objConn.DefaultDatabase = objRS.Fields("Catalog_Name")
        objRS.MoveNext
Loop

'Clean up
objRS.Close
objConn.Close
```

As shown in Figure 22.5, the relationship of the various ADOMD objects under the `Catalog` object is purely hierarchical and not complex.

FIGURE 22.5
The hierarchy of the Catalog *object in ADOMD is pretty straightforward.*

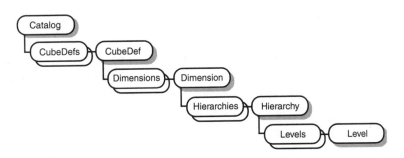

The following code iterates through all of the objects in the hierarchy under a catalog:

```
'Initialize ADO Objects
Dim objConn As New ADODB.Connection

'Initialize ADOMD Objects
Dim objCatalog As New ADOMD.Catalog
Dim objCubeDef As ADOMD.CubeDef
```

```
Dim objDimension As ADOMD.Dimension
Dim objHierarchy As ADOMD.Hierarchy
Dim objLevel As ADOMD.Level
Dim objMember As ADOMD.Member

'Establish Connection
objConn.Open "Data Source=SERVER;Provider=MSOLAP"

'Iterate through Catalog structure
Set objCatalog.ActiveConnection = objConn
For Each objCubeDef In objCatalog.CubeDefs
        For Each objDimension In objCubeDef.Dimensions
                For Each objHierarchy In objDimension.Hierarchies
                        For Each objLevel In objHierarchy.Levels
                                For Each objMember In objLevel.Members

                                Next objMember
                        Next objLevel
                Next objHierarchy
        Next objDimension
Next objCubeDef

'Clean Up
objConn.Close
```

The `Cellset` Object

While the `Catalog` object is the main object for retrieving information about the data structure, the `Cellset` object is the fundamental object for retrieving data itself. Like the recordset in ADO, the cellset holds the result of an ADOMD query (MDX) after it has been executed.

The process populating the `Cellset` object is simple. Specify the query and the connection, and execute the open method of the `Cellset` object. The query and the connection can either be set using the properties of the cellset or as parameters of the open method. The syntax of the cellset open method is

`Cellset.`**`Open`** `source,active connection`

The *source* parameter is a variant that evaluates to the MDX statement. The *active connection* parameter is a variant that evaluates to the connection string for an open ADO connection. It is permissible to pass a connection definition for *active connection*. In this case, a new connection is opened and the MDX statement is executed.

While both parameters are actually optional in the syntax of this method, if they are not included in the method call, they must be set as properties before the method is executed.

The following code segment establishes a connection with an OLAP Server (the default database because none is specified explicitly). A cellset is then opened with a simple MDX query.

```
Dim objConn As New ADODB.Connection
Dim objCellset As New ADOMD.Cellset

Dim strMDX as string

'Establish Connection
objConn.Open "Data Source=SERVER;Provider=MSOLAP"

'Execute a query
strMDX = "SELECT [Product Family].Members on Columns, _
[Gender].Members on Rows from Sales"
objCellset.Open strMDX, objConn

'Clean up
objCellset.Close
objConn.Close
```

After the `Cellset` object has been populated, a developer must navigate through the cellset to access the data and the structure of the data.

In the case of ADO recordsets, this process is accomplished by iterating through the rows of the recordset. Each row in a recordset has any number of common fields (columns), each of which contains a different piece of data.

Because of the multidimensional nature of a cellset, the structure of a cellset is more complex than a recordset. The object hierarchy under the cellset is shown in Figure 22.6

FIGURE 22.6

The Cellset *object hierarchy includes* Cell *and* Axes *collections.*

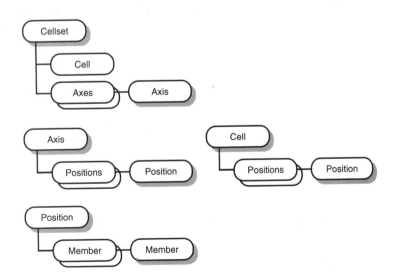

As Figure 22.6 shows, the `Cellset` object consists of `Cell` objects for each cell, the `Axes` collection composed of `Axis` objects, and a `Properties` collection. The `Cell` and `Axis` objects both have a `Positions` collection, and the `Position` and `Level` objects both have a `Members` collection.

Most of the `Cellset` object's properties and methods are familiar to developers who have some experience programming to the ADO interface. Tables 22.1 and 22.2 list the properties and methods of the `Cellset` object.

TABLE 22.1   Cellset Properties

Property	Description
ActiveConnection	Can be used to set or retrieve a variant containing the connection string or the connection object.
FilterAxis	Returns an Axis object consisting of the slicers used to retrieve the data. (Read-only)
Source	Contains the MDX query used to retrieve the data. Read/Write for cellsets before they are open. Read-only for an open cellset.
State	Returns a long integer indicating whether the cellset is open. (Read-only)
adStateClose	Closed cellset; value: 0
adStateOpen	Open cellset; value: 1

TABLE 22.2   Cellset Methods

Method	Description
Close	Closes an open cellset.
	`cellset.Close`
Open	Opens a cellset using an MDX query as the *source*.
	`cellset.Open Source,ActiveConnection`
Item	The `Item` method is used to retrieve a cell from within a `Cellset` object and create a `Cell` object.
	`Set Cell = Cellset.Item(positions)`

To retrieve data from within a `Cellset` object, it is necessary to directly reference the cell to be retrieved from the `Cellset` object.

Each individual cell exists at an intersection of the positions on the axes. This MDX query is used to retrieve a cellset in the example code that follows:

```
SELECT
 {[Product].[Product Family].Members} ON COLUMNS,
 CrossJoin({[Gender].[Gender].Members},
 {[Marital Status].[Marital Status].Members}) ON ROWS
FROM [Sales]
```

As shown in Figure 22.7, this query produces a cellset with two axes: Axes(0) and Axes(1). There are three positions on Axes(0), with a single member in each: Drink, Food, and Non-Consumables. There are four positions on Axis(1), and each position has two members [Female][Married], [Female][Single], [Male][Married], [Male][Single].

FIGURE 22.7

An MDX query produces a cellset result.

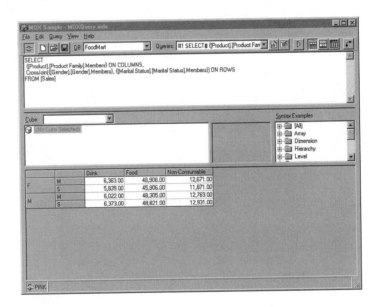

The following code segment establishes a connection, creates a cellset with the query shown previously, and iterates through the cellset to show its structure:

```
'Establish Connection
Dim objConn As New ADODB.Connection
objConn.Open "Data Source=SERVER;Provider=MSOLAP"

'Open a Cellset
Dim strMDX As String
strMDX = "SELECT [Product Family].Members on Columns, " &_
"CrossJoin({[Gender].[Gender].Members}, " &_
"{[Marital Status].[Marital Status].Members}) ON ROWS " &_
"FROM Sales"

Dim objCellset As New ADOMD.Cellset
objCellset.Open strMDX, objConn
```

```
Dim intColIndex As Integer
Dim intRowIndex As Integer
Dim objMember As ADOMD.Member
Dim objCell As ADOMD.Cell

For intColIndex = 0 To objCellset.Axes(0).Positions.Count - 1
    For intRowIndex = 0 To objCellset.Axes(1).Positions.Count - 1

        Debug.Print "---"

        'Print the column names
        For Each objMember In _
        objCellset.Axes(0).Positions(intColIndex).Members
            Debug.Print "Column:" & objMember.UniqueName
        Next objMember

        'Print the row names
        For Each objMember In _
        objCellset.Axes(1).Positions(intRowIndex).Members
            Debug.Print "Row:" & objMember.UniqueName
        Next objMember

        'Print the cell value
        Set objCell = objCellset(intColIndex, intRowIndex)
        Debug.Print objCell.Value


    Next intRowIndex
Next intColIndex

'Clean up
objCellset.Close
objConn.Close
```

While the example code does not include any dimensions on the Filter Axis, this information is easily accessible as members in the `FilterAxis` property of the `Cellset` object.

Using Local Cubes as the Data Source

Finally, Microsoft OLAP Services includes functionality for local cubes that exist outside of the OLAP Server to provide for offline data analysis. As discussed in Chapter 20, the PivotTable Service plays an important role in building local cubes and in managing access to the cubes (through cache management).

While the PivotTable Service performs a variety of functions, for developers of client applications, the following are of most interest:

- PivotTable Service functions as a multidimensional data provider.
- PivotTable Service allows local cubes to be created from OLAP Servers.
- PivotTable Service acts an OLAP client, allowing users offline access to multidimensional data on local computers.

From the perspective of OLAP client application development, the primary interface with a local cube is *not* significantly different than programming to an OLAP Server.

Similar to connecting to an OLAP Server, the connection string to a local cube file must contain the DataSource and Provider parameters. However, in the case of a local cube, the Data Source property contains the path to the *.cub file. For example:

```
Data Source = _
"c:\Program Files\OLAP Services\Samples\sales.cub";Provider=MSOLAP;
```

Once the connection is established, retrieving metadata information from the cube, executing MDX queries on the cube, and retrieving data sets on the cube are essentially the same as programming to an OLAP Server with the following exceptions:

- PivotTable Service works only with a single cube partition. Therefore, the Catalog object is not relevant.
- PivotTable Service does not have an intrinsic aggregation engine capable of recalculating aggregate values along levels of a dimension.
- PivotTable Service does not have functionality for defining users, roles, data access rules, virtual cubes, and global named members.

Summary

The goal of this chapter was to introduce the basic concepts needed to begin the process of building a client interface to OLAP Services.

Because ADOMD is a natural extension of ADO, understanding and implementing the ADOMD object model should not be a particularly difficult process for programmers experienced in building client applications for databases.

The Catalog and Cellset objects are the two most important parts of the ADOMD object model. As the next few chapters will show, the Catalog object is very useful in retrieving metadata information about the OLAP server. Understanding the Cellset object, which is similar to the Recordset object, is critical to building a user interface that accurately and effectively returns information to the user.

The next few chapters introduce techniques for building various types of client applications for OLAP Services, and the concepts introduced in this chapter will resurface periodically.

CHAPTER 23

Implementing Microsoft Excel as an OLAP Client

by Jim Pinkelman

IN THIS CHAPTER

When you decide to implement Microsoft OLAP Services, you should spend some time evaluating Microsoft Excel 2000 as an OLAP client for some of your users. This is particularly true if there is a version of Windows Office installed within the organization, and the users employ Excel for other business functions.

Excel 2000 (Excel 9.0) has tools named PivotTable and PivotChart that allow a user to manipulate data in a crosstab format. As implied by their names, PivotTable manipulates data within a table in a spreadsheet while PivotChart is used to show data graphically.

> **Note**
>
> Keep in mind that the PivotTable and PivotChart discussed in this chapter are add-in utilities for Office 2000 applications. They are *not* the same as the PivotTable Service, which is part of OLAP Services Architecture and serves as an OLAP data provider with cache capabilities.

This chapter introduces the Excel's PivotTable and PivotChart and discusses their capabilities and limitations with regard to accessing OLAP Services data. Additionally, this chapter also provides a discussion of the development process necessary to build an Excel add-in and presents some product alternatives to Microsoft's PivotTable tool.

Keep in mind that the purpose of this chapter is to discuss OLAP clients within Excel, and the functionality is typically less than that which can be achieved with a standalone client.

The PivotTable in Excel 2000

Excel 2000 is not the first version of Excel to contain the PivotTable. Excel 97 included PivotTable, but it was not a very capable tool and few people made use of it. In its previous version, before the release of OLAP Services, PivotTable was primarily used to display data from within a spreadsheet database or from relational databases in crosstab format.

Unfortunately, flat recordsets retrieved from relational databases and typical Excel databases do not translate particularly well into a pivot-type, or crosstab, reporting mechanism. In contrast, multidimensional data from OLAP Services does translate extremely well into a crosstab format. As a result, there was a strong incentive for Microsoft to update and upgrade PivotTable to coincide with the release of OLAP Services.

The discussion in this chapter is limited to the use of PivotTable as a thin client within Excel to access data stored in OLAP Services.

Accessing the PivotTable

Microsoft logically places access to the both the PivotTable and PivotChart under Data in
the Excel main menu. The PivotTable and PivotChart Report items in this menu activate
a wizard that walks the user through the initial process of adding a PivotTable or
PivotChart to an Excel worksheet.

> **Note**
>
> In addition to the PivotTable and PivotChart Wizard, there is a Get External
> Data item in the Data menu that also allows a user to connect and retrieve data
> from an OLAP data source. Also note that the basic steps in the wizard are the
> same whether you are creating a PivotTable or a PivotChart. In this example, a
> PivotTable is created.

The first step of the PivotTable and PivotChart Wizard (shown in Figure 23.1) prompts
the user to select a data source and either a PivotTable or PivotChart. OLAP Services is
considered an External Data Source.

FIGURE 23.1

*Indicate the
source of your
data and select
the kind of report
you want on the
wizard's first
screen.*

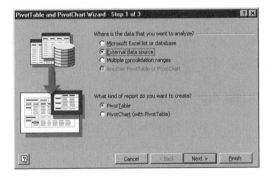

Step 2 (shown in Figure 23.2) of the wizard uses Microsoft Query to Get Data, or connect to a data provider, for the PivotTable. Click Get Data and you are presented with an
option to connect to an ODBC data source, to run an existing query, or to connect to an
OLAP cube.

FIGURE 23.2

*Specify the exter-
nal data in Step 2
of the wizard.*

First, a few words about existing queries. When you use this procedure to create a connection to an OLAP database or cube from within Excel, an .oqy file is created and
saved automatically. However, the .oqy file only stores the information necessary to re-
establish the connection with the data provider. It does not contain the query. Therefore,
when the wizard allows the user to open a query file, a connection to an OLAP data file
is opened, but a specific query is not opened.

For this example, choose the OLAP Cubes tab on the Choose Data Source dialog. To
establish a "New Data Source" that is an OLAP data provider, it is necessary to create a
name for the data source (see Figure 23.3), select an OLAP provider such as Microsoft
OLE DB Provider for OLAP Services, and connect to either an OLAP Server or cube file
(see Figure 23.4).

FIGURE 23.3

*Name your data
source and specify
the provider.*

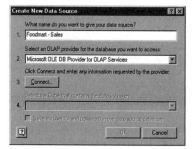

It is possible to use PivotTable as a thin client for either an OLAP Server or for an
offline cube file (.cub). To establish a connection to an OLAP Server, it is necessary to
specify the server, the database, and the cube on the Server.

In contrast, it is not necessary to explicitly define a database and cube when making a
connection to a .cub file, because these local cube files are based on a single cube.

FIGURE 23.4

Select the location of the data.

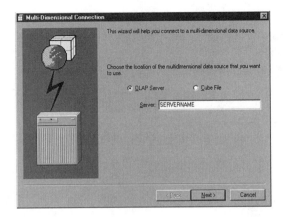

Screen shots of the database and cube selection are not shown, because they are merely simple select lists.

As described in the Chapter 22, "Programming Access to the OLAP Data Sources," security for the connection is managed through the NT operating system, so it is not necessary to provide an additional username and password in this wizard. And despite the cautions, a glance at the .oqy file shows that the username and password are not stored in the .oqy file.

The final step in the wizard (shown in Figure 23.5) is placing a PivotTable in the Excel spreadsheet, and optionally, selecting the data to be included in the PivotTable (Layout button), and the format of the PivotTable (Options button).

FIGURE 23.5

Place your PivotTable in the worksheet.

Populating the PivotTable is accomplished with the PivotTable toolbox. You are presented with all of the dimensions and measures available in the cube and a layout into which the dimensions and measures may be placed. As shown in the empty layout in Figure 23.6, there are four placeholders into which cube information can be placed. The four placeholders are

- Page Fields—These act as slicers, or filters, for the data. Because only members can be used as page fields, when a level or dimension is added to the page field drop area, the default member is used. Members from the Measures dimension cannot be added as page fields.

- Column Fields and Row Fields—These determine the data displayed on the columns and rows axes, respectively. These axes may contain any type of data from a cube structure except measures.

- Data Items—These determine the numerical data portion of the spreadsheet. Only members from the Measures dimension can be used as data items.

FIGURE 23.6

Placeholders are to be filled with cube information from the PivotTable toolbar.

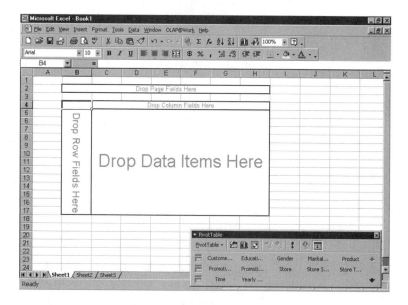

Figures 23.7 and 23.8 show the layout toolbar for PivotTable. The main body of the toolbar contains a scrolling list of the dimensions of the cube followed by a list of the members in the Measures dimension of the cube.

The icon at the far left of each row indicates the areas into which the dimension and measures can be placed. The icon represents the PivotTable on the spreadsheet. Notice that different areas of the icon are shaded to indicate where items from that row can be placed on the PivotTable.

FIGURE 23.7

*The PivotTable
toolbar shows the
cube dimensions
with icons at the
left showing
where the dimen-
sions can be
placed in the
PivotTable.*

FIGURE 23.8

*The icons left of
the cube measures
shown at the bot-
tom of the
PivotTable indi-
cate that measures
can be dropped on
to the PivotTable
as data items.*

Manipulating the PivotTable

Because the PivotTable is designed for nontechnical users, the interface uses simple drag-and-drop operations for basic access to data in a cube. First-time users should be able to intuitively learn simple operations quickly.

PivotTable allows multiple dimensions on the row and column axes, and multiple members as page fields. Drilldown operations are permitted using drop-down list boxes and by double-clicking members listed in either of the axes. Subtotals and grand totals are calculated and displayed automatically.

Format Report and Table Options are the primary menu items in the PivotTable toolbar for customizing the look and feel of the pivot table. Format Report provides a number of style templates from which the user can choose. Table Options enables the user to add or remove subtotals and grand totals, to decide how empty cells should be displayed, and a number of other formatting and data options.

Note

The PivotTable toolbar behaves like standard toolbars. To add or remove items, right-click on the toolbar and select Customize. Most of the important PivotTable commands can be found in the Data category.

The PivotTable in Use

At this point in the discussion a quick example is instructive. For this example, assume you are interested in the unit sales of products to customers of different genders in the first quarter of 1997.

1. Using the PivotTable toolbar, drag and drop the Gender dimension to the portion of the PivotTable that says "Drop Column Fields Here."

2. Drag and drop the Product dimension to the row fields area, and Drag and drop the Time dimension to the page fields area.

3. Scroll down in the PivotTable toolbar to the measures and drag Unit Sales to the data items area on the PivotTable.

After completing these steps, your PivotTable should look similar to the one shown in Figure 23.9.

FIGURE 23.9

This PivotTable shows Unit Sales of Product Families by customer gender for the year 1997.

To access the Q1 1997 data, expand the 1997 select list into a treeview, expand the 1997 node, select Q1, and click on OK. Notice that the data in the spreadsheet is automatically refreshed. The spreadsheet should now look like Figure 23.10.

Advanced OLAP Functions in the PivotTable

While some advanced functionality is provided in the Formulas and Field Settings menu items in the PivotTable toolbar, most advanced OLAP functionality is not available in PivotTable. To access the provided functions, right-click a row or column heading on the spreadsheet and select Field Settings from the popup menu.

While it is not within the scope of this book to explain the implementation of all available functions, it is useful to use the PivotTable example set up previously to demonstrate how advanced functions are added.

FIGURE 23.10

This PivotTable shows Unit Sales of Product Families by Customer Gender for the Q1 1997.

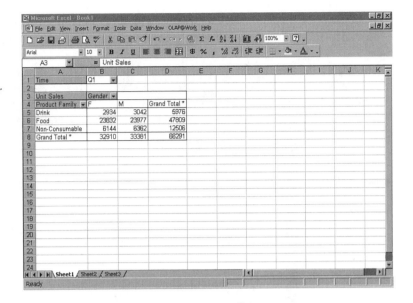

First, let's dig one level deeper into the product dimension. Instead of Product Families, assume you are interested in product departments. First expand the Product Family select list into a treeview, and expand each of the product family nodes. Now, as shown in Figure 23.11, select all of the product departments in each of product family.

FIGURE 23.11

The product departments are available under each of the product family members.

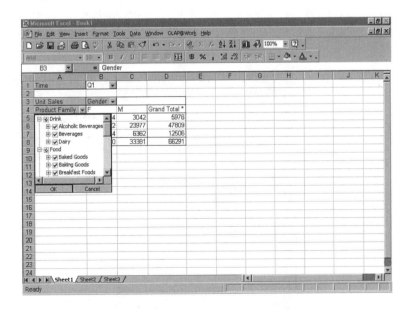

After clicking OK in the product family treeview, the PivotTable now will show all of the product departments grouped according to product family as shown in Figure 23.12.

	A	B	C	D	E
1	Time	Q1			
2					
3	Unit Sales		Gender		
4	Product Family	Product Department	F	M	Grand Total
5	Drink	Alcoholic Beverages	837	730	1567
6		Beverages	1649	1684	3333
7		Dairy	448	628	1076
8	Drink Total		2934	3042	5976
9	Food	Baked Goods	953	979	1932
10		Baking Goods	2452	2593	5045
11		Breakfast Foods	440	380	820
12		Canned Foods	2422	2315	4737
13		Canned Products	189	211	400
14		Dairy	1589	1673	3262
15		Deli	1508	1477	2985
16		Eggs	436	482	918
17		Frozen Foods	3218	3406	6624
18		Meat	182	209	391
19		Produce	4703	4796	9499
20		Seafood	209	203	412
21		Snack Foods	3951	3799	7750
22		Snacks	885	833	1718
23		Starchy Foods	695	621	1316
24	Food Total		23832	23977	47809

FIGURE 23.12
This PivotTable shows Unit Sales of Product Families and Product Departments by Customer Gender for the Q1 1997.

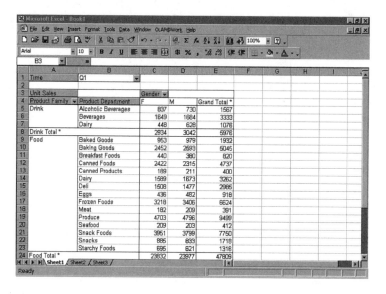

Finally, let's sort the product departments according to unit sales. Right-click the product department select list and choose Field Settings. When the PivotTable Field dialog appears, click the Advanced button. Choose the descending AutoSort option and sort on unit sales. Click OK, and the data in the PivotTable is automatically refreshed as shown in Figure 23.13. Notice that the sort did not break the hierarchy.

	A	B	C	D	E
1	Time	Q1			
2					
3	Unit Sales		Gender		
4	Product Family	Product Department	F	M	Grand Total
5	Drink	Beverages	1649	1684	3333
6		Alcoholic Beverages	837	730	1567
7		Dairy	448	628	1076
8	Drink Total		2934	3042	5976
9	Food	Produce	4703	4796	9499
10		Snack Foods	3951	3799	7750
11		Frozen Foods	3218	3406	6624
12		Baking Goods	2452	2593	5045
13		Canned Foods	2422	2315	4737
14		Dairy	1589	1673	3262
15		Deli	1508	1477	2985
16		Baked Goods	953	979	1932
17		Snacks	885	833	1718
18		Starchy Foods	695	621	1316
19		Eggs	436	482	918
20		Breakfast Foods	440	380	820
21		Seafood	209	203	412
22		Canned Products	189	211	400
23		Meat	182	209	391
24	Food Total		23832	23977	47809
25	Non-Consumable	Household	3362	3387	6749

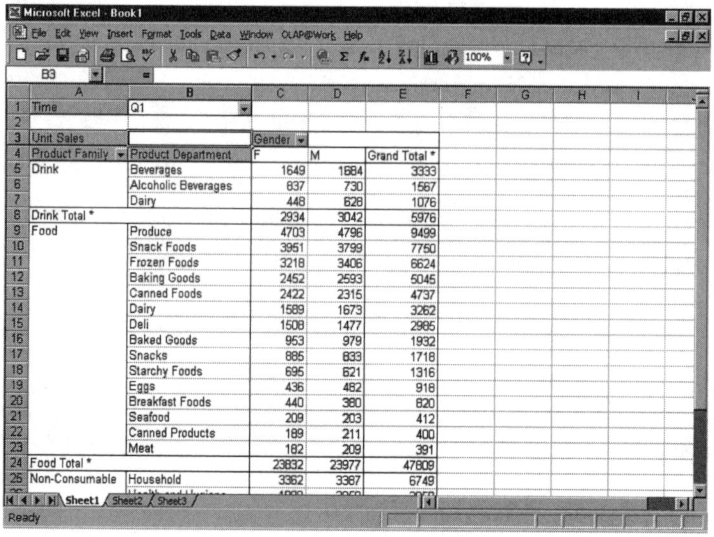

FIGURE 23.13
The Product Departments are sorted by Unit Sales by Customer Gender for the Q1 1997.

> **Note**
>
> Unlike the basic interface to add dimensions to rows and columns, I would not classify these additional, more complex functions as intuitive. In fact, they can be extremely confusing for even experienced users. To further complicate matters, in the current version of the PivotTable, help is not readily available.

Using the PivotChart

Underlying every PivotChart, there is a PivotTable that contains the values for the information in the chart. In most situations, it is practical for you to create a PivotTable first and then choose the PivotChart option from the PivotTable toolbar.

As with the PivotTable, there are four regions in PivotChart into which you can drag and drop dimensions, levels, and members. Figure 23.14 shows the different areas, which are

- Page Fields—These act as slicers, or filters, for the data.
- Category Fields and Series Fields—These determine the data displayed on the category axis (x-axis) and series axis (y-axis). Rows from the PivotTable translate to categories, while columns translate into the series.
- Data Items—These determine the numerical data portion of the spreadsheet. Members from the Measures dimension can be used as data items.

23

IMPLEMENTING
EXCEL AS AN
OLAP CLIENT

FIGURE 23.14

The PivotChart interface shows drop areas for the dimensions from the cube.

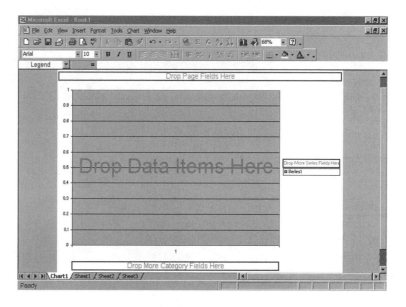

PivotChart provides functionality common in charting programs. Users can select from a variety of chart types and can format how data is displayed on the chart. Advanced functionality for sorting data, performing TopCount operations, and using formulas to manipulate cube data are also available.

Figure 23.15 shows the data generated in the example described previously.

FIGURE 23.15

This PivotChart shows Unit Sales of Product Families and Product Departments by Customer Gender for the Q1 1997.

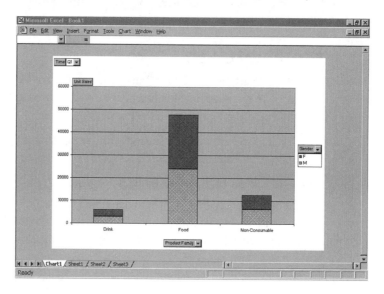

As Figure 23.16 shows, the chart becomes more complex as multiple dimensions are added to a single query axis.

FIGURE 23.16

A PivotChart can display multiple dimensions on a single axis.

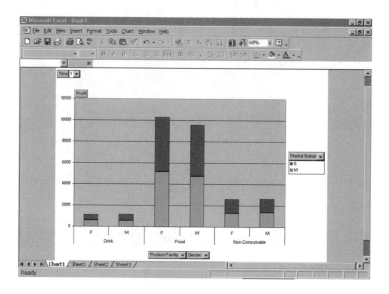

Building a Custom OLAP Client in Excel2000

In addition to PivotTable and PivotChart, there are a number of other methods of integrating OLAP data into Excel. Traditionally, two approaches are commonly used to extend Excel functionality:

- Building a single ActiveX control that can be added into an Excel spreadsheet. The ActiveX control contains functionality for connecting to the multidimensional data provider, for providing an interface to allow a user to compose a query, and to retrieve the data. Excel is used primarily as the method of displaying the resulting cellset to the user. The control would typically be built using a stand-alone programming language (like Visual Basic).

- Building multiple ActiveX controls with Visual Basic for Applications (VBA) for use within Excel. VBA code within these controls provides functionality to connect to the OLAP data provider and to allow you to create an OLAP query. The spreadsheet is used to display the data.

Chapter 25, "Building an OLAP Client Application with Visual Basic," discusses the subject of building standalone Visual Basic OLAP client applications. Because much of the information and code contained in that chapter could also be used to create an ActiveX control (the first method just described), the discussion that follows concentrates on using VBA to build controls within Excel.

The following sections walk you through the process of building an OLAP client with Excel. Because the primary goal here is to help you understand the development process, the resulting client application is very basic in its functionality. It is not elaborate or robust, and is not intended to be put in the hands of an end-user as is. Figure 23.17 shows the resulting application after a query has been run.

23

IMPLEMENTING
EXCEL AS AN
OLAP CLIENT

> **Note**
>
> The following discussion assumes that you have a basic understanding of VBA programming within Excel.

FIGURE 23.17

An OLAP client in Excel 2000 displays query results.

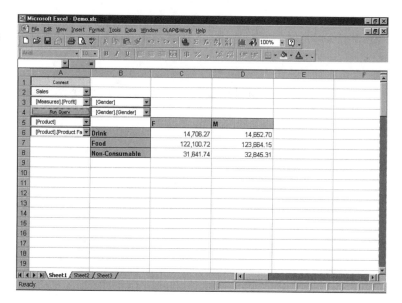

The Design Goals

The first step in building this application is to lay out the basic design requirements. In this case the requirements are simple:

- Connect to a predefined OLAP Server and database.
- Allow the user to select a cube from the database.
- Allow the user to select one measure from the Measures dimension to be used as the data.
- Allow the user to place one dimension on the row axis, and to specify a level within that dimension to retrieve members.
- Allow the user to place one dimension on the column axis, and to specify a level within that dimension to retrieve members.
- Allow the user to run a query after specifying the measure and the dimensions on the row and column axes.

Before building the control on the spreadsheet, you must add the necessary OLAP and data connection references into the VBAProject.

1. Open a new worksheet and select Macro from the Tools menu of Excel.
2. Select Visual Basic Editor to view the VBA programming interface.

3. Select References from the Tools menu of VBA. Use the resulting dialog to add the following two references to the project:

   Microsoft Active Data Objects (multidimensional) 1.0 Library

   Microsoft Active Data Objects 2.1 Library

> **Note**
>
> While Excel 2000 was used to build this demonstration application, Excel97 could also be used. The important necessary technical requirement is to be able to add ADO and ADOMD as references to the VBAProject.

Adding the ActiveX Controls to Excel

Because the design goals are primarily functional in nature, the controls to be used can be based directly on the design goals.

Open a new Excel worksheet and use the Toolbars item in the View menu to show the Controls toolbar in Excel. To add controls to the worksheet, simply left-click a control and then move to the worksheet to draw its location and size. To access the code behind a control, double-click on it.

Begin the development of this application by placing the following controls on a new worksheet.

- tglConnect (Toggle Button)
- cboCube (Combo Box)
- cboColDimension (Combo Box)
- cboColLevel (Combo Box)
- cboRowDimension (Combo Box)
- cboRowLevel (Combo Box)
- cboMeasures (Combo Box)
- cmdRun (Command Button)

Next, create the following variables in the declarations statement of the module.

```
'Worksheet Object
Dim shtDemo As Worksheet

'ADO Objects
Dim objConn As New ADODB.Connection
```

```
'ADOMD Objects
Dim objCellset As New ADOMD.Cellset
Dim objCatalog As New ADOMD.Catalog
Dim objCubeDef As ADOMD.CubeDef
Dim objDimension As ADOMD.Dimension
Dim objHierarchy As ADOMD.Hierarchy
Dim objLevel As ADOMD.Level
Dim objMember As ADOMD.Member
```

Using the concepts discussed in Chapter 22, "Programming Access to the OLAP Data Sources," the following code can be used to establish the data connection with the OLAP Server. Once the connection is established, the cube combo box is populated with a list of cubes from the specified database.

```
Private Sub tglConnect_Click()

If shtDemo Is Nothing Then
Set shtDemo = Sheet1
End If

'Establish Connection
If Not objConn.State = adStateOpen Then
    objConn.Open "Data Source=SERVER;Provider=MSOLAP;Catalog=Foodmart"
    tglConnect.Value = 1
    tglConnect.Caption = "Connected"
End If

'Iterate throught Catalog and populate the Cube combobox
Set objCatalog.ActiveConnection = objConn
cboCube.Clear
For Each objCubeDef In objCatalog.CubeDefs
    cboCube.AddItem objCubeDef.Name
Next objCubeDef
cboCube.ListIndex = 0

End sub
```

The last line in this segment of code selects the first cube in the database and causes the cboCube_Click event to be triggered. The procedure for this event, shown in Listing 23.1, can then be used to populate the columns and rows combo boxes with dimensions from the cube, and populate the measures combo box with members from the Measures level of the Members dimension.

LISTING 23.1   The cboClick Procedure

```
Private Sub cboCube_Click()

'Reset comboboxes
cboColDimension.Clear
cboRowDimension.Clear
cboMeasures.Clear

'Iterate through the cubes in the catalog
For Each objCubeDef In objCatalog.CubeDefs
    'If this is the selected cube
    If objCubeDef.Name = cboCube.List(cboCube.ListIndex) Then
        For Each objDimension In objCubeDef.Dimensions
        If objDimension.UniqueName <> "[Measures]" Then
            cboColDimension.AddItem objDimension.UniqueName
            cboRowDimension.AddItem objDimension.UniqueName
        Else
            For Each objHierarchy In objDimension.Hierarchies
                For Each objLevel In objHierarchy.Levels
                    For Each objMember In objLevel.Members
                        cboMeasures.AddItem objMember.UniqueName
                    Next objMember
                Next objLevel
            Next objHierarchy
        End If
        Next objDimension
    Exit For 'objCubeDef remains the selected cube
    End If
Next objCubeDef

'Set comboboxes
cboColDimension.ListIndex = 0
cboRowDimension.ListIndex = 1
cboMeasures.ListIndex = 0

End sub
```

The last three lines in this segment of code select the first dimension (Customers) for the column axis and the second dimension (Education Level) for the row axis. Finally, the first measure member is also chosen. When the column and row dimensions are selected, the cboColDimension_Click and cboRowDimension_Click events are triggered. The procedures for these two events are used to populate the cboColDimension and cboRowDimension combo boxes with the levels from the selected dimensions. The code for the cboColDimension_Click event is

```
Private Sub cboColDimension_Click()

cboColLevel.Clear
```

23

IMPLEMENTING
EXCEL AS AN
OLAP CLIENT

```
For Each objDimension In objCubeDef.Dimensions
    'Is this the selected dimension ?
    If objDimension.UniqueName = _
            cboColDimension.List(cboColDimension.ListIndex) Then
        cboColLevel.Clear
        For Each objHierarchy In objDimension.Hierarchies
            For Each objLevel In objHierarchy.Levels
                cboColLevel.AddItem objLevel.UniqueName
            Next objLevel
        Next objHierarchy
    End If
Next objDimension

cboColLevel.ListIndex = 0
cboColLevel.Enabled = True

End Sub
```

The code for the cboRowDimension_Click event is

```
Private Sub cboRowDimension_Click()

cboRowLevel.Clear
For Each objDimension In objCubeDef.Dimensions
    'Is this the selected dimension ?
    If objDimension.UniqueName = _
            cboRowDimension.List(cboRowDimension.ListIndex) Then
        cboRowLevel.Clear
        For Each objHierarchy In objDimension.Hierarchies
            For Each objLevel In objHierarchy.Levels
                cboRowLevel.AddItem objLevel.UniqueName
            Next objLevel
        Next objHierarchy
    End If
Next objDimension
cboRowLevel.ListIndex = 0
cboRowLevel.Enabled = True

End Sub
```

With the addition of some code to format the position and size of the controls, the previous code provides an interface that allows a user to

- Select a cube.
- Select a dimension and level for the column axis.
- Select a dimension and level for the row axis.
- Select a measure to use as the data.

After the user has accomplished all of these tasks, it is necessary to construct the MDX statement and execute it. The simple design goals of this tool were specifically chosen to allow for an MDX query to be easily written. There are no complex functions, no CrossJoin is necessary, and there is no need for calculated members.

The following code builds a query by using the .Members function on the levels to create sets for the column and row axes. It uses the cube name in the FROM clause. And it uses the measures members as a slicer in the WHERE clause. The query is then used with the open connection object to create a cellset with the results.

```
Private Sub cmdRun_Click()

Dim strMDXQuery As String
strMDXQuery = ""
strMDXQuery = "SELECT NON EMPTY "
strMDXQuery = strMDXQuery & cboColLevel.List(cboColLevel.ListIndex)
strMDXQuery = strMDXQuery & ".Members ON COLUMNS, "
strMDXQuery = strMDXQuery & "NON EMPTY "
strMDXQuery = strMDXQuery & cboRowLevel.List(cboRowLevel.ListIndex)
strMDXQuery = strMDXQuery & ".Members ON ROWS"
strMDXQuery = strMDXQuery & " FROM " & cboCube.List(cboCube.ListIndex)
strMDXQuery = strMDXQuery & " WHERE " & cboMeasures.List(cboMeasures.ListIndex)

'Close the previous cellset
If objCellset.State = adStateOpen Then
    objCellset.Close
End If

'Execute a query
On Error GoTo ErrInvalidMDX
objCellset.Open strMDXQuery, objConn

'Display the cellset
subDisplayCellset

Exit Sub

ErrInvalidMDX:
    MsgBox (Err.Description)
End Sub
```

Once the cellset object has been created, the data needs to be transferred from the cellset to the worksheet. The subroutine to accomplish this task is named subDisplayCellset and is called immediately after the cellset is created in the procedure previously shown.

The code in Listing 23.2 first clears out a portion of the spreadsheet of arbitrary size (25 columns by 95 rows). The procedure then undertakes the process of displaying the cellset in a region of cells such that the upper-left corner of the cellset is positioned in cell B5.

All of the column headers are placed and formatted in successive columns in row five; then all of the row headers are placed and formatted in successive rows in column B.

After the column and row headers are written, iteration is used to write the formatted value of each cell of the cellset into the appropriate cell of the spreadsheet.

LISTING 23.2   Writing the Cellset Values to the Worksheet

```
Private Sub subDisplayCellset()

Dim lintCols, lintRows As Integer
Dim objPosition As Position
Dim objMember As Member

'Clear out a region of the spreadsheet
shtDemo.Range("B5", "Z100").ClearContents
shtDemo.Range("B5", "Z100").Interior.Color = 16777215
shtDemo.Range("B5", "Z100").Borders.Color = 12632256
shtDemo.Range("B5", "Z100").Font.Bold = False

'Display the column headings
lintCols = 67
For Each objPosition In objCellset.Axes.item(0).Positions
    For Each objMember In objPosition.Members
        shtDemo.Range(Chr(lintCols) & "5").Value = objMember.Caption
        shtDemo.Range(Chr(lintCols) & "5").Interior.Color = 12632256
        shtDemo.Range(Chr(lintCols) & "5").Borders.Color = 0
        shtDemo.Range(Chr(lintCols) & "5").Font.Bold = True
        lintCols = lintCols + 1
    Next objMember
Next objPosition
lintCols = lintCols - 67

'Display the row headings
lintRows = 6
For Each objPosition In objCellset.Axes.item(1).Positions
    For Each objMember In objPosition.Members
        shtDemo.Range("B" & lintRows).Value = objMember.Caption
        shtDemo.Range("B" & lintRows).Interior.Color = 12632256
        shtDemo.Range("B" & lintRows).Borders.Color = 0
        shtDemo.Range("B" & lintRows).Font.Bold = True
        lintRows = lintRows + 1
    Next objMember
Next objPosition
lintRows = lintRows - 6

'Display the data
Dim objCell As ADOMD.Cell
Dim i, j As Integer
For i = 0 To lintRows - 1
```

```
    For j = 0 To lintCols - 1
        shtDemo.Range(Chr(67 + j) & (i + 6)).Value = _
                objCellset(j, i).FormattedValue
    Next j
Next i

'Close the cellset object
objCellset.Close

End Sub
```

Clearly this sample client is not extremely sophisticated or powerful. Instead, the intent was to provide an example of the relative ease with which Excel can be used as a simple OLAP client.

Summary

The primary reasons for considering Microsoft Excel 2000 for use as a client application for an OLAP Server are typical of the arguments used for using many Microsoft applications.

- It is comparatively inexpensive. PivotTable and PivotChart are part of Excel 2000, and many corporations have Office 2000 implementations in progress or in place.

- The learning curve is not particularly steep. An enormous number of business users are familiar with the look and feel of Excel, and they should not have difficulty learning the use of PivotTable for basic queries.

- PivotTable is integrated very well into Excel. In many cases, an OLAP user may have a need or a desire to use Excel for additional manipulation of the data.

It is clear that both the PivotTable and PivotChart were designed to allow users to get basic data from a multidimensional data provider into a spreadsheet quickly and easily. The user is shielded from the somewhat complex structure of the cube, the complexity of MDX queries, and the process of importing data into a spreadsheet.

Similarly, it is likely that any client application built to function within Excel will be somewhat limited in scope and power. Therefore, on the spectrum of OLAP functionality, these client tools typically occupy the low end—mainly because there are limits on the complexity of the queries that can be built. Ultimately, these limits are inherent in every OLAP client and are usually indicative of the audience at which the client tool is targeted.

Chapter 25, "Building an OLAP Client Application with Visual Basic," contains more information on building a more capable OLAP client that functions outside of the Microsoft Office suite.

23

IMPLEMENTING
EXCEL AS AN
OLAP CLIENT

Building an OLAP Web Client

by Jim Pinkelman

The Internet and corporate intranets provide excellent network infrastructures on which to base an OLAP application. This chapter provides you with an understanding of the development issues associated with building a Web-based client, and a start on the code necessary to build the client.

Because the fundamental goal here is to explain the critical concepts in building a Web client, the application built in this chapter is not overly complex. The name given to this application is "OLAP Web Client." By the end of the chapter you will understand the important steps in building a Web application and will be ready to begin building custom applications for your users' needs.

While a substantial number of Web applications are built with cgi programs on UNIX servers, the discussion in this chapter is based on Microsoft's IIS Server as the Web server. Building the Web application requires that the developer have a basic understanding of ADO and ADOMD connection objects, Microsoft OLAP Services, Active Server Pages, and html.

The chapter is divided to two main sections. The first section contains a discussion of the overall architecture of the application and the functional requirement of the various components. The second section presents the development of a Web application. Because the server prepares and sends the html page to the client, this discussion includes parts of both the client and the server components of the application as implemented using Active Server Pages (ASP) on IIS.

The Architecture for the Web Client

As is appropriate before making any development decisions, it is necessary to establish some development guidelines and decide on some design requirements.

Because the purpose of this chapter is educational in nature, simplicity and clarity drive the fundamental design objectives. Two important design objectives and assumptions are

- The client will be as "thin" as possible. ActiveX controls, Java applets, DHTML, and XML will not be used. (While there are not used here, these tools can be extremely effective in building real-world applications.)

- The server will make maximal use of Active Server Pages (ASP), and not use Web classes or custom server-side programming components.

If I were beginning the development of an OLAP Web client for a specific situation, with well-defined user requirements, use of more current Web programming techniques would be entirely appropriate.

The second critical assumption is the decision to limit the server-side programming to ASP. Deciding to use Microsoft's ISS Web server can be justified by the fact that the OLAP architecture being discussed here is almost entirely Microsoft-based. The decision to limit server-side programming to ASP is motivated by the goal for visibility into the programming code. Placing *all* of the server code in ASP pages is an effective method of achieving this visibility.

> **Note**
>
> The architecture used here and the development of the OLAP Web Client is one of many approaches that can be successful. This is neither the only nor the best method of deploying and OLAP client over the Web.

The functional requirements of OLAP Web Client are very simple. The application will

1. Connect with a server, database, and cube and display cube metadata to the user on a Web page.
2. Use html form components and variables to allow the user to specify the parameters of an MDX query. The user will not be required to directly create or edit the MDX query.
3. Provide limited capabilities for MDX functions.
4. Execute the MDX query and display the results to the user in an html table.

Figure 24.1 shows the overall architecture for this application.

As the figure shows, the client does not directly interface with the OLAP data provider. All interaction with the data server is conducted thought the Web server. By defining the architecture with this restriction, there is no need to establish an ADO connection between the client Web page and the data provider.

This approach has some advantages and some disadvantages. Most importantly, from a security perspective, all users assume the Windows NT identity of the Internet Guest Account. While this significantly simplifies the need to manage access to the data provider, it precludes the possibility of using only NT security to control the specific data to which each user has access. If the developer decides to allow a direct connection from the Web server to the OLAP server, configuring the network and the firewall to allow such access becomes a major design issue.

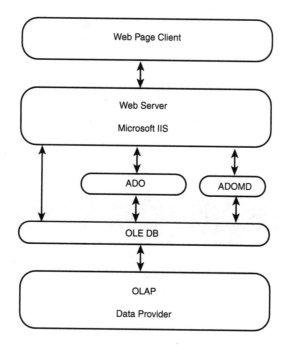

FIGURE 24.1

The Web page client, the Web server, and the OLAP data provider make up the three tiers of OLAP Web Client.

Figure 24.2 shows the primary data interfaces between the three tiers of the Web application.

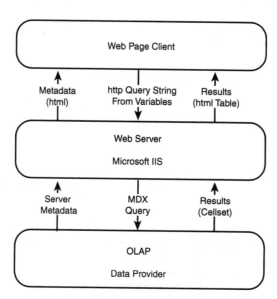

FIGURE 24.2

The complete OLAP Web application requires a series of sequential transactions between the three tiers.

To provide a more structured presentation of the Web client you are building in this chapter, the user interaction with the application is broken down into three sequential Web pages that collect and present the information necessary to execute the query. Figure 24.3 provides a simplified function representation of the relationship between the Web pages, the Web server, and the user.

FIGURE 24.3

The Web application is based on three sequential Web pages generated with Active Server Pages.

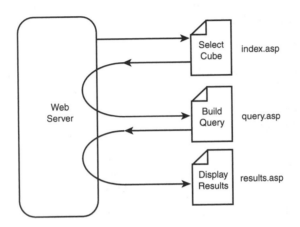

The discussion in the rest of this chapter is divided into three parts corresponding to the functional objectives of each of these Web pages. The function of the first page, index.asp, is to allow the user to select a cube and establish a connection to the cube. The second page, query.asp, retrieves and displays the structure of the cube and prompts the user to create a query. The final page, results.asp, displays the results to the user.

Developing the Web Application

As is show in Figure 24.3, the user interacts with three Web pages to retrieve data from the OLAP data provider. Each of these pages is discussed in subsequent subsections.

> **Note**
>
> It is important to note that the decision to use three pages in this particular application is completely arbitrary. The specific requirements of a project should determine the exact processes of the Web application as well as the number and role of the Web pages required by the application.

Connecting to the Server and Selecting the Cube

The first overall step in building OLAP Web Client is establishing a connection with the OLAP data provider, setting the database, and providing a list of cubes from which the user can select. These actions are accomplished with index.asp, which contains some server-side data access code and some standard html.

The specific approaches to each of these functions are as follows:

1. The Web server establishes the connection to the OLAP data source using the Internet Guest Account. No user interaction is required.
2. The Web server determines the database in the data source that will be exposed. No user interaction is required.
3. The Web server creates a Web page that contains an html form prompting the user to select a cube.
4. The user submits the form with the name of the cube to the server.

Figure 24.4 shows the interaction between the Web server and index.asp in accomplishing these functions.

FIGURE 24.4

The Web application establishes a connection to the OLAP data provider and sends a list of cubes to the user.

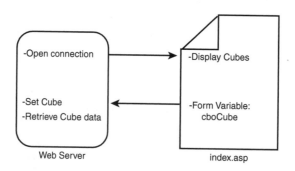

In implementing OLAP Web Client, it is necessary for the Web server to interact with the OLAP data provider in processing each of the three ASP pages. In terms of performance, the connection to the data source is the most taxing of these three tasks. To make this process more efficient, a single connection should be established for each user session through the use of session variables.

Place the following code in the global.asa file to create the connection and selects the FoodMart database.

```
<SCRIPT LANGUAGE=VBScript RUNAT=Server>

Sub Session_OnStart
```

```
'Establish the ADO connnection
Set Session("objConn") = Server.CreateObject("ADODB.Connection")
Session("objConn").Open _
("Data Source=ServerName;Provider=MSOLAP;Catalog=Foodmart")

'Specify the ADOMD catalog
Set Session("objCatalog") = Server.CreateObject("ADOMD.Catalog")
Set Session("objCatalog").ActiveConnection = Session("objConn")

End Sub

</SCRIPT>
```

After the connection to the server has been established, a list of cubes can be generated
and returned to the user. While this list could be returned in an applet or ActiveX control,
it is sent back as a select list within a form to keep the application simple. Figure 24.5
shows the index.asp Web page.

FIGURE 24.5

*Index.asp prompts
the user to select
a cube.*

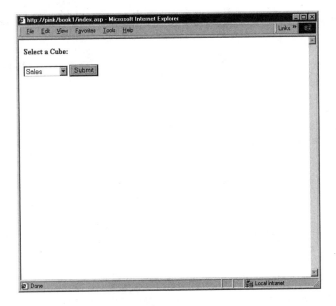

The following code shows how the ASP code in the index.asp file accomplishes this:

```
<html>
<head>
<meta NAME="GENERATOR" Content="Microsoft Visual Studio 6.0">
<title></title>
</head>
<body>
```

24

BUILDING AN
OLAP WEB
CLIENT

```
<H2>Select a Cube:  </H2>

<form method="POST" action="query.asp" name="cube">
<select name="cboCube" size="1">
<%For Each objCubeDef In Session("objCatalog").CubeDefs%>
  <option value="<%=objCubeDef.name%>"><%=objCubeDef.name%></option>
<%Next%>
</select>
<input type="submit" name="Submit" value="Submit">
</form>

</body>
</html>
```

Notice that the session variable created for the active catalog is used to access the cubes. As the next section describes, when this form is submitted to the server, the name of the cube is used to retrieve cube metadata.

Displaying the Metadata to Select the Query Parameters

As specified in the form tag, the variables submitted by the index.asp page are processed by query.asp, as shown in Figure 24.6

FIGURE 24.6

The Web application uses the selected cube to generate query.asp.

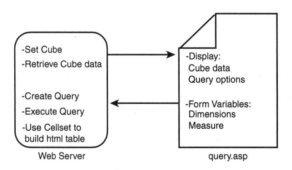

Because of the length and complexity of query.asp, I will present the code in three sections. The first segment contains the standard html header information and the code that creates the CubeDef based on the user cube selection on the index.asp page. This object is used throughout query.asp to retrieve dimension, level, and members.

```
<%@ Language=VBScript %>
<HTML>
<HEAD>
<META NAME="GENERATOR" Content="Microsoft Visual Studio 6.0">
</HEAD>
```

```
<BODY>

<%
'Declarations
dim intLevel

'Create the cube object
For Each objCubeDef In Session("objCatalog").CubeDefs
    if objCubeDef.name = Request.Form("cboCube") then exit for
Next
%>

<H2><%=objCubeDef.name%> Cube</H2>
```

The second code segment builds the html interface allowing the user to view cube dimensions and levels and to select the axes for each of the dimensions. Figure 24.7 shows the query.asp Web page created after the user has selected the sales cube.

FIGURE 24.7

The Web application generates query.asp from the Sales cube.

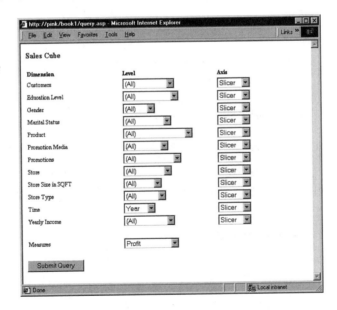

The code iterates through all the cube dimensions, with the exception of the Measures dimension. For each dimension a row in an html table is created. As Figure 24.7 shows, the first column contains the name of the dimension. The second column uses a select list to display the levels in the dimension and the members of the second level in the dimension. The third column contains a select list containing the axes of the query.

```
<form method="POST" action="results.asp" name="cube">

<table border=0>
```

```
 <tr align="left">
  <th width="200">Dimension</th>
  <th width="200">Level</th>
  <th>Axis</th></tr>

<%
'Print the cube dimensions in the first column
'Build a combobox from the levels in the second column
'Build a combobox for the axes in the third column

For Each objDim In objCubeDef.Dimensions
    If objDim.Name<>"Measures" then
        intLevel = 1
%>
 <tr>
  <td><%=objDim.Name%></td>

  <td><select name="<%=objDim.Name%>" size="1">
<%
    For Each objHie In objDim.Hierarchies
        For Each objLev In objHie.Levels
%>
          <option value="<%=objDim.UniqueName%>,
          <%=objLev.UniqueName%>.members"><%=objLev.name%></option>
<%
          if intLevel = 2 or objDim.name = "Time" then
              For Each objMem In objLev.Members
%>
                  <option value="<%=objDim.UniqueName%>,
                  <%=objMem.UniqueName%>">
                    - <%=objMem.name%></option>
<%
              Next
          end if
%>
              intLevel = intLevel + 1%>
<%      Next
    Next
%>
  </select></td>

<%'Build a combobox for the axes in the third column%>
  <td>
   <select name="<%=objDim.Name%>" size="1">
   <option value="Col">Column</option>
   <option value="Row">Row</option>
   <option value="Sli" selected>Slicer</option>
   </select>
  </td>
 </tr>
<%    End if%>
```

```
<%Next%>
</table>
```

Obviously, some important application decisions were made in building this page that impact the capabilities of this simple application. As is true with the development of all applications, the programmer must make decisions that strike a compromise between the capabilities the program provides to the user and the resources available to develop the program.

For the OLAP Web Client, I put some significant limitations on the capabilities available to the end-user to highlight the development process and to produce an application that fits well into the scope of this chapter. In building this Web-based OLAP application, some important design issues were encountered which are likely to be common in other development efforts.

One important design issue of this interface is that it only makes a subset of the cube metadata available to the user as potential query parameters. I decided to avoid the obvious performance problems associated with transferring thousands of members to a user's Web page.

A second important design issue of this application is that it does not allow the user to employ intrinsic MDX functions. In this case, the decision to exclude MDX functions was made purely because of the development constraints of this effort. Depending on the user requirements, it is probable that some of the MDX functions should be available. Implementing such functions as Sort(), Filter(), and .Children would not be particularly difficult in this situation. The use and syntax of these functions is discussed in Part IV of this book.

Finally, note that there is no capability for calculated members in OLAP Web Client. While adding such a capability would significantly enhance the power of the application, it would be technically very difficult to accomplish. An ActiveX control or Java applet would probably be the only effective method of implementing calculated members because of the complexity of the MDX syntax.

In almost all cases, the decisions a developer must make in building an application are influenced by available resources, available technology, and, most importantly, user requirements.

The query.asp code segment contains the code that displays the available measures to the user. For OLAP Web Client, only the members in the Measures dimension are available and, as discussed in the next section, the Measures member is always included as a slicer. The Measures dimension and level(s) are not available to the user.

24

BUILDING AN
OLAP WEB
CLIENT

```
<p></p>

<table border=0>
<%
For Each objDim In objCubeDef.Dimensions
    'For the measures dimension
    If objDim.Name="Measures" then
%>
 <tr>
  <td width=200><%=objDim.Name%></td>
  <td>
   <select name="<%=objDim.Name%>" size="1">
<%
      'Populate the select box with measure members
      For Each objHie In objDim.Hierarchies
        For Each objLev In objHie.Levels
           For Each objMem In objLev.Members
%>
                  <option value="<%=objMem.UniqueName%>">
                  <%=objMem.name%></option>
<%
           Next
        Next
     Next
%>
   </select>
  </td>
 </tr>
<%
    End if
Next
%>

</table>
<p></p>

<input type="submit" name="Submit">
</form>

</BODY>
</HTML>
```

> **Caution**
>
> Because these ASP pages contain a combination of html and VB script, they can
> be very difficult to read. The ASP code is much easier to read if it is displayed in
> a Web application programming environment where the text is color-coded.
> Microsoft's Visual InterDev is one such environment.

When the user completes his selections in query.asp and submits the form, one form variable for each dimension is submitted to the Web server. Parsing this form variable and generating the appropriate MDX query is accomplished in the results.asp page.

Building the Query and Displaying the Results

The two most challenging areas in building OLAP Web Client are providing an interface to the user for specifying the parameters of a query, and building the resulting MDX query string. Obviously, these two functions are related and in this particular application a conservative approach was taken with both.

As discussed in the previous section (query.asp), all of the cube's dimensions, all of the levels, and some of the members, are exposed to the user. After the user has selected query parameters from this information, the parameters must be combined to produce an MDX query.

The actual query string can be built either on the client or on the server. To build the query string on the client, either client-side script, an ActiveX control, or a Java applet must be used.

For this application, the MDX query is generated on the Web server. This decision was made with the goals of a thin, simple client in mind and to take advantage of the power and stability of the server platform.

Therefore, the query.asp page generates a number of form variables that are passed to the server with a standard submit action. It is the role of the Web server, through the next ASP page (results.asp), to transform these form variables into a query.

To complete the development of this application, it is necessary to

1. Accept the form variables submitted in the query.asp.
2. Convert this information into an MDX query.
3. Execute the query.
4. Send the results back to the user.

Figure 24.8 shows the status of a typical query.asp page just before it is submitted to the Web server.

24

BUILDING AN
OLAP WEB
CLIENT

FIGURE 24.8

*The user is ready
to submit a
query.asp page.*

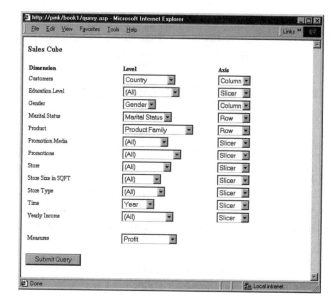

Notice that there are two dimensions on the columns axis, Customer and Gender, and the `[Customers].[Country]` and `[Gender].[Gender]` levels have been selected. There are also two dimensions on the rows axis, Marital Status and Product, and the `[Marital Status].[Marital Status]` and `[Product].[Product Family]` levels have been selected. All other dimensions are submitted as slicers, including the selected Measures member, Profit.

From the perspective of the Web server these variables are received as a series of 12 form variables as shown:

```
Customers = [Customers], [Customers].[Country].members, Col
Time = [Time], [Time].[Year].members, Sli
Education Level = [Education Level],
    [Education Level].[(All)].members, Sli
Store Size in SQFT = [Store Size in SQFT],
    [Store Size in SQFT].[(All)].members, Sli
Gender = [Gender], [Gender].[Gender].members, Col
Marital Status = [Marital Status],
    [Marital Status].[Marital Status].members, Row
Measures = [Measures].[Profit]
Product = [Product], [Product].[Product Family].members, Row
Promotion Media = [Promotion Media], [Promotion Media].[(All)].members, Sli
Promotions = [Promotions], [Promotions].[(All)].members, Sli
Store = [Store], [Store].[(All)].members, Sli
Store Type = [Store Type], [Store Type].[(All)].members, Sli
Submit = Submit Query
Yearly Income = [Yearly Income], [Yearly Income].[(All)].members, Sli
```

Each form variable has three comma-separated pieces of information:

1. The dimension

2. The level (with a `.members` suffix)

3. A column, row, or slicer designation

The Web server converts these form variables into the results.asp page, as shown in Figure 24.9.

FIGURE 24.9

The Web server uses the form variable from query.asp to build results.asp.

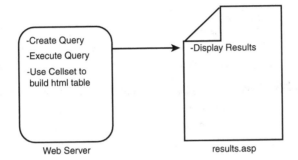

The query results are shown in Figure 24.10 as they are displayed in the Web page generated by the Web server.

FIGURE 24.10

The Web server generates an MDX query and returns the data in an html table.

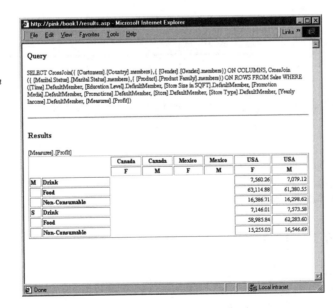

Use the code in Listing 24.1 as the first portion of results.asp. The function of this portion of the code is to parse the form variables and construct an MDX query string.

Because the form variables can be treated as a collection, the code necessary to dynamically iterate through the dimensions is straightforward. The first iteration loop is made to retrieve all of the dimensions with the exception of the Measures dimension, which is parsed in a second loop.

As each dimension is read, it is placed in the columns clause, the rows clause, or the slicers clause of the MDX query.

When multiple dimensions are placed in either the columns or rows axes, they must be combined with a CrossJoin() function. Because a CrossJoin() function must be used for each different dimension, nested CrossJoins are likely in complex queries.

Combining dimensions in the slicers, or WHERE, clause is less complex because a comma-separated list is the only requirement. Recall that only members can be used as slicers. Therefore, if the user chooses a dimension to add, the .DefaultMember expression must be added, and if a level is chosen, the dimension must be used instead.

Finally, the member from the Measures dimension is also used to construct a measure clause.

When the column, row, slicer, and measure clauses are finished, they are combined into a complete MDX statement.

LISTING 24.1 Constructing the Query

```
<%@ Language=VBScript %>
<HTML>
<HEAD>
<META NAME="GENERATOR" Content="Microsoft Visual Studio 6.0">
</HEAD>
<BODY>

<%
'Build Query
dim dimension, level, axis
dim colClause, rowClause, sliClause, meaClause
dim strKey

For Each Key In Request.Form
    if Key <> "Measures" and Key <> "Submit" then
        strKey = Request.Form(Key)
        dimension = left(strKey,instr(strKey,",")-1)
        strKey= mid(strKey,instr(strKey,",")+1)
        level= mid(strKey,instr(strKey," ")+1, _
```

```
                    len(strKey)-5-instr(strKey," "))
          strKey= mid(strKey,instr(strKey,",")+1)
          axis=mid(strKey,2)

          if axis = "Col" then
              if colClause = "" then
                  colClause = colClause & "{" & Level & "}"
              else
                  colClause = "CrossJoin(" & colClause
                  colClause = colClause & ",{" & Level & "}" & ")"
              end if
          end if

          if axis = "Row" then
              if rowClause = "" then
                  rowClause = rowClause & "{" & Level & "}"
              else
                  rowClause = "CrossJoin(" & rowClause
                  rowClause = rowClause & ",{" & Level & "}" & ")"
              end if
          end if

          if axis = "Sli" then
              if instr(Level,".members") <>0 then
                  sliClause = sliClause & Dimension & ".DefaultMember, "
              else
                  sliClause = sliClause & Level & ", "
              end if
          end if f

      else
          if Key = "Measures" then
              meaClause = Request.Form(Key)
          end if
      end if
Next

strMDX = "SELECT " & colClause & " ON COLUMNS, "
strMDX = strMDX & rowClause & " ON ROWS "
strMDX = strMDX & "FROM Sales "
strMDX = strMDX & "WHERE " & "(" & sliClause
strMDX = left(strMDX,len(strMDX)-2) & ", "
strMDX = strMDX & meaClause & ")"


Response.Write("<H2>Query</H2>")
Response.Write(strMDX)
Response.Write("<p><hr></p>")
```

The second code segment of results.asp is shown in Listing 24.2. This code executes the MDX query and translates the information from the resulting cellset object into an html table.

The session variable created for the connection to the OLAP Server is used to execute the MDX query and create the cellset object, objCellset.

The process of translating the cellset into an html table is not particularly difficult, but it is slightly confusing. You may want to review the discussion on the ADOMD cellset object presented in Chapter 22 when implementing this portion of the Web application.

The process is confusing because the html table must be created sequentially row-by-row. In contrast, the cellset has a multidimensional structure that does not translate directly into a flat table. However, presenting the results of the query in a crosstab is an important aspect of this Web application.

LISTING 24.2 Creating the Results Table

```
'Create the cellset with the results of the query
Set objCellset = Server.CreateObject("ADOMD.Cellset")
objCellset.Open strMDX, Session("objConn")

dim intColDim,intRowDim,intColPos,intRowPos

'Dimensions on the columns and rows axes
intColDim = objCellset.Axes(0).DimensionCount-1
intRowDim = objCellset.Axes(1).DimensionCount-1

'Positions on the columns and rows axes
intColPos = objCellset.Axes(0).Positions.Count - 1
intRowPos = objCellset.Axes(1).Positions.Count - 1

Response.Write("<H2>Results</H2>")
Response.Write(meaClause)
Response.Write chr(13) & "<Table width=100% border=1>" & chr(13)

'COLUMN HEADERS - Start
'Write a column header row for each dimension
For h = 0 to intColDim
    Response.Write "<tr>"

    'Blank column for each fixed row
    For i = 0 to intRowDim
        Response.Write "<td></td>" & chr(13)
    Next

    'Write the column headers
    For j = 0 To intColPos
```

```
            Response.Write "<th>"
            Response.Write objCellset.Axes(0).Positions(j).Members(h).Caption
            Response.Write "</th>"
    Next

    Response.Write "</tr>"
Next
'COLUMN HEADERS - End

'ROWS - Start
'Create an array to store row header information
Dim strRows()
Dim intArray,index

intArray=0
For a = 1 To intRowDim
    intArray = intArray+(intRowPos+1)
Next
intArray = intArray-1
ReDim strRows(intArray)
index=0

For j = 0 To intRowPos
  Response.Write "<tr>"

  'Write the row header(s)
  For h = 0 to intRowDim
    If h = intRowDim then
      Response.Write "<td><b>"
      Response.Write objCellset.Axes(1).Positions(j).Members(h).Caption
      Response.Write "</B></TD>"
    Else
      strRows(index) = objCellset.Axes(1).Positions(j).Members(h).Caption
      If index < intRowDim then
        Response.Write "<td><b>"
        Response.Write objCellset.Axes(1).Positions(j).Members(h).Caption
        Response.Write "</b></td>"
        index = index + 1
      Else
        If strRows(index) = strRows(index - intRowDim) then
          Response.Write "<td> </td>"
          index = index + 1
        Else
          Response.Write "<td><b>"
          Response.Write _
          objCellset.Axes(1).Positions(j).Members(h).Caption
          Response.Write "</b></td>"
          index = index + 1
        End if
```

continues

LISTING 24.2 continued

```
      End if
    End if
  Next

  'Write the values into the cells
  For k = 0 To intColPos
    Response.Write "<td align=right>"
    Response.Write "<font size=-1>"
    Response.Write objCellset(k, j).FormattedValue
    Response.Write "</font>"
    Response.Write "</td>"
  Next
  Response.Write "</tr>"
Next
'ROWS - End

Response.Write "</table>"
%>


</BODY>
</HTML>
```

Notice that the code constructs the html table row-by-row. The column headers are built first, and then each row of data is built. While the "headers" for the columns and rows are distinct properties in the cellset (Members.Caption), they are simply cells in the html table.

Finally, note that the data from the cellset is retrieved with objCellset(k, j).FormattedValue.

Summary

This chapter was intended to provide you with a basic understanding of the process of developing an OLAP application for deployment on the Web. After reading this chapter you should have an appreciation and understanding of some of the major issues in developing a Web-based OLAP client.

As you would expect, when the objective is to build an extremely powerful Web client, the development project becomes significantly more complex. The inherent technical limitations of Web pages and the browser's interface with the Web server place important restrictions on the development effort. Security constraints make it challenging to establish a connection between the client and the server. And, in many situations the interface between the data consumer and provider is more complex than in a typical client-server environment.

However, as this chapter demonstrates, building basic OLAP capabilities into a Web site is not a difficult project. In fact, a useful, functional Web client can be developed and deployed relatively simply. Furthermore, in many cases a basic Web application will meet a good portion of initial user requirements whose queries are not particularly complex.

Building an OLAP Client Application with Visual Basic

by Jim Pinkelman

IN THIS CHAPTER

The goal of this chapter is to educate the reader on the important aspects of developing a client application for Microsoft OLAP Services. Most of the topics discussed are applicable in a variety of development environments.

While there are many alternatives for building a custom OLAP client, Microsoft Visual Basic (VB) has the largest development community. For this reason, it was chosen as the language for the discussion in this chapter.

The project in this chapter is based on a simple two-tier architecture consisting of the client application and the OLAP data provider. The sample application you develop is called DemoOLAPClient.

> **Note**
>
> One of the most basic goals of the sample application you build in this chapter is to provide an interface that does *not* require the user to directly create or edit MDX statements.

This chapter is written with the assumption that you have an intermediate level of Windows programming experience somewhat equivalent to Visual Basic.

The Scope of the Project

Before diving into the code, it is important to understand the architecture in which this application is built and to lay out a set of high-level requirements for the client application.

The project is based on a simple two-tier architecture consisting of the client application and the OLAP data provider. Figure 25.1 shows a simple functional diagram of the application's architecture.

As the figure shows, ADO is an integral layer in the interface between the client and the server.

There are three primary, distinct interactions that occur between the client and the server in DemoOLAPClient, as shown in Figure 25.2. These interactions are

- Transferring metadata from the server to the client
- Submitting an MDX statement to the server
- Retrieving the results of the query in a cellset

FIGURE 25.1

A simple OLAP client-server application requires two tiers.

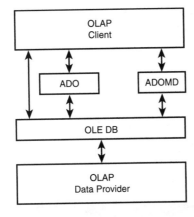

FIGURE 25.2

ADO and OLE DB are the two interface layers between the OLAP client and server.

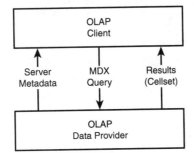

The basic requirements for DemoOLAPClient are

- A point-and-click user interface that does not require the user to know any MDX
- Read-only access to the data provider

It is also useful to make some simplifying assumptions and create some design guidelines regarding the capabilities of the client application. These assumptions are

- There are no requirements for client-side processing of data (sorting or max/min, for instance).
- Design simplicity will be a major goal, and the VB project will have a minimal number of forms, modules, and so on.

Client Functionality

The development of the OLAP client in this chapter is divided into two main efforts. First, you develop a simple client that is able to perform the most critical, basic capabilities. This section discusses the required basic capability and walks you through the process of developing the client from start to finish.

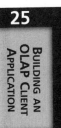

Developing the basic OLAP client requires the following:

1. Interfacing with the OLAP server to obtain metadata and displaying the appropriate metadata to the user.

2. Providing an interface that allows the user to select from the cube's metadata and create an MDX query.

3. Executing the MDX query and displaying the results.

For simplicity, the basic OLAP client will consist of a single form and all code for the client will be part of this form. As you may expect, the form module is named frmMain and saved as a file named Main.frm.

Note

It is obvious that in building most VB applications, a single form module is inadequate, inefficient, and atypical. However, keep in mind that the goal here is to introduce the concepts and functions that need to be considered in developing an OLAP client. The goal is not to build the best OLAP client.

Interfacing with the OLAP Server

The first step in building the OLAP client is the development of the initial interface between the client and the server. The client application must be able to establish a connection to the OLAP data provider, retrieve metadata, and display the metadata to the user. The first set of controls added to the form provide this functionality.

The next few sections discuss the VB development necessary to accomplish these functions. To provide a reference for this discussion, Figure 25.3 shows the state of frmMain after these controls have been added.

First, use the menu editor to create a File menu with a single item (Exit) to exit the application:

```
Private Sub mnuExit_Click()
    End
End Sub
```

Next, place the controls listed in Table 25.1 on the form.

FIGURE 25.3

After adding an initial set of controls, frmMain *should look similar to this.*

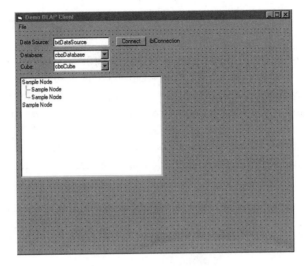

TABLE 25.1   Controls for frmMain

Name	Control	Component Required
lblDataSource	Label	
lblDatabase	Label	
lblCube	Label	
txtDataSource	TextBox	
cboDatabase	ComboBox	
cboCube	ComboBox	
cmdConnect	CommandButton	
lblConnection	Label	
tvwCube	TreeView	MSXOMCTL.OCX

The code associated with these controls is discussed in the following sections.

Opening an ADOMD Connection and Retrieving Metadata

Over the past two years Microsoft has made a concerted effort to improve and extend its components to access structured data. Two of the more important results of those efforts are the ADO and ADOMD object models. As discussed in Chapter 22, " Programming

Access to the OLAP Data Sources," these provide a simple, powerful, and efficient interface to structured data.

For most OLAP client development efforts, it is very difficult to find rationale against using ADO and ADOMD. To use ADO and ADOMD in this application, it is necessary to establish a reference to a type library and/or dynamic link library to access the ADO objects. Depending on the version of ADO you have installed, the appropriate reference will be similar to MSADO20.tlb or MSADO25.dll, and MSADOMD.dll. In VB these references are available in the References selection of the Project menu as "Microsoft ActiveX Data Objects 2.0 Library," and "Microsoft ActiveX Data Objects (Multidimensional) 1.0 Library."

Because this client is intentionally simple in its functionality, the connection to the OLAP data provider is straightforward. First, include the following code segment in the declarations section of the form module to initialize a set of ADO and ADOMD module variables.

```
Option Explicit

'Initialize ADO Objects
Dim objConn As New ADODB.Connection

'Initialize ADOMD Objects
Dim objCatalog As New ADOMD.Catalog
Dim objCubeDef As ADOMD.CubeDef
Dim objDimension As ADOMD.Dimension
Dim objHierarchy As ADOMD.Hierarchy
Dim objLevel As ADOMD.Level
Dim objMember As ADOMD.Member
```

To establish the data connection, the user types the name of the OLAP Server into the Data Source textbox (txtDataSource) and clicks the Connect command button (cmdCommand). The cmdConnect_Click event contains the code that establishes the connection.

The first part of following segment of code opens a connection and updates the label describing the connection state (lblConnection). If the connection is unable to be opened, execution of the subroutine is terminated.

The second part of the segment retrieves a list of databases, or MD catalogs, from the OLAP server and populates a combo box with the database names (cboDatabase). After the names of all databases are retrieved, the first database is selected as active and the recordset containing the list of databases is destroyed.

```
Private Sub cmdConnect_Click()
```

```
Me.MousePointer = vbHourglass

Dim intResult As Integer

'Establish Connection
Dim strConnect As String
objConn.Open ("Data Source=" & txtDataSource & ";Provider=MSOLAP")
If objConn.State = adStateOpen Then
    lblConnection.Caption = "Connected to " _
    & objConn.Properties("Data Source")
Else
    lblConnection.Caption = "Unable  to Connect"
    Me.MousePointer = vbDefault
    Exit Sub
End If

'Populate cboDatabase with databases (Catalogs) from the data source
cboDatabase.Clear
Dim objRS As New Recordset
Set objRS = objConn.OpenSchema(adSchemaCatalogs)
Do Until objRS.EOF
    cboDatabase.AddItem objRS.Fields("Catalog_Name")
    objRS.MoveNext
Loop

'Select the first database in the list
cboDatabase.ListIndex = 0

'Clean up
objRS.Close

Me.MousePointer = vbDefault

End Sub
```

When the first database in the combo box is selected (cboDatabase.ListIndex = 0), the cboDatabase_Click event can be used to generate a list of cubes within the selected database. Place the following code in the cboDatabase_Click event.

```
Private Sub cboDatabase_Click()

Me.MousePointer = vbHourglass

'Set the default database for the connection to the selected DB
objConn.DefaultDatabase = cboDatabase.List(cboDatabase.ListIndex)

'Populate cboCube with cubes from the database
cboCube.Clear
Set objCatalog.ActiveConnection = objConn
For Each objCubeDef In objCatalog.CubeDefs
    cboCube.AddItem objCubeDef.Name
```

```
Next objCubeDef
cboCube.ListIndex = 0

Me.MousePointer = vbDefault

End Sub
```

This segment of code has two purposes. First it sets the default database for the active connection, and the module-level object variable, objCatalog, is set. In doing so, all subsequent commands sent through the connection will be executed on this database. All metadata from the connection will be limited to the default database and all queries will be executed on the default database.

The second purpose of this subroutine is the population of the cube combo box (cboCube) with all cubes in the default database. The ADOMD Catalog object (objCatalog), the CubeDef object (objCubeDef), and the CubeDefs collection are used here. Finally, the first cube in the database is selected (cboDatabase.ListIndex = 0) and the cboDatabase_Click event occurs.

Displaying Dimensions, Hierarchies, Levels, and Members

Whenever the user chooses a cube (the cboCube_Click event), it is necessary to retrieve the metadata (the dimensions, hierarchies, levels, and members) and display it.

An experienced VB developer could use a number of techniques for displaying the information within a cube. Combo boxes, list boxes, treeview controls, and grids are all components that could be used.

For this application, however, I chose the treeview control because its structure corresponds well to the hierarchical nature of information stored in a multidimensional OLAP data provider. Microsoft's standard treeview control is used to display the dimensions, hierarchies, levels, and members within a cube.

To place the treeview control on the form, it is first necessary to add Windows Common Controls (MSCOMCTL.OCX or COMCTL32.OCX) as a component to the project.

To populate the treeview with high-level information from the cube, place the following segment of code in the cboCube_Click event.

```
Private Sub cboCube_Click()

Me.MousePointer = vbHourglass

Dim objNode, objNodeChild As Node
```

```
'Loop through each cube in the module variable objCatalog
For Each objCubeDef In objCatalog.CubeDefs
    'Determine if this is the selected cube
    If cboCube.List(cboCube.ListIndex) = objCubeDef.Name Then
        'Clear tvwCube
        tvwCube.Nodes.Clear
        'Add a node for this cube
        Set objNode = tvwCube.Nodes.Add(, , , objCubeDef.Name)
        objNode.Tag = "Cube"
        For Each objDimension In objCubeDef.Dimensions
            'Add a node for this dimension
            Set objNodeChild = tvwCube.Nodes.Add(objNode, tvwChild)
            objNodeChild.Text = objDimension.UniqueName
            objNodeChild.Tag = "Dimension"
            'Add a dummy node
            Set objNodeChild = tvwCube.Nodes.Add(objNodeChild, tvwChild)
        Next objDimension
        Exit For
    End If
Next objCubeDef

objNode.Expanded = True

'Clean up
Set objDimension = Nothing
Set objNodeChild = Nothing
Set objNodeChild = Nothing

Me.MousePointer = vbDefault

End Sub
```

This segment of code loops through each cube in the catalog to set the module variable, `objCube`, to the cube selected by the user. The treeview control, `tvwCube`, is reset and a node is created for the cube and child nodes are created for each dimension in the cube. A dummy node is added as a child to each dimension so that it displays the expand symbol (by default a plus sign in a box).

The text of each node is set to the unique name of the cube object while the tag of each node is set to the type of cube object (such as cube or dimension).

After the user has connected to the server, selected a database, and selected a cube, the interface should look like the one shown in Figure 25.4.

The remaining functionality that needs to be added to the treeview is population of the dimension nodes with hierarchies, levels, and members. This is accomplished in two distinct steps. First, when the dimension node is expanded, all hierarchies and levels (but not the members) in the dimension will be retrieved. Second, only when a level is expanded will the members be retrieved.

FIGURE 25.4

The OLAP client has established a simple connection to the OLAP server and retrieved some metadata.

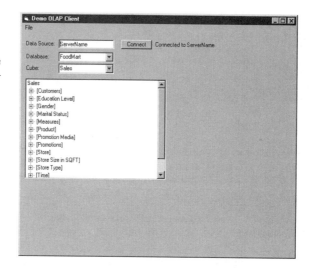

The rationale for this approach lies in the difference in the number of hierarchies and levels and the potential number of the members. In most operational cubes, the number of hierarchies and levels within a dimension will be relatively small, usually less than 20. In contrast, the number of members in a level will have a large range. There could be as few as 1 or 2 members or as many as thousands or millions of members.

Place all of the code for populating nodes in the tvwCube_Expand event:

```
Private Sub tvwCube_Expand(ByVal Node As MSComctlLib.Node)

    'Determine if the node is populated
    Select Case Node.Children

    Case 0: 'There are no child nodes, node cannot be expanded, exit sub

        Me.MousePointer = vbDefault
        Exit Sub

    Case 1: 'There is one child node, expand the node

        Dim objNode, objNodeChild, objNodeGrChild As Node

        If Node.Child.Tag = "" Then
            'The single child node is empty, delete it
            tvwCube.Nodes.Remove Node.Child.Index
        Else
            'The node is already populated, exit sub
            Exit Sub
        End If
```

```
Me.MousePointer = vbHourglass

'Populate the node
Select Case Node.Tag

Case "Dimension": 'Dimension node is being expanded
    For Each objDimension In objCubeDef.Dimensions
        If objDimension.UniqueName = Node.Text Then
            For Each objHierarchy In objDimension.Hierarchies
                'Add a node for this hierarchy
                Set objNodeChild = _
                tvwCube.Nodes.Add(Node, tvwChild)
                objNodeChild.Text = objHierarchy.UniqueName
                objNodeChild.Tag = "Hierarchy"
                For Each objLevel In objHierarchy.Levels
                    'Add a node for this level
                    Set objNodeGrChild = _
                    tvwCube.Nodes.Add(objNodeChild, tvwChild)
                    objNodeGrChild.Text = objLevel.UniqueName
                    objNodeGrChild.Tag = "Level"
                    'Add a dummy node
                    Set objNodeGrChild = _
                    tvwCube.Nodes.Add(objNodeGrChild, tvwChild)
                Next objLevel
            Next objHierarchy
            Exit For
        End If
    Next objDimension

Case "Level": 'Level node is being expanded
    For Each objDimension In objCubeDef.Dimensions
        For Each objHierarchy In objDimension.Hierarchies
            For Each objLevel In objHierarchy.Levels
                If objLevel.UniqueName = Node.Text Then
                    For Each objMember In objLevel.Members
                        'Add a node for this member
                        Set objNodeChild = _
                        tvwCube.Nodes.Add(Node, tvwChild)
                        objNodeChild.Text = objMember.UniqueName
                        objNodeChild.Tag = "Member"
                    Next objMember
                    Exit For
                End If
            Next objLevel
        Next objHierarchy
    Next objDimension

Case Else: 'Node other than dimension or level is being expanded

End Select
```

```
        Me.MousePointer = vbDefault

    Case Else: 'There is more than one child node, exit the sub
        Exit Sub

    End Select

End Sub
```

The first section of code in this subroutine tests the node to see if it has any child nodes. The IF and SELECT statements are used to determine the state of the node being expanded.

If there are zero child nodes, if there is a single non-empty child node, or if there are multiple child nodes, the parent node has already been populated with valid nodes and no change to the treeview is necessary.

If there is a single child node that is empty, it is a dummy node. The subroutine removes the dummy node and proceeds to populate the node with children. If the parent node is a dimension, all hierarchies and levels in the dimension are retrieved and added. If the parent node is a level, all members in the level are retrieved and added to the tvwCube.

> **Note**
>
> Depending on the characteristics of the cube, some caution should be used when programming this portion of the OLAP client. As mentioned previously, there could be thousands or millions of members. Retrieving all of the members, adding them as nodes to the treeview control, and displaying the member nodes could over-task the processor or exceed allowable memory limits.

Figure 25.5 shows the OLAP client when the Customers dimension has been partially populated and displayed.

> **Note**
>
> The FoodMart database that is installed with OLAP Services has only one hierarchy in each dimension. When a dimension only has a single hierarchy, omitting the hierarchy from display in the treeview is suggested. The MDX sample application included with OLAP services uses this approach.

FIGURE 25.5

The user has expanded the Customers dimension to display the hierarchy, the levels, and some members.

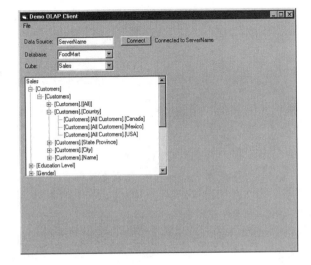

Building the Query

The next step in developing the OLAP client is creating the interface that allows the user to build a valid MDX query. The overriding design requirement for this client is that the user should not have to directly write or edit the MDX query.

For the basic OLAP client, the method of creating a query will be to select dimensions, hierarchies, levels, and members from the treeview and add them as columns, rows, and slicers. When any new item is added as a row, column, or slicer, it is necessary to generate a new MDX statement.

Add the following controls to frmMain. Figure 25.6 shows the three list boxes added.

Name	Control
lblColumns	Label
lblRows	Label
lblSlicers	Label
lstColumns	ListBox
lstRows	ListBox
lstSlicers	ListBox
cmdClearQuery	CommandButton
txtQuery	TextBox

FIGURE 25.6

Add the list boxes for the columns and rows axes and the slicer.

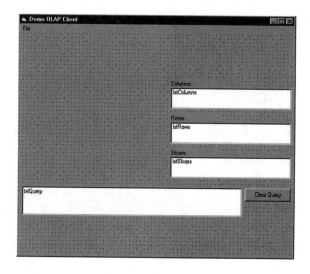

Now initialize the following module-level variables in the declarations section of `frmMain`.

```
'Initialize Treeview Objects
Dim objSelectedNode As Node
Dim strSelectedDim As String

'Initialize arrays for storing axis information
Dim strRowDims(1)
Dim strColDims(1)
Dim strSliDims(1)
```

While a drag-and-drop interface would probably be an effective technique of adding information from the treeview to the list boxes under each axis, a simpler approach using pop-up menus is employed in this application. Table 25.2 provides a list of the menus to add.

TABLE 25.2 Adding a Pop-up Menu

Name	Caption	Visible
mnuNodePopup	Node Pop-up Menu	False
..mnuAddAsColumn	Add as Column	True
..mnuAddAsRow	Add as Row	True
..mnuAddAsSlicer	Add as Slicer	True

When the user right-clicks any node in the treeview, the `tvwCube_NodeClick` event immediately occurs and the following code can be used to set a module variable equal to the node object:

```
Private Sub tvwCube_NodeClick(ByVal Node As MSComctlLib.Node)
    Set objSelectedNode = Node
End Sub
```

When the user releases the mouse button after selecting a node, the `tvwCube_MouseUp` event is triggered. This event is used to show the pop-up menu. Place the following code in the `tvwCube_MouseUp` event subroutine:

```
Private Sub tvwCube_MouseUp(Button As Integer, Shift As Integer, _
x As Single, y As Single)

If objSelectedNode Is Nothing Then Exit Sub
If Button = vbLeftButton Then Exit Sub

'Reset menu items
mnuAddAsColumn.Enabled = True
mnuAddAsRow.Enabled = True
mnuAddAsSlicer.Enabled = True

strSelectedDim = ""

Select Case objSelectedNode.Tag
Case "Cube"
    mnuAddAsColumn.Enabled = False
    mnuAddAsRow.Enabled = False
    mnuAddAsSlicer.Enabled = False

Case "Dimension":
    mnuAddAsSlicer.Enabled = False
    strSelectedDim = objSelectedNode.Text

Case "Hierarchy":
    mnuAddAsSlicer.Enabled = False
    strSelectedDim = objSelectedNode.Parent.Text

Case "Level":
    mnuAddAsSlicer.Enabled = False
    strSelectedDim = objSelectedNode.Parent.Parent.Text

Case "Member":
    strSelectedDim = objSelectedNode.Parent.Parent.Parent.Text

End Select

PopupMenu mnuNodePopup
subGenerateQuery

End Sub
```

This subroutine first verifies that a node has been selected and that the right mouse button has been clicked before activating the pop-up menu.

There are three items in the pop-up menu: Add as Column, Add as Row, and Add as Slicer. The main body of this subroutine first determines the type of cube item selected using the tag of the selected node. Based on the type of node (dimension, level, or member), the appropriate items in the pop-up menu are displayed. Also the module variable, strSelectedDim, is set to the parent dimension of the selected node.

Adding to the Rows and Columns Axes

The syntax of MDX statements specifies that the axes contain sets. As we will discuss in Chapter 27, "Building an MDX Query," the complexity of the sets can range from a single member to a series of tuples. In this simple client application, the primary area of difficulty in adding cube items to the rows and columns axes is logically converting the items to valid sets.

To accomplish this, the following guidelines are used:

- Cubes cannot be added to the rows and columns axes.
- When a dimension or hierarchy is added to the rows or columns axes, no MDX function is added. This results in a set created with the default member of the dimension to be used in the MDX query. For example, when the Customers dimension is added as a column, the resulting cellset returns a column for the default member of the customers dimension, [Customers].[All Customers].
- When a level is added to the rows or columns axes, the .members MDX function is added. This results in a set created with the members of the level to be used in the MDX query. For example, when the level [Product].[Product Family].members is added as a column, the resulting cellset has three columns, one for each member of the [Product].[Product Family] level.
- Finally, when a member is added to the rows or columns axes, no MDX function is added to the member. The resulting set consists of the single member. For example, when the member [Gender].[All Gender].[F] is added as a column, the resulting cellset returns a single column with the member [Gender].[All Gender].[F].

When the user right-clicks a dimension, hierarchy, level, or member, the code in the tvwCube_MouseUp event activates the pop-up menu with "Add as Column" and "Add as Row" enabled. The following two event subroutines add the selected item to the appropriate list box and add the .members function if appropriate.

```
Private Sub mnuAddAsColumn_Click()
```

```
If lstColumns.ListCount = 2 Then
    MsgBox "Maximum of two columns.", vbExclamation
Else
    If Not fctIsRow(strSelectedDim) And Not fctIsSli(strSelectedDim) Then
        strColDims(lstColumns.ListCount) = strSelectedDim
        Select Case objSelectedNode.Tag
        Case "Dimension":
            lstColumns.AddItem objSelectedNode.Text
        Case "Hierarchy":
            lstColumns.AddItem objSelectedNode.Text
        Case "Level":
            lstColumns.AddItem objSelectedNode.Text & ".members"
        Case "Member":
            lstColumns.AddItem objSelectedNode.Text
        End Select

    End If
End If


End Sub
Private Sub mnuAddAsRow_Click()


If lstRows.ListCount = 2 Then
    MsgBox "Maximum of two rows.", vbExclamation
Else
    If Not fctIsCol(strSelectedDim) And Not fctIsSli(strSelectedDim) Then
        strRowDims(lstRows.ListCount) = strSelectedDim
        Select Case objSelectedNode.Tag
        Case "Dimension":
            lstRows.AddItem objSelectedNode.Text
        Case "Hierarchy":
            lstRows.AddItem objSelectedNode.Text
        Case "Level":
            lstRows.AddItem objSelectedNode.Text & ".members"
        Case "Member":
            lstRows.AddItem objSelectedNode.Text
        End Select
    End If
End If

End Sub
```

Notice that these two subroutines perform two verifications before adding the selected node to the columns and rows list boxes. First, purely for simplicity in this application, the number of items in each list box is limited to two. While this may be an impractical limit in some real-world situations, it significantly simplifies the generation of the MDX statement for this application.

Second, the selection dimension is checked to determine if it has already been placed on the other axis or used as a slicer. The module string arrays `strColDims()`,`strRowDims()`, and strSliDims, and the following functions are used to verify the selected dimension is not already in use:

```
Private Function fctIsCol(strDim As String) As Boolean

    Dim i As Integer

    fctIsCol = False
    i = 0
    Do Until strColDims(i) = ""
        If strColDims(i) = strDim Then fctIsCol = True
        i = i + 1
        If i> UBound(strColDims) Then Exit Do
    Loop

End Function
Private Function fctIsRow(strDim As String) As Boolean

    Dim i As Integer

    fctIsRow = False
    i = 0
    Do Until strRowDims(i) = ""
        If strRowDims(i) = strDim Then fctIsRow = True
        i = i + 1
        If i> UBound(strRowDims) Then Exit Do
    Loop

End Function
Private Function fctIsSli(strDim As String) As Boolean

    Dim i As Integer

    fctIsSli = False
    i = 0
    Do Until strSliDims(i) = ""
        If strSliDims(i) = strDim Then fctIsSli = True
        i = i + 1
        If i> UBound(strSliDims) Then Exit Do
    Loop

End Function
```

Adding Slicers

As we'll discuss in Chapter 27 and demonstrate throughout Part V, "Programming the OLAP Client," of this book, only members of a cube can be used as a slicer. Therefore, the subroutine associated with tvwCube_MouseUp event contains code in which the "Add as Slicer" item on the pop-up menu is enabled only when the selected node is a member.

When the user selects a member to add as a slicer, the member is added to the slicers list box, lstSlicers. There is no need to apply any MDX function. The code for the mnuAddAsSlicer_Click event is relatively simple:

```
Private Sub mnuAddAsSlicer_Click()

If lstSlicers.ListCount = 2 Then
    MsgBox "Maximum of two slicers.", vbExclamation
Else
    If Not fctIsCol(strSelectedDim) And _
    Not fctIsRow(strSelectedDim) And _
    Not fctIsSli(strSelectedDim) Then
        strSliDims(lstSlicers.ListCount) = strSelectedDim
        lstSlicers.AddItem objSelectedNode.Text
    End If
End If

End Sub
```

Notice that this code segment includes a check to ensure that the parent dimension has not already been added to the columns or rows axes, or as a slicer.

Generating the MDX Query

The final major process in using the metadata in the cube to create a query is actually constructing the MDX query.

From a developer's perspective, building MDX queries is similar to building an SQL query. When the question is simple and the data structure is not complex, constructing the query string is usually not a difficult process. However, as most experienced developers will confirm, building complex query strings within an application for non-technical users can be extremely difficult.

The bottom line is that building a simple MDX query is not too difficult, while building a syntactically valid and functionally correct complex MDX statement can be very difficult. Building the user interface to accomplish this is also very difficult.

> **Tip**
>
> It is very possible that in building an OLAP client, programming the application to dynamically build a complex MDX queries could become the largest single functional task. I recommend closely monitoring Microsoft OLAP newsgroups and Web sites for tools, components, or SDKs that can perform this functionality. Two newsgroups which are particularly active are
> microsoft.public.sqlserver.olap and microsoft.public.data.oledb.olap.

Because the scope of this OLAP client is intentionally limited with a number of simplifying assumptions, the code necessary to construct the MDX statement will not be particularly complex.

There are four parts of the MDX query:

1. The ON COLUMNS part of the SELECT clause
2. The ON ROWS part of the SELECT clause
3. The FROM clause
4. The WHERE clause

To assemble the MDX query, create a subroutine named subGenerateQuery. Each of the
four parts in the subroutine builds a portion of the query.

```
Private Sub subGenerateQuery()

Dim i As Integer

Dim strMDX As String
strMDX = ""
strMDX = "SELECT "

'ON COLUMNS
Select Case lstColumns.ListCount

Case 0:

Case 1:
    strMDX = strMDX & "{"
    strMDX = strMDX & lstColumns.List(0)
    strMDX = strMDX & "}"
    strMDX = strMDX & " ON COLUMNS,"

Case 2:
    If strColDims(0) <> strColDims(1) Then
        'Two different dimensions, use a crossjoin
        strMDX = strMDX & "CrossJoin({"
        strMDX = strMDX & lstColumns.List(0)
        strMDX = strMDX & "},{"
        strMDX = strMDX & lstColumns.List(1)
        strMDX = strMDX & "})"

    Else
        'One dimension, comma-delimited list
        strMDX = strMDX & "{"
        strMDX = strMDX & lstColumns.List(0)
        strMDX = strMDX & ","
        strMDX = strMDX & lstColumns.List(1)
```

```
            strMDX = strMDX & "}"
        End If
        strMDX = strMDX & " ON COLUMNS,"

End Select

'ON ROWS
Select Case lstRows.ListCount

Case 0:

Case 1:
        strMDX = strMDX & "{"
        strMDX = strMDX & lstRows.List(0)
        strMDX = strMDX & "}"
        strMDX = strMDX & " ON ROWS "
Case 2:
        If strColDims(0) <> strColDims(1) Then
            'Two different dimensions, use a crossjoin
            strMDX = strMDX & "CrossJoin({"
            strMDX = strMDX & lstRows.List(0)
            strMDX = strMDX & "},{"
            strMDX = strMDX & lstRows.List(1)
            strMDX = strMDX & "})"

        Else
            'One dimension, comma-delimited list
            strMDX = strMDX & "{"
            strMDX = strMDX & lstRows.List(0)
            strMDX = strMDX & ","
            strMDX = strMDX & lstRows.List(1)
            strMDX = strMDX & "}"
        End If
        strMDX = strMDX & " ON ROWS "

End Select

'FROM
strMDX = strMDX & " FROM "
strMDX = strMDX & cboCube.List(cboCube.ListIndex)

'WHERE
If lstSlicers.List(0) <> "" Then
    strMDX = strMDX & " WHERE ("
    i = 0
    Do Until lstSlicers.List(i) = ""
        strMDX = strMDX & lstSlicers.List(i) & ", "
        i = i + 1
    Loop
    strMDX = Left(strMDX, Len(strMDX) - 2)
    strMDX = strMDX & ")"
```

```
End If

txtQuery.Text = strMDX

End Sub
```

This subroutine is straightforward because it primarily consists of simply building a query string piece by piece. Adding the crossjoin function is necessary when combining two different dimensions on either the columns or the rows axis. The slicer does not require the crossjoin operator because it can only contain a single member from each dimension.

Finally, the cmdClearQuery command button clears the axes, the slicers, and the current MDX query. Use the following code for the cmdClearQuery_Click event:

```
Private Sub cmdClearQuery_Click()

Dim i As Integer

For i = 0 To UBound(strColDims)
    strColDims(i) = ""
Next i

For i = 0 To UBound(strRowDims)
    strRowDims(i) = ""
Next i

For i = 0 To UBound(strSliDims)
    strSliDims(i) = ""
Next i

lstColumns.Clear
lstRows.Clear
lstSlicers.Clear

txtQuery.Text = ""

End Sub
```

Displaying the Results

There are a variety of techniques that could be used to display the results of a query to the user. As discussed in Chapter 23, " Implementing Microsoft Excel as an OLAP Client," when the OLAP client is embedded in Microsoft Excel, the Excel Worksheet is the logical container in which the results should be stored. When the client interface is hosted on a Web page, html tables, Java Applet grids, or ActiveX control-based grids are all valid choices for the results.

In this case, the client application is being developed in Visual Basic and any one of a number of grid controls would be a reasonable choice for display the results of a query.

While Microsoft includes a few grid controls with Visual Basic, MSFlexGrid is effective for this application, and it will be used to display the cellset. To use the MSFlexGrid, add the Microsoft FlexGrid Control (MSFLXGRD.OCX) to the project.

While Microsoft provides a number of datagrid components that can be bound to a recordset produced by an SQL query, it has not yet produced a grid control that can be bound to a cellset from an MDX query. Therefore it is necessary to iterate through the cellset and populate the grid control. Fortunately, this process is not particularly difficult because the structure of the cellset closely matches the structure of the grid.

Figure 25.7 shows the completed frmMain object after the MSFlexGrid control has been added to the form.

FIGURE 25.7

The MSFlexGrid control is added to the OLAP client.

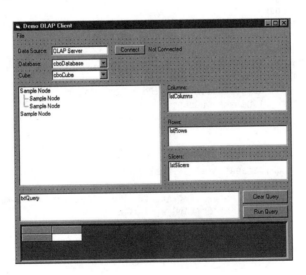

The following subroutine populates the grid when the user clicks the Run Query command button and triggers the cmdRun_Click event. The first significant step in the subroutine is the creation of the cellset using the MDX query and the open connection. After the cellset has been created, the subroutine has four functional segments:

- The first segment sets the number of columns, rows, fixed columns, and fixed rows for the grid.

- The second segment writes the names of the column headers into the fixed rows portion of each column.

- The third segment writes the names of the row headers into the fixed columns portion of each row.

- The fourth segment writes the actual data into the main body of the grid.

```vb
Private Sub cmdRun_Click()

Dim objCell As ADOMD.Cell
Dim objMember As ADOMD.Member
Dim objCellset As New ADOMD.Cellset

flxgrdResults.Clear
If txtQuery.Text = "" Then Exit Sub

'Create a cellset from the query
objCellset.Open txtQuery.Text, objConn

Dim intCol As Integer
Dim intRow As Integer
Dim i As Integer

'The columns and rows
flxgrdResults.Cols = objCellset.Axes(0).Positions.Count + _
    objCellset.Axes(1).DimensionCount
flxgrdResults.Rows = objCellset.Axes(1).Positions.Count + _
    objCellset.Axes(0).DimensionCount
flxgrdResults.FixedCols = objCellset.Axes(1).DimensionCount
flxgrdResults.FixedRows = objCellset.Axes(0).DimensionCount

'The column names
For intCol = 0 To objCellset.Axes(0).Positions.Count - 1
    intRow = 0
    For Each objMember In objCellset.Axes(0).Positions(intCol).Members
        flxgrdResults.TextMatrix(intRow, intCol + _
                flxgrdResults.FixedCols) = objMember
        intRow = intRow + 1
    Next objMember
Next intCol

'The row names
For intRow = 0 To objCellset.Axes(1).Positions.Count - 1
    intCol = 0
    For Each objMember In objCellset.Axes(1).Positions(intRow).Members
        flxgrdResults.TextMatrix(intRow + _
                flxgrdResults.FixedRows, intCol) = objMember
        intCol = intCol + 1
    Next objMember
Next intRow

'The data
For intCol = 0 To objCellset.Axes(0).Positions.Count - 1
```

```
    For intRow = 0 To objCellset.Axes(1).Positions.Count - 1
        Set objCell = objCellset(intCol, intRow)
        If Not IsNull(objCell.Value) Then
            flxgrdResults.TextMatrix(intRow + flxgrdResults.FixedRows, _
            intCol + flxgrdResults.FixedCols) = objCell.FormattedValue
        End If
    Next intRow
Next intCol

'Clean up
objCellset.Close

End Sub
```

Notice that this code segment navigates through the results of the query by making extensive use of the cellset.

Figure 25.8 shows the completed application after a simple MDX query has been generated and executed.

FIGURE 25.8

The completed OLAP client application shows the MDX query results.

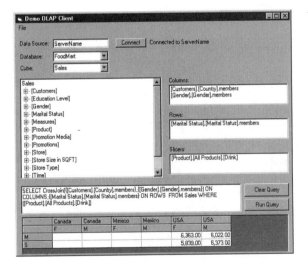

Summary

The goal of this chapter was to present the reader with a somewhat structured approach to building a very basic OLAP client. The development process was broken into three functional areas: retrieving metadata, building the query, and displaying the results.

The design requirements for this client were intentionally limited so that the discussion could focus on the fundamentals of the client instead of on specific features. The

25

BUILDING AN
OLAP CLIENT
APPLICATION

development of a fully functioning OLAP client is a large effort and entails a detailed definition and understanding of the users' requirements. Companies like Cognos, Business Objects, Seagate, and Brio spend many man-years developing such clients.

Finally, it should be noted that Microsoft distributes a sample OLAP client written in Visual Basic. It is named MDX Sample and can be installed when installing OLAP Services. This client is *not* meant for end users, because it requires extensive knowledge of the MDX language. However, it does provide developers an additional source of example code and it provides a tool for testing MDX queries. For more detailed information on MDX see Part VI of this book, "Querying with Multidimensional Expressions (MDX)."

Third-Party OLAP Clients

by Jim Pinkelman

For some situations, the best approach to deploying a Microsoft OLAP system is to use a third-party OLAP client to access the OLAP services.

The goal of this chapter is make the reader aware of applications, tools, and development tools that are available in the marketplace. Obviously, this discussion is only a snapshot of the current marketplace, and there will undoubtedly be significant changes and new products every year. While all of the OLAP client products are not discussed here, most of the products that have the largest market share are included.

I will discuss the features, strengths, and weaknesses of various products, but this is not intended to be a comprehensive evaluation of them.

> **Note**
>
> In the interest of full disclosures, the reader should be aware that the author works for Geppetto's Workshop L.L.C., a company that offers OLE DB for OLAP development tools.

This chapter is divided into two sections. The first section, "Standard Third-Party OLAP Clients," includes traditional, shrink-wrapped OLAP client products. The second section, "Third-Party Web and Add-In OLAP Clients," includes OLAP development products that can be used in building a custom OLAP application.

Standard Third-Party OLAP Clients

The following vendors provide OLAP clients that you can implement in a client-server environment. In some cases the products can also be deployed as Web-based clients.

Company	Client Name
Appsource Corp.	Wired Analyzer
Brio Technology, Inc.	BrioQuery
Cognos, Inc.	NovaView
Knosys, Inc.	ProClarity
Seagate Software, Inc.	Analysis

This is not a complete list of vendors who have OLAP applications. Microsoft has a number of dynamic locations on its Web site where it lists vendors with OLAP products. At this time, these Microsoft pages can be found at

http://www.microsoft.com/data/partners/products.htm

http://www.microsoft.com/industry/sql7/olap.htm

The following sections contain brief discussions of these products and vendors. The comments are more extensive for the products with demonstration versions available.

AppSource: Wired Analyzer

AppSource's OLAP client, is named Wired Analyzer.

Wired Analyzer is a standard OLAP client which allows crosstab analysis with multiple dimensions on each of the rows and columns axes. It also has the charting, printing, and export capabilities typical of OLAP clients.

Wired Analyzer offers access to standard OLAP functions such as ranking, sorting, and extensive navigation and drilldown capabilities in the cubes' levels and members.

As with most of the OLAP clients described here, the ability to use advanced features of Microsoft OLAP Services, including calculated members, using functions on sets of tuples, and time series analysis, is limited.

Information on Wired Analyzer can be found on the AppSource Web site at `http://www.appsource.com/`.

Brio: BrioQuery

Brio Technology offers a standalone client named BrioQuery for Microsoft OLAP Services, as well as a Web client named Brio.Insight.

Both BrioQuery and Brio.Insight employ a standard OLAP user interface that is similar to the majority of OLAP clients. The dimensions, levels, and members are shown in a treeview and are added to a query through a drag-and-drop interface.

Adding dimensions to the crosstab and navigating through dimensions and levels are both intuitive tasks, and therefore users can easily build and execute any basic query.

BrioQuery includes the basic OLAP functions to allow ranks, sorts, and filters. Access to more advanced Microsoft OLAP functions, like time series analysis and ranking and sorting sets of tuples is not yet available in this product.

Unfortunately, BrioInsight was not available for review.

Information on BrioQuery can be found on the Brio Web site at `http://www.brio.com/`.

Cognos: NovaView

Cognos offers a client tool for Microsoft OLAP Services called NovaView.

NovaView has a user interface with a very simple appearance. It includes both a spreadsheet view and a graphical view (shown in Figure 26.1). The dimensions and measures appear as a set of buttons. When a button for a dimension is pressed, the user can choose a member to slice the data. The dimensions and measures can be dragged and dropped onto the spreadsheet to change what is displayed on the rows and on the columns.

FIGURE 26.1

Cognos NovaView presents dimensions and measures with a set of buttons.

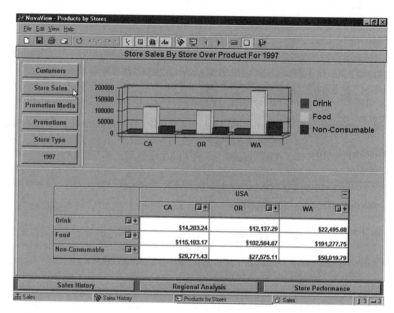

Version 2.0 of NovaView supports the write-back capability of OLAP Services, multiple hierarchies, member properties, slicer formulas, group formulas, and filtering by exception. Views of the data can be exported to Excel or to a Web page.

Information on NovaView can be found on the Cognos Web site at http://www.cognos.com/.

Knosys: ProClarity

Knosys offers a Windows OLAP client named ProClarity that has all of the basic features needed, and expected, in an OLAP client.

ProClarity features a user interface that is slightly unusual but rather easily mastered. Selecting dimension levels and members for use in a query is done through a tabbed treeview, and the results grid is updated when activated.

The main user interface screen for ProClarity is shown in Figure 26.2.

FIGURE 26.2

The user accesses the tabbed tree-view on the left side of the screen to build a query.

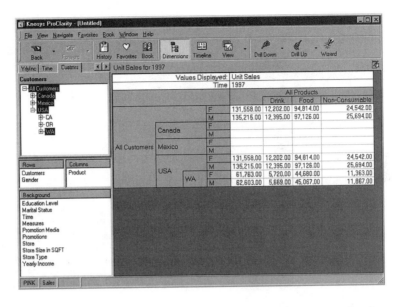

The treeview makes adding multiple dimensions to the rows and columns axes a simple process, and navigating among levels and members is more intuitive here than in other OLAP clients.

ProClarity implements sorting, top/bottom counts, and drillups and drilldowns extremely well. However, advanced MDX functions such as adding functions on sets, advanced numerical functions, and time series analysis functions are not in the first version of this product.

Knosys also offers ActiveX controls which can be used in the development of a custom OLAP Client application.

Information on ProClarity can be found on the Knosys Web site at
`http://www.knosysinc.com/`.

Seagate: Analysis

Seagate's standard windows OLAP client is named Analysis (it was formally called Worksheet). Figure 26.3 shows a Seagate's Analysis displaying a dataset of interest.

FIGURE 26.3

Analysis uses a crosstab to view data from an OLAP data provider.

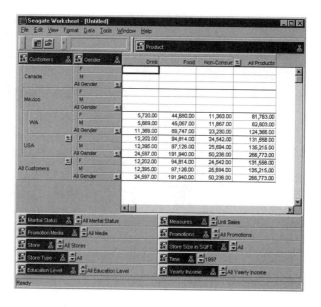

Seagate's Analysis product provides the basic capabilities one expects from a commercial grade OLAP client. Users can print the data, create charts with the data, and export the data to Excel or Lotus.

The user interface provides an intuitive method of building crosstab analyses by placing multiple dimensions on various axes and as slicers. The interface for navigating and selecting levels and members within a dimension is a bit unusual and may be difficult for new users to grasp.

On the other hand, users should have no problems implementing basic OLAP functions such as sorting, filtering, and top/bottom counts. Conversely, advanced functionality such as calculated members, functions on sets, numerical functions, and time series analysis functions are either nonexistent or very well hidden.

While it may take some time for non-technical users to master the user interface, technical users who have experience with OLAP concepts can become proficient with Analysis very quickly.

Information on Analysis can be found on the Seagate Software Web site at
http://www.seagatesoftware.com/.

Third-Party Web and Add-In OLAP Clients

A number of other vendors provide products that are not standard Windows OLAP Clients. This section discusses two Java Web applets which can be used as Web clients (dynasight and dbProbe), an OLE DB for OLAP SDK for building custom clients (AntMDX), and an Excel 2000 add-in OLAP interface (OLAP@Work).

Company	Client Name
Arcplan, Inc.	dynaSight
Geppetto's Workshop	AntMDX
Internetivity	dbProbe
OLAP@Work	OLAP@Work

arcplan: dynaSight

arcplan offers a Java applet that can be deployed with an ArcPlan Server and a Web server to access Microsoft OLAP Services. Figure 26.4 shows a screen shot of the dynaSight applet.

FIGURE 26.4

The dynaSight interface allows a user to explore measures along one dimension in a cube.

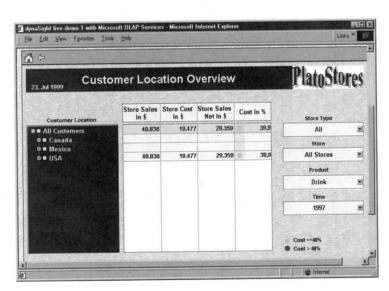

While the dynaSight applet is simple to use, the OLAP functionality is limited. The data is not presented in a crosstab, and it is not possible for the user to change the dimensions on the rows and columns axes or to add multiple dimensions to a single axis.

Based on the arcplan's demonstration version of dynaSight, user access to Microsoft's OLAP functions is very narrow. Sorting, filtering, tanking, and top/bottom counts are not apparent functions.

Information on dynaSight can be found on the arcplan Web site at `http://www.arc-plan.com/`.

Geppetto's Workshop: AntMDX

Geppetto's Workshop's AntMDX SDK is unique in the OLAP space. At this time, AntMDX is the only development tool available for Microsoft OLAP Services that dynamically generates MDX statements.

The AntMDX SDK consists of a Microsoft COM API containing objects for generating queries; AntQuery, a Visual Basic OLAP client (shown in Figure 26.5); and the VB source code for the client.

FIGURE 26.5

AntQuery is the VB Client provided with the AntMDX SDK.

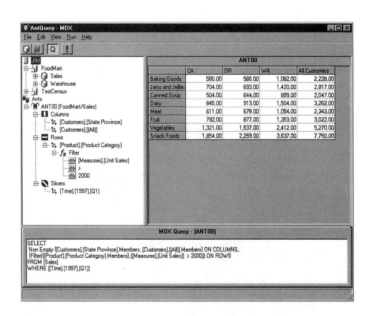

AntQuery is not a full-featured OLAP client, and it lacks printing, charting, and exporting functionality.

The user interface is very intuitive. Building simple queries is extremely easy and building more complex queries is a natural and logical extension.

Unlike other OLAP clients, AntQuery has no client-side processing capabilities. While this characteristic results in degraded performance for low-end queries, it is a much more stable and scalable approach because of extensive use of intrinsic MDX functions executed on the server.

Because the VB source code for the client is provided with the SDK, the OLAP client can be customized in any way desired.

Information on AntMDX can be found on the Geppetto's Workshop Web site at `http://www.geppetto.com/`.

Internetivity: dbProbe

Internetivity offers dbProbe, a Java OLAP client that functions on intranets, extranets, or the Internet. dbProbe is a single Java applet (approximately 300Kb) that provides the entire client user interface with the OLAP Server.

As seen in Figure 26.6, the user interface is a standard spreadsheet with printing, charting, and exporting capabilities.

FIGURE 26.6
dbProbe is implemented as a Java applet to be displayed in Web pages.

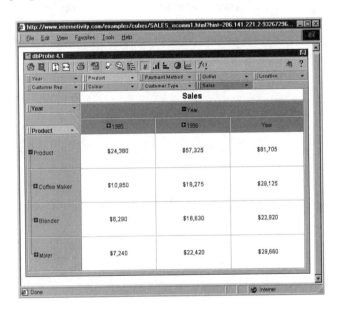

As with any OLAP product deployed over the Internet, the architecture for dbProbe has a critical impact on its capabilities and performance. Because Web clients have valid requirements to remain thin, client-side functionality is typically limited. dbProbe is no exception.

To its credit, dbProbe can be used to access data stored on a back-end data provider. It is also possible to download data with the html page.

Moving dimensions between axes and slicers and navigating and selecting levels and members within a dimension is very intuitive. dbProbe implements a look and feel that should be easily learned by most managers and executives.

Adding basic OLAP functions such as sorting, filtering, and drilling is simple. As one would expect with a thin Web client, advanced OLAP functionality such as calculated members, functions on sets, and time series analysis functions are not available.

Information on dbProbe can be found on the Internetivity Web site at `http://www.internetivity.com/`.

OLAP@Work: OLAP@Work

OLAP@Work provides a Microsoft Excel Add-in that allows a user to access an OLAP data provider through a wizard-style interface. At the current time, OLAP@Work's main competition in this market segment is Microsoft (with PivotTable and PivotChart). Figure 26.7 shows an example of data imported using OLAP@Work.

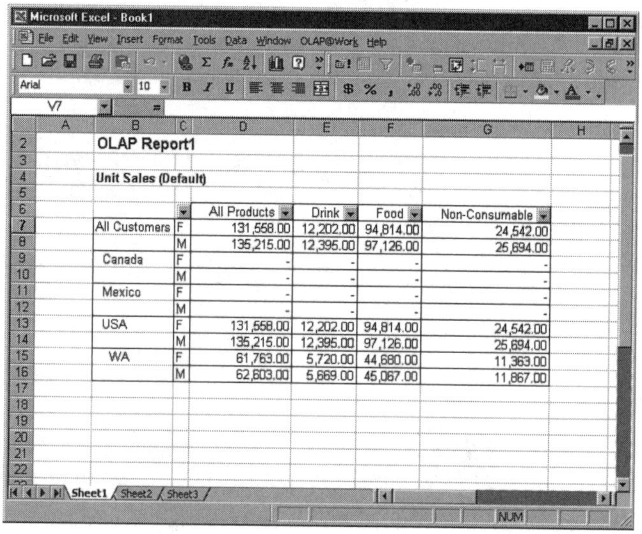

FIGURE 26.7

OLAP@Work's add-in for Excel allows browsing of OLAP cube data.

The most distinct advantage OLAP@Work's product has over traditional OLAP clients is the massive installed user base for Excel. The vast majority of business users are familiar with Excel and are comfortable interfacing with data in a spreadsheet.

26

Building a query with OLAP@Work involves navigating between selecting cube parameters in a dialog and the results in a spreadsheet. Novice users should not have too much difficulty building a simple query.

When compared to Microsoft's PivotTable, OLAP@Work's product is much more powerful, but the interface is less clean and the results are not as polished. For example, while OLAP@Work has both write-back capabilities and what-if analysis, initially building the simple query shown in Figure 26.7 required navigating through almost 15 dialogs.

Finally, it should be noted that OLAP@Work offers components that can be used in developing an OLAP client.

Information on OLAP@Work can be found on the Seagate Software's Web site at `http://www.olapatwork.com/`.

Summary

Based on the marketing literature from the vendors of OLAP clients, each has the "best" product and each is the "leading" vendor in the marketplace. Ignore it all.

Before you choose an OLAP client, clearly state and understand your user requirements and then research the features of the competing products. Download demonstration versions of the products and test the products over the Web.

A good way to begin your investigation of the available products is to visit the companies' Web sites. Most companies allow downloads of demo versions of the products and provide online demonstrations of their tools in action. (If they don't, call them and encourage them to do so.)

While it may not be advisable to base your final purchasing decision on a ten minute evaluation of a demo version, you will build a set of good questions for the vendors and begin to notice the differences in the products.

Ultimately, there are multiple options available, including developing a custom OLAP client. And as more companies build OLAP Server applications, the client products should get better and more plentiful.

Querying with Multidimensional Expressions (MDX)

PART
VI

IN THIS PART

Building an MDX Query

by Jim Pinkelman

In This Chapter

This chapter introduces the process of asking questions of Microsoft OLAP Servers. The material is also applicable to any provider or server that adheres to the OLE DB for OLAP specification.

This chapter introduces the basic syntax of an MDX statement, presents some of the most important, intrinsic functions available in the MDX language, and provides a number of examples describing some simple MDX queries.

While in some respects MDX is similar to SQL, it is different enough that transitioning the construct and syntax needs to be learned. Hopefully, this chapter will help the reader through the initial learning process.

Specifying the Axis and Slicer Dimensions

In its most basic form, an MDX statement has a very simple composition:

```
SELECT axis [,axis]
FROM cube
WHERE slicer [,slicer]
```

The SELECT clause is used to define *axis dimensions* and the WHERE clause is used to supply *slicer dimensions*. Before I begin a discussion of the axes and slicer dimensions, let's dispense with the FROM clause.

For the remainder of this chapter, and for the majority of Microsoft OLAP implementations in the foreseeable future, the FROM clause is easy. Put the name of the cube after the FROM statement, as these three examples show:

```
FROM Sales

FROM Warehouse

FROM Sales and Warehouse
```

It does not matter whether the cube is real or virtual, *cube* is simply the name of the cube.

Don't leave the FROM clause empty (no cube specified). Although there is a discussion of the "empty FROM clause" in the OLE DB for OLAP specification, it is currently necessary to specify the cube in the MDX statement. It is highly unlikely that the OLE DB for OLAP providers will implement adequate methods of dynamic cube selection and joined cubes until the 2.X versions of the servers.

What does a simple, actual MDX statement look like? If the user is interested in unit sales for each country for each year the MDX statement could be:

```
SELECT
 {[Gender].[Gender].Members} ON COLUMNS,
 {[Product].[Product Family].Members}  ON ROWS
FROM [Sales]
WHERE ([Measures].[Unit Sales])
```

With this MDX statement, the OLAP Server will use data from the Sales cube to construct a cellset of unit sales information with all genders along the columns axis (x-axis), and all product families along the rows axis (y-axis). The results of the query would produce the dataset shown in Figure 27.1.

FIGURE 27.1

A simple MDX query results in a crosstab view of cube data.

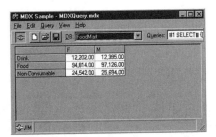

As mentioned earlier, this example uses the 'FoodMart' database installed with Microsoft OLAP Services. Figure 27.2 shows the structure of the FoodMart database, including the dimensions in the sales and warehouse cubes.

FIGURE 27.2

The structure of FoodMart database clearly shows its cubes and dimensions.

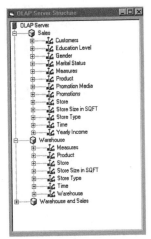

To complete the discussion of this example, notice that most of the cube dimensions were not specified in the MDX query. Any cube dimension not specified in the MDX statement is treated as a slicer dimension. Therefore, the following query is equivalent to the query listed above:

```
SELECT
  {[Gender].[Gender].Members} ON COLUMNS,
  {[Product].[Product Family].Members}  ON ROWS
FROM [Sales]
WHERE
  ([Measures].[Unit Sales],
  [Customers].[All Customers],
  [Education Level].[All Education Level],
  [Marital Status].[All Marital Status],
  [Promotion Media].[All Media],
  [Promotions].[All Promotions],
  [Store].[All Stores],
  [Store Size in SQFT].[All],
  [Store Type].[All],
  [Yearly Income].[All Yearly Income],
```

> **Note**
>
> In all of the preceding queries, all of the expressions have used unique names. By definition, the unique name of an object always contains an unambiguous reference within a cube. Although it complicates the syntax of an MDX statement, I highly recommend the use of unique names.
>
> The examples in the next few chapters will use a combination of unique names such as ([Time].[1997]) and simple names such as 1997. Using simple names allows for less complex MDX statements which are more useful as learning tools.

The Axis Dimensions in the SELECT Clause

For the vast majority of simple MDX statements, most of the action is in the SELECT clause. If the cube is viewed as an n-dimension data structure, this clause specifies the edge(s) of the cube to return.

In the previous example, the query specifies two dimensions, or edges, of interest. The country level of the customers dimension is returned on the columns axis, and the year level of the time dimension is returned on the rows axis.

If the user wants to view data about products for each gender, the user chooses these two dimensions as axis dimensions. The preceding example shows the results when the dimensions are placed on the column and row axes, and the following example demonstrates the results when they are placed on the same axis (rows). Figure 27.3 shows how multiple dimensions are displayed on a single axis.

```
SELECT
 {[Measures].[Unit Sales]} ON COLUMNS,
 CrossJoin({[Product].[Product Family].Members},
 {[Gender].[Gender].Members}) ON ROWS
FROM [Sales]
```

FIGURE 27.3

Multiple dimensions on a single axis produce these results.

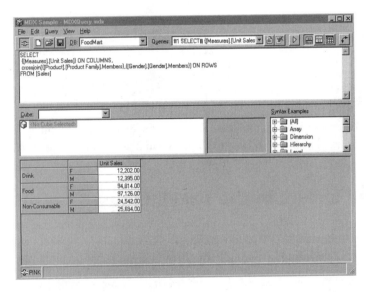

Either approach is valid, and resultset is the same in each case. But notice that in the last query, the two dimensions are combined in the rows axis and are joined with the CROSSJOIN function.

The basic structure of the SELECT clause is as follows:

```
SELECT    set ON axis_name,
    set ON axis_name,
    set ON axis_name
```

COLUMNS	or	AXIS(0)
ROWS	or	AXIS(1)
PAGES	or	AXIS(2)
SECTIONS	or	AXIS(3)
CHAPTERS	or	AXIS(4)
AXIS(*index*)	or	AXIS(5)

The following query contains multiple axes:

```
SELECT
  {[Customers].[Country].Members} ON COLUMNS,
  {[Time].[Year].Members} ON ROWS,
  {[Product].[Product Family].Members} ON PAGES,
  {[Gender].[Gender].Members} ON SECTIONS
FROM [Sales]
WHERE ([Measures].[Unit Sales])
```

An equivalent query would read:

```
SELECT
  {[Customers].[Country].Members} ON AXIS(0),
  {[Time].[Year].Members} ON AXIS(1),
  {[Product].[Product Family].Members} ON AXIS(2),
  {[Gender].[Gender].Members} ON AXIS(3)
FROM [Sales]
WHERE ([Measures].[Unit Sales])
```

The majority of the examples in this book contain only the columns and the rows axes. This is consistent with what most of us see in practice where the OLAP consumers programs rarely support more than two axes.

The Slicers in the WHERE Clause

The syntax of the WHERE clause and the use of slicer dimensions are more simple than the axis dimensions. The slicer dimensions contain the single members with which the cube is filtered or "sliced."

For example, if the user is only interested in data from a specific year, or information about a specific product, or results from a specific geographic region, the specification of these slicer dimensions are most appropriate in the WHERE clause.

The Contents of the Axes

Before we can discuss the contents of an axis, we need to define some terminology and how the terms are used in the context of queries.

- *member*—A member is an item in a dimension and corresponds to a specific piece of data. All of the following are members in the Sales cube:

  ```
  [Time].[1997]
  [Customers].[All Customers].[Mexico].[Mexico]
  [Product].[All Products].[Drink]
  ```

- *tuple*—A tuple is a collection of members from different dimensions. (It is acceptable for a tuple to contain only a single member from a single dimension.) It is standard practice to enclose a tuple in parentheses. The following are tuples:

```
([Time].[1997], [Product].[All Products].[Drink])
```

```
(1997, Drink)
```

```
(1997, [Customers].[All Customers].[Mexico].[Mexico])
```

- *set*—A set is a collection of tuples. There are a number of ways of creating and expressing a set. It is standard practice to enclose a set in curly brackets. The following are all sets:

```
{[Time].[1997], [Time].[1998], [Time].[1999]}
```

```
{1997, 1998, 1999}
```

```
{1990:1999}     (The colon(:) is an inclusive range.)
```

```
{(1997, Drink), (1998, Drink)}
```

An axis contains a set (a collection of tuples). Therefore, any of the preceding sets is valid as the *axis* portion of the SELECT clause.

The Data Hierarchy

For the vast majority of MDX statements, the context of the query will be limited to a single cube. While the structure of data within an OLAP Server has been discussed in earlier portions of this book, it is useful to review how all data within a cube is divided into the following relationships:

```
Dimensions
    Hierarchies
        Levels
            Members
```

Product information is frequently stored in cubes, and the following shows how product data could fit into the structure defined above. (Note that this example deviates slightly from the FoodMart database, which does not use any hierarchies.)

```
Product                             Dimension
    Function                        Hierarchy
        Product Family              Level
            Drink                   Member
            Food                    Member
            Non-Consumable          Member
        Product Department          Level
        Product Category            Level
        Brand Name                  Level
        Product Name                Level
```

```
Source                    Hierarchy
        Manufacturer      Level
        Product Name      Level
```

MDX Functions and Expressions

There is some ambiguity in the literature regarding these two particular terms. In this part of the book, the term function is used in its traditional manner to refer to a specific operation being performed on some set of data (Sum(), TopCount()). The term expression will be used to describe syntax in which the function is placed after the cube parameter ([1997].children, [Products].DefaultMember). The two syntactic forms for operations are:

```
Customers.Country.Members
```

```
CrossJoin(Customers.Country.Members, Gender.Members)
```

Whatever you may choose to call them, becoming familiar with the use and syntax of the intrinsic set of MDX functions is critical to building powerful, effective, and correct MDX queries are written. A good portion of this chapter as well as the next is focused on explaining the use and providing examples of these functions.

The tables below list some of the most important functions available in Microsoft OLAP Services. The chapter in which they are discussed is also indicated. Although all expressions are not discussed in detail in Chapters 27 or 28, all are covered in Chapter 30, "MDX Reference." This list is organized by general functionality, while the main list of functions in the MDX Reference Chapter is alphabetical.

TABLE 27.1 MDX Set Value Expressions

Set Value Expressions	Chapter 27	Chapter 28
<>.Members	*	
<>.children	*	
Descendants()	*	
Order()	*	
Hierarchize()	*	
BottomCount()	*	
BottomPercent()	*	
BottomSum()	*	
TopCount()	*	
TopPercent()	*	

Set Value Expressions	Chapter 27	Chapter 28
TopSum()	*	
Filter()	*	
Union()	*	
Distinct()	*	
Except()	*	
CrossJoin()	*	
Generate()		*

TABLE 27.2 MDX Tuple Value Expressions

Tuple Value Expressions	Chapter 27	Chapter 28
<>.currentmember		*
<>.item		*

TABLE 27.3 MDX Member Value Expressions

Member Value Expressions	Chapter 27	Chapter 28
parent		*
.firstchild		*
.lastchild		*
prevmember		*
.nextmember		*
.lead		*
.currentmember		*
.firstsibling		*
.lastsibling		*
Ancestor()		*
Cousin()		*

27

BUILDING AN
MDX QUERY

TABLE 27.4   MDX Numeric Functions

Numeric Functions	Chapter 27	Chapter 28
Sum()		*
Aggregate()		*
Count()		*
Avg()		*
Median()		*
Min()		*
Max()		*
Var()		*
StdDev()		*
Rank()		*

TABLE 27.5   MDX Time Series Functions

Time Series Functions	Chapter 27	Chapter 28
PeriodsToDate()		*
YTD()		*
MTD ()		*
WTD ()		*
DTD ()		*
LastPeriods()		*
ParallelPeriod()		*
OpeningPeriod()		*

TABLE 27.6   MDX Time Series Analysis Functions

Time Series Analysis	Chapter 27	Chapter 28
Covariance()		*
Correlation()		*
LinRegIntercept()		*
LinRegSlope()		*
LinRegVariance()		*
LinRegR2()		*
LinRegPoint()		*

> **Note**
>
> Expressions are not case sensitive; `topcount()`, `TopCount()`, and `TOPCOUNT()` all work. In this section of the book the case of expressions is dictated by readability. `LinRegIntercept`, for instance, is more likely to be used instead of `LINREGINTERCEPT`, because at a glance it is easier to decipher the meaning of `LinRegIntercept`.

At this time it is useful to introduce two important functions which are part of the MDX language. The `.Members` function and the `CrossJoin` function allow us to expand the scope of the SELECT clause significantly.

The `.Members` Expression

A particularly useful MDX expression is `.Members`. This expression is used to retrieve a set of enumerated members from a dimension, hierarchy, or level. The syntax is simple:

`dimension.Members`

`hierarchy.Members`

`level.Members`

Therefore, the following MDX statement results in all unit sales information for all members (years, quarters, months, and so on) in the FoodMart Sales cube.

```
SELECT
 {[Time].Members} ON COLUMNS
FROM [Sales]
WHERE ([Measures].[Unit Sales])
```

> **Note**
>
> Some caution should be exercised when using the `.Members` expression on a dimension. Because it produces a dataset with *all* of the members of a dimension, the resulting cellset can be very large. The following MDX query results in a very large dataset because there are a large number of customers and products.

When executed, the following query provides a clear demonstration of the danger:

```
SELECT
  {[Customers].Members} ON COLUMNS,
  {[Product].Members} ON ROWS
FROM [Sales]
WHERE ([Measures].[Unit Sales])
```

> **Note**
>
> The .children expression is similar to the .Members expression but it can only be used on members. It produces a set consisting of members one level lower than the member on which it is used.

The CrossJoin() Function

The CrossJoin() function is used to generate the cross-product of two input sets. If two sets exist in two independent dimensions, the CrossJoin operator creates a new set consisting of all of the combinations of the members in the two dimensions. The syntax of the CrossJoin is:

```
crossjoin(set1,set2)
```

In the Sales cube, there are three members at the country level of the Customers dimension: Canada, Mexico, and USA. There are two members at the gender level of the Gender dimension: F and M. The CrossJoin() function is used to create a set of all combinations of these two sets.

```
CrossJoin(customers.country.Members, gender.gender.Members)
```

produces the following six combinations:

```
{(Canada,F),(Canada,M),(Mexico,F),(Mexico,M),(USA,F),(USA,M)}
```

Because the syntax of the CrossJoin is limited to two sets, it is necessary to nest CrossJoin statements when combining three dimensions.

```
CrossJoin(
  {[Customers].[Country].Members},
  CrossJoin({[Gender].[Gender].Members}, {[Product].[Product Family].Members})
  )
```

This axis specification will produce a total of 18 combinations. The product family level of the Product dimension contains 3 members: Drink, Food, and Non-consumable. The first 4 of these 18 combinations are

```
{(Canada,F,Drink),
 (Canada,F,Food),(Canada,F,Non-Consumable),
(Canada,M,Drink), etc.
```

CrossJoin is an extremely useful function for decision-making processes because it directly enables requests such as "Show me the total sales by state for the past five years." In fact, the functionality inherent in the CrossJoin, and its absence in SQL, is one of the reasons it is appropriate to build an alternative query language.

> **Note**
>
> CrossJoin does exist in SQL server, but doesn't have the same functionality.

Note that the two sets used in the CrossJoin function must be from the different dimensions. If the goal is to combine members of the product dimension with other members of the product dimension, the Union() function is appropriate. As discussed later in this chapter, the Union() function is similar to CrossJoin but it is used to combine items from the same dimension.

```
union([Product Family].Members, [Product Category].Members)
```

is valid, while

```
crossjoin([Product Family].Members, [Product Category].Members)
```

is invalid.

Some Simple Examples

You are now armed with a basic understanding of the syntax of an MDX query, the structure of a data cube, and three simple methods—.member, .children, and CrossJoin()—of operating on the information in a cube.

A few examples should fill in part of the big picture at this time. Each of these examples includes an MDX query, the resulting dataset, and a brief discussion of the query. All of them are based on the FoodMart Sales cube.

Example #1

The intent of the first MDX example query is to view the total unit sales of customers in the USA in each of the product departments.

Figure 27.4 shows the dataset resulting from the following MDX query:

```
SELECT
  {[Customers].[All Customers].[USA].Children} ON COLUMNS,
  {[Product].[Product Department].Members} ON ROWS
FROM [Sales]
WHERE ([Measures].[Unit Sales])
```

This query includes only a single dimension on the axes and on the slicer. To get the states within the USA, the member [Customers].[All Customers].[USA] is placed on the columns axis with the .Children function. This returns a set of members one level below USA.

The Rows dimension consists of a level, [Product].[Product Department], with a .Members function. This results in a set of members at the product department level.

Finally, the unit sales member from the Measures dimension is included on the slicer dimension so that the dataset will consist of unit sales figures.

FIGURE 27.4

Here is the dataset resulting from the Example #1 basic MDX query.

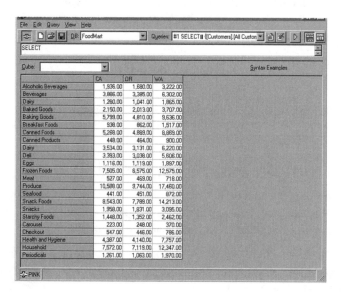

Example #2

This second example demonstrates the uses of the `CrossJoin` function in the query:

```
SELECT
 CrossJoin({[Gender].[Gender].Members},
 {[Time].[Year].Members}) ON COLUMNS,
 {[Measures].Members} ON ROWS
FROM [Sales]
```

This query crossjoins the Gender and the Time dimensions to produce data in which the data for each gender is broken into two years in this cube. Figure 27.5 shows the resulting dataset.

The two specific sets that are within the `CrossJoin` are the two members of the gender level of the Gender dimension, and the two years in the year level of the Time dimension.

The set of all members of the Measures dimension is included on the rows axis.

There is no member explicitly added as a slicer in this query.

FIGURE 27.5

The `CrossJoin()` *function in Example #2 produces this dataset.*

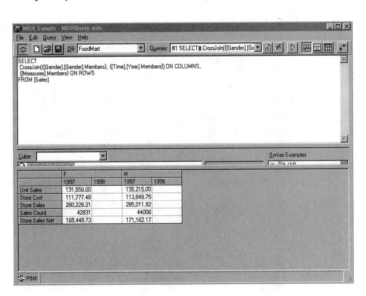

Example #3

This final example query specifies six of the cube dimensions:

```
SELECT
 {[Time].[Year].Members} ON COLUMNS,
 CrossJoin({[Marital Status].[Marital Status].Members},
          {[Promotion Media].[Media Type].Members}) ON ROWS
FROM [Sales]
WHERE ([Customers].[All Customers].[USA].[CA], [Gender].[All Gender].[M])
```

The column axis contains a set of all members [Time].[Year]. The rows axis contains a CrossJoin where the members of the marital status level are combined with the members of the media type level. As Figure 27.6 shows, this results in many tuples on the rows axis.

The slicer dimension contains two members from two different dimensions. As you will see in the more advanced MDX queries discussed in Chapter 28, "Advanced MDX Queries," the slicers are implemented on the cube prior to the execution of functions in the axes.

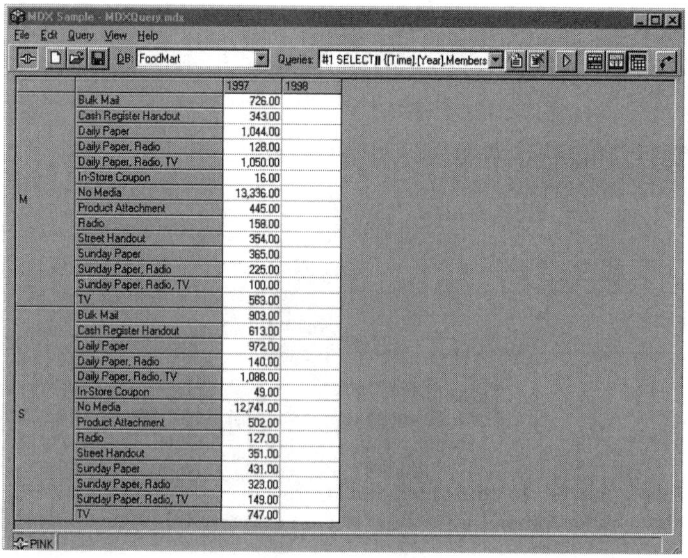

FIGURE 27.6

The Example #3 query, which uses six dimensions, produces these results.

Additional Important MDX Functions

The .Member and CrossJoin() operators are the most frequently used functions because they are almost always necessary when adding cube entities to a query. This section describes a second set of important MDX operators for performing data analyses.

The Order() Function

The Order() function provides sorting capabilities within the MDX language. When the Order expression is used, it can either sort within the natural hierarchy (ASC and BDESC), or it can sort without the hierarchy (BASC and BDESC). The "B" indicates "break" hierarchy. The syntax for the Order()function is

```
Order(set,string expression [,ASC ¦ DESC ¦ BASC ¦ BDESC])
```

or

```
Order(set,numeric expression [,ASC ¦ DESC ¦ BASC ¦ BDESC])
```

The Order() function ranks the items in the *set*, and as these two alternatives show, either a *string expression* or a *numeric expression* can be used as the criterion for the ranking. Although the order specification (ASC, DESC, and so on) is optional, it is wise to use it to avoid ambiguous MDX queries. If it is omitted, ASC is the default.

The following MDX clause returns all promotion media types sorted in descending order. BDESC causes the hierarchy in the product category to be ignored in the sort order.

```
{Order([Promotion Media].[Media Type].Members,[Unit Sales],BDESC)}
```

Note that the sort from this query will be performed according to unit sales for all customers, all education levels, all genders, and so on. In other words, none of the other dimensions is filtered. This can lead to some deceptive query results. For example, the following query

```
SELECT
 {[Marital Status].[All Marital Status].[S]} ON COLUMNS,
 {Order({[Promotion Media].[Media Type].Members},
 [Unit Sales],BDESC)} ON ROWS
FROM [Sales]
```

produces the dataset shown in Figure 27.7.

FIGURE 27.7

The Order() *function can produce results which appear to be incorrect.*

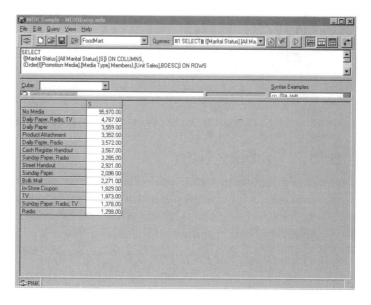

While it appears that the Order() function did not produce in a correct sort, the sort was actually performed using the [All Marital Status] member, *not* the [Marital Status].[All Marital Status].[S] member. The dataset shown in Figure 27.8 confirms this.

FIGURE 27.8

The sort is performed using the [All Marital Status] *member.*

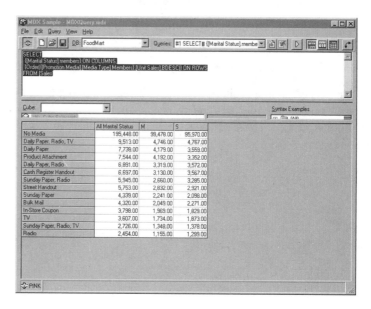

To ensure the `Order()` function correctly sorts data in the intend way, there are two options for sorting on a specific member. First, the numeric expression in the `Order()` function can be altered to include the name of the member to use as the sort criterion. Instead of

```
[Unit Sales]
```

in the `Order()` function, use

```
([Marital Status].[All Marital Status].[S],[Unit Sales]).
```

For example,

```
{Order([Promotion Media].[Media Type].Members,
 ([Marital Status].[All Marital Status].[S],[Unit Sales]),BDESC)}
```

The other option is to remove the `[Marital Status].[All Marital Status].[S]` member from the columns axis and add it as a slicer in the WHERE clause in the MDX query:

```
SELECT
 {[Customers]} ON COLUMNS,
 {Order({[Promotion Media].[Media Type].Members},
 [Unit Sales],BDESC)} ON ROWS
FROM [Sales]
WHERE ([Marital Status].[All Marital Status].[S])
```

The `Hierarchize()` Function

The `Hierarchize()` function is used to sort members by their natural order as defined in the cube's data structure. The syntax is simple:

```
Hierarchize(set)
```

For example, In the case of the store's dimension in the FoodMart Sales cube, the natural hierarchy within a level is alphabetically-based. Therefore, when this function is applied to a set of members in the store dimension, the results will be sorted first by the hierarchy, then by level, and then alphabetically within a level. The statement

```
{Hierarchize({
  [Store].[All Stores].[USA].[CA].children,
  [Store].[All Stores].[Canada].[BC],
  [Store].[All Stores].[USA],
  [Store].[All Stores].[USA].[OR],
  [Store].[All Stores].[Mexico].[Guerrero].children})}
```

produces a set in which the following members are returned and ordered as shown here:

```
[Store].[All Stores].[BC]
[Store].[All Stores].[Mexico].[Guerrero].[Acapulco]
```

```
[Store].[All Stores].[USA]
[Store].[All Stores].[USA].[OR].[Beverly Hills]
[Store].[All Stores].[USA].[OR].[Los Angeles]
[Store].[All Stores].[USA].[OR].[San Diego]
[Store].[All Stores].[USA].[OR].[San Francisco]
[Store].[All Stores].[USA].[OR]
```

Notice that because the `Hierarchize()` function first sorts by the level [Store].[Store Country] all members from Canada are first, followed by all members from Mexico, and then all members from USA. Within each country, members are sorted first according to the level, [Store].[Store State]; and within each state members are sorted alphabetically by [Store].[Store City].

All members are sorted as if the applicable parent is present in the set, even if the parent is not. In the preceding example, [BC] is listed first even though [Canada] is not present.

The `TopCount()` and `BottomCount()` Functions

The `TopCount()` and `BottomCount()` functions provide rank functionality critical in a decision support and data analysis environment. These expressions sort a *set* based on a *numerical expression* and pick the top *index* items based on rank order. The syntax for the expressions is

`TopCount(set,index,numeric expression)`

`BottomCount(set,index,numeric expression)`

Both of these expressions break the natural hierarchy of the set. Also note that these functions return only the index number of items even in the case of equivalent numerical expressions (that is, where there are ties.).

The following MDX query results in the top five product categories in unit sales listed in descending order:

```
SELECT
  {[Unit Sales]} ON COLUMNS,
  {TopCount({[Product Category].Members}, 5,[Unit Sales])} ON ROWS
FROM [Sales]
```

The single most confusing aspect of these functions is the criteria used for the sorting process. Similar to the order function, these functions operate on the default member if it is not explicitly defined.

The `TopPercent()` and `BottomPercent()` Functions

The `TopPercent()` and `BottomPercent()` functions sort a *set* based on a *numerical expression* and pick the items such that their contribution to the total is at least *percentage*. These functions are applicable in decision support situations where the goal is to find the top contributors to a particular measure. The syntax of the functions is

`TopPercent(set,percentage,numeric expression)`

`BottomPercent(set, percentage,numeric expression)`

In the FoodMart sales cube, the following query shows that the total store sales for all stores is equal to $565,238.13.

```
SELECT
 {[Measures].[Store Sales]} ON COLUMNS,
 {[Store]} ON ROWS
FROM [Sales]
```

There are a total of 24 stores in this cube, and to find the stores whose sales make up 80% of the total sales, the MDX query would be:

```
SELECT
 {[Measures].[Store Sales]} ON COLUMNS,
 {TopPercent({[Store].[Store Name].Members}, 80,
 [Measures].[Store Sales])} ON ROWS
FROM [Sales]
```

Both the `TopPercent()` and the `BottomPercent()` functions break the natural hierarchy of the set.

The `TopSum()` and `BottomSum()` Functions

The `TopSum()` and `BottomSum()` expressions sort a *set* based on a *numerical expression* and pick the items such that their contribution to the total is at least *value*. The syntax of the functions is

`TopSum(set,value,numeric expression)`

`BottomSum(set,value,numeric expression)`

As mentioned previously, in the FoodMart sales cube, the total store sales for all stores is equal $565,238.13. Assume a manager wants to reduce the total number of stores and decides to close all stores that did not contribute to the first $530,000 in sales.

To find the stores with the lowest sales that add up to the bottom $35,238.13, the MDX query would be:

27

BUILDING AN
MDX QUERY

```
SELECT
 {[Measures].[Store Sales]} ON COLUMNS,
 {BottomSum({[Store].[Store Name].Members},
 35238.13, [Measures].[Store Sales])} ON ROWS
FROM [Sales]
```

Both the `TopSum()` and the `BottomSum()` functions break the natural hierarchy of the set.

The `Filter()` Function

The `Filter()`function is used to filter a set based on a particular condition. The syntax for this function is

```
Filter(set,search condition)
```

The basic use of this function is straightforward. The following MDX clause returns a set of product categories whose sales count was greater than 1000:

```
{Filter({[Product].[Product Category].Members},([Sales Count])> 1000)}
```

The following are two more complex examples:

The set of product categories whose sales count in stores in Washington was greater than 1000:

```
{Filter({[Product].[Product Category].Members},
```

```
([Store].[Store State].[WA],[Sales Count])> 1000)}
```

The set of stores whose 1998 unit sales is less than 1997 unit sales:

```
{Filter({[Store].[Store Name].Members},([1998],[Unit Sales]) < ([1997],[Unit
Sales]))}
```

All of the normal comparison operators (=,>, <, <>,>=, and <=) are valid for use with the `Filter()` function.

`Filter()` Versus Slicer

In some respects, the `Filter()`function and the slicer axis have similar purposes. The difference between the two is that the `Filter()` function defines the members in a set, while slicers determine a slice of the cube returned from a query.

While the differences in syntax can be subtle, the disparity of the resulting dataset can be significant. The two queries shown below highlight the differences. The first query uses a filter to produce a set consisting of all product departments where the unit sales for female customers is greater than $10,000. The data returned is the unit sales for all customers, male and female. Figure 27.9 shows the results of this query.

```
SELECT
 {[Measures].[Unit Sales]} ON COLUMNS,
 {Filter({[Product].[Product Department].Members},
 ([Gender].[All Gender].[F],[Measures].[Unit Sales]) > 10000)} ON ROWS
FROM [Sales]
```

FIGURE 27.9

The Filter() *function produces a set of product departments meeting the Filter criteria.*

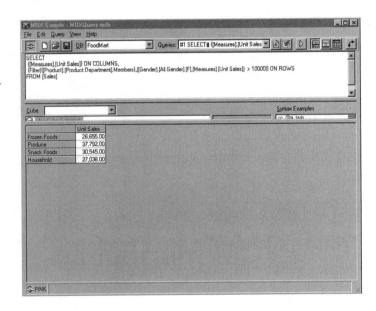

The second query includes both a slicer and a filter. Because the slicer is applied first, only female customer data can be returned.

```
SELECT
 {[Measures].[Unit Sales]} ON COLUMNS,
 {filter({[Product].[Product Department].Members},
 [Measures].[Unit Sales]> 10000)} ON ROWS
FROM [Sales]
WHERE ([Gender].[All Gender].[F])
```

As seen in Figure 27.10, the results of this query are similar to the first in that the set returned on the rows axis consists of product departments for which unit sales to females is greater than $10,000. However, the slicer on female customers causes the data returned to be only for females, not all customers as in the first query.

Figure 27.11 shows a data set that included the results of both queries. Notice that the first query returns the first column, while the second query returns the second column.

27

BUILDING AN
MDX QUERY

FIGURE 27.10

The slicer limits the resulting data to female customers only.

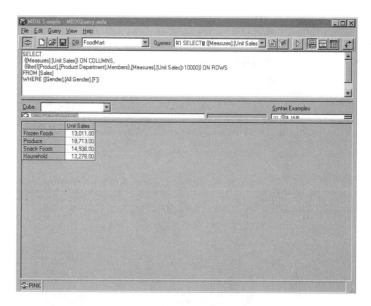

FIGURE 27.11

This dataset results from a simple MDX query.

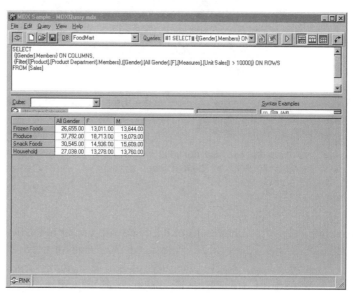

The important distinction to keep in mind is that the Filter() function is used to control the members in a set, while slicers are used to control the resulting dataset.

The Union() Function

The Union() function combines two sets into one. The syntax is

```
Union(set1,set2[,[All]])
```

By default, the Union() function eliminates all duplicates from the resulting set. The [All] flag can be used to retain the duplicates.

In practical use, the Union() function is frequently unnecessary because it can be accomplished with a comma-separated list of the sets to be joined. For example,

```
union({Food},{Drink},[All])
```

is equivalent to

```
{Food, Drink}
```

The ability of the Union() function to eliminate duplicates is its most useful characteristic. The MDX clause

```
Union(
  {filter([Store Name].Members,([Drink],[unit sales])>2000)},
  {filter([Store Name].Members,([Food],[unit sales])>15000)}
  )
```

produces a set in which stores that meet either requirement are included, but the stores that meet both filter requirements are included only once. When used in a manner such as this, the Union() function is comparable to the concept of "or" in mathematics. This is an important capability if the goal is to count the stores.

Note that the two sets used in the Union() function must be from the same dimensions. If the goal is to combine members of the product dimension with members of the time dimension, the CrossJoin() function is appropriate. For instance,

```
CrossJoin([Product Family].Members,[Year].Members)
```

is valid, while

```
Union([Product Family].Members,[Year].Members)
```

is invalid.

The Intersect() Function

The Intersect() function compares two sets and produces a set consisting of members in both sets. The syntax is

```
intersect(set1>,set2[,[All]])
```

Unless the [All] flag is included, all duplicates are eliminated from the set prior to the intersection process. Although the following use is not very practical, it demonstrates the functionality of Intersect. The set produced by

```
intersect({drink},{food, drink})
```

is equivalent to

```
{drink}
```

A more practical example that parallels the preceding Union() example is the following MDX clause:

```
intersect(
  {filter([Store Name].Members,([Drink],[unit sales])>2000)},
  {filter([Store Name].Members,([Food],[unit sales])>15000)}
  )
```

This Intersect() function creates a set of members that meet both filter requirements. When used in a manner such as this, the Intersect() function is comparable to the concept of "and" in mathematics.

The Distinct() Function

The most direct method of eliminating duplicates from a set is to use the Distinct() function. The syntax is

```
Distinct(set)
```

As with the other methods of eliminating duplicates, the second member of a duplicate is discarded. Although the following use is not very practical, it demonstrates the functionality of the Distinct() function. The set produced by

```
distinct({drink, food, drink})
```

is equivalent to

```
{drink, food}
```

The Except() Function

The Except() function finds the difference between two sets. The syntax is

```
Except(set1,set2[,[All]])
```

This function compares the first set to the second set and returns a set consisting of members of the first set that are not in the second set. Once again, a contrived example makes the function clear. In this example, two sets of stores are compared:

```
Except({[Store 1],[Store 2],[Store 3],[Store 4]}, {[Store 2],[Store 5]})
```

The resulting set is

```
{[Store 1],[Store 3],[Store 4]}
```

In practice, the most common use of this function is to remove particular members from a set. For example, the MDX clause

```
except({[Store Name].Members},
{[Store].[All Stores].[USA].[WA].[Seattle].children})
```

returns a set of all store names except stores in Seattle.

Including the [All] flag results in all duplicates being retained.

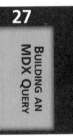

The NON EMPTY Keyword

Within most cubes, there are numerous cases in which there is no data at a particular intersection of dimensions. For example, in the FoodMart Sales cube, there is no data for the customers in Canada and Mexico and there is no data for the year 1998.

As shown in Figure 27.12, the following query results in a data set in which there are cells with null values.

```
SELECT
 {[Customers].[Country].Members} ON COLUMNS,
 {[Time].[Year].Members} ON ROWS
FROM [Sales]
```

FIGURE 27.12

*Some queries
return data sets
with null values
cells.*

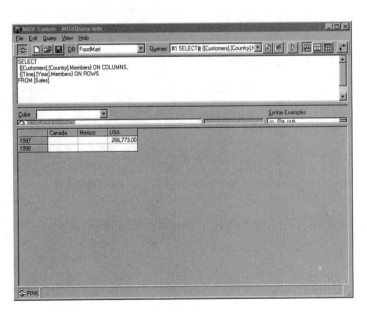

Depending on the situation, there are situations in which it is important that the user see that there are null cells in a data set. This may indicate that data is not being collected for a particular segment of the cube. In a different situation, the user may only wish to see cells that have data. This would probably be the case for extremely sparse data sets.

The NON EMPTY keyword in an MDX query allows these empty cells to be filtered out of the dataset. NON EMPTY is used on an entire axis and in the MDX query it precedes the *axis specification*.

```
NON EMPTY axis specification ON axis
```

For example, to filter out tuples with all empty cells in a column, the NON EMPTY keyword is placed before the column axis clause.

```
NON EMPTY {[Customers].[Country].Members} ON COLUMNS,
```

To remove all empty cells in a query with both columns and rows, use NON EMPTY on each axis.

```
SELECT
 NON EMPTY {[Customers].[Country].Members} ON COLUMNS,
 NON EMPTY {[Time].[Year].Members} ON ROWS
FROM [Sales]
```

Figure 27.13 shows how the NON EMPTY keyword affects the results of the query shown previously.

FIGURE 27.13

Use the NON EMPTY *keyword to eliminate nulls from a dataset.*

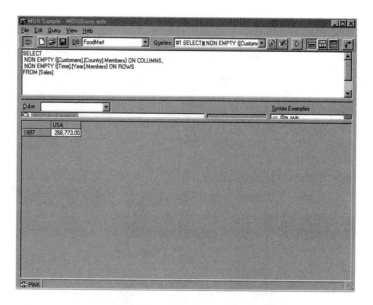

Practical Examples

While the material in this chapter discusses only the most fundamental aspects of the MDX language, these basic functions and concepts provide the foundation for many of the important requirements of an OLAP or decision support system.

To close out this chapter, some examples are presented and discussed. The examples combine the capabilities of the expressions discussed in this chapter for typical OLAP functionality. As with the previous examples, each of these includes an MDX query, the resulting dataset, and a brief discussion of the query. All of them are based on the FoodMart Sales cube.

Example of `TopCount()` on a Part of an Axis

This query is motivated by a desire to determine which products married women are most likely to purchase and the sales of these same products to married men.

```
SELECT
 {[Gender].Members} ON COLUMNS,
 {TopCount({[Product].[Product Name].Members},
 10,([Gender].[Gender].[F], [Measures].[Unit Sales]))} ON ROWS
FROM [Sales]
WHERE ([Marital Status].[All Marital Status].[M],[Measures].[Unit Sales])
```

The columns axis contains all members of the gender dimension, [All Gender], [F], and [M]. [All Gender] is included because the `.Members` function was placed on the gender dimension instead of on the [Gender].[Gender] level.

The fundamental set in the rows axis consists of names of products (members of the [Product].[Product Name] level). In this query the `TopCount()` function is used to examine some of the products. Of specific interest here are the top 10 products in unit sales purchased by females. Therefore, the index in the `TopCount()` function is 10, and the numeric expression is the tuple ([Gender].[Gender].[F], [Measures].[Unit Sales]).

The slicer contains the two members explicitly defined, [Marital Status].[All Marital Status].[M] and [Measures].[Unit Sales], because only data with these characteristics is desired.

The results of the query are shown in Figure 27.14.

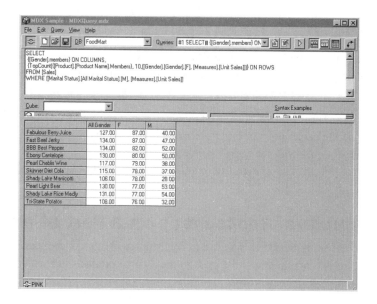

Finally, it is important to realize that the set on the rows axis is found by ranking the products by unit sales to female customers.

Example of Simultaneous Use of `TopCount()` and `BottomCount()`

The next example examines the unit sales of the various product categories in the USA and the three states this cube contains for the USA.

```
SELECT
 {[Customers].[All Customers].[USA],
 [Customers].[All Customers].[USA].Children} ON COLUMNS,
 {TopCount({[Product].[Product Category].Members},
 5, [Measures].[Unit Sales]),
 BottomCount({[Product].[Product Category].Members},
 5, [Measures].[Unit Sales])} ON ROWS
FROM [Sales]
```

The columns axis contains the members from the customers dimension. The single member, `{[Customers].[All Customers].[USA]`, is specified and the children of USA, `[Customers].[All Customers].[USA].Children`, are combined in a comma-separated list to make up the set.

The product categories are included on the rows axis in a comma-separated list where different operators are used to specify a particular subset of the [Product].[Product Category].Members set. Unit sales is used as the measure with which to select the top five product categories and the bottom five product categories.

The results of this query are shown in Figure 27.15.

FIGURE 27.15

The dataset resulting from the query where there is an implicit union of two sets operated on by functions.

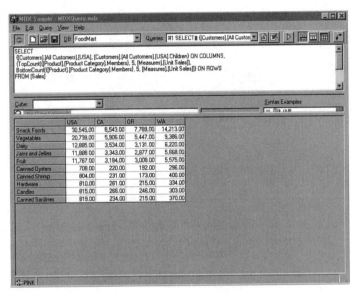

Notice that in this query, the measure is never specified. Although unit sales is used for TopCount() and BottomCount(), there is no measure explicitly defined in either the columns or rows axes, or in the slicer. When a dimension is not specified, the default member is returned. Because unit sales is the default member in measures, it is used to produce the results.

Example of Nested Functions

The final example is motivated by a search for product lines that may need to be discontinued. Products that are sold in high numbers but produce very little profit are considered for elimination because of the overhead associated with carrying the products.

```
SELECT
 {[Measures].[Profit], [Measures].[Sales Count]} ON COLUMNS,
 {TopCount(
  {Filter({[Product].[Product Name].Members}, [Measures].[Profit]<100)}
  , 15, [Measures].[Sales Count])} ON ROWS
FROM [Sales]
WHERE ([Time].[1997])
```

The query produces a dataset where the two measures of interest, profit and sales count, are included on the columns axis. The slicer specifies the year of interest, 1997.

Two nested functions have been used on the product name level to obtain a set of candidate products on the rows axis.

The inner function, `Filter()`, is executed first. It creates a set of products with profits of less than $100. The number of products that meet this criterion is unknown. The outer function, `TopCount()`, selects the 15 products within this set that have the highest sales count. Figure 27.16 shows the resulting set sorted in descending order of sales count.

FIGURE 27.16

The dataset produced by a query with nested functions.

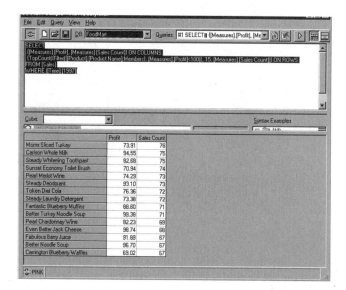

Summary

The goal of this chapter was to lay the foundation for building MDX queries to access data stored in Microsoft OLAP Services.

While there was a significant amount of detailed information provided in this chapter, there were some high-level concepts discussed. After completing this chapter, you should understand the following:

- The general structure of an MDX is a SELECT clause in which the axes are specified, a FROM clause where the cube is specified, and a SELECT clause that is used to filter the data.

- The multidimensional nature of cubes and MDX allows for multiple dimensions to be specified on a single axis, but does not permit using a dimension on more than one axis.

- MDX functions (sometimes referred to as expressions) are the primary tools for manipulating the dimensions on the axes and the data within the cube. As such, mastering the use of functions is a critical skill.

Another group of MDX functions and some more advanced OLAP concepts are introduced in Chapter 28, "Advanced MDX Queries."

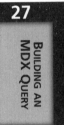

27

BUILDING AN
MDX QUERY

Advanced MDX Queries

by Jim Pinkelman

This chapter provides the information necessary to implement more advanced OLAP functionality based on more advanced MDX queries. In general, each section in the chapter discusses a particular topic and covers any functions relevant to that function.

The topics include building temporary members using calculated members and calculated sets; building queries based on member properties; using numerical functions (sum, count, and so on); formatting the results of a query; using time functions (year-to-date, count, and so on); and using user-defined functions.

Using the WITH Clause

Because of its usefulness, the WITH clause is the first concept that a user should master after learning the basics of MDX. Build a calculated member or set in an MDX statement by placing a WITH clause at the beginning of the MDX statement. The WITH clause defines members or sets that can then be used in the SELECT or WHERE clause of the MDX statement.

The placement of the WITH clause in an MDX query is as follows:

```
WITH formula
SELECT axis [, axis...]
FROM cube
WHERE slicer
```

It is important to keep in mind that the calculated members and sets that are defined within a WITH clause are limited only to the scope of the MDX statement. In other words, one MDX statement cannot refer to the calculated member defined in a different statement.

> **Note**
>
> Calculated members and calculated sets are also referred to as named members and named sets.

The WITH Clause and Calculated Members

Short of programming, there are two common methods of creating calculated members. The first involves the calculated member builder in the OLAP manager and was explained in Chapter 15, "Creating Cubes." As was discussed in that chapter, calculated members built with this technique are real-time in their calculation and are global in scope. They can be used like any other member in the normal syntax of an MDX statement.

The FoodMart sales cube has a global calculated member named profit as a measure. Profit is defined as:

```
[Measures].[Store Sales]-[Measures].[Store Cost]
```

As shown in the following MDX statement, syntactically, profit appears as any other standard member.

```
SELECT
 {[Gender].[Gender].Members} ON COLUMNS,
 {[Product].[Product Family].Members}  ON ROWS
FROM [Sales]
WHERE ([Measures].[Profit])
```

The second method of creating a calculated member is to use the WITH clause. To define a member in the WITH clause, you must specify the name of the member and the formula needed to calculate the member.

Using the WITH clause, a query equivalent to the previous one is

```
WITH member
 [Measures].[Store Profit] as
'([Measures].[Store Sales]-[Measures].[Store Cost])'
SELECT
 {[Gender].[Gender].Members} ON COLUMNS,
 {[Product].[Product Family].Members}  ON ROWS
FROM [Sales]
WHERE ([Measures].[Store Profit])
```

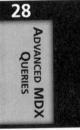

28

ADVANCED MDX
QUERIES

In this case, the WITH clause is used to define a single calculated member. The name of the calculated member is defined as [Measures].[Store Profit], which is used later in the query. Store Profit is defined as Store Sales minus Store Cost, which is enclosed in single quotation marks.

The results of the two queries are identical and are shown in Figure 28.1.

You can perform basic arithmetic operations as a formula in the WITH clause, and you can use members other than measures in the WITH clause. The following query creates a new member as the addition of California and Oregon customers:

```
With Member
 [Customers].[CA and OR] As
 '[Customers].[All Customers].[USA].[CA] +
 [Customers].[All Customers].[USA].[OR]'
SELECT
 {[Measures].[Unit Sales], [Measures].[Store Cost]} ON COLUMNS,
 {[Customers].[All Customers].[USA].Children,
 [Customers].[CA and OR]} ON ROWS
FROM [Sales]
```

FIGURE 28.1

The calculated member defined in the cube is global in scope.

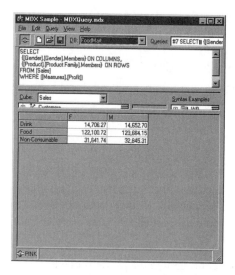

Figure 28.2 shows that the calculated member in the query is applicable for multiple measures.

FIGURE 28.2

Dataset resulting from an MDX query using a WITH *clause.*

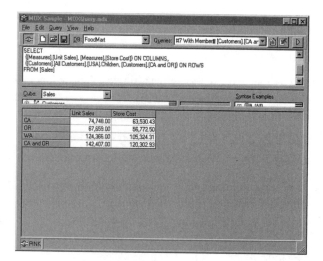

WITH is used only once in an MDX query, but it is possible to define multiple calculated members in a single WITH clause. For example, the following MDX query specifies a calculated member on both the columns and the rows axes:

```
With
Member [Customers].[CA and OR]
As '[Customers].[All Customers].[USA].[CA] +
```

```
[Customers].[All Customers].[USA].[OR]'
Member [Product].[Consumables]
 As  '[Product].[All Products].[Drink]+[Product].[All Products].[Food]'
SELECT
 {[Customers].[All Customers].[USA].[WA],
  [Customers].[CA and OR],
  [Customers].[All Customers].[USA]} ON COLUMNS,
 {[Product].[Product Family].[Non-Consumable],
  [Product].[Consumables]} ON ROWS
FROM [Sales]
```

> **Note**
>
> As explained in the next section, because this query uses calculated members of both axes, it is somewhat ambiguous. This ambiguity lies in the fact that the OLAP server performs these calculations at runtime and the order in which the calculations are performed affect the results. This can lead to errors interpreting the results in these situations.

28

ADVANCED MDX
QUERIES

Figure 28.3 shows the results of this query.

FIGURE 28.3

Multiple calculated members can be used in an MDX query.

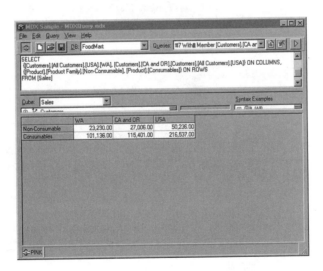

Creating calculated members using the WITH clause will be used extensively throughout this chapter because it is necessary to implement many of the arithmetic functions and advanced time-related functions available in MDX.

Solve Order and Calculated Members

For complex analyses, it is not unlikely that MDX statements could have calculated members on both the columns and the rows axes. In such a situation, a potential problem arises. An example is the most effective method of explaining.

The following MDX statement is used to examine the unit sales of the various product families for each gender:

```
WITH
 Member [Gender].[Gender Difference] As
 '[Gender].[All Gender].[M]-[Gender].[All Gender].[F]'
 Member [Product].[Non-Con. Share] As
 '[Product].[All Products].[Non-Consumable]/[Product].[All Products]'
SELECT
 {[Gender].[Gender].Members, [Gender].[Gender Difference]} ON COLUMNS,
 {[Product].[Product Family].Members,
  [Product].[All Products],
  [Product].[Non-Con. Share]} ON ROWS
FROM [Sales]
```

The results of this query are seen in Figure 28.4.

FIGURE 28.4

Calculated members are used on both axes in this query.

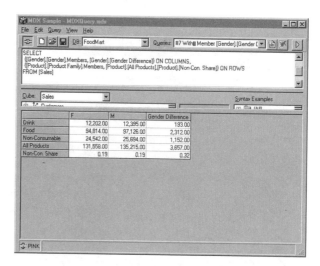

The problem encountered here involves the cell at the intersection of the two calculated members; in this case, the bottom row, last column. Notice that the value in this cell is 0.32 and is obtained by dividing 1,152 by 3,657. In other words, this cell is the Non-Con. Share of the Gender Difference.

The ambiguity lies in the fact that this cell could alternately have been calculated as the Gender Difference of the Non-Con. Share, or 0.19 minus 0.19.

The previous MDX statement should be written in one of two forms. The following query produces the results shown in Figure 28.5:

```
With
 Member [Gender].[Gender Difference] As
 '[Gender].[All Gender].[M]-[Gender].[All Gender].[F]',
 Solve_Order=1
 Member [Product].[Non-Con. Share] As
 '[Product].[All Products].[Non-Consumable]/[Product].[All Products]',
 Solve_Order=2
SELECT
 {[Gender].[Gender].Members, [Gender].[Gender Difference]} ON COLUMNS,
 {[Product].[Product Family].Members,
  [Product].[All Products],
  [Product].[Non-Con. Share]} ON ROWS
FROM [Sales]
```

FIGURE 28.5

This query produces the Non-Consumables Share of the Gender Difference.

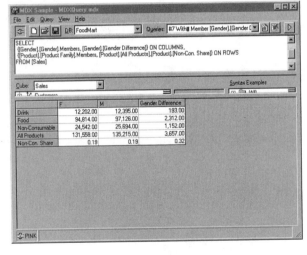

In contrast, this next query produces the results shown in Figure 28.6.

```
With
 Member [Gender].[Gender Difference] As
 '[Gender].[All Gender].[M]-[Gender].[All Gender].[F]',
 Solve_Order=2
 Member [Product].[Non-Con. Share] As
 '[Product].[All Products].[Non-Consumable]/[Product].[All Products]',
 Solve_Order=1
SELECT
 {[Gender].[Gender].Members, [Gender].[Gender Difference]} ON COLUMNS,
```

```
  {[Product].[Product Family].Members,
   [Product].[All Products],
   [Product].[Non-Con. Share]} ON ROWS
FROM [Sales]
```

FIGURE 28.6

This query produces the Gender Difference of the Non-Conumables Share.

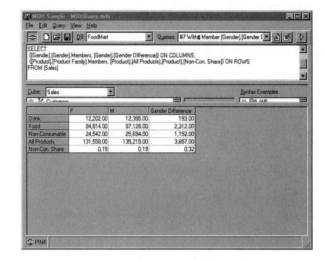

The WITH Clause and Calculated Sets

In addition to creating calculated members in an MDX query, it is possible to create calculated sets.

The syntax of a calculated set is equivalent to that of a calculated member. To define a set in the WITH clause, it is necessary to specify the name of the set and the formula needed to calculate the set. The formula for the calculated set can contain standard MDX functions.

```
WITH
 Set [Marital by Gender]
 as 'CrossJoin({[All Gender].Children},{[All Marital Status].Children})'
SELECT
 {[Measures].[Unit Sales]} ON COLUMNS,
 {[Marital by Gender]} ON ROWS
FROM [Sales]
```

The expected results of this query are shown in Figure 28.7.

Calculated sets are most useful when they are used in conjunction with intrinsic MDX functions. The following query creates a calculated set equivalent to the previous query, and then uses the ORDER function to order each of the tuples resulting from the crossjoin.

FIGURE 28.7

A calculated set in an MDX query produces these results.

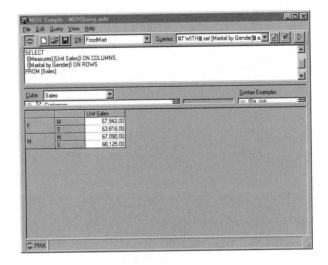

WITH
```
 Set [Marital by Gender]
 as 'CrossJoin({[All Gender].Children},{[All Marital Status].Children}) '
SELECT
 {[Measures].[Unit Sales]} ON COLUMNS,
 {Order([Marital by Gender],[Unit Sales],BDESC)} ON ROWS
FROM [Sales]
```

As Figure 28.8 shows, this query allows the user to rank each combination of gender/marital status by unit sales.

FIGURE 28.8

Using an MDX function on a calculated set to rank tuples.

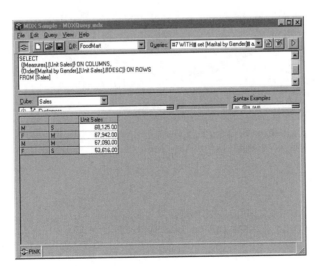

28

ADVANCED MDX
QUERIES

Numerical Functions

One of the major strengths of Microsoft OLAP Services is its rich set of mathematical and analytical functions. The existence of these intrinsic analytical MDX functions within the query language is one of the most significant advantages of MDX over SQL when it comes to OLAP functionality.

Unlike the functions discussed in the last chapter, the functions covered here are implemented in the context of calculated members. These functions are typically used to create a new member by manipulating existing sets or members.

> **Caution**
>
> Incorrectly using numerical functions on measures is a classic pitfall in implementing and using OLAP systems. Some measures are non-additive, and using functions like Sum() and Average() on these measures is not valid. Inventory is an obvious example of a non-additive measure. If you sum inventory levels over a time period, you have created a meaningless results set.

The Sum() Function

The Sum() function returns the sum of a numeric expression over a set. The syntax is

```
Sum(set[,numeric expression])
```

Although the numeric expression is optional, it is recommended that it always be included to avoid ambiguity. A typical use of the Sum() function is seen in this MDX query:

```
WITH
 Member [Time].[1st Half of 1997] as
 'Sum({[Time].[1997].[Q1], [Time].[1997].[Q2]}, [Unit Sales])'
 Member [Time].[2nd Half of 1997] as
 'Sum({[Time].[1997].[Q3], [Time].[1997].[Q4]}, [Unit Sales])'
SELECT
 {[Product].[Product Family].Members} ON COLUMNS,
 {[Time].[1st Half of 1997],
  [Time].[2nd Half of 1997],
  [Time].[1997]} ON ROWS
FROM [Sales]
WHERE ([Measures].[Unit Sales])
```

This query results in the dataset shown in Figure 28.9.

FIGURE 28.9

This dataset is returned as the result of using the Sum() *function.*

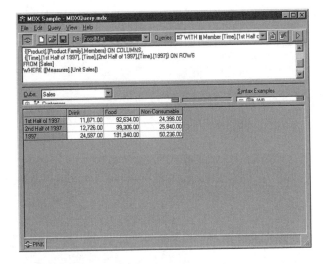

If the numeric expression is not included, the summed value is determined by the remaining portion of the MDX statement. For example, in the following MDX query, the numeric expression is not included and [Sales Count] is used on the slicer axis. As a result, [Sales Count] is the summed value.

```
WITH
 Member [Time].[1st Half of 1997] as
 'Sum({[Time].[1997].[Q1], [Time].[1997].[Q2]})'
 Member [Time].[2nd Half of 1997] as
 'Sum({[Time].[1997].[Q3], [Time].[1997].[Q4]})'
SELECT
 {[Product].[Product Family].Members} ON COLUMNS,
 {[Time].[1st Half of 1997],
  [Time].[2nd Half of 1997],
  [Time].[1997]} ON ROWS
FROM [Sales]
WHERE ([Measures].[Sales Count])
```

The Count() Function

The Count() function returns the number of tuples in a set. The syntax is

```
Count(set[, EXCLUDEEMPTY ¦ INCLUDEEMPTY])
```

By default, empty cells are counted. If empty cells are to be excluded from the count, use the EXCLUDEEMPTY keyword. The following query uses a calculated member to count the number of customers who bought products in each of the various product departments:

```
WITH
 Member [Customers].[Customer Count] as
```

```
'Count({[Customers].[Name].Members},EXCLUDEEMPTY)'
SELECT
 {[Customers].[Customer Count]}  ON COLUMNS,
 {Order([Product].[Product Department].Members,
  [Customers].[Customer Count],BDESC)} ON ROWS
FROM [Sales]
```

As seen in Figure 28.10, the query also uses the Order() function to rank the product departments according to customer count.

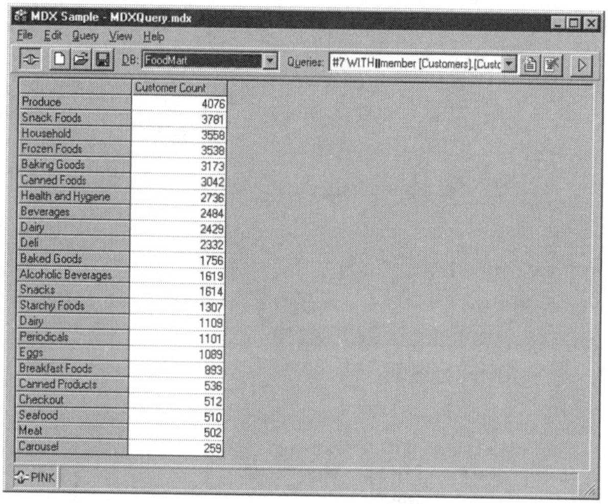

FIGURE 28.10

The Order()
*function ranks the
results of a query
using the* Count()
function.

> ### Caution
>
> Do not misconstrue the use of COUNT() here with DISTINCT COUNT(). The query shown will count a customer twice if he made two purchases. The DISTINCT function is discussed further in Chapter 30, MDX Reference.

The Avg() Function

The Avg() (average) function returns the average of the tuples in a set based on the value of the numeric expression. The syntax is

Avg(*set*[,*numeric expression*])

The results of this query, shown in Figure 28.11, demonstrate that the average function does not include empty cells when performing its calculation.

```
WITH
 Member [Customers].[Country Avg] as
 'Avg({[Customers].[Country].members},[Sales Count])'
SELECT
 {[Customers].[Country].members,[Customers].[Country Avg]}  ON COLUMNS,
 [Product].[Product family].members ON ROWS
FROM [Sales]
WHERE [Sales Count]
```

FIGURE 28.11

The Avg() *function does not include empty cells in its calculation.*

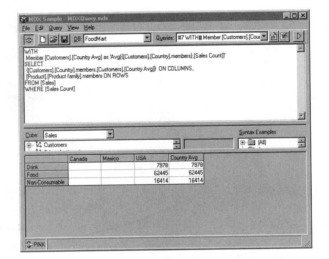

The following query provides a more complex example where averages are calculated for the set on the columns axis and the set on the rows axis:

```
WITH
 Member [Customers].[State Avg] as
 'Avg({[Customers].[Country].[USA].children},[Sales Count])'
 Member [Product].[Product Family Avg] as
 'Avg({[Product].[Product Family].members},[Sales Count])'
SELECT
 {[Customers].[USA].children,[Customers].[State Avg]}  ON COLUMNS,
 {[Product].[Product Family].members,
  [Product].[Product Family Avg] } ON ROWS
FROM [Sales]
WHERE ([Sales Count],[Time].[1997].[Q1].[1])
```

The results of this query are shown in Figure 28.12.

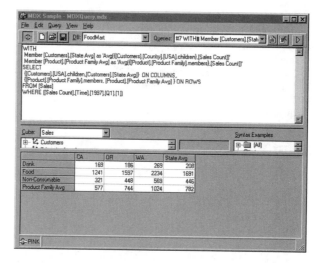

FIGURE 28.12

Use of the Avg() *function can be more complex.*

Time Series Functions

Time series functions provide a variety of capabilities critical to advanced data analysis and decision-support systems. This section discusses all of the functions related to the analysis of data using time as a variable. These functions are placed into two groups for this discussion. The first group contains a variety of basic functions for manipulating levels, members, and values within a cube. The second group contains the time series analysis functions that are used to perform linear regression and classical statistical analysis.

> **Note**
>
> Many of these functions are commonly used with the Time dimension. In most situations, the Time dimension is called Time, but this in not always the case. More importantly, when Microsoft OLAP Services applies these functions, the literal name of the dimension is irrelevant. Instead, a dimension is considered a time dimension if the DIMENSION_TYPE property is set to MD_DIMTYPE_TIME.

Miscellaneous Time Functions

The primary purpose of the following time functions is to navigate within the time dimension. For example, find the next year, use the last month in the quarter, or use the same period in the next year.

The YTD(), QTD(), MTD(), WTD() Functions

Year-to-date YTD(), quarter-to-date QTD(), month-to-date MTD(), and week-to-date WTD() functions all operate on a *member*. These functions return a set consisting of all members up to and including the specified *member*. The set begins with the first time period and ends with the *member* time period. Only *members* that are at the same level as the *member* are returned.

The syntax of this function is

```
YTD(member),
QTD(member),
MTD(member),
WTD(member)
```

Using the FoodMart sales cube, the following examples provide enough information to explain the use of these functions.

This first example produces the set of quarters from the first quarter in 1997 through the third:

```
YTD([Time].[1997].[Q3])
```

yields

```
{[Time].[1997].[Q1], [Time].[1997].[Q2], [Time].[1997].[Q3]}
```

The second example produces the set of months from the first month in 1997 through the fifth:

```
YTD([Time].[1997].[Q2].[5])
```

yields

```
{[Time].[1997].[Q1].[1],
 [Time].[1997].[Q1].[2],
 [Time].[1997].[Q1].[3],
 [Time].[1997].[Q2].[4],
 [Time].[1997].[Q2].[5]}
```

This third example produces the set of months from the first month in the second quarter of 1997 through the fifth month.

```
QTD([Time].[1997].[Q2].[5])
```

yields

```
{[Time].[1997].[Q2].[4] , [Time].[1997].[Q2].[5]}
```

Although this last example is not practical, it is included for completeness and produces the set of months from the first month in the fifth month of 1997 through the fifth month of 1997.

28

ADVANCED MDX QUERIES

```
MTD([Time].[1997].[Q2].[5])
```

yields

```
{[Time].[1997].[Q2].[5]}
```

These functions are very useful in retrieving members within a time period without having to explicitly define the members. They should be implemented in situations where the user is interested in a running sum up through a time period. For example, every day the user may be interested in the sales to date in the current quarter.

The `PeriodsToDate()` Function

The `PeriodsToDate()` function is similar to the *x*TD functions just described. However, the syntax includes the specification on a level:

```
PERIODSTODATE([level.[,member]])
```

This function returns a set of members up to and including the specified *member* that is within the specified *level*. For example, the following statement produces a set of months within the quarter of the specified month:

```
PERIODSTODATE([Time].[Quarter],[Time].[1997].[Q3].[9])
```

yields

```
{[Time].[1997].[Q3].[7], [Time].[1997].[Q3].[8], [Time].[1997].[Q3].[9]}
```

It is interesting to note that both of the parameters in this function are optional. As a result, three distinct syntax configurations are permissible.

If neither the *level* nor the *member* is specified, the *level* is the parent level of `Time.CurrentMember` and the *member* is `Time.CurrentMember`:

```
PERIODSTODATE()
```

If the *level* is specified and the *member* is not specified, the *member* is `dimension.CurrentMember`. The *dimension* is the parent dimension of the specified *level*:

```
PERIODSTODATE(level)
```

To avoid ambiguity and avoid potential problems, it is recommended that both the `level` and the *member* be specified:

```
PERIODSTODATE(level,member)
```

The `LastPeriods()` Function

The `LastPeriods()` function is used to generate a set of members up to and including the specified *member*. While the `PeriodsToDate` function returns all members back to the beginning of a period, `LastPeriods()` returns the number of members specified by an *index* value. The syntax is

```
LASTPERIODS(index[,member])
```

The set generated by `LastPeriods()` will cross the boundaries of periods. For example:

```
LastPeriods(4,[Time].[1998].[Q1].[2])
```

yields

```
{[Time].[1997].[Q4].[11],
 [Time].[1997].[Q4].[12],
 [Time].[1998].[Q1].[1],
 [Time].[1998].[Q1].[2]}
```

If the *member* is not included, `Time.CurrentMember` is used.

Time Series Analysis Functions

Microsoft OLAP Services offers a set of functions that perform simple linear regression functions using the least squares method. These functions perform a least squares fit of numerical values for a given set.

> **Note**
>
> While it is clearly not within the scope of this book to discuss linear regression in any detail, it is worth putting the concept in context. As discussed in this section and as implemented in Microsoft OLAP Services, Linear Regression is the classical statistics technique of modeling the relationship between two variables. All of the concepts, terms, and techniques used in statistical analysis in this modeling process are applicable here.

In the following examples, the MDX linear regression functions are used to analyze the effect of store sales on profits in the FoodMart sales cube. The linear regression equation is $y = ax + b$, where a is the slope of the line and b is the y-intercept value.

The following query retrieves sales and profit data from each month in 1997. The results are shown in Figure 28.13.

28

ADVANCED MDX
QUERIES

```
SELECT
  {[Measures].[Store Sales], [Measures].[Profit]} ON COLUMNS,
  {Descendants([Time].[1997], [Time].[Month],SELF)} ON ROWS
FROM [Sales]
```

FIGURE 28.13

A simple query produces 1997 monthly store sales and profits.

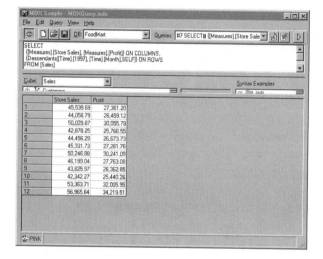

Using Microsoft Excel, a simple least squares fit of the estimating equation is shown in Figure 28.14.

FIGURE 28.14

A chart shows the least squares fit of store sales versus profits.

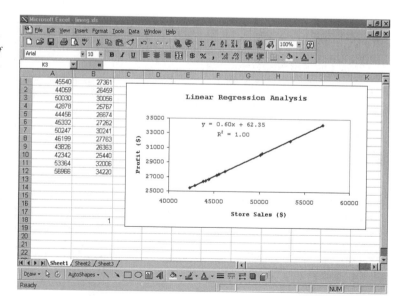

> **Note**
>
> The particular example is a bit contrived because profit is defined in the cube as a calculated member equal to store sales minus store cost. Furthermore, to generate the data in the FoodMart cube, store sales are consistently two and a half times store costs. As a result, the correlation between store sales and profit equals one—this is usually an unrealistically high correlation between random variables.

Finally, like the numerical functions discussed earlier, because the linear regression functions return numeric values (and not sets), they can only be used with calculated members. They can only be used in the WITH clause not the SELECT clause.

The `LinRegIntercept()` Function

The `LinRegIntercept()` function calculates the y-intercept of the regression line (b in y = ax + b). The syntax is

```
LinRegIntercept(set,numeric expression[,numeric expression])
```

This syntax is common to all of the linear regression functions. The function uses the *set* to obtain the numerical values used for the axes of the estimating equation. The first *numeric expression* is used as the y-axis, or dependent variable, and the second *numeric expression* is used as the x-axis, or independent variable.

In the case where the second *numerical value* is omitted, the members of the *set* are used for the x-axis. This situation occurs only with the time dimension where the members have numeric value equivalents.

The following statement returns 2.51, the y-intercept of the regression line as shown in Figure 28.14:

```
LinRegIntercept(
 {Descendants([Time].[1997], [Time].[Month],SELF)},
  [Measures].[Profit], [Measures].[Store Sales]
 )
```

> **Note**
>
> When performing the curve fit, null, text, and logical values are ignored; zero values are used.

The `LinRegSlope()` Function

The `LinRegSlope()` function calculates the slope of the regression line (a in $y = ax + b$). The syntax is

```
LinRegSlope(set,numeric expression[,numeric expression])
```

The following clause returns 62.37, the slope of the regression line:

```
LinRegSlope(
  {Descendants([Time].[1997], [Time].[Month],SELF)},
  [Measures].[Profit], [Measures].[Store Sales]
  )
```

The `LinRegVariance()` Function

The `LinRegVariance()` function calculates the variance of the regression line in the curve fit. The syntax is

```
LinRegVariance(set,numeric expression[,numeric expression])
```

The following clause returns a variance value of 864.42:

```
LinRegVariance(
  {Descendants([Time].[1997], [Time].[Month],SELF)},
  [Measures].[Profit], [Measures].[Store Sales]
  )
```

The `LinRegR2()` Function

The `LinRegR2()` function calculates the coefficient of determination (R^2) for the regression line. The syntax is

```
LinRegR2(set,numeric expression[,numeric expression])
```

The following clause returns 1.00, the coefficient of determination of this regression line.

```
LinRegR2(
  {Descendants([Time].[1997], [Time].[Month],SELF)},
  [Measures].[Profit], [Measures].[Store Sales]
)
```

The `Correlation()` Function

The `Correlation()` function calculates the coefficient of correlation (R) for the regression line. The syntax is

```
Correlation(set,numeric expression[,numeric expression])
```

The following clause returns 1.00, the coefficient of correlation of this regression line:

```
Correlation(
 {Descendants([Time].[1997], [Time].[Month],SELF)},
 [Measures].[Profit], [Measures].[Store Sales]
)
```

The `Covariance()` Function

The `Covariance()` function calculates the covariance of a regression line using the biased population. The syntax is

```
Covariance(set,numeric expression[,numeric expression])
```

The following clause returns 11,432,611.66, the covariance of the regression line.

```
Covariance(
 {Descendants([Time].[1997], [Time].[Month],SELF)},
 [Measures].[Profit], [Measures].[Store Sales]
)
```

The `LinRegPoint()` Function

The `LinRegPoint()` function is used to estimate a y, or dependent, value. The function requires an x, or independent, value and the data necessary to perform a curve fit. As a result, the syntax of the `LinRegPoint()` function varies slightly from the other linear regression functions. The syntax is

```
LinRegR2(numeric expression, set,
 numeric expression[,numeric expression])
```

The first *numeric expression* is the x-value, while the *set* is used to build the data set for the curve fit. As with all of the other linear regression functions, the first *numeric expression* is the y-axis and the second numeric expression is the x-axis.

The following clause estimates the profit (y-axis) given store sales of $55,000 (x-axis). Based on the slope and y-intercept values, the regression line is $y = (0.6)(x) + 62.37$. For store sales of $55,000, the estimated profit is $33,035.08.

```
LinRegPoint(
 55000,{Descendants([Time].[1997],[Time].[Month],SELF)},
 [Measures].[Profit],[Measures].[Store Sales]
)
```

Summary

The following MDX statement calculates all of the linear regression values:

```
With
 Member [Measures].[Slope] as
 'LinRegSlope({Descendants([1997], [Month])},
  [Profit], [Store Sales])'
 Member [Measures].[Intercept] as
```

28

ADVANCED MDX
QUERIES

```
'LinRegIntercept({Descendants([1997], [Month])},
 [Profit],[Store Sales])'
Member [Measures].[Variance] as
'LinRegVariance({Descendants([1997], [Month])},
 [Sales Count], [Store Sales])'
Member [Measures].[R2] as
'LinRegR2({Descendants([1997], [Month])},
 [Sales Count], [Store Sales])'
Member [Measures].[Correlation] as
'Correlation({Descendants([1997], [Month])},
 [Sales Count], [Store Sales])'
Member [Measures].[Covariance] as
'Covariance({Descendants([1997], [Month])},
 [Profit], [Store Sales])'
Member [Measures].[Point] as
'LinRegPoint(55000,{Descendants([1997], [Month])},
 [Profit], [Store Sales])'
SELECT
{[Time].[1997]} ON COLUMNS,
{[Slope],[Intercept],[Variance],[R2],[Correlation],
 [Covariance],[Point]} ON ROWS
FROM [Sales]
```

The results are shown in Figure 28.15.

FIGURE 28.15

A linear regression analysis of store sales and profit is displayed.

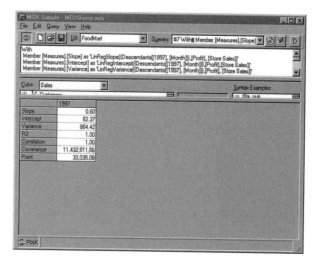

Miscellaneous MDX Functions

There are a number of MDX functions that were not covered in Chapter 27. The most important of these functions are discussed here and the rest are presented in Chapter 30, "MDX Reference."

The Generate() Function

The Generate() function provides capabilities to derive a set by repeatedly applying a set expression to a defined set. The basic syntax is

```
Generate(set, set expression)
```

When executed, the Generate() function applies the *set expression* to each member in the *set*. When the very simple example that follows is run, the *set expression* Customers.CurrentMember.Children is applied to each member of the [Customers].[Country] level.

```
{Generate([Customers].[Country].members,
  Customers.CurrentMember.Children)}
```

The set produced is equivalent to the set produced by the following clause:

```
{[Customers].[Country].[Canada].children,
 [Customers].[Country].[Mexico].children,
 [Customers].[Country].[USA].children}
```

The actual set is

```
{[BC],[DF],[Guerrero],[Jalisco],[Mexico],[Oaxaca],
 [Sinaloa],[Veracruz],[Yucatan],[Zacatecas],[CA],[OR],[WA]}
```

Clearly, more practical applications exist for the generate functions. The following MDX statement is used to find the top five cities in CA and WA as measured by Unit Sales:

```
SELECT
{[Measures].[Unit Sales]} ON COLUMNS,
{Generate
  ({[Customers].[All Customers].[USA].[CA],
    [Customers].[All Customers].[USA].[WA]},
    TopCount(Descendants(Customers.CurrentMember,[Customers].[City]),
    5,[Measures].[Unit Sales])
  )} ON ROWS
FROM [Sales]
```

The following MDX statement produces the exact same result, as shown in Figure 28.16:

```
SELECT
 {[Measures].[Unit Sales]} ON COLUMNS,
 {TopCount(
  {[Customers].[All Customers].[USA].[CA].Children},
   5, [Measures].[Unit Sales]),
  TopCount(
  {[Customers].[All Customers].[USA].[WA].Children},
   5, [Measures].[Unit Sales])} ON ROWS
FROM [Sales]
```

FIGURE 28.16

*Two different
queries produce
the same results.*

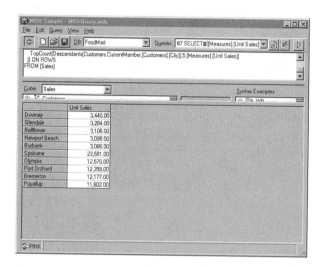

As these two queries demonstrate, the MDX language allows for multiple approaches to the same questions. And in this specific example, the second query which does not use the Generate() function is probably less complex to construct for most users. However, while the syntax for the Generate() function is complex, there are situations where its use is the most concise method of implementing certain functionality.

Consider the following MDX statement that finds the single customer in each city who has the highest unit sales. To accomplish this same goal without the use of the Generate() function, it would be necessary to apply the TopCount() function explicitly for each city in the cube. The resulting MDX query would be very time-consuming to create and extremely long.

```
SELECT
{[Measures].[Unit Sales]} ON COLUMNS,
{Generate
  (
    {[Customers].[City].members},
    TopCount(Descendants(Customers.CurrentMember,[Customers].[Name]),
    1,[Measures].[Unit Sales])
  )} ON ROWS
FROM [Sales]
```

Finally, if CurrentMember is not used to relate the *set* to the *set expression*, the Generate() function simply produces a replication of the *set expression* for each tuple in the *set*.

The `.CurrentMember` Expression

As described above, the `.CurrentMember` expression is used when iterating through a dimension (as is frequently done with the `Generate` function). During an iteration `.CurrentMember` returns the specified member associated with a particular iterative step. Usually that member is then operated on by a function. The syntax of the `CurrentMember` function is

```
dimension.CurrentMember
```

The `.PrevMember` and `.NextMember` Expressions

These two expressions allow access to the previous and next members within the same level as the *member* upon which these operate. In the FoodMart sales cube there are three countries in the customer dimension. In their natural hierarchical order, these members are: Canada, Mexico, and USA. Therefore,

```
[Customers].[All Customers].[Mexico].NextMember
```

yields

```
[Customers].[All Customers].[USA]
```

while

```
[Customers].[All Customers].[Mexico].PrevMember
```

yields

```
[Customers].[All Customers].[Canada]
```

and

```
[Customers].[All Customers].[USA].NextMember
```

yields an empty set.

And

```
[Customers].[All Customers].[Canada].PrevMember
```

yields an empty set.

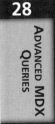

Parent

The `Parent` function simply gives the parent of the member. The parent is one level higher than the *member* upon which this function operates. Once again using the `Customers` dimension in the FoodMart sales cube,

```
[Customers].[All Customers].[USA].Parent
```

yields an empty set.

```
[Customers].[All Customers].[USA].Parent
```

yields

```
[Customers].[All Customers]
```

while

```
[Customers].[All Customers].[USA].[CA].Parent
```

yields

```
[Customers].[All Customers].[USA]
```

The .FirstChild and .LastChild Expressions

These two expressions allow access to the first and last members one level below the *member* upon which they operate. In the FoodMart sales cube, there are three members that are children to the member USA. In their natural hierarchical order these members are CA, OR, and WA. Therefore,

```
[Customers].[All Customers].[USA].FirstChild
```

yields

```
[Customers].[All Customers].[USA].[CA]
```

and

```
[Customers].[All Customers].[USA].LastChild
```

yields

```
[Customers].[All Customers].[USA].[WA]
```

The Descendants() Function

The Descendants() function is a powerful tool for navigating between the levels of a cube's dimensions. It builds a set at the specified level using the dimension of the specified member. The syntax is

```
Descendants(member, level[,flag])
```

The optional *flag* determines whether descendants at a particular level are included in the returned set. The following examples provide the clearest method of learning how this function operates.

As a reminder, in the FoodMart sales cube, the levels within the Customers dimension in descending order are Country, State Province, Cities, and Name.

```
Descendants([Customers].[All Customers].[USA],
  [Customers].[State Province])
```

yields a set of states in the USA. While

```
Descendants([Customers].[All Customers].[USA], [Customers].[Name])
```

yields a set of customers in the USA.

If no *flag* is included, the set will consist only of members at the specified level. The available flags and their effects are described in Table 28.1.

TABLE 28.1 Flags for the Descendants Function

Flag	Description
SELF	Default. Only members at *level* are returned.
AFTER	All descendant members below *level* are returned.
BEFORE	All descendant members between the *member* level and *level* are returned. Does not return members from the *level*.
BEFORE_AND_AFTER	All descendant members below the *member* level are returned. Does not return members from the *level*.
SELF_AND_AFTER	All descendant members at and below *level* are returned.
SELF_AND_BEFORE	All descendant members between the *member* level and *level* are returned.
SELF_BEFORE_AFTER	All descendant members below the *member* level are returned.

28

Using Member Properties in MDX Queries

When a cube is built in Microsoft's OLAP manager, there are two methods of exposing the data in the columns of a dimension table. The most common method is to define the column as a level, and to use the data in that column as members. The second method is to define the column as a level and to specify member properties of that level. Member properties correspond to other columns in the same dimension table. Typically member properties are created on columns that are not important enough to be defined as levels and are less frequently accessed by users.

For example, the store dimension of the FoodMart sales cube has four levels: store country, store state, store city, and store name. These levels are directly dependent on columns in the store table in the underlying star schema relational database. Figure 28.17 shows the structure in the store table.

FIGURE 28.17

The Store table in the FoodMart database has four levels.

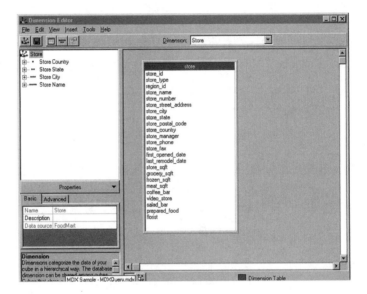

Each row of the table contains data on a particular store and each column is the piece of data stored. When the cube was constructed, a decision was made to use geographic information about the store as one of the cube's axes. In making this decision, 4 of the columns of the table were included in the cube and 20 of the columns were left out. This decision was made to limit the size of the cube.

What about the 20 remaining columns? The OLAP administrator could choose to expose additional columns as "properties." In the case of the FoodMart sales cube, 3 of the 20 columns are used as properties: store manager, store sqft, and store type.

The appropriate syntax for accessing property values is

```
member.Properties("property name")
```

However, it is critical to realize that the result of this function is always a string—it cannot be used as a set.

The two most common implementations of member properties are to

- Use the string in a filter operation.
- Convert the property into a value in a calculated member.

The following MDX statement includes a filter using the store manager member property.

```
SELECT
 {[Customers]} ON COLUMNS,
 Filter([Store].[Store Name].Members,
 [Store].CurrentMember.Properties("Store Manager")="Smith") ON ROWS
FROM [Sales]
```

The results are shown in Figure 28.18.

FIGURE 28.18

This query shows how to filter data using a member property.

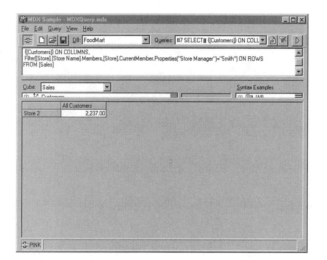

Formatting the Results of an MDX Query

MDX provides for a number of functions to control the formatting of the data returned from an MDX query. The syntax used in format expressions is similar to the syntax commonly used in programming (Excel and SQL, for instance).

Formatting values in an MDX query is accomplished in the WITH clause using calculated members. The formatting specification follows the formula. For example, the following MDX query includes a format string:

```
WITH member
 [Measures].[Store Profit]
 as '([Measures].[Store Sales]-[Measures].[Store Cost])', format = '#.000'
SELECT
 {[Gender].[Gender].Members} ON COLUMNS,
 {[Product].[Product Family].Members}  ON ROWS
```

```
FROM [Sales]
WHERE ([Measures].[Store Profit])
```

As Figure 28.20 shows, this format string controls the numeric values in the dataset.

FIGURE 28.20

*Values can be for-
matted within the
syntax of an MDX
query.*

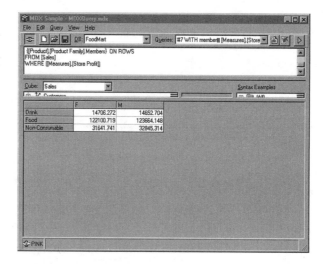

There are format expressions for both numeric values and character values.

Numeric format expressions can have 1–4 sections, each of which contains formatting instructions for a certain type of numeric value. Each section is separated by semicolons. The table below describes each section in a format expression.

TABLE 28.2 Sections of a Format Expression

# of Sections	Comment
1 section	The format expression applies to all numeric values. Example: '#,###.0'
2 sections	The first section applies to positive values and zero values.
	The second section applies to negative values. Example: '#,###.0;(#,###.0)'
3 sections	The first section applies to positive values.
	The second section applies to negative values.
	The third section applies to zero values. Example: '$#.00;($#.00);\z\e\r\o'
4 sections	The first section applies to positive values and zeros.
	The second section applies to negative values.
	The third section applies to zero values.
	The fourth section applies to null values. Example:
	'$#.00;($#.00);\z\e\r\o;\n\u\l\l'

Tables 28.3–28.5 detail the most frequently used formatting characters (a complete list is provided in Chapter 29).

The characters in Table 28.3 are applicable when formatting numeric values.

TABLE 28.3   Formatting Numeric Functions

Character	Description
0	Placeholder that displays a digit or a zero.
#	Placeholder that displays a digit or nothing.
.	Placeholder for decimal.
%	Placeholder for percentage. The value is multiplied by 100 before the placeholder is inserted.
,	Thousands separator.
E- E+ e- e+	Scientific format.
- + $ ( )	Used to display any of these literal characters.
\	Used to display the specific character that follows the backslash.
"string"	Used to display the string inside the double quotation marks.

The characters in Table 28.4 are applicable when formatting date/time values.

TABLE 28.4   Formatting Dates and Times

Character	Description
:	Time separator.
/	Date separator.
s, ss	Displays the second without a leading zero (s, 0-59), or with a leading zero (ss, 00-59).
n, nn	Displays the minute without a leading zero (n, 0-59), or with a leading zero (nn, 00-59).
h, hh	Displays the hour without a leading zero (m, 0-12), or with a leading zero (mm, 00-23).
d, dd	Displays the day without a leading zero (d, 1-31), or with a leading zero (dd, 01-31).
m, mm	Displays the month without a leading zero (m, 1-12), or with a leading zero (mm, 01-12).

continues

28

ADVANCED MDX QUERIES

TABLE 28.4 continued

Character	Description
mmm, mmmm	Displays the month as an abbreviation (Jan-Dec), or as a full month name (January-December).
y	Displays the day of the year (1-366).
yy, yyyy	Displays the year as a two-digit number (yy, 00-99), or as a four-digit number (yyyy, 1000-9999).
Dddddd	Displays the data formatted according to the long date setting of the system. Usually this format is mmmm dd, yyyy.
tttttt	Displays the data formatted according to the default time format of the system. Usually this format is h:nn:ss.

The characters in Table 28.5 are applicable when formatting character strings.

TABLE 28.5 Formatting Character Strings

Character	Description
@	Placeholder that displays a character or a space. Placeholders fill from right to left by default.
&	Placeholder that displays a character or nothing. Placeholders fill from right to left by default.
<	Forces all characters to be in lowercase format.
>	Forces all characters to be in uppercase format.
!	Changes fill of placeholders from right to left (the default) to left to right.

Business Cases

This last section of the chapter puts some of the pieces of the MDX puzzle together. For the most part, the previous two chapters have presented material in small sections designed to explain a single function or group of functions. This section is devoted to common business situations and questions that OLAP systems are intended to address.

The particular queries are not extraordinarily complex, but they do address questions that are commonly asked.

Market Share Analysis

The ability to perform market share analysis is a great demonstration of the benefits of Microsoft's OLAP Services and the power of the MDX language.

Market share analysis is an examination of the relative contribution of a specified member (or members) to a total of a group of members. It is common to examine the percentage a particular group contributes to the whole.

Once again, using the FoodMart sales cube, the unit sales of both California customers and USA customers are returned by the following query, and the results are shown in Figure 28.21.

```
SELECT
 {[Measures].[Unit Sales]} ON COLUMNS,
 {[Customers].[All Customers].[USA].[CA],
  [Customers].[All Customers].[USA]} ON ROWS
FROM [Sales]
```

FIGURE 28.21

Unit sales in California and USA are the basis for a market share analysis.

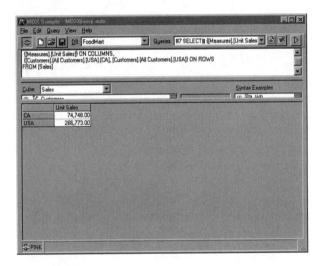

As you might expect, if you were interested in the relative percentage of California unit sales to that of the total unit sales in the USA, you would construct a simple calculated member, such as the following code example demonstrates. Its results are shown in Figure 28.22.

```
With
 Member [Customers].[CA Share of USA] As
 '[Customers].[All Customers].[USA].[CA]/
  [Customers].[All Customers].[USA]'
SELECT
```

```
{[Measures].[Unit Sales]} ON COLUMNS,
{[Customers].[All Customers].[USA].[CA],
 [Customers].[All Customers].[USA],
 [Customers].[CA Share of USA]} ON ROWS
FROM [Sales]
```

FIGURE 28.22

California unit sales are compared to USA unit sales to determine the California market share.

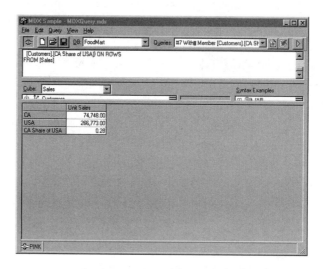

As the following query (and Figure 28.23) shows, this simple use of a calculated member remains valid and useful as other dimensions or members are included in the query:

```
With
 Member [Customers].[CA Share of USA] As
 '[Customers].[All Customers].[USA].[CA]/
 [Customers].[All Customers].[USA]'
SELECT
 CrossJoin({[Measures].[Unit Sales], [Measures].[Store Cost]},
  {[Gender].[Gender].Members}) ON COLUMNS,
{[Customers].[All Customers].[USA].[CA],
 [Customers].[All Customers].[USA],
 [Customers].[CA Share of USA]} ON ROWS
FROM [Sales]
WHERE ([Time].[1997].[Q1], [Product].[All Products].[Drink])
```

While this approach is not complex, it is very limited in its usefulness. Extrapolate this simple situation to one in which you want to examine the market share of each of the 50 states. Defining 50 different calculated members is not an efficient approach.

FIGURE 28.23

A more elaborate query returns the unit sales of drink product by gender in California and the USA for the first quarter of 1997.

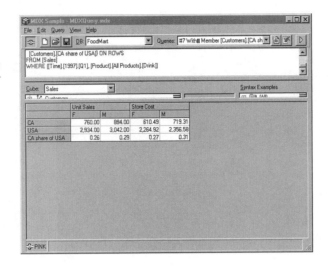

There is a much more powerful technique available. The following query contains a market share calculated member on the columns axis. The formula for market share is

```
'[Measures].[Unit Sales]/([Measures].[Unit Sales],
 [Product].[All Products])'
```

When this expression is executed within the query, the unit sales (the numerator) of each tuple on the rows axis is divided by the unit sales of all products (the denominator), as the following code shows, and as shown in Figure 28.24.

```
WITH
 Member [Measures].[Market Share] As
'([Measures].[Unit Sales],Product.CurrentMember)/
 ([Measures].[Unit Sales],[Product].[All Products])'
SELECT
 {[Measures].[Unit Sales],[Measures].[Market Share]} on columns,
 {[Product].[Product Department].Members,
  [Product].[All Products]} on rows
FROM Sales
```

Percentage Change Over Time

The time functions described earlier are one of the significant advantages MDX has over SQL. Some of the most frequently encountered questions in OLAP implementation involve the change in a quantity over a period of time. How do sales in the latest period compare to last period? How do they compare to the same period last year?

The most direct method of determining this information is to build specific calculated members that perform the necessary arithmetic.

28

ADVANCED MDX
QUERIES

FIGURE 28.24

A simple calculated member executed in a query results in product department market share data.

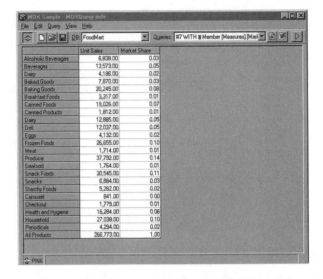

> **Note**
>
> Because it has data for both 1997 and 1998, the warehouse cube in the FoodMart database is used for these examples.

For example, the following code compares the 1997 unit sales to the 1998 unit sales. The results of the query are shown in Figure 28.25.

```
With
 Member [Time].[Yearly Growth] As
 '[Time].[1998]/[Time].[1997]',format='00.0%'
SELECT
{[Product].[Product Family].Members} ON COLUMNS,
 {[Time].[Year].Members, [Time].[Yearly Growth]} ON ROWS
FROM [Warehouse]
```

While this approach is direct, it is not particularly flexible. A more generic approach can be implemented with the `PrevMember()` and the `ParallelPeriods()` functions.

Consider a situation in which you want to examine the percentage growth each month over the previous month for the time span of an entire year. Instead of building 12 explicit calculated members, a generic approach can be used.

FIGURE 28.25

The query produces the percentage of growth in unit sales from 1997 to 1998.

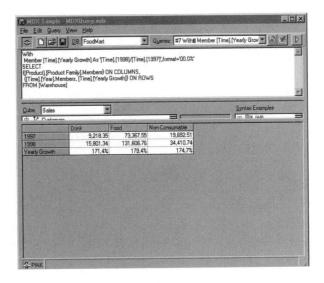

When comparing the values over consecutive time periods, the `PrevMember()` function is appropriate, as this code shows, and as shown in Figure 28.26:

```
With
 Member [Measures].[Monthly Growth] As
 '([Measures].[Units Shipped],Time.CurrentMember)/
 ([Measures].[Units Shipped],Time.CurrentMember.PrevMember)',
  format='00.0%'
SELECT
 {[Measures].[Units Shipped],[Measures].[Monthly Growth]} ON COLUMNS,
 {Descendants([Time].[1998], [Time].[Month],SELF)} ON ROWS
FROM [Warehouse]
```

FIGURE 28.26

This query shows the percentage growth in units shipped for consecutive months in 1998.

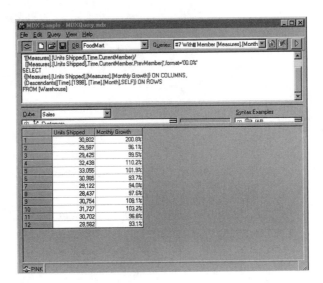

You can use a similar approach to calculate the percentage growth from one period to a parallel period using the `ParallelPeriods()` function. The following MDX statement calculates the percentage change in units shipped for each month in 1998 compared to the equivalent month in 1997.

```
With
 Member [Measures].[Monthly Growth] As
 '([Measures].[Units Shipped],Time.CurrentMember)/
  ([Measures].[Units Shipped],ParallelPeriod([Time].[Year]))',
   format='00.0%'
SELECT
 {[Measures].[Monthly Growth]} ON COLUMNS,
 {Descendants([Time].[1998], [Time].[Month],SELF)} ON ROWS
FROM [Warehouse]
```

The results of this query are shown in Figure 28.27. The 135.6% increase in units shipped in January, for instance, comes from data in the cube that 22,722 units shipped in January 1997 and 30,802 units shipped in January 1998.

FIGURE 28.27

The query produces the percentage growth in units shipped per month, 1998 over 1997.

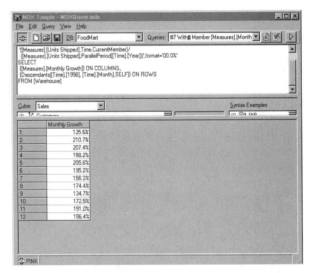

Summary

The underlying goal of this chapter was to get readers far enough up the learning curve that they can begin to attack their specific implementation issues with a good fundamental basis in MDX.

It is difficult to convey the usefulness and power of named members. Like the MDX language itself, a simple statement is usually easy to construct and easy to understand.

However, programming with named members quickly leads to the point where the statements are difficult to construct, complex to understand, and hard to debug.

It is unreasonable to expect that a single chapter in a book would address any more than a small fraction of the potential questions and problems that arise in building MDX statements. However, this chapter provides some useful information regarding the use of numeric, time, and time series functions.

The next chapter describes the use of SQL in querying Microsoft OLAP Services. Most developers will find that SQL is more of an exception than the rule in this environment. However, there are some situations where it can be useful.

28

ADVANCED MDX QUERIES

CHAPTER 29

Using SQL Queries on the OLAP Server

by Jim Pinkelman

IN THIS CHAPTER

Summary Microsoft OLAP Services also provides for the capability of executing SQL queries. As the last two chapters have demonstrated, when queries built in multidimensional expressions (MDX) are executed, OLAP Services returns a multidimensional dataset acting as a multidimensional data provider. In contrast, when SQL queries are executed, OLAP Services returns a flattened rowset acting as a tabular data provider.

As with MDX queries, SQL queries are executed using either an OLE DB or an ADO connection. The process of establishing these connections is common to both MDX and SQL.

This chapter contains a brief discussion of the syntax of these SQL statements.

> **Note**
>
> This chapter is intended to cover the use of SQL to retrieve data. Using SQL statements with PivotTable Services to build cubes is covered in Chapter 20.

Basic SQL Syntax

The basic syntax of an SQL statement for OLAP services is no different than a standard SQL statement, as shown here:

```
SELECT select list
FROM from clause
[WHERE where clause]
[GROUP BY group by clause]
```

The *select list* consists of a comma-separated list of levels and members from the measures dimension. Only levels and measure members are permissible. Because levels of a cube are defined with columns from a dimension table in the underlying star schema, using levels in the *select list* is logical. Similarly, measure members are defined with columns from the fact table, and therefore, they also can be included in the *select list*. In contrast, members from all other dimensions cannot be included in a *select list* because they are defined from the row data in the columns of dimension tables.

The *from clause* simply contains the name of the cube. When SQL is executed on OLAP Services, the cube functions as the single table from which all data is retrieved.

The *where clause* includes only levels and members from the measures dimension.

The *group by clause* includes only levels and members from the measures dimension.

Finally, it is possible to include the keyword DISTINCT in the select clause.

```
SELECT DISTINCT select list
```

Microsoft acknowledges the following three "operational issues" regarding the use of the DISTINCT keyword and the *group by clause*.

- Neither the DISTINCT keyword nor the *group by clause* can be used if the *select list* contains members.

- DISTINCT may also cause some problems with levels in which duplicate rows can be returned. This problem is most likely to arise when the parent level or the root level contains more than one member. To avoid this situation, explicitly include all parents, and include as columns all dimensions with root levels having more than one member.

- The DISTINCT keyword and the *group by clause* may return duplicate rows if the server contains more than one segment.

SQL Functionality

OLAP Services only supports a subset of the overall SQL command syntax. As presented in the previous section, the FROM clause and the GROUP BY clause are simple and implemented at the most basic level. Because there are no joins necessary, the syntax in these two clauses is not complex. However, it is possible to use the SELECT clause and the WHERE toward more advanced functionality.

While the *select list* primarily consists of a list of column names, it can also include the DISTINCT clause as described above; it can include identifiers for the column names; and it can include aggregate functions COUNT¦MIN¦MAX¦SUM.

The following series of statements provide progressive, more complex (and powerful) use of SQL to retrieve data from a cube.

This first query returns the product family for all 86,805 rows of sales transactions:

```
SELECT [Product Family]
FROM Sales
```

This next query returns each different product family that has a sales transaction.

```
SELECT DISTINCT [Product Family]
FROM Sales
```

As seen in Figure 29.1, because there are three different and distinct product families, this query returns three rows.

29

USING SQL
QUERIES ON THE
OLAP SERVER

FIGURE 29.1

Using the
DISTINCT *keyword
returns each
distinct product
family.*

As this next example shows, it is also permissible to use an identifier to name the output column. This next query returns three rows (shown in Figure 29.2) for each different product department involved in the sales transactions.

```
SELECT DISTINCT [Product Family] as [Prod. Family.]
FROM Sales
```

FIGURE 29.2

*An identifier is
used to name the
output column.*

SQL statements with aggregate function are processed as expected by OLAP Services. The following query returns three rows with two columns.

```
SELECT
  [Product Family] as [Prod. Family.],
  SUM([Unit Sales])
FROM Sales
GROUP BY [Product Family]
```

As shown in Figure 29.3, the first column contains the distinct product families (because of the GROUP BY clause), and the second column contains the cumulative unit sales for each product department.

FIGURE 29.3

Including an aggregate function returns a column of appropriate numbers.

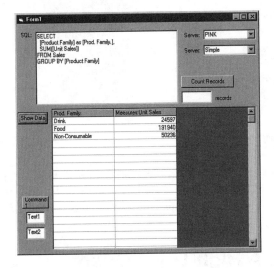

This next example extends the previous query by adding filter conditions. As in the previous query, three rows with two columns are returned, but the data is different in this case because of the WHERE clause.

```
SELECT
  [Product Family],
  SUM([Unit Sales])
FROM Sales
WHERE ([Store State] = 'OR') AND ([Year]='1997')
GROUP BY [Product Family]
```

The results of this query are shown in Figure 29.4.

From the perspective of the OLAP client, the cube functions similar to one very large fact table. Because of this fact, it is not necessary to explicitly define joins in SQL or in MDX queries. One of the primary functions of the OLAP Services engine is to transform a query that refers to a single cube into a query or set of queries in which the table's names and joins exist. In performing this function, OLAP Services removes a significant level of complexity from query generation.

29

USING SQL QUERIES ON THE OLAP SERVER

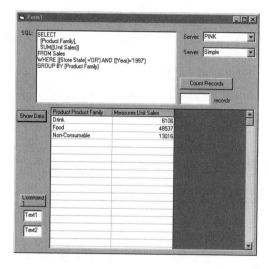

SQL Examples

To gain more insight into the execution of SQL statements with OLAP Services, it is useful to compare how SQL and MDX are applied to more real-world situations. The following four examples are make this comparison and demonstrate more complex SQL statements.

Example #1: A High-Level Query

It is important to keep in mind that when you use SQL as the query language, you **do not** employ two major capabilities of OLAP Services—aggregation and default members. As a result, a simple SQL query does not produce an aggregated result and does not use the default member, while a simple MDX query uses both.

This first example compares two simple, similar queries. The first is written in SQL, the second in MDX. Despite the fact that these two queries are similar in syntax and content, the performance and the results of the queries are radically different.

The SQL statement is:

```
SELECT
  [Gender].[Gender],
  [Product].[Product Family],
  [Measures].[Unit Sales]
FROM [Sales]
```

The recordset created with the SQL statement has 86,805 records, a portion of which is shown in Figure 29.5. Each row in the fact table is returned with three fields—gender, product family, and unit sales. The result transaction records are essentially useless from an OLAP perspective.

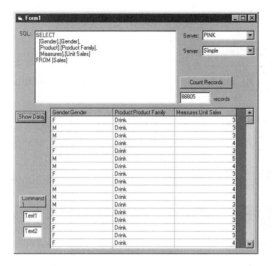

A similar, simple MDX statement is:

```
SELECT
 {[Gender].[Gender].Members} ON COLUMNS,
 {[Product].[Product Family].Members} ON ROWS
FROM [Sales]
WHERE ([Measures].[Unit Sales])
```

The dataset generated with the MDX statement has two columns, three rows, and six data points (see Figure 29.6). In contrast to the SQL recordset, the data returned from the MDX statement is extremely useful because of its aggregate nature.

To aggregate data within an SQL statement, it is necessary to use both the GROUP BY clause, and the Sum() function within the SELECT clause. The following SQL statement sums the unit sales data using the Gender column and the Product Family column.

```
SELECT
  [Product].[Product Family],
  [Gender].[Gender],
  Sum([Unit Sales])
FROM [Sales]
GROUP BY
  [Product].[Product Family] ,
  [Gender].[Gender]
```

The recordset resulting from this query is shown in Figure 29.7.

FIGURE 29.6

The MDX state-ment returns aggregate data.

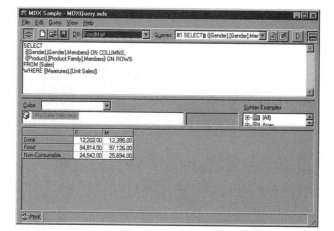

FIGURE 29.7

Aggregation of records with an SQL statement requires the GROUP BY clause.

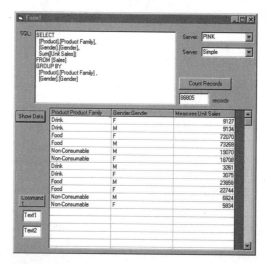

Note

Notice the fact that the resulting recordset returns 12 rows and is not complete-ly aggregated. This is a bug. As discussed earlier in this chapter, this is one of the "operational issues" identified by Microsoft OLAP Services.

The important concept to learn from this example is that it is necessary to explicitly define the aggregation to be performed when an SQL query is created. In contrast, MDX queries use an implicit aggregation when they are executed.

Example #2: A Low-Level Query

While the intent of the queries in Example #1 is to view highly aggregated data, this example is intended to compare the use of SQL and MDX when the goal is to retrieve transaction-level data.

To retrieve low-level data with a SQL statement, it is necessary to use a series of search or filter conditions in the WHERE clause. The following query retrieves specific records from the cube.

```
SELECT
  [Customers].[Name],
  [Store].[Store Name],
  [Measures].[Unit Sales]
FROM Sales
WHERE [Promotions].[Promotion Name]='No Promotion'
  AND [Time].[Month]='1'
  AND [Marital Status].[Marital Status]='M'
  AND [Gender].[Gender]='M'
  AND [Product].[Product Family]='Drink'
  AND [Education Level]='Bachelors Degree'
  AND [Yearly Income].[Yearly Income]='$30K - $50K'
  AND [Promotion Media].[Media Type]='No Media'
```

The resulting recordset is shown in Figure 29.8.

FIGURE 29.8

Using the WHERE clause in a SQL query retrieves detailed data.

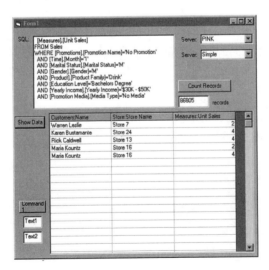

29

USING SQL
QUERIES ON THE
OLAP SERVER

An equivalent query written in MDX is actually very similar to the SQL statement. The MDX statement is:

```
SELECT
  {[Measures].[Unit Sales]} ON COLUMNS,
  Non Empty
  {CrossJoin([Customers].[Name].Members,[Store].[Store Name].members)}
  ON ROWS
FROM [Sales]
WHERE(
  [Time].[1997].[Q1].[1],
  [Marital Status].[All Marital Status].[M],
  [Gender].[All Gender].[M],
  [Product].[All Products].[Drink],
  [Education Level].[All Education Level].[Bachelors Degree],
  [Yearly Income].[All Yearly Income].[$30K - $50K],
  [Promotions].[All Promotions].[No Promotion],
  [Promotion Media].[All Media].[No Media])
```

It is **extremely** important to observe that this MDX query uses the keyword Non Empty
on the rows axis. Because the [Customers].[Name] level contains 10,281 members and
the [Store].[Store Name] level contains 24 members, the crossjoin of
[Customers].[Name] and [Store Name] produces a set of 246,744 tuples. If Non Empty
were not included on the rows axis, it would list all 246,744 tuples as rows.

However, in this case, because of the conditions in the WHERE clause of the MDX query,
all but four of these tuples have a null value for [Unit Sales]. The Non Empty clause
specifies that only non-empty tuples be returned, and the resulting dataset is shown in
Figure 29.9.

FIGURE 29.9

*Using the WHERE
clause in an MDX
query to retrieve
detailed data.*

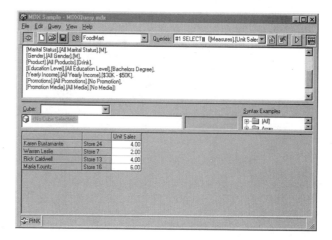

Example #3: A Typical OLAP Query

Some of the usefulness of OLAP Services is its ability to quickly retrieve aggregate data and display it directly in a crosstab format. This example shows a typical, simple MDX statement and the results.

The MDX statement retrieves the aggregate sum of all measures and displays them for each combination of product family and gender. Additionally, there is a slicer used to filter out all sales data generated while a promotion was active.

```
SELECT
 {[Measures].Members} ON COLUMNS,
 CrossJoin({[Product].[Product Family].Members}, {[Gender].[Gender].Members}) ON
ROWS
FROM [Sales]
WHERE ([Promotions].[All Promotions].[No Promotion])
```

The resulting recordset is shown in Figure 29.10.

FIGURE 29.10

The results of a typical MDX query are displayed.

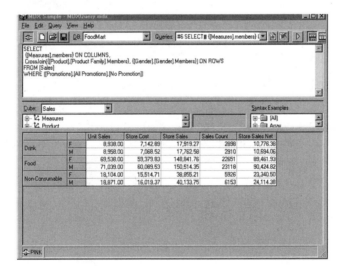

To write an equivalent SQL query it is necessary to specify all measures individually and construct an aggregate for each. The SQL statement must also contain a GROUP BY clause to perform the necessary aggregation.

The following SQL statement produces a recordset similar to the dataset produced by the MDX statement shown above.

```
SELECT
 [Product Family] as [Prod Family],
 [Gender] as [Gender],
```

```
  Sum([Unit Sales]),
  Sum([Store Cost]),
  Sum([Store Sales]),
  Sum([Sales Count]),
  Sum([Store Sales])
FROM Sales
WHERE ([Promotion Name]='No Promotion')
GROUP BY
  [Product Family],[Gender]
```

> **Note**
>
> It is important to note that the execution time of these two queries is approximately equivalent because both use the same OLAP cube. If the cube is configured to function as MOLAP system, the performance should be excellent because the information is pre-compiled. In contrast, if the cube is configured to function in a ROLAP mode, where the underlying relational database is needed, the performance will depend on the power of the RDBMS.

Example #4: Using a Stored Procedure with OLAP Services

Finally, Microsoft allows linking to an OLAP Server from within the SQL server database management system. This is accomplished with the use of the system stored procedure `sp_addlinkedserver`, and allows for the execution of distributed queries against OLE DB data sources connected to the linked OLAP server.

There are two methods of creating a linked server. The first method is to execute the following stored procedure with the appropriate parameters (for example, use the name of the desired server and database as the data source and the catalog).

```
EXEC sp_addlinkedserver
  @server='olap_server',
  @srvproduct='',
  @provider='MSOLAP',
  @datasrc='server',
  @catalog='foodmart'
```

The second method is to use the SQL Server Enterprise Manager. Register a server and expand the security node below the server. Right-click the linked servers node and follow the simple process of creating a linked server. Name the linked server; choose the Provider for OLAP Services; name the OLAP Server as the data source, and specify the catalog.

After you have successfully created a linked server, you can execute queries against it.

The following SQL statement could be executed on the linked server you just created.

```
SELECT *
FROM OPENQUERY (olap_server,
'SELECT [Store Name] FROM sales GROUP BY [Store Name]')
```

Summary

This chapter serves two purposes. First, it provides some information regarding the differences and similarities between SQL and MDX queries. Second, it forms the basis of a development technique that could be useful in solving specific problems encountered in the field.

The reader should make a point to understand the fundamental difference between MDX and SQL when submitting simple queries. Typically, an OLAP cube is configured so that MDX uses a high level of aggregation by default. In contrast, SQL returns granular data unless aggregation is explicitly defined.

MDX Reference

by Jim Pinkelman

In This Chapter

This chapter lists the functions and expressions which are available in Microsoft OLAP Services. While some of these functions are discussed in either Chapter 27 or 28, this list is comprehensive.

Throughout this chapter, the term function is used in its traditional manner to refer to a specific operation being performed on some set of data (Sum(), TopCount()). The term expression will be used to describe syntax in which the function is placed after the cube parameter ([1997].Children, [Products].DefaultMember).

MDX Functions and Expressions

The functions are listed in alphabetical order. Each contains a definition of the syntax of the function, a description of how the function operates, and an example of how the function is used. When functions use flags, these are also discussed.

Unless otherwise indicated, all examples use the FoodMart Sales cube that is available with the installation of Microsoft OLAP Services.

The AddCalculatedMembers() Function

Syntax: AddCalculatedMembers(*set*)

Description: The AddCalculatedMembers() function creates a set consisting of all members, including all calculated members within the specified *set*.

Example: The following statement produces a set consisting of both members and calculated members from the Measures dimension.

```
AddCalculatedMembers([Measures].Members)
```

yields

```
{[Profit], [Sales Average], [Unit Sales], [Store Cost], [Store Sales],
[Sales Count], [Store Sales Net]}
```

The Aggregate() Function

Syntax: Aggregate(*set*[, *numeric expression*])

Description: The Aggregate() function returns a numeric value using a variable aggregate function. The aggregate function is chosen based on the context of the query. Sum, max, min, and count are all available aggregate functions.

Example: Assuming two members, SumProfit and MaxProfit, have been added to the Measures dimension, the following statement uses Aggregate() to produce two different aggregate calculations (sum and max). Note that while the aggregate function can only be used in the WITH clause to create a calculated member, it cannot be used *on* a calculated member.

```
WITH MEMBER [Customers].[Total] as [sr]
AGGREGATE({[Customers].[CA],[Customers].[WA]})
SELECT {[Measures].[SumProfit], [Measures].[MaxProfit]} ON COLUMNS,
 {[Customers].[CA],[Customers].[WA]} ON ROWS FROM Sales
```

The Ancestor() Function

Syntax: Ancestor(*member*, *level*)

Description: The Ancestor() function retrieves the member at the specified level that is the ancestor (parent, parent of parent, and so on) of the specified member.

Example: The following statement produces the set consisting of the single member that is the ancestor of wine at the product department level.

```
Ancestor([Product].[All Products].[Drink].
[Alcoholic Beverages].[Beer and Wine].[Wine],
[Product].[Product Department])
```

yields

```
{[Product].[Product Department].[Alcoholic Beverages]}
```

The Avg() Function

Syntax: Avg(*set*[, *numeric expression*])

Description: The Avg() function returns the average of the tuples in the *set* based on the value of the *numeric expression*. Because this function returns a numeric value, it is almost exclusively used in building calculated members.

Example: The following statement produces a numeric value equal to the average sales count for each country.

```
Avg({[Customers].[Country].Members},[Sales Count])
```

The BottomCount() Function

Syntax: BottomCount(*set* ,*index* ,*numeric expression*)

Description: The BottomCount() function sorts the specified *set* based on the *numeric expression* in ascending rank order. It then creates a set using the top *index* items.

In the case of a tie between items, the hierarchy, or natural order, is used to return only *index* items. Other than ties, the hierarchy is ignored when performing this function. While information in other axes is not applied before the sort, slicers are applied prior to the sort.

Example: The following statement produces a set of the five product categories with the lowest unit sales listed in ascending order.

```
BottomCount({[Product Category].Members}, 5,[Unit Sales])
```

The BottomPercent() Function

Syntax: BottomPercent(*set, percentage, numeric expression*)

Description: The BottomPercent() function sorts the specified set based on the *numeric expression* in ascending rank order. It then builds a set of members from the top of the list such that the total of the members is at least *percentage* of the total set.

In the case of a tie between items, the highest items in the hierarchy, or natural order, are returned. Other than ties, the hierarchy is ignored when performing this function. While information in other axes is not applied before the sort, slicers are applied prior to the sort.

Example: The following statement sorts the set of all 24 stores, and builds a set of the stores with the lowest sales whose store sales make up the bottom 20% ($113,047.63) of the total store sales ($565,238.13).

```
BottomPercent({[Store].[Store Name].Members},
20, [Measures].[Store Sales])
```

The BottomSum() Function

Syntax: BottomSum(*set, value, numeric expression*)

Description: The BottomSum() function sorts the specified set based on the *numeric expression* in ascending rank order. It then builds a set of members from the top of the list such that the total of the members is at least equal to the specified *value*.

In the case of a tie between items, the highest items in the hierarchy, or natural order, are returned. Other than ties, the hierarchy is ignored when performing this function. While information in other axes is not applied before the sort, slicers are applied prior to the sort.

Example: The following statement sorts the set of all 24 stores, and builds a set of the stores with the lowest sales whose store sales add up at least $100,000.

```
BottomSum({[Store].[Store Name].Members},
100000, [Measures].[Store Sales])
```

The .Children Expression

Syntax: *member*.Children

Description: The .Children expression produces a set consisting of all members one level lower in the hierarchy than the specified *member*. The parent of all members in the resulting set is the specified *member*.

Example: The following statement produces the set of all members one level below USA whose parent is USA.

```
[Customers].[All Customers].[USA].Children
```

yields

```
{[CA],[OR],[WA]}
```

The ClosingPeriod() Function

Syntax: ClosingPeriod([*level*[, *member*]])

Description: The ClosingPeriod() function returns the last sibling among the descendants of a member at a level.

Example: The following statement returns the member at the month level that is the last period in the [1997].[Q1].

```
{ClosingPeriod([Time].[Month], [Time].[1997].[Q1])}
```

yields

```
{[Time].[1997].[Q1].[3]}
```

The CoalesceEmpty() Function

Syntax: CoalesceEmpty(*value expression*[,*value expression*])

Description: The CoalesceEmpty() function changes an empty cell into a string or a number specified by the value expression.

Example: Instead of returning an empty cell for unit sales in Canada and Mexico, the following statement returns cells with a zero.

```
With Member [Measures].[Sales]
 as 'CoalesceEmpty([Measures].[Unit Sales], 0)'
SELECT
```

```
{[Measures].[Sales]} on columns,
[Customers].[Country].members on rows
FROM Sales
```

The `Correlation()` Function

Syntax: `Correlation(set, numeric expression[,numeric expression])`

Description: The `Correlation()` function calculates the coefficient of correlation for a regression line. The function uses the *set* to obtain the numerical values used for the axes of the estimating equation. The first *numeric expression* is used as the y-axis, or dependent variable, and the second *numeric expression* is used as the x-axis, or independent variable.

When the second *numeric expression* is omitted, the members of the *set* are used for the x-axis. This situation occurs only with the Time dimension where the members have numeric value equivalents.

The `Correlation()` function ignores empty cells, cells containing text, and cells containing logical values. Cells with zero values are used in the calculation.

Example: The following statement produces a numeric value of `1.00`, the coefficient of correlation of the regression line where `[Profit]` is the y-axis and `[Store Sales]` is the x-axis for the months of 1997.

```
Correlation({Descendants([Time].[1997], [Month],SELF)},
[Profit], [Store Sales])
```

The `Count()` Function

Syntax: `Count(set[, EXCLUDEEMPTY ¦ INCLUDEEMPTY])`

Description: The `Count()` function returns the number of tuples in the specified *set*. `Count()` returns a numeric value.

By default, empty cells are counted (`INCLUDEEMPTY`). If empty cells are to be excluded from the count, use the `EXCLUDEEMPTY` keyword.

Example: The following statement produces a numeric value equal to the number of customer names. Note that in the FoodMart sales cube, this function will count a customer name for each purchase, and a single customer will be counted multiple times if he has made multiple purchases. (Also see the `Distinct` function.)

```
Count({[Customers].[Name].Members},EXCLUDEEMPTY)
```

The Cousin() Function

Syntax: Cousin(*member1*, *member2*)

Description: The Cousin() function returns a member that is a descendent under *member2* with the same relative relationship defined in *member1*.

The cousin function uses the level/member relationship defined in *Member1* to retrieve a member with the same relationship for *Member2*. The example shown below explains it best.

Example: The following statement produces the member below 1997 that has the same relationship with 1997 as the seventh month ([7]) has with 1998.

```
Cousin([Time].[1998].[Q3].[7],[1997])
```

yields

```
{[1997].[Q3].[7]}
```

While

```
Cousin([Product].[All Products].[Drink].[Alcoholic Beverages],[Food])
```

yields

```
[Product].[All Products].[Food].[Baked Goods]
```

because Alcoholic Beverages and Baked Goods are the first members under Drink and Food respectively.

The Covariance() Function

Syntax: Covariance(*set*, *numeric expression*[,*numeric expression*])

Description: The Covariance() function calculates the covariance of a regression line using the biased population. The function uses the *set* to obtain the numerical values used for the axes of the estimating equation. The first *numeric expression* is used as the y-axis, or dependent variable, and the second *numeric expression* is used as the x-axis, or independent variable.

When the second *numeric expression* is omitted, the members of the *set* are used for the x-axis. This situation occurs only with the Time dimension where the members have numeric value equivalents.

The Covariance() function ignores empty cells, cells containing text, and cells containing logical values. Cells with zero values are used in the calculation.

Example: The following statement produces a numeric value equal to the covariance of the regression line where [Profit] is the y-axis and [Store Sales] is the x-axis for the months of 1997.

```
Covariance({Descendants([Time].[1997],
[Month],SELF)}, [Profit], [Store Sales])
```

The CovarianceN() Function

Syntax: CovarianceN(*set, numeric expression*[,*numeric expression*])

Description: The CovarianceN() function calculates the covariance of a regression line using the unbiased population. The function uses the *set* to obtain the numerical values used for the axes of the estimating equation. The first *numeric expression* is used as the y-axis, or dependent variable, and the second *numeric expression* is used as the x-axis, or independent variable.

When the second *numeric expression* is omitted, the members of the *set* are used for the x-axis. This situation occurs only with the Time dimension where the members have numeric value equivalents.

The CovarianceN() function ignores empty cells, cells containing text, and cells containing logical values. Cells with zero values are used in the calculation.

Example: The following statement produces a numeric value equal to covariance of the regression line where [Profit] is the y-axis and [Store Sales] is the x-axis for the months of 1997.

```
CovarianceN({Descendants([Time].[1997],
[Month],SELF)}, [Profit], [Store Sales])
```

The CrossJoin() Function

Syntax: CrossJoin(*set1, set2*)

Description: The CrossJoin() function returns a set of tuples generated by the cross-product of the two specified input sets, *set1* and *set2*.

In other words, the CrossJoin() function creates a new set consisting of all of the combinations of the members in the two dimensions. The two input sets must exist in two independent dimensions.

Example: The following statement produces a set of all combinations of countries and genders. There are three members at the country level of the customers dimension (Canada, Mexico, and USA), and there are two members at the gender level of the gender dimension (F and M).

```
CrossJoin([Customers].[Country].Members, [Gender].[Gender].Members)
```

yields

```
{(Canada,F),(Canada,M),(Mexico,F),(Mexico,M),(USA,F),(USA,M)}
```

The .CurrentMember Expression

Syntax: *dimension*.CurrentMember

Description: The CurrentMember() function is used when iterating through a dimension (as is frequently done with the Generate() function). During an iteration, CurrentMember() returns the specified member associated with the current iterative step.

Example: The following statement produces a set by iterating through each member of the [Customers].[Country] level and applying the .Children function.

```
Generate([Customers].[Country].Members,
[Customers].CurrentMember.Children)
```

is equivalent to

```
{[Customers].[Canada].Children, [Customers].[Mexico].Children,
[Customers].[USA].Children}
```

The .DefaultMember Expression

Syntax: *dimension*.DefaultMember

Description: The .DefaultMember expression returns the member that is defined as the default member in the cube. In many cases the default member is usually defined as one of the members in the top level of a dimension or as All.

Example: The following statement returns the default member in the Time dimension.

```
[Time].DefaultMember
```

yields

```
[Time].[1997]
```

The Descendants() Function

Syntax: Descendants(*member*, *level*[, *DESC_FLAG*])

Description: The Descendants() function returns a set at the specified *level* using the dimension of the specified *member*.

The optional *DESC_FLAG* determines whether descendants at a particular level are included in the returned set. If no flag is included, the set will consist only of members at the specified level. Here are descriptions of the available flags and their effects:

Flag	Description
SELF	Default. Only members at *level* are returned.
AFTER	All descendant members below *level* are returned.
BEFORE	All descendant members between the *member* level and *level* are returned. Does not return members from the *level*.
BEFORE_AND_AFTER	All descendant members below the *member* level are returned. Does not return members from the *level*.
SELF_AND_AFTER	All descendant members at and below *level* are returned.
SELF_AND_BEFORE	All descendant members between the *member* level and *level* are returned.
SELF_BEFORE_AFTER	All descendant members below the *member* level are returned.

Example: The following statement produces a set of all states in the USA from the customer dimension.

```
Descendants([Customers].[All Customers].[USA],
[Customers].[State Province])
```

yields

```
{[Customers].[CA],[Customers].[OR],[Customers].[WA]}
```

The .Dimension Expression

Syntax: *hierarchy*.Dimension

level.Dimension

member.Dimension

Description: The .Dimension expression returns the dimension in which the specified *level* or *member* exists. The expression *hierarchy*.Dimension returns the hierarchy.

Example: The following statement returns the [Product], the dimension within which the level Drink exists.

```
[Drink].Dimension
```

yields

```
[Product]
```

The `Dimensions()` Function

Syntax: Dimensions(*numeric expression*)

Dimensions(*string expression*)

Description: The Dimensions() function returns the dimension specified by the *numeric expression* or *string expression*.

The *numeric expression* is the zero-based position of the dimension within the cube, while the *string expression* is the string equivalent of the dimension name. Note that the Measures dimension is always Dimensions(0).

Example: The following statement returns the [Store] dimension because it is the first dimension defined in the FoodMart sales cube.

```
Both Dimensions(1) and Dimensions("Store")
```

yield

```
[Store]
```

The `Distinct()` Function

Syntax: Distinct(*set*)

Description: The Distinct() function produces a set of members in which all duplicates from the original *set* are eliminated. By default, the first member of a duplicate pair of members is retained.

Example: The following statement eliminates the second occurrence of [Drink] in the original set.

```
Distinct({[Drink],[Food],[Drink]})
```

yields

```
{[Drink],[Food]}
```

The `DrilldownLevel()` Function

Syntax: DrilldownLevel(*set*[,*level*])

Description: The DrilldownLevel() function returns the original specified *set* and all of the children of the members of the *set* if the member is at the specified *level*.

If the optional *level* is not specified, the level of the lowest level member of the specified *set* is used. The resulting set follows the natural order.

As is true of most of the drill functions, `DrilldownLevel()` was created to allow a developer to directly translate a user's action into an MDX function.

Example: The following statement produces a set where Drink and Food are not drilled into (because they are not at the product department level), and Deli and Snacks are drilled into (because they *are* at the product department level).

```
DrilldownLevel({[Drink],[Food],[Deli],[Snacks]},
[Product].[Product Department])
```

yields

```
{[Drink],[Food],[Deli] ,[Meat] ,[Side Dishes],[Snacks],[Candy]}
```

An alternate syntax, `DrilldownLevel(set, ,index)`, which uses an *index* parameter, is also permissible when the set consists of tuples. When it is employed, the *index* is used to determine the dimension to be drilled using a zero-based numeric position in the set.

Example: The following statement produces a set of tuples containing 1997, the children of Drink and Food, and Female.

```
DrilldownLevel({([1997],[Drink] ,[F]),([1997],[Food],[F])},,1)
```

is equivalent to

```
Crossjoin({Crossjoin({[1997]},{[Drink],[Drink].Children,
[Food],[Food].Children})},{[F]})
```

The `DrilldownLevelBottom()` Function

Syntax: `DrilldownLevelBottom(set, count,[, level][, numeric expression)`

Description: The `DrilldownLevelBottom()` function drills down into the bottom *count* members of the *set* if the member is at the specified *level*. The *numeric expression* is used to rank the set in descending order.

As is true of most of the drill functions, `DrilldownLevelBottom ()` was created to allow a developer to directly translate a user's action into an MDX function.

Example: The following statement builds a set of all members in the `[Product Family]` and the single child with the lowest `[Unit Sales]` from each of these members.

```
DrilldownLevelBottom({[Product Family].members},1,,[Unit Sales])
```

The `DrilldownLevelTop()` Function

Syntax: `DrilldownLevelTop(set, count,[, level][, numeric expression)`

Description: The DrilldownLevelTop() function drills down into the top *count* members of the *set* if the member is at the specified *level*. The *numeric expression* is used to rank the set in descending order.

As is true of most of the drill functions, DrilldownLevelTop() was created to allow a developer to directly translate a user's action into an MDX function.

Example: The following statement builds a set of all members in the [Product Family] and the single child with the highest [Unit Sales] from each of these members.

DrilldownLevelTop({[Product Family].members},1,,[Unit Sales])

The DrilldownMember() Function

Syntax: DrilldownMember(*set1*, *set2*,[, RECURSIVE])

Description: The DrilldownMember() function drills into each member of *set1* that is also present in *set2*. If the RECURSIVE flag is used, the drilldown operation compares the resulting set with *set2* at each of the recursive steps. It is permissible for *set1* to contain tuples, in which case the results set contains tuples.

When implementing this function, the developer will find that *set1* is most often a subset of *set2*.

As is true of most of the drill functions, DrilldownLevel() was created to allow a developer to directly translate a user's action into an MDX function.

Example: The following statement drills into [Drink] because it is present in the [Product Family].members set.

DrilldownMember({[Drink]},{[Product Family].members})

yields

{[Drink],[Alcoholic Beverages],[Beverages],[Dairy]}

The DrilldownMemberBottom() Function

Syntax: DrilldownMember(*set1*, *set2*, *count*, [, *numeric expression*][, RECURSIVE])

Description: The DrilldownMember() function drills into each member of *set1* that is also present in *set2*. The results set is limited to the bottom *count* members based on the *numeric expression*. If the RECURSIVE flag is used, the drilldown operation compares the resulting set with *set2* at each of the recursive steps. It is permissible for *set1* to contain tuples, in which case the results set contains tuples.

30

MDX REFERENCE

When implementing this function, the developer will find that *set1* is most often a subset of *set2*.

As is true of most of the drill functions, DrilldownLevel() was created to allow a developer to directly translate a user's action into an MDX function.

Example: The following statement drills into [Drink] because it is present in the [Product Family].members set. It returns the two children of [Drink] that have the lowest [Unit Sales].

```
DrilldownMemberBottom({[Drink]},{[Product Family].members},
2, [Unit Sales])
```

yields

```
{[Drink],[Alcoholic Beverages],[Dairy]}
```

The DrilldownMemberTop() Function

Syntax: DrilldownMemberTop(*set1, set2, count*, [, *numeric expression*][, RECURSIVE])

Description: The DrilldownLevel() function returns the original specified *set* and all of the children of the members of the *set* if the member is at the specified *level*.

As is true of most of the drill functions, DrilldownLevel() was created to allow a developer to directly translate a user's action into an MDX function.

Example: The following statement drills into [Drink] because it is present in the [Product Family].members set. It returns the two children of [Drink] that have the highest [Unit Sales].

```
DrilldownMemberTop ({[Drink]},{[Product Family].members}, 2, [Unit Sales])
```

yields

```
{[Drink], [Beverages], [Alcoholic Beverages]}
```

The DrillupLevel() Function

Syntax: DrillupLevel(*set*[, *level*])

Description: The DrillupLevel() function drills up each member of the *set* that is below the specified *level*. If the *level* is not specified, it is assumed to be one level below the member of the *set* with the lowest level.

As is true of most of the drill functions, DrilldownLevel() was created to allow a developer to directly translate a user's action into an MDX function.

Example: The following statement drills up [Beverly Hills] because it is below the [Customers].[State Province] level.

```
DrillupLevel ({[Customers].[USA],[Customers].[CA],
[Customers].[Beverly Hills]}, [Customers].[State Province])
```

yields

```
{[USA],[CA]}
```

The DrillupMember() Function

Syntax: DrillupMember(*set1*, *set2*)

Description: The DrillupMember() function drills up all members in *set1* that are present in *set2*. When implementing this function, the developer will find that *set2* is most often a subset of *set1*.

As is true of most of the drill functions, DrilldownLevel() was created to allow a developer to directly translate a user's action into an MDX function.

Example: The following statement drills up members in *set1* that are also present in *set2*.

```
DrillupMember({[Customers].[Canada], [Customers].[USA],
[Customers].[WA], [Customers].[CA], [Customers].[Beverly Hills]},
{[Customers].[CA]})
```

yields

```
{[Canada],[USA],[WA],[CA]}
```

The Except() Function

Syntax: Except(*set1*, *set2*[, ALL])

Description: The Except() function produces a set consisting of the differences between the *set1* and *set2*. The set resulting from this function consists of members of the *set1* which are not in *set2*. By default, duplicates are eliminated, but the optional ALL can be used to retain duplicates.

Example: The following statement builds a set consisting of the members in *set1* that are not in *set2*.

```
Except({[Store 1], [Store 2], [Store 3], [Store 4]},
{[Store 2], [Store 5], [Store 6]})
```

yields

```
{[Store 1],[Store 3],[Store 4]}
```

The `Filter()` Function

Syntax: Filter(*set, search condition*)

Description: The `Filter()` function is used to filter a *set* based on a particular *search condition*.

Example: The following statement returns a set of product categories whose sales count is greater than 1000. The members in the set are arranged in their natural order.

```
{Filter({[Product Category].Members},([Sales Count])> 1000)}
```

The `.FirstChild` Expression

Syntax: *member*.FirstChild

Description: The `.FirstChild` expression returns the first child of the specified *member*.

Example: The following statement returns the first child of [USA].

```
{[Customers].[USA].FirstChild}
```

yields

```
{[Customers].[USA].[CA]}
```

The `.FirstSibling` Expression

Syntax: *member*.FirstSibling

Description: The `.FirstSibling` expression returns the first child of the parent of the *member*.

Example: The following statement returns the first state in [Customers].[USA].

```
{[Customers].[OR].FirstSibling}
```

yields

```
{[Customers].[CA]}
```

The `Generate()` Function

Syntax: Generate(*set, set expression[, ALL]*)

Description: The `Generate()` function provides a set by repeatedly applying the *set expression* to each member of the *set* provided.

By default, duplicates in the generated set are removed. If the optional ALL flag is used, the duplicates are retained.

Example: The following statement returns a set where the `Customers.CurrentMember.Children` is applied to each member of a set consisting of members of the `[Customers].[Country]` level.

```
{Generate([Customers].[Country].members,
Customers.CurrentMember.Children)}
```

is equivalent to

```
{[Customers].[Country].[Canada].children,
[Customers].[Country].[Mexico].children,
[Customers].[Country].[USA].children}
```

The `Head()` Function

Syntax: Head(*set*[, *numeric expression*])

Description: The `Head()` function returns the first *numeric expression* elements of the *set*. If omitted, *numeric expression* is assumed to be 1.

Example: The following statement returns the first two elements of the *set*.

```
Head({[USA],[CA],[WA],[Canada]}, 2)
```

yields

```
{[USA],[CA]}
```

The `Hierarchize()` Function

Syntax: Hierarchize(*set*)

Description: The `Hierarchize()` function is used to sort members by their natural order as defined in the cube's data structure. All duplicates in the specified set are retained.

Example: The customer dimension in the FoodMart Sales cube has a natural hierarchy that is alphabetically ordered. When `Hierarchize()` is applied to a set of customer members, the resulting set is sorted first by the hierarchy, then by level, and then alphabetically within a level. The statement

```
{Hierarchize({
  [Store].[All Stores].[USA].[CA].children,
  [Store].[All Stores].[Canada].[BC],
  [Store].[All Stores].[USA],
  [Store].[All Stores].[USA].[OR],
  [Store].[All Stores].[Mexico].[Guerrero].children})}
```

yields

```
{[BC],[Acapulco], [USA], [Beverly Hills], [Los Angeles],
[San Diego], [San Francisco], [OR]}
```

The `.Hierarchy` Expression

Syntax: *level*`.Hierarchy`

> *member*`.Hierarchy`

Description: The `.Hierarchy` expression returns the hierarchy of the specified *level* or *member*.

Example: The following statement returns [`All Products`], the hierarchy in which [`Drink`] exists.

```
[Product].[Product Family].[Drink].Hierarchy
```

yields

```
[Product].[All Products]
```

The `Iif()` Function

Syntax:

```
IIf(logical expression, numeric expression1, numeric expression2)

IIf(logical expression, string expression1, string expression2)
```

Description: The `Iif()` function returns one of two values based on a logical test. If the test is true, *numeric expression1 or string expression1* is returned. Otherwise, *numeric expression2 or string expression2* is returned.

Example: The best method of understanding the `Iif()` function is to use it in the context of an entire MDX query. The following query produces a cellset with three columns and two rows. The columns are the countries Canada, Mexico, and USA. The first row is unit sales. USA is the only country with a unit sales value. Both Canada and Mexico have empty cells for unit sales. The second row contains the calculated member that examines the unit sales for each country and assumes a value of "`No`" or "`Yes`". In this example, Canada and Mexico have "`No`" written in the second row because neither country has recorded unit sales. USA has "`Yes`" in the second row.

```
With Member [Measures].[Any Sales?]
 as 'iif(IsEmpty([Unit Sales]),"No","Yes")'
SELECT
Customers.[Country].members ON COLUMNS,
{[Unit Sales],[Measures].[Any Sales?]} ON ROWS
FROM Sales
```

The `Intersect()` Function

Syntax: `Intersect(set1, set2[, ALL])`

Description: The `Intersect()` function compares two sets and produces a set consisting of members that are in both of the original sets. Unless the optional `ALL` flag is included, all duplicates are eliminated from the sets prior to the intersection process.

Example: The following statement intersects two sets with members from the Product Family level.

```
Intersect({Drink}, {[Food],[Drink]})
```

yields

```
{[Drink]}
```

The `IsEmpty()` Function

Syntax: `IsEmpty(value expression)`

Description: The `IsEmpty()` function returns true if the `value expression` evaluates to an empty cell.

Example: The use of the `IsEmpty()` function is frequently used with the conditional `Iif()` function. The following query checks each cell to determine if is an empty cell and produces a "No" or "Yes" appropriately. The columns in the resulting cellset are the countries Canada, Mexico, and USA, and the first row is unit sales. In the cube, USA is the only country with a non-empty value for unit sales, because both Canada and Mexico have empty cells for unit sales.

The second row contains the calculated member that examines the unit sales for each country and assumes a value of "No" or "Yes". In this example, Canada and Mexico have "No" written in the second row because neither country has recorded unit sales, while USA has "Yes".

```
With Member [Measures].[Any Sales?]
 as 'iif(IsEmpty([Unit Sales]),"No","Yes")'
SELECT
Customers.[Country].members ON COLUMNS,
{[Unit Sales],[Measures].[Any Sales?]} ON ROWS
FROM Sales
```

The `.Item` Expression

Syntax: `tuple.Item(numeric expression)`

```
set.Item(string expression[,string expression …])
```

30

MDX REFERENCE

Description: In the first syntax, the `.Item` expression returns a member from the *tuple* based on the zero-based *numeric expression* position.

In the second syntax, the `.Item` expression returns the tuple from the *set*, as specified by the *string expression*.

Example: The following statement returns the second tuple in the set.

```
{[Product Family].Members.Item(1)}
```

yields

```
{[Food]}
```

while

```
{[Product Family].Members.Item("Food")}
```

yields

```
{[Food]}
```

The `.Lag()` Function

Syntax: *member*.Lag(*numeric expression*)

Description: The `.Lag()` function returns a member that is *numeric expression* positions before *member* in the *member*'s dimension. The positions of the members are zero-based and based on their natural order. In contrast, the `.Lead()` function returns a member after the specified *member*.

Example: The following statement returns the third month before `[1997].[Q2].[5]`.

```
[Time].[1997].[Q2].[5].Lag(3)
```

yields

```
[1997].[Q1].[2]
```

The `.LastChild` Expression

Syntax: *member*.LastChild

Description: The `.LastChild` expression returns the last child of the specified *member*.

Example: The following statement returns the last child of `[USA]`.

```
{[Customers].[USA].LastChild}
```

yields

```
{[Customers].[USA].[WA]}
```

The `LastPeriods()` Function

Syntax: LastPeriods(*index*[, *member*])

Description: The `LastPeriods()` function generates a set of members up to and including the specified *member*. While the `PeriodsToDate()` function returns all members back to the beginning of a period, `LastPeriods()` returns the number of members specified by an *index* value.

While it is not recommended, if the optional [*member*] is omitted, then `Time.CurrentMember` is used.

If the *index* is zero an empty set is returned.

Future periods can be obtained by using an *index* which is negative. For example, an index of –3 would yield the next three periods beginning with the specified *member*.

The set generated by `LastPeriods()` can cross the boundaries of periods.

Example: The following statement produces a set of the last two months within the first quarter ending with the specified month.

```
LastPeriods(2,[Time].[1998].[Q1].[3])
```

yields

```
{[Time].[1998].[Q1].[2],[Time].[1998].[Q1].[3]}
```

The `.LastSibling` Expression

Syntax: *member*.LastSibling

Description: The `.LastSibling` expression returns the last child of the parent of the *member*.

Example: The following statement returns the first state in [Customers].[USA].

```
{[Customers].[OR].LastSibling}
```

yields

```
{[Customers].[WA]}
```

The `.Lead()` Function

Syntax: *member*.Lead(*numeric expression*)

Description: The `.Lead()` function returns a member that is *numeric expression* positions after the *member* in the *member*'s dimension. The positions of the members are zero-based and based on their natural order. In contrast, the `.Lag()` function returns a member before the specified *member*.

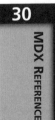

Example: The following statement returns the third month after `[1997].[Q2].[5]`.

```
[Time].[1997].[Q2].[5].Lead(3)
```

yields

```
[1997].[Q3].[8]
```

The `.Level` Expression

Syntax: *member*`.Level`

Description: The `.Level` expression returns the level of the specified *member*.

Example: The following statement returns the level in which `[Bag Stuffers]` exists.

```
[Promotions].[All Promotions].[Bag Stuffers].Level
```

yields

```
[Promotions].[Promotion Name]
```

The `Levels()` Function

Syntax: `Levels(`*string expression*`)`

               dimension`.Levels(`*numeric expression*`)`

Description: As shown in the first syntax, the `Levels()` function returns the level specified by the *string expression*.

In the second syntax, the `.Levels()` function returns the level from the *dimension* based on the zero-based *numeric expression* position.

Example: Both of the following statements return the Month Level in the Time dimension.

```
Both Levels("Month") and Time.Levels(2) yield the level
[Time].[Month]
```

The `LinRegIntercept()` Function

Syntax: `LinRegIntercept(`*set, numeric expression*`[, `*numeric expression*`])`

Description: The `LinRegIntercept()` function calculates the y-intercept of the regression line (b in y = ax +b). The function uses the *set* to obtain the numerical values used for the axes of the estimating equation. The first *numeric expression* is used as the y-axis, or dependent variable, and the second *numeric expression* is used as the x-axis, or independent variable.

When the second *numeric expression* is omitted, the members of the *set* are used for the x-axis. This situation occurs only with the Time dimension where the members have numeric value equivalents.

Example: The following statement returns a numeric value of 62.37, the y-intercept of the regression line where [Profit] is the y-axis and [Store Sales] is the x-axis for the months of 1997.

```
LinRegIntercept({Descendants([Time].[1997],
[Time].[Month],SELF)}, [Profit], [Store Sales])
```

The `LinRegPoint()` Function

Syntax: LinRegPoint(*numeric expression, set, numeric expression[, numeric expression]*)

Description: The LinRegPoint() function is used to estimate a dependent (y) value given an estimating regression line. The function requires an independent value (x) and the data necessary to perform a curve fit. The syntax of the LinRegPoint() function varies slightly from the other linear regression functions.

The first *numeric expression* is the x value, while the *set* is used to build the data set for the curve fit. As with all of the other linear regression functions, the first *numeric expression* is the y-axis and the second *numeric expression* is the x-axis.

Example: The following clause estimates the profit (y-axis) given store sales of $55,000 (x-axis). Based on the slope and y-intercept values, the regression line is y = (0.60)(x) + 62.37. For store sales of $55,000, the estimated profit is $33,035.08. (Beware of rounding errors!)

```
LinRegPoint(55000,{Descendants([Time].[1997],
[Time].[Month], SELF)}, [Profit], [Store Sales])
```

The `LinRegR2()` Function

Syntax: LinRegR2(*set, numeric expression[, numeric expression]*)

Description: The LinRegR2() function calculates the coefficient of determination (R^2) for the regression line. The function uses the *set* to obtain the numerical values used for the axes of the estimating equation. The first *numeric expression* is used as the y-axis, or dependent variable, and the second *numeric expression* is used as the x-axis, or independent variable.

When the second *numeric expression* is omitted, the members of the *set* are used for the x-axis. This situation occurs only with the time dimension where the members have numeric value equivalents.

30

MDX REFERENCE

Example: The following statement returns a numeric value of 1.00, the coefficient of determination of the regression line where [Profit] is the y-axis and [Store Sales] is the x-axis for the months of 1997.

```
LinRegR2({Descendants([Time].[1997],
[Time].[Month],SELF)}, [Profit], [Store Sales])
```

The `LinRegSlope()` Function

Syntax: LinRegSlope(*set, numeric expression[, numeric expression]*)

Description: The LinRegSlope() function calculates the slope of the regression line (b in y = ax +b). The function uses the *set* to obtain the numerical values used for the axes of the estimating equation. The first *numeric expression* is used as the y-axis, or dependent variable, and the second *numeric expression* is used as the x-axis, or independent variable.

When the second *numeric expression* is omitted, the members of the *set* are used for the x-axis. This situation occurs only with the Time dimension where the members have numeric value equivalents.

Example: The following statement returns a numeric value of 0.60, the slope of the regression line where [Profit] is the y-axis and [Store Sales] is the x-axis for the months of 1997.

```
LinRegSlope({Descendants([Time].[1997],
 [Time].[Month],SELF)}, [Profit], [Store Sales])
```

The `LinRegVariance()` Function

Syntax: LinRegVariance(*set, numeric expression[, numeric expression]*)

Description: The LinRegSlope() function calculates the variance of the regression line in the curve fit. The function uses the *set* to obtain the numerical values used for the axes of the estimating equation. The first *numeric expression* is used as the y-axis, or dependent variable, and the second *numeric expression* is used as the x-axis, or independent variable.

When the second *numeric expression* is omitted, the members of the *set* are used for the x-axis. This situation occurs only with the Time dimension where the members have numeric value equivalents.

Example: The following clause returns a numeric value of 864.42, the variance of the regression line where [Profit] is the y-axis and [Store Sales] is the x-axis for the months of 1997.

```
LinRegVariance({Descendants([Time].[1997],
[Time].[Month],SELF)}, [Profit], [Store Sales])
```

The Max() Function

Syntax: Max(*set*[, *numeric expression*])

Description: The Max() function returns the maximum value of the *numeric expression* for the members of the *set*. Because this function returns a numeric value, it is almost exclusively used in building calculated members. Empty cells are ignored in this calculation.

Example: The following statement returns the unit sales value for the month with the maximum unit sales.

```
Max([Month].Members,[Unit Sales])
```

yields

```
26,796.00
```

which is the unit sales for [1997].[Q4].[12], the month with the maximum unit sales.

The Median() Function

Syntax: Median(*set*[, *numeric expression*])

Description: The Median() function returns the median value of the *numeric expression* for the members of the *set*. Because this function returns a numeric value, it is almost exclusively used in building calculated members. Empty cells are ignored in this calculation.

Example: The following statement returns the median unit sales value for all of the months.

```
Median([Month].Members,[Unit Sales])
```

yields

```
21,489.00
```

The .Members Expression

Syntax: *dimension*.Members

    hierarchy.Members

    level.Members

30

MDX REFERENCE

Description: .Members is a particularly useful MDX expression that provides a simple method of a complete drilldown. This expression returns a set of enumerated members from within a dimension, hierarchy, or level.

Example: The following statement results in a set of all members of the Time dimension from each level. Each time period (years, quarters, and months) is included in the set.

```
[Time].Members
```

The Members() Function

Syntax: Members(*string expression*)

Description: The Members() function returns the member specified by the *string expression*.

Example: The following statement returns the member [Product].[All Products].[Drink].

```
Members("Drink")
```

The Min() Function

Syntax: Min(*set*[, *numeric expression*])

Description: The Min() function returns the minimum value of the *numeric expression* for the members of the *set*. Because this function returns a numeric value, it is almost exclusively used in building calculated members. Empty cells are ignored in this calculation.

Example: The following statement returns the unit sales value for the month with the minimum unit sales.

```
Min([Month].Members,[Unit Sales])
```

yields

```
19,958.00
```

which is the unit sales for [1997].[Q4].[10], the month with the minimum unit sales.

The MTD() Function

Syntax: MTD([*member*])

Description: The MTD() function, month-to-date, operates on a *member* of the Time dimension, and returns a set beginning with the first time period of the month and ending with the *member* time period. The set consists of all members up to and including the specified *member*. Only members that are at the same level as the *member* are returned.

Although it is not recommended, if no member is specified, the default member is Time.CurrentMember.

Example: If day is a level in the Time dimension, the following statement returns a set of days from the first day in [1997].[Q2].[5] to [1997].[Q2].[5].[3].

```
MTD([Time].[1997].[Q2].[5].[3])
```

yields

```
{[1997].[Q2].[5].[1], [1997].[Q2].[5].[2], [1997].[Q2].[5].[3]}
```

The .Name Expression

Syntax: *dimension*.Name

          hierarchy.Name

          level.Name

          member.Name

Description: The .Name expression returns the name of the *dimension*, *hierarchy*, *level*, or *member*. Because this function returns a string value, it is almost exclusively used in building calculated members.

Example: The following statement returns the string equal to the parent of [CA].

```
[Customers].[All Customers].[USA].[CA].Parent.Name
```

yields

```
"[Customers].[All Customers].[USA]"
```

The .NextMember Expression

Syntax: *member*.NextMember

Description: The .NextMember expression uses the natural order of a level to retrieve the next member within the same level as the *member* upon which .NextMember operates.

Example: In the FoodMart Sales cube, the three members of the [Customers].[Country] level are Canada, Mexico, and USA in their natural order. The following statement retrieves the member USA.

```
[Customers].[All Customers].[Mexico].NextMember
```

yields

```
[Customers].[All Customers].[USA]
```

The NON EMPTY Keyword

Syntax: NON EMPTY *axis specification* ON *axis*

Description: Depending on the situation, it may be important for the end user to see that there is no data at these points or the user may want to see only cells in which there are data.

The NON EMPTY keyword in an MDX query allows these empty cells to be filtered out of the dataset. NON EMPTY is used on an entire axis and, in the MDX query, it precedes the *axis specification*.

Example: In the FoodMart Sales cube, there are three countries, Canada, Mexico, and USA and two years, 1997 and 1998. There are six combinations of these two dimensions. Of the six combinations, only {USA, 1997} has a value. All other combinations result in NULL values.

Therefore, the following query returns a cellset with six cells, five of which are empty.

```
SELECT
 {[Customers].[Country].Members} ON COLUMNS,
 {[Time].[Year].Members} ON ROWS
FROM [Sales]
```

Adding the NON EMPTY keyword to this query returns a cellset with only one cell.

```
SELECT
NON EMPTY {[Customers].[Country].Members} ON COLUMNS,
NON EMPTY {[Time].[Year].Members} ON ROWS
FROM [Sales]
```

The OpeningPeriod() Function

Syntax: OpeningPeriod([*level*[, *member*]])

Description: The OpeningPeriod() function returns the first sibling among the descendants of a *member* at a *level*.

Example: The following statement returns the member at the month level that is the last period in [1997].[Q1].

```
{OpeningPeriod([Time].[Month], [Time].[1997].[Q1])}
```

yields

```
{[Time].[1997].[Q1].[1]}
```

The Order() Function

Syntax:

```
Order(set, string expression [,ASC ¦ DESC ¦ BASC ¦ BDESC])

Order(set, numeric expression [,ASC ¦ DESC ¦ BASC ¦ BDESC])
```

Description: The Order() function provides sorting capabilities within the MDX language. The sort can either be performed within the natural hierarchy (ASC and DESC), or it can ignore the hierarchy (BASC and BDESC). The leading "B" indicates break hierarchy.

When a hierarchized order is used, the members at each level of the dimension are sorted relative to other members of the same level. Therefore, if CA sales are greater than OR sales, Beverly Hills, CA will always precede Portland, OR. When a non- hierarchized order is used, all members in the set are sorted independently of the level in which they reside. Therefore, if Portland, OR Sales are greater than CA, Portland will precede California.

Example: The following statement returns a set of all product categories types sorted in descending order. The measure [Unit Sales] is used as the sorting criteria, and because BDESC is used, the natural hierarchy in the product category is ignored when the sort is performed.

```
Order([Product].[Product Category].Members,[Unit Sales],BDESC)
```

The .Ordinal Expression

Syntax: *level*.Ordinal

Description: The .Ordinal expression returns the zero-based ordinal value associated with the specified *level*.

Example: The following statement returns an ordinal value of 2 because product department is the third level in the product dimension.

```
[Product].[Product Department].Ordinal
```

The ParallelPeriod() Function

Syntax: ParallelPeriod([*level*[, *numeric expression*[, *member*]]])

30

MDX REFERENCE

Description: The `ParallelPeriod()` function starts by taking the ancestor of specified *member* at specified *level*. It then lags the sibling of that *level* by the *numeric expression* to find a parallel period of the original *member*.

This function is typically used with times series operations.

The default member is `Time.CurrentMember` if a level is not specified. If a level is specified, the default member is *dimension*.`CurrentMember` where *member*'s *dimension* is used.

The default *numeric expression* is 1, and the default *level* is the level of the parent of the *member*.

Example: The following statement finds a parallel member to [1997].[Q2].[5] in the previous quarter.

```
ParallelPeriod([Quarter],1,[Time].[1997].[Q2].[5])
```

yields

```
[Time].[1997].[Q1].[2]
```

The `.Parent` Expression

Syntax: *member*.`Parent`

Description: The `.Parent` expression retrieves the parent member of the specified *member*. The parent is one level higher than the *member* upon which this function operates.

Example: The following statement retrieves the parent member of the member `[Customers].[All Customers].[USA]`.

```
[Customers].[All Customers].[USA].[CA].Parent
```

yields

```
[Customers].[All Customers].[USA]
```

The `PeriodsToDate()` Function

Syntax: `PeriodsToDate([`*level*`[,`*member*`]])`

Description: The `PeriodsToDate()` function is similar to the other to-date functions. However, the syntax includes the specification on a level. This function returns a set of members up to and including the specified *member* that are within the specified *level*.

Although it is not recommended, if no member is specified, the default member is `Time.CurrentMember`.

Example: The following statement produces a set of months within the quarter of the specified month.

```
PeriodsToDate([Time].[Quarter],[Time].[1997].[Q3].[8])
```

yields

```
{[Time].[1997].[Q3].[7], [Time].[1997].[Q3].[8]}
```

The .PrevMember Expression

Syntax: *member*.PrevMember

Description: The .PrevMember expression uses the natural order of a level to retrieve the next member within the same level as the *member* upon which .PrevMember operates.

Example: In the FoodMart Sales cube, the three members of the [Customers].[Country] level are Canada, Mexico, and USA in their natural order. The following statement retrieves the member Canada.

```
Example: [Customers].[All Customers].[Mexico].PrevMember
```

yields

```
[Customers].[All Customers].[Canada]
```

The QTD() Function

Syntax: QTD([*member*])

Description: The QTD() function, quarter-to-date, operates on a *member* of the Time dimension, and returns a set beginning with the first time period of the quarter and ending with the *member* time period. The set consists of all members up to and including the specified *member*. Only members that are at the same level as the *member* are returned.

Although it is not recommended, if no member is specified, the default member is Time.CurrentMember.

Example: The following statement returns a set of months from the first month in [1997].[Q2] through [1997].[Q2].[5].

```
QTD([Time].[1997].[Q2].[5])
```

yields

```
{[Time].[1997].[Q2].[4] , [Time].[1997].[Q2].[5]}
```

The Rank() Function

Syntax: Rank(*tuple*, *set*)

Description: The Rank() function returns the one-based rank of the specified *tuple* in the *set*.

Example: The following statement returns 3 because the tuple ([CA],[F]) is the third tuple in the set.

```
Rank(([CA],[F]),{([CA],[M]), ([OR],[F]), ([CA],[F]), ([WA],[F])}
```

The SetToStr() Function

Syntax: SetToStr(*set*)

Description: The SetToStr() function builds a string from the specified *set*. The result of this function is a string.

Example: The following statement creates a string listing the two members of the [Gender].[Gender] level.

```
SetToStr([Gender].[Gender].members)
```

yields

```
"[Gender].[All Gender].[F], Gender].[All Gender].[M]"
```

The Stddev() or Stdev() Function

Syntax: Stddev(*set*[, *numeric expression*])

Description: The Stddev() and Stdev() functions return the unbiased standard deviation of the *numeric expression* for the members of the *set*. These functions can be used interchangeably. Because this function returns a numeric value, it is almost exclusively used in building calculated members. Empty cells are ignored in this calculation.

Example: The following statement returns the standard deviation of the unit sales value for all of the months.

```
Stddev([Month].Members,[Unit Sales])
```

yields

```
2,168.82
```

The `StddevP()` or `StdevP()` Function

Syntax: StddevP(*set*[, *numeric expression*])

Description: The StddevP() and StdevP() functions return the biased standard deviation of the *numeric expression* for the members of the *set*. These functions can be used interchangeably. Because this function returns a numeric value, it is almost exclusively used in building calculated members. Empty cells are ignored in this calculation.

Example: The following statement returns the biased standard deviation of the unit sales value for all of the months.

```
StddevP([Month].Members,[Unit Sales])
```

yields

```
2,076.49
```

The `StripCalculatedMembers()` Function

Syntax: StripCalculatedMembers(*set*)

Description: The StripCalculatedMembers() returns the set resulting from removing all calculated members from the specified *set*.

Example: The following statement removes the calculated member, Profit, from the set.

```
StripCalculatedMembers({[Profit],[Store Sales Net]})
```

yields

```
{[Store Sales Net]}
```

The `StrToSet()` Function

Syntax: StrToSet(*string expression*)

Description: The StrToSet() function creates a set from the *string expression*.

Example: The following statement creates a set consisting of the product family members.

```
StrToSet("[Product Family].Members")
```

yields

```
{[Drink],[Food],[Non-Consumables]}
```

30

MDX REFERENCE

The `StrToTuple()` Function

Syntax: StrToTuple(*string expression*)

Description: The StrToTuple() function creates a tuple from the *string expression*.

Example: The following statement creates a tuple consisting of [1997] and [Drink].

```
StrToTuple("([1997],[Drink])")
```

yields

```
([1997],[Drink])
```

The `Subset()` Function

Syntax: Subset(*set, start*[, *count*])

Description: The Subset() function constructs a set by iterating through the elements in the specified *set* and adding them to the new set. The iteration is zero-based; it begins with *start* and continues for *count* iterations. If the optional *count* is not specified, the iteration continues to the end of the set.

Example: The following statement iterates through the set of states beginning with the second state and making two iterations.

```
Subset({[CA],[OR],[WA]},1,2)
```

yields

```
{[OR],[WA]}
```

The `Sum()` Function

Syntax: Sum(*set*[,*numeric expression*])

Description: The Sum() function returns the sum of a *numeric expression* over a *set*. Although the *numeric expression* is optional, it is recommended that it always be included to avoid ambiguity. Sum() returns a numeric value.

Example: The following statement totals the [Units Sales] of the first two quarters of [Time].[1997]

```
Sum({[Time].[1997].[Q1], [Time].[1997].[Q2]}, [Unit Sales])
```

The `ToggleDrillState()` Function

Syntax: ToggleDrillState(*Set1, Set2*[, RECURSIVE])

Description: The `ToggleDrillState()` function reverses the drill state of every member in *Set2* that is also in *Set1*. If the member in *Set1* has descendants, the DrillUpMember() function is applied. Conversely if the member in *Set1* has no descendants, the `DrillDownMember()` function is applied.

As is true of most of the drill functions, `ToggleDrillState()` was created to allow a developer to directly translate a user's action into an MDX function.

Example: The following statement drills down into CA because it is present in *Set2* and does not have descendants in *Set1*. Neither OR or WA are drilled into because they are not present in *Set2*.

```
ToggleDrillState({[Customers].[USA].Children},{[Customers].[USA].[CA]})
```

is equivalent to

```
{[Customers].[USA].[CA], [Customers].[USA].[CA].Children,
[Customers].[USA].[OR], [Customers].[USA].[WA]}
```

The `Tail()` Function

Syntax: Tail(*set*[, *count*])

Example: The following statement builds a set with the last two members of the original set.

```
Tail({[CA],[OR],[WA]},2)
```

yields

```
{[OR],[WA]}
```

The `TopCount()` Function

Syntax: TopCount(*set* ,*index* ,*numeric expression*)

Description: The `TopCount()` function sorts the specified *set* based on the *numeric expression* in descending rank order. It then creates a set using the top *index* items.

In the case of a tie between items, the hierarchy, or natural order is used to return only *index* items. Other than ties, the hierarchy is ignored when performing this function. While information in other axes is not applied before the sort, slicers are applied prior to the sort.

Example: The following statement produces a set of the five product categories with the highest unit sales listed in descending order.

```
TopCount({[Product Category].Members}, 5,[Unit Sales])
```

30

MDX REFERENCE

The `TopPercent()` Function

Syntax: TopPercent(*set, percentage, numeric expression*)

Description: The TopPercent() function sorts the specified *set* based on the *numeric expression* in descending rank order. It then builds a set of members from the top of the list such that the total of the members is at least *percentage* of the total set.

Example: The following statement sorts the set of all 24 stores, and builds a set of the stores with the highest sales whose store sales make up the top 80% ($452,190.50) of the total store sales ($565,238.13).

```
TopPercent({[Store].[Store Name].Members}, 80, [Measures].[Store Sales])
```

The `TopSum()` Function

Syntax: TopSum(*set, value, numeric expression*)

Description: The TopSum() function sorts the specified *set* based on the *numeric expression* in descending rank order. It then builds a set of members from the top of the list such that the total of the members is at least equal to the specified *value*.

In the case of a tie between items, the highest items in the hierarchy, or natural order, are returned. Other than ties, the hierarchy is ignored when performing this function. While information in other axes is not applied before the sort, slicers are applied prior to the sort.

Example: The following statement sorts the set of all 24 stores, and builds a set of the stores with the highest sales whose store sales add up at least $500,000.

```
TopSum({[Store].[Store Name].Members}, 500000, [Measures].[Store Sales])
```

The `TupleToStr()` Function

Syntax: TupleToStr(*tuple*)

Description: The TupleToStr() function builds a string from the specified *tuple*.

Example: The following statement creates a string from the tuple ([Drink],[WA]).

```
SetToStr([Drink],[WA])
```

yields

```
"([Drink],[WA])"
```

The Union() Function

Syntax: Union(*set1*, *set2*[, ALL])

Description: The Union() function combines two sets into one. The original sets must be from the same dimension. By default, the Union() function eliminates all duplicates from the resulting set. The optional ALL flag can be used to retain the duplicates.

Example: The following statement combines two members from the Product Family level.

```
Union({Food}, {Drink}, ALL)
```

yields

```
{[Food], [Drink]}
```

The .UniqueName Expression

Syntax: *dimension*.UniqueName

      level.UniqueName

      member.UniqueName

Description: The .UniqueName expression returns the unique name of a *dimension*, *level*, or *member*. The UniqueName is defined when the cube is created and is unique within the database.

Example: The following returns the unique name of the product department named "Alcoholic Beverages."

```
[Alcoholic Beverages].UniqueName
```

yields

```
[Product].[All Products].[Drink].[Alcoholic Beverages]
```

The Var() or Variance() Function

Syntax: Var(*set*[, *numeric expression*])

Description: The Var () and Variance() functions return the unbiased variance of the *numeric expression* for the members of the *set*. These functions can be used interchangeably. Because this function returns a numeric value, it is almost exclusively used in building calculated members. Empty cells are ignored in this calculation.

Example: The following statement returns the variance of the unit sales value for all of the months.

```
Var([Month].Members,[Unit Sales])
```

yields

```
4,703,798.08
```

The `VarP()` or `VarianceP()` Function

Syntax: VarP(*set*[, *numeric expression*])

Description: The VarP () and VarianceP() functions return the biased variance of the *numeric expression* for the members of the *set*. These functions can be used interchangeably. Because this function returns a numeric value, it is almost exclusively used in building calculated members. Empty cells are ignored in this calculation.

Example: The following statement returns the biased variance of the unit sales value for all of the months.

```
VarP([Month].Members,[Unit Sales])
```

yields

```
4,311,814.91
```

The `WTD()` Function

Syntax: WTD(*member*)

Description: The WTD() function, week-to-date, operates on a *member* of the Time dimension, and returns a set beginning with the first time period of the week and ending with the *member* time period. The set consists of all members up to and including the specified *member*. Only members on the same level as *member* are returned.

Although it is not recommended, if no member is specified, the default member is Time.CurrentMember.

Example: If weeks and days are levels in the time dimension, the following statement returns a set of days from the first day of the week [1997].[4] to the third day of [1997].[4].

```
WTD([Time].[1997].[4].[3])
```

yields

```
{[Time].[1997].[4].[1], [Time].[1997].[4].[2], [Time].[1997].[4].[3]}
```

The YTD() Function

Syntax: YTD([*member*])

Description: The YTD() function, year-to-date, operates on a *member* of the Time dimension, and returns a set beginning with the first time period of the year and ending with the *member* time period. The set consists of all members up to and including the specified *member*. Only members that are at the same level as *member* are returned.

Although it is not recommended, if no member is specified, the default member is Time.CurrentMember.

Example: The following statement returns a set of all quarters in 1997 up to and including the third quarter.

```
YTD([Time].[1997].[Q3])
```

yields

```
{[Time].[1997].[Q1], [Time].[1997].[Q2], [Time].[1997].[Q3]}
```

MDX Functions and Expressions by Functionality

The following listing is my attempt at grouping the MDX functions by their general functionality. These listings make it possible to see all of the numerical functions at a glance.

Dimension, Hierarchy, Level Functions and Expressions

.Dimension expression

Dimensions() function

.Hierarchy expression

.Level expression

Levels() function

Drill Functions

DrilldownLevel() function

DrilldownLevelBottom() function

DrilldownLevelTop() function

DrilldownMember() function

DrilldownMemberBottom() function

30

MDX REFERENCE

DrilldownMemberTop() function

DrillupLevel() function

DrillupMember() function

ToggleDrillState() function

Logical Functions

IiF() function

IsEmpty() function

Member Functions and Expressions

Ancestor() function

ClosingPeriod() function

Cousin() function

.CurrentMember expression

.DefaultMember expression

.FirstChild expression

.FirstSibling expression

.Item expression

.Lag() function

.LastChild expression

.LastSibling expression

.Lead() function

Members() function

.NextMember expression

OpeningPeriod() function

ParallelPeriod() function

.Parent expression

.PrevMember expression

Numeric Functions and Expressions

Aggregate() function

Avg() function

Count() function

Iif() function

Max() function

Median() function

Min() function

.Ordinal expression

Rank() function

Sum() function

Set Functions and Expressions

AddCalculatedMembers() function

BottomCount() function

BottomPercent() function

BottomSum() function

.Children expression

CrossJoin() function

Descendants() function

Distinct() function

Except() function

Filter() function

Generate() function

Head() function

Hierarchize() function

Intersect() function

.Members expression

Order() function

StripCalculatedMembers() function

StrToSet() function

Subset() function

Tail() function

TopCount() function

TopPercent() function

TopSum() function

Union() function

String Functions and Expressions

CoalesceEmpty() function

.Name expression

SetToStr() function

TupleToStr() function

.UniqueName expression

Time Functions

LastPeriods() function

MTD() function

PeriodsToDate() function

QTD() function

WTD() function

YTD() function

Time Series Analysis Functions

Correlation() function

Covariance() function

CovarianceN() function

LinRegIntercept() function

LinRegPoint() function

LinRegR2() function

LinRegSlope() function

LinRegVariance() function

Stddev() function

StddevP() function

Stdev() function

StdevP() function

Var() function

Variance() function

VarianceP() function

VarP() function

Tuple Functions and Expressions

.Item expression

StrToTuple() function

Summary

Clearly, a rich set of functions is defined in the MDX language. In fact, despite the fact that MDX OLAP clients have been in development for almost two years, there are no current clients that allow easy access to all of the functions.

Finally, expect the list of functions to grow as the OLE DB for OLAP specification becomes more widely accepted, more mature, and as users demand more diverse functionality out of their OLAP applications.

Managing a Data Warehousing System

PART VII

IN THIS PART

Performance Issues

by Russell Darroch and Shane Swamer

In This Chapter

CHAPTER 31

Some people do not get much of a kick out of talking about performance issues—by and large, such people are called "users" or "clients," and their only interest in performance is whether it is fast or not. These people simply expect it to happen! For those of us who support SQL and OLAP server systems, the topic is somewhat more intriguing and deserves specific attention.

As a user of Microsoft OLAP Services, one of the main considerations that you need to think about is the manner in which you will achieve top performance in your OLAP environment. There are many ways in which performance is affected in a normal working environment. This chapter should in many ways be the first chapter that you read on OLAP Server and Microsoft SQL Server. However, without the previous parts of the book under your belt, this chapter would make far less sense and probably prove less useful.

There are many areas that require consideration in producing a high-efficiency working environment for OLAP Services. In this chapter I will canvas the range of these topics which you need to plan for, think about, and apply in order to make your OLAP environment a top-performing one.

The following list identifies the key concerns in this chapter:

- Choosing Your Hardware
- Configuring the OLAP Server
- Cube Design and Management

The successful achievement of a top-performing environment for OLAP Server is the primary consideration here with two exceptions. First, I have separated the discussion of indexing, as it is so central to performance. Indexing is instead covered in Chapter 32. Second, I have not focussed on Microsoft SQL Server 7.0 performance and tuning as such; that topic is covered in depth in other excellent books like *Inside Microsoft SQL Server 7.0* by Ron Soukup and Kalen Delaney, and *Sams Teach Yourself Microsoft SQL Server 7.0 in 21 Days* by Rick Sawtell and Richard Waymire.

Choosing Your Hardware

I have started the discussion on performance in this slightly unusual way because the absolute starting point for performance is the purchase of your hardware. I'm making some assumptions. First, I assume you have read this far because you are seriously involved in OLAP and its daily use or you will be so involved. Second, I assume that your focus on OLAP is more from the software side than the hardware side. Third, you are, if you are working in a corporate or government environment, likely to be "given" hardware.

In my experience, many organizations often under-specify their hardware when it is outside of the mainframe arena. In the OLAP and data warehouse space, the focus of the tools and the processing has been on large environments until recently; now that we have data warehousing in the Windows NT environment things need to be re-thought by most organizations. When moving OLAP activities to "mere PCs" (as one person put it), there is still a wide range of choice as to what to purchase.

To achieve a top-performing OLAP environment, you need to actively get involved in the planning, design, and purchase of the hardware on which you will be working. The purchase of hardware is the most fundamental performance choice that can be made. While it is possible to fix some hardware later on in a project, it is often inefficient. Consequently, gird your loins and prepare to do battle with the bean counters in your company or with the IT purchasing people! Such discussions may require great diplomacy on your part (something I'm not always good at) and even greater persistence in the face of negative responses.

The short form of what we are about to discuss is this: **Buy the largest, fastest, most loaded-with-RAM computer that your company budget can afford**. Disk configurations are also very important but will depend a bit on your performance and RAID strategies. As OLAP a la Microsoft becomes better understood, it will be used more and more intensely in any company that implements it. Be prepared for such growth from Day One and you will save yourself a lot of grief as the processing load on your server increases.

In each of the following areas you can achieve particular types of performance gains for your OLAP environment. Because the hardware market changes almost by the hour, I have generally not specified particular models in this discussion.

> **Note**
>
> When I set up my first Microsoft Training center in 1988, I spent a fortune on what were then the absolutely top-end Compaq 386 Deskpro machines—those machines actually remained useful for eight years! Many people advised me against such a strategy and subsequent business associates made purchases that wasted a great deal of money. It is my firm opinion that you should always buy as "high" as you can and then you can sit back for at least a couple of machine generations and enjoy the spectacle of watching those who bought "cheap".

When planning your hardware purchases, you need to do some serious capacity planning and you probably will need to become a pretty serious social researcher in seeking out your client's estimates of his requirements for his data marts and data warehouses. Good luck!

Dedicated Servers

I begin this discussion with servers because one of your most critical decisions depends on whether you are buying a server specifically for OLAP work or whether you are going to load up a server with multiple Microsoft BackOffice products. In either event, the guidelines for the boxes themselves are similar; however, strategically it is important to start at the more fundamental level.

In order to make your OLAP environment sing and dance you should, if you possibly can, purchase separate servers for each major function.

> **Tip**
>
> Remember that Microsoft BackOffice is fundamentally designed around the principal that commodity hardware is (relatively) cheap and that servers with dedicated functions that can talk to each other are the preferred solution. While it is possible to pile up multiple BackOffice products on a single server, it is not what either Microsoft or any responsible Microsoft Solution Provider would recommend.

So, the first task is to work out what the job(s) require. What is the distribution of work likely to be between OLTP (On Line Transaction Processing) uses of SQL Server, traditional decision support (DSS) application requirements, and data warehousing and OLAP requirements? In each case you will almost certainly find that there are good performance reasons for having multiple servers. OLTP, DSS, and OLAP tend to fundamentally conflict with each other from a performance standpoint.

If at all possible, get a separate server for your OLAP work so that it is dedicated to processing OLAP queries and serving cubes stored on that server. Use other servers for normal SQL processing and ensure that the network across which they communicate is fast and reliable for the purposes of updating your cubes, warehouses, and marts. If you have multiple major warehouses or marts in your company, be prepared to split them across multiple servers as the use of them grows. Even though a particular server might have started out as a great solution, it is unlikely to remain so as processing loads increase, the data volume grows, and the users become ever more aware of just how much information can come out of a well-run data warehouse and OLAP environment. (Needless to say such patterns thrill the hearts of hardware vendors and their shareholders alike!) You may find that you have to argue strongly for such a purchasing strategy, but in the end it will pay off handsomely in performance terms. So, buy a machine that will be dedicated to your OLAP work. Plan to put your normal SQL work on one or more other machines. Doing otherwise is false economy and will cost you more in the long run in a production environment.

> **Tip**
>
> For development work such a separation is not so critical and you can more easily overlap SQL and OLAP work, providing of course that you have sufficient RAM and CPU capacities. If you work in a development/test/production type of framework, your test machines should be identical to your production machines in every way possible.

The actual physical capacity of your OLAP machine needs to be carefully worked out, as I will discuss shortly.

With that general strategy in mind, let us turn to the more mundane issues of the hardware components themselves.

CPUs

There are many excellent servers on the market which have fast processors. The simple truth is that you should always buy ones that are as fast as you can afford. Today's fastest processor will, with absolute certainty, be out of date within a few months (to see some of the directions anticipated by Intel, visit its Web site at www.intel.com). As I write, the "high end" of the Intel CPU world for commodity hardware is the Xeon 550MHz processor. At the same time, Intel and HP have just announced details of the instruction sets for IA-64 chips and the expectation is that sometime in the year 2000 we will see the first of these Merced chips.

In most corporate environments today it is routine to have multiprocessor servers for almost any purpose. Whether you are a government department or a private company, large or small, SMP (symmetric multiprocessor) servers are available at reasonable prices from all major hardware vendors. You should plan on getting as many CPUs as you can afford for your OLAP work, but at the very least you should get a two-CPU server. Single CPU boxes are adequate for many smaller businesses but the fact is that the price differential for single- and dual-processor boxes makes it easy to put in at least a dual-CPU server, even in a smaller business, for very little difference in price.

If you are working in larger OLAP and data warehouse environments, you should seriously consider purchasing servers with 4, 8 or more CPUs. How high you go in your CPU count depends very much on budget and processing loads—and to justify the purchase of very high-end machines, you will almost certainly need to do some serious testing on test servers which you can normally arrange through vendors. Vendors such as Sequent (www.sequent.com) provide options with up to 120 CPUs running in multiserver clusters—serious computing that rivals any mainframe environment for price performance. (The Sequent Web site has excellent white papers on issues of interest to OLAP and data warehousing.)

> **Note**
>
> Historical note: In addition to these developments there are a number of mainframe vendors also working on NT-based solutions. Vendors engaged in such exploratory projects with Microsoft include Amdahl, NEC, and Hitachi.

For most businesses, the use of 4- or 8-CPU systems in a cluster arrangement provides more than sufficient computer power for excellent daily production work.

> **Tip**
>
> Many systems permit you to add processors after market, either by filling sockets in the server's motherboard or by adding additional processor boards to the server. On some systems (Compaq Proliant models, for example) such upgrades are relatively simple, while on other systems it is far less easy. Compaq provides special management software that lets you upgrade working systems with minimum hassle. Many vendors do not have equivalent software, and upgrading processors on an NT system requires manual hacking of the registry and other manual adjustments to the system, all of which are a bit "ugly."

Unfortunately there are no real guidelines once you enter this space; the essence of the argument is to buy at the highest level you can manage and which you and your advisors think is sensible for the OLAP activities anticipated.

Recommendation: Aim to get, at the very least, a dual-processor system for OLAP work and plan to have it as a dedicated server for OLAP and data warehousing. Get the fastest processors you can afford. If you run a mission-critical system that must be up all the time, then you should budget for a cluster solution such as those that are readily available from Compaq and Hewlett Packard.

Memory

You should also plan to get as much memory as you can afford, but at the very least plan to have at least 512MB for a decent OLAP Server system.

Fortunately RAM is fairly cheap and is likely to remain so. In serious production systems for OLAP and data warehouse work, it is increasingly the case that systems are running 1 gigabyte of RAM or more. Systems with 2 or more gigabytes of RAM are also more and more common.

The fundamental issue is that SQL Server and OLAP Server are designed to use RAM whenever possible and so it is literally the case that the more you have the better your system will run, almost without doing anything else. I'll talk more about performance tuning and RAM later in the chapter in the section on "OLAP Server Configuration Options".

Recommendation: Get all the RAM you can afford but, at the absolute minimum, you should get at least 512MB in production systems.

Disks

As you know from previous chapters, data warehousing requires more storage space than the OLTP systems from which the data warehouses and marts collect their base data.

Many people do not understand the difference between an IDE drive and an ultra-wide, hot-swappable SCSI drive, and you may encounter such people in your company when planning the hardware purchases. While it is true that one can buy a 14GB IDE hard drive for about $300 today, a comparable serious-production hot swappable SCSI drive from Compaq is still around $2,000 for a 9GB drive—quite a difference, but the difference is worth considerable peace of mind when you are running a 7×24 production warehouse system.

You will need to plan your disk capacity most carefully. Disk space is used for swap files, for tempdb, for writing changes to tables, for storing indexes, and for cube storage. In a data warehouse environment, you may have significant requirements well beyond your OLTP systems.

To estimate the storage requirements of an OLAP system, you need to remember that the fact table (discussed in Chapter 5, "The Star Schema") will constitute the majority of your storage needs, often 97–99 percent of it. Within your fact table the granularity has a major impact on storage needs—the finer the grain, the more storage required. It is useful to consider the following types of values to estimate the size you require.

Volume of transactions/unit time

Size of data row/transaction

Size of measures within rows

For example, consider a fact-table–based inventory where the data are updated on a regular basis as follows:

Years of hourly data:	10 years
Number of warehouses:	40
Average number of inventory items moved per hour per store:	100
Number of rows in the fact table:	(10×365×24)×100×40=350400000 rows
Assume that:	Key values take 4 bytes
	There are 8 keys
	There are 10 measures of 4 bytes each
Estimate fact table rows:	(8×4)+(10×)=72 bytes/row
Estimate fact table size:	72×350400000=25228800000 bytes or more than 25GB

As you can see, the data volume becomes significant; if you were to double the size of the rows or use an 8-byte datatype, your space requirements would become 50 gigabytes.

Planning for your data warehouse and its growth requires some serious estimates of the actual data volumes that you will be storing, so you can buy disks accordingly.

In many data warehouse situations I am also assuming that you will be running a RAID 5 storage system (hardware-based, of course!) and you will need to size your system with that in mind as well.

In the end, the amount of disk space you need will depend on all the factors previously mentioned, data sizes of keys and measures, frequency of additions to the warehouse's fact table, and number of sources. You may want to create an Excel template worksheet for such estimations.

Recommendation: Buy top-quality hard disks from a reputable major hardware vendor. They should be SCSI disks and should ideally be hot swappable in servers with the ability to run standby disks (the Compaq Proliant 5500 series, for example). They are more expensive than disks you would use at home but remember that they contain your corporate data, the loss of which could be enormously more costly than the disks themselves.

Network

While networks are not of primary interest in this book, they merit a quick word.

The network on which you run your data warehouse should be as fast as possible so that all updates happen quickly to your OLTP systems and to your data warehouse when it updates from the OLTP (or other) systems.

These days, 100Mb networks are routine, but you must ensure that your network adapters can actually run at this speed as well; many older cards cannot. For best response across the network, all adapters should be checked and their configurations should be verified as well. As some of you know, it is all too easy to get an incorrect adapter driver or to misconfigure its duplex or speed settings. If this is not an area in which you have adequate expertise, I recommend that you work closely with a network administrator to ensure that your system will run as fast as possible.

There are other issues that have more to do with network use. If you are running massive imports or exports across the LAN, you may cause bottlenecks that interfere with your normal data warehouse or data mart processing. While this is not a central issue for this book, you should ensure that you do not have conflicting requirements on your network which would degrade performance of your data warehouse or data marts. Clearly it is crucial that such import/export work be scheduled (usually after hours) when it will not interfere excessively with normal work processing. Similarly, if you are doing backups across your network they should also be scheduled at appropriate times.

Workstation Hardware

Workstations have somewhat different requirements than do servers. At the workstation level, while Microsoft SQL 7.0 and OLAP Server have been designed to work on all platforms from Windows 95 to Windows 2000 Professional, there are still some important guidelines to consider.

CPUs

As with servers, buy the fastest CPU that you can afford. Because the workstation machine is likely to be used for more than just OLAP analysis purposes, it is important that it can handle the processing requests from all the applications running on it.

With the advent of laptops that have the equivalent CPU power to desktop units, it is safe to talk about these as though they were the same. (Strictly speaking, the desktop choices are still running ahead of the laptop capabilities, but once we get to CPU speeds of 300MHz or greater, the significance of the differences is relatively trivial.)

Whether you are running Windows 95 or Windows 2000 Professional, you will derive clear benefits from fast processors, particularly for OLAP analysis work.

If you are working in an environment with older workstations, consider moving them to non-OLAP workers and provide your OLAP users with newer, faster machines. If you are going to use existing workstations, be sure that they have sufficient RAM and hard disk space.

> **Tip**
>
> If you do move machines between OLAP and non-OLAP workers, rather than doing replacements, be sure to explain the movement of workstations properly to staff. Failure to do so may result in needless antagonism from staff getting the "old" machines since almost everyone these days is aware of the real costs of desktop units (that is, cheap!).

The minimum workstation that you should consider for OLAP work is a Pentium 100MHz, but most workstations purchased in the last two years would be at this spec or higher.

> **Warning**
>
> Although Microsoft has been pretty "up front" about the requirements for Windows 2000 products, I am sure it is still going to catch people by surprise: If you don't have Pentium systems with at least 64MB of RAM and at least 600MB of free hard disk space, you are not going to be able to load or use Windows 2000.

> **Note**
>
> History note: Back in 1986-88 Microsoft spent considerable time cautioning users that they should buy more RAM, at least 2MB worth! When software demanded higher levels of RAM, people still complained that they hadn't been warned. It will probably happen again but it isn't for lack of Microsoft providing the warning of increased hardware requirements.

Recommendation: Provide your OLAP users with laptops or desktops that have fast CPUs (300MHz or better). If you have laptop users, provide them with proper docking stations, keyboards, and monitors for when they are doing non-mobile work.

Memory

Memory is, even on laptops and workstations, still of major importance in the processing of SQL Server and OLAP Server. Whether you are running the full products or are just running PivotTable Services applications, you will benefit from every byte of RAM that you can afford.

For a working system it is important to have at a minimum 64MB of RAM. It is preferable to have more than that. Many laptops have upper limits of 190MB of RAM or thereabouts; desktop machines often will take at least 512MB or more.

If you are doing OLAP work on your laptop or desktop system, it is best to get as much as you can afford and cram into the system.

Recommendation: For workstation use put at least 128MB of RAM into your system. There is a remarkable difference between 64MB and 128MB of RAM when you start checking performance values. If you are going to be running full desktop editions of SQL Server and OLAP Server, you will want to have as much RAM as you can for the same reasons as discussed under the server memory topic earlier in this chapter. If you are using laptops as desktops, provide real keyboards, mice, and monitors in addition to proper docking stations—your users will be far more comfortable and efficient.

Disks

For your workstation you should also plan for the capacity requirements of OLAP work. If you are going to be using off-line storage of cubes (as discussed in Chapter 20, "The PivotTable Service"), you need to take that into account.

Generally, workstations connected to a network have access to network drives and local storage is not an issue (unless the network drives have limited capacity or quotas). Mobile users are a slightly special case and should be treated accordingly.

> **Tip**
>
> Under Windows 2000 it is possible to set quotas on drive space for individual users. This can prove to be a mixed blessing if users are accustomed to the lack of quotas on NT systems. Nevertheless, network administrators will need to provide sufficient capacity for users choosing to use "local" storage. True mobile users who disconnect will need sufficient clear disk space for their cubes.

Recommendation: For mobile OLAP users, provide laptops with at least 3GB hard disks, preferably larger.

Network

If your workstations are constantly connected, presumably you need only worry about the connection to the LAN. However, it isn't quite this simple. In many companies when machines are upgraded, the old network card is moved from the old machine to the new machine. This can produce an unintended performance bottleneck, as the old cards may not be able to run at the full capacity of today's networks (100Mb).

Most mobile users have either docking stations with real NICs or PC Card Ethernet adapters. For the most part these are running at speeds designed to cope with modern networks; however, you should check if users are relying on such adapters that are more than two years old.

Recommendation: Be sure that your network adapters are sufficiently recent to run at the speed of your network. Ensure that they are all installed with the absolutely correct driver—an incorrect driver might work but can have serious performance impact. Be sure also that all network hubs and switches are running at the right speeds and configured properly.

Special Consideration for Mobile Users

If you are have mobile users, it is important to be sure that they have a fast dialup connection capability. As mobile users may need to periodically connect and update their information in either SQL Server or OLAP Server, they should be running 56K modems for dialup purposes.

Recommendation: Get the best combination of fast CPU, large amount of RAM, and high-capacity hard disk as well as a good, large, clear screen for your mobile OLAP users.

Network Considerations

The network side of things is pretty straightforward for OLAP Server. Just make sure it is a fast, reliable network! In the normal course of events it must handle a considerable amount of update traffic between your OLTP systems and your OLAP systems. Most modern network topologies will meet the needs of your system.

However, having said that, it should be noted that almost any network can be degraded in unintended ways. Misconfiguration of switches and hubs can occur, wrong drivers can impact the performance of network adapters, and faulty links can cause data loss and inconsistencies.

Network Interface Cards (NICs)

Network adapters should be fast and reliable. By choosing mainstream (brandname) products, you should be safe for both quality of the product and the availability of the correct (and latest!) drivers for the NICs. Do not assume that the driver you got with the adapter is the best one—often there are later versions of drivers for adapters.

When older machines are upgraded, be sure that their NICs are not moved to newer, faster machines unless you are certain that they are of sufficiently recent origin that they will run at today's network speeds.

Network Protocols

Ensure that your system is running the correct protocols for your network, hardware, and operating systems mixture. SQL Server installations load Named Pipes, Multiprotocol (TCP/IP), and TCP/IP sockets by default, but other network libraries must be specifically loaded if you are running on other networks. It is best to leave the defaults as they are because SQL Server and OLAP Server use different protocols under a variety of processing conditions. See your SQL Books on Line for a detailed discussion of protocols.

OLAP Server Configuration Options

One of the initial mistakes users of Microsoft OLAP Server can make is to assume that it simply uses the SQL Server settings for memory management.

Unfortunately this is not the case. In the OLAP Manager console, select your OLAP Server and then right-click Properties. The dialog shown in Figure 31.1 appears.

FIGURE 31.1

The OLAP Server Properties dialog allows you to configure the server environment.

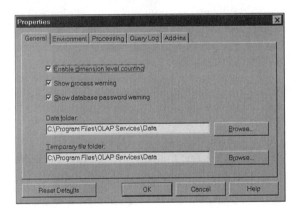

Within the Properties dialog exist a number of settings affecting server configuration. I'll examine each of these in turn.

Environment Settings

You can set memory settings and performance settings on the Environment tab of the Properties dialog, shown in Figure 31.2.

FIGURE 31.2

Settings for memory and performance can be managed from the Environment tab of the Properties dialog.

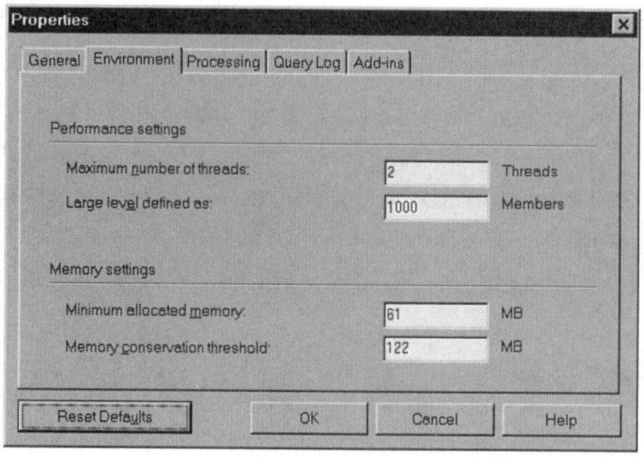

Memory Settings

Two specific values of memory are important for OLAP Server. These can be managed through the interface shown in Figure 31.2.

First, there is the Minimum Allocated Memory setting. This setting means that your OLAP Server will get at a minimum the amount of memory that you specify here. By default, OLAP Server allocates itself half of your machine's total memory but it may well use more than this for processing your OLAP work. Clearly the more total memory you have, the more that OLAP Server can give itself to work with.

Second, there is a setting for the Memory Conservation Threshold, which provides OLAP Server with a value that it works toward. As it approaches this value, it becomes more efficient in its use of the memory with which it is working. The default value for this setting is simply all of the computer's memory. You may set this to other values that are less than the total, but OLAP is free to use more memory if it requires it.

As you can see, the "tuning" of memory for OLAP is only partially under your direct control. This may change in future versions of the product. With the current version of OLAP Server, it is another indication that you should consider using a dedicated server for your OLAP requirements so that nothing else contends with it for memory usage.

Recommendation: Use the default values for the memory settings unless you have extremely large amounts of RAM (more than 512MB). The more RAM you have, the happier your OLAP Server will be and the faster it will do its memory-based processing.

Performance Settings

OLAP Server also allows you to adjust the number of threads that are used for processing.

As with the memory settings, these values can be adjusted on the Environment tab in the Properties window. Two settings can be varied, the number of threads and the value of the large level settings for Dimension members.

The first of these, Maximum Number of Threads, allows you to specify how many processing threads can be used at any one time to work with the CPU in the computer. The default number of threads is twice the number of CPUs (for example, if you have a single CPU, the default thread count is 2).

By providing more threads to OLAP Server, it is possible to increase the processing throughput for the server machine, as long as the CPU can handle the load. The maximum number of threads that can be specified is 1000.

In general, a larger number of threads will allow OLAP server to process its work load more quickly but if the processor itself bottlenecks, or if other processes are competing with OLAP server, it is unlikely that setting thread count to a very high value will provide much benefit. Setting this level depends on tracking the performance using the Performance Monitor.

The second item that can be set for performance tuning is the number of members that are considered to constitute a "Large Level". The value is the minimum value that constitutes a large level dimension; the default value is 1000. What this means is that when information is requested of OLAP Server from a client machine, the entire dimension (levels) information is sent to the client if the number of members in the dimension is no larger than this value.

If you do not want excessive network traffic and processing overhead, you should set this to a smaller value; if you know that you do have large dimensions, you may need to increase the value. Unfortunately Microsoft has not, as yet, provided any guidelines on this particular measure so it requires testing and monitoring in order to determine the effects of changing this value.

Processing Settings

Three settings exist on the Processing tab of the Properties dialog, shown in Figure 31.3. These settings are OLE DB Timeout, Read-Ahead Buffer Size, and Process Buffer Size.

OLE DB Timeout

When working with data sources it is possible to set a timeout value, which determines how long OLAP Services will wait for the connection to occur.

Valid values are from 0 to 10,000 seconds. The 0 value indicates that the timeout is disabled and OLAP Services basically will wait forever.

FIGURE 31.3

Set processing parameters by modifying values on the Processing tab of the Properties dialog.

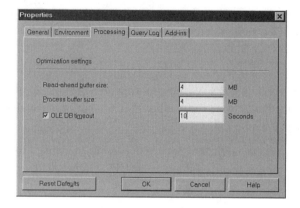

This setting interacts with the one specified for the data source itself. The Connection timeout takes precedence if it is shorter than the OLE DB Timeout setting, but if the latter is shorter, it takes precedence. If no Connection timeout is specified for the Data Link properties, the OLE DB value is used.

The timeout values affect your overall processing efficiency because the connection timeouts tend to indicate (by succeeding or failing) that there are other problems with your network or your data links.

Read-Ahead Buffer Size

This setting controls the amount of RAM set aside for the reading of data into memory. The default value is 4MB and this should be a good starting point. However, if you have lots of RAM and a large database then you will probably want to increase this value to support better read-ahead efficiency.

Process Buffer Size

The process buffer provides space for the actual processing work, and the larger it is the fewer I/Os that will be required. Here too the default value is 4MB but you almost certainly will want to increase this to gain processing efficiency. The more RAM you have available the larger you are likely to want to make this value. Unfortunately, at the time of writing, Microsoft has not provided guidelines on this, so you will need to experiment and check your performance counters in Performance Monitor to see how much you can reduce the I/O traffic.

Design Your Cube to Maximize Performance

The design and implementation of the cube plays a large role in both the processing and query performance. Care must be taken in the design or you will risk undoing the benefits provided by the hardware and server configuration.

Choose the Smallest Datatype

The choice of datatypes will have an impact on your OLAP Server's performance since the smaller the datatype, the smaller the storage requirements for your base data and the faster the server can "cover the ground" to retrieve data.

To maximize processing efficiency, always select the smallest datatype that will hold your data correctly. In particular, you should avoid using Unicode datatypes if they are not actually required by your application environment.

Keep the Schema Simple

Schemas were discussed extensively in Chapter 5, but it is worth remembering in the context of this performance discussion that when you build your schema, you should keep the design as simple as possible. Generally, the more complex the cube, the more work the server must perform to process the cube. The number of dimensions and measures directly affect the number of aggregations needed to create the cube. Every extra dimension, member, and measure adds to the processing and storage load on your OLAP Server.

The basic rule of thumb is to keep your cubes as simple as possible, but at the same time design them to address a coherent set of issues so that you do not need multiple similar cubes.

Use shared dimensions where you can. They will make your designs more efficient as well.

You may also want to put different parts of your cubes on multiple partitions so that different types of processing and storage can be used as a function of query intensity and frequency.

Most of the performance issues associated with these matters are addressed in Chapter 15, "Creating Cubes."

It is best to use a star schema rather than a snowflaked schema to reduce the number and complexity of joins that OLAP server must do to process queries against your cube.

Cube Processing Versus Query Performance

The manner of aggregation of cubes is always a trade-off for speed, efficiency, and storage space. Fast query performance requires a high number of aggregations. A large number of aggregations requires more processing time to process the aggregations and more storage space in which to store the aggregations. When designing your cube, you must carefully examine the needs of your solution. If there is a narrow processing window or limited disk resources, query response time may have to suffer. If query performance is your top priority, then more disk space and a larger processing window will be required. Once you have analyzed your needs, you are ready to manage the trade-off that exists between processing and query performance by selecting your storage type and number of aggregations.

Storage Types

There are three basic storage types in an OLAP Server. Each type provides particular advantages and disadvantages. The fundamental advantage of Microsoft OLAP Server is that you have all the major options available to you rather than being restricted to a particular mode of storage. This gives you a flexible system that can be managed to provide an excellent trade-off between speed and storage requirements, which is the fundamental compromise you must make.

In order to discuss this, we need to take a quick look at the three types of storage, ROLAP, MOLAP, and HOLAP.

ROLAP

Relational OLAP (ROLAP) refers to the storage of cubes in a relational database (which some people would say was obvious from the name!) and this in turn has particular characteristics that need to be taken into account.

In ROLAP storage, you as the designer have elected to keep your base data in the relational database itself, in the original fact table, and to refer to it whenever you need to know about an aggregation. The aggregations themselves are stored in tables in the relational database. Through this mechanism it is possible to store aggregations and base data (remember these are still in the fact table) in a fairly efficient manner as far as space goes. However, the compromise with this method is that the retrieval of information and the response of your cube queries will be slower, since OLAP Server may have to retrieve data from the fact table for some aggregations as the aggregations requested may not exist in the relational aggregate tables.

MOLAP

Multidimensional OLAP (MOLAP) enables you to store the base data and the aggregations themselves in the same storage structure. By keeping a copy of the base data and the aggregations in the same place you achieve excellent response times to queries at the expense of space on your system.

MOLAP provides the fastest response times to cube queries but the penalty is that you will consume significant amounts of disk space. This may be particularly problematic on portable systems for mobile users.

Your choices to control this depend on your trade-off between the percentage of aggregations that you want to store (remember our discussion about data explosion) and the speed you require for response times to your queries. As various people over the years have observed, there is no such thing as a free lunch; there is always a cost somewhere in the system.

HOLAP

One of the distinctive features of Microsoft SQL Server and OLAP Server is that it provides you with the option of having a mixture of MOLAP and ROLAP storage, known as *Hybrid OLAP* (HOLAP). To some degree this came about because of customer requests.

Tip

Unlike some companies in the database space who like to "tell you how it is," Microsoft has a pretty good track record of asking customers for their opinions and for feedback. Microsoft uses various mechanisms, including focus groups, customer surveys, market research (interviews, independent studies, questionnaires, and so forth), beta testing, and Web responses. If you ever have something that you want to say, go to the Web site and find the "Write Us" option on the home page—and do so! Alternatively, you can email your comments to `mswish@microsoft.com`. There are email aliases for things like `officewish@microsoft.com`, `sqlwish@microsoft.com`, and so on.

If you have unlimited disk space, you can have fantastic response by storing all your aggregations and base data in MOLAP. Unfortunately, not all of us have bottomless pockets for purchasing and must make some choices as to speed versus disk storage. So, consider HOLAP, which allows you to store your aggregations in MOLAP data stores while permitting you to save space by leaving base data in the relational databases (ROLAP) in your OLAP Server. You *can* have your OLAP cake and eat it, too.

The summary of your storage options and issues looks like this:

Storage Type	Advantage	Disadvantage
ROLAP	Conserves disk space	Slows response time
ROLAP	Does not store redundant data	Must calculate aggregations from the base data which are in a relational store
ROLAP	Works well for infrequent queries	Works poorly for frequent queries
MOLAP	Stores great detail for both base data and aggregations	Requires significant disk space for redundant data
MOLAP	Works well for frequent queries	Provides needless detail for infrequent queries
HOLAP	Allows placement of aggregations and data in the most appropriate type of storage	Requires you to more actively manage the system by choosing what balance is required between MOLAP and ROLAP
HOLAP	Smaller cubes than MOLAP	Slower response for some queries
HOLAP	Faster response to queries than ROLAP	Requires more storage space than ROLAP
HOLAP	Gives great compromise	Requires more active management and madministrative overhead

> **Tip**
>
> As you design your storage choices, keep in the mind the so-called "80/20" rule. You can get enormous efficiency by using 80 percent as a cutoff for your aggregations which will require only about 20 percent as much storage space as if you had specified 100 percent! Follow the next section to check this yourself.

Using the Storage Design Wizard

The Storage Design Wizard focuses on the actual allocation of storage for aggregations. OLAP Server uses a number of mechanisms to keep storage requirements under control within this framework. These mechanisms include the following:

- Empty cells are not stored.

- Compression is used on cells that contain data.

- Special algorithms are used to create aggregations efficiently for summaries of data.

As you have seen, there are three fundamental storage types to work with in this environment. The purpose of this wizard is to help you manage these storage alternatives.

When you start the wizard, you have the option of not showing the startup screen (shown in Figure 31.4); this screen is basically a welcome and serves no other purpose.

FIGURE 31.4

One of the most useful tools for performance is the Storage Design Wizard. Note that the introductory screen can be disabled.

The wizard's next screen (shown in Figure 31.5) tells you if aggregations already exist. If they do, the wizard shows the type of storage, the space used by the aggregations, and the number of aggregations, and gives you the option of replacing them or adding to them. In the following screen (see Figure 31.6), you need to select the type of storage that you would like to use; the screen provides a reminder of the advantages of each type—MOLAP, ROLAP, and HOLAP.

The wizard's next screen, shown in Figure 31.7, is where you select which way you would like to do the aggregations—by storage space, by performance gain, or by making decisions manually as you watch the aggregation graph. Generally, the best option is to set a percentage performance gain that is calculated according to the following formula:

```
PercentGain = 100 * (QTimeMAX - QTimeTARGET) / (QTimeMAX - QTimeMIN)
```

FIGURE 31.5

The wizard tells you whether aggregations already exist and, if so, allows you to replace or add to them.

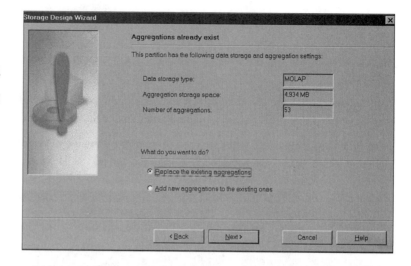

FIGURE 31.6

You select your storage method on this screen.

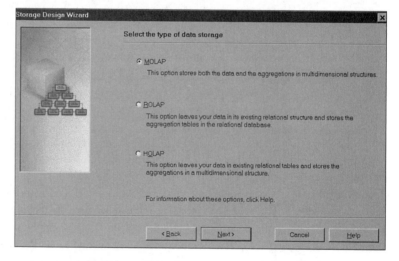

This allows you to choose the trade-off between space and performance. The important thing to remember is that the higher your performance gain between maximum and minimum query times, the larger your storage requirements will be. Notice that you can play with this screen, reset it, and try different values. On the FoodMart Sales cube, for example, a 50 percent performance gain (shown in Figure 31.7) requires 3.2MB storage and calculates 53 aggregations while an 80 percent gain requires 21.3MB but provides 117 aggregations. A 25 percent performance gain uses a mere 0.3MB but only gets 30 aggregations! Bottom line, you need to play with this wizard and decide which you want, speed or space saving. Figure 31.8 shows this calculation with an 80 percent performance

gain. Run the same process yourself to see what the values are for 100 percent performance gain—you may be surprised. (Be sure to notice that the scale of the graph changes as you modify your processing settings!)

FIGURE 31.7

The graph shows the results of running the aggregations (using MOLAP) with performance gain set to 50 percent.

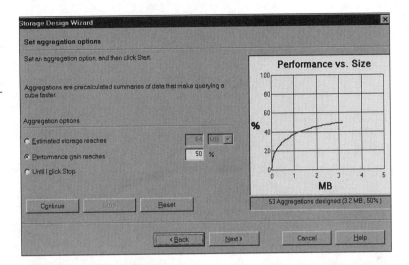

FIGURE 31.8

Increasing the performance gain to 80 percent also increases storage and the total number of aggregations.

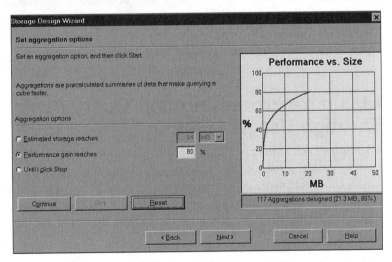

The final screen (see Figure 31.9) lets you decide to process the cube immediately or at some time in the future. You may want to postpone the processing until you have designed all of your storage and made some estimates as to how much storage will be required overall.

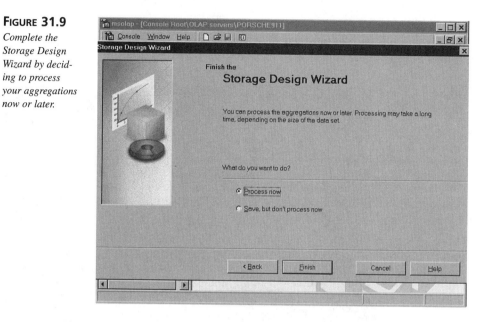

FIGURE 31.9

*Complete the
Storage Design
Wizard by decid-
ing to process
your aggregations
now or later.*

Recommendation: Work with the Storage Design Wizard to see how the aggregation, size, and storage method dynamics work. Make your decision based on the response patterns that you would like—this is really your choice of fundamental storage type, and after you have made the choice between MOLAP, ROLAP or HOLAP, you can decide on the balance between aggregations and space.

Maximize Processing and Query Performance Through Usage Analysis

Microsoft OLAP Server provides some very good tools for analyzing your usage and tuning your aggregations to match your usage. With the Usage Analysis Wizard, you can review the actual queries that are being executed against the cube. The Usage-Based Optimization Wizard takes this a step further and creates aggregations based on the usage history. With these wizards, you can customize your solution to the query needs of your users.

The Usage Analysis Wizard

The Usage Analysis Wizard makes it possible to do extensive examinations of patterns of cube querying, which in turn provides you a mechanism for tuning your OLAP cubes.

The wizard provides table reports and graphical reports of the queries executed against the server. Tables 31.1 and 31.2 give a summary of these reports.

TABLE 31.1 Usage Analysis Wizard Table Reports

Report Type	*What It Does*
Query Run-time	Shows how long queries take to run; summarized in table form, longest to shortest times.
Query Frequency	Shows how often queries are run; also listed in table form from most frequent to least frequent.
Active Users	Shows which users are active and which queries they use; data in table form from most used queries by user to least used.

TABLE 31.2 Usage Analysis Wizard Graphical Reports

Report Type	*What It Does*
Query Response	Shows a bar graph, which portrays the distribution of the response times for all queries.
Query by Hour	Provides a bar graph that shows numbers of queries processed per hour.
Query by Date	Bar graphs the total numbers of queries sent to the server grouped by date.

To run this wizard, do the following:

1. Locate and select the cube in OLAP Server Manager that you want to analyze.

2. Right-click the cube and select the Usage Analysis Wizard from the popup menu. The screen shown in Figure 31.10 appears.

FIGURE 31.10

The Usage Analysis Wizard gives you many combinations of options.

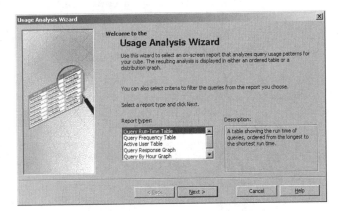

3. Select the type of report that you would like to see. The screens that follow will depend on your selection, because each of these reports has multiple filter factors that can be specified. The option screen for an analysis based on a date range report is shown in Figure 31.11.

FIGURE 31.11

Select the optional filter factors for each analysis that you want to run. There are literally thousands of possible combinations.

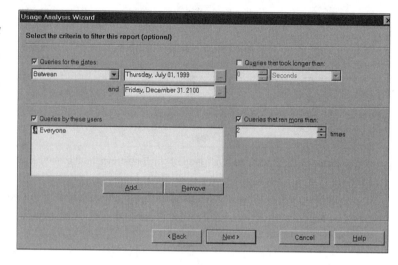

Notice that the date ranges will do for most of us—until December 31, 2100! You can select users, query run times, and query frequencies among other things.

This is very much a tool to "play" with. As you get more experience with your cubes and your users, you will have more data to work with here and gain a better sense of just what the query patterns are in your data warehouse or environment. This will help you to decide on processing tuning. The filters allow you to tune the aggregations to your specific needs. If there are a few important users that need immediate query response, then filter the wizard to concentrate solely on their queries.

On the wizard's final screen you can choose to delete the queries that you have examined from the query log. Be sure to notice that you cannot save the report generated by this wizard.

Tip

Be sure to edit the properties of your OLAP Server and set the query log frequency to 1. If you stay with the Microsoft default of 10, you may be wondering why the query log report seems to be missing some of the queries you just executed.

The Usage-Based Optimization Wizard

You can use the information accumulated by OLAP Server to further optimize the aggregations in the cube by the query processing which has been done against your OLAP cube. The Usage-Based Optimization Wizard allows you to maximize both processing and query performance. The OLAP Server stores a log of all queries executed against the server. OLAP Server can then create aggregations to satisfy the queries executed against the server. This provides a solution in which less processing time and disk space is required since fewer aggregations will be needed to satisfy user requests.

To run the Usage-Based Optimization Wizard, do the following:

1. Locate and select the cube in OLAP Server Manager that you wish to analyze.

2. Right-click the cube and select the Usage-Based Optimization Wizard from the pop-up menu. The wizard's first screen (see Figure 31.12) appears.

FIGURE 31.12

If someone (or you!) has turned off the introductory screen for this wizard, you will see the screen shown in Figure 13.13 instead.

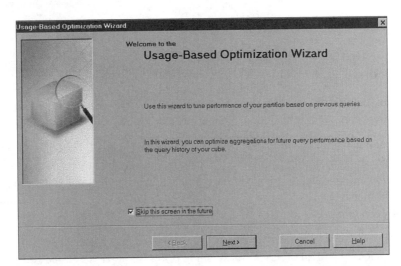

Note

If you want to have the introductory screen activated, select the Back button (notice that it is active) and uncheck the Skip This Screen in the Figure checkbox on the introductory screen.

While the interface for this wizard looks similar to the Usage Analysis wizard, there are some key differences. As Figure 31.13 shows, there is an option for running the optimization against queries that have been run against MOLAP, ROLAP, or the server cache. If you have cubes with multiple partitions, you also have the option to choose to optimize particular partitions.

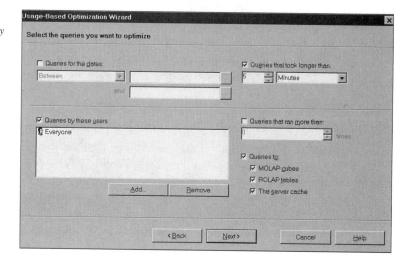

By running optimization against the server cache, the wizard only looks at queries that were completed in the cache without reference to the storage structures.

At this point the wizard takes you to the Storage Design Wizard interface and you process the cube as you did before, but this time the processing is driven by the queries you have elected to include in the optimization analysis so far. You have the same fundamental control as you had before in the choices of storage, optimization criteria, and when to process.

I would advise replacing previous aggregations rather than appending to existing aggregations. The goal of usage-based tuning is to save processing time and disk requirements by choosing those aggregations that meet the normal usage patterns. Simply appending the aggregations to the existing aggregations will not save space or processing time. However, if processing time and storage space are not issues, simply append the aggregations to obtain a query performance increase. Through this wizard you have now reached a compromise in the processing versus query performance trade-off. You have minimized processing issues while attempting to maximize query performance for your users.

Summary

In this chapter I have identified the key areas where performance of your OLAP Server can be affected. I have not reproduced all of the cautions that are documented in the Books On Line for OLAP Server with regard to processing and reprocessing cubes in particular. You should search on the word "caution" to locate these items for your review. In many cases your activities on a cube will have performance impact in both the literal sense of inhibiting your users because the cube is either unavailable or technically obsolete (because a newer cube is being generated) and in the figurative sense that your work on the cube will use processing resources in competition with your users' doing their analytic work.

From configuration of your server to processing and updating of your cubes, you need to understand, plan, and manage your OLAP data warehouse and data marts in a deliberate and careful manner. These guidelines should assist you in that endeavor. The one element that I have left out of this discussion is the use of indexes in your data warehouse environment; that is the topic of the next chapter.

Indexing

by Kevin Viers

CHAPTER 32

This chapter provides a look into how indexing plays a part in a data warehousing and OLAP scenario. In most instances, the OLAP databases that you create with Microsoft OLAP Services are based on an underlying relational data source. The indexing strategy implemented within the relational data source can have a dramatic impact on the performance and overall success of your OLAP installation. This chapter presents basic information about indexing and general indexing strategies along with a look at how those indexing strategies affect an OLAP Services implementation. Additionally, this chapter discusses some tools that are provided in SQL Server 7.0 to facilitate your indexing decisions.

Indexing Overview

It is important that you have a solid understanding of what indexes are and how they are used within a traditional relational database environment. This section gives you the basic information about indexes and their implementation. The discussion of indexes within this chapter is centered on indexing in a SQL Server 7.0 environment. The concepts discussed, however, are applicable in almost any relational database environment.

Understanding Indexes

The most resource-intensive operation that your database performs is disk I/O. Every time the database reads a record in a table, it requires a disk I/O operation. The best way to improve performance in the database is to limit the amount of disk I/O that is needed for any operation. An index is a physical structure within a database that is used to speed the retrieval of data from a table by reducing the amount of disk I/O required to perform the retrieval.

> **Note**
>
> To understand how indexes can affect disk I/O it is helpful to understand a little about how SQL Server stores data. The smallest unit of storage used by SQL Server is a data page. Each read of a data page requires one CPU clock cycle. In SQL Server 6.5, each data page was only 2K in size. This meant that every time SQL Server had to read 2K worth of data it had to spend a CPU cycle. SQL Server 7.0 has increased the data page size from 2K to 8K meaning that each CPU cycle can now read more data, thus improving performance. Additionally SQL Server 7.0 has improved its data storage management so that it can read up to 8 data pages at a time, allowing it to effectively read 64K of data with each CPU cycle. While SQL Server 7.0 has introduced significant performance improvements, the bottom line is that disk I/O is still an expensive exercise.

An index is created as a separate physical storage structure that contains the value of the indexed column(s) along with a pointer to the physical location of the rest of the row of data. The indexed values are stored in sorted order. When a query containing an indexed column is issued, the database reads the index until it finds the appropriate data value and then goes directly to the row in the table without having to scan the entire table. Because the index values are stored in order, the database stops reading the index once the value no longer matches the requested value.

You can apply as many as 249 indexes on a table within SQL Server 7.0. However, every index that is created takes up space and can have significant performance implications on other operations within the database. Although indexes speed up data retrieval, they actually slow the performance of INSERT, DELETE, and UPDATE operations. The reason for this is that every time data is updated in a table, every index that has been created on that table must be updated as well. For this reason, it is critical that you understand how your database is being used to determine an appropriate indexing strategy.

Physical Implementation

In SQL Server, indexes are implemented as B-Tree structures. As its name implies, a B-Tree structure consists of a collection of data pages that loosely resemble a tree. In other words, a B-Tree structure consists of root level, one or more branches or intermediate levels, and a set of leaf levels. Figure 32.1 illustrates the B-Tree structure.

FIGURE 32.1

A B-Tree index structure has a root level, one or more branches (intermediate level), and "leaves," the third level.

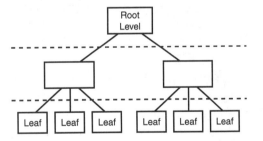

The B-Tree structure enables SQL Server to quickly find data by traversing the levels of the tree. In other words, at each level within the tree, SQL Server will be pointed to a specific branch at the level below until it reaches the data it is seeking. By using a B-Tree, the worst case scenario would have SQL Server reading only half of the data contained in the index.

Each level within the B-Tree structure is made up of physical data pages. These data pages contain the values of indexed columns along with pointers to the physical data page location of the data rows. There are two basic types of indexes used in SQL Server, clustered and nonclustered.

Clustered Indexes

A clustered index is one in which the physical data pages that contain the table data are stored in sorted order based on the index column and are contained in the leaf pages of the B-Tree structure. Because the actual data pages are physically sorted on the index column, you can only have one clustered index per table. Whenever a clustered index is created, the data pages must be resorted, which can often create a tremendous amount of disk I/O.

Nonclustered Indexes

A nonclustered index does not affect the physical storage of the data pages that hold the table data. Rather, the nonclustered index is created as a separate data storage area that contains the values of the indexed column(s) and pointers to the physical data pages that are stored in the leaf pages of the B-Tree structure. If a clustered index exists along with a nonclustered index, the pointers point to the clustered index leaf pages that contain the appropriate data.

Composite Indexes

A composite index can be either clustered or nonclustered but it is based on more than one column. This type of index is useful when querying a table with multiple columns in a WHERE clause provided those columns are all contained within the index. The problem with composite indexes is that they are physically larger than single-column indexes, taking up more data pages, and their use can result in increased disk I/O.

Covering Indexes

A covering index describes a situation where all columns that are involved within a query (including the selected columns) are contained in an index. Because all of the values are stored on the index pages, the database only has to read the index pages and does not have to go to the table data pages to return the data. Prior to SQL Server 7.0, the only way to achieve a covering index was to use composite indexes on all relevant columns. SQL Server 7.0 supports index intersection, which enables it to use multiple single-column indexes to achieve index covering.

General Indexing Considerations

Now that you understand how indexes work and how they are implemented in SQL Server, let's take a look at some general guidelines that you should keep in mind when developing an indexing strategy. Keep in mind that these suggestions are general "rules of thumb."

- Keep the number of indexes reasonable. Usually no more than 3 or 4 indexes per table are recommended.

- Don't index small tables (few rows).

- Don't index tables with extremely high transaction processing volumes. Any table that is continually updated is a poor candidate for indexing.

- Keep indexes narrow. Try not to place indexes on large (greater than 30 bytes) columns.

- Good index columns are typically those that are frequently used in joins, those that are used in ORDER BY and GROUP BY operations, and those that are used in aggregate functions (SUM, AVG, and so on).

When you have determined that you want to index a column or columns, you need to decide whether a clustered or nonclustered index is appropriate. Table 32.1 lists some general guidelines.

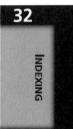

TABLE 32.1 When To Use Clustered or Nonclustered Indexes

Clustered Indexes	Nonclustered Indexes
Columns containing many duplicate values	Primary key columns or columns containing unique values
Columns referenced in ORDER BY and GROUP BY clauses	Columns used in aggregate functions (SUM, AVG, and so on)
Columns used in JOIN operations (other than the primary key)	Foreign key columns
Columns used in range searches	Columns used in single row lookups

Indexing in a Data Warehousing Environment

Until now, I have been discussing indexing in very generic terms as it relates to any relational database system. Now let's look at indexing as it relates to a data warehousing environment and how your indexing strategies may be altered to accommodate the unique needs of this environment.

OLTP Versus Data Warehousing

As I discussed earlier, indexing is really a double-edged sword. While indexes can bring tremendous benefits by speeding data retrieval operations, they can cause equally disastrous performance problems when trying to update data. As a result, your indexing strategy is highly dependent on the type of application that is accessing your database.

On-Line Transaction Processing (OLTP) applications typically involve a heavy volume of data updates within a database. Consider a sales database that has to record a new transaction record with every sale that occurs. Databases that are used to service OLTP applications typically require a very conservative indexing strategy that limits index creation to only those indexes that are absolutely necessary.

Data warehouses, on the other hand, are specifically designed for the retrieval and aggregation of data. Speedy data retrieval is often the most important element of a successful data warehouse implementation. As a result, most data warehouses employ a very aggressive indexing strategy, where almost every column that can be requested is indexed. Because data warehouses are primarily read-only environments, the indexes do not have to be updated often. The following sections examine indexing for a data warehouse in more detail.

Indexing the Star Schema

Most data warehouses are based on the star schema. As you learned in Chapter 5, "The Star Schema," this is a database schema that consists of one or more fact tables that hold detail transaction level data and a set of related dimension tables that provide definition to your transactional data. In general, the dimension tables each contain a primary key that is a foreign key into the fact table.

The most common indexing strategy for a star schema is to create a nonclustered index on the primary key of each dimension table and a nonclustered index on each of the foreign keys contained in the fact table. Before SQL Server 7.0 introduced the concept of index intersection, it was also recommended that one or more composite indexes containing various combinations of foreign keys be created on the fact table. Indeed, it is not uncommon in some data warehouses to find indexes on virtually every column and every combination of columns that could possibly be requested.

Performance Implications

There is a downside to overindexing a data warehouse. First of all, many of the indexes that are created will not be used. This results in a lot of wasted space in the database. Of course, storage is cheap these days so wasted space may not that big of a concern. The real performance issue with indexing a data warehousing is the burden that the indexes place on the load process.

Most data warehouses contain read-only snapshots of data. The data warehouses are loaded on a periodic basis (hourly, nightly, weekly, and so forth). Each time the data warehouse is loaded, the indexes reduce the performance of the load. Remember that every record that is added to the data warehouse requires each index created on the table to be updated. This can often result in exaggerated load time.

Indexing and OLAP Services

Now take a look at how indexing applies to your Microsoft OLAP Services implementation. In particular, I will focus on how OLAP Services utilizes indexes within your relational data stores and on the performance implications of various OLAP storage strategies.

In most instances, your OLAP database is built using a relational data warehouse as its underlying data source. As a result, the indexing strategy that is put in place within your data warehouse has implications in your OLAP implementation. There are two primary areas where indexing plays a part in OLAP performance: cube processing and data retrieval. The following sections examine each area in more detail.

Cube Processing

The primary performance benefit provided by OLAP Services is the pre-aggregation or summarization of data that is done when you create and process a cube in an OLAP database. This pre-aggregated data allows OLAP Services to respond to user queries efficiently without having to calculate data on-the-fly. In order to process the cube, OLAP Services has to perform several SELECT statements against the underlying data source. Many of these operations include the SUM aggregate function and GROUP BY clauses. As is the case with any query issued to a database, the indexes in place have a tremendous impact on the performance of these queries.

The way that OLAP Services utilizes indexes depends on the storage mode you choose for your cube. The storage mode also has an effect on how indexes impact OLAP performance when processing a cube.

MOLAP

In the MOLAP storage mode, OLAP Services copies all of the underlying relational data into a proprietary multidimensional data store. All aggregations that are created on the fact data are also created and stored within a multidimensional data store. Once the cube has been processed, OLAP Services does not select data from the relational data store again until the cube is reprocessed. In other words, all user requests for data are satisfied from within the multidimensional data store.

The impact of indexes when using MOLAP storage is limited to the initial load of data from the relational database into the multidimensional database. Processing a cube using MOLAP storage results in a single SELECT statement being executed on the relational database. This statement consists of all data columns from each specified dimension table and the fact table. The presence of indexes on the fact table and the dimension tables have a significant impact on how quickly the initial data load can happen. If the tables are not indexed on the join columns, costly table scans occur.

Once the data has been selected from the relational database, OLAP Services applies its own indexing scheme to the multidimensional data. This indexing scheme is a bitmap indexing scheme that is completely controlled by OLAP Services.

ROLAP

In the ROLAP storage mode, OLAP Services leaves all underlying detail data in its original relational data store. All aggregations that are created are stored in relational tables, which are created and populated while the cube is being processed. As you might imagine, indexing strategy plays a significant role in cube processing performance when using the ROLAP storage mode.

To help understand the implications of indexing when processing a cube using ROLAP storage mode, consider the following example. Figure 32.2 shows the dialog box that results from processing a ROLAP cube with aggregations.

FIGURE 32.2

The Cube Processing Status dialog lets you view what happens during processing.

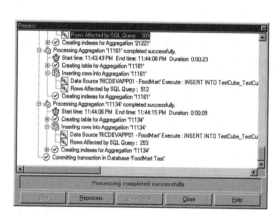

As you can see, each aggregation created by OLAP Services results in the creation of a table. The table is populated by an INSERT INTO statement containing a subquery. The subquery consists of a SELECT statement with several SUM and GROUP BY clauses. In this example, I want to make sure that each column in the SUM and GROUP BY clauses is indexed. Additionally, each column that is represented in the JOIN operation should be indexed.

OLAP Services generates indexes on all aggregation tables that it creates. You can look at the cube processing dialog box to determine what indexes were built on the aggregation tables. In most cases OLAP Services creates nonclustered indexes on one or more of the aggregation columns and, in some cases, composite indexes on all of the columns. Because all user requests for data are answered from the relational data store it is very important that the tables be adequately indexed.

HOLAP

In the HOLAP storage mode, OLAP Services leaves all of the underlying detail data in the relational data store, but creates all aggregations in the multidimensional data store. The implications of your indexing strategy are much the same as they are when using MOLAP storage mode. The primary difference is that only data chosen for aggregation is selected from the relational data store.

Data Retrieval

In addition to cube processing, indexing has implications when OLAP Services retrieves data in response to user queries. As I mentioned before, if your cube is based on the MOLAP storage mode, all user requests are satisfied from within the multidimensional data store. Because all indexing within the multidimensional store is managed by OLAP Services, indexing isn't much of a consideration for an administrator.

If your cube is using either the ROLAP or HOLAP storage mode, data retrieval activities can be impacted by your indexing strategy. When a user requests data from a cube, OLAP Services first tries to satisfy that request from all existing aggregations. If an aggregation (or combination of aggregations) satisfies the user query, OLAP Services returns the aggregated data immediately. Because all of the aggregations created by OLAP Services are indexed, query response time is generally fast.

If, however, a user query cannot be satisfied from an existing aggregation, OLAP Services retrieves the data and performs any necessary calculations on the underlying relational detail data. This usually results in a complex SELECT statement with multiple SUM and GROUP BY clauses. As you can imagine, the indexes that exist (or don't exist) on the detail data tables have an impact on query response time.

SQL Server 7.0 Indexing Tools

Appropriate index design has always been one of the most challenging aspects of managing a database. Balancing the trade-off between fast data retrieval and slow data update is particularly difficult. Add to that the complexities of understanding data distribution (the uniqueness of values in your data) and the myriad ways users try to request data, and you can see that designing a perfect indexing strategy is close to impossible.

In an effort to help administrators create effective indexing strategies, SQL Server 7.0 has introduced some tools that are definitely recommended. You can use the SQL Server Profiler and the Index Tuning Wizard to help you define an indexing strategy for your data warehouse and OLAP implementation.

SQL Server Profiler

The SQL Server Profiler is a tool that allows you to capture information about your SQL Server activity. For example, you can use it to trace all of the SQL statements that are being executed against your SQL Server. A good idea to help develop an indexing strategy for your data warehouse is to use the SQL Server Profiler to capture a trace while you are processing your cube. This enables you to analyze the queries that are being sent to your database.

To launch the SQL Server Profiler, double-click the SQL Server Profiler icon in the SQL Server program group. Then choose File, New, Trace to open the Trace Properties dialog box (shown in Figure 32.3).

FIGURE 32.3

The Trace Properties dialog is one place to develop an indexing strategy.

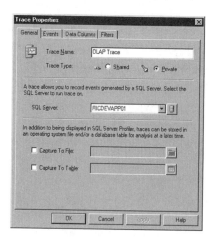

In the Trace Properties dialog, enter a name for your trace and specify the SQL Server on which you want to run the trace. Make sure this is the SQL Server on which your data warehouse resides—more specifically, the server on which your OLAP data source resides. Check the Capture to File checkbox and enter a filename to save your trace. This file becomes the workload file that can be analyzed by the Index Tuning Wizard.

The Events, Data Columns, and Filters tabs in the Trace Properties dialog allow you to further refine what you want to trace. You can specify that the trace only records certain events or that certain users and applications are excluded from the trace. A full discussion of all available options in the SQL Server Profiler is beyond the scope of this chapter.

Once you click OK in the Trace Properties dialog, the Profiler begins to record all activity occurring against the specified SQL Server. This may include SQL statements, connections, stored procedures, and other events. Once the trace is running, go to your OLAP Server and process your cube. When you process the cube, all commands sent to the SLQ Server are captured in your trace file. When the cube processing has completed, go to the Profiler and stop the trace. You now have a workload file that can be analyzed by the SQL Server Index Tuning Wizard to help recommend indexes.

Index Tuning Wizard

This section is not intended to be a complete reference on using the Index Tuning Wizard, rather it is intended to provide you with a brief introduction to a very useful SQL Server 7.0 tool. For a more detailed look at this tool and SQL Server 7.0 indexing in general, check out *Microsoft SQL Server 7.0 Unleashed* or *Microsoft SQL Server 7.0 DBA Survival Guide*.

Launch the Index Tuning Wizard from the SQL Server Profiler: choose Tools, Index Tuning Wizard. The Index Tuning Wizard starts. Click Next to bypass the introduction screen; the next screen is shown in Figure 32.4.

FIGURE 32.4

Begin by selecting the Server and Database you want to analyze.

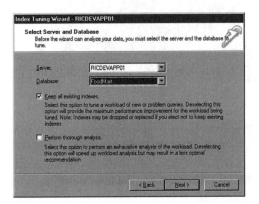

Enter the name of the SQL Server and the database that is to be analyzed. Because you are going to analyze a workload of new queries, you can leave the options as checked. Once you have entered the server and database, click Next. The next dialog, shown in Figure 32.5, appears.

Make sure the I Have a Saved Workload File radio button is selected and click Next. The dialog shown in Figure 32.6 appears.

FIGURE 32.5

Identify a workload for the wizard.

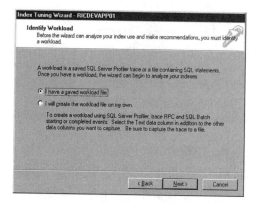

FIGURE 32.6

Next, specify the workload file to be analyzed.

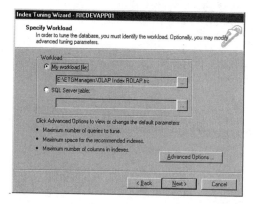

Browse to the location of the .trc file that you created using the SQL Server Profiler. This is the workload file that the Index Tuning Wizard will analyze. Click Next to go to the dialog shown in Figure 32.7.

FIGURE 32.7

Select the specific tables you want analyzed.

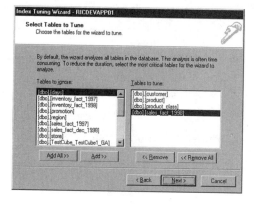

This dialog allows you to specify that you only want certain tables analyzed for index recommendations. For example, if only some of your data warehouse tables are involved in your cube design, you can choose to include only those tables in the index analysis. This can help speed up the recommendation process. Click Next and the dialog shown in Figure 32.8 appears.

FIGURE 32.8

The wizard displays its indexing recommendations for improved performance by your workload.

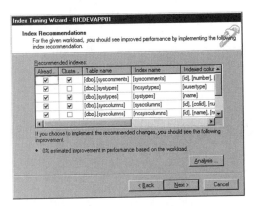

Once the Index Tuning Wizard has analyzed your workload file, it presents you with a set of recommendations for applying indexes to the tables. This analysis tells you whether an index already exists. In some cases, the Index Tuning Wizard does not recommend any additional indexes. This does not necessarily mean there are no other indexes that would be helpful. The Index Tuning Wizard does the best it can based on the queries that it finds in your workload file. This tool helps you to easily identify any obvious indexes that may be missing on your underlying data warehouse tables.

Once the Index Tuning Wizard has made recommendations, you can choose to implement those changes immediately or schedule the changes for later. The wizard creates the indexes for you if you choose to accept the recommendations.

The Index Tuning Wizard should be used as a starting point for defining an indexing strategy and not as an end point. In other words, you want to analyze the data and how it is being accessed on an on-going basis.

Summary

This chapter has covered some basic indexing concepts as they relate to a data warehouse and OLAP environment. It is by no means an exhaustive discussion of indexing and indexing strategies. That discussion could be the topic of an entire book.

The bottom line is that while indexes speed up data retrieval, they consume space and can degrade performance on data update activities. It is the job of the administrator to balance those two competing forces to create an indexing scheme that enables the best possible end-user performance while keeping the data load and cube-processing performance at an acceptable level. SQL Server provides some tools to help you manage that balancing act, but they are no replacement for an administrator's knowledge and understanding of indexes and how they relate to an OLAP Services environment.

OLAP Security

by Kevin Viers

IN THIS CHAPTER

CHAPTER 33

Just as it is in any other database engine, security is a critical component of a successful implementation of OLAP Services. Unfortunately, the shipping version of OLAP Services has very minimal security capabilities—it allows you to grant or deny access to specific users or groups of users at the cube level only. This means that users can access any of the data within a cube or none of the data within a cube.

This level of security is probably inadequate for a production-quality OLAP solution. In an effort to provide a more robust security environment, Microsoft has released Service Pack 1 for OLAP Services. It makes some significant enhancements to the Decision Support Object model to enable you to create cell-level security within a cube. This means that you can grant or deny access to specific members and measures within a cube to a user or group of users.

The first part of this chapter focuses on the basic security capabilities that are provided in the shipping version of OLAP Services. This functionality remains intact and is not changed by applying Service Pack 1. The remainder of the chapter focuses on the more advanced topic of adding cell-level security to your OLAP databases.

Integrated Windows NT Security

The first level of any security scheme is user authentication. Before you even begin to determine what data a user should or should not be able to view within an OLAP database, you need to determine whether the user should have access to the OLAP Services server. OLAP Services employs integrated Windows NT security for this authentication process.

In order to have access to OLAP Services, a user must be a member of the domain under which the OLAP Services was installed or be a member of one of its trusted domains.

The OLAP Administrators Group

When OLAP Services is installed, it creates a local NT group called OLAP Administrators on the server on which it is installed. By default, the user account under which the OLAP Services is installed becomes a member of that group. You can add other users to this group as long as they are part of the same or another trusted domain. This is done through the Windows NT User Manager. There is no interface within OLAP Manager to add users to the OLAP Administrators group. Those users will then have Administrator privileges on the OLAP Server. Be aware that any user who is a member of the OLAP Administrator group will have full access to all cube data regardless of any specific roles or permissions that you apply through OLAP Manager.

OLAP Roles

Now that you understand that OLAP Services uses basic NT authentication to allow users to access the server, you need to understand how to restrict access to the specific OLAP databases and cubes within those databases. The primary mechanism for creating this level of security is the role. A role provides a way to map NT user accounts and groups to specific security roles within an OLAP database.

Roles are defined at the database level and are not shared across databases. You may define as many roles as you like within each OLAP database. Once the roles have been defined at the database level, you can assign those roles to those cubes for which you want to apply security.

> **Note**
>
> The default behavior for OLAP Services as it is shipped is that all users who can be authenticated are granted read access to any database for which no role exists. Installing Service Pack 1 will change this default behavior. When Service Pack 1 is installed, you must explicitly define a role in the database and assign a user to that role to allow that user access to that database.

Access Control

As I mentioned previously, the shipped version of OLAP Services provides a minimal architecture to apply security to your OLAP data. Each role that you create can be assigned one of two levels of access control. Those access control levels are

- Read—This is the base level of security access and, as its name implies, allows users to browse data within the cube. The user can browse cell-level data as well as metadata about the cube structures. When you create a role and assign the role to a cube, the default access level is read.

- Read/Write—This access level applies only to those cubes that are write-enabled. Take a look at Chapter 17, "Partitioning Cubes and Administering OLAP Server," for more information about write-enabled cubes. When this level of access is specified, the user has full read capabilities plus the ability to modify data in a write-enabled cube.

In addition to read and read/write permissions, some users can also have Administration privileges on a database. This access level allows user access to the OLAP Manager interface with the ability to process data in a cube including refreshing data, changing cube and dimension structures, partitioning, and all other administrative activities pertaining to the OLAP database. By default, the user account under which OLAP Services is installed is the only user account with Admin privileges against all OLAP databases. Additionally, any user who has been added to the OLAP Administrator group will have Admin ability. There is no interface within OLAP Manager to assign Admin privileges to a user.

The following sections explain in more detail how to use the OLAP Manager interface to create and manage roles for your OLAP databases.

Creating Roles

Creating a role using the OLAP Manager is a very straightforward process. Remember that you must create roles first at the database level. An OLAP database can contain many roles and not all of those roles need to be assigned to individual cubes.

To create a new role for your OLAP database:

1. Expand the database in the OLAP Manager.
2. Expand the Library folder.
3. Highlight the Roles folder and right-click to display a shortcut menu.
4. Choose New Role from the shortcut menu. The dialog shown in Figure 33.1 appears.

FIGURE 33.1

Name your role in the Create a Database Role dialog.

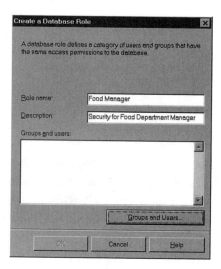

Once you have given the role a name and a description, you need to add users to the role. The role within an OLAP database is tightly integrated with NT Security, which means you can add any users or groups that exist in your NT Domain structure. To add users to the role, click the Groups and Users button; the dialog shown in Figure 33.2 appears.

FIGURE 33.2

Use the Add Users and Groups dialog to add users.

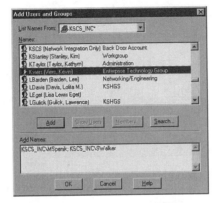

Choose any users or groups that you want to add to the role and click Add. You can modify the list of users and groups that belong to the role at any time by right-clicking the role in the OLAP Server Manager and choosing Edit.

> **Note**
>
> When a user makes a connection to the OLAP Server, he is authenticated using NT Security. The OLAP Server assigns roles to the user based on his NT logon. This means that if you are using OLAP Services in an intranet or Internet environment using IIS, you need to make sure the anonymous Web user account is assigned to the appropriate role. A user can be a member of many roles. If you want to restrict a user from accessing a particular cube, you must make sure that he is not a member of any role that has access to the cube.

When the role is created in the database, it does not have any access permissions associated with it. Essentially the role does not provide any security until it is assigned to a cube.

Assigning Roles to Cubes

To assign roles to specific cubes, expand the database in the Server Manager, expand the Cubes folder, highlight the desired cube, and then right-click to display a shortcut menu. Choose Manage Roles from the shortcut menu; the dialog shown in Figure 33.3 appears.

FIGURE 33.3

The Manage Roles dialog.

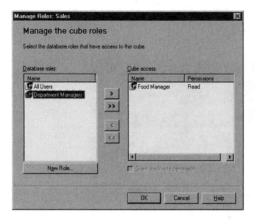

All the roles that have been created in the database where the cube resides are found in the Database Roles list. You can add as many roles as you need to the cube. Simply select the roles you want to add and click the arrow buttons to add them to the cube. Any member of any role that is assigned to the cube will have read access to that cube.

If your cube is write-enabled, you can check the Grant Read/Write Permission check box to allow selected roles to write data to the cube.

> **Note**
>
> You may be wondering how you can grant Admin privileges to a role. Administrator privileges allow users to process cubes, alter cube structures, and so on. You cannot explicitly grant Admin privileges to a role through the user interface. Only users who are members of the OLAP Administrators NT group on the OLAP Services machine are allowed Admin privileges to the cubes. If a user is a member of this group, he automatically has Admin access to the cubes regardless of any roles that are assigned.

Under the Hood

Just like everything else in OLAP Services, you can use the Decision Support Objects (DSO) to create roles and assign those roles to a cube within your applications. OLAP Services security is implemented via the Role interface of the DSO object model. The Role interface supports two objects, `clsCubeRole` and `clsDatabaseRole`. The `clsDataBase` and `clsCube` objects that are exposed through the MDStore interface contain Roles collections. As you might imagine, the Roles collections of each of these objects contain all of the roles that have been created for a given database and assigned to a given cube.

Assigning users or groups to the role is done at the database level and is implemented through the `UsersList` property of the `clsDatabaseRole` object. The `UsersList` property contains a string that lists all NT user accounts or groups that are part of the role. The actual security level for a cube is implemented through the `SetPermissions` method of the `clsCubeRole` object. Both the `UsersList` property and the `SetPermissions` method are exposed through the Role interface.

The example shown in Listing 33.1 illustrates how you can use DSO to create a role in the FoodMart database and assign that role to the Sales cube with read access. To use Visual Basic to implement DSO, you must make sure that Decision Support Objects is included in Project References. For a more detailed explanation of programming with DSO, refer to chapter 18, "Decision Support Objects".

LISTING 33.1   Creating and Assigning Roles

```
Private Sub Form_Load()

Dim lsRoleName as String
LsRoleName = "New Role"

'Declare all of your DSO variables.

Dim dsoServer As DSO.Server
Dim dsoDatabase As DSO.MDStore
Dim dsoCube As DSO.MDStore
Dim dsoRole As DSO.Role

'Make a connection to the OLAP Server on which you want to create the role.

Set dsoServer = New DSO.Server
DsoServer.Connect ("LocalHost")

'Get the target OLAP Database and Cube.  Note that both the
'database and cube objects are exposed through the MDStores
'interface in the DSO object model

Set dsoDatabase = dsoServer.MDStores("FoodMart")
Set dsoCube = dsoDatabase.MDStores("Sales")

'Create the new role in the database

'make sure role does not already exist in the database, add role to the
'database, assign users to the role, and update the role definition
If Not dsoDatabase.Roles.Find(lsRoleName) Then

    dsoDatabase.Roles.AddNew(lsRoleName)
    Set dsoRole = dsoDatabase.Roles(lsRoleName)
```

continues

LISTING 33.1   continued

```
        dsoRole.UsersList = "MASTER\kviers;"                        dsoRole.Update
End If

'Assign the role to the target Cube and set access permission
' to read permission

If Not dsoCube.Roles.Find(lsRoleName) Then
dsoCube.Roles.AddNew(lsRoleName)                dsoRole.SetPermissions "Access",
"R"             DsoCube.Update
End If

'Close connection with OLAP Server

dsoServer.CloseServer

End Sub
```

This example illustrates how easy it is to implement roles using DSO. The UsersList property simply contains a semicolon-separated list of valid NT user or group names that will be added to the role. You can add as many users or groups to this list as you need. The shipped version of OLAP Services only supports one permission per role. Obviously, this security model is not robust enough for most production environments.

With the Service Pack 1 for OLAP Services, Microsoft has expanded the Role interface so that it contains a collection of permissions and not just a single permission. In this way, you are able to implement cell-level security. The remainder of this chapter discusses how to implement cell-level security in your OLAP applications.

Cell-Level Security

The ability to restrict access to the individual data elements within a cube is a vital part of any OLAP application. This concept, known as cell-level security, enables you to create cubes that contain all your relevant data and then restrict access to that data based on various data-related criteria.

The most obvious example of why you need cell-level security is seen when examining sensitive data such as salary information. You may want to create a cube that contains salary data for a department within your organization. Obviously, only certain individuals within the department will need access to that data, while virtually every individual within the department will need access to other data contained within the cube. Without cell-level security, the only way to achieve this level of security would be to create multiple cubes for each type of user and then physically slice the data partitions to restrict certain data from users. This solution creates an administrative nightmare, redundant data storage, and any number of other disadvantages.

To solve this problem, OLAP Services Service Pack 1 enables you to define a set of permissions for each role you create that will allow various levels of access to specific data elements within your cubes. Each cube can be assigned many roles and each role can have a more granular permission assigned to restrict cell-level data access. The following sections explain in more detail how to do this within your applications.

> **Note**
>
> All the cell-level security must be applied programmatically. The discussions in the following sections of this chapter are based on custom Visual Basic applications that expose the DSO object model to implement the cell-level security rules. As of the publication of this book, OLAP Services does not have a GUI interface built in to the OLAP Manager to apply cell-level security. It is possible, however, to write a custom add-in that would enable you to apply cell-level security through the OLAP Manager interface. For more information about programming with DSO and creating custom add-ins for OLAP Manager, refer to Chapter 18, "Decision Support Objects," and Chapter 19, "Developing an Add-In Program for OLAP Services."

33

OLAP SECURITY

Implementation

Security is handled through the Role interface in the DSO object model. In the original shipped version of OLAP Services, the role object only contained a single property called Permissions to hold either read, write, or Admin access privileges for a given role. That security applied to the entire cube so that a user had to be a member of a role that was assigned to a cube to read all of the data within the cube. If a user had access to the cube, the user could access all of the data within the cube. The OLAP Services Service Pack 1 enhances the object model so that role objects assigned to a cube now contain a collection of permissions properties and not simply a single property. Each permission property stores rules for granting access to cell values based on various conditions.

The basic implementation of a permission for a role is an MDX statement that evaluates to true or false. Chapter 27, "Building an MDX Query," provides a more detailed discussion of the MDX syntax. Any valid MDX statement that returns a Boolean value can be used as the source for a cell-level permission. The permissions are applied by using the

`SetPermissions` method that is exposed through the Role interface. The syntax is as follows:

```
Role.SetPermissions(PermissionsKey As String, _

    PermissionsExpression As String) As Boolean
```

Within this syntax the `PermissionsKey` is a string that represents the permission level to enforce on the cell. The available permission levels and their associated `PermissionsKey` values are shown in Table 33.1 and are discussed in more detail in the next section on Permissions.

TABLE 33.1 Permissions Keys for the `SetPermissions` Method

PermissionsKey	*Access Level*
`CellRead`	Read Permission
`CellReadContingent`	Contingent Read Permission
`CellWrite`	Write Permission

`PermissionsExpression` is a string that contains an MDX statement that returns either 1 (true) or 0 (false). Whenever a user attempts to access a cell, the `PermissionsExpression` is evaluated. If the `PermissionsExpression` evaluates to true, access to the cell is granted; otherwise access is denied. The following is an example MDX statement that will restrict certain users from seeing any salary data:

```
Iif (Measures.CurrentMember.Name = "Salary", 0, 1)
```

When this statement is evaluated, it will equate to false (0) only when the "Salary" measure is being requested. As a result, the salary will not be displayed to the user when this permission is in effect.

Permissions

There are three possible permission levels that you can grant at the cell level. Those permission levels are

- Read Permission—This level allows users to read the data values within a cell based on a set of criteria that is defined by the `PermissionsExpression`.
- Contingent Read Permission—This level applies only to calculated members. It enables you to set read access to a cell that returns calculated members as long as the underlying data cells are readable.
- Write Permission—This level allows a cell to be written. It is only applicable for a write-enabled cube.

The key to understanding the cell-level permissions is to understand that each cell permission level can have only one rule per role. In other words, you can only define one MDX statement to determine whether or not to grant read access to a cell. Whenever a user application requests data from an OLAP cube, the server evaluates the rules for every cell that is requested. The outcome of that rule evaluation determines if an individual cell is returned.

The easiest way to understand these concepts is to work with some examples. The following sections provide code samples that can be used to set cell-level permissions and illustrate the results using the MDX sample application. All code examples are based on using Visual Basic 6 with the Decision Support Objects reference set. In order to implement the VB application, you must be logged on as a member of the OLAP Administrators group.

Read Permission

Probably the most common thing you will want to do within your security scheme is to set read access to specific cells. Remember that each role can only have one access rule defined for read access to the cell data. To implement this example, create a role called Food Manager in the FoodMart database. Add to this role a user who is NOT a member of the OLAP Administrators group. Assign that role to the Sales cube and remove the All Users role from the cube. You need to remove the All Users role because it contains everyone and its security settings may override your role.

The following example will set a cell read permission for the Food Manager role that only allows access to the measures relating to the Food department. Create a new Visual Basic project and add the code in Listing 33.2 to the Form_Load() procedure.

LISTING 33.2 Setting Read Permissions at the Cell Level

```
Private Sub Form_Load()

Dim lsRoleName as String
LsRoleName = "Food Manager"

'Declare all of your DSO variables.

Dim dsoServer As DSO.Server
Dim dsoDatabase As DSO.MDStore
Dim dsoCube As DSO.MDStore
Dim dsoRole As DSO.Role

'Make a connection to the OLAP Server
```

continues

33

OLAP SECURITY

LISTING 33.2 continued

```
Set dsoServer = New DSO.Server
DsoServer.Connect ("LocalHost")

'Get the target OLAP Database and Cube.

Set dsoDatabase = dsoServer.MDStores("FoodMart")
Set dsoCube = dsoDatabaser.MDStores("Sales")
Set dsoRole = dsoCube.Roles(lsRoleName)

'Set read permission

Dim sPermission As String
SPermission = "Iif(Ancestor(Current.Member, _
    [Product Family]).Name = ""Food"",1,0)"
dsoRole.SetPermissions "CellRead", sPermission

'Update Cube and Close connection with OLAP Server

dsoCube.Update
dsoServer.CloseServer

End Sub
```

When you run this form, the rule is applied to the Food Manager role. When any user who is a member of this role attempts to access data, the rule is evaluated for every cell requested. In this example, only data that is associated with the Food member of the Product dimension will be readable. All other data will not be accessible. To test this example, log on as a member of the Food Manager role and run the MDX sample application. Figure 33.4 shows the results of a query against the cube.

FIGURE 33.4

Results of a query against a cube with security in place.

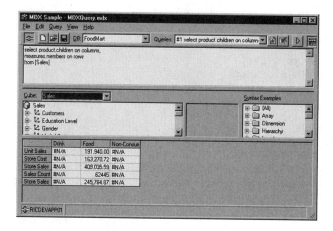

Notice that all data values other than those associated with "Food" return a #N/A. This is the standard result returned when read access is denied to a cell. If you want to switch the permission so that only data pertaining to Food is denied while all other access is granted, rewrite the *SetPermissions* statement as follows:

```
'Set read permission

Dim sPermission As String
SPermission = "Iif(Ancestor(Current.Member, _
    [Product Family]).Name = ""Food"",0,1)"
dsoRole.SetPermissions "CellRead", sPermission
```

The results of applying this permission are illustrated in Figure 33.5.

FIGURE 33.5

Changing access permissions produces different query results.

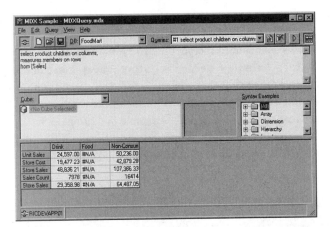

Caution

Be very careful about how you build your permission rules. In a typical security scenario, most administrators tend to lock everything down and then grant access to resources as needed. If you take this approach when applying cell-level security to a cube, you can get burned. In other words, if you apply a permissions rule that will only evaluate to TRUE when a given condition exists, then all other data will be denied to the user. This can have consequences if you don't create your MDX statement correctly. A safer approach is to create permission rules that will evaluate to FALSE only when a given condition exists. This has the effect of keeping all data accessible except those cells for which you explicitly want to deny access. It is up to the administrator to determine the security

continues

strategy that is most appropriate, but you must be careful. Consider the following:

Case 1: SetPermissions "CellRead", "Iif(1=2,1,0) "

Case 2: SetPermissions "CellRead",,"Iif(1=2,0,1) "

The condition "1=2" can never be satisfied; therefore in Case 1 all data will be denied to the user and in Case 2 all data in the cube will be accessible to the user.

Contingent Read Permission

The contingent read cell permission is only applicable to calculated members. Calculated members are derived from the data values of underlying members. For example, the Sales cube contains a calculated member called Profit. This calculated member is defined as `Measures.[Store Sales]` - `Measures.[Store Cost]`. You can assign the contingent read cell access rule to the cells that contain Profit. This means that OLAP Services will return the cells corresponding to Profit only if the underlying members Store Sales and Store Cost have read access. Consider the example in Listing 33.3.

LISTING 33.3 Setting Contingent Read Permission at the Cell Level

```
Private Sub Form_Load()

Dim lsRoleName as String
LsRoleName = "Food Manager"

'Declare all of your DSO variables.

Dim dsoServer As DSO.Server
Dim dsoDatabase As DSO.MDStore
Dim dsoCube As DSO.MDStore
Dim dsoRole As DSO.Role

'Make a connection to the OLAP Server

Set dsoServer = New DSO.Server
DsoServer.Connect ("LocalHost")

'Get the target OLAP Database and Cube.

Set dsoDatabase = dsoServer.MDStores("FoodMart")
Set dsoCube = dsoServer.MDStores("Sales")
Set dsoRole = dsoCube.Roles(lsRoleName)
```

```
'Set read permission on Store Sales and Store Cost

Dim sPermission As String
sPermission = "Iif(((Measures.CurrentMember.Name = ""Store Sales"")"
sPermission = sPermission & _
        " or (Measures.CurrentMember.Name = ""Store Cost""))"
sPermission = sPermission & _
        " and (Ancestor(Store.CurrentMember,[Store State]).Name = ""CA""),1,0)"
dsoRole.SetPermissions "CellRead",sPermission


'Set contingent read permission on Profit

sPermission = "Iif(Measures.CurrentMember.Name = "Profit",1,0) "
dsoRole.SetPermissions "CellReadContingent", sPermission

'Update Cube and Close connection with OLAP Server

dsoCube.Update
dsoServer.CloseServer

End Sub
```

In this example, we set a cell read permission rule to only allow read access to the Store Cost and Store Sales measures where the Store State dimension is California. By setting the contingent read permission rule on cells containing the Profit measure, you are telling OLAP Services to return those cells containing Profit as long as the underlying measures have appropriate read access.

The results of applying this permission are illustrated in Figure 33.6.

FIGURE 33.6

A query against data that has contingent read permission rules applied returns different results.

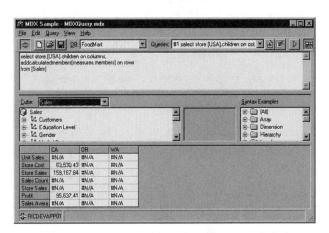

33

OLAP SECURITY

Write Permission

The last type of cell-level permission is write permission. If you are dealing with a write-enabled cube, you can set permission rules to allow or deny specific write access to cells within the cube. Suppose you write-enable the sales cube and you only want people to be able to update the Store Cost measure within the cube. Listing 33.4 illustrates how to apply this permission rule.

LISTING 33.4   Setting Write Permission at the Cell Level

```
Private Sub Form_Load()

Dim lsRoleName as String
LsRoleName = "Food Manager"

'Declare all of your DSO variables.

Dim dsoServer As DSO.Server
Dim dsoDatabase As DSO.MDStore
Dim dsoCube As DSO.MDStore
Dim dsoRole As DSO.Role

'Make a connection to the OLAP Server

Set dsoServer = New DSO.Server
DsoServer.Connect ("LocalHost")

'Get the target OLAP Database and Cube.

Set dsoDatabase = dsoServer.MDStores("FoodMart")
Set dsoCube = dsoServer.MDStores("Sales")
Set dsoRole = dsoCube.Roles(lsRoleName)

'Set write permission for the Store Cost measure

Dim sPermission As String
sPermission = "Iif(Measures.CurrentMember.Name = ""Store Cost"",1,0)"
dsoRole.SetPermissions "CellWrite",sPermission


'Update Cube and Close connection with OLAP Server

dsoCube.Update
dsoServer.CloseServer

End Sub
```

This security can only be tested with an application that supports cube write-back. The MDX sample application and the Excel 2000 Pivot Table Service currently do not support cube write-back. If you have a custom-written or third-party client application that supports write-back to OLAP Services cubes, these security rules will work.

> **Caution**
>
> Be careful when you have users assigned to more than one role. A user can be assigned to many roles. If you define read-access permissions to a cell in one role and try to deny read access to the same cell in another role, the results are unpredictable. This is only the case if the same user is a member of both roles. The best strategy is to create separate roles for each type of cell access you need to manage and never assign the same user to two roles with conflicting cell-level security.

Order of Operations

It is important to understand the order in which OLAP Services will evaluate security rules so as to determine whether to return a cell value. This can have an impact when you plan your security strategy.

If a client application requests read access to a cell, the following are evaluated:

- If there are no read-access rules defined for the role, OLAP does not perform any further checks and returns the value of the cell.

- If a read-access rule applies to the cell, the rule is evaluated. If the condition is satisfied, OLAP Services returns the value of the cell and no further checks are performed.

- If a contingent-read-access rule applies to the cell, the rule is evaluated. If the condition is satisfied, OLAP Services returns the value of the cell and no further checks are performed.

- If the cell contains a calculated member (defined by the client application and not in the OLAP cube structure), OLAP Services returns the value of the cell.

- If none of the above conditions is satisfied, OLAP Services returns an error.

The following is the default security behavior:

- If no read-access or contingent-read-access rules are present, read access is granted to all cells within the cube.

- If no write-access rules are present, and the role has read/write permission on the parent cube, write access to all cells is granted.

Summary

As in any other database environment, security is an important component of rolling out a production-ready OLAP application. Microsoft has provided an enhanced capability to apply granular security within the cube structure itself. The security is still relatively basic, as you can only define one rule for each type of security permission within a role. If you need more sophisticated security, you have to apply that security on the client application. This can be accomplished using many of the same concepts discussed in this chapter.

Metadata

by Russell Darroch

One of the new "in" words of the era is *metadata*. Once reserved for the intelligentsia tucked away in remote college and university campuses somewhere in snowbound Minnesota (at least that's where I first heard the word metadata—in a philosophy class), it has become a feature of everyday discussion in the OLAP arena. Unfortunately, like all such language that becomes commonplace, the term is not always used properly. This chapter is designed to help you gain a better feel for what metadata means in the context of OLAP Server and Microsoft SQL Server 7.0.

Metadata areas in Microsoft SQL Server and OLAP services are based on more general issues that are thoroughly described in discussions of Microsoft Repository. The general underlying themes that you should become familiar with include the concepts of information models, the Unified Modeling Language, the Open Information Model (OIM), and specific submodels (for databases, OLAP and others). Each topic discussed in this chapter has an associated modeling language and OIM submodel. I return to these in more detail at the end of the chapter.

Metadata Definitions and Concepts

Metadata, often defined as data about data, are the sets of defining information that allow you to talk to the components of the system, in this case, OLAP services and related technology components.

Datum, Data, Meta...

Throughout this chapter, I will try to use the words *metadata* and *metadatum* properly. It has become a neverending battle with editors, courseware authors, and others, within Microsoft and elsewhere, over the proper use of the words *datum*, *data*, *metadatum*, and *metadata*. Having acquired a minor in linguistics/psycholinguistics years ago, I have always understood that language evolves and changes, but I have to say that with a science background, the current use and abuse of the word *data*, particularly in the computing industry, grates every time I hear it. Today people routinely refer to both the singular and plural with the word *data* and hardly use the word *datum* at all. Datum is singular, data is plural, and so it goes for metadatum and metadata. The elegance of language is part of its appeal and should be treasured, not destroyed.

--rkd

If you look in the glossary for OLAP Books Online, you will not find the word *metadatum* at all. You will find the word *metadata* defined as

> Information about the nature of data or the structure of data. This can range from the information about particular features or characteristics of columns, dimensions, or cubes or any other object used to refer to data within a particular frame of reference. In this case the frame of reference is OLAP Server and Microsoft SQL Server.

Now as you can see, this is pretty broad. Basically, metadata are the pieces of information about data items themselves, structure of data items, aspects of OLAP objects such as cubes, dimensions, members, hierarchies, and virtual cubes along with a host of others. Each metadatum provides a piece of information about the particular item in question. The collection of metadata about an object or piece of data should completely define it, in all aspects.

As mentioned in Chapter 18, "Decision Support Objects," the Decision Support Object model is rich in metadata, which can be used to define the particular activities and relationships of the objects themselves and the data that they in turn handle.

In this chapter I will explore the various places in which metadata are used within the broader context of OLAP services, English Query, and SQL Server. This is not intended to be a comprehensive, exhaustive analysis of each and every place metadata are used to refer to features of data or objects, but I do aim to give you a good feel for how broadly the term is used.

As indicated earlier, the Microsoft Repository gets a lot of focus when talking about metadata because, for all intents and purposes, that is the main place where such data are stored within the environments in which we are interested. We have already examined some of these ideas in Chapter 13, "Using the Repository in Data Transformations."

Let us look at the breadth of usage first and then I'll return to the role of Microsoft Repository and the Unified Modeling Language Model in all of this. In the meantime, I recommend that you go to msdn.microsoft.com/repository and download the latest version of the Repository SDK (2.1b at the time of writing) so that you can explore it when you finish the chapter.

When you have downloaded the SDK you will find about two dozen references to metadata in the documentation. The most crucial concept in those references is the distinction drawn between data and metadata, or between "types" and "instances." Types refer to the characteristics (properties, classes) of data, while instances refer to the actual data used by software users, the use of data properties, and particular values. The point is made that the distinction is not rigid; this is an understatement.

34

METADATA

I will try to stick to the low road of data and metadata in the very particular environment of Microsoft software, and SQL Server, OLAP Service, and Repository in particular, and leave the extensive metaphysical arguments for you and your friends to pursue around a cozy fire or campfire while sipping a good (Australian!!) red wine.

Uses of Metadata in SQL Server

While OLAP is the primary focus, metadata occur in the context of Microsoft SQL Server. If you search on the word *metadata* in SQL Server Books Online, you will find 152 references, compared to the 44 references you find when you search the OLAP Books Online.

The modeling languages on which the metadata of SQL Server are based are the Database Model (Dbm) and the SQL Server Model (Sql).

In the context of SQL Server itself, data are usually thought of as the particular items stored within the rows and cells of your database tables. But even here the ease of definitive statements is elusive: The contents of cells in system tables are, in fact, usually metadata, while information in the cells of normal tables are generally data.

The system catalog keeps track of names, sizes, locations, and other key information about databases, database files, logical names, physical path references, and so on. These are metadata about databases. The actual data of databases are the contents of the user database, the records of information about the objects of each table, relationship, and the measures and descriptors recorded therein. For example, the logical name of a database (such as Northwind) is one piece of information about a physical file (such as c:\mssql7\data\northwnd.mdf) that contains data for a specific database.

In the SQL Server environment, if you start with the idea that everything that is descriptive and not core user data is metadata, you are probably not too far from the truth. Each and every thing within SQL Server that describes parts of the environment can be considered metadata of a sort. There are quite a few places within the product where these metadata are articulated quite explicitly. Let me show you some examples.

Metadata Use in DTS

Data Transformation Services (DTS) uses metadata in many ways to describe packages, data handling done by packages, sources, destinations, and other key characteristics. Metadata are used to store the information in a repository database that may be referenced by DTS itself, by other providers such as third-party products, and for purposes of tracking data lineage.

Versioning can also be traced in the metadata about a DTS package, enabling you to keep track of modifications in a direct and easy manner.

Other metadata used within the DTS context include information such as column names in source and destination tables; table names; data types including size, scale and precision; nullability; and indexes. If you are writing code to translate information between source and destination, the metadata about the language type are also stored.

One of the key concepts to remember is that, almost without exception, the handling of metadata is done through particular tools and interfaces or directly through the programmatic handling of objects and their associated properties, classes, and methods. The metadata are handled by the special tools of SQL Enterprise Manager, the DTS Package Designer, the Replication wizards, and so on. You seldom, if ever, will work directly with the Repository and the metadata stored therein. Even when using the Repository SDK itself, you "talk to" the metadata through the special tools of the Repository Browser.

In the SQL Server context, you can see this most clearly under the Data Transformation Services branch in Enterprise Manager, as shown in Figure 34.1.

FIGURE 34.1
*SQL Server
Enterprise
Manager shows
the location of the
most direct meta-
data interfaces
within it.*

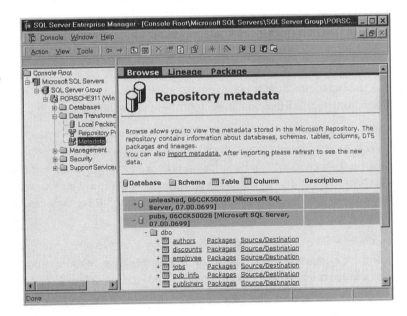

Metadata Use in Creating SQL Jobs

When you create jobs within SQL Server, the jobs and job steps are all made up from descriptive information, or metadata, which includes details of the processes to be done in the job step, the operators to be notified (if any), and the other details of precedence, dependence, and scheduling that may also be involved in the job.

Metadata Use in Result Sets

The details of the data being returned through a particular result set again get down to basics—column information, data size, type, precision, and so forth. For example, through its API catalog functions, ODBC provides metadata to the applications that are using ODBC as their data-handling mechanism.

When an application is well designed and efficient, it almost certainly has metadata referencing done in such a way that code does not have to be rewritten with every little change in the metadata about the base tables in the database. On the other hand, if you were to hard-code references to metadata about column definitions, you would almost certainly have to rewrite parts of the applications when you changed a column, even if it was just a matter of changing its nullability or its precision. This would make it very tedious to manage result sets for such a hard-coded application. In general, you want to develop code that does not require such fundamental rewriting just to modify a column.

Metadata Use in Distributed Queries

Another instance in SQL Server where you would use metadata is in the development of distributed queries. The references to the linked servers are metadata about the locations and sources for the distributed queries to work with. One of the SQLOLEDB interfaces that returns such information is the IDBSchemaRowset interface.

Other information used by distributed queries in terms of their particular references to objects, tables, procedures, or other Transact-SQL items are also metadata. In the end, the data from the distributed queries are returned to you by using metadata to locate the data sources, return it to your client application, and know which servers are involved and whether they are all SQL Servers or a mixture of DB2, Oracle, and SQL Server sources.

Just in case you are wondering if I forgot about error messages, you can sleep soundly. There are even references to metadata in error messages. With regard to distributed queries, you might on some occasion see Error 7356, which is described as

> Error 7356. Severity Level 16. OLE DB provider '%ls' supplied inconsistent metadata for a column. Metadata information was changed at execution time. [Note: '%ls' would be replaced by a specific reference in the actual error message sent to the client]

Explanation

This error indicates that there was inconsistent metadata reported by the provider on a given table between compilation time and execution time of the query. This typically occurs because the provider returns inconsistent metadata between the OLE DB schema rowset COLUMNS (during compilation) and that metadata reported by the IColumnsInfo interface on the table's rowset.

Action

Consult SQL Server Profiler to determine which table column caused this error.

There are a few similar error messages that will refer you back to metadata as well. To review these, search on "metadata" and "error" together in Books Online.

Use of Metadata with Server Cursors

When server cursors are being implemented, they are also referenced through metadata information. There are two methods of retrieving the metadata.

First, metadata can be obtained through the particular API being used; data about the nature and state of the cursor can be retrieved through a number of APIs, including

- ADO
- ODBC
- OLE DB
- DB-Library

Second, metadata are retrieved through the normal use of Transact SQL in the form of triggers and stored procedures to gather information about cursors. This information enables you to work with the cursor in the manner which most suits your purposes, including deciding which type of cursor should be used in a particular situation.

Use of Metadata in Full-Text Indexing

One of the newest features of SQL Server is also an excellent example of the use of metadata. With full-text indexing we can now easily retrieve information from all kinds of textual data with speed and ease. The mechanisms that enable this to happen are, guess what, metadata!

When a database is enabled for full-text indexing, a variety of metadata items are created to make it possible to store indexing information and provide retrieval of the indexed items. In particular, the catalog structures and references are created in the database, the tables that are being indexed are marked, and references are created, so that the indexing service, Microsoft Search, knows what to do and where to do it.

34

METADATA

Metadata to the rescue again! As you can see, once we are talking about data about data, we are right back into metadata territory.

Uses of Metadata in OLAP Services

OLAP services and its components use metadata heavily. This is not an accident. The complexities of OLAP require that we have a rich descriptive language and model. As the discussions of DSO in Chapter 18 show, there are many objects, properties, classes, and interfaces involved in managing cubes, virtual cubes, dimensions, hierarchies, members, and measures. These special components of the OLAP world are described in the OLAP Model (Olp) of the Unified Modeling Language (Uml).

To sufficiently describe and manage all of these is, as in the SQL Server environment, an operation dependent on metadata. The data to describe cubes alone are extensive and, used along with the PivotTable Service metadata, give extensive control over the cubes and the querying of them.

Each aspect of the cube, the data storage type, its structure, and its aggregations, is managed through metadata. In OLAP, this information is also stored normally in a relational data store, either in a JET database or a SQL database (MSDB).

Both the server- and client-side caches store information whenever querying is done in an OLAP environment. The information managed through the cache is a mixture of data and metadata, and this is part of what makes the architecture so powerful. When queries are run against the server, the query engine checks to see what is in the cache and then uses this information to decide what is already in the cache and what else needs to be retrieved from storage. Smart caching between the client and the server means that only data that must be retrieved are handled; what is in cache is used and only has to be refreshed if the query is actually different from a previous one.

When planning your OLAP environment, you should store related cubes and dimensions within the same database so that the metadata may be used most efficiently. This will enable the most effective use of data on sources, roles, cubes and virtual cubes.

In working with OLAP, one of the new concepts you need to grasp fairly quickly is that whenever you change the metadata of a cube or virtual cube, you must reprocess the cube to ensure that it is consistent with the changed metadata and resultant structures, aggregates, dimensions and measures. The point is that we tend to think of updating things when data change; here we need to ensure that updating is done when metadata change. You must be alert to such situations, whether it is the change in a dimension structure or a revised cube definition. By and large, Microsoft OLAP is pretty helpful in reminding you that something has changed, but there may be times when this will not happen automatically and you must to be aware of the need to refresh the cube or virtual cube.

I also want to remind you that when you develop programs that are custom add-ins built on DSO, there are many opportunities to leverage off of the rich metadata information to create reports and analyses of the metadata as well as of the data.

Just as data are critical to your OLAP work, so too are your metadata. It is important to back them up, and you may want to build additional add-ins to help manage this aspect of your OLAP server. This is important primarily if you want customized solutions; it is easy enough to use the standard environment to ensure that your critical backups are done in a timely manner.

Your metadata are potentially of significance to others who would like to know about the structure of your data or your company. Just as with other aspects of SQL Server and OLAP services, you can control the access to your metadata so that it remains secure. Remember that security is only really an option under the NTFS, which is what I am presuming you are using; if not, you cannot really implement security in any meaningful sense.

> **Caution**
>
> With every passing day there are a few more devious, some would say twisted, minds who think it is "fun" to break into systems, crack passwords, and destroy corporate data. You should always ensure that you have all levels of security properly implemented in your data warehouse—physical, firewall, and file and share level security. You should keep an eye on the additional security features incorporated in Windows 2000 products and in the future versions of SQL Server that can then build on the Windows 2000 architecture to provide you even greater peace of mind.

34

METADATA

You should consider carefully who has full (admin) access to your metadata. The descriptive data alone could give a competitor a good set of clues as to what your business focuses on in its analyses of both data marts and data warehouses. You do not need to have the data to make some educated guesses about the focus and purpose of strategic analyses, so I recommend that you only allow access to that level of information to the appropriate people within your organization.

Wherever you turn within Microsoft OLAP, metadata are in use. Your task as a developer/user is to become familiar with the breadth and depth of this powerful system of describing and controlling data and to become a true power user of Microsoft Repository and related tools.

Uses of Metadata in English Query

The English Query, in which you build natural language queries against relational and multidimensional data stores, is built upon an object model and an information model designed specifically by Microsoft to fit tightly with Microsoft Repository and its associated metadata capabilities.

The model used for metadata in English Query is the Semantic Information Model (Sim), a special subset that allows interaction with databases without reference to a specific data manipulation language. This particular model is an extension of the Dbm model mentioned earlier and can interact in this case with both the Sql and the Olp models.

At the time of release of SQL Server 7.0, the English Query tool could only be used directly against the normal relational database model (Dbm and Sql). Since then, the English Query tool has been enhanced and was shown at TechEd99 working against the OLAP environment, which was always part of the plan. To work with the OLAP environment, the English Query tool has been greatly improved in order to handle not only the metadata for normal relational queries but also the special requirements of the multidimensional query language.

Metadata describe the domains, entities, and attributes—as well as relationships, actions, and synonyms—in English Query. There are two additional uses of the metadata with this tool. First, the metadata allow the mapping of database schema to a particular semantic model that can then be used by a linguistic processor (English Query engine) to interpret the natural language against the underlying database structure and data.

The second use of the metadata is to provide a way of exporting, in a consistent and meaningful manner, the English Query models that a developer creates into Repository for the storage of the metadata. The special tool for this is called the English Query Exporter (EQE). The importance of this capability is that as other third-parties develop additional tools to work with OLAP and SQL Server, they will also be able to work with the English Query models developed in the Microsoft English Query environment and extend them as they want.

The most thrilling aspect of this extensibility is that, with time, it is likely that there will be a rich, multiple language set of semantic models which will enable the use of a query in any of the main languages against your data warehouse. Now that's exciting!

I now turn to the generic issues with metadata as represented in the Unified Modeling Language and the Microsoft Repository.

Microsoft Repository and Metadata

Microsoft Repository is fundamentally just a tool for storing (in an agreed and systematic manner) the various information models that can be created based on a standard language.

Microsoft has worked with industry partners over the last several years to achieve an agreed-upon structure and standard for the Repository. The Repository is fundamentally a purpose-built relational database that holds metadata and maintains, for any particular information model, the specific data details of the metadata items, the relationships between elements of the metadata, and any other modeling elements required by the particular model. When I say that Repository is "just" this, do not underestimate its value. Such an agreed-upon standard provides all parties with a tremendous capability to provide consistent standards, guidelines, and, in turn, tools, to work against any information model and its object incarnations in an agreed, predictable, and efficient manner. This is an extremely significant benefit to the entire information industry, particularly in the database arena, in terms of development, ease of use, and interaction between vendors' technologies. Let us look at the main elements of this system.

The Unified Modeling Language

There has been an agreement among industry members to work with Microsoft and others on an Open Information Model (OIM). With all major vendors and parties involved in the discussion and development of such a standard, it has helped the industry to progress rapidly on interoperability in many areas.

To fully appreciate the complexity of this, I urge you to read the documentation for the Repository SDK as mentioned before. In essence, there is a special Repository Type Information Model (RTIM) that is part of the OIM. With the libraries and shared interfaces that these support, it is possible for you to build your own applications in Visual Basic or Visual C++ for use with the Microsoft Visual Modeler tool set. Within each of the areas available under the Uml, you can build applications to work with particular types of metadata for a specific subject matter.

34

METADATA

The nature of the Uml is an agreed set of guidelines and language components that explains how to describe models, components, objects, interfaces and other key aspects of metadata for particular extensions to the OIM.

The inherent problem in a multi-object universe is that each object (or model) is unique but at the same time we want to use them to interact with each other. The Uml provides sets of rules, agreed-upon descriptive mechanisms, and user-defined types that allow for the common storage of information in a format that can be shared. The particular implementation through Microsoft Repository enables the sharing of information in a manner that permits the co-evolution of models by various vendors in a storage environment that contains both the elements described and descriptions of how to describe elements. This means that

- The OIM is stored along with the information to which it refers. Since this is self-descriptive, it makes it possible to use queries against the model to modify processing behavior.
- Interfaces encapsulate the stored information completely, which in turn makes it easy to change the model and have the changes to data evolve as necessary. Vendors can write their particular extensions to models to tailor interfaces for their own use. Extensions provide the customization without tampering with the interface itself.

If used properly, this can have enormous benefits for both intra-vendor and inter-vendor application and tools development projects and products.

Extensions to the UML

Uml itself is a particular implementation of the UML (Unified Modeling Language version 1.0) conceptual model. There are many ways of extending the Uml, and the industry, working with Microsoft, has produced a significant number of extensions that are of particular interest to those of us who work with databases, data warehousing, and tools such as English Query. These are in addition to tools produced by other vendors, as mentioned in Chapter 21, "Other OLE DB for OLAP Servers."

The major extensions at present to the UML are listed in an abbreviated summary form in Table 34.1.

Table 34.1 A List of Major Extensions to the UML

Model Prefix	Description
RTIM	Repository Type Information Model. This is the meta meta model—the language in which the other information models (or meta models) are defined.
Uml	Unified Modeling Language Model. This information model represents the conceptual Unified Modeling Language (UML) 1.0 model, an industry standard for analyzing, specifying, designing, constructing, and visualizing the artifacts of a software system.
Umx	Uml Extension Model. A set of generic extensions to the Uml model, and a realization of some of the predefined stereotypes in UML 1.0.
Dtm	Data Type Model. A set of Uml model extensions that supply numerous common data types.
Cde	Component Description Model. A set of generic component-related Uml model extensions describing runtime (executable) components and their specifications.
Com	COM (Component Object Model) Model. A set of COM-specific extensions to the Cde and Dtm models.
Gen	Generic Model. A set of general-purpose interfaces, relevant across diverse information models.
Dbm	Database Model. A set of extensions to the Uml model covering generic database concepts.
Sql	SQL Server Model. A set of Microsoft SQL Server-specific extensions to the Dbm model.
Ocl	Oracle Model. A set of Oracle-specific extensions to the Dbm model.
Db2	DB2 Model. A set of DB2-specific extensions to the Dbm model.
Ifx	Informix Model. A set of Informix-specific extensions to the Dbm model.
Tfm	Database Transformation Model. Describes transformations for moving data between databases.
Olp	OLAP Model. An extension of the Dbm model describing multidimensional databases.
Sim	Semantic Information Model. An extension of the Dbm model that enables users to interact with database data without learning data manipulation languages.

34

METADATA

There is a set of specific relationships and dependencies between these extensions, as shown in Figure 34.2.

FIGURE 34.2

This figure shows the systematic dependencies between extensions to the Uml as developed in Microsoft Repository.

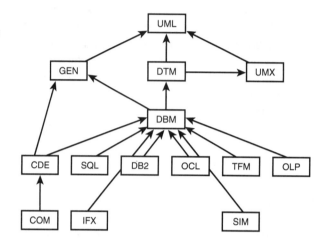

If you were to build your own model, you would have to establish the various components in the same manner as these were built. This would include developing, through the Model Development Kit, the following types of model elements:

- Class—COM class that implements interfaces
- Interface—Models semantically related behaviors and relationships, properties, and methods
- Association—Relationship between interfaces
- Aggregation—Also known as containment, represents inclusions between interfaces
- Inheritance—An interface's special use of another interface's characteristics, properties, and relationships
- Refinement—Relationship from a class to an interface
- Implication—Indicates dependency of an interface on another interface; required because COM does not allow multiple inheritance
- Dependency—The generic term; refinement and implication are both versions of dependency

All of these may be drawn in the Microsoft Visual Modeler within Microsoft Visual Studio. You can attach the information from your information model properties that are required to make it consistent with the UML.

Each and every component of the model has its own metadata and needs to be represented in full detail. To see how this is done, look at "Metadata for the Information Model Package" in the Repository SDK.

And Now That You Have So Much Spare Time...

I have endeavored to give you a good introductory "feel" for the types of things that can be done with the Repository implementation of UML. There are as many variants on this as there are ideas for particular models of any specific kind—that pretty much limits it to your imagination.

If you have found this introduction intriguing, I urge you to stock up on peanut butter sandwiches, pizza, or whatever else is your favorite programming food, grab some suitable drinks to go with it, download the latest SDK, and start reading and experimenting. If you get nothing else out of the exercise, you will acquire an even better "gut feel" for how a model is put together, the nature of the logic, and the requirements for a coherent representation of any model, just by working through the examples in the SDK.

It is quite possible that you have reached this point and decided that Repository SDK is not for you. If that is so, I feel that I have failed—and no author likes that feeling. Repository is inherently intriguing and enticing but it requires specific, dedicated learning and reading time, and to get the full "feel" for it you really do have to play with it. So, if you aren't feeling sufficiently intrigued by now, perhaps you should flag this chapter and come back to it when the mood, the candles, and the music are just right. Like many things on which we now rely in our daily work with databases and data warehouses, the sophistication of the tools in the SDK are worthy of your time and attention in their own right, but that they assist in your daily understanding of the use of metadata within Microsoft SQL Server, OLAP Services, and English Query is a clear bonus.

> **Note**
>
> Search on www.amazon.com. You will find that metadata has some interesting associations in the book world for furthering your appreciation of just how broadly the word is used today.

34

METADATA

Summary

Metadata play a significant role in the understanding of how Microsoft SQL Server and OLAP "hang together" and provide a deeper appreciation of the power of data about data. This chapter has supplied a variety of pointers to where such metadata are used and the tools with which you can work. All I have done here is expose the tip of a very large knowledge iceberg. There is a great deal that can be learned specifically about metadata, Microsoft Repository, and other tools that can be used—including the entirety of the Visual Studio Enterprise Edition, for those who feel ready for an extra challenge!

INDEX

G

X-Z

Other Related Titles

Microsoft SQL Server 7 DBA Survival Guide
Mark Spenik and Orryn Sledge
ISBN: 0-672-31226-3
$49.99 USA/$74.95 CAN

Roger Jennings' Database Developer's Guide with Visual Basic 6
Roger Jennings
0-672-31063-5
$59.99 US /$89.95 CAN

Building Enterprise Solutions with Visual Studio 6
G.A. Sullivan
0-672-31489-4
$49.99 US/$74.95 CAN

Sams Teach Yourself Database Programming with Visual Basic 6 in 24 Hours
Dan Rahmel
0-672-31412-6
$19.99 US /$29.95 CAN

Sams Teach Yourself Excel 2000 Programming in 21 Days
Matthew Harris
0-672-31543-2
$29.99 US / $44.95 CAN

Sams Teach Yourself Visual Basic 6 in 21 Days, Professional Reference Edition
Greg Perry
0-672-31542-4
$49.99 US/$74.95 CAN

Sams Teach Yourself Windows NT Server in 21 Days
Peter Davis
ISBN: 0-672-31555-6
$29.99 USA/$44.95 CAN

Sams Teach Yourself Linux in 24 Hours, Second Edition
Bill Ball
0-672-31526-2
$24.99 US/ $37.95

Maximum Security, Second Edition
Anonymous
0-672-31341-3
$49.99 US / $71.95 CAN

Roger Jennings' Database Workshop: Microsoft Transaction Server 2.0
Stephen Gray and Rick Lievano
ISBN: 0-672-31130-5
$39.99 USA/$59.95 CAN

Sams Teach Yourself SQL Server 7 in 21 Days
Richard Waymire
0-672-31290-5
$39.99 US / $59.95 CAN

SAMS

www.samspublishing.com

All prices are subject to change.

Get FREE books and more...when you register this book online for our Personal Bookshelf Program

http://register.samspublishing.com/

SAMS

 Register online and you can sign up for our *FREE Personal Bookshelf Program*...unlimited access to the electronic version of more than 200 complete computer books—immediately! That means you'll have 100,000 pages of valuable information onscreen, at your fingertips!

 Plus, you can access product support, including complimentary downloads, technical support files, book-focused links, companion Web sites, author sites, and more!

 And you'll be automatically registered to receive a *FREE subscription to a weekly email newsletter* to help you stay current with news, announcements, sample book chapters, and special events, including sweepstakes, contests, and various product giveaways!

 We value your comments! Best of all, the entire registration process takes only a few minutes to complete, so go online and get the greatest value going—absolutely FREE!

Don't Miss Out On This Great Opportunity!

Sams is a brand of Macmillan Computer Publishing USA.

For more information, please visit *www.mcp.com*